P9-DFP-241

lonely planet

Southwest France

John King
Julia Wilkinson

LONELY PLANET PUBLICATIONS
Melbourne • Oakland • London • Paris

SOUTHWEST FRANCE

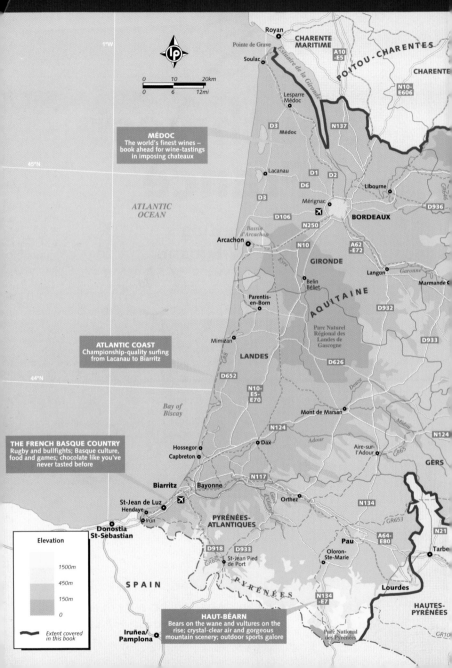

SOUTHWEST FRANCE

Royan
CHARENTE MARITIME
Pointe de Grave
A10-E5
Soulac
POITOU-CHARENTES
CHARENTE
N10-E606
Lesparre Médoc
N137

MÉDOC
The world's finest wines –
book ahead for wine-tastings
in imposing chateaux

D3
Médoc
Lacanau
D1 D2
D6
Libourne
D936
D3
Mérignac
D106
N250
BORDEAUX
ATLANTIC OCEAN
Bassin d'Arcachon
N10
Arcachon
A62-E72
GIRONDE
Langon
Garonne
Marmande
Belin Béliet
AQUITAINE
Parentis-en-Born
D932
Parc Naturel Régional des Landes de Gascogne
D933

ATLANTIC COAST
Championship-quality surfing
from Lacanau to Biarritz

Mimizan
LANDES
D626
D652
N10-E5-E70
Bay of Biscay
Mont de Marsan
N124
Adour
N124
Dax
Aire-sur-l'Adour
GERS
Hossegor
Capbreton

THE FRENCH BASQUE COUNTRY
Rugby and bullfights; Basque culture,
food and games; chocolate like you've
never tasted before

Biarritz
Bayonne
N117
Orthez
N134
St-Jean de Luz
Hendaye
Irún
PYRÉNÉES-ATLANTIQUES
Pau
A64-E80
N21
Donostia St-Sebastian
Tarbe
Oloron-Ste-Marie

Elevation
1500m
450m
150m
0

D918 D933
St-Jean Pied de Port
SPAIN
Lourdes
PYRÉNÉES
HAUTES-PYRÉNÉES
N134-E7

Extent covered in this book

Iruñea Pamplona

HAUT-BÉARN
Bears on the wane and vultures on the
rise; crystal-clear air and gorgeous
mountain scenery; outdoor sports galore

Parc National des Pyrénées
GR10

SOUTHWEST FRANCE

VÉZÈRE VALLEY
Concentration of world-class prehistoric cave art, including Font-de-Gaume and the replica Lascaux II

DORDOGNE VALLEY
Majestic river lined with redoubtable chateaux, ideal for riverboats, canoes and kayaks

ROCAMADOUR
Dramatic, cliff-hugging pilgrimage site for 800 years, with chapels, shrines and souvenir shops galore

CAHORS
Laid-back, historic capital of the Lot, near the delightful Lot and Célé Valleys and the famous Grotte du Pech Merle

CHEMIN DE ST-JACQUES
One of Europe's great medieval pilgrimage trails, to Santiago de Compostela in Spain, marked en route by numerous Unesco World Heritage Sites

TOULOUSE
Sunny, Spanish-flavoured city; France's biggest, most complete Romanesque structure; elegant town houses borne of the woad trade

Angoulême
D939
Parc Naturel Régional du Périgord Limousin
Brântôme
N21
Périgueux
La Forêt de la Double
DORDOGNE
Bergerac
Ste-Foy-la-Grande
LOT-ET-GARONNE
Villeneuve-sur-Lot
Lauzerte
TARN-ET-GARONNE
N21
Agen
A62-E72
N113
Moissac
Montauban
Condom
N21
Auch
MIDI-PYRÉNÉES
Mirande
St-Gaudens
D929
Bagnères de Luchon
PYRÉNÉES
ARIÈGE
Foix
D117
Quillan

LIMOUSIN
AUVERGNE
CORRÈZE
Brive-la-Gaillarde
D60
Sarlat-la-Canéda
D47
CANTAL
MASSIF CENTRAL
Rocamadour
N20
LOT
Cahors
AVEYRON
N140
Villefranche de Rouergue
Rodez
A20
Cordes-sur-Ciel
N88
Albi
A68
TARN
N112
Castres
Parc Naturel Régional du Haut Languedoc
Mazamet
LOZÈRE
Montagne Noire
TOULOUSE
HAUTE-GARONNE
A62-E9-E72
A64-E80
A61-E80
N113
Carcassonne
AUDE
N20-E9
LANGUEDOC-ROUSSILLON

Southwest France
2nd edition – March 2002
First published – April 2000

Published by
Lonely Planet Publications Pty Ltd ABN 36 005 607 983
90 Maribyrnong St, Footscray, Victoria 3011, Australia

Lonely Planet Offices
Australia Locked Bag 1, Footscray, Victoria 3011
USA 150 Linden St, Oakland, CA 94607
UK 10a Spring Place, London NW5 3BH
France 1 rue du Dahomey, 75011 Paris

Photographs
Many of the images in this guide are available for licensing from
Lonely Planet Images.
email: lpi@lonelyplanet.com.au
Web site: www.lonelyplanetimages.com

Front cover photograph
A man with plenty of boules, Richard Passmore (Tony Stone Images)

ISBN 1 86450 382 3

text & maps © Lonely Planet Publications Pty Ltd 2002
photos © photographers as indicated 2002

GR and PR are trademarks of the FFRP (Fédération Française de la
Randonée Pédestre).

Printed through Colorcraft Ltd, Hong Kong
Printed in China

Although the authors
and Lonely Planet try
to make the informa-
tion as accurate as
possible, we accept
no responsibility for
any loss, injury or
inconvenience sus-
tained by anyone
using this book.

2   Contents – Text

Contents – Text

Contents – Maps

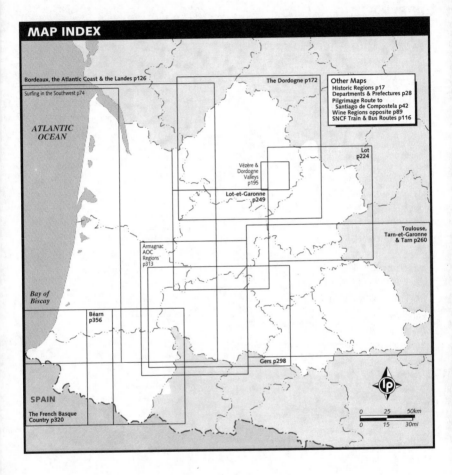

MAP INDEX

Bordeaux, the Atlantic Coast & the Landes p126

The Dordogne p172

Other Maps
Historic Regions p17
Departments & Prefectures p28
Pilgrimage Route to
    Santiago de Compostela p42
Wine Regions opposite p89
SNCF Train & Bus Routes p116

Surfing in the Southwest p74

ATLANTIC
OCEAN

Vézère &
Dordogne
Valleys
p195

Lot
p224

Lot-et-Garonne
p249

Toulouse,
Tarn-et-Garonne
& Tarn p260

Armagnac
AOC
Regions
p313

Bay of
Biscay

Béarn
p356

Gers p298

SPAIN

The French Basque
Country p320

0   25   50km
0   15   30mi

The Authors

Julia Wilkinson

Julia was first introduced to Southwest France as a child of 11 when her parents invested their hearts and savings into a tiny cottage in Périgord Noir. She has since been back almost every year, more recently with her own two children. After years spent in Hong Kong as a freelance travel writer and photographer and long spells on the road – authoring Lonely Planet's *Lisbon*, co-authoring *Portugal* and contributing to *Western Europe*, *Mediterranean Europe* and *Europe on a shoestring* – there is always the reward of a return to this magical corner of France.

John King

John grew up in the USA, and in earlier 'incarnations' has been a university physics teacher and an environmental consultant. In 1984 he headed off for a look at China, ended up living there for half a year, and never quite came home. John took up travel writing in 1988 with the 1st edition of Lonely Planet's *Karakoram Highway*. He is also co-author of Lonely Planet's *Pakistan*, *Czech & Slovak Republics*, *Prague*, *Portugal* and *Wales*, and was co-author of early editions of *Russia, Ukraine & Belarus* and *Central Asia*. He is also a contributor to *Western Europe* and *Mediterranean Europe*. John lives with his wife Julia Wilkinson and their two children in southwest England.

FROM THE AUTHORS

Julia would like to thank Ann Noon and colleagues at the London office of Maison de la France, the French tourism organisation; Cécile Ha and Marie-Yvonne Holley at the Comité Régional du Tourisme d'Aquitaine; Karine Lacour at the Conseil Régional d'Aquitaine; Martine Bouchet of the Comité Départemental du Tourisme du Lot; Anne Fernandez of the Comité Départemental du Tourisme du Lot-et-Garonne; Benoît Parayre at the Mairie, Bordeaux; and staff at regional Offices du Tourisme, particularly Erick Thillet at Bergerac, Estelle at Sarlat-la-Canéda and Sandrine Lesizza at Villeneuve-sur-Lot.

For patience and excellent help, John especially thanks Christian Mercurol and François Caussarieu at the Pau office of the Comité Départemental du Tourisme Béarn-Pays Basque; Catherine Tierce, Marie-Thérèse Pech and Veronique Mazac at the Toulouse tourist office; Christian Rivière in Albi; and Isabelle Forget in St-Jean de Luz. Other tourism officials who made a big difference are Hélène Barrere (Bayonne tourist office), Christiane

Bonnat (Comité Départemental du Tourisme Béarn-Pays Basque) and Maylis Garrouteigt (Biarritz tourist office).

Thanks to Alain Bonhomme and Paul François for information and insights on Toulouse, to Andy Fisher for saving John's bacon in Bayonne, and to Mme Agest who was in the Bedous tourist office at just the right time. Peter Mills and Charles Page at Rail Europe provided timely help as always, as did Anna-Lisa Morris at Air France.

This Book

This is the second edition of LP's *Southwest France* guide. John King and Julia Wilkinson wrote the first edition and updated the second.

From the Publisher

This edition of *Southwest France* was produced in Lonely Planet's London office. Charlotte Beech was the coordinating editor. Arabella Shepherd, Sam Trafford and Claire Hornshaw helped with editing and proofing. Fiona Christie handled the mapping, with assistance from Angie Watts. Fiona also designed and laid out the book. Annika Roojun designed the cover and Lachlan Ross drew the back-cover map. Lonely Planet Images provided the photographs and the illustrations were drawn by Jane Smith, Nicky Caven, Lisa Borg and Martin Harris. Emma Koch updated the language chapter, and Rachel Suddart lent her expertise to the Getting There & Away chapter. Special thanks to Amanda Canning as resident style guru, and especially to Tim Ryder and Sara Yorke for their endless calm, know-how and encouragement.

Thanks

Many thanks to the travellers who used the last edition and contacted us with helpful hints, advice and interesting anecdotes:

Tad Boniecki, Alyson & David Hilbourne, Kim & Daryl Hughes, Bob Lee Tze Yen, Helga Robinson, Andrew Sumner, Claire Wilhelm, Roxane Winkler, Rusty Wyrick, Sophie Jacques, Stephen Beck.

Foreword

ABOUT LONELY PLANET GUIDEBOOKS

The story begins with a classic travel adventure: Tony and Maureen Wheeler's 1972 journey across Europe and Asia to Australia. Useful information about the overland trail did not exist at that time, so Tony and Maureen published the first Lonely Planet guidebook to meet a growing need.

From a kitchen table, then from a tiny office in Melbourne (Australia), Lonely Planet has become the largest independent travel publisher in the world, an international company with offices in Melbourne, Oakland (USA), London (UK) and Paris (France).

Today Lonely Planet guidebooks cover the globe. There is an ever-growing list of books and there's information in a variety of forms and media. Some things haven't changed. The main aim is still to help make it possible for adventurous travellers to get out there – to explore and better understand the world.

At Lonely Planet we believe travellers can make a positive contribution to the countries they visit – if they respect their host communities and spend their money wisely. Since 1986 a percentage of the income from each book has been donated to aid projects and human rights campaigns.

Updates Lonely Planet thoroughly updates each guidebook as often as possible. This usually means there are around two years between editions, although for more unusual or more stable destinations the gap can be longer. Check the imprint page (following the colour map at the beginning of the book) for publication dates.

Between editions up-to-date information is available in two free newsletters – the paper *Planet Talk* and email *Comet* (to subscribe, contact any Lonely Planet office) – and on our Web site at www.lonelyplanet.com. The *Upgrades* section of the Web site covers a number of important and volatile destinations and is regularly updated by Lonely Planet authors. *Scoop* covers news and current affairs relevant to travellers. And, lastly, the *Thorn Tree* bulletin board and *Postcards* section of the site carry unverified, but fascinating, reports from travellers.

Correspondence The process of creating new editions begins with the letters, postcards and emails received from travellers. This correspondence often includes suggestions, criticisms and comments about the current editions. Interesting excerpts are immediately passed on via newsletters and the Web site, and everything goes to our authors to be verified when they're researching on the road. We're keen to get more feedback from organisations or individuals who represent communities visited by travellers.

Lonely Planet gathers information for everyone who's curious about the planet – and especially for those who explore it first-hand. Through guidebooks, phrasebooks, activity guides, maps, literature, newsletters, image library, TV series and Web site we act as an information exchange for a worldwide community of travellers.

Research Authors aim to gather sufficient practical information to enable travellers to make informed choices and to make the mechanics of a journey run smoothly. They also research historical and cultural background to help enrich the travel experience and allow travellers to understand and respond appropriately to cultural and environmental issues.

Authors don't stay in every hotel because that would mean spending a couple of months in each medium-sized city and, no, they don't eat at every restaurant because that would mean stretching belts beyond capacity. They do visit hotels and restaurants to check standards and prices, but feedback based on readers' direct experiences can be very helpful.

Many of our authors work undercover, others aren't so secretive. None of them accept freebies in exchange for positive write-ups. And none of our guidebooks contain any advertising.

Production Authors submit their raw manuscripts and maps to offices in Australia, USA, UK or France. Editors and cartographers – all experienced travellers themselves – then begin the process of assembling the pieces. When the book finally hits the shops, some things are already out of date, we start getting feedback from readers and the process begins again …

WARNING & REQUEST

Things change – prices go up, schedules change, good places go bad and bad places go bankrupt – nothing stays the same. So, if you find things better or worse, recently opened or long since closed, please tell us and help make the next edition even more accurate and useful. We genuinely value all the feedback we receive. A well-travelled team reads and acknowledges every letter, postcard and email and ensures that every morsel of information finds its way to the appropriate authors, editors and cartographers for verification.

Everyone who writes to us will find their name in the next edition of the appropriate guidebook. They will also receive the latest issue of *Planet Talk*, our quarterly printed newsletter, or *Comet*, our monthly email newsletter. Subscriptions to both newsletters are free. The very best contributions will be rewarded with a free guidebook.

Excerpts from your correspondence may appear in new editions of Lonely Planet guidebooks, the Lonely Planet Web site, *Planet Talk* or *Comet*, so please let us know if you *don't* want your letter published or your name acknowledged.

Send all correspondence to the Lonely Planet office closest to you:

Australia: Locked Bag 1, Footscray, Victoria 3011
USA: 150 Linden St, Oakland, CA 94607
UK: 10A Spring Place, London NW5 3BH
France: 1 rue du Dahomey, 75011 Paris

Or email us at: talk2us@lonelyplanet.com.au

For news, views and updates see our Web site: www.lonelyplanet.com

HOW TO USE A LONELY PLANET GUIDEBOOK

The best way to use a Lonely Planet guidebook is any way you choose. At Lonely Planet we believe the most memorable travel experiences are often those that are unexpected, and the finest discoveries are those you make yourself. Guidebooks are not intended to be used as if they provide a detailed set of infallible instructions!

Contents All Lonely Planet guidebooks follow roughly the same format. The Facts about the Destination chapters or sections give background information ranging from history to weather. Facts for the Visitor gives practical information on issues like visas and health. Getting There & Away gives a brief starting point for researching travel to and from the destination. Getting Around gives an overview of the transport options when you arrive.

The peculiar demands of each destination determine how subsequent chapters are broken up, but some things remain constant. We always start with background, then proceed to sights, places to stay, places to eat, entertainment, getting there and away, and getting around information – in that order.

Heading Hierarchy Lonely Planet headings are used in a strict hierarchical structure that can be visualised as a set of Russian dolls. Each heading (and its following text) is encompassed by any preceding heading that is higher on the hierarchical ladder.

Entry Points We do not assume guidebooks will be read from beginning to end, but that people will dip into them. The traditional entry points are the list of contents and the index. In addition, however, some books have a complete list of maps and an index map illustrating map coverage.

There may also be a colour map that shows highlights. These highlights are dealt with in greater detail in the Facts for the Visitor chapter, along with planning questions and suggested itineraries. Each chapter covering a geographical region usually begins with a locator map and another list of highlights. Once you find something of interest in a list of highlights, turn to the index.

Maps Maps play a crucial role in Lonely Planet guidebooks and include a huge amount of information. A legend is printed on the back page. We seek to have complete consistency between maps and text, and to have every important place in the text captured on a map. Map key numbers usually start in the top left corner.

Although inclusion in a guidebook usually implies a recommendation we cannot list every good place. Exclusion does not necessarily imply criticism. In fact there are a number of reasons why we might exclude a place – sometimes it is simply inappropriate to encourage an influx of travellers.

Introduction

Imagine you were heading to Southwest France for a holiday 700 years ago. Bad timing: You would have been in the thick of the Hundred Years' War between England and France, one of Europe's longest-running wars, over control of the rich lands of Aquitaine (and other areas in the north). Castles and chateaux changed hands almost daily and revolutionary new *bastides* (fortified towns) were being built everywhere. Even if you had delayed your visit by a couple of centuries, you would have found warfare, this time between Catholics and Protestants, resulting in widespread destruction.

But go back a few millennia – 15,000 years or so – and you would step into one of the world's finest art galleries: caves decorated with fantastic carvings and paintings of bison, mammoth and deer.

It's prehistoric cave art like this that has given Southwest France much of its fame. But the additional legacy of those turbulent medieval days – the restored chateaux and bastides – makes an impressive backdrop to what has become one of the most tranquil and unspoiled corners of France. For since the 16th century, nothing much has matched the drama of those days. Indeed, time moves so slowly that pre-Revolutionary place names are preferred to the modern departmental ones – Périgord instead of Dordogne, Gascony for the Gers, Pays Basque and Béarn rather than Pyrénées-Atlantiques. The medieval *langue d'oc* (Occitan language) is spoken alongside French in a few places. Modern-day Gascons still live off the reputations of their swashbuckling ancestors. Rural parts of the French Basque country

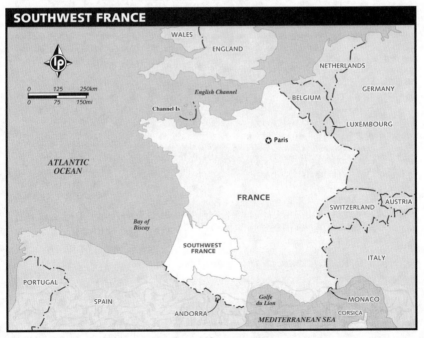

SOUTHWEST FRANCE

and Béarn still look (and the locals still live) as they must have centuries ago.

This slow touch of time has given the people of the southwest a chance to relish life, particularly when it comes to food. In this gourmand heartland, the cuisine is both rich (no more so than *foie gras* and *confit d'oie*) and simple, distinguished by truffles, mushrooms, nuts and fruit. The quality wines of the Bordeaux region are the world's finest, and hundreds of other vineyards produce top-class vintages. You're unlikely to move very far or fast on this kind of culinary trail.

Public transport helps you adjust to the pace, with limited services to remote areas. You're better off on foot or a bike (the Lot *département*, or administrative department, alone has some 3000km of signposted paths). Many trails follow the pilgrimage routes to Spain's Santiago de Compostela, from whose 13th-century heyday have come dozens of ecclesiastical monuments (33 in

Southwest France are now Unesco World Heritage Sites). The Atlantic coast offers different distractions: 250km of sandy beaches and world-class surfing. Or you can drift down the region's waterways in a houseboat.

Of course it's not all rural calm; Bordeaux and Toulouse are the region's largest, liveliest cities, high-tech industrial and aeronautical centres. But the soul of Southwest France is in the countryside – where the calendar is marked by truffle and foie-gras markets, the gathering of grapes, tobacco or maize, or simply the chance to share some home-made *eau de vie*. It's a lifestyle that epitomises *la France profonde*. The tranquillity masks the sad reality of depopulation, however, with many villages struggling to survive. But tourism is bringing new revenues and, provided it doesn't abuse the hospitality on offer, may help keep this richly endowed corner of France on its slow, special way for many more centuries.

Facts about Southwest France

HISTORY
Early Inhabitants

In no other region of the world is there such rich evidence of early human habitation and artistic skill as in Southwest France. The best known artefacts are the cave paintings of Lascaux (near Montignac), created some 16,000 years ago, but Lower Palaeolithic *Homo erectus* was probably hunting in the western Pyrénées as long as 450,000 years ago.

The Neanderthals of the Middle Palaeolithic period took the stage 150,000 years ago, only to disappear without a trace 35,000 years ago. Though thuggish in appearance – short and stocky with jutting jawbones and elongated heads – Neanderthals were cleverer than *Homo erectus*, producing sophisticated tools, using fire skilfully, and often burying their dead with special rituals. Their so-called Mousterian culture got its name from a site at Le Moustier in Périgord, where a skeleton and flint implements were found in 1909.

However, the real talent belonged to the *Homo sapiens sapiens* Cro-Magnon people. Similar to us in appearance – tall and upright with long limbs and nimble hands – they flourished from the Upper Palaeolithic to the Neolithic periods, roughly 35,000 to 6000 years ago. They employed their hunting skills to kill reindeer, bison, horse and mammoth, and their artistic skills to produce some of the world's finest cave art, such as in the area around the Cro-Magnon cave shelter near Les Eyzies in Périgord, where three skeletons were found in 1868 (one of the first prehistoric excavations to take place in France).

So prolific were the Cro-Magnons that several distinct subcultures have been defined. The early Périgordian and Aurignacian cultures – the latter named after Aurignac in the Haute-Garonne, where early discoveries were made – bone and horn tools, wooden spears and bead necklaces. Most exciting were the first-known cave decorations: tiny, fleshy female figurines (most notably the so-called *Vénus à la Corne,* 'Venus with a Horn'), tracings in black or red of their own hands (as at Grotte du Pech Merle in the Lot) and rudimentary animal sketches.

The people of the Cro-Magnon Solutrean culture (from about 20,000 to 15,000 BC), well represented in the Dordogne, focused more on tools than art, producing slim flint blades, stone and wood weapons, and the world's first sewing needles, complete with eyes.

This was a period of intense cold – the end of the last Ice Age – and the Cro-Magnons increasingly retreated to caves and rock shelters, plentiful in Périgord's Vézère Valley. Here, during the period of the Magdalenian Culture (named after discoveries at La Madeleine near Les Eyzies, roughly 15,000 to 9000 BC, they produced their finest art, crafting superb bone-and-ivory implements, and carving, engraving or painting increasingly realistic animal and hunting scenes in caves throughout the region. See the boxed text 'The Painted Caves of the Southwest' in Arts later in this chapter. For more on Lascaux itself, see the Dordogne chapter.

The Cro-Magnons also enjoyed music and dance, performed fertility rituals and other ceremonies, and had fairly complex social patterns. However, with the climatic warming that forced reindeer herds northwards in search of lichen, the nomadic Cro-Magnon hunter-artists drifted after them and the area's cave art came to an end.

After the undistinguished Mesolithic period came the Neolithic period, about 7500 to 3000 years ago. The warmer climate saw the rise of farming (crops included wheat, barley and lentils), stock rearing and trading, and a more sedentary life. This was Europe's first real civilisation, with a sophisticated culture (including evidence of extraordinary astronomical knowledge) and a well organised, probably matriarchal, society. The most intriguing reminders of this time are the megaliths that still dot the area, especially the Lot, the Dordogne and the western Pyrénées.

Another leap came with the metalworking cultures. By 2500 BC, descendants of Indo-European tribes from the Aegean were making copper tools and weapons on both sides of the Alps, with the Artenac people establishing a foothold around Bordeaux. Waves of newcomers included a tribe the Romans called the Aquitanii, who appeared around the 7th century BC. More significant, however, were the Celts.

Celts & Romans

The Celts spread across modern-day France (known in Roman times as Gaul) and by 600 BC were trading with the Greeks along Neolithic trade routes. One of these, among Europe's oldest trading roads, ran from the Atlantic to the Mediterranean via Pau near the Spanish border. Settlements were generally either hilltop fortifications or larger *oppida* (defensive towns) with political, economic and religious functions.

It wasn't long before the Gauls came into conflict with the Romans who, by the 2nd century BC, had put their military toe in at Tolosa (Toulouse) and begun edging northwards. In 56 BC Burdigala (Bordeaux) was captured by Julius Caesar's colleague Crassus. Four years later the Gauls, under Vercingétorix, were finally defeated by Caesar himself at a still-disputed location in the Lot or Périgord.

South and east of the Garonne, on both sides of the Pyrénées, lived a more ancient, pre-Celtic people, the Vascones, called Novempopulanii ('Nine Tribes') by the Romans. The Vascones put up stiff military and cultural resistance – just as their descendants, the Basques and the Gascons, do today.

In AD 16, the Romans created the new province of Aquitania, spanning almost the entire southwest from the River Loire to the Pyrénées. They introduced new crops such as walnuts, chestnuts and wine grapes and built spa resorts (for example at Dax) and lavish villas, such as the one excavated at Séviac in the Gers. Flourishing centres included Tolosa, Burdigala, Vesunna (Périgueux) and Divona Cadurcorum (Cahors). Early in the 4th century AD, Christianity arrived.

These deceptively prosperous times (the heavily taxed poor, no better than slaves, just got poorer) came to an end soon afterwards. Germanic tribes, the Franks and the Alemanni, were already sweeping in from the east and by the early 5th century the more powerful Vandals and Visigoths arrived, snapping the already weakened Roman rule. In 507 the Franks got the upper hand, chasing the Visigoths into Spain.

The Merovingians & Carolingians

The Christianised Franks adopted important elements of Gallo-Roman civilisation but lacked the Romans' authoritarian skills. When the Moors swept across the Pyrénées in the early 700s and seized Bordeaux, it was the ambitious Charles Martel who defeated them (at Poitiers in 732). He was a member of the powerful Pepin family, mayors of the palace, who increasingly took control from the Frankish Merovingian dynasty and, in defeating the Moors, laid the foundations for his own Carolingian dynasty. His grandson,

Take That, Roland

The earliest surviving work of French literature, the 11th-century *Chanson de Roland* (Song of Roland), is an epic ballad recounting the death of the larger-than-life knight. The character in question was ambushed in the Pyrénées in 778 on the way back from his uncle Charlemagne's campaign against the Moors in Spain. Numerous local legends mirror this tale and the Pyrénées abound in natural landmarks said to have been made by Roland's sword Durandal, his foot, or whatever else stirred the imagination. Little real historical information is available on the man, but what there is suggests that the ambush was laid by angry Basques. The ballad's substitution of Muslims as the villains simply may have been a battle cry for the Crusades, which kicked off at about the same time.

Charlemagne, considerably expanded the boundaries of the Frankish Empire and mollified the rebellious Duchy of Aquitaine by giving it the title of kingdom.

In the 9th century, ferocious Vikings began raiding the western coast, sacking Bordeaux in 848 and Bayonne in 862, and penetrating inland as far as Toulouse. By the time they were pushed back to what is now Normandy in 982, the southwest was fragmenting into independent feudal states. The Vascones south of the Pyrénées had already founded their own little kingdom of Navarre, and in the 10th century the baronies of Périgord (Mareuil, Bourdeilles, Beynac and Biron) were established. As the millennium dawned, the feudal states had spawned a patchwork of prosperous towns.

The Middle Ages

The most notable development at the start of the Middle Ages was the appearance of *bastides,* fortified new towns built by rich feudal lords anxious to protect their fiefdoms (see the special section 'Bastides & Châteaux' later in the chapter). The increasingly powerful Church also began to express its power in mortar and stone: Fabulous churches and abbeys appeared all over the region (notably at Chancelade and Cadouin), often funded by the Cistercian order or by local lords – especially the powerful counts of Toulouse and dukes of Aquitaine.

In a parallel artistic vein, the region's many post-Roman dialects – collectively known as Langue d'Oc (also known as Occitan) – appeared for the first time in poetry, notably troubadour poetry (for more information see Literature under Arts later in this chapter), which served as a cultural and political focus for the so-called Occitan people.

It was the granddaughter of one of the finest troubadour poets (Guillaume IX, duke of Aquitaine) who was to turn the region on its historical head. As the sole heir to Aquitaine's vast lands and wealth, the beautiful but strong-willed Eleanor was hot property on the royal marriage market, good enough for the king of France himself. But 15 years of marriage to the lacklustre Louis VII ended in annulment in 1152, and

with hardly a fare-thee-well Eleanor married Henry Plantagenet, count of Anjou (see the boxed text 'Eleanor of Aquitaine' for more details).

When Henry became king of England, Eleanor's dowry of Aquitaine and Gascony – a third of France – fell under English rule. The sting in the arrangement was that Henry, as duke of Aquitaine, had to pay homage to the king of France. The subsequent rivalry between France and England for control of Aquitaine and the vast English territories elsewhere in France (including Anjou, Lorraine and Normandy) would last three centuries.

England vs France

The petty battles to consolidate English rule, often instigated by Eleanor's son, Richard the Lion-Heart (see the boxed text), were background noise to an otherwise orderly, well liked English administration.

But in the 13th century the Albigensian Crusade was launched to subjugate the wealthy and independent-minded counts of Toulouse on the pretext of evicting Cathar heretics from Toulouse, Albi and the Languedoc. Simon de Montfort led an

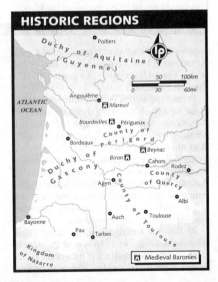

HISTORIC REGIONS

Eleanor of Aquitaine

JANE SMITH

It was thanks to the beautiful and wealthy Eleanor of Aquitaine that France, and particularly the southwest, was rocked by the Hundred Years' War. Born in 1122 to Guillaume X, duke of Aquitaine, she was his only heir, and in 1137 her considerable wealth (including one of the largest domains in France) became part of the French Crown when she married Louis VII.

Although she bore him two daughters and influenced him greatly, Eleanor never much fancied the dull Louis who for his part was so annoyed by her flirtatious behaviour during the Second Crusade that he annulled the marriage in 1152. The ink had hardly dried on the paper when 30-something Eleanor (who still had possession of Aquitaine) found her true love: 19-year-old Henry Plantagenet, duke of Normandy and count of Anjou. In 1154 he became King Henry II of England, thereby bringing vast areas of French land under the control of the English Crown and sparking off centuries of rivalry between the French and the English.

Eleanor's sons were a lousy lot (see the boxed text on her favourite, 'Richard the Lion-Heart'). Her support of their revolt against their father – support that was probably borne of fury at her husband's infidelities – cost her her freedom for many years: Henry had her imprisoned in England and it was only on his death in 1189 that she returned to Aquitaine, to act as Richard's administrator while he was engaged in the Third Crusade.

In addition to managerial prowess, Eleanor had enormous cultural and social influence. A whole new chivalric attitude towards women was promoted at her brilliant court in Poitiers, where the novel idea that men belonged to women was celebrated in troubadour poetry.

After a jaunt across the Pyrénées at the age of 80 to fetch her granddaughter Blanche from the court at Castile for marriage to the son of the French king, she retired to her castle on the isle of Oléron. She died in 1204 at the abbey-church of Fontevrault, eulogised by the nuns as a queen 'who surpassed almost all the queens of the world'.

---

especially vicious campaign against Count Raymond VI of Toulouse (see the boxed text 'The Albigensian Crusade' in the Toulouse chapter).

French power was now uncomfortably close to the Plantagenet English rulers in Aquitaine, and the two sparred with increasing ferocity. In 1337, outright war – the start of what came to be called the Hundred Years' War – became inevitable when Philippe VI ordered the confiscation of Aquitaine on the pretext that Edward III had defaulted in his feudal service. Battles soon raged, with bastides and castles changing sides from one year to the next.

At first the English had the upper hand, winning at Crécy in 1346 and at Poitiers in 1356 – the latter under the infamous Black Prince, Edward III's eldest son, who heaped insult on injury by capturing the French king, Jean II. As part of Jean's ransom, Aquitaine was officially ceded to the English crown in 1360. After some confused negotiations, the Black Prince installed himself as Aquitaine's new duke.

In 1370, France wrested back control of Aquitaine and a series of truces began. The 15th century, however, dawned with a new round of claims from the English. In 1415, Henry V defeated the French at Agincourt and five years later was recognised as king of France.

It took the legendary Joan of Arc (Jeanne d'Arc) to rally the French behind Charles VII. By 1450, Aquitaine had been recaptured, with Bordeaux falling in 1451. The final battle of the Hundred Years' War was fought at Castillon-la-Bataille (near St-

Émilion) two years later. The English had been booted out of Aquitaine forever (well, at least until the tourists arrived).

Repression & Religious Persecution

The 16th century ushered in a new wave of warfare thanks to the spread of Protestantism and the radical ideas of Luther and Calvin. The southwest – already disgruntled by repressive French rule – embraced the new ideas with enthusiasm. Protestant communities first emerged in the 1530s in Agen and Béarn and by 1560 conflicts between these 'Huguenots' and supporters of the Catholic League (a national anti-Huguenot movement) were erupting like brush fires. Many Protestants were massacred in Cahors (which, like Périgueux, was a staunch supporter of the Catholic League) and expelled from Toulouse. However, Bergerac, Ste-Foy-la-Grande, Figeac and Montauban all emerged as fiercely pro-Protestant, supported by the bigoted Jeanne d'Albret of Navarre, the tiny Gascon kingdom that encompassed Béarn.

By 1562, the Wars of Religion had witnessed atrocities everywhere (Cahors suffered a particularly nasty Protestant attack in 1580). The most visible result of this brutal war was severe damage to churches and other religious icons, but feuds between families, villages and regions left scars that would last for decades.

Protestantism, and its power in the southwest, took the spotlight in 1584 when Jeanne d'Albret's Huguenot son, Henri, inherited the French throne as Henri IV. Only after years of suspicious assassinations was his throne secure. Even then, Catholic Parisians remained hostile. After diplomatically converting tó Catholicism in 1593, Henri issued the Edict of Nantes in 1598, mandating religious tolerance and an end to the Wars of Religion.

Richard the Lion-Heart

Richard Coeur de Lion is one of Aquitaine's most colourful historical characters. Regarded as a hero thanks to his prowess in the Third Crusade, he was a talented troubadour, and probably gay. He was also an unreconstructed cad, with 'little or no filial piety, foresight, or sense of responsibility', as one historian put it.

Born in 1157 to Henry II and Eleanor of Aquitaine, he was given the duchy of Aquitaine when he was 11 and officially crowned duke four years later. At 16 he joined forces with his equally unfilial brothers (and his mother) in a revolt against his father. He later submitted, turning his attention instead to bullying the barons of Aquitaine. So obnoxious was his money-grabbing harassment that in 1183 the whole region rose up against him, enlisting the help of Richard's older brother Henry, the 'Young King', whose sudden death fortuitously ended the fighting.

Richard was now heir to the English throne (and to all England's French possessions). Refusing his father's request to give Aquitaine to his younger brother, he sought the support of Philippe II of France and in 1189 joined forces with him to defeat Henry once and for all. The elderly, weakened king died later that year and Richard inherited the English throne.

Obsessed with recapturing Jerusalem, he plundered his late father's treasury and set sail to lead the Third Crusade. His military exploits, his quarrels with French, German and English crusaders and his subsequent captivity on his way home became the stuff of legend.

Greed and arrogance did him in at the age of 42. Back in France in 1199 (he spent only six months of his 'reign' in England and reputedly couldn't even speak English), he learned of a hoard of treasure hidden by the viscount of Limoges in his castle at Châlus. Richard besieged the castle but during the fighting his armour was pierced by an arrow from a new type of long-range cross-bow.

He was, ironically, buried beside his parents in the abbey of Fontevrault. Or rather, his body was buried there; his entrails were interred in Châlus and his heart in Rouen. As for the archer who killed him, he was flayed alive.

Revolts & Revolution

This was hardly the end of internal conflicts, however. *Croquants* – disgruntled peasants of Périgord and Quercy – had revolted against high rents and taxes in the mid-1590s and did so again in 1637. Louis XIII and his ruthless minister, Cardinal Richelieu, were intent on forcing absolute obedience to the monarchy: Béarn's independence was quashed in 1620, and the Croquant movement and other civil disturbances were crushed.

While the king's soldiers made life a misery for peasants – billeting themselves wherever they wished, pillaging and raping when it suited them – these were good times for the nobility, who ploughed high rents into many a splendid new chateau. Toulouse found wealth from the manufacture of *le pastel* (dyer's woad) and from markets opened up by the new Canal du Midi (see the boxed text 'Les Canaux des Deux Mers' in the Getting Around chapter). Bordeaux augmented healthy wine revenues with a disreputable slave trade with the Americas.

When the young Louis XIV, Le Roi Soleil (The Sun King), came on the scene in 1643 assisted by another powerful cardinal, Mazarin, the drive for absolute monarchy went into high gear. A series of urban revolts, sparked in Paris in 1648 and known as Les Frondes (after the word for a sling), spread across the land and Mazarin was temporarily forced to flee for his life. One by one, these uprisings were quashed, with Bordeaux the last of the Frondes' cities to submit, in 1653. In 1660 the young Louis took a year-long tour of his lands before his gala marriage to the Spanish princess Marie Thérèse (Maria Teresa) in St-Jean de Luz.

In 1685, the king earned the everlasting hatred of Protestants by revoking the Edict of Nantes. Brutal persecution drove many Huguenots into exile in England, Prussia, the Netherlands and North America. Only the fiercely monarchist Basques were allowed a measure of independence, while the southwestern provinces were largely ruled by *intendants* (governors) from Paris. Some, such as the Marquis de Tourny, who instigated major town-planning projects in Bordeaux and Périgueux, made lasting contributions; others were bitterly resented.

As the 18th century progressed, new economic and social circumstances rendered the *ancien regime* (old order) dangerously out of step with the needs of the country. The regime was further weakened by the anti-establishment and anticlerical ideas of the Enlightenment. In the rural southwest, general unrest over rising prices and falling wages, as well as a booming population (in Quercy it rose by 70% between 1700 and 1786) helped to pave the way for the collapse of the regime in 1789, when the urban masses of Paris took to the streets and launched the Revolution.

Among the Revolution's first victims were the Girondins, a faction of moderate republican deputies from Bordeaux, representatives of the upper-mercantile class, who lost power to the radical Jacobins. However, after the Reign of Terror had finally wound down in 1794 (with the loss of some 17,000 heads), it was the Girondins' brand of moderation that won the day.

Napoleon & the Dawn of the Republics

Meanwhile, Napoleon Bonaparte was winning glorious successes in a military campaign against Austria. On his return to an unstable Paris in 1799 he assumed power. By 1804, he had himself crowned emperor of the French and launched a series of wars against his European neighbours to consolidate and legitimise his authority. He also instituted a number of important reforms, including a reorganisation of the judicial system and the promulgation of a new legal code, the Code Napoleon (or civil code), which still forms the basis of the French legal system to this day. A Périgordian from Domme, Jacques de Maleville, was one of its authors.

Among Napoleon's most loyal fans were the people of Périgord and the Lot, who sent thousands of their young men (including several who became high-ranking generals) to join his Grande Armée. Many met their end in Napoleon's disastrous Russian campaign of 1812; two years later the allied armies forced Napoleon to abdicate. Though he returned briefly for a 'Hundred Days' of power, his fate was sealed when his forces were defeated by the English under the Duke of Wellington at Waterloo in 1815.

After these excitements, the southwest sank into obscurity and poverty. Bordeaux, which had suffered from the allies' blockade and the abolition of the slave trade, plunged to an all-time low. In 1851, Louis Napoleon, Napoleon's nephew, took advantage of the political instability to lead a coup d'etat and proclaim himself Emperor Napoleon III, ushering in the Second Empire.

During this period, France enjoyed significant economic growth and even the southwest claimed Napoleon III's attention. His major achievement here was to transform the once-desolate Landes – a region of marshy swamps, encroaching sand and poor soil – into Europe's largest pine forest. He and his Spanish wife, Eugénie, spent holidays in Biarritz and the Basque region, turning them into fashionable resorts. Thermal spas also gained popularity, with Pau a favourite among English visitors.

The tourist trade became an essential new revenue-earner, especially vital after a phylloxera epidemic in 1868 that nearly wiped out the region's entire wine production, a body-blow to an area already struggling to survive. Despite the arrival of the railway in the 1850s, young men left in their thousands to seek their fortunes elsewhere. Village populations dwindled with alarming speed. With the onset of the World Wars, the decline quickened.

The World Wars

Like his uncle, Napoleon III led his Empire to its end after a series of inadvisable wars. In 1870 the Prussians inflicted a humiliating defeat on the French, forcing the government to negotiate an armistice and hold elections.

After a rocky start, the Third Republic launched into an era known as the *belle époque* (beautiful age), with the introduction of Art Nouveau architecture, a whole field of 'isms' from Impressionism onwards and advances in science and engineering. In the southwest, Bordeaux picked itself up, boosted by a brief reign as the nation's capital in 1870 (twice more, in times of war, it was to serve as a temporary capital, in 1914 and 1940). When France entered WWI, however, the southwest suffered terribly, each village losing at least a third of its young men to the war.

After WWI there followed a brief respite, during which the southwest made headlines with the discovery of various important prehistoric sites, culminating in 1940, with the stunning paintings of Lascaux cave. But the country was soon engulfed in conflict once again; within a year of declaring war on Germany in 1939, France had fallen. Bordeaux was the scene of the armistice with Hitler in June 1940.

The Germans divided France into a directly occupied zone (the north and the entire Atlantic Coast) and a puppet state based in the spa town of Vichy. For four years, the southwest, like the rest of France, dealt in varying ways with the Occupation. A small minority joined the underground Résistance. Many in the Basque region smuggled escapees into Spain and Allied agents into France; indeed, Spaniards (half a million of whom had fled to Southwest France after Franco's onslaught on the Spanish Basque country in 1937) constituted a large proportion of the area's Résistance.

Almost every town and village has its memorial to those who died before and during the Occupation. Several suffered particularly badly, especially at the end of the war when the Germans launched a wave of revenge attacks against the Résistance, who had become increasingly effective from their hideaways in the caves and *causses* (limestone plateaus) of Quercy and Périgord.

Liberation of the southwest came in August 1944. A former Résistance fighter, Jacques Chaban-Delmas, became deputy, and later mayor, of Bordeaux. Less worthy post-war officials included a former general secretary of Gironde, Maurice Papon, appointed *préfet* (prefect) of the Landes in 1945 and later chief of police in Paris and minister in Giscard d'Estaing's government. In 1983, it was revealed that he had been a Nazi collaborator. Only in April 1998 was he finally tried and found guilty.

Post-War Revival

After the German capitulation, Général Charles de Gaulle, who had set up a French government-in-exile in London, returned to head a provisional government.

After an unsuccessful attempt to quash a nationalist uprising in Algeria (whose population included over a million French settlers), civil war seemed to loom. De Gaulle drafted a new constitution, launching the Fifth Republic in 1958. In 1962, after troubles in Algeria had escalated, he gave the country its independence. Some 750,000 *pieds noirs* (literally 'black feet', as Algerian-born French are known in France) flooded into France. The southwest hosted many of them and their continued presence – along with descendants of refugees from the Spanish Civil War – gives the area a distinctive diversity.

Economically, the area's biggest postwar boom has been in Toulouse, which has become the base for Aérospatiale, Airbus and the French space agency, and a lively rival to Bordeaux, which regained some of the limelight by hosting several football matches in the 1998 World Cup.

And what of the rural hinterland? The ongoing exodus of the young and the depopulation of villages has been offset slightly by the arrival of thousands of foreign settlers from the Netherlands, Germany and particularly England, who since the 1960s have established a multitude of holiday homes here. Indeed, tourism is today's lifeblood for many regions, especially the Dordogne.

With the election in 1981 of the Socialist François Mitterand, several measures were introduced that affected the region. In particular, a decentralisation program created the modern-day *régions* (administrative regions) of Aquitaine and Midi-Pyrénées, providing the first steps away from centuries of heavy-handed Parisian control.

GEOGRAPHY

The area covered by this guide, roughly 65,700 sq km (about 12% of France's land area), spans what is known as the Bassin Aquitaine (Aquitaine Basin). It is embraced to the north by valley-crossed limestone plateaus, to the north-east by the foothills of the Massif Central and to the south by the Pyrénées (see the following Geology section). An extraordinary diversity of landscapes is to be found here.

Some 230km of fine, sandy Atlantic coastline (known as La Côte d'Argent, or The Silver Coast) stretches arrow-straight from Pointe de Grave (100km north of Bordeaux) almost to the Spanish border. Here is Europe's longest, highest sand dune belt, surmounted by the 114m-high Dune du Pilat and broken only by the Bassin d'Arcachon, a 250-sq-km inland sea. Southwards and inland lies the 14,000-sq-km plain of the Landes, a mix of dunes, marshland and nearly a million hectares of pine and oak plantations. It was established in the 19th century to hold back the encroaching sand, and is Europe's largest cultivated forest.

Behind the Landes' dunes lies a mosaic of lakes and lagoons, whose often-turbulent outlets to the sea provide locations for some of the southwest's finest watersports. The lakes themselves, from Étang d'Hourtin-Carcans (at 16km, France's longest lake) in the north to Étang d'Orx in the south, offer calmer activities and havens for wildlife.

Inland, one of France's five major rivers – the 575km-long Garonne – rises in the Pyrénées and shapes 56,000 sq km of the southwest before emptying into the Atlantic at Europe's largest estuary, the Estuaire de la Gironde. Garonne's tributaries include some of the country's loveliest waterways: the Dordogne, Lot and Tarn. Others are the Vézère, Dronne and Isle (all in the *département* – or administrative department – of the Dordogne), Aveyron (in Tarn-et-Garonne), Grande Leyre (in Gironde; called the Eyre or Leyre in lower reaches), and Gers and Baïse (in the Gers). Little wonder the Romans called this region Aquitania (land of waters).

The region's other major river, the Adour, also rises in the Pyrénées, crossing the southern Landes to the sea at Bayonne. Its major branches – the Nive, Oloron and Pau – drain the Pyrénées-Atlantiques department. An artificial waterway that has become part of the landscape is the body comprising the Canal du Midi and Canal

Latéral à la Garonne (see the boxed text 'Les Canaux des Deux Mers' in the Getting Around chapter).

GEOLOGY
Of the mighty 450km Pyrénées range defining the France-Spain border, this book covers only the western arm, known as the Haut-Béarn. This part of the range, scored by picturesque and fertile valleys, rises highest at Pic du Midi d'Ossau (2884m), near the border south of Pau.

A Muddle of Names

In Roman times, Aquitania was a vast area extending as far north as the Loire and east to the Massif Central. The kingdom of Aquitaine declared by Charlemagne corresponds to the modern *départements* (administrative departments) of Gironde, most of Lot-et-Garonne, the Dordogne, Lot and Aveyron. It also acquired the alias Guyenne, or Guienne, around the time the English arrived (because, say some, the Anglo-Saxons couldn't pronounce 'Aquitaine').

When Henry II married Eleanor of Aquitaine, her dowry also included Gascony (roughly corresponding to the modern departments of Gers and Landes). By this time, though reference was still made to 'Aquitaine', it no longer actually existed as a political entity. Its various provinces, which changed hands continually during the Hundred Years' War – included Poitou (the area west of Poitiers), Guyenne, Gascony and several smaller provinces.

Aquitaine has recently been revived as one of France's 22 *régions* (regions), made up of the Dordogne, Gironde, Landes, Lot-et-Garonne and Pyrénées-Atlantiques departments.

Other historical names that still pop up occasionally are Quercy (a part of Guyenne during the Middle Ages, and corresponding to modern-day Lot and most of Tarn-et-Garonne), Languedoc (east of the Garonne, including Toulouse and Armagnac, stretching from the Pyrénées – including Béarn – to Agen), and Périgord (synonymous with the modern department of the Dordogne).

Equally dramatic formations are revealed in the Lot's causses – monumental, 1000m-high limestone plateaus separating lush, deeply cut gorges. The causses host several splendid clifftop villages, such as Rocamadour, and hide a network of caves and subterranean waterways quite at odds with the almost semi-desert conditions on the surface. A spectacular example is the Gouffre de Padirac (in the Causse de Gramat, near Rocamadour) where a navigable river flows 103m below ground level.

Lining the wide, looping valleys of the Rivers Vézère and Dordogne in Périgord are hard, cave-riddled limestone cliffs that have given shelter since prehistoric times. Towards Brive-la-Gaillarde, these ridges peter out in a depression of sandstone and schist.

CLIMATE
Like most of France, the southwest has a temperate, Atlantic-influenced climate. Rainfall is below the countrywide average, owing to the influence of the Massif Central, and summers are warmer and often punctuated by dramatic thunderstorms. The hottest months are July and August, with average daytime temperatures of about 25°C.

Winter temperatures drop to around 10°C in December and January; chill winds make this season particularly harsh on the high plateaus. In the Haut-Béarn there's enough snow for skiers from December to March or April, though weather in the foothills is quite mild – indeed, Pau is famed for its year-round mild climate.

The mountains see as much as 1000mm of rain each year, compared with Toulouse's 656mm. Elsewhere in the southwest the heaviest rains usually occur in spring and late autumn, with fog and frost common in Périgord in spring. In November 1999, the country's worst floods of the century (following a year's worth of rain in just 24 hours) affected the Tarn and neighbouring coastal departments, and resulted in some 22 deaths. They were followed in late-December by violent 120mph storms that felled over 300 million trees nationwide, hitting the southwest (particularly northern Dordogne) hard.

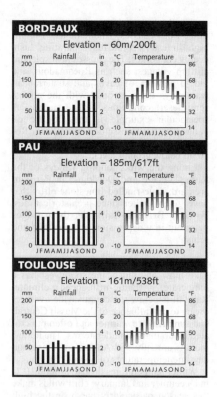

BORDEAUX
Elevation – 60m/200ft

PAU
Elevation – 185m/617ft

TOULOUSE
Elevation – 161m/538ft

ECOLOGY & ENVIRONMENT

The southwest is loved by French and foreigners alike for its rural traditions and tranquillity – an image of *'la France profonde'*, to quote the late President Mitterand. But depopulation is rapidly destroying the bucolic picture. In Périgord alone, the number of farmers has dwindled in 20 years from 104,000 to 32,000.

To forestall this social 'desertification' the government has encouraged farmers to be more responsible for the environment in return for subsidies. Tourism, not agriculture, however, may be the only answer. Many deserted farms have been lovingly restored by foreigners; *ferme auberges* (farm restaurants) and *tables d'hôtes* (meals in private houses) provide income for small family farms; and the summer tourist invasion guarantees a

healthy revenue for many service providers. The downside is increased pollution and small-town resources stretched to their limit. For information on how to avoid adding to this problem, see Responsible Tourism in the Facts for the Visitor chapter.

Large-scale industry is mostly limited to Bordeaux and Toulouse, although several paper factories make their presence felt elsewhere, for example at Condat in the Dordogne and Mimizan on the Atlantic Coast. Nuclear power stations loom over the landscape at Blaye (47km north of Bordeaux on the Gironde Estuary) and Golfech (21km up the Garonne from Agen).

Among projects threatening the local environment are a proposed 30,000-tonnes-per-year toxic waste incinerator at Graulhet, south-west of Albi and a nuclear waste dump near Latronquiere south-east of St-Céré. Most controversial is the E7, a proposed four-lane highway to run up Béarn's beautiful vallée d'Aspe, threatening its fragile lifestyle and France's last community of indigenous bears (see Endangered Species in the following Flora & Fauna section).

Local environmental organisations include Association 24 pour la Sauvegarde d'Environnement (☎ 05 53 46 78 17, 10 bis rue Louis Blanc, 24000 Périgueux) and two branches of Les Amis de la Terre (Friends of the Earth; ☎/fax 05 61 55 36 70, [e] midipyrenees@amisdelaterre.org, 7 rue des Novars, 31300 Toulouse; and ☎ 05 53 08 55 45, [e] amiterre@micronet.fr, 2 chemin de Maisonneuve, 24000 Périgueux).

FLORA & FAUNA
Flora

Wildflowers – especially springtime orchids – thrive in the meadows and alluvial plains of Périgord, devoted largely to cattle grazing, tobacco and maize, walnut and chestnut plantations and geese farms. Look for early purple orchids, white and narrow-leafed helleborines, greater butterfly, bee and lady orchids. Holm oaks flourish, especially in Périgord Noir.

The sparse soil of the limestone plateaus (see the Geology section earlier in this chapter) supports only stunted oak and maple, and occasional juniper shrubs and lavender. Forest plantations are mainly of beech, oak, spruce and pine, while maritime pine, cork oak, ilex, hibiscus and black cypress dominate the vast Landes forest. Along many riverbanks, poplars and willows are common (poplars were traditionally planted for a daughter's dowry). The forests' treasure of wild mushrooms is highly prized by locals (see the special Food & Wine section for details of how to enjoy this local delicacy). Many forests still bear the scars of the devastating December 1999 storms (see under Climate).

Fauna

Thanks largely to a regional passion for *la chasse* – the hunt (see Treatment of Animals under Society & Conduct later in this chapter) – there is far less fauna in many areas than you would expect. Only the network of caves is safe, and is home to millions of bats, beetles and millipedes.

One animal on the increase is the *sanglier* (wild boar). Recent annual culls (some 350,000 in 1998) have hardly dented an estimated nine-fold increase over the last 25 years. Reasons include deliberate re-stocking to keep hunters happy and falling numbers of hunters with the general rural exodus.

Animals and birds stand a better chance in the regional parks: The Parc National des Pyrénées hosts vultures and wild bears as well as thousands of lizards, and the Parc Naturel Régional du Haut-Languedoc is home to many mouflon (wild mountain sheep). The Parc Naturel Régional des Landes de Gascogne includes the marshy saltwater and freshwater Parc Ornithologique du Teich, a major nesting ground and stopover for migratory birds. Over 280 different species have been identified here, including 13 species of duck and a host of breeding species, such as purple heron, bittern, spotted crake and Savi's warbler. Migrants include white and black storks, night heron, osprey, common crane and several species of tern.

The lakes along the Côte d'Argent (especially the Étang de Cousseau) are havens for birdlife and waterfowl (as well as deer, genets, terrapins and the rarely seen otter). Such freshwater wildlife is, however, increasingly threatened by the aggressive giant Californian Bullfrog *(Rana catesbeiana)*, released as a joke in a pond near Libourne some 20 years ago and now rampant throughout the Gironde, eating indigenous frogs, fish, lizards and even some small birds.

Escaping its clutches are the many birds of prey – including black kite, goshawk and short-toed eagle – found in the forests of Périgord Noir and along the Dordogne. Other birds in the area include nightingale, melodious warbler, red-backed shrike, crag martin and middle-spotted woodpecker.

For guided bird-watching tours and other information, contact Maison de la Nature du Bassin d'Arcachon (see under Parc Naturel Régional des Landes de Gascogne in the Bordeaux, the Atlantic Coast & the Landes chapter) or the regional office of La Ligue pour la Protection des Oiseaux (LPO; ☎/fax 05 56 91 33 81, ⓔ aquitaine@lpo-birdlife.asso.fr), 3 rue de Tauzia, 33800 Bordeaux.

Endangered Species

Otters, which were once abundant in the southwest, have fallen victim to trappers. The Pyrenean ibex and several species of bats are endangered. A quarter of the fish species are also in trouble. The brown bear, 300 of whom roamed the Pyrénées in the 1930s, has fallen in number to fewer than 15. A proposed highway through the vallée d'Aspe (see Ecology & Environment earlier) could finish them off.

Some animals have returned from the

LISA BORG

Tourism and forest management are edging the brown bear perilously close to extinction.

edge of extinction thanks to re-introduction programs, including one at a private reserve called La Falaise au Vautours in Béarn's vallée d'Ossau. Alpine dwellers such as the chamois (a mountain antelope) plus the *bouquetin* (a type of ibex) were widely hunted until the founding of the Pyrénées and other national parks.

In the French Basque country (Pays Basque) a unique, tiny horse called the *pottok* is down to its last 200 (although there are many crossbreeds). Traditionally popular with smugglers and circus-owners, the sturdy pottok – which stands an average 1.25m high – is now the focus of a program (Pottok 2000) launched by l'Association Nationale du Pottok (ANAP) to establish a core of purebreds. If you want to see a pottok, head for La Maison du Pottok, in Bidarray (see The French Basque Country chapter for details) or the two-day fair of pottoks held in Espelette in January.

National & Regional Parks

Within the region covered by this book lie a section of a national park, two regional natural parks and parts of two others. For further information on the regional parks contact the Fédération des Parcs Naturels Régionaux de France (☎ 01 44 90 86 20, fax 01 45 22 70 78, e info@parcs-naturels -regionaux.tm.fr, w www.parcs-naturels -regionaux.tm.fr), 4 rue de Stockholm, 75008 Paris.

Parc National des Pyrénées This 457-sq-km park, created in 1967, spans the Hautes-Pyrénées for about 100km along the Franco-Spanish border, eastwards from Béarn's vallée d'Aspe. It's bordered by a 2060-sq-km buffer zone where controlled development is permitted. Roughly 40% of the park is in the scope of this book, in the Pyrénées-Atlantiques department. On the Spanish side is the 150-sq-km Parque Nacional de Ordesa y Monte Perdido.

The main park office (☎ 05 62 44 36 60, fax 05 62 44 36 70) is at 59 rue de Pau, 65000 Tarbes, in the Hautes-Pyrénées department. A visitor centre should have opened in Laruns by the time you read this.

Parc Naturel Régional des Landes de Gascogne This 2620-sq-km park in the Landes was founded in 1970 to protect the area's valuable pine forests, marshlands and birdlife. The flat terrain and well marked trails make this an attractive destination for cyclists. Other points of interest are the three sites of the Ecomusée de la Grande Lande: an open-air ethnological museum at Marquèze, a resin workshop in Luxey and a museum of religious heritage and popular beliefs at Moustey (see the Bordeaux, the Atlantic Coast & the Landes chapter).

Park headquarters (☎ 05 56 88 06 06, fax 05 56 88 12 72, e info@parc-landes-de -gascogne.fr) are at 22 av d'Aliénor, 33830 Belin-Béliet, 30km south-east of Arcachon. For information on species, and on guided visits by canoe, kayak or on foot, contact the Maison de la Nature du Bassin d'Arcachon (☎ 05 56 22 80 93, fax 05 56 22 69 43), rue du Port, Le Teich.

Parc Naturel Régional des Causses du Quercy This new park between Cahors and Figeac was created in 1999 and features some of the most dramatic landscapes and geology in the southwest: high limestone plateaus or causses, and deeply carved valleys, chasms and underground rivers, and stony hillsides threaded by dry-stone walls. A severely depopulated area, it nevertheless includes several big tourist attractions, notably Rocamadour and Grotte du Pech Merle (see under Lot in the Lot & Lot-et-Garonne chapter), and is particularly attractive to walkers, speleologists and cyclists.

The park's head office (☎ 05 65 24 20 50, fax 05 65 24 20 59, e pnr.quercy@wanadoo .fr) is in Le Bourg, Labastide-Murat.

Parc Naturel Régional du Haut-Languedoc Founded in 1973 to protect the natural beauty of this isolated and economically deprived region, the heavily forested, 2606-sq-km park straddles the border between the Tarn and Hérault departments (the latter in the Languedoc-Roussillon region). Highlights on the Tarn side include the Montagne Noire range south of Castres, home to mouflon and several species of eagle, and the bizarre granite outcrops of the Sidobre, north-east of Castres.

The park office (☎ 04 67 97 38 22, fax 04 67 97 38 18) is at 13 rue du Cloître, 34220 St-Pons de Thomières (Hérault).

Parc Naturel Régional du Périgord-Limousin Overlapping the departments of the Dordogne and Haute-Vienne (the latter in the Limousin region), this 1800-sq-km park was only founded in 1998. Its many lakes and marshy areas host a rich variety of birdlife, mammals (including deer, otters and bats) and numerous species of orchid. Park headquarters (☎ 05 53 60 34 65, fax 05 53 60 39 13, e perilim.perigord@wanadoo.fr) are at 24300 Abjat-sur-Bandiat (Dordogne).

GOVERNMENT & POLITICS
France is divided into 22 regions, each subdivided into departments. This book covers all of the Aquitaine region, most departments of the Midi-Pyrénées region and a corner of the Limousin region's Corrèze department. Though pre-Revolution regional names are still often used (see the boxed text 'A Muddle of Names' earlier in this chapter) each department's two-digit code is the official last word; see the boxed text 'What's Your Number?' for details.

Each region and each department has a *conseil régional/général* (elected council), with limited powers, based at the region's capital city and departmental main town. The seat of the conseil général is called a *préfecture* (prefecture) where the government's representative, the *préfet* (prefect), is based. Each department is split into smaller *arrondissements* (districts), whose main towns are *sous-préfecture* (sub-prefectures), themselves divided into *cantons* (parishes) and smaller *communes* (villages), the basic administrative unit of local government. Each commune is presided over by a *maire* (mayor) based in a *mairie* or *hôtel de ville* (town hall).

The present national government is a Socialist-led coalition of Socialists, Communists and Greens under Parti Socialiste (PS) Prime Minister, Lionel Jospin. Jospin governs in awkward *cohabitation* with the right-

What's Your Number?

These are the official codes for the departments that feature in this book. They appear as the first two digits of each department's postcodes, and as the last two numbers on all its car numberplates. If the last three digits of a town's postcode are zeros it indicates that this is a *préfecture* (prefecture).

region	department	code
Aquitaine	Dordogne	24
	Gironde	33
	Landes	40
	Lot-et-Garonne	47
	Pyrénées-Atlantiques	64
Midi-Pyrénées	Gers	32
	Haute-Garonne	31
	Lot	46
	Tarn	81
	Tarn-et-Garonne	82
Limousin	Corrèze	19

wing Gaullist president, Jacques Chirac (elected in 1995). Despite pervasive strikes (especially by SNCF) and the controversial introduction of the 35-hour working week, Jospin is currently on a high, thanks to a fast-growing economy and falling unemployment. The next presidential and legislative elections are both due in summer 2002.

Traditionally, the southwest (particularly the Dordogne) is a leftist stronghold. In the 2001 municipal elections (when the Left did poorly nationwide) six of the 10 departments covered by this book remained Socialist. Even Toulouse, a traditionally right-wing fief, only narrowly escaped falling to the Left (it elected the centre-right Philippe Douste-Blazy), though Bordeaux's mayor, the former Gaullist prime minister Alain Juppé, was comfortably re-elected.

ECONOMY
The tranquil, heavily rural southwest has some unexpected economic statistics, not least the fact that it is Europe's leading aerospace region, with all branches of the

DEPARTMENTS & PREFECTURES

aeronautics industry represented and annual sales of €3.7 billion (US$3.3 billion).

While Bordeaux is a European centre for components testing, a world leader in rocket motors and France's largest exporter of auto parts and equipment, it is rival Toulouse that captures the aeronautics limelight. Four Aérospatiale factories, responsible for Concorde, Airbus and ATR (regional transport planes), make this Europe's aeronautics capital. Also here is the National Space Center, responsible for the development of the Ariane rocket.

Of course agriculture is still a major player. Aquitaine contributes more to the national agricultural economy than any other region (11.6%), with 8% of its workforce in agriculture – almost twice the national average. Aquitaine is the world's leading producer of foie gras and *vins d'appellation d'origine contrôlée* (AOC; the highest French wine classification), and it is the leading national producer of maize, strawberries and prunes. Other southwestern specialities, such as truffles and walnuts, continue to make a major contribution, though truffle production is a fraction of what it used to be.

Midi-Pyrénées' most important products include yarn and carded wool, garlic and seeds. The Toulouse region's seed research and production labs are among France's best. Although of diminishing economic clout, fishing continues at certain places along the Atlantic Coast and the Gironde Estuary, while the modernised port of Bordeaux is a major hub on the Gironde Estuary, with six harbour sites – including the oil port and container terminal of Bordeaux-le-Verdon.

The paper industry of the heavily forested Landes is of major importance: This region is the world's leading producer of laid kraft paper, and Europe's main source of fluff pulp.

Finally, tourism is increasingly influential. Some six million tourists a year visit Aquitaine, a million of them foreigners. The service industry is the region's biggest employer and is set to grow steadily as agriculture declines.

POPULATION & PEOPLE

Southwest France is home to about five million people (a small percentage of the 59-million national population), 2.9/2.5 million of them in Aquitaine/Midi-Pyrénées. The greatest density of population – 129 per sq km – is in Gironde, though overall density is just 70 per sq km in Aquitaine and 55 per sq km in Midi-Pyrénées (the national average is 108 per sq km). Most sparsely inhabited are the Lot and Landes, with just over 30 people per sq km.

Surprisingly, though, seven out of 10 Aquitainians live in an urban environment. The two largest urban concentrations in Southwest France are in Toulouse (741,000, including the suburbs) and in Bordeaux (735,000). Toulouse is also one of France's fastest-growing cities.

Despite a rural exodus (see Ecology & Environment earlier in this chapter), the population of both Aquitaine and Midi-Pyrénées is growing steadily at 0.44% per year (the national rate is 0.37%). Between 1990 and 2020, Aquitaine's population is expected to increase by 15%, one of the biggest spurts in the country (this is especially true of the increasingly popular Atlantic Coast). As in the rest of France, the elderly of the whole region are a growing faction (15.4% are 60 or over).

The number of resident foreigners is low compared with the national average of 6.3%. For example, 2.8% are foreigners in the Dordogne, mostly from Portugal and Morocco, with a concentration of British expatriates in the Ribérac and Eymet areas. Lot-et-Garonne has one of the highest figures with 5.5% of its 305,400 residents hailing from Spain, Italy, Portugal or Morocco. Most foreigners arrived as immigrants in search of work after WWI, or during the 1950s and '60s as the French colonial empire collapsed. There appear to be few problems with racism in the region, although many French harbour hidden prejudices. In a recent nationwide poll, 20% admitted having some racist or xenophobic views.

ARTS
Literature
Medieval The most famous literary era in Southwest France was also the earliest. Between the 11th and 13th centuries, a new form of lyric poetry emerged from the feudal courts of Aquitaine, expressed in song by troubadours. These poet-musicians invented melodies in the native Langue d'Oc rather than in Latin, the literary language of the Middle Ages. They created new rhythms and poetic forms, mostly songs (accompanied on the lute) lamenting unrequited love. The earliest known troubadour was Guillaume IX (1071–1127), duke of Aquitaine.

Encouraged by royal patronage (Eleanor of Aquitaine, granddaughter of Guillaume IX, was a leading light), troubadours continued to write of chivalry and courtly love right into the 13th century when the Albigensian Crusade wreaked havoc on the region's nobility. The troubadours' legacy remained, however, and influenced medieval secular music and many later poets, including the 20th-century American Ezra Pound.

16th Century Pierre de Bourdeilles (pseudonym Brantôme), born in 1540, was a courtier and lascivious soldier of fortune

The Troubadours of the Dordogne

No wonder Henry Miller called the Dordogne 'the cradle of the poets'. It was here that some of the finest troubadour poets flourished in the 12th century – notably Arnaut Daniel (Ribérac), Elias Carels (Sarlat), Arnaut de Mareuil (Mareuil), Girault de Borneil (Excideuil) and Bertrand de Born (Hautefort).

Not all specialised in love: Bertrand de Born was notorious for bloodthirsty songs of war and biting satirical ballads (called *sirventès*), which made him as many enemies as fans. Indeed, he almost lost his life when a furious King Henry II accused him of provoking his eldest son, Henry (known as the 'Young King') into battle against his brother (Richard the Lion-Heart) and King Henry himself. It was de Born's moving lament for the Young King (who died during the conflict) that led Henry II to pardon him.

who, rather ironically, became Abbot of Brantôme. After a fall from his horse in the 1580s put a stop to his martial wanderings, he retired to the abbey and wrote two works, *Les Vies des Hommes Illustres et Grands Capitaines* (The Lives of Illustrious Men and Great Commanders) and the spicier *Les Vies des Dames Galantes* (The Lives of the Courtesans). The latter brought him fame, though many consider his enthusiastic descriptions of war and bravery superior.

The region's best-known writer had a different attitude to life: Michel Eyquem de Montaigne (1533–92) was born (and died) at Château de Montaigne near St-Émilion. A brilliant student, he was brought up speaking only Latin until he was six and was then educated by a French-speaking Scottish humanist, George Buchanan. He practised law in Bordeaux until he was 39, when, disgusted by the hypocrisy of it all and the cruelty of the Wars of Religion, he retired to the family chateau and started to write *essaies* – literally 'attempts' – a new genre which was to be his literary legacy. Montaigne's philosophy of life was, however, even more revolutionary. The true aim of life, he proclaimed, was:

> not to win, or to write books, or to gain battles and lands, but to live orderly and tranquilly. To live properly is our great and glorious masterpiece.

He put his philosophy into practice as mayor of Bordeaux, valiantly trying to reconcile Protestants and Catholics.

Montaigne's greatest friend, Étienne de la Boétie, born in Sarlat in 1530, was a skilful counsellor in the Bordeaux regional *parlement* (court of law), and a writer of sonnets. He's most famous, however, for his impassioned work *Contr'un* (literally 'Against One', better known as 'A Discourse on Voluntary Servitude'), a remarkable treatise on liberty he wrote at the age of 18 and which later influenced Jean-Jacques Rousseau. The essay's argument – that the sycophants and supporters of a tyrant are as evil and guilty as the tyrant himself – was nothing short of subversive at that time. Montaigne's moving 'Essay on Friendship', written when Boétie died at the tragically early age of 32, now tends to overshadow Boétie's work.

17th & 18th Centuries Another gently tolerant humanist followed in Montaigne's footsteps: François de Salignac de la Mothe-Fénelon (1651–1715) trained as a priest and in 1689 became tutor to Louis XIV's dull grandson, the duke of Burgundy. Some years earlier Fénelon had inherited the priory-deanery of Carennac from his uncle and it was there, tradition has it, that he wrote *Télémaque,* an educational allegory for the duke about truth and virtue, based on the legends of Odysseus and his son Telemachus. Though the novel led to nothing but trouble for him it eventually received due praise and was reprinted over 180 times.

Baron Charles Louis de Montesquieu (1689–1755) was a vine-grower, magistrate and eventually deputy president of the Bordeaux court of law. A liberal political philosopher and writer, he became best-known for his seminal *L'Esprit des Lois* (The Spirit of the Law; 1748), a masterpiece of political theory. In his day he became equally famous for satirical works such as *Lettres Persanes* (Persian Letters), mocking Parisian civilisation, social classes and the reign of Louis XIV.

19th & 20th Centuries The story of a peasant, written by a humble citizen of Périgord, is perhaps the region's most relevant work of literature. Eugène Le Roy was the son of the steward of Château de Hautefort. After a Paris education, funded by the baron of Hautefort, he joined the finance department and became a tax-collector in Montignac. A passionate republican, concerned about the hard life of his fellow Périgourdins, he briefly lost his job because of his views. By the time he took up his pen, religious tolerance and equality were declining under a new wave of ultra-royalists, powerful clergy and nobility. Published in 1899, his *Jacquou le Croquant* – recalling the Croquant peasant rebels of the 15th and 16th centuries – tells the bitter tale of a young peasant boy struggling against injustice and fighting for revenge. What makes this and Le Roy's other novels still so popular in Périgord is his lovingly detailed portrait of the region; here is a true local who knew the ways of the people and was fluent in the *patois* or local dialect which colours the text.

No literary work since then has shown such an attachment to the area, though several outstanding writers emerged during this time: André Herzog (1885–1967) lived in Périgord after WWI and wrote enthusiastically about the region under the pen-name André Maurois. François Mauriac (1885–1970), born and brought up in Bordeaux and the nearby Garonne Valley until his early 20s when he left for Paris, won the 1952 Nobel prize for Literature. Although he had little affection for his home town, he loved the Landes forests, which feature in his novels *Le Mystère Fronenac* (set in St-Symphorien)

and, more oppressively, in *Thérèse Desqueyroux*. One of the Basque country's most famous poets and novelists is also from this era: Francis Jammes (1868–1938) who lived many years in Orthez (and died in Hasparren), wrote a dozen books, including *Clara d'Ellébeuse*.

As for *Cyrano de Bergerac* – Edmond Rostand's sad and successful 1897 verse play about a large-nosed swordsman and poet – it actually has little to do with the town of Bergerac. Even his real, 17th-century namesake, one Savinien de Cyrano de Bergerac, is believed to have come from near Paris and only visited Bergerac.

Architecture
Prehistoric France's earliest monuments are stone megaliths erected in Neolithic times (from about 4000 to 2400 BC), ranging from simple menhirs (huge standing stones) to dolmens (several vertical stones topped by a horizontal slab). There are several striking examples in the Lot (eg, at Gramat, Cajarc and Puy l'Evêque). The Pierre de Grimann, near Sabres, is the Landes' most famous dolmen, while the Dolmen du Blanc, south of Beaumont in the Dordogne, is still an eerily impressive sight.

Gallo-Roman Southwest France's richest Gallo-Roman remains are in the two main oppida of the time: Vesunna (now Périgueux), elegant capital of the Gallic Petrocorii tribe, and Burdigala (Bordeaux), capital of Aquitania.

Remains at Vesunna include stones from its amphitheatre, part of a defensive wall and a tower from a temple dedicated to the goddess of the city. In Bordeaux (which still has two main Gallo-Roman roads, rue Ste-Catherine and rue de la Porte Dijeaux), the most impressive Roman site is the Palais Gallien, the ruins of a huge 3rd-century amphitheatre. The Musée d'Aquitaine has a superb collection of mosaics, steles and amphora, decorated ceramics and some striking statues. Another noteworthy site is the remains of a 4th-century Roman aristocrat's luxurious country home, at Séviac near Montréal (Gers).

Romanesque A religious and economic revival in the 11th century saw much fine construction in the Romanesque style, so called because of the adoption of features such as vaulting and round arches from Gallo-Roman architecture. Romanesque buildings typically have heavy walls, few windows and a simplicity of ornamentation bordering on the austere.

Christianity had been fostered in Périgord in the 9th century by Charlemagne who supported the Benedictines' new monasteries (such as at Sarlat and Brantôme). In the 11th to 13th centuries such religious orders flourished, building churches and abbeys throughout the region, for example at Belvès, Périgueux, Moissac and St-Sever (Benedictine); Cadouin (Cistercian); Sergeac (Knights Templar); St-Cyprien, St-Amand de Coly and St-Jean de Côle (Augustinian). The surging popularity of the pilgrimage to Santiago de Compostela – and the financial benefits from catering for the thousands of pilgrims – generated many grand Romanesque projects, notably Toulouse's Basilique St-Sernin, Europe's largest Romanesque church.

Certain features make Périgordian Romanesque distinctive, particularly the use of a Byzantine dome for the vaulting. Believed to be an influence brought back from the crusades, it can be seen on over 60 churches in the region and is particularly impressive in Périgueux's Cathédrale St-Front (with five domes over a Greek-cross plan) and Souillac's Église Ste-Marie. Many churches in northern Périgord are built of golden-hued sandstone and roofed with slabs of the region's limestone. One of the finest of these is at St-Léon-sur-Vézère, with a perfect harmony of radiating chapels, arcade bell tower and domed transept.

Elsewhere in the southwest, for example at Martel and Moissac, the Languedoc school of sculpture inspired flamboyant sculptural decorations (see Sculpture later in this section). In a reflection of the uncertainty of the times, several churches (notably St-Amand de Coly in the Dordogne) are more fortress than church, exhibiting Romanesque austerity at its most extreme.

The region's best secular Romanesque architecture is represented by parts of various castles, notably Beynac and Biron, Bourdeilles and Castelnaud.

Gothic In the 12th to 15th centuries the southwest continued to develop its own architectural styles, notably the so-called Southern Gothic. In churches this was distinguished by a single wide nave with no transept, catering to a post-Albigensian trend of preaching to vast congregations, including pilgrims en route to Santiago de Compostela.

The only outstanding Northern Gothic monument in the region is Bayonne's Cathédrale Ste-Marie, with typical radiating chapels and a long spacious nave. The more common Languedoc (or Toulouse) style favoured the use of brick and was also distinguished by a wide *clocher-mur* (literally 'bell-wall') on the facade, most impressively on Toulouse's Basilique St-Sernin. Albi's massive Cathédrale Ste-Cécile is one of the southwest's best representatives of Southern Gothic with its single nave, dark and huge, and buttresses sheltering a dozen chapels.

Several striking Gothic monuments from the 15th century are in Bordeaux, including the Basilique St-Michel's hexagonal belfry (Tour St Michel). The region also has many castles with Gothic features and decorated town houses such as Figeac's Hôtel de la Monnaie and Martel's Hôtel de la Raymondie.

Cahors' Pont Valentré, built in the mid-14th century, is the most striking example of the region's military architecture, while the most outstanding secular architecture from this era is that of the bastides (see the special section) that first appeared in the 13th century.

Renaissance The Renaissance, which started in Italy in the early 15th century, aimed for a rebirth of classical Greek and Roman culture. In the boom years following the end of the Hundred Years' War, the southwest embraced the new style enthusiastically.

[continued on page 36]

Bastides & Chateaux

JULIA WILKINSON

INGRID RODDIS

Title page: The facade of Château des Milandes, Périgord Noir, once home to the colourful Josephine Baker. (Photograph: Sally Dillon)

Top: The dominating ruin of Château de Bonaguil, west of Cahors

Bottom: Medieval bastide, Larressingle

BASTIDES & CHATEAUX

Bastides

Southwest France isn't just famous for its food and wine. Its turbulent medieval history spurred the development of dozens of planned, fortified towns known as *bastides*. Even today, these are remarkable for their aesthetic appeal and fine design – superb examples of town planning.

During the 11th and 12th centuries country life for the average villager was no bed of roses. Lucky were those who lived in the few purpose-built, fortified rural towns that existed at the time – *sauvetés* or *sauveterres* (sanctuary-towns, usually founded by ecclesiastical officials) and *castelnaus* (villages that grew up around the chateaux of local lords). Most people were stuck in isolated hamlets or roamed the countryside in search of work. Brigands created a sense of insecurity everywhere except in the few big towns, notably Albi, Auch and Toulouse. Survival – let alone economic development – was a hazardous affair.

The first bastides (from the Occitan *bastida*, literally a group of buildings) appeared in the mid-13th century around Albi and Toulouse, probably in response to the Albigensian Crusade and a general urge for public order. Another likely catalyst was that *seigneurs* (local lords) saw fortified 'new towns' – typically big enough for 2000 people – as a way to attract the countryside's more-or-less rootless population with promises of work and stability, thus firming up their own power bases and, into the bargain, generating a regular revenue from taxes and rent.

These seigneurs often formed partnerships with the other powerful landowning body of the time – the Church, whose abbeys granted them land to build their bastides, in return for a cut of the revenues. The Cistercians in particular were frequent co-founders. This underlying economic motive was unprecedented for towns at this time.

Cordes-sur-Ciel, near Albi, claims to be the earliest bastide, founded in 1222 by the count of Toulouse. Within 150 years there were over 300 of these rigidly-planned towns across the southwest. Though most were built for commercial reasons, many soon took on military importance. Indeed one of their leading proponents, Edward I of England, built bastides such as Beaumont and Monpazier specifically to counter the French threat in the Hundred Years' War – including Villeréal and Monflanquin, founded by the indefatigable French bastide-builder, Alphonse de Poitiers, third son of Louis VIII. Some bastides, such as Domme, were repeatedly refortified with ramparts, gateways and walls. Bastides were fought over and changed hands frequently in the war.

These towns were built on empty sites, cleared forest or in places where a small community already existed. They always followed a grid pattern, usually square or rectangular (as at Monpazier or Montauban), although the local topography sometimes allowed or demanded an oval or circular variation (as at Monflanquin). Their plans were set forth in a charter, together with regulations on the management and taxation of the town. The chessboard design made them easy to administer, creating a simple fiscal map for the tax-collector.

The design of bastides implied an unprecedented openness to trade. Many had especially wide streets (for carts), criss-crossed by narrow pedestrian streets that led out to the fields. There was always a market square or *place* in the centre, often with a timber-roofed *halle* where weekly markets took place (larger annual fairs were usually held on common land outside the bastide). Merchants later erected *cornières* (covered, arcaded passageways) for their shops around the market place. There were designated plots for houses and gardens, with allotments outside the town for further cultivation such as vines (cereal crops were grown in larger plots in the surrounding countryside).

The entire town was enclosed within gated walls. During the war-torn 14th century, many bastides erected stronger defensive walls and ramparts. The church – no longer always at the centre of the settlement since commerce was now the pivot of life – was also often fortified.

To entice people into these newfangled towns, they were offered certain privileges, including protection in times of attack, exemption from military service, and various tax breaks (the name of one bastide, Villefranche, comes from *ville franche de taxes ordinaires*, or 'town free of ordinary taxes'). Regular market fairs were another major financial attraction. Peasants were often lured from rival seigneurs' lands with promises of freedom and the protection of a new, powerful master. Some seigneurs had to build bastides just to keep their labour force: Cancon, founded in 1255, was one such bastide.

In return, new arrivals had to build their houses – one plot per family – within a set time and pay their rents to a bailiff who also dispensed justice. In some places, such as Libourne, settlers were recruited by force, but mostly bastides grew naturally. Founders of course saw to it that they profited from the arrangement – not only from the rents levied but also from various tolls: Even passing visitors were charged.

Some bastides were obliterated in the Hundred Years' War and the Wars of Religion, and some decimated by plague or famine in the 14th century, but many survive to this day, either grown into cities (eg, Villeneuve-sur-Lot, Libourne and Montauban), or surviving in elegant simplicity (eg, Domme, Monpazier, Monflanquin and the unusual circular Fourcès). The region has several museums devoted to the bastide era, including one at Monflanquin (described in the Lot chapter) and another at Labastide d'Armagnac (see the Gers chapter).

JANE SMITH

Left: Intimate, arcaded passageways are a common feature of bastide market squares.

Chateaux

Southwest France isn't in the same league as the Loire Valley when it comes to pretty chateaux, but it does have many impressive fortified chateaux, thanks to the military necessities of the Albigensian Crusade, the Hundred Years' War and the Wars of Religion. The Dordogne department boasts about its '1001 chateaux' (although many of these are mere manor houses or fortified farmhouses with 'chateau' names).

Some of the earliest constructions, from the 12th and 13th centuries, consisted largely of tall, fortified towers, as at the now-ruined Château de Commarque (Dordogne). From the 14th century onwards, chateaux began acquiring sophisticated defences, including imposing keeps (as at Châteaux de Beynac and Bourdeilles, in the Dordogne), barbicans and portcullises, ramparts and towers, double-perimeter walls and massive gateways. The incredibly well fortified Castelnau-Bretenoux (Lot) is a prime example, while Château de Biron (Dordogne) has a bloody history to go with all its fortifications. Some, such as Château de Bonaguil (Lot), although fortified to the hilt, never saw conflict, but many in the Osse Valley (Gers) were ruined from the constant battles.

The 16th century introduced graceful Renaissance architecture to the region. One of France's earliest examples of the style is an immense wing of the Château de Gramont (Gers). But times were still troubled, largely thanks to the Wars of Religion, so even the finest Renaissance chateaux – some of them, like Puyguilhem and Jumilhac-le-Grand (Dordogne) and Montal (Lot) reminiscent of the most elegant Loire versions – still had their arrow-slits and barbicans. For some chateaux owners, a keep or portcullis was little more than a status symbol; the imposing Hautefort (Dordogne) is a fine example.

Many of the region's chateaux have been fiddled with so often during their lifetimes that no specific style can be attached to them: Château de Biron, first built in the 11th century, has everything from a redesigned medieval keep to a Renaissance chapel, while Les Châteaux de Bruniquel (Tarn-et-Garonne) is an entire complex of castles and eras, from the 13th to 19th centuries. Some, like Château de Cassaigne (Gers), were built, and remain, as little more than country houses. Others are now famous more for their owners than their architecture – for example, the Château des Milandes (Dordogne), once the home of music-hall star Josephine Baker. A few, like Château d'Abbadie near Hendaye (French Basque country), are actually neo-Gothic creations from the 1860s.

Lastly there are the chateaux that don't exist at all. A good many of the resonant chateaux names on the region's prestigious wine labels refer simply to the estate where the wine is produced or the facilities where it's aged – a centuries-old convention. The Médoc *does* have some genuine and quite fabulous private chateaux, though the most you'll ever see of them is their wine cellars. One exception is the Château de Monbazillac (Dordogne), where you can taste its famous sweet, rich wine *and* look in on a fine 16th-century chateau.

[continued from page 32]

The most striking examples of civil Renaissance architecture are the beautiful mansions built by the wealthy textile and woad merchants of Toulouse and Albi in the mid-15th to mid-16th centuries – for example Albi's Hôtel de Reynès and Toulouse's Hôtel d'Assézat. In the Dordogne, similar Renaissance flourishes are best seen in Périgueux's old town and in Sarlat (eg, the Hôtel de Malleville and the Maison de la Boétie). Other sites with Renaissance touches include the graceful 16th-century chateaux of Montal and Puyguilhem, typical of chateaux in the Loire Valley.

An ecclesiastical Renaissance masterpiece is the stained glass and the carved oak choir stalls of Auch's Cathédrale Ste-Marie.

Baroque & Classical During the baroque period, from the end of the 16th century to the late 18th century, architects of the region followed Parisian models, introducing few original touches. Bordeaux, which underwent major urban redevelopment in the 18th century, has some of the finest work from this era, including the Église Notre Dame.

Bordeaux also best represents the style of 18th-century classical architecture, reflecting the Louis XVI style inspired by the art of antiquity. The city's Grand Théâtre is one of France's finest classical buildings. Also impressive is the restored Palais de la Bourse (Stock Exchange). Among the region's chateaux, Hautefort best exemplifies the classical style, merging harmoniously with Renaissance features, while in the Basque country churches are distinguished by their massive, gabled or tiered belfries.

19th & 20th Century Neoclassical architecture, which remained in vogue from about 1740 to the early 19th century, is demonstrated by many of the Gironde wine country's *chartreuses* (small chateaux). The 19th-century popularity of seaside resorts such as Arcachon, Biarritz and Hendaye led to an outburst of more whimsical luxury villas, casinos and spas, copying styles from almost every era and European country. It was also in this region (especially in Biarritz and Dax), that the Art Deco movement was taken up most enthusiastically.

Many ecclesiastical projects that took place in the late 19th century were restorations – often controversial – of ancient monuments. Paul Abadie's Second Empire-style restoration (more a complete rebuilding) of the once-Romanesque Cathédrale St-Front in Périgueux still arouses passionate indignation. Contemporary projects, such as Bordeaux's Cité Mondiale business centre and the concrete glass-and-steel Meriadeck District Administrative Centre, have also failed to win general approval.

Vernacular Architecture Traditional domestic architecture is very distinctive in the southwest. On the limestone plateaus of the Lot, the white limestone houses have thick walls to protect against the wind while in the valleys, houses often feature towers and a *cave* (an underground cellar) traditionally used for cattle and nowadays mostly used for storing wine and produce. In the Dordogne (especially Périgord Noir) the golden limestone houses have steeply pitched roofs covered with *lauzes* (limestone slabs), whereas typical houses in the Toulouse and Albi areas are nearly always made of brick and traditionally plastered with pink stucco, their gently sloping roofs covered in brick tiles. *Les maisons labourdines,* the large, traditional half-timbered wood and stone houses of the Basque country, have tiled or slate roofs and an extensive porch, and the wooden beams are painted red or blue.

Throughout the region you'll come across charming *pigeonniers* (dovecotes), often free-standing, some resting on stone columns. Originally used as much for collecting droppings (a valuable manure) as for housing the pigeons themselves, they were also a status symbol: Landowners had to buy the right to keep pigeons.

More mysterious are small, round, drystone huts called *bories, cabanes* or *gariottes,* usually tucked away in isolated fields. They're believed to have been used for storage (as they still are today) but no-one knows quite when they first appeared.

The Painted Caves of the Southwest

There are more prehistoric decorated caves in Southwest France than anywhere else in the world, over a hundred of them, mostly concentrated in the Vézère and Lot Valleys. The extraordinary paintings of horses and reindeer, buffalo, bison and mammoth found in these caves date from between 35,000 and 10,000 BC and were discovered largely in the late 19th to mid-20th century. They are to be found most famously in Lascaux (Montignac), Font de Gaume (Les Eyzies), Pech Merle (Cabrerets), Rouffignac and Cougnac (Gourdon). Even now, new sites are being discovered. In 1998 and 1999 extraordinary engravings of animals and – most unusually – women, were revealed in caves at Montcabrier (near Cahors) and Faycelles (near Figeac; both in the Lot).

In the early days of archaeology, such cave art was thought to be fake, but in 1895, the Grotte de la Mouthe (Les Eyzies) was discovered, which contained not only paintings and engravings, but also a prehistoric lantern. This forced sceptics to accept that Upper Palaeolithic *Homo sapiens sapiens* – particularly Cro-Magnons of the Magdalenian period (15,000 to 9000 BC) – had indeed produced these subtle and beautiful works, full of symbolism and three-dimensional effects.

Just why is this area so blessed with prehistoric art? And why did the Cro-Magnons retreat into these dark recesses and tunnels to paint (they never lived in these galleries)? The area's many limestone shelters and caves were certainly ideal sites (and preserved the art for millennia afterwards). Perhaps, too, increasing pressure on resources in this Late Ice Age environment (a surge in population growth leading to more intensive hunting by smaller groups of hunters) made these people look towards more ritual and creative approaches to finding food. Certainly, much of the most striking cave art is about hunting animals.

However, since only about 15% of the works depict wounded animals, many art historians argue that these paintings must have had other purposes than hunting magic – perhaps to initiate children into adulthood (prehistoric adolescent footprints are still visible in Pech Merle), or as models for human social groups centred on pregnant women (there are many pregnant horses and bison to be seen). Perhaps the work helped forge alliances between far-flung tribes when they met for ceremonial gatherings (hundreds of ornaments discovered near Les Eyzies suggest such meetings). Was it a way to record stories and beliefs about man and nature? Or, dare one ask, was it simply for the pleasure of painting?

Theories abound, but there's no question about the breathtaking impact of the art itself, especially when seen *in situ* (as at Pech Merle and Font de Gaume, among the few painted caves still open to the public). The paintings are coloured red, brown or yellow (from ochres of iron oxide) or black (from manganese dioxide). These natural pigments were probably applied by the dim light of oil lamps with fingers, feathers or brushes, or even blown through a tube, as suggested by the early handprints at Pech Merle. Most impressive is the way the natural contours of the rock are often used to depict the shape of an animal – a protruding belly or sweeping hump, or the length of a mammoth's tusk. Several paintings, perhaps produced thousands of years apart, may overlap. Many combine engraving with painting.

With good reason, the finest of all the area's grottoes is the most famous: the 'Hall of Bulls' at Lascaux (now partly recreated in the replica Lascaux II), where four huge bulls rampage through a fantastic frieze of horses, stags, ox and deer. This, said Henri Breuil, the local priest and art historian who discovered many of the caves, is 'the Sistine Chapel of prehistoric art' (for more information on the Lascaux caves see under Montignac in the Dordogne chapter).

Painting

Prehistoric Southwest France's finest and unique contributions to the arts are the extraordinary prehistoric paintings, discovered in the 20th century, in the limestone caves of the Dordogne and the Lot (see the boxed text).

Medieval & Later Frescoes and murals are the most remarkable artworks of this period, notably in Cahors' Cathédrale St-Étienne, whose west dome is covered with frescoes from the 14th century. Many of the region's small, Romanesque churches also have fine frescoes, notably the splendid 15th-century frescoes at Allemans du Dropt near Duras. The Hundred Years' War and Wars of Religion seriously hampered the development of French painting in the region. Most French Renaissance painters copied Italian models with little passion or inspiration.

19th Century Two big names stand out in this century – Henri de Toulouse-Lautrec and Jean-Dominique-Auguste Ingres. They couldn't have been more different. Ingres was born in 1780 in Montauban, the son of a painter and musician. From an early age he produced perfectly executed portraits and huge neoclassical works, many of them commissioned by Napoleon. Criticised first for his sensual nudes and later for what was seen as an over-meticulous, stuffy approach, it's his skill as a draughtsman and his intimate, daring portraits that are particularly recognised today.

Toulouse-Lautrec was born in Albi in 1864, to a French count and his German wife. He moved to Paris when he was 18 and flung himself with such enthusiasm into the city's debauched low life that by the age of 37 he was dead, of alcoholism and syphilis. By then he was already famous for his lithographs and posters depicting bars and nightclubs. His hometown never featured in his work, though he often visited Arcachon (where he had a seaside villa and shocked the neighbours by swimming naked in the sea) and the nearby family home, the Château de Malromé, where he died in 1901.

Both home towns have good museums that are dedicated to the work of their prodigal sons – the Musée Toulouse-Lautrec in Albi and the Musée Ingres in Montauban.

20th Century French painting in the 20th century has been characterised by a bewildering diversity of styles, including fauvism and cubism, expressionism and surrealism. While the southwest produced no stars in these genres (though André Lothe produced good cubist-figurative works), it did become home to a leading painter-turned-tapestry maker, Jean Lurçat (see the boxed text in the Lot chapter).

The region has several good museums of 20th-century and contemporary art, notably Bordeaux's Musée d'Art Contemporain, the Maison des Arts Georges Pompidou in Cajarc and the Musée Despiau-Wlérick in Mont de Marsan (for more information on this see the following Sculpture section).

Sculpture

At the end of the 11th century, sculptors began to decorate the portals, capitals, altars and fonts of Romanesque churches, illustrating Bible stories, moral tales and the lives of the saints for the illiterate. The most outstanding examples are found in Moissac and Toulouse, both centres of Romanesque sculpture that came to influence the region as a whole. The richly decorated tympana, cloisters and doorway of Moissac's abbey and Toulouse's Basilique St-Sernin gave birth to other work, notably in churches at Carennac, Martel, Beaulieu-sur-Dordogne and Cahors in the Lot. Striking, too, is the 12th-century portal of Souillac's Église Ste-Marie, especially its famously stylised figure of the prophet Isaiah, so alive it looks as if he's dancing. A fine collection of the works of the Toulouse school is displayed in Toulouse's Musée des Augustins.

As well as adorning churches, sculpture in the following centuries was commissioned for the tombs of the nobility (eg, in the church at Espagnac Ste-Eulalie) and for life-size representations of biblical scenes (as in the cloisters of Carennac's Église St-Pierre).

The Renaissance era is best exemplified by the delicate reliefs on the facade of the Château de Montal and on its fantastic stairway. The elaborately decorated doorways of the Hôtel d'Assézat in Toulouse reflect the revival of interest in stone sculpture on secular buildings at this time.

The region's two leading sculptors of the 19th and 20th centuries were students of Rodin: Émile Antoine Bourdelle (1861–1929), from Montauban, produced similarly powerful busts and figures, and Charles

Despiau (1874–1946), from Mont de Marsan, created a more original style, especially in his nudes and female busts. Robert Wlérik (1882–1944), also from Mont de Marsan, became famous for his work on the equestrian statue of Maréchal Foch in Paris. The Musée Despiau-Wlérick in Mont de Marsan is the only one in France devoted to modern figurative sculpture and displays works by over a hundred artists.

Another unusual museum, Musée Zadkine in the remote village of Les Arques (between Gourdon and Puy l'Evêque in the Lot) houses works by the Cubist sculptor, Ossip Zadkine, who lived here in the 1930s.

Music

Although the region has only produced one musical giant – composer Maurice Ravel (1875–1937) who was born in the Basque country's Ciboure – it does host a vibrant musical scene.

Toulouse's Orchestre National du Capitole, based at La Halle aux Grains, is a 104-strong national orchestra that performs some 40 concerts a year in Toulouse plus 15 in the region. In Bordeaux, the 117-strong Orchestre National Bordeaux Aquitaine, based at the Grand Théâtre, is a vital part of the city's musical life. (Check the Web site, W www.opera-bordeaux.com, for details of their concerts plus performances by the Opéra de Bordeaux). A highly regarded classical music festival in the region is the Festival du Périgord Noir in August.

There are dozens of more unusual groups, from the amateur Tarbes-based Mandolines de Bigorre, or the Castres-based La Saltarelle (who perform Renaissance songs, dance and music), to the various outfits performing traditional Basque music at festivals such as Musique en Côte Basque in St-Jean de Luz in August. Jazz is big in the region, too (see the boxed text 'Jazz Bonanza' in the Facts for the Visitor chapter for details of festivals). Bordelaise jazz pianist, Pierre Buzon, and Toulouse-based Zanbla are names to watch, the latter often performing a fusion of jazz, Latin rhythms and a *soupçon de swing*.

On the rock scene, you can choose from the hard rock of Toulouse's Black Swan, the pop-influenced Calc in Bordeaux or the pop-rock sounds of Zed from Auch.

Theatre, Dance & Cinema

In addition to highbrow groups such as Théâtre National Bordeaux-Aquitaine, you can catch some great street theatre in the region – Toulouse-based 12 Balles dans la Peau have been popping up all over the place since 1985, while Bordeaux-based Le Théâtre du Chapeau specialises in clowning around. Theatre festivals abound: Le Festival de Pau (late June) presents everything from comedy to Brecht, while Sarlat's Festival des Jeux du Théâtre (late July) is an open-air event that has been going strong for 50 years. One of the most appealing events is the Festival International du Mime Actuel, held in Périgueux (early August).

Heavyweight dance companies include the Biarritz-based Centre Chorégraphique National/Ballet, established in 1998. For some distinctive traditional dances, check out groups such as Pau-based Menestrèrs Gascons or Les Tortues Véloces from Langoiran (Gironde) whose dancers and musicians can demonstrate a perfect *rondeau* or *bourrée*. Some of the finest Basque music and dance is on display during Biarritz's Fête Bi Harriz Lau Xori (late March).

The region's only claim to cinematic fame is that Cadouin was the birthplace of the late-19th-century cinematographer, Louis Delluc. The Oscar-award-winning *Chocolat,* based on the novel by Joanne Harris, which was set in Gascogny (see Books in Facts for the Visitor chapter), was actually filmed in Burgundy because the director found the Gascon locations 'too scenic and pretty'. But the recent Hollywood blockbuster, *The Musketeer,* featuring Catherine Deneuve, *was* shot in the area, making use of various chateaux in the Midi-Pyrénées. Two major regional film festivals are the Festival du Film, held during early November in Sarlat, and the Festival de Cinéma au Féminin held in Arcachon in late September.

SOCIETY & CONDUCT
Traditional Culture
Throughout the region, passion for football and rugby are eroding support for the traditional games of *pelote* and *boules,* although in the French Basque country and the Landes there's still considerable support for their unique versions of the *corrida* and *les courses landaises* (bullfighting). For more information on traditional Basque sports, see Spectator Sports in the Facts for the Visitor chapter. The stilt-walking shepherds of the Landes (see the boxed text 'On Your Stilts' in the Bordeaux, the Atlantic Coast & the Landes chapter) are long gone, but some 20 folklore groups keep the practice alive, many appearing at festivals where the region's *bandas* (traditional brass bands) also perform.

Many rural traditions quietly continue everywhere, including celebratory dinners (invariably for the menfolk) held at the end of the fruit and grape harvests and at the close of the hunting season. During the winter truffle and foie gras season, markets are at their traditional best.

Dos & Don'ts
To generalise somewhat rashly, the River Garonne is the Mason-Dixon Line of social conduct, with more reserve to the north and more gusto to the south. Influenced perhaps by centuries of English rule, the folk of Périgord and Quercy – no-one would dream of identifying themselves by the modern department names such as Dordogne and Lot – exhibit almost courtly politeness and hospitality. South of the Garonne there is considerable pride in being a real 'Gascon' – honest, brave, down-to-earth, with a passionate *joie de vivre*. The Basques have an even stronger cultural identity, manifest in their own language, traditions and lingering desire for independence.

Some historical understanding is an important prerequisite to correct small-talk in Southwest France. Everyone laughs about how the English are conquering Aquitaine for a second time by buying up old farmhouses as holiday homes, but the rural depopulation and loss of land can be sensitive issues. Among the elderly you will still find

considerable emotion about WWII. This was, after all, one of the strongest bastions of the Résistance and the scene of many Nazi atrocities at the war's end.

Talk about food and wine, however, and you're on safe ground everywhere in this gourmand heartland. You may find wine connoisseurs a little stuffy in Bordeaux but there's no snobbery in the hinterland, where the locals often finish their soup by splashing in some house red wine, a practice known as *chabrol*. If you're invited to aperitifs in a local home, you'll be pressed to drink – and drink, and drink. And if you're lucky enough to be invited to a Périgordian home for dinner, you'll need to fast beforehand to get through the dozen courses. A suitable gift for such occasions is a bunch of flowers (but not chrysanthemums, which are only brought to cemeteries).

Women should expect lots of kisses on greeting country folk – as many as four quick pecks (not lingering, slurpy kisses) may be exchanged among family or friends, starting with the right cheek. In cities, two tends to be the norm. Men – and women if they are strangers – nearly always exchange handshakes, though it's cool for young women to exchange kisses even with strangers. Little kids always give – and get – kisses.

Even if you're not on kissing terms, it's essential to greet all and sundry with a *Bonjour, monsieur/madame/mademoiselle.* French people are delightfully cordial to one another and will typically acknowledge everyone at large with a *bonjour* or a *m'sieur/m'dame* when walking into a shop or cafe, and with a *merci, monsieur..., au revoir* when leaving. Both *s'il vous plait* and *merci* (please and thank you) should be used liberally if you want to give a good impression of your foreign manners.

Treatment of Animals
Hunting Traditions in the southwest are among the strongest in the country, with *la chasse* (the hunt) considered a right of the common man entrenched since the Revolution. Out of the country's 1.5 million hunters, Gironde boasts the largest number of any department – over 60,000, many of

whom head for the woods with their dogs as soon as the hunting season opens.

Others lie in wait in specially constructed hides for migratory birds to pass overhead. Especially popular are *tourterelle* (turtle-doves), which are illegally hunted (especially in the Médoc) from early May, and *palombes* (wood-pigeons), which are a particular passion in northern Aquitaine in October. Box and clap nets are used throughout Aquitaine to catch these as well as skylarks. An estimated 50,000 ortolan buntings and some 350,000 chaffinches and bramblings are illegally trapped each year in the region. Some 24 migratory species of rare or declining status are annually at risk.

Until 2000, the hunters had things pretty much their own way, with a hunting season lasting longer than anywhere else in the EU (from 14 July to 28 February) and an increasingly militant 1.6-million-strong hunting lobby with its own political party, the Chasse Pech Nature Tradition, which won 7% of the vote in the 1999 European elections. In April 2000, however, a bill was finally introduced to bring the migratory bird-hunting season in line with EU directives, restricting it to 1 September through until 31 January. Inevitably, the pro-hunting lobby is incensed, although environmentalists argue that the law still does not go far enough on other issues to meet EU requirements.

Anti-hunting campaigns continue to be active throughout France, chiefly by the Rassemblement des Opposants à la Chasse (ROC; ☎ 01 43 36 04 72, or locally ☎ 05 53 03 24 55, e infos@roc.asso.fr, w www.roc.asso.fr) and also La Ligue pour la Protection des Oiseaux (LPO; see Flora & Fauna earlier in this chapter for contact details).

Foie Gras The issue of *le gavage* – the force-feeding of geese to make foie gras – also rouses strong feelings, though mostly among foreign visitors horrified at the sight of a funnel being thrust down a goose's neck. However, foie gras is one of the region's major income-earners and unlikely to be banned on the basis of foreign sensitivities.

Geese are force-fed on boiled maize or corn three times daily for three weeks to increase the quality and size of their livers to a massive 1.3kg. Ducks are also subjected to the practice. Battery farming is used in many cases, though the best foie gras comes from free-range geese. See the special Food & Wine section for more background information.

Bullfighting Spanish-style bullfighting is at its most popular in the Landes and the Gers, where fights take place regularly during the July to September season. There appear to be few protesters or anti-bullfighting movements, though the gentler bull-running competition called *les courses landaises* attracts a sizable following too. See Spectator Sports in the Facts for the Visitor chapter for more details.

RELIGION

Some 80% of French people identify themselves as Catholic but, though most have been baptised, relatively few attend church. This is certainly true in the southwest, where you'll invariably find only the elderly attending mass in village churches.

There's also a strong Protestant following here, especially in Béarn, where the first of France's Protestant communities appeared in the 1530s, encouraged by its staunchly Protestant ruler, Jeanne d'Albret. The 1598 Edict of Nantes decreeing religious tolerance put an official end to the Wars of Religion that had torn the region apart, but Catholic–Protestant hostilities still simmered and, when the edict was revoked in 1685, some 300,000 Protestants fled out of France, founding major communities in England, Prussia, the Netherlands and North America.

Nationally some 1.8% of French people are Protestant. Orthez, a former capital of Béarn, has an unusually high figure (10% of the population), while the communities of some isolated villages in the Ossau and Aspe Valleys are as much as 50% Protestant. The French refer to a Protestant church as a *temple,* and Protestants are apt to be offended if you call their church an *église.* See the Béarn chapter for details about Orthez's good

The Pilgrims of St-Jacques

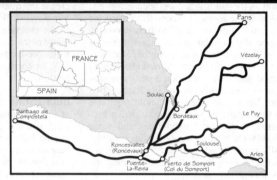

It all began two thousand years ago, when King Herod beheaded James the Great, making him the first apostle to be martyred for his beliefs. A legend grew that he had been buried on the coast of Galicia in north-western Spain. As luck would have it, his tomb was 'discovered' in the early 9th century just when the flagging Christian forces of Spain needed some help against the Moors; St James (Santiago in Spanish) proved his worth by appearing on a white horse at the battle of Clavijo in 844, helping to defeat the Moors.

A church was built on the site of his tomb, the town of Compostela grew around it and within a few years the first pilgrims arrived at this *campus stelae in finis terrae* (field of stars at the world's end). By the Middle Ages, the trickle had turned into a flood of two million visitors per year.

In France the Jacquets, as the pilgrims were called (from Jacques, the French name for James), used a network of routes – four main ones and various branches like the coastal route from Soulac – which converged at Pyrénéan passes including Roncevaux and Col du Somport. The journey evolved into a series of mini-pilgrimages taking weeks or months, with detours to other shrines en route.

New churches were built to cater for (and skim money from) the passing faithful, and hospices and hostels were established by the Benedictine monks of Cluny, the Knights' Templars and the Hospitallers of St John. In the 12th century, the first-ever tourist guide appeared, the *Codex Calixtinus*, written in Latin by a French monk to clue pilgrims in on the best holy spots and hostels, and on avoiding the 'barbarous Basques'. It was, of course, a bestseller.

Thanks to the Wars of Religion and to the more ambitious ideals of the Renaissance, the popularity of the pilgrimage began to wane by the 17th century, but today its popularity is again on the rise, with tens of thousands making it over the Pyrénées to Santiago de Compostela each year. Unesco has designated the whole route a World Heritage Site, with 69 monuments currently listed, of which 50 are in France and 33 within the scope of this book. Tourist boards now market the routes (Aquitaine has the lion's share) and walkers' topoguides exist for each section of the route.

For further information, check the Web site of Les Amis de St-Jacques, W www.amis-st-jacques.org, which lists numerous regional associations including those in Southwest France. In the UK, the Confraternity of St James (☎ 020-7403 4500, fax 7407 1468, W www.csj.org.uk, 1 Talbot Yard, Borough High St, London SE1 1YP), holds seminars and publishes a useful guide to the route. Among many outfits organising pilgrimage walks is La Pèlerine (☎ 04 66 69 60 87, fax 04 66 69 60 90, e pelerine.randonnee@wanadoo.fr, W www.lapelerine.doc), Romagnac F, 43580 St-Vénérand.

Musée du Protestantisme Béarnais. There is also a small Musée du Protestantisme en Haute-Languedoc in Ferrières (Tarn).

Bordeaux, Toulouse and some larger towns have small Muslim and Jewish communities. Islam is France's second religion, with about four million adherents nationally. France's 650,000-strong Jewish community is Europe's largest. Above the Périgord Noir village of St-Léon-sur-Vézère is a well established Tibetan Buddhist centre (with resident Tibetan monks), which attracts many visitors and has even hosted a visit by the Dalai Lama (see the boxed text 'Meditation on the Côte de Jor' in the Dordogne chapter).

LANGUAGE

French is one of the great languages of the world; a language of society, culture and diplomacy. Being able to speak some French will broaden your travel experience and ensure you are treated with great appreciation. It is the mother tongue of about 75 million people around the world. The total number of French speakers, including those who use it as a second language, is estimated as more than 200 million. For more information about the French language, some useful words and phrases and a food glossary, see the Language chapter later in this book.

Pride and perseverance have ensured the survival of local dialects in the region of Southwest France (although it is unlikely you will hear anything but standard French being spoken). In 1998, the PM, Lionel Jospin, tried to change the law to permit official use of regional languages but this was opposed by the right-wing president.

Dialects of Southwest France

The origins of Euskara (the Basque language) are still shrouded in mystery. Some scholars believe it to be related to languages from the Caucasus, others link it to languages from Africa, and still others highlight similarities with languages from Asia, Japanese for example. Despite the successive invasions of the Gauls and the Romans, Basque has managed to survive to the present day and is still spoken by about one million people in France and Spain. The French Basque country is north of the Pyrénées. Centuries of neglect and marginalisation, combined with two centuries of French republicanism and 40 years of Spanish fascism, pushed Basque to the brink of extinction but pride in the language has resulted in its preservation. There is now a television station in France that broadcasts entirely in Basque.

The generic term of 'Occitan' refers to the variety of dialects that are spoken over a large territory in the south of France, spreading from the area north of Bordeaux to the region south of Grenoble, and even extending partially into northern Italy. As the language of the troubadours, Occitan enjoyed great literary prestige during the Middle Ages. However, economic and religious imperialism from the north resulted in the Parisian dialect being imposed in administrative spheres. Occitan has no standard and so reference is often made to the individual varieties: Provençal, Gascon, Limousin, Languedocien and so on. Recent estimates suggest there are around eight million speakers, of which two million still use the language every day.

Facts for the Visitor

PLANNING
When to Go
Mid-season, during spring (April to June) and autumn (September to October), is the best time to visit the southwest. In the high season (July and August, and sometimes June and September too) – especially in the Dordogne and at the Atlantic resorts – temperatures soar, rooms are scarce or wildly overpriced, bus services dwindle, roads are choked and local markets are awash with tour groups. But these months are also the best for water sports, beaches, high-elevation trekking and festivals (see Public Holidays & Special Events later in this chapter) – and a few sights, restaurants, shops, tourist offices and camp sites are only open at this time.

Spring brings cool to mild temperatures, a landscape bursting with wild flowers, and mid-season rates for accommodation – but beware the weekends of Easter and Pentecost (the seventh Sunday after Easter) when it's high season again. In autumn, the *vendange* (grape harvest) and walnut-gathering make a fascinating backdrop to forays into the Médoc wine area and the Dordogne – but be prepared for dramatic thunderstorms in late September. Spring and autumn are the best low-elevation walking and cycling seasons.

Winter is when skiers head to the Pyrénées and truffle-lovers go to markets in the Dordogne and Lot. In January a great many hotels, restaurants and cultural sites close down altogether.

During school holidays (see the boxed text 'School Holidays' in the Getting Around

---

Highlights

Some things that you really shouldn't miss when travelling in the southwest – a visit to a prehistoric painted cave, for instance, and a splurge on the region's superb food. Here are a few specific recommendations:

Prehistoric Art
Gaze in wonder at the 15,000- to 20,000-year-old paintings and carvings at Font de Gaume (Les Eyzies), Pech Merle (Cabrerets) and Cougnac (Gourdon). The replica Lascaux II cave is worth a visit too (book ahead in the high season).

Romanesque Art
Track down wonderful Romanesque carved stone in Toulouse's Basilique St-Sernin, Souillac's Abbaye Ste-Marie, Cahors' Cathédrale St-Étienne, Moissac's Abbaye St-Pierre, the Cathédrale Notre Dame at Lescar (Pau) and Abbaye-Église St-Sever near Mont de Marsan.

Outdoor Activities
See the region from a different point of view: canoe the Dordogne or the Lot, pedal the well marked bike trails of Gironde or the Landes, or ride a horse almost anywhere. Surfers will find some of Europe's best beaches at Lacanau, Biscarosse, Hossegor and Anglet. The Haut-Béarn offers high-elevation treks, parasailing, fishing, white-water rafting, skiing and more.

Bastides
Discover the charming atmosphere of these orderly, medieval 'new towns' – at their best at Monpazier, Monflanquin, Villeréal, Domme, Montauban and Cordes-sur-Ciel.

chapter) crowds again mushroom and room prices soar.

On Sundays and public holidays, many small towns seem to shut down completely, leaving you gasping for a coffee and a baguette – though *boulangeries* (bakeries) often open on Sunday morning (and close all day Monday).

Maps

Quality regional maps are widely available outside France. Many bookstores stock locally relevant regional maps, and you can also find a wide selection in the Fnac stores in Bordeaux, Toulouse and Pau. Town maps are easily found on arrival – at tourist offices, bigger newsagents (often called Maison de la Presse), bookshops and some newspaper kiosks.

Road Maps Michelin does the best road maps. Its red-jacketed *Southern France* (No 919) map covers the whole of the region at 1:1,000,000 (1cm = 10km). More detailed and useful for drivers are yellow-jacketed maps at 1:200,000 (1cm = 2km). The fat *Aquitaine* (No 234) and *Midi-Pyrénées* (No 235) cover the region, as does a series of seven more manageable maps (Nos 71, 75, 78, 79, 82, 83 and 85). AA Publishing in the UK produces marginally more readable, 1:180,000 equivalents of the Aquitaine and Midi-Pyrénées maps.

Tourist Maps The best topographic maps are published by the Institut Géographique National (IGN). They're sold in better bookshops, and through IGN's French-language Web site, Ⓦ www.ign.fr.

Walkers will like IGN's 1:25,000 (1cm = 250m) Séries Bleue maps (€7); in many tourist zones these are being replaced with the TOP 25 series (€9), which contain more information – for example, on trails and sports facilities. Nature trails and fishing, walking and bathing spots feature on the

Highlights

Chateaux & Fortresses
Take your pick of truly beautiful chateaux – notably the Renaissance marvels of Puyguilhem and Montal – and hugely fortified hilltop castles of the Hundred Years' War, such as Beynac-et-Cazenac and Biron. Château de Hautefort and the redoubtable Château de Castelnaud are impressive, too.

Museums
Bordeaux's Musée d'Aquitaine surveys Southwest France's treasures from all ages. Bayonne's Musée Bonnat is a treasure-trove of 19th-century art. Auch's Musée des Jacobins is one of France's best provincial museums. Maison des Arts Georges Pompidou (Cajarc) is a surprising contemporary art gallery in the back of beyond. For modern figurative sculpture, the Musée Despiau-Wlérick (Mont de Marsan) is the only one of its kind in France.

Views & Landscapes
Marvel at nature's work on the Dune du Pilat (Arcachon), Gouffre de Padirac (Padirac) or the Needles of Ansabère (vallée d'Aspe, Béarn). Have your camera ready at the hilltop sites of Albi, Rocamadour and St-Cirq Lapopie, and the beautiful old towns of Sarlat-la-Canéda, Martel and Carennac. Dream away the hours in the serene Célé and Vézère Valleys.

Regional Food
You haven't discovered the southwest until you've tasted an *omelette aux truffes* (truffle omelette), *pâté de foie gras* (goose-liver pâté), *confit de canard* (duck preserved in its own fat, cooked until crisp), Agen prunes and Bayonne chocolate. Pick up walnuts (or walnut cake or oil), honey, strawberries and goat cheese at weekly markets throughout the region.

1:50,000 (1cm = 500m) Séries Plein-Air maps. Covering a wider area and more suitable for cyclists are the 1:100,000 (1cm = 1km) Séries Verte maps, or their tourist versions in the TOP 100 series (both €4.90).

Other publishers start with these maps and add details. Walkers may also like the Guide Franck maps showing short walks around specific areas (eg, Bergerac, Périgueux and Sarlat in the Circuits Pedestres Périgord series). Families with young children should look for Les Sentiers d'Emilie en... series, suggesting gentle walks in specific areas.

A handsome series of big IGN *département* (administrative department) maps from 1:100,000 to 1:140,000 (€4.90) are crammed with topographic detail, roads, political boundaries, town plans and a town index. Similar ones in IGN's Découvertes Régionales series (€5.35) include *Aquitaine* (1:250,000), *Dordogne* (1:125,000), *Midi-Pyrénées* (1:275,000) and the *Pyrénées-Atlantiques* (1:125,000).

Several 1:1,000,000 IGN maps (€4.90) are useful for overall planning: *France – Grand Randonnée* (No 903) shows long-distance GR trails (see Walking later in this chapter); *France – VTT & Randonnées Cyclos* (No 906) indicates dozens of rural bicycle tours; and *France – Canöe-Kayak et Sports d'Eau Vive* (No 905) is useful for water-sports enthusiasts.

City Maps Free tourist-office *plans* (street maps) range from superb to useless. Michelin's *Guide Rouge,* or Red Guide (see Guidebooks under Books later in this chapter) has maps for larger cities, towns and resorts showing one-way streets and numbered town entry points; this is coordinated with Michelin's yellow-jacketed 1:200,000 road maps.

Blay-Foldex publishes *plans-guides* (city map-guides) for Agen, Albi, Arcachon, Bayonne, Bordeaux, Brive-la-Gaillarde, Cahors, Montauban, Pau, Périgueux and Toulouse, costing from €3 to €5.

What to Bring

Bring as little as possible; forgotten items can be purchased practically anywhere. If you'll be on the move a lot, or even just humping everything between hotels and stations, a backpack is the way to carry it. An internal-frame pack whose straps can be zipped inside can be made to resemble a nylon suitcase; some have exterior pouches that zip off to become daypacks.

Hostellers must provide their own towels and soap. Bedding is almost always provided or available for hire, though you might want to have your own sheet bag. You'll also sleep easier with your own padlock on the storage locker often provided by hostels.

Other items to consider are a torch (flashlight), an adapter plug (for electrical appliances such as an immersion heater for preparing tea), a universal bath/sink plug (a plastic camera-film canister sometimes works), a few clothes pegs and premoistened towelettes. Essential items for surviving the July and August sun are a water bottle, sunglasses, sun hat, suncream (including sunblock) and after-sun lotion. Among its other uses, a big cotton handkerchief can be soaked in fountains and used to cool off. Bring a warm sweater in spring or autumn and a small collapsible umbrella in any season.

RESPONSIBLE TOURISM

The summertime tourist invasion of the southwest brings environmental and social stress: narrow rural roads are clogged with cars and tour buses, pretty villages lack the infrastructure to cope with the crowds, and locals may hardly get a look-in at popular markets and summer festivals.

You can reduce your own impact by travelling by train, bike (on your own or on small group tours) or even on foot, instead of in a car. You can do even better, and keep your own stress level down, by lingering longer in a smaller number of places, and by visiting during the low or mid-season when everything is less fraught and your euros are more appreciated. Choosing *camping à la ferme* (farm camp sites) or *chambres d'hôte* (B&Bs) over chain hotels gives locals a bigger share of what you spend (for more information see Accommodation later in this chapter). Buying *produits du terroir* (local, home-made produce) straight from the farm or a small-town market rather than the supermarket or a tourist shop also helps the local populace.

When exploring the Vézère and Lot Valleys, and their prehistoric cave sites, remember that it's illegal in many areas to dig for fossils, flints or other artefacts. The locals have been doing it for decades, of course, but then it's their land.

TOURIST OFFICES
Local Tourist Offices
Nearly every city, town and village has an *office de tourisme* (a tourist office run by local government) or *syndicat d'initiative* (a tourist office established by a local merchants' association). These are excellent resources and almost always have maps and accommodation information. A few will also book hotels or exchange foreign currency.

There are also *comités départemental du tourisme* (CDT; departmental offices) where you can pick up general information, though they're more administrative and less user-friendly than the local offices:

CDT Béarn-Pays Basque
Bayonne: (☎ 05 59 46 52 52, fax 05 59 46 52 46, e cdf@cg64.fr) 4 allée des Platanes, 64108 Bayonne
Pau: (☎ 05 59 30 01 30, fax 05 59 84 10 13) Maison du Tourisme, 22 ter rue JJ-de-Monaix, 64000 Pau
CDT Corrèze (☎ 05 55 29 98 78, fax 05 55 29 98 79, e cdt.correze@wanadoo.fr) quai Baluze, 19000 Tulle
CDT Dordogne (☎ 05 53 35 50 24, fax 05 53 09 51 41, e dordogne.perigord.tourisme@wanadoo.fr) 25 rue du Président Wilson, 24000 Périgueux
CDT Gers (☎ 05 62 05 95 95, fax 05 62 05 02 16, e cdtdugers@wanadoo.fr) 7 rue Diderot, BP 106, 32002 Auch
CDT Gironde (☎ 05 56 52 61 40, fax 05 56 81 09 99, e tourisme@gironde.com) 21 cours de l'Intendance, 33000 Bordeaux
CDT Landes (☎ 05 58 06 89 89, fax 05 58 06 90 90, e cdt.landes@wanadoo.fr) 4 av Aristide Briand, BP 407, 40012 Mont de Marsan
CDT Lot (☎ 05 65 35 07 09, fax 05 65 23 92 76, e cdt47@wanadoo.fr) 107 quai Cavaignac, BP 7, 46001 Cahors

CDT Lot-et-Garonne (☎ 05 53 66 14 14, fax 05 53 68 25 42, e c.d.t@wanadoo.fr) 4 rue André Chénier, BP 158, 47005 Agen
CDT Tarn (☎ 05 63 77 32 10, fax 05 63 77 32 32, e cdt_du_tarn@wanadoo.fr) 41 rue Porta, BP 225, 81006 Albi
CDT Tarn-et-Garonne (☎ 05 63 21 79 09, fax 05 63 66 80 36, e cdt82@wanadoo.fr) 7 blvd Midi-Pyrénées, 82000 Montauban

Operating independently but in association with most departmental offices is a leisure-booking organisation called Loisirs Accueil France (W www.loisirsaccueilfrance.com), which can arrange activities, courses, tours, meals, accommodation and more. Each local tourist office will have contact details.

There are also two regional offices, though they're mainly administrative: Comité Régional du Tourisme d'Aquitaine (☎ 05 56 01 70 00, fax 05 56 01 70 07, e tourisme@cr-aquitaine.fr), Cité Mondiale, 23 Parvis des Chatrons, 33000 Bordeaux; and Comité Régional du Tourisme de Midi-Pyrénées (☎ 05 61 13 55 55, fax 05 61 47 17 16, e promotion.crtmp@wanadoo.fr), 54 blvd de l'Embouchure, BP 2166, 31022 Toulouse.

French Tourist Offices Abroad
Information on the southwest is also available from French government tourist offices abroad:

Australia
(☎ 02-9231 5244, fax 9221 8682, e frencht@ozemail.com.au) 22nd floor, 25 Bligh St, Sydney, NSW 2000
Belgium
(☎ 0902 88 025, fax 02 502 3829, e info@france-tourisme.be) 21 av de la Toison d'Or, 1050 Brussels
Canada
(☎ 514-288 4264, fax 845 4868, e mfrance@mtl.net) 1981 McGill College Ave, Suite 490, Montreal, Que H3A 2W9
Germany
Frankfurt-am-Main: (☎ 069-758 021, fax 745 556, e maison_de_la_france@tonline.de) Westendstrasse 47, 60325 Frankfurt-am-Main
Berlin: (☎ 030-218 2064, fax 214 1238) Keithstrasse 2-4, 10787 Berlin
Ireland
(☎ 01-703 4046, fax 874 7324) 35 Lower Abbey St, Dublin 1

Italy
(☎ 166 116 216, fax 02 58 48 62 21, **e** info@
turismofrancese.it) Via Larga 7, 20122 Milan
Netherlands
(☎ 0900 112 2332, fax 020-620 3339,
e informatie@fransverkeersbureau.nl)
Prinsengracht 670, 1017 KX Amsterdam
South Africa
(☎ 011-880 8062, fax 880 7722, **e** mdfsa@
frenchdoor.co.za) Oxford Manor, 1st floor, 196
Oxford Rd, Illovo 2196
Spain
(☎ 91 541 8808, fax 91 541 2412,
e maisondelafrance@mad.sericom.es) Alcalá
63, 28014 Madrid
Switzerland
Zürich: (☎ 01-211 3085, fax 212 1644,
e tourismefrance@bluewin.ch) Löwenstrasse
59, 8023 Zürich
Geneva: (☎ 022-732 8610, fax 731 5873,
e mdlfgva@ bluewin.ch) 2 rue Thalberg,
1201 Geneva
UK
(☎ 0906 824 4123, fax 020-7493 6594,
e info@mdlf.co.uk) 178 Piccadilly, London
W1V 0AL
USA
New York: (☎ 212-838 7800, fax 838 7855,
e info@francetourism.com) 444 Madison
Ave, 16th floor, New York, NY 10022-6903
Chicago: (☎ 312-751 7800, fax 337 6339,
e fgto@mcs.net) 676 North Michigan Ave,
Chicago, IL 60611-2819
Beverly Hills: (☎ 310-271 6665, fax 276 2835,
e fgtola@juno.com) 9454 Wiltshire Blvd,
Suite 715, Beverly Hills, CA 90212-2967

These and other French tourist offices
around the world are listed in the Web site
W www.franceguide.com.

VISAS & DOCUMENTS
Passport
The law requires everyone in France, including tourists, to carry identification at all
times. For foreign visitors this means a
passport or national ID card. Your passport
must be valid for three months beyond the
date of your departure from France.

Visas
Tourist Visas The general requirements
for entry to France also apply to other
signatories of the 1990 Schengen Convention on the abolition of mutual border con-

trols (Austria, Belgium, Denmark, Finland,
France, Germany, Greece, Iceland, Italy,
Luxembourg, the Netherlands, Norway, Por-
tugal, Spain and Sweden).

Citizens of any Schengen country can visit
any other Schengen country – including
France – without a visa, as can citizens of all
other EU countries, ie, UK and Ireland. Citizens of Australia, Canada, Israel, Japan, New
Zealand, Switzerland and the USA, among
others, can also visit without a visa, though
they should first check regulations with the
consulate of each Schengen country they plan
to visit, or with the EU information office in
Brussels (☎ 02 295 1780). A visa issued by
one Schengen country is generally valid for
travel in all the others, although individual
Schengen countries may impose additional
restrictions on certain nationalities.

The standard tourist visa issued by France
and other Schengen countries is the 'Schengen short-stay visa', good for a visit of up to
90 days within six months of the visa date.
You must apply for it in your country of residence. You'll need your passport; evidence
of funds, medical insurance, hotel bookings
and return travel; two passport-size photos;
and the visa fee in cash. The fee for a stay of
one to 30 days is about €30, and from 31 to
90 days is about €40, converted to the currency of your home country. Visas are usually issued on the spot.

Tourist visas cannot be extended except
in emergencies (such as medical problems).
If you have an urgent problem you could try
consulting your own nearest consular office
in France, or the nearest *préfecture* (prefecture – see the following section).

Long-Stay Visas & Permits If you'd like
to work or study in France, or stay for over
90 days, apply for the appropriate *séjour*
(long-stay) visa. Unless you're an EU citizen, it's difficult to get a visa allowing you
to work in France, although student-visa
holders can apply for permission to work
part time (ask at your place of study). For
any long-stay visa, begin the paperwork in
your home country several months before
you plan to leave.

If you're issued with a visa for a stay of

six months or more, you'll probably have to apply for a *carte de séjour* (residence permit) within eight days of arrival in France. You'll need it to work legally. Getting it is almost automatic for EU nationals, but almost impossible for anyone else except full-time students. Ask at your place of study or at the local prefecture, *sous-préfecture* (sub-prefecture), *mairie* or *hôtel de ville* (city or town hall) or *commissariat* (police station). The prefectures have visa sections that also handle cartes de séjour:

Dordogne (☎ 05 53 02 24 24) 2 rue Paul Courrier, Périgueux
Gironde (☎ 05 56 90 60 60) esplanade Charles de Gaulle, Bordeaux
Haute-Garonne (☎ 05 34 45 34 45) place St-Étienne, Toulouse
Landes (☎ 05 58 06 58 06) 26 rue Victor Hugo, Mont de Marsan
Lot (☎ 05 65 23 10 00) Cité Bessières, Cahors
Lot-et-Garonne (☎ 05 53 77 60 47) place Verdun, Agen
Pyrénées-Atlantiques (☎ 05 59 98 24 24) 2 rue du Maréchal Joffre, Pau

Travel Insurance

Make sure you take out a comprehensive travel-insurance policy covering you for medical expenses and luggage theft or loss, and for cancellation or delays in travel arrangements. The policies handled by student travel organisations are usually good value. Some offer lower and higher medical expense options; go for as much as you can afford. Some are cheaper if you forgo cover for lost baggage.

Buy travel insurance as early as possible; if you buy it the week before you fly, you may find, for example, that you're not covered for flight delays caused by industrial action.

Paying for your ticket with a credit card often provides limited travel accident insurance, and you may be able to reclaim the payment if the operator doesn't deliver.

Driving Licence & Permits

Driving licences from EU countries are valid in France. So are many non-European licences, but it's still a good idea to bring an International Driving Permit (IDP). This is a multilingual translation of the details on your local licence; it's not valid unless accompanied by the original. An IDP can be obtained for a small fee from your local motoring association – take a passport photo and a valid licence.

Hostel Cards

A Hostelling International (HI) card is only necessary at official *auberges de jeunesse* (youth hostels). You can buy one at most French hostels for €10.65/15.25 if you're aged under/over 26. A family card costs €22.80. See the HI Web site (W www.iyhf.org) for further details.

Student, Youth & Teachers Cards

The International Student Identity Card (ISIC) and Teachers Card (ITIC) can pay for themselves through half-price admissions and discounted air and ferry tickets. Valid for one year, they're available for the equivalent of about €9.60 from youth-oriented travel agencies such as usit Campus, STA Travel, Council Travel and Travel CUTS, as well as France-based OTU Voyages and Accueil des Jeunes en France (AJF).

Youth-card schemes Euro<26 and IYTC provide more general discounts – for example, in shops and cinemas – and for some accommodation and travel. Also valid for a year, they're available for about €11.20. Visit the Web site W www.istc.org for details on ISIC, ITIC and IYTC, or W www.euro26.org for more on Euro<26.

France's own Carte Jeunes (€18.30 for one year) is available to anyone under 26 who has been in France for at least six months. You can obtain it from youth-travel agencies and BIJs (see the boxed text 'Bureaux d'Information Jeunesse' later in this chapter).

Seniors Cards

With the Rail Plus Card (€19.20), which replaces the old Rail Europe Senior Card, those aged 60 and over get up to 25% off any international rail journey. To be eligible you first need a local senior citizens' railcard; in the UK this is called a Senior Railcard (£18) and is sold, along with Rail Plus Cards, at major stations, through rail companies or from Rail Europe (☎ 0870 584 8848).

SNCF offers the Carte Sénior (€44.20) to those aged over 60, good for reductions of 25% to 50% on domestic train tickets. For details, see SNCF Discounts & Passes under Train in the Getting There & Away chapter.

Discounts are available for people aged over 60 at most museums, galleries and public theatres.

Camping Card International (CCI)

The CCI can be presented instead of your passport at camping grounds affiliated to the Federation Internationale de Camping et de Caravanning (FICC). It guarantees insurance coverage for any damage you may cause, and is sometimes good for discounts. It's available to members of most national motoring clubs except in the USA; the RAC in the UK charges members £4 for one.

Bicycle Information

If you're cycling around France on your own machine, proof of ownership and a written description and a photograph of it will help police if it's stolen.

Copies

All important documents (passport data page and visa page, credit cards, travel insurance policy, air/bus/train tickets, driving licence, etc) should be photocopied before you leave home. Leave one copy with someone at home and keep another with you, separate from the originals. Other copies you might want to carry include travellers cheque numbers (plus telephone numbers for cancelling cheques and credit cards) and any documents related to possible employment.

EMBASSIES & CONSULATES
French Embassies & Consulates

France's diplomatic and consular representatives abroad include:

Australia
Embassy: (☎ 02-6216 0100, fax 6216 0127, e embassy@france.net.au) 6 Perth Ave, Yarralumla, ACT 2600
Consulate: (☎ 03-9820 0921, fax 9820 9363, e cgmelb@france.net.au) 492 St Kilda Rd, Level 4, Melbourne, Vic 3004
Consulate: (☎ 02-9261 5779, fax 9283 1210, e gsydney@france.net.au) 20th floor, St Martin's Tower, 31 Market St, Sydney, NSW 2000

Belgium
Embassy: (☎ 02 548 8711, fax 02 513 6871, e amba@ambafrance.be) 65 rue Ducale, 1000 Brussels
Consulate: (☎ 02 229 8500, fax 02 229 8510, e consulat.france@skynet.bruxelles.be) 12A place de Louvain, 1000 Brussels 82

Canada
Embassy: (☎ 613-789 1795, fax 562 3735, e consulat@amba-ottowa.fr) 42 Sussex Drive, Ottawa, Ont K1M 2C9
Consulate: (☎ 514-878 4385, fax 878 3981, e fsltmral@cam.org) 26th floor, 1 place Ville Marie, Montreal, Que H3B 4S3
Consulate: (☎ 416-925 8041, fax 925 3076, e fsltto@idirect.com) 130 Bloor St West, Suite 400, Toronto, Ont M5S 1N5

Germany
Embassy: (☎ 030-20 639 000, fax 639 010) Kochstrasse 6-7, 10969 Berlin
Consulate: (☎ 030-885 902 43, fax 882 5295), Kurfürstendamm 211, 10719 Berlin
Consulate: (☎ 089-419 4110, fax 030-419 41141) Möhlstrasse 5, 81675 Munich

Ireland
Embassy & Consulate: (☎ 01-260 1666, fax 283 0178, e consul@ambafrance.ie) 36 Ailesbury Rd, Ballsbridge, Dublin 4

Italy
Embassy: (☎ 06 686 011, fax 06 860 1360, e france-italia@france-italia.it) Piazza Farnese 67, 00186 Rome
Consulate: (☎ 06 6880 6437, fax 06 6860 1260, e consulfrance-rome@iol.it) Via Giulia 251, 00186 Rome

Netherlands
Embassy: (☎ 070-312 5800, fax 312 5854) Smidsplein 1, 2514 BT, The Hague
Consulate: (☎ 020-624 8346, fax 626 0841, e consulfr@euronet.nl) Vijzelgracht 2, 1000 HA Amsterdam

New Zealand
Embassy & Consulate: (☎ 04-384 2555, fax 384 2577, e consulfrance@actrix.gen.nz) Rural Bank Building, 34–42 Manners Street, Wellington

Spain
Embassy: (☎ 91 423 8900, fax 91 423 8901) Calle de Salustiano, Olozaga 9, 28001 Madrid

Consulate: (☎ 91 700 7800, fax 91 700 7801,
[e] creire@consulfrance-madrid.org) Calle
Marques de la Enseñada 10, 28004 Madrid
Consulate: (☎ 93 270 3000, fax 93 270 0349,
[e] info@consulat-france.org) Ronda Universi-
tat 22, 08007 Barcelona
Switzerland
Embassy: (☎ 031-359 2111, fax 352 2191,
[e] ambassade.fr@iprolink.ch) Schlosshalden-
strasse 46, 3006 Berne
Consulate: (☎ 022-319 0000, fax 319 0072,
[e] consulat.france@ties.itu.int) 11 rue Imbert
Galloix, 1205 Geneva
Consulate: (☎ 01-268 8585, fax 268 8500,
[e] consulat.france.zurich@swissonline.ch)
Mühlebachstrasse 7, 8008 Zürich
UK
Embassy: (☎ 020-7201 1000, fax 7201 1004,
[e] press@ambafrance.org) 58 Knightsbridge,
London SW1X 7JT
Consulate: (☎ 020-7838 2000, fax 7838 2018)
21 Cromwell Rd, London SW7 2EN
Visa Section: (☎ 020-7838 2051) 6A
Cromwell Place, London SW7 2EW
USA
Embassy: (☎ 202-944 6000, fax 944 6166,
[e] visas-washington@amb-wash.fr) 4101
Reservoir Rd NW, Washington DC 20007
Consulate: (☎ 212-606 3600/88, fax 606 3620,
[e] visa@franceconsulatny.org) 934 Fifth Ave,
New York, NY 10021
Consulate: (☎ 415-397 4330, fax 433 8357,
[e] consul-general@accueil-sfo.org) 540 Bush
St, San Francisco, CA 94108.
Other consulates are located in Atlanta,
Boston, Chicago, Houston, Los Angeles,
Miami and New Orleans.

Consulates in Southwest France

It's important to realise what your embassy
or consulate can and can't do to help you if
you get into trouble. Generally speaking, it
won't be much help if the trouble you're in
is your own fault or if you end up in jail
after committing a crime locally. Remember that you're bound by the laws of the
country you're in.

In genuine emergencies you might get
some assistance, but only if other channels
have been exhausted. If you need to get home
urgently, a free ticket is exceedingly unlikely:
you'd be expected to have insurance. If your
money and documents are stolen you might
get help with a new passport, but a loan for
onward travel is out of the question.

Few consular offices nowadays keep letters for travellers or maintain a reading
room with newspapers from back home.

All foreign embassies are in Paris, but the
following countries have consular offices
(some open by appointment only) in Southwest France:

Algeria
Bordeaux: (☎ 05 56 99 03 36) 41 rue F
Despagent, 33000 Bordeaux
Toulouse: (☎ 05 61 62 97 07) 23 rue Arnaud-
Vidal, 31000 Toulouse
Belgium
Bordeaux: (☎ 05 56 52 29 49) 12 cours
Balguerie Stuttenberg, 33000 Bordeaux
Toulouse: (☎ 05 61 52 67 93) 3 rue Mage,
31000 Toulouse
Canada
(☎ 05 61 99 30 16) 30 blvd de Strasbourg,
31000 Toulouse
Germany
Bordeaux: (☎ 05 56 17 12 22, fax 05 56 42 32
65, [e] cansabordeaux@wanadoo.fr) 377 blvd
Président Wilson, 33200 Bordeaux
Toulouse: (☎/fax 05 61 52 35 56) 24 rue de
Metz, 31000 Toulouse
Italy
(☎ 05 34 45 48 48) 13 rue d'Alsace-Lorraine,
31000 Toulouse
Netherlands
(☎ 05 61 13 64 94) 4th floor, 54 bis rue
d'Alsace-Lorraine, 31000 Toulouse
Portugal
Bordeaux: (☎ 05 56 00 68 20) 11 rue H Rodel,
33000 Bordeaux
Toulouse: (☎ 05 61 80 43 45) 22 av Camille
Pujol, 31500 Toulouse
Bayonne: (☎ 05 59 25 55 97) 6 rue Jacques
Lafitte, 64100 Bayonne
Spain
Bordeaux: (☎ 05 56 52 80 20, fax 05 56 81 88
43) 1 rue Notre Dame, 33000 Bordeaux
Toulouse: (☎ 05 61 52 05 50) 16 rue Ste-
Anne, 31000 Toulouse
Bayonne: (☎ 05 59 59 03 91) Résidence du
Parc, 4 blvd du BAB, 64100 Bayonne
Pau: (☎ 05 59 27 32 40) place Royale, 64000
Pau
Switzerland
Bordeaux: (☎ 05 56 52 18 65) 14 cours Xavier
Arnozan, 33080 Bordeaux
Toulouse: (☎ 05 61 40 45 33) 36 allées de
Bellefontaine, 31081 Toulouse
Tunisia
(☎ 05 61 63 61 61, fax 05 61 63 48 00) 19
allées Jean-Jaurès, 31000 Toulouse

UK
Bordeaux: (☎ 05 57 22 21 10, fax 05 56 08 33 12) 353 blvd Président Wilson, 33073 Bordeaux
Toulouse: (☎ 05 61 15 02 02) 20 chemin de Laporte, 31300 Toulouse

USA
Bordeaux: (☎ 05 56 48 63 80, fax 05 56 51 61 97) 10 place de la Bourse, 33025 Bordeaux
Toulouse: (☎ 05 34 31 36 50, fax 05 34 41 16 19) 25 allées Jean-Jaurès, 31000 Toulouse

CUSTOMS

The usual allowances apply to duty-free goods purchased at airports or on ferries outside the EU: tobacco (200 cigarettes, 50 cigars or 250g of loose tobacco), alcohol (1L of strong liquor or 2L of less than 22% alcohol by volume; 2L of wine), coffee (500g or 200g of extracts) and perfume (50g of perfume and 0.25L of eau de toilette).

Do not confuse these with duty-paid items (including alcohol and tobacco) bought at normal shops in another EU country and brought into France. In this case the allowances are more generous: 800 cigarettes, 200 cigars or 1kg of loose tobacco; 10L of spirits (more than 22% alcohol by volume), 20L of fortified wine or aperitif, 90L of wine or 110L of beer.

Duty-free shopping within the EU was abolished in 1999.

MONEY
Currency

As this book is published, France is in the throes of a painful transition – from one currency to another. The French franc (FF) ceased to be the national currency on 1 January 2002, when it was replaced by the euro (€), the new shared currency of 12 EU countries. The dual circulation period ended on 28 February 2002, and all francs should have been exchanged by 30 June 2002. *Mon dieu!*

One euro is divided into 100 cents. Euro coins (in denominations of one, two, five, 10, 20 and 50 cents, and €1 and €2) and notes (€5, €10, €20, €50, €100, €200 and €500) are usable throughout the 'euro-zone' – including Austria, Belgium, France, Finland, Germany, Greece, Ireland, Italy, Luxembourg, the Netherlands, Portugal and Spain.

In this period of confusion, check your bills carefully to make sure that any conversion has been calculated correctly. We give all prices in euros in this book.

Exchange Rates

The EU has its own dedicated euro Web site: Ⓦ europa.eu.int/euro. You can also check the currency converter at Ⓦ www .oanda.com for current rates.

country	unit		euro
Australia	A$1	=	€0.59
Canada	C$1	=	€0.74
Japan	¥100	=	€0.92
New Zealand	NZ$1	=	€0.48
UK	£1	=	€1.63
USA	US$1	=	€1.13

Exchanging Money

Cash Cash is not a safe way to carry money. What's more, banks tend to pay more for travellers cheques than for cash. Still, it's smart to carry a small stash of cash – the equivalent of perhaps US$100 – for emergencies. Bring low-denomination notes: fear of counterfeits makes banks and others reluctant to accept US$100 notes. Post offices often offer the best cash exchange rates and accept banknotes in a variety of currencies.

During the euro transition period from 1 January to 30 June 2002, if you have soon-to-be-obsolete banknotes from euro-zone countries, swap them for euro notes at banks rather than at private currency exchanges. Exchanges, faced with extra charges to sell those old notes back to the banks, may pass those charges on in the form of higher commissions or poorer rates.

Travellers Cheques & Eurocheques

Most banks charge a commission to exchange travellers cheques, typically €4 to €5 per transaction, or a percentage fee for large sums. The post office charges 1.5% (minimum €3.80) for euro-zone cheques; US dollar cheques are cashed for free. The American Express (AmEx) office in Bordeaux charges nothing for AmEx cheques, but 3% (minimum €6.10) for other brands. The whole business should go more smoothly if you have cheques in euros.

Eurocheques, available if you have a European bank account, are guaranteed up to a certain limit. When cashing them you must show your signed Eurocheque card. Many hotels and merchants refuse to accept Eurocheques because of the relatively large commissions, and most French banks no longer accept them either.

Lost or Stolen Travellers Cheques If your AmEx travellers cheques are lost or stolen in France, call toll-free ☎ 08 00 90 86 00; reimbursement can be made at the AmEx office (☎ 05 56 00 63 33, fax 05 56 00 63 39), 14 cours d'Intendance in Bordeaux. If you lose your Thomas Cook travellers cheques, call toll-free ☎ 08 00 90 83 30; they'll tell you the nearest bank where you can get a refund.

ATMs In French, automated teller machines (ATMs) are *distributeurs automatiques de billets* (DABs) or *points d'argent*. ATM cards can give you direct access to cash reserves back home at a superior exchange rate. Although French banks limit the size of a transaction (typically €100 to €300), only your home bank charges commission (typically about 1.5%). Most ATMs are linked to the international Cirrus and Maestro networks.

Credit Cards Visa (Carte Bleue) is the most widely accepted credit card, followed by MasterCard (Access or Eurocard). AmEx cards are not very useful except at particularly upmarket establishments, but they do allow you to get cash at certain ATMs and at the AmEx office in Bordeaux (see the preceding section on Lost or Stolen Travellers Cheques).

Taking along two different credit cards (stashed in different wallets) is safer than taking one, as it may be impossible to replace a lost Visa or MasterCard until you get home (AmEx and Diners Club International offer on-the-spot replacement).

Lost or Stolen Cards If your Visa card is lost or stolen, Carte Bleue (☎ 08 36 69 08 80 or 08 00 90 20 33, 24 hours) can freeze the account; to replace the card you must deal with the issuer. Report a lost MasterCard, Access or Eurocard to Eurocard France (☎ 01 45 67 53 53) and if possible to the issuer; for cards from the USA, call ☎ 1 314 275 6690.

For a lost or stolen AmEx card, call ☎ 01 47 77 70 00 or ☎ 01 47 77 72 00, both staffed 24 hours. In an emergency, AmEx card holders from the USA can call collect to the USA at ☎ 202-783 7474 or 202-677 2442; replacements can be arranged at the AmEx office in Bordeaux (see Lost or Stolen Travellers Cheques earlier in this section).

Report a lost Diners Club card on ☎ 01 47 62 75 75.

International Transfers Telegraphic transfers are inexpensive but slow. It's quicker and easier to have money wired via AmEx in Bordeaux (at a cost of US$50 for US$1000). Western Union's Money Transfer system (☎ 01 43 54 46 12) and Thomas Cook's MoneyGram service (☎ 08 00 90 83 30) are also popular.

Exchange Bureaus In Bordeaux and Toulouse, private *bureaux de change* are faster, open longer and usually give better rates than the banks, but shop around before changing large amounts.

Costs

The worst time to come if you want to save money is in July or August, when accommodation prices soar and some places even require that you take *demi-pension* (half-board). Outside the high season, if you stay in camp sites, hostels or budget hotels and have more picnics than restaurant meals, you can get by for about €28 (US$25) a day per person (€40/US$35 during July and August).

Travelling with someone else immediately slashes costs, since single rooms, if they're offered at all, cost the same or only a little less than doubles. Triples and quads are the cheapest per person and usually offer the most comfort for the money.

You can cut costs dramatically at mealtimes, too. Baguette-and-cheese picnics are a pauper's banquet, and carrying a water bottle saves you forking over €3 for a canned drink. For other money-saving ideas see the boxed text 'Keeping Costs & Stress Down' later in this chapter.

If you're travelling with kids you'll save a bundle with family tickets to museums and other attractions.

Cyclists who camp out and cook on their own stoves can pare costs down as low as €23 (US$20) per day.

Discounts Museums, cinemas, SNCF, ferry companies and other institutions offer a range of price breaks to young people, students and senior travellers; for example, see under Visas & Documents earlier in this chapter for information on discount cards. Look for the words *demi-tarif* (half-price) or *tarif réduit* (reduced price), and ask even if you don't see them.

Freebies Admission to most municipal and regional museums is free on the first Sunday of each month. Nearly all galleries, palaces, museums, gardens and other cultural attractions are free on the third weekend in September during France's Journées du Patrimoine (Days of Patrimony).

Tipping & Bargaining

French law requires that restaurant, cafe and hotel bills include a service charge (usually around 10%), so a *pourboire* (tip) is neither necessary nor expected. Most people leave an extra 5% or so anyway, unless the service has been dire. Taxi drivers appreciate a similar amount. The normal tip for service station attendants who do your windows and check your tyres is around €1. Tip lavatory attendants a few cents.

Little bargaining goes on in the region's markets.

Taxes & Refunds

France's Value Added Tax, called *taxe sur la valeur ajoutée* (TVA), is 19.6% on most goods except food, medicine and books, for which it's 5.5%. Prices are rarely given without TVA.

If you're not an EU resident, you can get a refund on most of the TVA you have paid, provided you're over the age of 15, you'll be spending less than six months in France and you purchase goods worth at least €185 (tax included, and not more than 10 of the same item) at a single shop – and provided the shop offers *vente en détaxe* (duty-free sales), usually indicated by a sign on the door or at the till.

Present your passport at the time of purchase and ask for a *bordereau de détaxe* (export sales invoice). When you leave France or another EU country, ensure that customs officials validate all three pages of the bordereau; the green sheet is your receipt. You'll receive a transfer of funds in your home country.

If you're flying directly out of the EU from Bordeaux or Toulouse, certain stores can arrange for you to receive your refund as you leave the country, but you must arrange this at the time of purchase. When you arrive at the airport, customs will validate your bordereau and tell you which *douane de détaxe* (customs refund exchange bureau window) to go to for your refund.

POST & COMMUNICATIONS
Post

The French postal service is fast (next-day delivery for most domestic letters), reliable, bureaucratic and expensive. Post offices are signposted *La Poste*; older branches may be marked with the letters PTT (Postes, Télégraphes, Téléphones). To mail things, go to a postal window marked *toutes opérations*.

Postal Rates Domestic letters up to 20g cost €0.46. From France, by *service ordinaire*, postcards and letters up to 20g cost €0.46 within the EU, €0.58 to most of the rest of Europe, €0.59 to Africa, €0.67 to the USA, Canada and the Middle East, €0.75 to Asia and €0.79 to Australasia. *Enveloppes prétimbrées* (aerogrammes) always cost €0.76. France's worldwide express mail delivery service, Chronopost, costs a fortune.

Sending parcels overseas is costly since nearly everything international now goes by air; keep your parcel under 2kg for the cheapest *service économique* (economy) rates (taking around 10 days) – for example, €7.47 within the EU, €10.21 to the USA and Canada, and €17.38 to Australasia. An under-publicised seamail service called *livre/brochure* is available for books – a parcel under 5kg costs €8.23 to the UK or €13.72 to the USA or Australasia, and delivery takes about a month.

Timbres (stamps) are sold at post offices, both at windows and from coin-operated machines. You can pay at the window with a credit card at bigger post offices. Most shops selling postcards also sell stamps.

Sending & Receiving Mail When addressing mail to a French destination, do it the French way: the *nom de famille* (surname or family name) in capital letters first, followed by the *prénom* (first name) in lower case. The house number is followed by a comma, and generic terms such as 'rue' are not capitalised. 'Cedex' after the city or town name means mail is collected at the post office rather than delivered to the door.

Poste-restante mail not addressed to a particular branch goes to the city's *recette principale* (main post office). To send it to another branch of the post office (this book mentions and maps some centrally located ones), include the street address noted in the text.

Telephone
Most public telephones now accept France Telecom *télécartes* (magnetic-strip phone-cards), sold for about €7.40 or €14.80 at post offices, *tabacs* (tobacconists), supermarket checkout counters and SNCF ticket windows.

Alternatively, you can choose from a range of other cards, sold for about €7.60 or €15.30 at many tabacs, which have a secret PIN number (obtained by scratching the card) that you dial in order to make a call. These tend to be better value for international calls than France Telecom's, but are poor value for local calls.

Lonely Planet's eKno Communication Card is aimed at independent travellers and offers competitive international rates, messaging services, free email and travel information. You can join online at [W] www.ekno .lonelyplanet.com, or by phone from France at ☎ 08 00 91 26 77; to use eKno from France, dial ☎ 08 00 91 20 66.

Calling Southwest France from Abroad French telephone numbers all have 10 digits. To call anywhere in France from abroad, dial your country's international access code, followed by ☎ 33 (France's country code) and the full number, dropping the first 0.

Calling Abroad from Southwest France To call abroad from France, dial ☎ 00 (France's international access code), followed by the country code, area code (dropping the initial zero if there is one) and local number.

Country-Direct Numbers You can make international reverse-charge (collect) or person-to-person calls to many countries from France by dialling a number that connects you directly to an operator in the particular country. The connection to the operator is toll-free, so you can call from a public telephone without a télécarte or coin.

Australia	☎ 08 00 99 00 61 (Telstra)
	☎ 08 00 99 20 61 (Optus)
Canada	☎ 08 00 99 00 16
Ireland	☎ 08 00 99 03 53
Netherlands	☎ 08 00 99 00 31
New Zealand	☎ 08 00 99 00 64
South Africa	☎ 08 00 99 00 27
UK	☎ 08 00 99 00 44 (BT)
	☎ 08 00 99 09 44 (Cable & Wireless)
USA	☎ 08 00 99 00 11 (AT&T)
	☎ 08 00 99 00 19 (MCI)
	☎ 08 00 99 00 87 (Sprint)
	☎ 08 00 99 00 13 (Worldcom)

For other countries, see the reference pages at the back of the local *Pages Jaunes* (Yellow Pages).

Enquiries The number for domestic enquiries is ☎ 12, and if your French is no good you can usually ask for an operator who speaks your language. For international enquiries dial ☎ 3212. Both are free calls from public phones, though not from private ones.

International Rates The cheapest time to call home is during reduced tariff periods – generally weekday evenings from 7pm to 8am (7pm to 1pm for calls to North America), and all day on weekends and public holidays.

The cost of a three-minute call to other EU countries, and to the USA and Canada, is about €0.75 (€0.50 during reduced-tariff periods). A three-minute call to Australia or New Zealand would cost about €1.95/1.45.

Domestic Tariffs The cheapest time to call is from 7pm to 8am on weekday evenings, and all day on weekends and public holidays.

Local calls cost €0.11 for the first three minutes, plus €0.02/0.04 per minute thereafter during reduced-tariff/normal periods. National calls (beyond about 30km) cost €0.11 for the first 39 seconds, and then €0.06/0.12 per minute thereafter. A three-minute call to Paris from anywhere in Southwest France, for example, would cost about €0.25/0.39.

A 10-digit number that starts with ☎ 06 indicates a mobile phone, and therefore an expensive number to call.

Note that a call made from a hotel-room telephone is usually very much more expensive than the same call from a public telephone.

Toll-Free Numbers Country Direct numbers and toll-free *numéros verts* (literally, 'green numbers', whose 10 digits begin with ☎ 08 00), can be dialled from public phones without a télécarte or coins. For a list of toll-free emergency numbers, see Emergencies later in this chapter.

Mobile Phones France uses the Global System for Mobile Communications (GSM) 900/1800, which is compatible with the rest of Europe and Australia but not with the North American GSM 1900 or the totally different system in Japan (though some North Americans have GSM 1900/900 phones that do work in France). If you have a GSM phone, check with your service provider about using it in France, and beware of calls being routed internationally (which works out as very expensive for a 'local' call).

Minitel

Minitel is a telephone-connected, computerised information service peculiar to France, set up in the 1980s. It's expensive to use and is being given a run for its money by the Internet. Coordinates consist of four digits (eg, 3611, 3614, 3615) and a string of letters. We have not included Minitel addresses in this book except those that may represent an especially cheap or easy route, or the only one.

However, France Telecom has an electronic directory that you can access in some post offices. 3611 is the prefix for general address and telephone enquiries. 3615 SNCF and 3615 TER provide train information.

Fax

Virtually all town post offices can send and receive *télécopies* or *téléfaxes* (domestic and international faxes), telexes and telegrams. To send a one-page fax costs about €4.60 to the UK, and about €7.60 to North America or Australasia.

Email & Internet Access

The cheapest places to access the Internet are the many state-funded youth resource centres called Bureaux d'Information Jeunesse (BIJ) or, in Toulouse and Bordeaux, Centres Régionaux d'Information Jeunesse (CRIJ); see the boxed text 'Bureaux d'Information Jeunesse' later in this chapter. Typical online rates are about €3 per hour, though many BIJs have periods or days when access is free (and booking ahead is essential); we list these under individual towns. These facilities are intended for the use of young French people, so please don't overuse or misuse them.

The number of cybercafes in the region is small but growing. Typical rates are from about €4 to €5 per hour.

The French postal service is installing 'Cyberposte' terminals in larger post offices, with payment by special magnetic card (€7.60 per hour initially, €4.55 per hour upon 'recharge' of the card). In tourist offices, cafes and other public spots you'll see France Telecom terminals where you can surf via Telecom's own server, Wanadoo, and pay for it with a télécarte; access is billed by the minute at rates equivalent to €7.20/9 per hour using a 120/50-unit card.

If you've got your own laptop and modem, and an account with a server that has local access points in France, you should be able to log on from your hotel room for the cost of a local or long-distance call. You'll need an *adapteur* (adapter) between your telephone plug and the standard T-shaped French receptacle. You can pick these up at a local electronics shop, or from a Web-based dealer such as Magellan's (W www.magellans.com) or Konexx (W www.konexx.com). If the telephone is hard-wired into the wall, ask if you can plug into the hotel's fax line. You're best off with a reputable 'global' modem.

DIGITAL RESOURCES

The World Wide Web is a rich resource for travellers. You can research your trip, hunt down bargain air fares, book hotels, check on weather conditions or chat with locals and other travellers about the best places to visit (or avoid!).

A good place to start is the Lonely Planet Web site (W www.lonelyplanet.com). Here you'll find information on travelling to most places on earth, postcards from other travellers and the Thorn Tree bulletin board, where you can ask questions before you go or dispense advice when you get back. You can also find travel news and updates to many of LP's most popular guidebooks. The subWWWay section links you to useful travel resources elsewhere on the Web.

France-specific sites worth checking out include:

Maison de la France The multilingual site of the French national tourism board, with background information, events, activities, accommodation, transport, package tours and more.
W www.franceguide.com

France Sud-Ouest With features, events, weather reports and good links to other regional-interest sites.
W www.francesudouest.com

Terres Occitanes A comprehensive site for those with an interest in the region's renascent Occitan culture.
W www.terresoccitanes.com

BOOKS

As a general rule, books are published in different editions by different publishers in different countries. Thus it's possible for a book to be a hardcover rarity in one country but readily available in paperback in another. Fortunately, bookshops and libraries

---

Internet en Français

If you surf the Web in France, you may have to do it in French. The following is a bit of useful French cyber-speak:

aide	help
cancel or *annuler*	cancel
coller	paste
copier	copy
couper	cut
edition	edit
fermer	close
fichier	file
ouvrir	open
précédent	back/preceding
quitter or *abandon*	exit
signet	bookmark
suivant	forward/next
vue	view

The '@' symbol is spoken as *arobase*, and 'dot' is *point*. Before French email addresses (whose accents can, in general, be safely ignored), you often see *mél*, short for *message électronique*.

search by title or author, so your local bookshop or library is best able to advise you on the availability of books recommended here. The following list is limited to works still in print and generally available in paperback.

Lonely Planet

Lonely Planet publishes guides to *France*, *Western Europe* and *Mediterranean Europe*, which include chapters covering Southwest France. It also publishes *Cycling France* and *Walking in France* for self-propelled visitors, *World Food France* for foodies and a handy *French phrasebook*.

Guidebooks

Michelin publishes the annual *Guide Rouge* (or Red Guide), rating France's hotels and, more famously, its restaurants with one, two or three stars. The annual *Guide Gault Millau France* awards up to four *toques rouges* (red chefs' caps) to restaurants offering exceptionally creative cuisine, and *toques blanches* (white chefs' caps) to those with good modern or traditional cuisine. Gault Millau is said to be quicker at picking up-and-coming restaurants. An English edition is available.

Travel

Freda White's *Three Rivers of France: Dordogne, Lot, Tarn* (1962) is a much-admired classic; although details are often out of date, its perceptive comments and local knowledge remain unbeatable. *Down the Dordogne*, by Michael Brown, describes the author's often-amusing adventures as he follows the river on foot from its source to Bordeaux. An out-of-print book worth looking for is *A Guide to the Dordogne*, by James Bentley, with fascinating background information on regional history, cuisine, art and literature, and a gazetteer of even the tiniest hamlets.

History & Politics

The Hundred Years' War, by Christopher Allmand, is a comparative study of how people in England and France coped with this interminable conflict. Historian Desmond Seward takes an Anglocentric look in his

book of the same name. A third work with the same title by Robin Neillands is an easier read, geared for travellers and, for a change, is biased towards the French.

Eleanor of Aquitaine, by Marion Meade, is a colourful, engrossing account of the life of this powerful woman. A new biography with the same title by Alison Weir is packed with details about Eleanor's personal life and times. *The Albigensian Crusade*, by Jonathan Sumption, examines the background to the 13th-century repression of Catharism, which set the seal on the future of Toulouse and Languedoc.

The Josephine Baker Story, by Ean Wood, recounts the story of the legendary cabaret-dancer, undercover agent and adoptive mother. *Vichy France and the Resistance*, by Harry R Kedward, is a recognised classic on this period. *Das Reich: The March of the 2nd SS Panzer Division Through France*, by Max Hastings, chillingly follows the movements of a German armoured division through the Dordogne and Limousin in 1944.

A classic on the history and culture of the Basques, especially on the French side, is Rodney Gallop's *A Book of the Basques*. First published in the 1930s, it remains one of the most readable attempts to explain the Basques to the rest of the world.

Art & Architecture

The Cambridge Illustrated History of Prehistoric Art, by Paul Bahn, is a beautifully illustrated survey which gives generous treatment to the cave carvings and paintings of Southwest France. *The Shamans of Prehistory: Trance & Magic in the Painted Caves*, by rock-art expert Jean Clottes, will annoy many an art historian with its argument that the region's Cro-Magnon cave art is the work of shamans. Aimed at children and illustrated with photos and computer imagery, Patricia Lauber's *Painters of the Caves* describes how the cave painters lived, ate and painted.

Jean-Auguste-Dominique Ingres, by Robert Rosenblum, is a biography of the enigmatic painter and son of Montauban. *Toulouse-Lautrec: A Life*, by Julia Frey, is a scholarly but sympathetic appraisal of the Albi-born artist.

Food & Wine

James Bentley's affectionate *Life & Food in the Dordogne* reveals how and why this region became famous for its cuisine, with recipes, personal anecdotes (Bentley lived in the area for years) and historical snippets. Paula Wolfert's *The Cooking of South West France* brings the region's people and food to life in her acclaimed cookery book. Jeanne Strang's *Goose Fat and Garlic* is another classic on the subject.

A Taste of Périgord, by Helen Raimes, paints an evocative picture of local life, while offering over 200 recipes, many (in true local style) requiring only simple, inexpensive ingredients. *Dordogne Gastronomique,* by Vicky Jones, is a richly photographed tome with some great recipes and absorbing cultural detail. Another visual delight is *The Joy of Truffles,* mixing the history of this elusive tuber with recipes and tips on how to find truffles yourself.

The most comprehensive guide to Bordeaux wines is David Peppercorn's *The Wines of Bordeaux,* featuring not only the famous vineyards but local brews that become our favourite *vins de table.* Paul and Jeanne Strang are here again with *Wines of Southwest France,* a guide to the region's 200-plus wineries, plus a generous look at its history and personalities.

Fiction

William Golding's extraordinary *The Inheritors* evokes a Neanderthal tribe's bewildered, dying days as it encounters a new race – the Cro-Magnon – in its land, seen through the eyes of a young Neanderthal man. The craggy landscape, described in twig-and-branch detail, is very reminiscent of the Périgord's limestone valleys.

Sir Arthur Conan Doyle's gripping historical novel, *The White Company,* recounts the adventures of an English monk who learns about chivalry, battle and bravado during the Hundred Years' War – a great read for kids and adults alike.

Joanne Harris' best-selling and magical

Chocolat tells of the transformation of a conservative Gascon village by a mysteriously gifted *chocolatiere* (chocolate maker) who arrives out of nowhere. See under Cinema in the Facts about Southwest France chapter for more about the film that followed.

General

The Most Beautiful Villages of the Dordogne is a lavish coffee-table book with text by James Bentley and photographs by Hugh Palmer. *Pétanque – The French Game of Boules,* by Garth Freeman, will give you a rolling start on this ancient, gentle and well loved game.

NEWSPAPERS & MAGAZINES

The major regional daily newspapers are *Sud Ouest* in Aquitaine and *La Depêche du Midi* in the Midi-Pyrénées, each with various regional editions or inserts. Regional weeklies include *La Semaine du Pays Basque* and *La République des Pyrénées.* The *News* (W www.french-news.com) is a monthly English-language newspaper 'for residents and lovers of France', published from Périgueux with features, tips and columns of expat interest.

International daily newspapers, such as the *Guardian* and the *Times,* the *International Herald Tribune,* the *Washington Post* and *USA Today* are widely available in tourist centres. Foreign magazines, such as the *Economist,* are on sale in Bordeaux and Toulouse.

RADIO

Radio France broadcasts via a network of stations, five of them national: France Bleu, France Culture, France Info (a 24-hour news station at 105.5MHz FM throughout the southwest), France Inter and France Musiques. FM pop-music stations include Fun Radio, Skyrock and Nostalgie, heavy on phone-ins and wisecracking DJs.

A big voice in the southwest is Toulouse-based Sud Radio. Radio Liberté, originating from Ribérac (Dordogne) at 96.1MHz FM, has expat-aimed, English-language programming at 12.15pm weekdays, with local events, weather, sports and news. For a mix of programming in Occitan and other languages (including English) try Radio Occitanie at 98.3MHz FM, from 6am to midnight daily.

English-language broadcasts of the BBC World Service and Voice of America (VOA) can be picked up on some medium-wave and short-wave frequencies. A reliable BBC short-wave frequency at night is 6195KHz.

TV

The country's major national TV channels are France 2 (news, entertainment, education), France 3 (regional programs) and La Cinquième (cartoons, game shows, documentaries). The big private stations are Canal+ (a pay channel with lots of films, both foreign and French), TF1 (France's most popular station, with news, sports and variety) and M6 (drama, music, news). MCM is France's answer to MTV.

Toulouse has its own channel, TLT Télé-Toulouse, with exclusively local programming. Upmarket hotels often offer Canal+ and access to CNN, BBC Prime, Sky and other English-language networks.

VIDEO SYSTEMS

Unlike the rest of Western Europe and Australia, which use PAL, and the USA and Canada which both use NTSC, France uses SECAM. Non-SECAM TVs won't work in France; nor can French videotapes be played on video recorders and TVs that lack a SECAM capability.

PHOTOGRAPHY & VIDEO

Colour-print and *diapositive* (slide) film are widely available in supermarkets, photo shops and Fnac stores, as are camcorder video cartridges (see the preceding section). To err on the side of caution, do not to put unprocessed film through airport scanners, as some powerful new machines may damage it.

In summer, avoid snapping at noon when glare is strongest. Photography is rarely forbidden, except in museums, art galleries and some churches. When photographing people, ask permission; if needs be, just smile and point at your camera and they'll get the picture – as you probably will.

TIME

French time is GMT/UTC plus one hour, except during daylight-saving time (from the last Sunday in March to the last Sunday in October) when it's GMT/UTC plus two hours. The UK and France are always one hour apart – when it's 6pm in London, it's 7pm in Bordeaux. New York is six hours behind (earlier than) France.

France uses the 24-hour clock. Times are written with an 'h' between hour and minutes – for example, 15h30 for 3.30pm.

ELECTRICITY

France runs on 220V, 50Hz AC. Old-style wall sockets take two round pins. Newer sockets accept fatter prongs and have a protruding earth (ground) pin. Many old-style sockets are recessed so the newer round plugs cannot be used in them; to avoid getting stuck with an up-to-date appliance in an out-of-date hotel, carry an adapter.

WEIGHTS & MEASURES

France uses the metric system. When writing numbers of four or more digits the French use full stops (periods) or spaces, rather than commas. For example, one million is 1.000.000 or 1 000 000. The decimal place is indicated with a comma, so English 1.75 becomes French 1,75.

LAUNDRY

Most towns have a *laverie libre-service* (unstaffed, self-service laundrette), usually open daily; they're noted in the individual chapters. Typical charges for a 6kg to 7kg load are about €4, plus €0.30/75 for five/12 minutes of drying.

TOILETS

Public toilets, signposted *toilettes* or WC, are scarce, though you can usually find a free one in the *mairie* (town hall) or the market hall, open even when the rest of the building isn't. Some car parks and public squares have coin-operated, self-flushing toilet booths (€0.15 to €0.30) – disconcerting things that look like they might trap you inside. At staffed toilets, expect to pay €0.30 to €0.75 for a wad of toilet paper.

The easiest option may be to use the facilities in a cafe or restaurant – preferably after ordering a drink or snack, though most proprietors aren't fussed if you don't. Ask, *est-ce que je peux utiliser les toilettes, s'il vous plaît?*

Bashful males take note: Some toilets are semi-mixed, with urinals and washbasins in a common area through which all and sundry pass to reach the closed stalls. Older establishments often have squat loos, with flushing mechanisms that can soak your shoes if you're not quick.

Few public toilets, except at airports and newer bus and train stations, are wheelchair-accessible.

Bidets

A bidet is a porcelain fixture that looks like a shallow toilet with a pop-up stopper. Originally conceived for the personal hygiene of aristocratic women, its primary purpose is for washing the genitals and anal area, though uses have expanded to everything from soaking your feet to hand-washing your laundry.

HEALTH

The southwest is a healthy place. Your main risks are sunburn, foot blisters, insect bites and upset stomach from eating and drinking too much.

Predeparture Planning

Immunisations Innoculations are not required to travel to France. A few routine vaccinations are recommended whether you're travelling or not: polio (usually administered during childhood), tetanus and diphtheria (usually administered together during childhood, with a booster shot every 10 years), and sometimes measles. All vaccinations should be recorded on an International Health Certificate, available from your doctor or government health department.

Health Insurance Citizens of EU countries are covered for emergency medical treatment throughout the EU on presentation of an E111 certificate, though charges are likely for medications, dental work and

secondary examinations including x-rays and laboratory tests. Ask about the E111 at your national health service or travel agent at least a few weeks before you go. In the UK you can get the forms at the post office. Claims must be submitted to a local *caisse primaire d'assurance-maladie* (sickness insurance office) before you leave France.

Most travel insurance policies also include medical coverage. For important suggestions about travel insurance, see Visas & Documents earlier in this chapter.

Other Preparations Ensure you're basically healthy before you start travelling. If you're going on a long trip make sure your teeth are OK. If you wear glasses take a spare pair and your prescription. If you require a particular medication take an adequate supply, as it may not be available locally. Take part of the packaging showing the generic name, rather than the brand, which will make getting replacements easier (and cheaper). It's a good idea to have a legible prescription or letter from your doctor to show that you legally use the medication, to avoid any problems.

Medical Treatment in France

Major hospitals are indicated on the maps in this book and their addresses and phone numbers are mentioned in the text. Tourist offices and hotels can put you onto a reliable doctor or dentist.

Public Health System Anyone (including a foreigner) who is sick can receive treatment in the *service des urgences* (casualty ward or emergency room) of any public hospital. Hospitals try to have people who speak English in casualty wards, but it's not always the case. If necessary, the hospital will call in an interpreter. It's a good idea to request a copy of any diagnosis – in English, if possible – for your doctor back home.

Treatment for illness or injury in a public hospital is cheaper in France than in many other western countries. A consultation costs about €25 (more on Sunday, public holidays and at night). Blood tests and other procedures each have a standard fee. Full hospitalisation costs from €450 a day. Hospitals usually ask that visitors from abroad settle accounts immediately after receiving treatment.

Dental Care Most major hospitals offer emergency dental services.

Pharmacies French pharmacies are usually marked by a green cross. *Pharmacien(ne)s* (pharmacists) can often suggest treatments for minor ailments.

If you're prescribed a medication in French, make sure you understand the dosage, frequency and timing. Ask for a copy of the *ordonnance* (prescription) for your records. During mushroom-picking season (autumn), pharmacies act as a mushroom-identifying service (see Poisonous Mushrooms under Dangers & Annoyances later in this chapter).

Pharmacies coordinate their closures so that a town isn't left without a place to buy medication. Details on the nearest *pharmacie de garde* (pharmacy on weekend and night duty) are posted on all pharmacy doors. There are 24-hour pharmacies in Bordeaux and Toulouse.

Basic Rules

Everyday Health Normal body temperature is 37°C (98.6°F); more than 2°C (4°F) higher indicates a high fever. The normal adult pulse rate is 60 to 100 beats per minute (children 80–100, babies 100–140). As a general rule the pulse increases about 20 beats per minute for each 1°C (2°F) rise in fever. Respiration (breathing) rate is also an indicator of illness. Count the number of breaths per minute: between 12 and 20 is normal for adults and older children (up to 30 for younger children, 40 for babies). People with a high fever or serious respiratory illness breathe more quickly than normal. More than 40 shallow breaths a minute may indicate pneumonia.

Water Tap water all over France is safe to drink. Fountain water isn't always *eau potable* (drinkable). In rural areas, beware of natural water sources. A burbling stream may

---

Medical Kit Check List

Following is a list of items you should consider including in your medical kit – consult your pharmacist for brands available in your country.

☐ **Aspirin or paracetamol (acetaminophen in the USA)** – for pain or fever

☐ **Antihistamine** – for allergies, eg, hay fever; to ease the itch from insect bites or stings; and to prevent motion sickness

☐ **Cold and flu tablets, throat lozenges and nasal decongestant**

☐ **Multivitamins** – consider for long trips, when dietary vitamin intake may be inadequate

☐ **Antibiotics** – consider including these if you're travelling well off the beaten track; see your doctor, as they must be prescribed, and carry the prescription with you

☐ **Loperamide or diphenoxylate** – 'blockers' for diarrhoea

☐ **Prochlorperazine or metaclopramide** – for nausea and vomiting

☐ **Rehydration mixture** – to prevent dehydration, which may occur, for example, during bouts of diarrhoea; particularly important when travelling with children

☐ **Insect repellent, sunscreen, lip balm and eye drops**

☐ **Calamine lotion, sting relief spray or aloe vera** – to ease irritation from sunburn and insect bites or stings

☐ **Antifungal cream or powder** – for fungal skin infections and thrush

☐ **Antiseptic (such as povidone-iodine)** – for cuts and grazes

☐ **Bandages, Band-Aids (plasters) and other wound dressings**

☐ **Scissors, tweezers and a thermometer** – note that mercury thermometers are prohibited by airlines

---

appear crystal clear, but it's inadvisable to drink untreated water unless you're at the source and can see it coming out of the rocks.

The simplest way of purifying water is to boil it thoroughly. At high altitude water boils at a lower temperature, so germs are less likely to be killed. Boil it for longer in these environments.

It's very easy to not drink enough liquids, particularly on hot summer days or at high altitude. Don't rely on thirst to indicate when you should drink. Not needing to urinate or very dark-yellow urine is a danger sign. Carrying your own water bottle is wise.

Environmental Hazards

Fungal Infections Fungal infections occur more commonly in hot weather and are usually found on the scalp, between the toes or fingers, in the groin and on the body (ringworm). You get ringworm (which is a fungal infection, not a worm) from infected animals or other people. Moisture encourages these infections.

To prevent fungal infections wear loose, comfortable clothes, avoid artificial fibres, wash frequently and dry carefully. If you do get an infection, wash the infected area at least daily with a disinfectant or medicated soap and water, then rinse and dry well. Apply an antifungal cream or powder such as Tolnifate (Tinaderm). Try to expose the infected area to air or sunlight as much as possible; wash all towels and underwear in hot water, change them often and let them dry in the sun.

Heat Exhaustion Dehydration and salt deficiency can cause heat exhaustion. Take time to acclimatise to the high temperatures, drink sufficient liquids and do not do anything too physically demanding.

Salt deficiency is characterised by fatigue, lethargy, headaches, giddiness and muscle cramps; salt tablets may help, but adding extra salt to your food is better.

Prickly Heat This is an itchy rash caused by excessive perspiration trapped under the skin. It usually strikes people who have just arrived in a hot climate. Keeping cool, bathing often, drying the skin and using a mild talcum or prickly heat powder or resorting to air-conditioning may help.

Sunburn You can get sunburned surprisingly quickly, even through cloud. Use a sunscreen, hat and barrier cream for your nose and lips. Calamine lotion or Stingose are good for mild sunburn. Protect your eyes with good-quality sunglasses, particularly if you will be spending time near water, sand or snow.

Hay Fever Sufferers of hay fever should be aware that the pollen count is especially high in May and June.

Infectious Diseases

Diarrhoea Simple things, such as a change of water, food or climate, can all cause a mild bout of diarrhoea, but a few rushed toilet trips with no other symptoms is not indicative of a major problem.

Dehydration is the main danger with any diarrhoea, particularly in children or the elderly, as it can occur quickly. Fluid replacement (at least equal to the volume being lost) is most important. Weak black tea with a little sugar, soda water, or soft drinks allowed to go flat and diluted 50% with clean water are all good. Keep drinking small amounts often. Stick to a bland diet as you recover.

Hepatitis There are almost 300 million carriers of hepatitis B in the world. It's spread by contact with infected blood, blood products or body fluids, for example through sexual contact, unsterilised needles and blood transfusions, or contact with blood via small breaks in the skin. Other risk situations include having a shave, a tattoo, or having your body pierced with contaminated equipment. You should seek medical advice, but there is not much you can do apart from resting, drinking lots of fluids and eating lightly.

AIDS & HIV The Human Immunodeficiency Virus (VIH in French), develops into AIDS, or Acquired Immune Deficiency Syndrome (SIDA in French), which is a fatal disease. HIV is a major problem in many countries. Any exposure to blood, blood products or body fluids may put an individual at risk. The disease is often transmitted through sexual contact or dirty needles – vaccinations, acupuncture, tattooing and body piercing can be as dangerous as intravenous drug use. HIV/AIDS can also be spread through

64 Facts for the Visitor – Health

infected blood transfusions, but French hospitals use blood that has been screened.

Fear of infection with HIV should never preclude treatment for serious medical conditions.

Information For information on free and anonymous *centres de dépistage* (HIV-testing centres) in France, ring the 24-hour SIDA Info Service toll-free (☎ 08 00 84 08 00).

AIDES (Association de Prévention, Information, Lutte contre le SIDA; W www.aides .org) is a national AIDS-prevention and help organisation. Its regional centres include AIDES Midi-Pyrénées (☎ 05 34 40 22 60, fax 05 34 40 22 61, e aidesmp@aol.com), 122 rue du Général Bourbaki, Toulouse; and AIDES Aquitaine (☎ 05 56 24 33 33, fax 05 56 98 93 10, e gironde@aidesaquitaine .com), 173 bis rue Judaïque, Bordeaux.

Sexually Transmitted Diseases Gonorrhoea, herpes and syphilis are among these diseases; sores, blisters or rashes around the genitals, discharges or pain when urinating are common symptoms. Syphilis symptoms eventually disappear but the disease continues and can cause severe problems in later years. In some STDs, such as wart virus or chlamydia, symptoms may be less marked or absent, especially in women.

While sexual abstinence is the only 100% effective prevention, using condoms is also effective. The different STDs each require specific antibiotics. There is no cure for herpes or AIDS.

Condoms All pharmacies carry *préservatifs* (condoms) and condom dispensers are increasingly common in public areas, such as brasseries, discotheques and WCs in cafes and petrol stations. Condoms conforming to French government standards are marked NF *(norme française)* in black on a white oval inside a red and blue rectangle.

Cuts, Bites & Stings
Rabies This is a potentially fatal viral infection found in many countries. Animals can be infected and it is their saliva that carries the virus. Any bite, scratch or even lick from a warm-blooded, furry animal should be cleaned immediately and thoroughly. Medical help should be sought promptly to receive a course of injections to prevent the onset of symptoms and death.

Insect Bites & Stings Bee and wasp stings are usually painful rather than dangerous. However, in people who are allergic to them severe breathing difficulties may occur and they may require urgent medical care. Calamine lotion or Stingose spray will give relief and ice packs will reduce the pain and swelling.

Ticks Check all over your body if you have been walking through a potentially tick-infested area, as ticks can cause skin infections and other more serious diseases. If a tick is found attached, press down around the tick's head with tweezers, grab the head and gently pull upwards. Avoid pulling the rear of the body as this may squeeze the tick's gut contents through the attached mouth parts into the skin, increasing the risk of infection and disease. Smearing chemicals on the tick will not make it let go and is not recommended.

Women's Health
Sexually transmitted diseases are a major cause of vaginal problems. Symptoms include a smelly discharge, painful intercourse and sometimes a burning sensation when urinating. Medical attention should be sought and sexual partners must also be treated. Remember that in addition to these diseases HIV or hepatitis B may also be acquired during exposure.

Antibiotic use, sweating, synthetic underwear and contraceptive pills can lead to fungal vaginal infections when travelling in hot climates. Good personal hygiene, loose-fitting clothes and cotton underwear will help to prevent them.

Fungal infections, characterised by a rash, itch and discharge, can be treated with a vinegar or lemon juice douche, or with yogurt. Nystatin, miconazole or clotrimazole pessaries or vaginal cream are the usual over-the-counter treatment.

The vines and rolling hills of Entre-deux-Mers

Vines destined to become fine wines

Bottles of quality St-Émilion tipple

Château Latour, Bordeaux

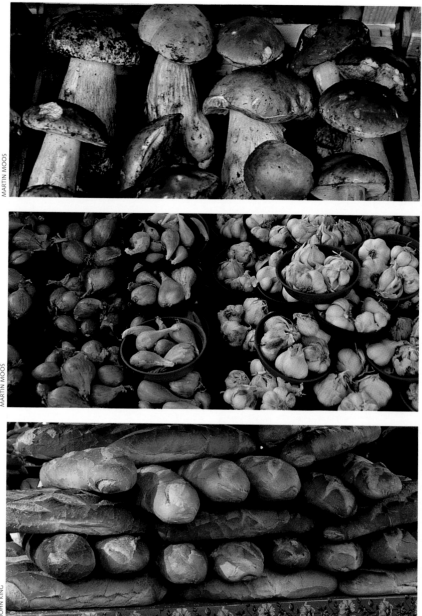

MARTIN MOOS

MARTIN MOOS

JOHN KING

There's no shortage of flavoursome fresh food to be found in French markets. Mushrooms, garlic, onions and delicious crusty bread are all common sights.

WOMEN TRAVELLERS

Some French men have clearly given little thought to the concept of *harcèlement sexuel* (sexual harassment), and believe that leering at a passing woman is paying her a compliment. Women needn't walk around in fear, however. Suave stares are about as adventurous as most French men get, with women rarely being physically assaulted on the street or touched up in bars. Still, as in any country, the best way to avoid trouble is to be conscious of your surroundings, avoid going out alone at night and to recognise potentially risky situations: deserted streets, lonely beaches or dark corners of big-city train stations.

Of course, it's not just French men that women travellers have to worry about. While solo women travellers attract little unwanted attention in the rural southwest, popular Atlantic coastal resorts attract macho personalities of all nationalities. Again, common sense is your best protection.

Topless sunbathing is not generally interpreted as deliberately provocative.

Organisations

The Centre d'Information sur les Droits de la Femme (CIDF) – including offices in Bordeaux (☎ 05 56 44 30 30, 5 rue Jean-Jacques Rousseau) and Toulouse (☎ 05 61 52 83 59, 95 grande rue St-Michel) – is the leading women's information and advice centre. Although geared to assisting with family or marital problems it can also offer practical support and information (eg, contacts for creches and baby-sitters), job assistance and general advice.

The national rape-crisis hotline is ☎ 08 00 05 95 95.

GAY & LESBIAN TRAVELLERS

France is one of Europe's most liberal countries regarding homosexuality, in part because of the French tradition of tolerance towards people living outside conventional social codes. In October 1999 the government passed the Civil Solidarity Pact, giving legal and fiscal (eg, tax and property) rights to unmarried couples including homosexuals.

The southwest's biggest gay communities are in Toulouse and Bordeaux. The lesbian scene is less public and is centred mainly in women's cafes and bars.

Several publications give a good overview of the scene in (and beyond) the southwest. The free *Gay Friendly France: Liberté, Egalité, Diversité* can be ordered from Gay Friendly France, c/o French Government Tourist Office, PO Box 386, Bohemia, NY 11716, USA (or **e** info@francetourism .com). The annual, French/English-language *Guide Gai Pied* (€12.05) lists cafes, bars, shops and gay organisations; order it on the Web at **W** www.gaipied.fr. At bookstores or newsstands in major towns you can find national, monthly gay publications such as *Gay, 3 Keller* and *Lesbia*.

Web sites geared specifically for homosexual travellers include:

Lonely Planet Up-to-date advice from recent visitors.
   W www.lonelyplanet.com.au/thorntree/gay/topics
Out and About A spin-off from the gay travel magazine *Out and About*, with information on the scene in various cities plus a calendar of events.
   W www.outandabout.com
Guidemag Gay-friendly hotels, bars and nightclubs.
   W www.guidemag.com/travel
New York University Everything from nightclubs and bookstores to gay community centres.
   W www.nyu.edu/pages/sls/travel/gltravel
La France Gaie et Lesbienne Listings in Toulouse and elsewhere.
   W www.france.qrd.org
Association Motocycliste Alternative Site of AMA (a long-established organisation for gay and lesbian bikers in the south of France), with details of regional meetings and biking activities.
   W www.multimania.com/motard

Organisations

In addition to the following there are also AIDS-awareness and help groups in Toulouse and Bordeaux – see the Health section earlier in this chapter.

Maison de l'Homosocialité (☎/fax 05 56 01 12 03) 30 rue Paul Bert, Bordeaux. A social centre organising debates and activities; see Bordeaux for details.

Wake Up! (☎ 06 21 48 40 83, e wake-up@gay .com) A Bordeaux association for gay and lesbian students.

CRIPS Aquitaine (☎ 05 57 57 18 80, fax 05 57 57 18 82) Université de Bordeaux II, 3ter place de la Victoire. Aquitaine's centre for regional news and AIDS awareness, open 9am to 6pm Monday to Thursday.

Lesbian & Gay Pride Bordeaux (☎ 06 14 56 45 01, fax 05 56 91 03 58) Organises Bordeaux's Gay Pride march in early June (variable date).

Gais et Lesbiennes en Marche (☎ 06 11 87 38 81, fax 05 34 60 18 66, e gelem@citiweb.net) apt 530, 34 rue Paul Decamps, Toulouse. Defends the rights of gays and takes part in many gay events, notably the Gay Pride march in June.

Le Centre Gai et Lesbien de Toulouse (☎ 05 61 62 30 62) 4 rue de Belfort. Toulouse's main drop-in gay centre, and home to other gay associations; open 5pm to 8pm Monday to Friday and 3pm to 8pm at weekends.

Bagdam Espace Lesbien (☎ 05 61 53 55 48) 1 rue de la Fonderie. Toulouse's main lesbian help-centre; organises the annual Printemps Lesbien in April and May, with films, meetings and discussions.

Association Gay et Lesbienne de Soutien Santé et Divertissement (☎ 05 53 70 48 58, fax 05 53 70 12 21) 13 rue Etienne Marcel, Villeneuve-sur-Lot. A gay/lesbian organisation active in the Lot and neighbouring departments.

DISABLED TRAVELLERS

The southwest is not user-friendly for *handicapés* (disabled people). Kerb ramps are scarce, older public facilities and budget hotels lack lifts and the hilltop villages of the Lot and Dordogne are a nightmare in a wheelchair. And you can practically forget the prehistoric caves for which the region is so famous.

But all is not lost. Many two- or three-star hotels are equipped with lifts; Michelin's *Guide Rouge* indicates hotels with facilities for disabled people, while *Gîtes Accessibles aux Personnes Handicapées* (€9.15 from Gîtes de France) lists regional *gîtes ruraux* (country cottages) and chambres d'hôte with disabled access (for more information see Accommodation later in this chapter).

SNCF has made efforts to make its trains accessible. *Fauteuil roulant* (wheelchair

travellers) are welcome on all trains provided they make a reservation by phone or at a station at least a few hours before departure; arrival stations can also be alerted. A wheelchair symbol in timetables indicates stations with facilities for the disabled. See SNCF's free *Guide du Voyageur à Mobilité Réduite,* or contact SNCF Accessibilité at toll-free ☎ 08 00 15 47 53 for details.

At mainline train stations, SOS Voyageurs (Toulouse ☎ 05 61 62 27 30, Bordeaux ☎ 05 56 92 24 31) – a voluntary group usually run by retirees – offers to elderly and/or disabled travellers.

Toulouse and Bordeaux airports have wheelchair access and assistance (eg, allocated parking spaces); tell the airline in advance of your requirements and they'll make arrangements to help you on board. Europcar has a few adapted cars for hire through its Bordeaux and Toulouse offices. Eurostar (see the Getting There & Away chapter) offers wheelchair passengers 1st-class travel for 2nd-class fares, and most ferry companies have facilities for the disabled.

For an overview of facilities available to the disabled, see *European Holidays and Travel Abroad: A Guide for Disabled People,* published by the Royal Association for Disability & Rehabilitation (RADAR; ☎ 020-7250 3222), 12 City Forum, 250 City Rd, London EC1V 8AF. The Paris-based Association des Paralysés de France (☎ 01 40 78 69 00) also has details of wheelchair-friendly accommodation.

SENIOR TRAVELLERS

Senior citizens (in what the French call *le troisième âge,* the third age) are entitled to discounts, for example, on public transport and museum admission charges, provided they show proof of their age. In some cases an official-looking card or pass might move things along (see Seniors' Cards under Visas & Documents earlier in this chapter).

See the preceding section on Disabled Travellers for additional resources.

TRAVEL WITH CHILDREN

Successful travel with children requires planning and effort. Don't overdo things;

trying to see too much can cause problems. Include the kids in the planning. Balance a day traipsing around bastides or Romanesque churches with a canoe trip, swimming at a *base de loisir* (leisure complex) or a theme-park outing.

Many towns, such as Lacanau, Lourdes, Périgueux, St-Émilion, Rocamadour and Domme, cater for kids (and foot-weary parents) with 'Le Petit Train Touristique' – electric trains that trundle round the town and can perk up a day's sightseeing. If these are a hit, look out for other special train rides in the region (see the boxed text 'Tops for Kids'). If you're into walking, Les Sentiers d'Emilie en... is a series of walking guides that offers family-friendly route suggestions.

Nature-loving kids might enjoy Fermes des Découverte (Discovery Farms), part of the Bienvenue à la Ferme (Welcome to the Farm) program; ask at tourist offices. Gîtes d'Enfants is a program of one-week stays on vetted farms, with full board and activities, for groups of children aged from four to 10 or six to 13, and marketed by Gîtes de France (see under Accommodation later in this chapter). A similar program for kids aged under seven is L'Accueil Toboggan (contact the Comité Régional de Midi-Pyrénées; for details see under Tourist Offices earlier in this chapter).

Getting around the region is easiest with a car. Most car-rental firms have children's safety seats for hire at a nominal cost (book in advance). Highchairs and cots (cribs) are standard in most restaurants and hotels, though numbers are limited. The choice of baby food, infant formulas, disposable nappies (diapers) and the like is as great in French supermarkets as it is back home.

Eating out can be a nightmare at upmarket restaurants: French children are trained from an early age to sit still while their parents enjoy their multiple-course meals. Foreign tourists can be just as child-intolerant. Save your nerves and choose a place with an outdoor *terrasse* where the kids can flick bread across the table without the maitre d' glaring. Some readers recommend the restaurants in shopping centres such as Car-

Tops for Kids

Here are some suggestions to keep the kids happy. Details can be found under relevant town listings.

Amusement & Theme Parks
Walibi Parc d'Attractions (Agen); Prehisto Parc (Tursac); Le Thot (Thonac); Village du Bournat (Le Bugue); Musée en Plein Air du Quercy (Cabrerets).

Historic Sights, Caves & Great Musums
Cité de l'Espace (Space Park Museum/Planetarium, Toulouse); Croiseur Le Colbert (navy cruiser, Bordeaux); Château de Castelnaud (Beynac-et-Cazenac); Château de Biron, (near Monpazier); Rouffignac Cave (Rouffignac); Gouffre de Padirac (near Rocamadour); Interactive Museum of Bastides (Monflanquin).

Outdoor Thrills & Spills
Biking on easy trails in the Gironde and along the Atlantic Coast (see the Bordeaux, the Atlantic Coast & the Landes chapter); canoeing and kayaking along the Dordogne and Lot rivers; horse-riding practically everywhere; rock-climbing or potholing in the Lot.

Fun Train Rides
Steam train from Martel (Lot) and the coastal ride from Pointe de Grave to Soulac (Atlantic Coast); cog-wheel railway up La Rhune Mountain (French Basque country); century-old train from Sabres to Marquèze (the Landes); Le Petit Train d'Artouste in the Vallée d'Ossau (Béarn).

✹ ✹ ✹ ✹ ✹ ✹ ✹ ✹ ✹ ✹ ✹ ✹ ✹

refour and Mammouth (on the outskirts of larger towns and usually open). The authors' kids found that rural *fermes auberges* and *tables d'hôte*, and many small village restaurants, were far more fun, especially when there were hens, pigs, dogs or cats to play with once the first course had been gulped down.

Most tourist offices will have a list of suitable *gardes d'enfants* (baby-sitting services) and creches in the area. It may also be worth looking in at local Bureaux d'Information Jeunesse (see the boxed text 'Bureaux d'Information Jeunesse' later in this chapter) as many will have noticeboards that list similar services. Lonely Planet's *Travel with Children* is another good source of general information.

DANGERS & ANNOYANCES

For emergency numbers see under Telephone in the Post & Communications section earlier in this chapter.

Theft

The southwest is a pretty safe place. The biggest problem for tourists is *vol* (theft), especially from easily identifiable rental cars. Other common problems are pickpocketing and bag-snatching (not just handbags but daypacks), particularly in crowded train stations, cinemas, rush-hour public buses and even tourist offices. Keep an eye on your bags and always keep your money, credit cards, tickets, passport, driving licence and other important documents in a belt or pouch worn inside your clothes. Keep enough money for the day in a separate wallet.

If you leave your bags at a left-luggage office or luggage locker at a train station, treat the claim chit or locker code like cash. Daypack snatchers have taken stolen chits to the train station and claimed the rest of their victims' belongings.

Theft from hotel rooms is less common but it's still unwise to leave your valuables in your room. In hostels, lock nonvaluables in the locker provided and take everything valuable with you. Upmarket hotels have *coffres* (safes).

Cops

There are two kinds of law enforcers in France. *Gendarmes* – the ones with the traditional pill-box hats – are quasi-military police under the Ministry of Defence and are usually the only law enforcers in the countryside. Their headquarters is called a *gendarmerie*. *Police*, who wear soft caps and come under the umbrella of the Ministry of the Interior, are found only in the cities and larger towns, at the *commissariat de police*.

With the possible exceptions of Toulouse and Bordeaux, you will find few of either who can speak much English. In a medical emergency you'll have better luck at a hospital, since doctors are required to study English.

The Hunt

Throughout the southwest, gun-toting Frenchmen are on the move during the hunting season (September to January), making walking a potentially hazardous activity, especially in areas signposted *chasseurs* (hunters) or *chasse gardé* (beware hunting) and especially if you're dressed in anything that might remind a short-sighted hunter of a deer or wild boar. Accidents do happen (some 50 French hunters die each year after being shot by other hunters) so beware of wandering into remote forests or woodland areas at this time.

Poisonous Mushrooms

Mushroom hunting is a passion in the southwest. Pick by all means, but eat nothing until it has been positively identified. Most pharmacies will offer a mushroom-identifying service. In the Bordeaux region there is even a hotline (☎ 05 56 96 40 80) you can call for advice on what to do if you suspect mushroom poisoning.

Coastal Dangers

There are strong undertows and currents along the Atlantic coast. If you sleep on a beach, ensure that you're above the high-tide mark! The Centre d'Essai des Landes, between Biscarosse and Mimizan, is a missile testing area and strictly off-limits.

Smoke

Serious nonsmokers should consider holidaying in another country – or at least sticking to outdoor dining areas. Many French people smoke like Vesuvius, and even in the region's very few no-smoking restaurants some still cheerfully light up.

EMERGENCIES

When you ring ☎ 15, the 24-hour dispatchers at the Service d'Aide Médicale d'Urgence (SAMU; Emergency Medical Aid Service) will send a private ambulance (€40 to €45) or, if necessary, a mobile intensive-care unit. For less serious problems, SAMU can dispatch a doctor for a house call. If you'd prefer to be taken to a particular hospital, mention this to the ambulance crew, as otherwise they will go to the nearest. You must pay cash at the time, although in emergency cases (those requiring intensive-care units), billing is taken care of later.

The following emergency numbers are toll-free:

EU-wide Emergency number	☎ 112
SAMU medical treatment/ambulance	☎ 15
Police	☎ 17
Fire Brigade	☎ 18

LEGAL MATTERS

The police are allowed to search anyone at any time, regardless of whether there is an obvious reason to do so.

As elsewhere in the EU, laws are tough when it comes to drink-driving. The acceptable blood-alcohol limit is 0.05%, with drivers who exceed this amount facing fines of up to €5000 and even jail terms. Licences can be immediately suspended.

Importing or exporting drugs can lead to a jail sentence of between 10 and 30 years. The fine for possession of drugs for personal use can be as high as €80,000. If you litter, you risk a €150 fine.

BUSINESS HOURS

Museums and shops (but not cinemas, restaurants or boulangeries) are closed on public holidays. On Sunday, a boulangerie is usually about all that is open (morning only) and public transport services are less frequent or nonexistent.

Hotels, restaurants, cinemas, cultural institutions and shops usually close for a few weeks or longer in winter for their congé annuel (annual closure) – though most office workers go on holiday en masse in August. For information on the high/low seasons see 'When to Go' under Planning earlier in this chapter. The majority of shops open at 9am or 10am. Village shops close for a long lunch between 2pm and 4pm.

Commercial banks are generally open from 8am or 9am to sometime between 11.30am and 1pm, and from 1.30pm or 2pm to 4.30pm or 5pm Monday to Friday. Many banks in towns with Saturday markets open on Saturday and then close on Monday.

PUBLIC HOLIDAYS & SPECIAL EVENTS
French National Holidays

The following jours fériés (public holidays) are observed throughout France and are often a cue for festivities that spill into the streets.

New Year's Day (Jour de l'An) 1 January
Easter Sunday (Pâques) Late March/April
Easter Monday (Lundi de Pâques) Late March/April
May Day (Fête du Travail) 1 May
Victory Day (Victoire) Celebrating the Allied victory in Europe that ended WWII, 1945; 8 May
Ascension Thursday (L'Ascension) A national holiday celebrated on the 40th day after Easter.
Pentecost/Whit Sunday (Pentecôte) A national holiday celebrated on the seventh Sunday after Easter. Mid-May to mid-June
Whit Monday (Lundi de Pentecôte)
Bastille Day/National Day (Fête Nationale) 14 July
Assumption Day (L'Assomption) 15 August
All Saints' Day (La Toussaint) 1 November
Remembrance Day (L'Onze Novembre) In celebration of the WWI armistice; 11 November
Christmas (Noël) 25 December

The holidays celebrated with greatest gusto are Bastille Day and May Day; on the latter, many people (especially kids) sell muguets (lilies of the valley), which are said to bring good luck.

When a holiday falls on a Tuesday or Thursday you'll probably find it linked to the nearest weekend to make a four-day break. The doors of banks are a good place to look for announcements of upcoming long weekends.

The following are not public holidays in France: Shrove Tuesday (Mardi Gras; the day before the first day of Lent); Jeudi Saint (Maundy – or Holy – Thursday) and Vendredi Saint (Good Friday) just before Easter; and Boxing Day (26 December).

Regional Festivals

The southwest offers a feast of festivals, with scores of annual events – plus, of course, any excuse to celebrate the region's most beloved pastime – the preparation and eating of food. Regional and most departmental tourist offices have detailed information on local events. Here are a few highlights:

February

Carnaval A major event on the religious calendar, with festivities all over France during the last few days before Lent (about six weeks before Easter); Albi's celebrations are especially grand, with folk groups, bands and processions.

April

Printemps des Musées All of France's state-run museums are open for free on the first Sunday in April.

Festival de Flamenco Béarn echoes to the sound of stamping feet for 15 days in early April, Pau.

Weekend Portes Ouvertes dans les Châteaux du Médoc Winemakers around the region open their cellars and fermenting rooms to present the latest vintages for a weekend in early April, Médoc.

Festival Européen des Cerfs-Volants European kite festival on a weekend in late April, Hossegor.

May

Fête de St-Sicaire A traditional fair held on 1 May, complete with food stalls and fairground, Brantôme.

Alors Chante A festival of traditional French songs during the week before Easter, Montauban.

Fête de la Montagne The Mountain Festival, a gathering of professionals and organisations introducing the Haut-Béarn through trips, films and traditional Ossau music, on the first weekend in May, Laruns.

Bandas à Condom Two days of European marching bands and high jinks on the second weekend of May, Condom.

Fête des Corridas Bullfight fever over Pentecost weekend, Vic Fézensac.

Formula 3000 Grand Prix A high-gear event over Pentecost weekend, Pau.

Foire International de Bordeaux The region's biggest trade fair, with art and craft exhibits, music and dance, in mid-May.

Danses des 7 Provinces Basque Dance troupes come from all over the Spanish and French Basque country in late May or early June, St-Jean de Luz.

June

Festival International de Théâtre d'Enfants A four-day children's drama festival in early June, Toulouse.

Festival de Pau A three-week extravaganza of drama, dance and music from mid-June to early July, Pau.

Jazz Bonanza

Southwest France loves its jazz. During the summer you can find jazz festivals everywhere. Here are some of the best:

Festival de Jazz Two days in early July, Oloron-Ste-Marie.

Festival de Jazz five days in mid-July, Villeneuve-sur-Lot.

Jazz à Montauban 10 days from mid-July, Montauban.

Souillac en Jazz Four days in mid-July, Souillac.

Jazz aux Remparts Six days in mid-July, Bayonne.

Festival de Jazz d'Albi Last week of July, Albi.

Jazz au Marciac 10 days in mid-August, Marciac.

✹ ✹ ✹ ✹ ✹ ✹ ✹ ✹ ✹ ✹ ✹ ✹

Fête de la Musique The world's biggest free music event. All of France lets its hair down with music from drum 'n' bass to symphony concerts, in venues of every kind, 21 June.

Printemps de Cahors A three-week celebration of the visual arts, including outdoor night-time shows, from mid-June to early July in Cahors' old town.

July

Fête de Flamenco A celebration of flamenco music and dance for a week following the first Monday in July, Mont de Marsan.

Fête Ossaloise An evening of traditional song and dance, usually on the first Saturday in July during the annual movement of sheep to the high valleys, Laruns.

Festival Garonne Concerts, theatre and dance celebrating the River Garonne during the first fortnight in July, Toulouse.

Biarritz Surf Festival A week-long event with competitions, demonstrations, films and concerts, mid-July.

Festival de Blues A popular blues event for four days in mid-July, Cahors.

Festival de Country Music Country tunes, Western dancing and hot-air balloons from Thursday to Sunday closest to Bastille Day, Mirande.

Festival du Haut Quercy Three weeks of sacred music, choral and instrumental works, Martel and Rocamadour.

Fêtes du Grand Fauconnier A two-day medieval fair, with traditional markets, costumes and parades in mid-July, Cordes-sur-Ciel.

Festival du Périgord Noir A celebrated series of classical concerts in churches and chateaux around the region, mid-July to late August.

Festival du Folklore Also called the Festival de Montignac, a week-long celebration of international folk music and dance in late July, Montignac.

Fête du Vin A hugely popular three-day wine festival, held in late July on Bordeaux's river bank.

Festival du Folklore 1½ weeks of international dance, music and theatre in late July and early August of even-numbered years, Oloron-Ste-Marie.

Festival Goya No, not Goya paintings but Latin and North African music, held over two weeks from July to mid-August, Castres.

Festival Musiques et Paroles en Ribéracois World music, classical and jazz performances, from mid-July to mid-August, Ribérac.

Fête de la Madeleine Parades, concerts, bullfights, *courses landaises* and an airshow, for six days from the Saturday after Bastille Day, Mont de Marsan.

August

Festival International du Mime Actuel A week-long international mime festival in early August, Périgueux.

Fête du Vin A wine fair in the appropriately named town of Buzet (near Nérac), early August.

Fêtes de Bayonne Five days of Basque music, bullfights, a float parade and rugby matches starting on the first Wednesday of August, Bayonne.

Grande Semaine de Pélote Basque Pélote fever in the second week of August in villages throughout the French Basque country.

Festival de Force Basque One of the largest displays of Basque muscle-power, including rock-lifting and tug-of-war, in mid-August, St-Palais; similar events take place throughout the region during July and August.

Hossegor Rip Curl Pro World surfing championships at the end of August, Hossegor.

Sinfonia en Périgord A two-week celebration of baroque music with performances in abbeys and chateaux, late August to early September, Périgueux.

September

Jour des Monuments Historiques Free admission to historic buildings all over France on the second Sunday in September.

Jurade de St-Émilion The start of the wine harvest is proclaimed by the Wine Brotherhood of St-Émilion on the third Sunday of September.

Fête des Montgolfiades A two-day hot-air balloon fiesta at the end of September, Rocamadour.

Aqui Parlem Nostra Linga

If you understand that, you'll feel right at home when La Félibrée kicks off in Périgord on the first Sunday in July. This celebration of southern France's ancient Occitan language, music and traditions is held in a different village each year, a practice dating back to the 19th century when the Félibrée society was founded by a group of poets and writers in reaction to the central government's attempts to suppress regional cultures. It's still a driving force in keeping Occitan traditions alive.

In 2001, when Périgueux hosted the event, the town was decorated with 150,000 paper flowers, they presented a mass in Occitan and a typical Périgord lunch (called a *taluda*), plus they put on an open-air pageant and 10 days of musical and dramatic activities. Smaller towns can't match that, but at any Félibrée you're likely to see townsfolk dressed in traditional costume and bands playing instruments such as the hurdy-gurdy to accompany songs in the Langue d'Oc (language of Occitan).

❋ ❋ ❋ ❋ ❋ ❋ ❋ ❋ ❋ ❋ ❋ ❋

October

La Cita A celebration of Latin American film and culture during the first week of October, Biarritz.

Jazz sur Son 31 International jazz festival ('31' refers to the Haute-Garonne department) in October, Toulouse.

Medieval fair & Foire aux Fromages Period costume, traditional music and the judging of the vallée d'Ossau's famous summer cheeses on the first weekend in October, Laruns.

Fête du Piment The French Basque country's last big bash of the year, with a blessing of the peppers and the crowning of a Knight of the Pimento, on the last weekend in October, Espelette.

Reef Biarritz Surf Trophée Surfing's 'Masters', in late October or early November (dates vary), Biarritz.

November

Festival du Film Held in early November, Sarlat.

Fête de Ste-Catherine A religious festival accompanied by agricultural and gastronomic fairs all over the region, late November.

Journées de la Danse Traditionelle en Midi-Pyrénées Concerts and courses on the theme of Occitan traditional dance during the third week of November of odd-numbered years, Toulouse.

ACTIVITIES

Southwest France offers an array of outdoor pursuits to please the most adventurous tastes. On the Atlantic coast you may surf, swim, scuba dive or pamper yourself with a fortnight of thalassotherapy (see under Spas & Thalassotherapy, later in this section). You can climb the canyons of the Haut-Béarn (part of the Basses-Pyrénées), jump off them with a paraglider, fly over them in a hot-air balloon or, in winter, ski down some of them. You can pilot a houseboat on, or drop a fishing line into, a network of canals and calm rivers, or you can kayak, raft or go canyoning down the frisky streams of the Béarn and the Tarn. The limestone of Périgord is honeycombed with caves to explore. And you can walk, ride a bike or gallop all over the place.

Most departmental tourist offices and many municipal ones in Southwest France publish their own *guide loisirs* (leisure guide) booklets, listing things to do and local outfits who will help you do them. Loisirs Accueil France, a leisure services organisation with branches in each department (see Tourist Offices earlier in this chapter), also has details of activities and courses. Numerous travel agencies run thematic tours built around cycling, walking and other activities; for contact details see Organised Tours in the Getting There & Away chapter.

Cycling

The French take their cycling seriously; whole parts of the country – including the Pyrénées in Southwest France – almost grind to a halt during the annual Tour de France (see Spectator Sports later in this chapter).

Pedalling Southwest France is tremendously popular, both by touring *vélo* (bicycle) and also by *vélo tout-terrain* (VTT; mountain bike). The richly picturesque back roads of the Dordogne and the easy coastal trails of the Landes are big favourites with visitors. Also popular are the foothills of the Pyrénées, including the Basque country. There are few killer hills, except in Haut-Béarn.

You can hire VTTs in most larger towns for €10 to €16 per day, or €40 to €80 per week (around a third less for touring bikes). VTTs are permitted on some GR trails (see Walking), but take care not to startle walkers. VTTs are forbidden off-road in the Parc National des Pyrénées, so keep to the *pistes cyclable* (cycling paths).

Many local cycling clubs organise tours that are open to visitors; look for their announcements in tourist offices or, just ahead of the events, on roadside signs. Many tourist offices sell itineraries (some in English) compiled by these clubs, and each department publishes its own guide to cyclable trails. Didier-Richard publishes Les guides VTT, a series of cyclists' topo-guides (in French).

For information on road rules, cycling organisations, bicycle transport and rental, see the Bicycle section of the Getting Around chapter. See Organised Tours in the Getting There & Away chapter for bicycle tours. Places that rent bikes are noted under city or town listings.

Walking

Southwest France is criss-crossed by hiking trails. No permits are needed for walking, though there are restrictions on where you can camp, especially in the Parc National des Pyrénées.

The best-known trails are *sentiers de grande randonnée,* long-distance footpaths whose names begin with 'GR', marked by red and white stripes on everything from trees and rocks to walls and posts. The GR6 crosses the Dordogne from west to east, while the GR36 threads together the Dordogne, Lot and Tarn departments. The popular GR10 spans the Pyrénées from the Mediterranean to the Atlantic, and the GR8 runs down the Aquitaine coast. The GR65 and its branches take in many of the pilgrim routes to Santiago de Compostela (see the boxed text 'The Pilgrims of St-Jacques' under Religion in the Facts about Southwest France chapter) across the Lot, Tarn-et-Garonne, Gers and the French Basque country.

Most *grandes randonnées de pays* (GRP), marked yellow and red, are loop trails designed for a close, multi-day look at one area. Shorter day-hike trails are *sentiers de petites randonnées* (PR) or *sentiers de pays;* many of these are circular too.

The Fédération Française de Randonnée Pédestre (FFRP; W www.ffrp.asso.fr), which marks and maintains GR, GRP and PR trails, also publishes excellent French-language 'topoguides' about them, with trail conditions, flora, fauna, villages, camp sites, accommodation and other general information. Local topoguides are also available. *The Way of Saint James,* from Cicerone Walking Guides, is a detailed, two-part, English-language guide to the famous GR65. Larger bookshops and tourist offices stock many of these. Also check out Lonely Planet's own *Walking in France.*

For information on maps, see Planning earlier in this chapter. For information on *refuges, gîtes d'étape* and other overnight accommodation for walkers, see Accommodation later in this chapter. If the weather looks dodgy, contact Météo Consult (☎ 08 36 68 12 34, W www.meteoconsult.fr).

Surfing

The coast of Gironde, the Landes and the French Basque country is dotted with prime surfing beaches, many of which are actually championship quality (see the boxed text 'Surfing in the Southwest'). Surfing first arrived here during the 1950s and the first World Surfing Championships to be held in Europe took place in 1968 at Anglet on the Basque coast.

Surfing is a year-round activity, though conditions tend to be best (and crowds minimal) during September and October. Aquitaine's tidal variations are extreme, with miserable conditions often turning brilliant an hour later. The top spots, or adjacent towns, have surf schools, surf shops, gear *location* (rental) and a brisk social scene. Surf schools cater for every level.

You can rent a surfboard for €12 to €23 per day, or a bodyboard for less. Individual surfing lessons cost €20 to €45 per hour. A cheaper option is to do a group course – for example, attending five half-day sessions for €250 to €400. The youth hostel

at Anglet offers course-plus-accommodation packages. A week with half board in the high season costs €306 (€280 if you're camping).

Sailing & Windsurfing

Voile (sailing) and *planche à voile* (windsurfing) are popular wherever there's water and a breeze. The big coastal lakes and basins of Gironde and the Landes (Hourtin Carcans, Lacanau, Arcachon, Cazaux, Sanguinet, Biscarosse Parentis, Aureilhan, Léon, Soustons and Hossegor) are especially good, and it's easy to rent gear and take lessons in the area.

Scuba Diving & Snorkelling

The Atlantic coast and its inshore lakes and basins (see the preceding Sailing & Windsurfing section) offer attractive opportunities for *plongée* (diving). Shops and clubs where you can hire equipment or take a diving course are listed in the relevant regional chapters.

Swimming

The Atlantic coast abounds in fine, sandy beaches; good places to start are those listed in the boxed text 'Surfing in the Southwest' overleaf. In France, any beach not signposted as private is open to the public.

Topless bathing for women is pretty normal in France; if others are doing it, you can assume it's OK. The Atlantic coast is also well endowed with nude beaches, some of them associated with naturist camp sites.

River & White-Water Sports

In summer, local agencies organise serene canoe and kayak trips on every river of any size in Southwest France, complete with drop-off and pick-up services.

For more serious *eau-vive* (white-water) junkies, these and other outfits also run day and multiday kayak and raft trips on frisky streams such as the lower Aveyron (along the border between the Tarn-et-Garonne and Tarn departments), the Ossau, Oloron and Pau in Béarn, and the Nive in the French Basque country. We note such outfits in the regional chapters. The Fédération Française

Surfing in the Southwest

No two surfers agree on the best swells, but a good starting point would be the beaches that have consistently served as past world surfing championship venues – for example, Lacanau in Gironde, Biscarrosse and Hossegor in the Landes, and Anglet in the French Basque Country.

Following is a rundown of Aquitaine's better surfing beaches. Those that have been preferred venues for national or world championships in the past are shown by (*). Those with spots suitable for novices are shown by (+). Those with dubious water quality are shown by (=). Be aware that each beach may consist of several spots (surfing locations) of varying quality. Note that many of these spots have no lifeguards.

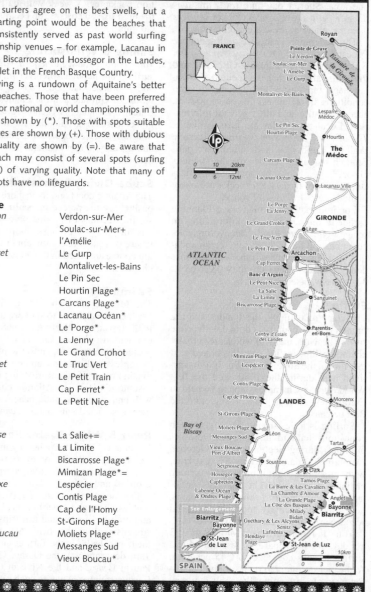

Gironde

Le Verdon	Verdon-sur-Mer
Soulac	Soulac-sur-Mer+
	l'Amélie
Montalivet	Le Gurp
	Montalivet-les-Bains
Hourtin	Le Pin Sec
	Hourtin Plage*
Carcans	Carcans Plage*
Lacanau	Lacanau Océan*
Lège	Le Porge*
	La Jenny
	Le Grand Crohot
Cap-Ferret	Le Truc Vert
	Le Petit Train
	Cap Ferret*
	Le Petit Nice

Landes

Biscarrosse	La Salie+=
	La Limite
	Biscarrosse Plage*
Mimizan	Mimizan Plage*=
Lit-et-Mixe	Lespécier
	Contis Plage
	Cap de l'Homy
St-Girons	St-Girons Plage
Vieux-Boucau	Moliets Plage*
	Messanges Sud
	Vieux Boucau*

Surfing in the Southwest

Seignosse	Seignosse*
Hossegor	Hossegor*
Capbreton	Capbreton*=
Labenne	Labenne Océan
	Ondres Plage
Boucau	Tarnos Plage=

French Basque Country

Anglet	La Barre*
	Les Cavaliers
	Plages d'Anglet
	Sables d'Or
	VVF
	La Chambre d'Amour
Biarritz	La Grande Plage*
	La Côte des Basques
	Milady
Bidart	Bidart
Guéthary	Guéthary*
	Les Alcyons
	Senix
	Lafiténia
St-Jean de Luz	Erromardie
	Ste-Barbe
	Ciboure
	Socoa
Hendaye	Hendaye-Plage+=

MARTIN HARRIS

Southwest France has world-class surf for fledgling surfer and pro alike.

More Information

For surf conditions (in French), contact Swell Line (☎ 08 36 68 40 64). Those with Internet access can see live video footage of the waves at Lacanau, Hossegor or Anglet at ⓦ www.swell-line.com. For information on surf clubs and competition dates, contact the Fédération Française du Surf (☎ 05 58 43 55 88, fax 05 58 43 60 57), 30 impasse Digue Nord, BP 28, 40150 Hossegor.

The Stormrider Guide: Europe, an atlas of European surfing, has 80 pages of maps and information on the Aquitaine coast. It's sold for £25 by Low Pressure (☎/fax 01288-359867, ⓔ mail@lowpressure .co.uk), 2 Efford Farm, Bude, Cornwall EX23 8LP, UK; and at the Low Pressure shop (☎ 020-7792 3134), 23 Kensington Park Rd, London W11 2EU.

Surf Etiquette

Surfers may look like seaborne anarchists, but they have their own unwritten safety rules, among them:

- On the way out, stay clear of anyone on a wave and never let go of your board.
- Hanging around where waves break puts you and others at risk.
- When there are many people on a wave, priority goes to the first on the peak or, if that's not clear, to the first surfer to stand or the first bodyboarder to go.
- Don't surf between blue flags, which mark swimmers-only zones.

de Canoë-Kayak (☎ 01 45 11 08 50, fax 01 48 86 13 25, ⓦ www.ffcanoe.asso.fr), 87 Quai de la Marne, 94340 Joinville le Pont, Paris, has information on canoeing and kayaking clubs around the country.

Hydrospeed is white-water rafting without the raft. Participants are equipped only with a sturdy individual board, wetsuit and helmet. Canyoning tackles all the challenges offered by a river canyon: trekking, swimming, abseiling and rock climbing. A few agencies, as noted in the regional chapters, offer programs for visitors in these high-adrenalin activities.

Parasailing
Parapente (parasailing or paragliding) is popular throughout France. Conditions are best in the Pyrénées; there are two schools of parasailing to be found at Accous in the vallée d'Aspe (see Activities under Haut-Béarn in the Béarn chapter). A *baptême en parapente* (tandem introductory flight) costs about €60.

Other ways to ride the thermals are *vol à voile* (gliding) and *vol libre* (hang-gliding). For information on gliding clubs in France, contact the Paris-based Fédération Française de Vol à Voile (☎ 01 45 44 04 78, fax 01 45 44 71 93, ⓦ www.ffvv.org). Add a motor to a hang-glider and you have an *ultraléger motorisé* (ULM; microlight). A *baptême en ULM* costs around €30.

Rock Climbing
In Béarn alone there are at least half a dozen reliable companies who can teach you *escalade* (rock climbing) and show you where to do it, for around €25/40 per half-/full-day. The Dordogne and Lot have a few similar outfits – usually those offering canoe and kayak trips too.

Caving
The scientific study of caves, *spéléologie,* was pioneered by a Frenchman named Édouard-André Martel in the late 19th century. The word also refers to the sport of cave exploration, which has adapted many of the skills of divers and rock climbers. In return for the weird and breathtaking places

they wriggle into, 'spelunkers' must adjust to long periods in cold, wet, dark and very cramped places. Claustrophobes need not apply. The limestone grottoes of the Dordogne are a spelunker's dream and many of the same companies who run treks and climbing expeditions will take you underground for similar prices. Haut-Béarn is also full of explorable caves.

Horse Riding
Équitation (horse riding) is a popular pastime everywhere. Look for roadside signs to *centres hippiques* (equestrian centres) offering *promenades à cheval* (horseback rides). We also list a number of centres in each regional chapter. Typical rates are from €12 to €15 per hour or €25 to €40 per half-day; many places also have ponies for children at lower rates, and some organise thematic and multiday trips. Note that a few places are reservation-only, and that some are open only in July and August. Some GR and GRP trails (see Walking earlier in this section) are open to horses.

Canal Boating
One of the calmest ways to see the southwest is to pilot a houseboat along its canals and navigable rivers, whose often tree-lined channels pass through some of Europe's loveliest countryside. Europe's oldest-functioning canal system is the Canal du Midi, which with the Canal Latéral à la Garonne provides a continuous route between the Atlantic and the Mediterranean. Branching from this are navigable stretches of the Garonne, Baïse, Lot and Tarn. See under Boat in the Getting Around chapter for more on how to hire your own boat.

Fishing
Pêche (angling) in France requires not only a *carte de pêche* (fishing licence) but a familiarity with seasons, sizes, catch limits and other regulations that vary between regions, between streams and between species. Licences, issued by local fishing associations (but often valid for other areas), are sold in tackle shops; cheaper tourist licences, good for short summer periods, are

also available. Most tourist offices and tackle shops have details on regulations and on local fishing organisations.

The southwest's best fishing areas are the Bassin d'Arachon and nearby lakes (Gironde), the French Basque country and Béarn. The Gironde tourist board (see Information under Bordeaux in the Bordeaux, The Atlantic Coast & The Landes chapter) keeps track of good sites. For information on camp sites and other accommodation tailored to anglers in the French Basque country and Béarn, contact the Association du Tourisme Pêche des Pyrénées-Atlantiques (☎ 05 59 39 98 00, fax 05 59 39 43 97) in Oloron-Ste-Marie.

Skiing & Snowboarding
Southwest France's few ski resorts are in Haut-Béarn (see the Béarn chapter). With wetter, heavier snow than in the Alps, and less of it, these resorts are best suited to beginners and intermediates. The ski season generally lasts from December to March or April, with the best conditions in January and February. The slopes get crowded during the February/March school holidays.

Bird-Watching
The great near-shore lakes and basins of Gironde and the Landes offer an unparalleled look at migratory and resident waterbirds. You can pay visits year round to Gironde's Parc Ornithologique du Teich on the Bassin d'Arcachon. Important *réserve naturelles* (nature reserves), which can be visited at certain times of the year in the Landes are Marais d'Orx (Labenne), Étang Noir (Seignosse) and Courant d'Huchet (Léon).

Golf
The continent's first golf club was founded in Pau in 1856 by five Scottish aristocrats, and France's finest old golf courses are all in the southwest. Details about these and others (there are some 50 in Aquitaine alone) are listed in a free booklet called *Golf in France,* available from overseas offices of Maison de la France (see Tourist Offices earlier in this chapter). Or contact

the Fédération Française de Golf (☎ 01 41 49 77 00, fax 01 41 49 77 01), 68 rue Anatole France, 92309 Levallois-Peret, Paris.

Naturism
The region's many *naturiste* (nudist) centres – all family oriented – are listed in a brochure called *Naturism in France,* available at most tourist offices. On the Atlantic coast there are three in Gironde and one in the Landes; inland, the Dordogne has five, the Gers and Haute-Garonne two each, and Lot-et-Garonne and Lot one each. They range from small rural camp sites to holiday villages complete with cinemas, tennis courts and shops. Most are open from April to October, some year round.

Visitors must have an International Naturist Federation (INF) *passeport naturiste,* available at many naturist holiday centres, or a membership card from a naturist club. The Fédération Française de Naturisme (☎ 01 47 64 32 82, fax 01 47 64 32 63), 65 rue de Tocqueville, 75017 Paris, is a source of further information.

Spas & Thalassotherapy
For over a century, the French have been keen fans of *thermalisme* (water cures), for which visitors with ailments ranging from rheumatism to serious internal disorders flock to hot-spring resorts. Once the domain of the wealthy, spa centres now offer fitness packages aimed at a broad range of income and age. Most of the region's spas, numbering about a dozen, are in south-western Landes and the Haut-Béarn. Dax is a major centre for information on thermalism; contact the tourist office there.

A salty variant is *thalassothérapie,* which is based on the curative properties of sea water and a marine climate. Overseas offices of Maison de la France (see Tourist Offices earlier in this chapter) have a free booklet, *Thalassotherapy in France,* which has information on treatments and centres. There are four major centres to be found on the Basque coast. A six-day program (the minimum recommended) for two, with accommodation and half-board, ranges from €265 to €300 per day.

Leisure Complexes

Many towns with limited history or architecture to offer visitors have climbed aboard the leisure bandwagon, building their own *bases de loisirs* (leisure complexes) around artificial lakes or at a wide place in the nearest river. With canoes, swimming pools, windsurfers, water slides, pedal-boats, dryland sports facilities and programs for young people, they can be great outlets if you're travelling with energetic kids.

COURSES

A great souvenir that won't take up any space in your luggage is a skill you can take home with you. Of course an obvious subject is French, but in this heartland of fine food and fine wines, how about cookery or wine-tasting?

The following courses are taught in French, unless stated otherwise. Multiday courses include accommodation and full board, unless otherwise noted. Comprehensive listings of courses of all kinds are maintained by the departmental affiliates of Loisirs Accueil France (for details see Tourist Offices earlier in this chapter) and available through local tourist offices.

Language

Of course there's no better place to learn French than in France, and a formal course – anything from an intensive two weeks to three months or more – is a good way to cement what you're learning out on the street.

Overseas offices of Maison de la France (see Tourist Offices earlier in this chapter) have lots of information on studying French in France. Following are some reliable private schools with a choice of courses for foreigners; most can either provide, or help you find, accommodation too.

Alliance Française de Bordeaux (☎/fax 05 56 79 32 80, ⓔ alliance.bordeaux@alliance-bordeaux .org, ⓦ www.alliance-bordeaux.org) 38 rue Ferrère, 33000 Bordeaux. Summer two-week or one-month intensives; other courses during the rest of the year.
Alliance Française de Toulouse (☎ 05 34 45 26 10, fax 05 34 45 26 11, ⓔ af.toulouse@wanadoo .fr, ⓦ www.alliance-toulouse.org) 9 place du Capitole, 31000 Toulouse. Summer four-week intensives at all levels; other courses during the rest of the year.
BLS (☎ 05 56 51 00 76, fax 05 56 51 76 15, ⓔ info@bls-frenchcourses.com, ⓦ www.bls -frenchcourses.com) 42 rue Lafaurie de Monbadon, 33000 Bordeaux. One-week to one-year courses at all levels, plus a teenage summer program in Biarritz.
Centre d'Études de Langues (☎ 05 59 46 58 00, fax 05 59 46 59 73, ⓔ ccf@bayonne.cci.fr) Centre Consulaire de Formation, 50–51 allées Marines, 64102 Bayonne. Month-long introductory courses.
Institut d'Études Françaises pour Étudiants Étrangers (☎ 05 59 92 32 22, fax 05 59 92 32 65, ⓔ ief@univ-pau.fr, ⓦ www.univ-pau.fr) Faculté des Lettres, Université de Pau et des Pays de l'Adour, av du Doyen Poplawski, 64013 Pau. General and tailored courses.
Langue Onze Sud-Ouest (☎ 05 61 54 11 69, fax 05 63 58 41 30, ⓔ sudouest@langue-onze .asso.fr, ⓦ www.langue-onze.asso.fr/sudouest) 16 rue Coupeau, 31500 Toulouse. Two- to four-week classes year round, plus intensive summer courses.

Cookery

Why not learn to prepare your own *magret de canard*, or get acquainted with the mysterious truffle? Multiday courses include accommodation and full board, except as indicated.

Hôtel de la Reine Jeanne (☎ 05 59 67 00 76, fax 05 59 69 09 63) 44 rue de Bourg Vieux, 64300 Orthez, Béarn. A three-day course that focuses on foie gras.
Latitude (☎ 05 65 30 25 76, fax 05 65 31 29 73, ⓔ barbara@latitude.org, ⓦ www.latitude.org) La Toulzanie, 46330 St Martin Labouval, Lot. 'A Taste of Southwest France', a one-week course featuring culinary/social history of the region and visits to farmers and local cooks.
Le Tourisme Basque (☎ 05 59 26 23 87, fax 05 59 26 18 82) 100 rue Gambetta, 64500 St-Jean de Luz, Pyrénées-Atlantiques. Four-day courses in Basque cuisine.
Office du Tourisme de Sarlat (☎ 05 53 31 45 45, fax 05 53 59 19 44) place de la Liberté, BP 114, 24203 Sarlat. Information on two- to four-day courses specialising in foie gras, truffles and the cuisine of Périgord Noir.
Service Loisirs Accueil Dordogne (☎ 05 53 35 50 24, fax 05 53 09 51 41, ⓔ dordogne.perigord .tourisme@wanadoo.fr) 25 rue du Président Wilson, 24009 Périgueux. Information on

courses featuring mushrooms, truffles, cuisine du canard and the cuisine of Périgord.

Service Loisirs Accueil Lot (☎ 05 65 53 20 90, fax 05 65 53 20 94, [e] loisirs.accueil.lot@ wanadoo.fr) Maison du Tourisme, Place F Mitterand, 46000 Cahors. Information on courses, including week-long introduction to Quercy cuisine, October to May.

Shaw Guide's online annual Guide to Cooking Schools (W www.shawguides.com) includes schools in the Dordogne and the French Basque country. For information on a combined cycling-and-cooking tour of the Bordeaux area, see Organised Tours in the Getting There & Away chapter.

Oenology & Wine Tasting

The following private institutions and tourist offices will walk you through the minefield of subjectivity that is wine-tasting, and help you to appreciate the best (and avoid the worst) of the region's wines.

L'École du Vin, Conseil Interprofessionel du Vin de Bordeaux (CIVB; ☎ 05 56 00 22 66, fax 05 56 00 22 82, [e] ecole@vins-bordeaux.fr, W www.vins-bordeaux.fr) 3 cours du 30 Juillet, 33075 Bordeaux. Multilingual weekend to three-day courses on Bordeaux wines from the leading Bordeaux wine organisation.

Maison du Tourisme de la Gironde (☎ 05 56 52 61 40, fax 05 56 81 09 99, [e] tourisme@gironde .com, W www.tourisme-gironde.cg33.fr) 21 cours de l'Intendance, 33000 Bordeaux. Information on weekend courses.

Maison du Tourisme et du Vin de Pauillac (☎ 05 56 59 03 08, fax 05 56 59 23 38, [e] tour ismeetvindepauillac@wanadoo.fr) La Verrerie, 33250 Pauillac. Information on afternoon or evening wine-tasting sessions or longer courses.

Maison des Vins (CIVRB; ☎ 05 53 63 57 57, fax 05 53 63 01 30, [e] vin.civrb@wanadoo.fr) 2 place du Docteur Cayla, 24100 Bergerac. Offers summer courses.

Fine Arts

In tourist office brochures or on signs by the roadside, *atelier* indicates workshops or studios where artists will show you what they do and how they do it, in the hope that you'll buy some of it. At a few of these, such as the ones noted here, you can arrange classes. Where details in the following list

are not specific, it indicates that the artist may tailor the length and content of a class to your interests.

Aletta Baker van der Have (☎ 05 53 59 60 85, fax 05 53 28 10 00, [e] alettaglass@free.fr) Les Communaux, Chapelle Aubareil (near Sarlat). Decorative stained-glass; individual or group courses.

Service Loisirs Accueil Dordogne (see under Cookery) One-week course in decoration (eg, mural patina, decorated furniture) and painting under Luc Fouquet (☎ 05 53 29 75 02) in Sarlat.

Christine Robert (☎ 05 53 61 04 81) Pottery courses (afternoons open to children) in Limeuil.

Service Loisirs Accueil Lot (see under Cookery) Five-day group course in traditional stained-glass window-making, near Gramat.

Atelier Créac (☎ 05 63 41 82 66) Le Cambou, 81800 Mézens (Tarn). Wood and stone sculpture and weaving (week-long and weekend courses, year round).

Atelier du Chemin Vert (☎ 05 63 75 03 58, fax 05 63 75 29 67) 81470 Lacroisille (Tarn). One- or two-week summer courses in watercolour, oil painting, drawing, sculpture, casting and jewellery, in a restored Occitan farmhouse; English spoken.

Atelier Greschny (☎ 05 63 55 14 82 or 05 63 45 40 69) La Maurinié, 81430 Marsal (Tarn). Enamelling, icons, Byzantine-style art, by the family of late artist Nicolas Greschny.

Hélène & Francis Pratt, Painting School of Montmiral (☎ 05 63 33 13 11) rue de la Porte Neuve, 81140 Castelnau de Montmiral (Tarn). 15-day summer painting courses with visiting artists.

Latitude (see under Cookery). Techniques of cave art and tool-making with materials both ancient and modern; one-week course.

Suzanne Legallou (☎ 05 59 82 61 20) route de Marie Blanque, 64260 Bilhères, vallée d'Ossau (Béarn). Courses on ceramics.

Outdoor Activities

For information on classes in outdoor sports including surfing, caving, climbing, parasailing and riding, see Activities earlier in this chapter. For details of companies, see regional or individual town listings.

WORK

To work legally here you need a residence permit known as a carte de séjour (see Visas

Bureaux d'Information Jeunesse

Centres, Bureaux and Points d'Information Jeunesse form a countrywide network of state-funded resource offices with a wide range of information for young people on education, training, jobs, housing, health, sports, travel, events, discounts and more.

Bureaux d'Information Jeunesse (BIJ) are mainly located in departmental capitals, while smaller towns may have only a one-room Point d'Information Jeunesse (PIJ). Each regional capital has a big Centre Régional d'Information Jeunesse (CRIJ) with additional facilities, such as a library and a budget travel agency. CRIJs and most BIJs also offer Internet access at a modest rate, and at some it's free of charge during certain periods.

Foreign visitors are usually welcome to use these services. French-speaking visitors may also find them good places to meet young locals. We include details under individual town listings. The regional centres for Southwest France are:

Centre d'Information Jeunesse Aquitaine (☎ 05 56 56 00 56, fax 05 56 56 00 53, e cija@cija.net, w www.info-jeune.com) 5 rue Duffour Dubergier & 125 cours d'Alsace et Lorraine, 33000 Bordeaux
Centre Régional d'Information Jeunesse Toulouse Midi-Pyrénées (☎ 05 62 21 20 20, fax 05 61 27 28 29, e crij-tlse@crij.org, w www.crij.org) 17 rue de Metz, 31000 Toulouse

The Centre d'Information et de Documentation Jeunesse has a Web site (w www.cidj.asso.fr) with links to these and other regional centres.

& Documents earlier in this chapter). Non-EU nationals must also get an *autorisation de travail* (work permit) before arriving in France.

The government seems to tolerate undocumented workers helping out with some agricultural work, especially during harvests, though you get no workplace insurance protection in case of an accident, either to you or because of you. The national minimum wage for nonprofessionals is about €6 an hour, although employers willing to hire in the black are also apt to ignore minimum wage laws.

Over half of all French students take temporary jobs in July and August, so the competition is fierce at this time.

Tourist offices may direct you to departmental Chambres d'Agriculture, to growers' cooperatives, or to the nearest office of the Agence National pour l'Emploi (ANPE; w www.anpe.fr), France's national employment service. On Minitel, key in 3615 INFOJOBS. More accessible resources for temporary jobs are the ubiquitous BIJs in most sizeable towns. We have identified these in individual town listings. For more

on what these centres have to offer, see the boxed text 'Bureaux d'Information Jeunesse' under Email & Internet Access earlier in this chapter.

A good reference for those contemplating a working holiday is Susan Griffiths' classic handbook, *Work Your Way Around the World,* now in its 10th edition. Overseas Jobs Express (w www.overseasjobsexpress.co.uk) is an on-line 'newspaper' for international job-hunters.

Agricultural Work
Important items on the southwest's harvest calendar include apples (September), asparagus (March to June), cherries (June), maize (July to mid-August) and tobacco (late August and September). Many farmers prefer hiring people who know at least a bit of French.

Vendange The southwest's annual vendange happens largely in September, with southern varieties ripening in October or even later. The starting date in any given area changes from year to year, and is normally announced by the prefecture no more than a week before picking starts. Once started, it lasts just a couple of weeks. Food is usually supplied but accommodation is often not.

Work opportunities are shrinking as more and more vendanges are done by machine, though mechanical picking is disdained by the most prestigious chateaux. The most effective way of getting vendange work is to approach the various *domaines* (wine-producing estates) directly, from early May onwards. Tourist offices have lists of producers, as do the Maisons des Vins (see the Food & Wine section for contact details).

Building Restoration
Here's a summer job with a difference: help in the restoration of old buildings and monuments. Besides mixing concrete and carrying hods, you'll also learn about the finer aspects of the craft. The work is unpaid, but food and lodging are free. Contact Companions Bâtisseurs (☎ 05 63 72 59 64, e cb .france@wanadoo.fr), 2 rue Claude Bertholet, 81000 Castres (Tarn).

Au Pairing
Under the au pair system, single people aged between 18 and about 27 who are studying in France can live with a French family and receive lodging, full board and a bit of pocket money in exchange for childcare, light housework and perhaps teaching English to the children. Most families want native English speakers, but may also insist on some knowledge of French. The minimum commitment ranges from two to six months. EU residents can easily arrange for an au pair job after arriving in France; non-EU applicants must apply for an au pair visa before leaving home.

Beach Hawking & Busking
Selling goods and services on the beach is one way to make a few euros, but you'll have to sell a lot of ice cream to make a living. If you play an instrument or have some other talent in the performing arts, you could try busking – for example, as a street musician, actor, juggler or pavement artist. Talk to other street artists to avoid hassles

with the police, with ill-tempered shop owners and with other buskers.

Ski Resorts
The ski resorts in Haut-Béarn offer few work opportunities; if you contact a resort months in advance you might find some work in a hotel or restaurant.

ACCOMMODATION
Accommodation in the region gets expensive in summer, but with some foresight you can always find something to suit your budget. Municipal tourist offices usually maintain lists of accommodation over a wide price range; they'll help you find (and sometimes book) a place, though they scrupulously avoid making recommendations.

Most prices are seasonal. Many places give discounts for longer stays, but you usually need to ask. We use the following price categories for an establishment's most basic double with toilet and shower/bath: budget (to about €30); mid-range (from €30 to €60); top end (over €60). Unless noted, prices quoted are for *peak* season, and include taxes and service charges.

Advance reservations eliminate the headache of a hotel search and are especially useful if you're arriving late in the day. A simple call ahead, on the day (or even the morning) before you arrive, is often enough. Budget places are generally full by midday in summer, but they're rarely booked days or weeks ahead as with top-end accommodation.

Camping
Southwest France has hundreds of camp sites, many beautifully set on river banks, lakeshores, beaches or mountain sides. In out-of-the-way areas such as the Gers they can be surprisingly empty even in eminently campable June weather. Some are open only in summer, and most close for at least a few months in winter. North American visitors should be ready for a more cheek-by-jowl style of camping than they're used to at home. Camping outside designated sites is illegal, though it's tolerated in some places (but never in a national park).

Camp sites are rated with a system of one to four stars based on facilities and amenities. Separate tariffs are usually charged per person, per tent or caravan, per car or motorcycle and for electricity. Some places offer a *forfait* (package rate) for two people plus car and tent or caravan. Children aged up to about 12 enjoy big discounts. In this book we quote forfait prices if they're offered, or sample rates per adult, per pitch and/or per car.

Some camp sites are part of municipal *bases de loisirs* (leisure complexes), complete with kids' activities, artificial lakes, water slides, swimming pools and more. Some hostels (see Hostels later in this section) will let you pitch a tent in the garden. Most camping à la ferme is coordinated by Gîtes de France or Clévacances (see the following sections for contact details).

If you'll be doing lots of car camping, a good investment is the *Guide Officiel* of the Fédération Française de Camping et de Caravanning (€11.90), listing just about every site in the country. Michelin's multilingual *Camping & Caravanning* (€12.65) includes around one-third of them, in more detail. Free booklets published annually by Aquitaine and Midi-Pyrénées Comités Régionaux de Tourisme (see Tourist Offices earlier in this chapter for contact details) list most camp sites.

For information on the useful Camping Card International see under Visas & Documents earlier in this chapter.

Chambres d'Hôte

Chambres d'hôte are essentially B&Bs: rooms in private homes (often charming, traditional-style houses with gardens), rented by the night with breakfast included. Rates for a double room start at about €35 in the high season. An evening meal may be available for an extra charge. There may be quite a few of these around smaller towns with no other accommodation options, though they tend to be poorly advertised; you'll probably have to ask at the tourist office.

Many chambres d'hôte are represented by Gîtes de France (☎ 01 49 70 75 75, fax 01 42 81 28 53, [e] info@gites-de-france

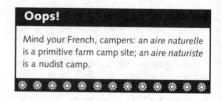

Oops!

Mind your French, campers: an *aire naturelle* is a primitive farm camp site; an *aire naturiste* is a nudist camp.

.fr, [w] www.gites-de-france.fr), 59 rue St-Lazare, 75439 Paris Cedex 09. This is a semi-private, national organisation that promotes, books and maintains standards of such accommodation. Contact them if you want to book ahead with some assurance, or look for their free booklets in tourist offices.

Self-Catering Accommodation

You have several options if you want to rent a place and do your own cooking, though you're likely to need your own transport. Such accommodation is usually rented by the week, and it's essential to book it well ahead in peak season.

Most popular is the *gîte rural,* a private farm building restored as furnished lodgings with kitchenette and bathroom. Weekly prices for a four-person gîte start at about €200 in June and September or €300 in July and August. A *meublé* is a furnished flat; those kitted out for tourists may be called *meublés de tourisme* or *meublés saisonniers.*

Local tourist offices often have listings, but you'll probably want to know about these long before you get there. Most gîtes ruraux are represented by – and can be booked through – Gîtes de France (see the preceding section on chambres d'hôte). A similar agency dealing mostly in flats and houses is Clévacances (☎ 05 61 13 55 66, fax 05 61 13 55 94, [e] infos@clevacances .com, [w] www.clevacances.com), 54 blvd de l'Embouchure, BP 2166, 31022 Toulouse. Both organisations work closely with departmental tourist offices, and publish annual listings, complete with photos.

Other self-catering options are the bungalows, chalets or fixed mobilehomes (suitable for four to eight people) available for rent at many camp sites – usually by the week and often for a longer season than for camping itself.

Refuges & Gîtes d'Étape

Refuges and *gîtes d'étape* offer simple, dormitory-style accommodation for walkers, horse-riders and mountaineers.

Refuges are simple mountain shelters run by park authorities or by private outfits, such as the Club Alpin Français. They're usually marked on walking maps and are often accessible only on foot. They're equipped with bunks, mattresses and blankets, but not sheets (though these are sometimes available to rent). Nightly rates are about €8 to €14 per person; meals are usually available for €12 to €15. Some may be partly open but unstaffed in winter.

Gîtes d'étape, better equipped and more comfortable than *refuges,* tend to be located in towns or villages. Some accommodate only pilgrims. Typical prices are €8 to €10 per person. Gîtes de France acts as agent for many gîtes d'étape, and publishes an annual compilation, *Gîtes d'Étape et de Séjour*.

Rando'Plume (☎ 05 62 90 09 92, fax 05 62 90 09 91) is the brand name of a kind of walkers' accommodation with ambience, a hybrid of gîte d'étape and hotel with two- to four-person en suite rooms, half board on offer, and extra facilities and services on demand. Typical per-person rates are €10 to €20. In the southwest they're concentrated in the Pyrénées-Atlantiques department.

For more information on mountain accommodation in the Pyrénées, check out *Hébergement en Montagne,* published by Association Randonnées Pyrénéennes, or visit W www.cimes-pyrenees.net on the Web.

Homestays

Students, young people and tourists can also stay with French families under an arrangement called *hébergement chez l'habitant* or *hôtes payants* (literally, 'paying guests'), under which you rent a room and have limited access to the family's kitchen and telephone. Rates for a single room with breakfast per day/week/month start at about €20/180/450. Tourist offices will have information on these.

Most language schools (see Courses earlier in this chapter) arrange homestays for their students. Hundreds of agencies in the USA and Europe arrange homestay accommodation in France; for a list, contact any overseas French tourist office (see Tourist Offices earlier in this chapter).

Hostels

Official youth hostels, called auberges de jeunesse, in Southwest France belong to the Fédération Unie des Auberges de Jeunesse (FUAJ), which grades them from one to four pine trees depending on facilities and whether breakfast is included.

At the time of writing the per-bed price for a bunk in a single-sex dormitory ranged from €6.85 to €11.30, independent of season. You must bring a sleeping sheet, or rent one for €2.90 per stay.

Camping is permitted at many hostels, at €4.55 per person per night. Where extra meals are available, continental breakfast is €2.90 and a midday or evening meal €7.60. Most hostels have kitchen facilities for use by guests. Guests are expected to pitch in with chores.

You'll need a Hostelling International card (see Visas & Documents earlier in this chapter). The maximum stay is three nights. Booking ahead is wise, especially in July and August; for a small fee your hostel can book you a bed in the next one. Smaller places may have a curfew. Find out more about each FUAJ hostel at the multilingual Web site W www.fuaj.org.

In university towns you may also find *foyers,* worker or student dormitories converted for use by travellers during summer holidays.

Hotels

Hotels are rated on a system of one to four stars, based on quantifiable criteria such as the size of the entry hall, rather than on the quality of service or cleanliness, so a one-star establishment may be more pleasant than some two- or three-star places. Prices tend to be the best indicators of such intangibles.

Most hotel rooms at mid-range and above have TVs and telephones. Breakfast is rarely included in room prices; expect an extra €4 to €6 (or more) for that. Breakfast at a nearby cafe will be cheaper and usually more pleasant. Some places in touristy areas require that you take breakfast, and a few insist on demi-pension – half board with breakfast plus either lunch or dinner.

Rather than an *oreiller* (pillow), beds in many lower-end places have only an uncomfortable, sausage-shaped bolster called a *traversin*. A *cabinet de toilette* is a little cubicle in the room, with washbasin, bidet and toilet.

Budget Expect €25 to €30 per night for a double with a washbasin (and often a bidet), with shared toilet and shower. A shower located in the hall (called a 'hall shower' in this book) may be free but sometimes costs €1 to €1.50 a go. Most budget hotels won't offer the cheapest option off the bat, but might show you something cheaper if you ask (eg, a top-floor room or one in poorer condition); most also have pricier rooms with toilet and shower or bath. Most demand pre-payment, but check out the room before parting with any cash. Prices stay the same year round.

Many budget hotels have no singles, only rooms with *un grand lit* (a double bed) costing the same for one or two guests. There is sometimes a very considerable jump in price if you want *lits séparés* or *lits jumeaux* (twin beds). Those with genuine singles usually charge at least 70% of the price of a double.

Thin-walled, unatmospheric but clean and dependable chain hotels in urban outskirts are good value for those passing through by car. Formule 1 (W www.hotel formule1.com) charges €24.40 for a three-bed room with shared shower and toilet. Première Classe (W www.premiereclasse .com), B&B (W www.hotel-bb.com) and Climat (W www.envergure.fr/climatdefra ncefr.html) also have rooms with attached shower and toilet.

Mid-Range & Top-End Some 350 one- and two-star hotels in Southwest France display the Logis de France logo and generally offer very good value (and good food). The Fédération Nationale des Logis de France (☎ 01 45 84 70 00, fax 01 45 83 59 66, e info@logis-de-france.fr, W www.logis-de-france.fr), 83 av d'Italie, 75013 Paris, publishes an annual guide (€15) to all of them. Expect to pay €30 to €50 for a room.

If you fancy staying the night in a chateau (€60 to €220 plus meals), check out Chateaux & Hotels of France (W www .chateauxethotels.com) or Relais & Chateaux (W www.relaischateaux.fr).

Mid-range and top-end hotels usually have seasonal prices (see When to Go under Planning earlier in this chapter).

FOOD

The southwest is made for foodies. Périgord, particularly, boasts among its specialities such luxuries as truffles and foie gras (liver of goose or duck). Though you may not be able to splash out on a truffle omelette every day, you can pick up other regional produce such as walnuts, strawberries and goat's cheese from the markets.

Even serious gourmands may find a Périgord meal too much to handle every day. Goose fat and walnut oil are basic to many regional recipes, making traditional meals sumptuous, filling affairs. A 'simple' family meal might feature home-made *pâté de canard* (duck pâté) or foie gras, topped with a slice of truffle, and followed by confit de canard. Even potatoes become delicacies as *pommes de terre sarladaises:* sizzling in goose fat, mixed with *cèpe* mushrooms, garlic and parsley.

Meals of the Day

Breakfast If you're accustomed to a big breakfast fry-up you're in for a shock. The traditional *petit déjeuner* (breakfast) is microscopic, usually a croissant or bread, sometimes with butter and jam, washed down with *café au lait* (coffee with lots of hot milk), strong black coffee or hot chocolate. Hotel breakfasts may include fruit juice and cereal.

Lunch & Dinner *Déjeuner* (lunch) is the day's main meal. It starts at noon and can last until 2.30pm or 3pm. Restaurants (but not brasseries; see Types of Eatery) close from about 3pm to 7pm and serve *dîner* (dinner) from 7.30pm to around 10pm. Most restaurants close on Sunday.

Lunch and dinner fare are similar: *entree* (starter), *plat principal* (main course), salad, cheese and/or dessert. Bread is usually free and freely available. *Boissons* (drinks) cost extra unless the *menu* says *boisson comprise*. If it says *vin compris* you'll probably get a small *pichet* (jug) of plain *vin de table*. The waiter will ask if you want to finish with coffee, which usually costs extra.

If you go the whole hog, this is the order in which courses are served:

Aperitif – pre-dinner drink plus nibbles
Entree – first course or starter; one or more
Plat principal – main course
Légumes – vegetables or potatoes, sometimes with the main course
Salade – usually just lettuce and dressing
Fromage – cheese
Dessert – anything from ice cream to gâteau
Fruit – fresh fruit to end the meal
Café – coffee of your choice
Digestif – after-dinner drink such as Armagnac or brandy

Types of Eatery
Restaurants & Brasseries Many restaurants offer excellent French meals for €25 to €30 – Michelin's *Guide Rouge* is full of them – but good, inexpensive restaurants are rare. Some of the best are attached to mid-range hotels (and most are open to non-residents). Another option for quick, hearty meals is the loose chain of Les Routiers (truckers' restaurants), usually found on the outskirts of towns and along major roads. The annual *Guide des Relais Routiers* (€18.30), available in major bookshops, lists every one.

While restaurants often specialise in one type of food (eg, regional, traditional or Vietnamese) and open only for lunch and dinner, brasseries (which often look like cafes) serve a wider selection, more cheaply, in a more casual atmosphere, all day long. Restaurant or brasserie lunch *menus* start at around €10. At €6 to €8, the plat du jour (dish of the day) is the best budget choice.

Menus & Menus
In French, *le menu* is a list of the dishes comprising a single complete meal. What English-speakers think of as a menu, ie, a folder or book listing all of a restaurant's available meals and dishes, is *la carte*. Throughout this book, *menu* is italicised whenever it is used in the French sense.

Evening *menus* (especially in restaurants) can cost from €10 to €60 per person.

Cafes & Bars The cafe is an integral part of French society; in the rural southwest the village cafe may double as bar, meeting place and bistro. Most can knock up a sandwich (half a baguette filled with cheese, ham or pâté) or *croque-monsieur* (toasted cheese and ham sandwich) for under €4. An urban cafe on a grand boulevard charges more than a place on a quiet side street, and all charge according to where you choose to take it: at the *comptoir* (standing by the counter; the cheapest option), in the *salle* (sitting at a table indoors) or on the *terrasse* (outside; the most expensive). But once you've ordered you can stay as long as you like, with no pressure to order anything more. The price of drinks usually goes up after about 8pm.

At busy or touristy cafes you may be asked to pay *l'addition* (the bill) when your drink arrives, but in most places you'll spend ages catching the waiter's attention so you can leave.

Salons de Thé & Creperies *Salons de thé* (tearooms) are trendy, somewhat pricey establishments serving quiches, salads, pies and pastries in addition to tea and coffee. *Creperies,* found everywhere and especially in tourist spots, specialise, of course, in *crepes* – ultra-thin pancakes with a sweet or savoury filling – or thicker, usually savoury versions called *galettes,* made with buckwheat flour.

Vegetarian You're in the wrong part of France for gourmet vegetarian fare – this is, after all, the land of foie gras. But it's also the land of truffles and wild mushrooms, asparagus and strawberries, walnuts and goat cheese. You can pick up a cornucopia of veggie fare at markets, and order salads (usually generous) or vegetarian entrees at restaurants. Creperies always have vegetarian options. If you eat fish, there's nearly always a good choice in restaurants. Dedicated vegetarian restaurants, and even vegetarian *menus*, are rare.

Ethnic Restaurants Toulouse, Bordeaux and other large towns invariably have Chinese, Indian and/or Vietnamese restaurants or stalls selling North African couscous and lamb kebabs. Even in rural markets you're likely to find a range of ethnic specialities such as Vietnamese spring rolls.

Self-Catering

If the cuisine of the southwest wasn't so tempting you could easily get by on daily gourmet picnics. It's easy to shop for delicious fresh bread, pastries, cheese, fruit, vegetables and prepared dishes from supermarkets, speciality shops and weekly markets. But don't leave it till Sunday afternoon or Monday when many food shops close.

A boulangerie or *dépôt de pain* (breadseller) is the essential first stop. In addition to the traditional *baguette* (long, thin loaf) and fatter, softer *pain,* you'll find *pain complet* (wholemeal), *pain de campagne* (country loaf) and *pain de seigle* (rye bread). Eat your baguette the same day or it will turn to stone; the other loaves keep longer. Many boulangeries also sell cakes and pastries; if not, find a *patisserie* (pastry shop) for *pain au chocolat* (chocolate croissant), *pain aux raisins* (spiral pastry filled with sultanas), *tarte aux fruits* (fruit tart) or *canelé* (Bordeaux's own custard pastry).

Speciality shops, not supermarkets, sell the best and ripest produce. Cheese is best from a *fromagerie* where you can *goûter* (taste) those you don't know or ask for recommendations. Shop for sliced cold meat, pâté, seafood salads, olives and spicy sausage at a *charcuterie* (delicatessen); you can always get just a few *tranches* (slices) of meat or *un petit bout* (small chunk) of sausage, or enough meat *pour une/deux personnes* (for one/two people). A *traiteur*

Keeping Costs & Stress Down

France can be hard work at mealtimes, because of the language barrier (and food names that are obscure even if you're fluent), widespread Sunday and/or Monday closures and generally quite high prices. Many travellers can end up living on picnics, snacks and takeaways, but it doesn't have to be this way.

- Look for brasseries, which are usually cheaper, quicker, more casual, open longer and serve bigger helpings than restaurants.
- Get the most for your money with the cheapest lunchtime *menu* or *menu du jour,* or a *formule* (choose any two courses from starter, main course and dessert), or just the plat du jour (dish of the day) with no accompaniments, and eat lightly in the evening when things cost more; avoid ordering a la carte (selecting courses individually).
- Arrive punctually at opening time to avoid long waits, to get that plat du jour before it runs out and to escape before the place fills with cigarette smoke.
- If you ask simply for water you may get expensive bottled mineral water – ask specifically for tap water *(une carafe d'eau* or *de l'eau de robinet);* and a *pichet* of house wine is usually a bit cheaper than beer.
- Skip dessert, which is usually pricey.
- Look for a *menu enfant* for children under 12.
- You'll nearly always find a *carte* (menu) posted outside, so you can see what's available before committing yourself.

sells ready-to-eat dishes. If there's a *marché couvert* (covered market, often known as the *halles* and open up to six days a week) you'll probably find such speciality shops inside. Anything else you need is probably at the local *épicerie* (grocery store) or *alimentation générale* (general food shop); though generally pricier than supermarkets, they're central, accessible and often open on days when other shops close.

Markets

Marchés en plein air (outdoor markets) are one of the great pleasures of Southwest France. Quite apart from the produce, they're a social rendezvous for everyone from elderly farmers who only venture into town for this event to itinerant artisans selling trinkets and jewellery.

Every town of any size has a weekly market, and many have two; we note good ones in the text. Here you'll find fresh local fruit and vegetables, home-made jams and honey, goat's cheese, walnut cake and oil, and pâté de foie gras. Local wines are on display (free tastings usually available), and local arts and crafts on sale. There's usually produce from other regions, too – olives and fish, mussels and oysters, garlic and herbs – and ready-to-eat roast chickens or seafood paellas.

There's no bargaining. Weighing is by hand scales, or not at all. Arrive early (around 8am) for the buzz and the best choice; by midday everyone starts packing up.

DRINKS

Alcohol consumption in France as a whole has dropped 20% since WWII, but the trend hasn't reached the southwest yet. Thanks to the major wine-growing regions of Bordeaux, Bergerac and Cahors, wine is not just a mealtime accompaniment but an anytime-at-all tipple. So too are home-made brews such as *vin de noix* (walnut wine) and *eau de vie* (literally, 'water of life'; see Aperitifs & Digestifs).

Nonalcoholic Drinks

Tap water in the southwest is safe to drink. Water in public fountains or streams often isn't drinkable, as indicated by *eau non potable* signs. In restaurants, ask for *de l'eau du robinet* (tap water) or you'll get pricey *eau de source* (mineral water), which comes *plate* (still) or *gazeuse* (fizzy).

Canned or bottled soft drinks are expensive (up to €3 in cafes). A cheaper option is a *sirop* (syrup) served with water or soda – *cassis* (blackcurrant), *grenadine* (pomegranate), *menthe* (mint) or *citron* (lemon). The most expensive choice is *citron* or *orange pressé* – freshly squeezed lemon or orange with iced water and sugar. For a refreshing alternative, try a *panaché* (shandy). If you want ice cubes *(des glaçons)* in your drink, you'll probably have to ask for them.

Coffee costs €1 to €1.50 a cup. Unless you specify otherwise, you get a small, strong, black espresso. For a bigger punch, ask for *un grand café* (double espresso). Milky versions include *un café crème* (espresso with steamed milk) and *un café au lait* (hot milk with a dash of coffee).

Thé (tea) and *chocolat chaud* (hot chocolate) are widely available. Kids like the cold chocolate bottled drink called *Cacolac*. *Tisane* (herbal tea, sometimes known as an infusion) is also popular, especially mint, *camomille* (camomile) or *tilleul* (lime).

Alcoholic Drinks

Wine See the special Food & Wine section.

Aperitifs & Digestifs You may get offered an aperitif at any time of the day, not just before a meal. Popular with men is *pastis* (also referred to by brand names such as Pernod and Ricard), a 90-proof aniseed drink that turns cloudy when mixed with water. Women are usually offered milder drinks such as sweet port, *kir* (white wine or vin de Cahors sweetened with cassis) or *pineau* (cognac and grape juice).

The southwest's home-grown, dry and pungent digestif, Armagnac (see the boxed text 'Armagnac' in the Gers chapter) is made from distilled white wine and often used to give regional sauces a bit of punch. *Floc de Gascogne,* made from Armagnac mixed with selected red or white wines, is like a sweet port, and served chilled as an aperitif. The

Basque country's own potent herbal liqueur, *izarra,* is now popular all over France.

Although eaux de vie – fiery brandies distilled from local fruits – are theoretically digestifs, they pop up as aperitifs too, especially if made by the patron himself. Popular versions are *eau de vie de prune* (plum brandy) and *eau de vie de framboise* (raspberry brandy) – both irresistible and deceptively potent.

Beer Beer is usually either Alsatian, or imported from Belgium or Germany. In cafes and pubs it's cheaper *à la pression* (on draught) than *en bouteille* (by the bottle) – just ask for *une pression* to get a *demi* (about 330mL) for €2 to €2.50. Prices may rise as the night wears on.

ENTERTAINMENT

Local tourist offices are the best source of information about what's on. Many of them publish their own monthly or seasonal listings of events. Several regional newspapers also carry comprehensive cinema, theatre and festival listings.

Fnac superstores are a good source for tickets for everything from opera to rock concerts. Most have a booking and ticket desk with a calendar of upcoming events. There are Fnacs with ticket desks in Bordeaux, Toulouse and Pau.

Music

Every city and many towns lay on at least one music festival each year (see Public Holidays & Special Events earlier in this chapter), some internationally known. The contemporary music scene is dominated by jazz (see the boxed text 'Jazz Bonanza' earlier in this chapter) and the sounds of Cuba, Brazil and Africa. The *chansons* (songs) of Edith Piaf, Georges Brassens and Belgian-born Jacques Brel have never gone out of style. On the classical side, Toulouse has its own well regarded symphony orchestra and a national chamber orchestra, Bordeaux boasts national and municipal orchestras and an opera company, and many smaller towns have their own orchestras. See the Arts section in the Facts about Southwest France chapter for details.

One of the simplest but most appealing musical manifestations we came across is the monthly Baïona Kantus, essentially a public Basque singalong, in Bayonne (with others in smaller towns of the French Basque country).

Bars, Discos & Clubs

Most departmental capitals have several cheerful bars with live or recorded blues, country, folk or rock music. *Discothèques* (discos) and *boîtes du nuit* (clubs), once rare beyond Bordeaux, Bayonne and Toulouse and the summer communities of the Atlantic coast, are now popping up in smaller towns too. Most don't hit their stride until at least midnight. Music (live or recorded) ranges from jazz to Latino to techno.

Cinema

You can see foreign films in their original language (with French subtitles) in selected cinemas in most bigger towns. Look for the letters v.o. (*version originale,* nondubbed) or v.o.s.t. (*version originale sous-titrée,* with subtitles) on cinema billboards. V.f. *(version française)* means the film has been dubbed into French. Count on paying €6 to €7.50 for a first-run film. Most French cinemas offer discounts to young people, students and people aged over 60, except at weekends. Many also give discounts to everyone on Wednesday.

SPECTATOR SPORTS

Southwesterners take their spectator sports seriously, although they and their northern cousins don't share the same priorities. Bullfighting stirs passions in the Landes, Gers and the French Basque country, along with a bloodless variant called *les courses landaises* (see Courses Landaises later in this section). The most popular contact sport is not football but rugby. The gentlest of pastimes – to play or to watch – is *pétanque,* or *boules.* And only in or near the Basque country will you find the unique menu of games and competitions known as *jeux Basques.*

Fnac superstores are a good source of rugby and football tickets.

[continued on page 97]

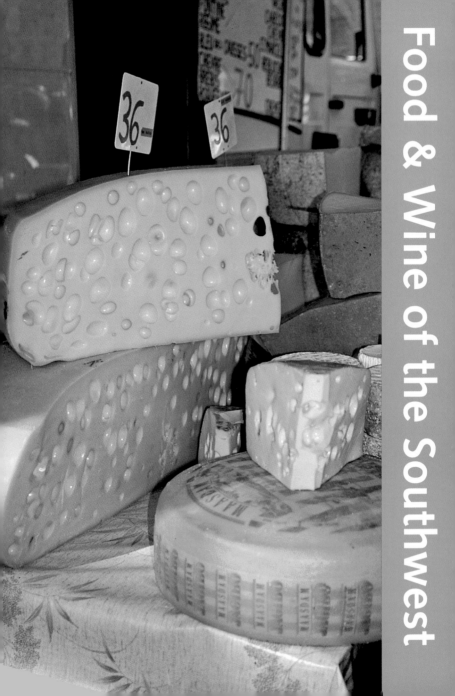

Food & Wine of the Southwest

WINE REGIONS OF SOUTHWEST FRANCE

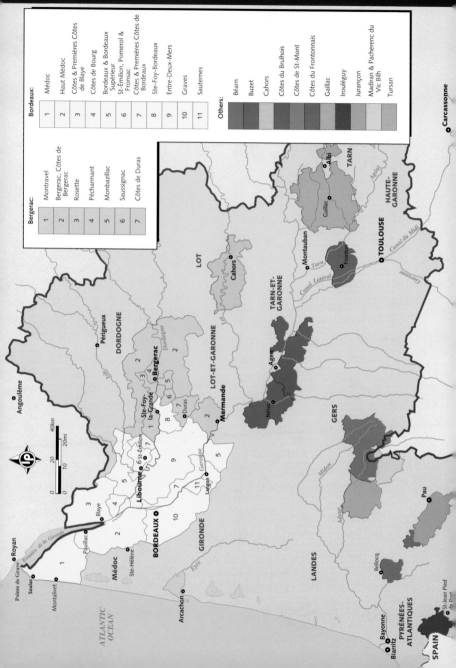

Bordeaux:

1	Médoc
2	Haut Médoc
3	Côtes & Premières Côtes de Blaye
4	Côtes de Bourg
5	Bordeaux & Bordeaux Supérieur
6	St-Émilion, Pomerol & Fronsac
7	Côtes & Premières Côtes de Bordeaux
8	Ste-Foy-Bordeaux
9	Entre-Deux-Mers
10	Graves
11	Sauternes

Others:

Béarn
Buzet
Cahors
Côtes du Brulhois
Côtes de St-Mont
Côtes du Frontonnais
Gaillac
Irouléguy
Jurançon
Madiran & Pacherenc du Vic Bilh
Tursan

Bergerac:

1	Montravel
2	Bergerac, Côtes de Bergerac
3	Rosette
4	Pécharmant
5	Montbazillac
6	Saussignac
7	Côtes de Duras

FOOD

The cuisines of Périgord, Gascony (the Gers and the Landes) and the French Basque country (Pays Basque) are among the richest and most diverse in the French culinary lexicon – *cuisine du terroir* (country cooking) at its best. While the French Basque country is a land apart, with a cuisine that's the spiciest in the land, Gascony and Périgord head the list of regional cuisines with an influence stretching nationwide. For this is the land of *truffes* (truffles) and *foie gras* (the fatty liver of goose or duck), luxuries that have made gourmands swoon for centuries: 'Heaven', exclaimed the Reverend Sydney Smith, 'is eating pâté de foie gras to the sound of trumpets.'

For information on cookery and wine-tasting courses see Courses in the Facts for the Visitor chapter.

Périgord & Gascony

The humble goose is central to the region's cuisine. In addition to foie gras, *confit d'oie* is perhaps the region's most traditional dish: goose legs and wings slowly cooked in their own fat and preserved in jars or earthenware pots, a pre-refrigerator technique also suitable for duck *(confit de canard)* and pork *(enchaud* or *enchaud Périgourdin)*.

The duck has its own prominence as steak-like *magret* or *maigret*, lightly roasted or grilled duck breast. Beef dishes are rare, apart from *tournedos,* a fillet in a foie gras and truffle sauce. You may come across game dishes such as *pâté de sanglier* (boar pâté) or *de faisan* (pheasant). Freshwater fish are popular, especially trout stuffed with foie gras or cooked with truffles.

Gascony favourites include *cassoulet,* a dish of confit de canard (or d'oie), sausages and broad beans (or green beans); and *agneau de causse,* lamb from Quercy's limestone plateaus, roasted with garlic. Sausages feature a lot: *boudin blanc* (soft chicken and veal sausage),

---

Potatoes, Sarlat-Style

Pommes de Terre Sarladaises

Serves 4

1kg potatoes (peeled)
2–3 tablespoons goose fat (or butter)
1 tablespoon finely chopped truffles or *cèpe* (cep) mushrooms
salt and pepper

Slice the potatoes, then wash and dry them. Heat the fat in a large frying pan, then add the potatoes, salt and pepper. Fry quickly for two minutes, reduce the heat and add the truffles. Cook only until the potatoes are ready (don't wait till they're mushy).

Truffles

Truffes, or truffles *(Tuber melanosporum)*, are edible, black, subterranean fungi that grow on the roots of certain oak and hazelnut trees. Known as 'the black diamonds of French cuisine' for their fabulous aroma and flavour, they are also notoriously difficult to grow, favouring certain soils and humidity levels, and not appearing until at least ten years after the trees have been planted. They vary from pea- to fist-sized.

JANE SMITH

They're also fiendishly difficult to find. Traditionally, sows were used to snuffle them out between November and March – apparently truffles smell like male pigs – but, since the sows tended to eat them, more trainable dogs have now become the trufflehunter's friend. Many *rabassaïres* (truffle hunters) first search for a telltale patch of scorched-looking earth, with a certain kind of bronze-coloured midge hovering above. Some use divining sticks.

Two centuries ago, truffles were so numerous that Christmas turkeys might be stuffed with up to 5kg of them. Even at the turn of the 20th century, over 1000 tonnes were harvested. During WWI truffle orchards were neglected and, despite all attempts to revive production, France is lucky to get 50 tonnes per year now (6 tonnes from the Dordogne department).

As a consequence they're pricey. A 100g specimen might fetch €45 at winter markets such as those at Périgueux, Sarlat or Montignac. They're graded from *extra* (top quality) to *deuxième choix* (second choice) and they're sold whole, or as *truffes en morceaux* (truffle pieces) or as *pelures* (truffle skins, for flavouring). Also useful for flavouring is *jus de truffes* (truffle juice).

Truffle fraud is common: White Italian truffles have been stained with walnut dye and passed off as the real thing. Chinese truffles have begun flooding the market at a quarter of the price of French ones, and artificial truffle flavouring has become the norm in many restaurants. However, there's no mistaking the real thing, renowned for its distinctive aroma.

Truffles are at their best when eaten fresh, and only keep for about a week. After eating one with a glass of good wine, said the famous French chef Brillat-Savarin, 'a man becomes more lovable, a woman more loving'. They're traditionally added to many sauces and dishes, and to foie gras and pâté, and are delicious sliced thinly into omelettes and salads. They can be preserved in Madeira or Armagnac with some loss of flavour.

To find out more, check out the Ecomusée de la Truffe in Sorges (see the boxed text in the Dordogne chapter).

saucisse de Toulouse (a fat sausage made with pork) and *andouillettes* (chitterling sausages). The prunes of Agen appear in several pork dishes, usually with a dose of wine.

JANE SMITH

Vegetarians may relish two of the region's finest and most essential ingredients − truffles and *cèpe* (cep) mushrooms − but they don't come cheaply. Truffles are edible subterranean fungi, snuffled out by trained dogs (see the boxed text). Cèpe *Bordelais (Boletus edulis)* − and the cheaper, less tasty *cèpe de pins (B. pinicola)* − are round-capped, fleshy mushrooms. They're harvested from early September to November (the profitable cèpe has become a controversial source of untaxed income, with villagers literally coming to blows over their right to scour the forests). Both kinds are used liberally in omelettes and stews, fried lightly in goose fat or *à la Périgourdine* (with bacon, herbs and grape juice), or, as in Sarlat, cooked in *verjus*, the acidic juice of unripe grapes (used since medieval times as a vinegar substitute). Other mushrooms that may feature in local dishes are the chanterelle *(Cantharellus cibarius)* and spongy *morilles* (yellow morel; *Morchella esculenta)*.

The Dordogne and Lot produce more walnuts than anywhere else in France, so these tasty nuts appear frequently in salads (such as *salade Landaise*), cakes and tarts or in walnut-oil salad dressings. Chestnut gateaux are yummy too, and chestnut purée figures in many desserts.

The region's only well known cheeses are *cabecou de Rocamadour*, made from sheeps' milk in spring and goats' milk in summer, and the French Basque country's similar *fromage de brebis* (ewe's-milk cheese). Among blue cheeses worth trying are *bleu de Quercy* from Figeac and Gourdon, and *bleu des Causses*, similar to Roquefort.

Abundant fruit everywhere ensures excellent *tartes aux fruits* (fruit tarts); prune *tourtières* are paper-thin, flaky-pastry tarts. Strawberries reign supreme (the Dordogne produces more than any other *département*, or administrative department, in France) and are available almost year round. Local varieties include long, super-sweet *garriguettes* and perfumed *marats des bois*, like tiny wild strawberries.

Local fruit often crowns a meal as a *digestif*, with apricots or cherries soaked in Armagnac or a fiery *eau de vie de prune*.

Foie Gras In the wild, geese are migrating birds, with an instinct to stuff themselves after the autumn moulting season to survive the long flight south. The ancient Egyptians were the first to take advantage of this tendency, force-feeding domestic geese to enlarge their tasty livers. The Romans fed theirs with figs and by the 16th century the French were doing it with corn.

A foie-gras 'industry' took off in the 1820s and is now a major

Shopping for Foie Gras

With so many varieties of foie gras on the market and so many shops selling them, it's easy to make a very expensive mistake. Read the small print: Some livers are actually imported. Priciest is foie gras d'oie (goose liver) but foie gras de canard (duck liver) is cheaper and may be just as tasty. Expect to pay at least €22 for 200g of best-quality mi-cuit foie gras d'oie, €15 for a 140g tin of pâté de foie gras or €12 for a 200g tin of bloc de foie gras d'oie. The best buys are often at small-town markets or direct from small producers.

bloc 100% de foie gras – from the processed livers of more than one bird (goose or duck)

délice de foie gras or **mousse 25% foie gras** – contains about 25% foie gras; the mousse is a puree, with the other 75% comprising various ingredients, from eggs to pork meat

foie gras au torchon – brandy-steeped livers rolled around truffles and poached in wine

foie gras entier – all or part of a single liver (goose or duck), cooked and preserved in *bocal* (jars) or *boîte de conserve* (tins)

parfait de foie gras – about 75% foie gras, the rest pork pâté

pâté de foie gras or **pâté périgourdin** – about 50% foie gras and 50% pork pâté or pork meat, often flavoured with truffles

mi-cuit – literally 'half-cooked', and must therefore be kept chilled

income-earner for farmers (and factories) in the southwest. Young geese and ducks destined for *gavage* (force-feeding) are allowed to range freely for between three and five months, fed with grain and alfalfa to expand the digestive system. They're then moved to a smaller enclosure and force-fed three times daily for around four weeks (three for ducks) with ground meal and then corn. It's usually done by hand with a simple funnel, though electric-powered force-feeders may be used. Proponents point to the birds' lack of distress, even claiming that they sometimes jostle to be first in the queue.

The process triples or even quadruples the weight of the birds' livers to between 700g and 900g for a goose and 400g to 500g for a duck. Livers produced by small farmers are usually sold fresh at weekly *marchés du gras*, common in the southwest from November to May.

Aficionados say goose liver is best served raw and chilled, with a glass of sweet Monbazillac. Next-best is *mi-cuit* (half-cooked), served with lemon, salt and pepper, verjus, white grapes and toast. Most of us will have to settle for pâté. See the boxed text 'Shopping for Foie Gras' for a guide to the options.

The Atlantic Coast & the Gironde

This area's most famous culinary contribution is probably sauce à la Bordelaise – a thick wine-based sauce with parsley, shallots and bone marrow, best with entrecôte à la Bordelaise (grilled steak) or agneau à *la Bordelaise* (lamb). More controversial is *palombe*. These wood pigeons are caught in their thousands while migrating through the region in October. Hunters like them *en salmis* (in a casserole or ragout), or roasted and flambeed in Armagnac.

Easier on the conscience is fish, which naturally features strongly in these coastal and estuary areas. From the Gironde estuary come shad, salmon and sturgeon, with ugly, eel-like *lamproies* (lampreys), a seasonal favourite. Topping the list of shellfish are the famous *huîtres* (oysters) of Arcachon. In Bordeaux they're often served with small sausages called *crépinettes*, while mussels are served in a garlic and wine or curry sauce.

Dessert specialities include peaches and plums from the Garonne Valley and prunes steeped in Armagnac. When you're in St-Émilion, don't miss the macaroons; in Bordeaux, look for small pastries called *canelé*.

French Basque Country

Food here is among France's spiciest, suffused with deep-red chillies. Two favourite peppery dishes are *piperade* – a piquant mixture of green peppers, tomatoes, garlic and whipped eggs – and *axoa d'Espelette*, a spicy veal stew with peppers and tomatoes. Salty *jambon de Bayonne* (Bayonne ham) is famous (and pricey), although most of it actually comes from around Orthez. Also special to the region are *loukinkos* (miniature garlic sausages) and *tripotxa* (a mutton blood pudding or little blood sausage). If that doesn't take your fancy, there's the ubiquitous *poulet Basquaise*, a tasty chicken stew with peppers, tomatoes, mushrooms and wine.

Soups are often as thick as stews. Try the chunky fish soup called *ttoro*, which includes scampi, hake, monkfish and conger eel. *Elzeckaria* is mostly vegetable, while *gabure* includes *trebuc* (preserved goose), *camot* (ham shank) and *coustoun* (pork ribs). Among fish

Piperade

Serves 2

2 onions (chopped)
1 tablespoon olive oil
2 cloves garlic (finely chopped)
500g tomatoes (chopped)
2 green peppers (chopped)
salt and pepper to taste
4 eggs, lightly beaten

Cook the onions in the oil over a low heat for 10 minutes, then add the garlic, the tomatoes and peppers. Season with salt and pepper and cook gently for another 15 minutes. Then pour the beaten eggs into the pan and stir until cooked. Lovely!

dishes, *koskera* (hake) is popular. *Thon Basquaise* is tuna grilled with peppers and tomatoes.

For dessert there's the obligatory *gateau Basque,* an almond cake filled with almond cream or cherry preserves and, from Bayonne, some of the best chocolate in France.

WINE

The southwest produces some of the world's finest wines, notably from Bordeaux, as well as many other less-august but eminently drinkable ones, principally from Bergerac, Monbazillac, Cahors and Jurançon (south-west of Pau). There are over 80 separate *vins d'appellation d'origine contrôlée* (AOCs – wines with the highest French wine classification) in the region. Following is a rundown of the better-known varieties. Refer to the map 'Wine Regions of Southwest France' for general locations.

LPP

Les Vignobles Bordelais

France's most famous region for fine wines is Bordeaux, which has an ideal soil and climate for their production. The 1130 sq km of vineyards contain over 5000 wine-producing chateaux (or estates). These typically produce around 30% of France's total AOC wine, classified into 57 different appellations.

Bordeaux wines have enjoyed a favourable reputation since Roman times. Britons (who call the reds claret) have long been major fans, although imports to the UK are falling. This is partly due to competition from 'New World' wines (from the USA, Australia, Chile and South Africa) but also because there's been a glut of mediocre Bordeaux wines during the past decade and some outrageously high prices for the best vintages. The widely hyped 2000 vintage, pronounced the best for a decade, has restored faith (and winemakers' fortunes): Indeed, the demand is so great that by spring 2003, when the wines hit the market, you'll probably have to fork out £200 a bottle for the most famous names.

Over 80% of Bordeaux wines are reds and rosés. The main grapes used are Merlot, Cabernet Sauvignon and Cabernet Franc. The whites are produced from Sauvignon, Sémillon and Muscadelle varieties. Many areas produce both whites and reds.

The appellations are often divided into seven 'families':

Bordeaux Supérieur and **Bordeaux** – fruity wines produced all over the area, labelled Supérieur if they have good ageing potential.
Côtes – include widely produced Côtes de Bordeaux, which can be enjoyed young, and soft, full-bodied reds and whites of Côtes de Bourg, Côtes and Premières Côtes de Blaye.
Médoc and **Graves** – produced from gravelly soil (hence the name Graves); fruity, ruby-red Médoc wines often need time to bring out their full potential.
Rosé, Clairet, Crémant and **Fine** – speciality wines: Bordeaux Rosé and the

slightly fuller-bodied Clairet are rosés, best enjoyed chilled and young; Crémant, a sparkling wine, ranges from dry to sweet; Fine de Bordeaux is a brandy made from white grapes.

St-Émilion, Pomerol and **Fronsac** – deep-red, rich wines; the lesser-known Pomerol has an outstanding bouquet, and Fronsac wines have a slightly spicy flavour.

Vins Blancs Moelleux et Liquoreux – sweet white wines best enjoyed with dessert; the most famous is Sauternes.

Vins Blanc Secs – popular, dry white wines, offering excellent value for money, especially crisp Graves and fruity Entre-Deux-Mers.

For more on wines of this region, visit the Web sites [w] www.bordeaux -wines.com and [w] www.medoc-wines.com.

Les Vignobles du Sud-Ouest
In the past, other wines of the southwest could only reach the port of Bordeaux (and wine-hungry export markets like England) on lengthy trips down the River Garonne in flat-bottomed boats called gabarres. As a result they were less well known than Bordeaux vintages. Nowadays, however, Bergerac, Pécharmant, Cahors, Côtes de Duras, Buzet and sweet, white Monbazillac are familiar names.

Bergerac is produced largely from Sauvignon grapes and comes in a dozen AOCs, both red and white. The reds can be drunk young and have a firm, fruity bouquet. The whites are dry and go well with seafood. Also included are sweeter Côtes de Bergerac Moelleux and Côtes de Montravel. **Pécharmant** reds are strong and full-bodied, best appreciated when they've matured.

Monbazillac is the area's supreme sweet white wine – golden, syrupy and very alcoholic, and an excellent accompaniment to foie gras or dessert. It's best drunk after a minimum of three years but can keep for up to 30 years.

Cahors wines are deep red, almost black, in colour, with a full-bodied, tannic flavour. Cahors wines from the chalky causse need up to 15 years to mature, while wines produced from the Lot Valley can be enjoyed after a year or so.

Distinctive, good-value reds are the **Côtes de Duras, Buzet** (near Nérac) and neighbouring **Côtes du Brulhois**. Lesser-known reds worth trying include those from **Gaillac** on the banks of the Tarn and the tannic **Madiran & Pacherenc du Vic Bilh, Côtes de St-Mont** and **Tursan** (north-east of Pau).

A mild climate and the protection of the mountains have enabled the grapes of **Béarn** and **Jurançon** (near Pau) to ripen right into November. The Jurançon whites come in both dry and sweet dessert varieties. The Béarn AOC vineyards produce red, white and rosé wines.

Also popular are the wines of **Irouléguy** near the Spanish border, ranging from full-bodied reds to fresh rosés.

Wine Tasting & Buying, Information & Tours
You can often buy wine straight from the winegrowers' caves or chais (wine cellars). Most will offer a dégustation (tasting), with the wine poured straight from enormous wood barrels or sparkling stainless-steel vats. It's

usually free, but you won't be popular if you sample several vintages and then leave without buying anything. Cellars often require that you buy *en vrac* (in bulk) – a 5L minimum is common. Be careful not to indulge in too many dégustations if you're driving: Bordeaux wines, in particular, are very strong.

Regional 'Maisons du Vin' are the best places to pick up information on which chateaux or chais are open for tours or tastings – see under Bordeaux, Pauillac and St Émilion (Bordeaux, the Atlantic Coast & the Landes chapter) and Cahors (Lot). For Béarn and Jurançon vineyards, contact Cave des Producteurs (☎ 05 59 21 57 03, fax 05 59 21 72 06), 53 av Henri IV, 6429 Gan; and for Irouléguy wines, contact Cave Cooperation des Vins d'Irouléguy (☎ 05 59 37 41 33), 64430 St-Étienne-de-Baïgorry.

Wine Lexicon

appellation d'origine contrôlée (AOC) – good to superb wines meeting stringent government regulations governing where, how and under what conditions the grapes are grown and the wine fermented and bottled

chai – local term for a winery/cellar

cuvée – a limited vintage

dégustation – wine tasting

domaine – wine-producing estate

grand cru – wine of recognised superior quality; literally 'great growth'

producteur – wine producer or grower, also known as a *vigneron*

vendange – grape harvest

vignoble – vineyard

vin délimité de qualité supérieure (VDQS) – good wine from a specific place or region

vin de pays – literally, 'country wine', of reasonable quality and generally drinkable

vin de table – table wine also known as *vin ordinaire*

vintage – the year or growing season in which a wine was produced

[continued from page 88]

Bullfighting

Corrida first appeared in France in 1851 at Vic-Fézensac (Gers), and this remains the centre of bullfighting in southern France (during its Pentecost weekend Fête des Corridas, accommodation is scarce all over the Gers). Other towns where the sport is big include Mont de Marsan and Dax in the Landes, and Estang in the Gers.

A bull, bred to be aggressive, matches wits with a team of French or Spanish toreros – banderilleros with small harpoons, mounted picadors with lances, and the matador, dressed like a flamenco dancer and armed with a sword, whose skill is measured by his cool pivots with the cape and the final swiftness of the kill. The spectacle is colourful and bloody, and the bull dies a drawn-out death, though there is as yet little debate about animal rights here (see the boxed text). Southwesterners regard the corrida as a passionate celebration of tradition, and make no apologies for it.

The main corrida season is from July through the first week in September. Major tournaments are held about half-a-dozen times each summer, with tickets selling for as little as €12 and as much as €70, depending on whether your seat is *soleil* (in the sun), *ombre et soleil* (mixed shade and sun) or *ombre* (in the shade – the most expensive).

Cruel?

Those who cannot help but see the *corrida* (bullfight), and even *courses landaises* (bull runs), as cruel sports can contact the following organisations for information and ideas for action:

People for the Ethical Treatment of Animals (PETA; ☎ 020-8870 3966, e info@petaeurope .org.uk, w www.petaeurope.org) PO Box 3169, London SW18 4WJ, UK

World Society for the Protection of Animals (WSPA; ☎ 020-7793 0540, e wspa@wspa .org.uk, w www.wspa.org.uk) 89 Albert Embankment, London SE1 7TP, UK

❀ ❀ ❀ ❀ ❀ ❀ ❀ ❀ ❀ ❀ ❀ ❀ ❀

Advance reservations are usually necessary; ask at the nearest tourist office.

Courses Landaises

Prior to some corridas (see the preceding Bullfighting section), the bulls were run through the streets to the arena and some daring villagers would run along with the bulls. This grew into a 'sport' in its own right and some towns in the far southwest still include a running of the bulls (or cows) in their annual festivals.

Laws in the 19th century required these to be confined and the modern result is *les courses landaises,* in which participants face cows – the Landes' own black, long-horned, ill-tempered variety – in an arena. Cattle ranches field teams of six *écarteurs* (dodgers) who goad the cows into charging and then dodge artfully or even jump over them. A jury awards points to each individual and/or team. To an outsider it may look like clowning around, but aficionados regard it as a sport of danger and grace.

Cycling

The Tour de France, started in 1903, is the world's most prestigious bicycle race. For three weeks each July, 189 of the world's top cyclists (in 21 teams of nine) take on a 3000km-plus route. The route changes each year, but always includes five or six days in the Alps and the Pyrénées, and always finishes down the Champs-Élysées in Paris.

Each daily stage is timed and the winner is the rider with the lowest accumulated time. Three special jerseys are awarded and re-awarded each day: the yellow one for race leader, the green one for points leader and the red polka dot one for the 'king of the mountains'. To win one, especially the yellow jersey, even for a day is certain to make headlines back home for that rider.

The 1999, 2000 and 2001 Tours were won by Lance Armstrong, the first American to win three successive Tours and only the sixth rider ever to do so.

Brightly clothed riders – many no doubt with their sights on the Tour de France – hurtle along the back roads of the southwest, year round. Visit the organiser's Web site at ⓦ www.letour.fr for information on the current or upcoming Tour.

Rugby

The game of rugby has been played with enthusiasm in France since 1900, nowhere more so than in the south, where the sport generally eclipses football in popularity.

Rugby union (15s) is most common. Favourite teams include Toulouse (who have been frequent national champions), Bayonne, Castres, Biarritz, Bordeaux, Brive-la-Gaillarde, Montauban, Mont de Marsan, Dax, Pau and Périgueux. Rugby league (13s), less popular in France on the whole, also has a loyal following here. The finals of the Championnat de France de Rugby take place in late May and early June.

Football

France's love affair with football (soccer) got a big boost when it hosted and won the 1998 World Cup, beating the reigning champions and tournament favourites, Brazil, by three goals to one in a one-sided final,

thanks to two goals from Zinedine Zidane and one from Emmanuel Petit. Millions of elated supporters celebrated on the streets of Paris and other cities.

Ironically, however, the 1995 Bosman decision – allowing European clubs to field as many European players as they like – has resulted in an exodus of French players (including Zidane and Petit) to clubs outside the country, where they're better paid.

Southwest France's biggest football club is Girondins de Bordeaux, although even here rugby has a bigger following. Two other regional clubs in good standing are at Toulouse and Brive-la-Gaillarde.

Pétanque

France's most popular traditional game is *pétanque,* or *boules,* usually played by village men on a rough gravel or sandy pitch called a *boulodrome,* scratched out on any handy patch of flat, shady ground. Some towns have purpose-built boulodromes. The favoured time is the cool of late afternoon, and spectators are always welcome.

Feet Tied & Bowled Out

Despite the seemingly informal nature of *pétanque* (a game resembling lawn bowls and played with metal balls on sandy ground), its rules are precise and inviolable.

Two to six people, divided into two teams, can play. Each player has three solid metal boules (two if there are six players), weighing between 650g and 800g and stamped with the hallmark of a licensed boule maker. The game revolves around the *cochonnet* (jack), a small wooden ball 25mm to 35mm in diameter. Each team takes it in turn to aim a boule at this marker, the idea being to land the boule as close to it as possible. The team with the closest boule wins the round; points are allocated by totting up how many boules the winner's team has closest to the marker (one point for each boule). The first to notch up 13 wins the match.

The team throwing the cochonnet (initially decided by a coin toss) has to throw it from within a small circle, 30cm to 50cm in diameter, scratched on the ground. It must be hurled 6m to 10m away. Each player aiming a boule must likewise stand in this circle, *pieds tanqués* (literally 'feet tied'), with both feet firmly on the ground. At the end of a round, a new circle is drawn, encompassing the cochonnet and determining the spot where the next round will start.

Underarm throwing is compulsory. Beyond that, players can choose to roll the boule along the ground (this is called *pointer*, 'to point'), or hurl it high in the air in the hope of it landing bang on top of an opponent's boule, sending it flying out of position. This flamboyant tactic (called *tirer*, 'to shoot') can turn an entire game around in a matter of seconds.

Throughout matches, boules are lovingly polished with a soft white cloth. Players unable to stoop to pick up their boules can lift them up with a magnet attached to a piece of string.

Nicola Williams

The object is to throw your boules (solid metal balls) as close as possible to the small coloured ball thrown at the start (see the boxed text 'Feet Tied & Bowled Out'). Despite its humble appearance, pétanque is a serious sport. Since their inception in 1959, the Pétanque Open World Championships have been won 19 times by France. There have been separate pétanque world championships for women and juniors since 1987.

Basque Sports

You know you're in the land of the Basque people when every town centre has a fronton, an outdoor concrete court with one tall, rounded wall, where any and all play variants of the traditional game of pilota (la pélote Basque in French). Pairs or teams of players volley with a small, rubber- or leather-covered ball against the wall, smacking it with their bare hands or with wooden racquets.

Less familiar are the extraordinary displays of male muscle-power known as indar jokoak (la force Basque in French) at certain festivals – not unlike the Scottish Highland Games.

For more on these and other Basque games see the introduction to the French Basque Country chapter. Local listings in that chapter include details on tournaments and games.

SHOPPING

Every town of any size has a weekly open-air market and regular big brocante (second-hand goods) and speciality markets. Not surprisingly, most products worth taking home are of the edible or drinkable variety. Refer to the special Food & Wine section for details on what's local and what's good.

Pâté de foie gras, as well as confits (conserves) of goose, duck and pork liver, are available almost everywhere. Keep an eye out, even on the remotest roads, for produits de la ferme signs. Fresh truffles are very expensive (up to €450 per kilogram) and only available in the winter months, at major truffle markets such as Périgueux or Ribérac. But you can find truffles preserved in Armagnac or tinned in truffle juice at souvenir and speciality food shops at any time of the year; these travel well and last a long time. You can also find pâté de foie gras flavoured with truffles for about €11 per 100g.

Another worthy farm product is local cheese – especially fromage de brebis (ewe's cheese) from the Pyrénées, aggressively marketed under the Ossau-Iraty label at roadside farms, fromageries and cooperatives in Béarn and the French Basque country. The finest of these are the rich summer cheeses of the vallée d'Ossau (see the boxed text 'Transhumance & Cheese' under Haut-Béarn in the Béarn chapter). Also from the Basque country comes jambon de Bayonne (Bayonne ham), the best of which bears the Ibaïona label. Tourist offices have lists of reliable local sellers.

Nut-lovers will like the Dordogne's walnut products. Walnut oil goes for around €5.50 for a 35cL bottle (though it only lasts a few months), and local markets have walnut cakes galore.

And of course there's wine, in enough varieties to make your head spin. Don't overlook very drinkable but less well known wines such as the reds of Pécharmant and Bergerac and the whites of Montravel and Jurançon (see the special section on Food & Wine for details). Other drinkables for which the southwest is known are the Armagnac of Gascony (Landes and Gers) and its mellower aperitif derivative, floc d'Armagnac (also called floc d'Armagnac). Izarra, the Basque Country's own potent herbal liqueur, is sold all over France.

Nonconsumables worth considering include locally made embroidery; Basque linen and cotton products; and espadrilles (fibre-soled cotton shoes in every style) for next to nothing. If you have a bit of money to spend, be the only one on your block with a makila, the splendid Basque aristocrat of walking sticks.

Non-EU residents may be able to get a rebate on some of France's value-added tax; see Taxes & Refunds under Money earlier in this chapter. American visitors take note: USA customs' regulations forbid the import of all edibles (including nonpasteurised cheeses, nuts and fruit) and plant products.

Getting There & Away

This chapter includes not only international connections but domestic transport to and from Southwest France. For information on transport between the towns of Southwest France, see the Getting Around chapter.

AIR

Unless otherwise noted, fares quoted are approximate return fares during the peak air-travel season, based on advertised rates at the time of writing. None constitutes a recommendation for any airline. In North America and Europe, peak season is roughly June to mid-September plus Christmas; 'shoulder' season is April to May and mid-September to October. In Australia and New Zealand, peak season is roughly December to January.

Airports & Airlines

Southwest France's two most important airports aren't in the southwest at all, but in Paris: Roissy Charles de Gaulle and Orly, served by most major international carriers. Although some airports in Southwest France call themselves 'international', most long-haul flights require a change of plane in Paris or another European capital such as London or Brussels.

On domestic routes from Paris to Southwest France, the leading carrier is Air France, the national airline (sometimes under the name of its domestic subsidiary, Régional Airlines), followed by Air Liberté.

The southwest's two main airports are to be found at Toulouse and Bordeaux. Together they have direct connections with over three dozen cities around France, Europe and North Africa. Agen, Bergerac, Biarritz, Castres, Lourdes, Pau and Périgueux all have smaller airports with direct connections to Paris and elsewhere in France. Biarritz also has direct connections from London (with Ryanair).

Two international airports outside the region but close enough to be useful gateways are at Carcassonne, 90km south-east

> ### Warning
>
> The information in this chapter is particularly vulnerable to change – prices for international travel are volatile, routes are introduced and cancelled, schedules change, special deals come and go, and rules and visa requirements are amended. At the time of writing several airlines were in difficulty and many routes had been cut or suspended. Check direct with the airline or a travel agent to make sure you understand how a fare works. In addition, the travel industry is highly competitive and there are many lurks and perks.
>
> The upshot is that you should get opinions, quotes and advice from as many airlines and travel agents as possible before you part with your cash. The details given in this chapter should be regarded as pointers and are not a substitute for your own careful, up-to-date research.

of Toulouse, and Tarbes (Tarbes-Ossun-Lourdes), 90km south-west of Auch.

Buying Tickets

The Internet is a useful resource for checking air fares, as most travel agencies and airlines have Web pages. There is also a growing number of online agents such as W www.travelocity.com and W www.deckchair.com. But a close watch on old-fashioned newspaper travel ads will turn up short-term bargains too.

In general there's little to be gained from going direct to the airlines. They release discounted tickets to selected travel agents and discount agencies, and these are often the best deals. For short-term travel you'll save by booking at least a few weeks ahead, travelling mid-week or staying away at least one Saturday night. Another money-saving tactic is to take an indirect flight with a third-country carrier.

Air France and some other carriers offer youth fares. Many discounted long-term travel tickets are valid for a year, allowing multiple stopovers with open dates. Round-the-World (RTW) tickets are comparable in price to ordinary long-haul return flights.

A good travel agent can tell you about all such deals, propose strategies for avoiding stopovers, and offer advice on everything from which airline has the best vegetarian food to the best travel insurance to bundle with your ticket.

But travel agents are getting a run for their money from the new breed of 'no-frills' airlines, which mostly sell direct – by telephone or online – and often for knock-down prices. However, these low fares are 'subject to availability', which means they can vary wildly according to date.

At the time of writing, two no-frills airlines that had links to Southwest France were Ryanair (to Biarritz and Carcassonne) and Buzz (to Bordeaux and Toulouse). These carriers often sell one-way tickets at half the return fare, making it easy to stitch together an 'open jaw' itinerary, flying into one city and out of another. The competition has forced many full-service airlines to offer their own conditional, limited-availability cheap fares.

You may find some very cheap flights advertised by obscure agencies. Most are honest and solvent, but there are rogue outfits, so keep your eyes open. Paying by credit card generally offers protection since most card issuers provide refunds if you don't get what you paid for. Similar protection comes from buying a ticket from a bonded agent, such as those covered by the Air Travel Organiser's Licence (ATOL; W www.atol.org.uk) scheme in the UK. Established agencies, such as those mentioned in this book, offer more security and are almost as competitive as you can get.

Travellers with Special Needs

If you have special requirements – you're in a wheelchair, taking the baby, vegetarian, terrified of flying – let the airline know when you book. Restate your needs when you reconfirm, and again when you check in at the airport.

With advance warning most international

Airline Booking Numbers

Air Afrique
Bordeaux ☎ 05 56 81 58 71
Air Algerie
Toulouse ☎ 05 61 23 32 34
Air France
☎ 08 20 82 08 20
Air Liberté
☎ 08 03 80 58 05
British Airways
☎ 08 25 82 54 00
Buzz
Paris ☎ 01 55 17 42 42
Crossair
☎ 08 20 83 08 30
Jersey European Airways
☎ 08 45 84 51 11
KLM
☎ 08 10 55 65 56
Lufthansa Airlines
☎ 08 02 02 00 30
Portugália
Bordeaux ☎ 05 56 34 58 40
Toulouse ☎ 05 34 60 55 44
Royal Air Maroc
Bordeaux ☎ 05 56 52 49 50
Toulouse ☎ 05 34 45 22 90
Ryanair
☎ 08 25 07 16 20
Tunis Air
Bordeaux ☎ 05 56 44 05 22
Toulouse ☎ 05 61 62 99 70

airports can provide escorts from check-in to the plane, and most have ramps, lifts, accessible toilets and telephones. Major carriers can arrange wheelchairs. Aircraft toilets present problems for wheelchair travellers, who should discuss this early on with the airline and/or their doctor. The Web site W www.everybody.co.uk has information on facilities offered by various airlines.

Guide dogs for the blind must often travel in a specially pressurised baggage compartment with other animals, and are subject to the same stiff quarantine laws as any other animal entering or returning to rabies-free countries such as the UK. Recent changes to UK quarantine laws allow animals arriving from elsewhere in the EU via certain routes

Air Travel Glossary

Alliances Many of the world's leading airlines are now intimately involved with each other, sharing everything from reservations systems and check-in to aircraft and frequent-flyer schemes. Opponents say that alliances restrict competition. Whatever the arguments, there is no doubt that big alliances are the way of the future.

Courier Fares Businesses often need to send urgent documents or freight securely and quickly. Courier companies hire people to accompany the package through customs and, in return, offer a discount ticket which is sometimes a bargain. However, you may have to surrender all your baggage allowance and take only carry-on luggage.

Fares Airlines traditionally offer 1st class (coded F), business class (coded J) and economy class (coded Y) tickets. These days there are so many promotional and discounted fares available that few passengers pay full fare.

Lost Tickets If you lose your airline ticket, an airline will usually treat it like a travellers cheque and, after inquiries, issue you with another one. Legally, however, an airline is entitled to treat it like cash and if you lose it then it's gone forever. Take very good care of your tickets.

Onward Tickets An entry requirement for many countries is that you have a ticket out of the country. If you're unsure of your next move, the easiest solution is to buy the cheapest onward ticket to a neighbouring country or a ticket from a reliable airline which can later be refunded if you do not use it.

Open-Jaw Tickets These are return tickets where you fly out to one place but return from another. If available, this can save you backtracking to your arrival point.

Overbooking Since every flight has some passengers who fail to show up, airlines often book more passengers than they have seats. Usually excess passengers make up for the no-shows, but occasionally somebody gets 'bumped' onto the next available flight. Guess who it is most likely to be? The passengers who check in late. If you do get 'bumped', you are normally offered some form of compensation.

Reconfirmation Some airlines require you to reconfirm your flight at least 72 hours prior to departure. Check your travel documents to see if this is the case.

Restrictions Discounted tickets often have various restrictions on them – such as needing to be paid for in advance and incurring a penalty to be altered or cancelled. Others are restrictions on the minimum and maximum period you must be away.

Round-the-World Tickets RTW tickets give you a limited period (usually a year) in which to circumnavigate the globe. You can go anywhere the carrying airlines go, as long as you don't backtrack. The number of stopovers or total number of separate flights is decided before you set off and they usually cost a bit more than a basic return flight.

Ticketless Travel Airlines are gradually waking up to the realisation that paper tickets are unnecessary encumbrances. On simple one-way or return trips, reservations details can be held on computer and the passenger merely shows ID to claim their seat.

Transferred Tickets Airline tickets cannot be transferred from one person to another. Travellers sometimes try to sell the return half of their ticket, but officials can ask you to prove that you are the person named on the ticket. On an international flight, tickets are compared with passports.

to avoid quarantine, provided they meet strict vaccination and other requirements (for details contact the UK Department for Environment, Food & Rural Affairs at ☎ 0870 241 1710, fax 020-7904 6834, e pets@ahvg.maff.gsi.gov.uk).

Children under two years normally travel for around 10% of the standard fare, as long as they don't occupy a seat. They don't get a baggage allowance. Bassinets or 'skycots' can usually be provided by the airline if requested in advance. Children between two and 12 years can usually occupy a seat for half to two-thirds the full fare, and do get a baggage allowance. Pushchairs can often be taken as hand luggage.

Airport Taxes
Imposed by both the country you're departing from and the country you're flying to – airport taxes are included in the price of your ticket. At the time of writing the tax for a one-way flight to France from the UK was about £14 or €24, and the tax on a domestic flight between Paris and Southwest France was about €19. Taxes are included in fares quoted here.

Other Parts of France
The variation in French domestic air fares is astonishing, depending on who you are, when you book and when you're travelling, among other things. Youth/student fares (with no restrictions or advance-booking requirements) are often available to under 26s and student-card holders. Travellers aged over 60, families and couples are entitled to some discounts. Generally speaking, unless you're eligible for one of these, it's cheaper to take the train.

Paris branches of reliable youth-oriented travel agencies include Accueil des Jeunes en France (AJF; ☎ 01 42 80 00 33), Council Travel (☎ 01 43 29 69 50, W www.counciltravel.com), OTU Voyages (☎ 08 20 81 78 17), Voyages Wasteels (☎ 08 25 88 70 06, W www.voyages-wasteels.fr) and usit Connect (☎ 01 44 55 32 60, W www.campustravel.com). Outside France, Air France representatives sell tickets for many domestic flights.

From Paris (mainly Orly), Air France has nearly three dozen flights a day to Toulouse and two dozen to Bordeaux (fewer at the weekend), plus daily or almost-daily connections to Agen, Bergerac, Biarritz, Castres, Lourdes, Pau and Périgueux. Air Liberté flies between Orly and Toulouse about eight times a day. Some rough examples of the best adult/youth return fares from Paris (taxes included) at the time of writing were €111/98 to Toulouse, €93/81 to Bordeaux, €162/131 to Périgueux and €140/110 to Biarritz. These adult fares (but not the youth fares) generally require about two weeks' advance booking and at least one Saturday night away.

To Toulouse and Bordeaux there are daily or almost-daily flights from Clermont-Ferrand, Lille, Lyons, Marseilles, Nantes, Nice, Rennes and Strasbourg. Additional connections to Toulouse are from Carcassonne, Metz-Nancy and Mulhouse-Basle. Other routes include Brest to Bordeaux, Montpellier to Bordeaux, Lyons to Biarritz, Clermont-Ferrand to Biarritz, Lyons to Pau and Nantes to Pau.

Continental Europe
The only direct scheduled flights to Southwest France from elsewhere in Continental Europe are to Toulouse, Bordeaux and Biarritz. Cities with daily or almost-daily connections to Toulouse include Amsterdam, Basle, Brussels, Frankfurt-am-Main, Geneva, Lisbon, Madrid, Milan and Munich. Daily or almost-daily links to Bordeaux include Barcelona, Basle, Bilbao, Brussels, Geneva, Lisbon, Madrid, Munich and Porto. Biarritz has once-weekly connections from Geneva and Helsinki.

Airfare specialists with branches around Germany include the Frankfurt-based STA Travel (☎ 069-70 30 35, W www.sta-travel.com) and Cologne-based usit Campus (☎ 01805 788336, W www.usitcampus.de). In Amsterdam try Malibu Travel (☎ 020-626 32 30). In Brussels, go to Acotra Student Travel Agency (☎ 02 512 86 07) or usit Connections (☎ 02 550 01 00, W www.connections.be); in Antwerp try WATS Reizen (☎ 03 226 16 26). In Madrid try

Barcelo Viajs (☎ 91 559 18 19), and in Lisbon consult with Wasteels (☎ 218 869 793).

Sample adult return fares for *direct* flights from various European centres at the time of writing include:

To Toulouse
Amsterdam €215, Madrid €210, Milan €260
To Bordeaux
Brussels €230, Lisbon €275, Munich €245

The UK & Ireland

Discount air travel is big business in London. Cheap fares appear in the Saturday *Independent* and *Sunday Times* travel sections and, in London, in *Time Out*, the *Evening Standard* and *TNT* (a free magazine available from bins outside Underground stations).

The UK's best-known bargain-ticket agencies are Trailfinders (☎ 020-7937 1234, W www.trailfinders.com), usit Campus (☎ 0870 240 1010, W www.usitcampus .co.uk), Travel CUTS (☎ 020-7792 3770) and STA Travel (☎ 020-7361 6161, W www .statravel.co.uk). All have branches throughout the UK, and usit Campus has outlets in many Hostelling International (HI) shops. In Ireland, reliable sources include usit Now (☎ 01-602 1600) and Trailfinders (☎ 01-677 7888, W www.trailfinders.com), both based in Dublin. SAGA Flights Service (☎ 01303-773 532, W www.saga.co.uk) has some bargains for travellers aged over 50.

From London, British Airways (BA; ☎ 08 45 773 3377, W www.britishairways.com) and Air France (☎ 0845 084 5111, W www .airfrance.fr) each fly daily direct to Toulouse; BA flies daily direct to Bordeaux; and KLM uk (☎ 0870 507 4074, W www.klmuk .com) flies daily via Amsterdam to Toulouse. The best available discounted return fare from London is about £70 to Toulouse or £100 to Bordeaux.

Also based in the UK, Buzz (☎ 0870 240 7070, W www.buzzaway.com) flies from London Stansted to Toulouse on Saturday and Sunday in July and August only (though future plans are up in the air) and to Bordeaux daily. High-season return fares start at £80.

British European Airways (☎ 0870 567 6676, W www.british-european.com) flies to Toulouse from Birmingham (£150, with connections from Belfast and Glasgow) on Sunday from mid-December to March, daily except Saturday from April to October and not at all from November to mid-December.

Dublin-based Ryanair (UK ☎ 0870 333 1231, Ireland ☎ 01-609 7881, W www.ryanair .ie) flies from London Stansted to Biarritz daily (from £45 return) and twice daily to Carcassonne (from £65). Connections from Dublin to Stansted start at about €32 return.

The USA & Canada

Discount travel agents in the USA and Canada are called consolidators, and can be found through the *Yellow Pages* or major newspapers. One leading consolidator is Ticket Planet (W www.ticketplanet.com). The *Los Angeles Times, New York Times,* San Francisco *Examiner,* Chicago *Tribune,* Toronto *Globe & Mail,* Toronto *Star,* Montreal *Gazette* and Vancouver *Sun* have weekly travel sections with ads and information.

Reliable flight specialists in the USA, with offices all over the country, include Council Travel (toll-free ☎ 1 800 226 8624, W www .counciltravel.com) and STA Travel (toll-free ☎ 1 800 777 0112/781 4040, W www .statravel.com). Nouvelles Frontières (W www .newfrontiers.com) has offices in New York and Los Angeles. Canada's best bargain-ticket agency is Travel CUTS/Voyages Campus (☎ 1 888 838 2887, W www.travelcuts .com). SAGA Holidays (☎ 1 800 343 0273, W www.saga.co.uk) offers bargain fares for travellers over age 50.

There are no direct flights from North America to Southwest France, but plenty via Paris, London and other European centres. You can fly from New York to Paris for as little as US$700/500 return in summer/ winter; equivalent fares from the west coast are about US$100 to US$150 higher. A direct flight from Toronto to Paris costs around C$1200/1100.

Australia & New Zealand

Cheap flights generally go via South-East Asian capitals; those from New Zealand sometimes stop in Australia, at one of the Pacific Islands or in Hawaii. The very cheapest flights may be on carriers, such as Emirates, which make two stops.

Check travel agency ads in the *Yellow Pages,* and in the Saturday travel sections of the *Sydney Morning Herald,* Melbourne's *The Age* or the *New Zealand Herald.* STA Travel and Flight Centres International, both with offices across Australia and New Zealand, are major dealers in cheap air fares. For the nearest office, contact STA (☎ 131 776 Australiawide, W www.statravel.com.au) or Flight Centres (☎ 131 600 Australiawide, W www.flightcentre.com.au or W www.flightcentre.com/nz).

Expect to pay about A$1800/3000 in the low/high season for a return ticket to the UK. RTW tickets are often real bargains, and can sometimes work out cheaper than turning around and coming back. RTWs including London start at about A$1720/1940 or NZ$2150/2200 for students/nonstudents.

LAND
Other Parts of France

Bus Forget about trying to get a bus from Paris to Southwest France. French transport policy is heavily lopsided in favour of the state-owned rail system, and inter-regional bus services are very limited. Take the train.

Train France's excellent rail network, run by the state-owned Société Nationale des Chemins de Fer (SNCF), reaches almost every part of the country. The network is very Paris-centred, with the most important lines radiating from the capital like the spokes of a wheel. While this makes for some tedious rail travel between towns on different 'spokes,' it means that getting almost anywhere from Paris is fast and easy.

SNCF's pride and joy is the world-famous TGV (teh-**zheh**-veh), short for *train à grande vitesse* (high-speed train). Thanks to the TGV, travel between some cities can be faster and easier by rail than by air, especially when airport transport is taken into account.

Southwest France is served by the TGV Atlantique service, which runs from Paris to Bordeaux (with a branch via Agen and Montauban to Toulouse), Facture (with a branch

to Arcachon), Dax (with a branch via Pau to Tarbes), and via Bayonne to the Spanish border at Hendaye/Irún. At the time of writing there were almost three dozen daily direct TGV services from Paris to Bordeaux, nine to Bayonne and five to Toulouse.

TGV *grandes lignes* (main lines) are also used by some slower, cheaper, non-TGV services. Other towns in the region are linked to these lines by *trains express régionaux* or TER (regional express trains). Many towns not on the SNCF network are linked with nearby railheads by SNCF or TER buses.

TGV Atlantique services depart from Paris' Gare Montparnasse, while all other services to Southwest France use the Gare d'Austerlitz. Track around Paris links the Atlantique line directly with the two other domestic TGV lines, TGV Nord and TGV Sud-Est (as well as with Roissy Charles de Gaulle airport).

Information Most larger stations have both ticket windows and enquiries/booking offices. Here you can pick up SNCF's free, pocket-size timetables. These can be daunting, with complex footnotes indicating the days on which each train runs. Some may *circule* (run) only on certain days or dates, or *tous les jours sauf* (every day except) Saturday, Sunday and/or *fêtes* (holidays). In the end you may be better off asking at the window.

SNCF's national enquiries/booking number is ☎ 08 36 35 35 35 (in French; 24 hours) or ☎ 08 36 35 35 39 (in English; 7am to 10pm daily). SNCF also has a user-friendly Web site, W www.sncf.com.

Services, Reservations & Tickets Most trains, including TGVs, have 1st- and 2nd-class sections. In this book we quote 2nd-class fares, which on non-TGV trains work out at about €8 to €10 per 100km for long trips, or €10 to €15 per 100km for short hops (compare this with car costs of €6 to €8 per 100km for petrol plus up to €6 to €7 per 100km for tolls). Travel in 1st class costs 50% more than 2nd class. Return tickets cost double the single-ticket price. Children aged under four travel free; those aged four to 11 travel half-price. Tickets bought on board the train command heavy surcharges.

A reservation fee, from €3 to €18 depending on the train, is mandatory for TGV travel and on certain other popular routes during holiday periods. Most overnight trains have *couchettes* (sleeping berths; six/four per 2nd/1st-class compartment) which must be booked ahead, for a €15 fee. These fees are included in the ticket price.

Reservations can be made up to two months in advance at major travel agencies, by telephone or online (see the preceding Information section), at any SNCF ticket office or at one of the automatic ticket vending machines in every station. Vending machines are of two kinds: touch-screen *billetteries automatiques* issue all types of tickets and accept cash or credit cards; *billetteries régionales* sell only regional tickets and accept only cash. A ticket bought with cash can be reimbursed (by anyone) for cash, so keep yours in a safe place. SNCF won't post tickets outside France.

Following are sample 2nd-class, one-way, full-price fares and journey times from Paris:

destination	TGV time	TGV fare	non-TGV time	non-TGV fare
Bayonne	5 hrs	€66.45	6½ hrs	€59.15
Bordeaux	3 hrs	€54.75	4½ hrs	€47.55
Brive-la-Gaillarde	n/a	n/a	4 hrs	€42.25
Toulouse	5½ hrs	€71.05	6½ hrs	€55.35

SNCF Discounts & Passes A range of 25%-off fares called Tarif Découverte automatically applies to: travellers aged 12 to 25, and those aged over 60; one to four adults travelling with a child under 12 years old; anyone taking a return journey of at least 200km and spending a Saturday night away; and any two people travelling together on a return journey. But they're available in limited numbers and tend to be scarce on busy days. They may also not apply during *périodes blancs* (high-traffic periods, publicised at stations).

Several one-year travel passes give 50% discounts: Carte 12-25 (€41.15) for travellers

---

What's the Orange Thingy For?

You risk an on-the-spot fine if you fail to validate your ticket before boarding the train. Time-stamp it in one of the orange *composteurs* (ticket-punching machines) at the platform entrance.

✹ ✹ ✹ ✹ ✹ ✹ ✹ ✹ ✹ ✹ ✹ ✹

---

aged 12 to 25, Carte Enfant Plus (€53.35) for one to four adults travelling with a child under 12 years old, and Carte Sénior (€44.20) for travellers aged over 60. The discount drops to 25% during périodes blancs, and is not valid for TGV services.

Rail Passes There are several passes for use on the European rail system, though you'd have to do a lot of train travel to make them worthwhile.

The **France Railpass** gives non-residents of France unlimited travel on the SNCF system for any three to nine days out of a month, plus discounts on SeaFrance Dover-Calais ferries. The 2nd-class, three-day pass costs the equivalent of £112/82 (adult/those under 26); each additional day of travel costs £20/13. There are also family, senior and child versions.

The **Inter-Rail Pass** is available to anyone resident in Europe for at least six months. There are eight passes, each for a different zone; for example, zone E includes France, Belgium, the Netherlands and Luxembourg. A pass for 22 consecutive days' travel costs £185/129.

The **Euro Domino Pass** is good for three to eight consecutive days within a month, in a specified European country. It too is only for those resident in Europe for at least six months. The price of a 2nd-class pass for France runs from £99/79 for three days to £198/159 for eight days.

For non-European residents, the **Eurailpass** is valid for unlimited travel (1st/2nd class for those aged over/under 26) in 17 European countries. Standard versions are good for 15 days (US$554) to three months (US$1558); 'flexi' versions allow a certain number of travel days per longer period.

In the UK you can get these and other passes from SNCF subsidiary Rail Europe (☎ 0870 5848 848, W www.raileurope.co.uk) and from specialist travel agencies. Contact Rail Europe in the USA at toll-free ☎ 1 888 4EURAIL or ☎ 1 888 274 8724; in Canada at toll-free ☎ 1 800 361-RAIL; or online at W www.raileurope.com. Several of these passes can also be booked at W www.europerailpass.co.uk, and Inter-Rail passes at W www.inter-rail.co.uk.

Even with these passes you must pay for seat and couchette reservations, and all supplements on express trains.

Left Luggage Most larger SNCF stations have a *consigne manuelle* (left-luggage office) where you pay by the day (€2.30 to €4.60 per bag); some also have a 72-hour computerised *consigne automatique*. Make sure you note its closing hours!

Auto Train Under SNCF's Auto Train scheme you can load your car or motorcycle on the train at certain stations and on certain days. Domestic routes to Southwest France run from Paris to Biarritz, Bordeaux, Brive-la-Gaillarde, Tarbes and Toulouse; and from several other parts of France to Biarritz and to Bordeaux. The price depends on route, season and vehicle size. To transport a small car from Paris to Bordeaux in the high/low season costs €130/84; a motorcycle costs €84/54. Cars are loaded on the train one hour before departure and unloaded 30 minutes after arrival. Contact SNCF or Rail Europe for details.

Car & Motorcycle The first rule for motoring down to Southwest France is: avoid it in July and August if you can, or prepare yourself for massive congestion, everywhere. This is when most of France goes on holiday. The second rule: Try to do your driving on Sunday, as lorries over 7.5 tonnes are prohibited from using any roads on this day (and on holidays).

The main motorway from Paris (via Orléans, Tours and Poitiers) to Bordeaux and the Spanish border at Hendaye has the European designation E5. To the French it's

Roads & Tolls in France

There are four types of intercity road in France.

Autoroutes, whose alphanumeric names begin with A, are multilane motorways, often with *aires de repos* (rest areas) with restaurants and pricey petrol stations. Most stretches are subject to road tolls, at about €6/4 per 100km for cars/motorcycles (see the Getting Around chapter for a table of tolls in Southwest France). Some have toll plazas every few dozen kilometres with machines that issue a ticket, which you hand over at a *péage* (toll booth) when you exit. You can pay in euro cash or by credit card.

Routes nationales, whose names begin with N (or RN on older maps and signs), are main highways; newer ones are wide and well marked.

Routes départmentales, designated by D, are secondary and tertiary local roads.

Routes communales are minor rural roads whose names sometimes begin with C.

Most autoroutes and many routes nationales also have European designations, beginning with E.

the A10 to Bordeaux, the N10 through most of the Landes, and the A63 from Dax to the border. A less congested route into the Dordogne from Poitiers is the Bis route (see the boxed text 'Bis' in the Getting Around chapter) E62/N147 to Bellac, D675 to Rochechouart, D901 to Châlus and N21 to Périgueux.

The main motorway south (via Limoges) to Toulouse branches at Orléans as the E9. Its French names are the A71 to Vierzon, the A20 to Brive-la-Gaillarde, a mixture of A20 and N20 onwards to Montauban, and the A62 to Toulouse. An alternative Bis route from Limoges is the D704/D15 to Châlus, N21 to Périgueux, D710 to Fumel and the D102, D2 and D927 to Montauban, and the A20/N20 to Toulouse.

Approximate road distances (assuming maximum use of motorways), travelling times and car tolls to Bordeaux from selected towns elsewhere in France include the following:

origin	distance (km)	time (hours)	toll (€)
Calais	867	8½	58
Paris	580	5½	41
Nantes	325	3½	17
Lyons	775	7½	49
Marseilles	642	6	35

And similarly, road distances, travelling times and tolls from other towns in France to Toulouse include:

origin	distance (km)	time (hours)	toll (€)
Calais	978	10	73
Paris	691	7	56
Nantes	566	5½	32
Lyons	532	5	35
Marseilles	399	4	21

For more information on routes to Channel ferry ports, see The UK under Sea in this chapter. For information on regional arteries, see the Getting Around chapter.

Continental Europe

Bus Several companies include Southwest France in their European routes.

Eurolines An association of companies that forms Europe's largest international bus network, Eurolines (☎ 08 36 69 52 52, 🄴 info@eurolines.fr, 🅦 www.eurolines.fr), links cities all over Western and Central Europe, Scandinavia and Morocco.

Buses are slower and less comfortable than trains, but cheaper, especially if you qualify for a 10 to 20% discount for those aged under 26 or 60 and over, or 30 to 40% discounts for children aged four to 12. During the summer it's a good idea to make reservations a few days in advance.

Eurolines' main offices in Southwest France are in Bordeaux (☎ 05 56 92 50 42) and Toulouse (☎ 05 61 26 40 04). Other stops in Southwest France are at Agen, Arcachon, Bayonne, Bergerac, Brive-la-Gaillarde, Cahors, Castets, Hossegor, Lourdes, Marmande,

Mimizan, Mont de Marsan, Montauban, Pau, Périgueux, Souillac, St-Jean de Luz, Tarbes and Villeneuve.

Among Eurolines affiliates around Europe are those in Amsterdam (☎ 020-560 8788), Barcelona (☎ 93 490 4000), Berlin (☎ 030-86 0960), Brussels (☎ 02 274 1350), Madrid (☎ 91 506 3360), Rome (☎ 06 440 4009) and Vienna (☎ 01-712 0453).

Following are some sample adult/youth one-way fares in the high season; return fares are about 15% lower than two singles.

Brussels-Bordeaux: €61/55
Copenhagen-Bordeaux: €105.50/95.50
Valencia-Bayonne: €62/55.50
Barcelona-Toulouse: €33.50/30.50

Intercars The company Intercars (🅦 www.intercars.fr) operates buses between towns in southern and Central Europe. Its main hub in Southwest France is at the main bus station in Toulouse (☎ 05 61 58 14 53). Some sample one-way fares (adult/youth) to Toulouse are from Madrid (€46.50/44), Porto (€84/81) and Berlin (€111/96). Discounts of up to 15% for those aged under 26 or 60 and over, and up to 50% for those aged from two to 12, are available.

Train Paris abounds with rail connections from all over Europe; other big border stations in France are at Lille, Metz, Strasbourg, Mulhouse, Lyons and Nice. Bordeaux has links, with a change at Irún/Hendaye, from Spain and Portugal – for example, three times a day from Madrid (9½ hours; €84 one way). Toulouse has links, with a change at Nice, from Italy – for example, twice daily from Milan (12½ hours; €122). A couchette costs about €25 extra.

You can book tickets with Rail Europe up to two months ahead; its European affiliates include:

Belgium
Rail Europe Benelux (☎ 02 534 4531)
Germany
Rail Europe Deutschland (☎ 069-9758 4661)
Italy
Rail Europe Italia (☎ 02 72 54 43 09)
Spain
Rail Europe España (☎ 91 542 2018)
Switzerland
Rail Europe Suisse (☎ 031-380 1921)

You can book direct with SNCF but they won't post tickets outside France. For more on SNCF see Train under Other Parts of France earlier in this chapter.

If you plan to travel widely by train, consider buying the *Thomas Cook European Timetable,* which gives a complete listing of train (and ferry) schedules, supplements and reservations information. It's updated monthly and is available from Thomas Cook outlets worldwide, and online at [W] www .thomascookpublishing.com/books.

Auto Train Auto Train (see Train in the earlier Other Parts of France section) permits the transport of cars by passenger train between certain European stations. International links to Southwest France include Germany (Berlin, Dusseldorf, Frankfurt-am-Main, Hamburg or Hildesheim to Bordeaux), Belgium (Brussels or Liège to Biarritz, Bordeaux, Brive-la-Gaillarde or Toulouse; and Brussels to Tarbes) and the Netherlands (Bois le Duc to Biarritz, Bordeaux, Brive-la-Gaillarde or Toulouse).

SNCF offices in France have Auto Train information, as do Rail Europe offices. For most international journeys you should book Auto Train at least two months in advance.

The UK
Bus Eurolines has direct, year-round bus services, two to four times weekly, from London's Victoria Coach Station, via the Dover-Calais Channel crossing. Sample adult/youth one-way fares during the peak season (July, August and Christmas holidays) include Paris (£32/29); Agen, Bordeaux, Montauban or Toulouse (£64/58); and Bayonne (£70/64). Nonpeak fares are around 10% less. Bookings can be made with Eurolines UK (☎ 0870 514 3219 or ☎ 01582-404511, fax 400694, [W] www.eurolines.co.uk), or at any National Express office.

Train The cheapest rail route from London to Southwest France is from Charing Cross station to Paris on a 'rail-sea-rail' ticket (crossing the Channel by ferry or SeaCat), with a change of trains (and stations) in Paris for the onward, non-TGV journey (see Train in the preceding Other Parts of France section). Tickets for this route can be purchased from travel agents, larger mainline stations or Connex (☎ 020-7904 5020). At the time of writing a full 2nd-class, one-way fare for London-Bordeaux was £71/60 (adult/youth).

Eurostar, the passenger service that goes from Waterloo station via the Channel Tunnel, doesn't go to Southwest France but you can take it to Lille and from there catch the TGV direct to Bordeaux (eight hours from London) or Toulouse (11½ hours). Full fares can be more than twice those for rail-sea-rail, but a nonrefundable, compulsory-return London-Bordeaux ticket costs £120 if you book a week ahead and stay at least one Saturday night. An unrestricted youth fare is £60/110 one way/return.

In the UK, both Eurostar and non-Eurostar tickets are available from travel agents, many mainline train stations, Rail Europe and Connex. For Eurostar information only, contact Eurostar (☎ 0870 5186 186 in the UK, ☎ 1 800 EUROSTAR in the USA and Canada, [W] www.eurostar.com).

Auto Train services (see Train under Other Parts of France earlier in this chapter) are available only within Continental Europe. French Motorail (☎ 0870 241 5415, [W] www.frenchmotorail.com), an Auto Train service combined with private couchette or sleeper and marketed from the UK by Rail Europe, links the ferry port of Calais directly with Brive-la-Gaillarde and Toulouse, from late May to mid-September.

Car & Motorcycle Your car or motorcycle can travel to France by ferry; for more information on ferries, see under Sea later in this chapter.

It can also arrive through the Channel Tunnel. Specially designed trains operated by Eurotunnel (☎ 0870 535 3535, [e] call centre@eurotunnel.com, [w] www.eurotunnel .com) serve as a kind of round-the-clock vehicle conveyor belt, departing up to four times hourly during the day and hourly at night. Customs and Immigration formalities take place before you drive onto the train. The trip between Calais and Folkestone takes 35 minutes.

A one-way/return fare for a small car plus passengers ranges from about £150/170 (winter) to £180/300 (mid-July to early September). Tickets are sold on an as-available basis at check-in, but are best bought at least a day in advance – and many promotional deals are only available in advance. The return fare for a bicycle plus its rider is £15.

SEA

No direct international ferries serve Southwest France, but there are many options linking the UK and Ireland to northern France, from where you can drive south, and some from the UK to northern Spain, not far from Bayonne and the French Basque country.

The boxed text has details of the main ferry companies. Each has a welter of fares depending on season, time of day and the size of your vehicle. Some winter tickets cost less than half as much as in the high season. The cost for a car may include extra passengers at no additional cost, so if you can hitch a ride it will cost you and the driver nothing extra. On longer crossings there are options for cabin accommodation. Rail passes aren't valid for most ferry travel, but some discounts are available for students and young people.

Following are some sample costs – standard high-season return fares for a single foot passenger and for one car plus driver – plus crossing times and frequencies. Wide

---

Ferries from the UK & Ireland

Following are contact details for ferry companies with services to France and Spain.

Brittany Ferries
 UK ☎ 0870 556 1600
 Ireland ☎ 021-4277 801
 [w] www.brittany-ferries.com
Condor Ferries
 UK ☎ 0845 345 2000
 [w] www.condorferries.co.uk
Hoverspeed
 UK ☎ 0870 240 8070
 [w] www.hoverspeed.co.uk
Irish Ferries
 Ireland ☎ 189 0313 131
 [w] www.irishferries.ie
 UK ☎ 0870 517 1717
 [w] www.irishferries.co.uk
P&O Portsmouth
 UK ☎ 0870 242 4999
 [w] www.poportsmouth.com
P&O Stena Line
 UK ☎ 0870 600 0600
 [w] www.posl.com
SeaFrance
 UK ☎ 0870 571 1711
 [w] www.seafrance.co.uk

A Web site offering good deals on ferry fares is [w] www.ferrysavers.co.uk.

---

variations reflect the absurdly volatile nature of pricing structures. With advance planning, flexibility on dates and some comparison shopping, you can beat these prices with special offers at all but the busiest times.

UK to Far Northern France

For drivers, the big drawback of these crossings is the lack of a straightforward route around Paris. Take the A16 and A28 to Rouen, and the N154 via Evreux and Chartres to the E5/A10 past Orléans.

Dover-Calais (P&O Stena)
 ferry £26/195; 1¼ hours; every hour or less
Dover-Calais (SeaFrance)
 ferry £34/375; 1½ hours; every one to two hours
Dover-Calais (Hoverspeed)
 SeaCat £24/245; 40 minutes; four to seven daily

UK to Normandy

By car from Dieppe, make your way to Rouen and see the suggestions in the previous UK to Far Northern France section. From Le Havre, Ouistreham or Cherbourg the most direct route southwards is from Caen on the N158 and N138 via Le Mans to Tours.

Newhaven-Dieppe (Hoverspeed)
  SeaCat £28/265; two hours; two to three daily late April to early September
Poole-Cherbourg (Brittany Ferries)
  ferry £56/190; 4¼ hours; one to three daily (plus one daily fast ferry between June and September; 2¼ hours)
Portsmouth-Cherbourg (P&O Portsmouth)
  ferry £46/242; five to 12 hours; six daily (Portsmouth Express fast ferry £50/258; 2¾ hours; two daily)
Portsmouth-Le Havre (P&O Portsmouth)
  ferry £70/196; five hours (eight hours overnight); three daily
Portsmouth-Ouistreham (Caen; Brittany Ferries)
  ferry £45/190; six hours; two to three daily

UK to Brittany

By car, drive to Rennes (on the N137 from St-Malo or the E50/N12 from Roscoff), and from there on the A83 to the A10 at Niort.

Portsmouth-St Malo (Brittany Ferries)
  ferry £48/216; nine hours; one or two daily
Poole-St Malo (via Guernsey and Jersey; Condor Ferries)
  catamaran £47/209; 4½ to 5½ hours; one daily
Plymouth-Roscoff (Brittany Ferries)
  ferry £46/200; six hours; one to three daily (one weekly from mid-November to March)

UK to Spain

The fastest route by car from Santander and Bilbao to Bayonne is via autoroutes E70/A8 and E5/A63.

Portsmouth-Bilbao (P&O Portsmouth)
  ferry £250/555 (including obligatory cabin); 29–35 hours; twice weekly
Plymouth-Santander (Brittany Ferries)
  ferry £112/436 including reclining seats; 24 hours; twice weekly (from mid-November to mid-March these sail from Poole or Portsmouth, about 31 hours)

Ireland to France

Cork-Roscoff (Brittany Ferries)
  ferry €98/344; 14 hours; one weekly, April to early October
Rosslare-Roscoff (Irish Ferries)
  ferry €177/563; 15 hours; every other day, summer only
Rosslare-Cherbourg (Irish Ferries)
  ferry €177/563; 17 hours; every other day April to August, two or three times weekly the rest of the year

RIVER & CANAL

The best-known inland water route into Southwest France is the beautiful Canal du Midi, running north-west to Toulouse from the Bassin de Thau (Thau Basin) on the Mediterranean coast. At Toulouse this meets the Canal Latéral à la Garonne, which parallels the River Garonne to within about 50km of Bordeaux. This canal system, plus the lower Garonne and the Gironde Estuary, comprises a 360km navigable waterway all the way from the Mediterranean to the Atlantic. Linked directly to it are navigable stretches of the Garonne, Dordogne, Lot, Baïse and Tarn Rivers.

See under Boat in the Getting Around chapter for details of self-navigated holidays on the water, and the boxed text 'Les Canaux des Deux Mers' in that chapter for background information on the canals.

ORGANISED TOURS

Following are details of some reliable tour operators offering special-interest or made-to-order tours to Southwest France. For organised activity programs, see Activities in the Facts for the Visitor chapter.

A good listing of the UK's most interesting specialist tour operators is the free *AITO Directory of Real Holidays,* an annual index of member companies of the Association of Independent Tour Operators. It's available from AITO (☎ 0870 751 8080, W www.aito .co.uk).

Cycling Tours

Cycling is perhaps the finest way to explore Southwest France and there are lots of outfits offering appealing ways to do it.

The UK's biggest cycling organisation is

the Cyclists' Touring Club (CTC; ☎ 01483-417217, fax 426994, e cycling@ctc.org.uk). Among good-value, not-for-profit tours run by and for CTC members there are usually several each year to Southwest France. These, and scores of commercial bicycle holiday outfits, are listed in the December issue of CTC's *Cycle Holiday Guide* magazine. See Cycling Organisations under Bicycle in the Getting Around chapter for more about the CTC.

Three good UK companies offering trips (some self-led) in the upper Dordogne Valley are ATG Oxford (☎ 01865-315678, fax 315697, W www.atg-oxford.co.uk), Exodus (☎ 020-8675 5550, fax 8673 0779, W www.exodus.co.uk) and Sherpa Expeditions (☎ 020-8577 2717, fax 8572 9788, W www.sherpaexpeditions.com). Bike Tours (☎ 01225-310859, fax 480132, W www.biketours.co.uk) has a challenging Bordeaux to Barcelona (mostly camping) trip via the Gers. The Chain Gang (☎ 020-7323 1730, fax 7323 1731, W www.thechaingang.co.uk) offers a more indulgent guided week's meander through the Bordelais vineyards, plus a Dordogne circular trip from Les Eyzies.

True to its name, Susi Madron's Cycling for Softies (☎ 0161-248 8282, fax 248 5140, W www.cycling-for-softies.co.uk) runs no-worries trips in the Dordogne and Garonne. Another operator with a wide selection of trips to the Dordogne and Lot is Headwater Holidays (☎ 01606-813333, fax 813334, W www.headwater-holidays.co.uk).

US-based Blue Marble Travel (☎ 973-326 9533, fax 326 8939, W www.bluemarble.org) runs one- to four-week trips in the Bordeaux area and Dordogne, and in the Basque country. Canada-based Butterfield & Robinson (toll-free ☎ 1 800 678 1147, fax 416-864 0541, W www.butterfield.com) offers upmarket tours (Biarritz-Bordeaux, Bordeaux-Souillac, Dordogne & Lot Valleys) featuring luxury accommodation and restaurants. Backroads (☎ 510-527 1555, fax 510-527 1444, W www.backroads.com) runs week-long walking and biking trips in the Dordogne and biking and multisports trips in the Bordeaux area.

See under Activities in the Facts for the Visitor chapter, and under Bicycle in the Getting Around chapter, for more on cycling in Southwest France.

Walking Tours

The UK has many walking specialists with good small-group packages. Pyrenees Adventures (☎/fax 01433-621498, W www.pyreneesadventures.com) runs escorted tours in the hilly Basque country from its base near St-Jean Pied de Port. A gentle rural itinerary in the Lot is offered by Walking Safari Company (☎ 01572-821330, fax 821072, W www.walkeurope.com). For a week-long guided boating, cycling, walking and camping trip to the Rocamadour area east of Souillac, contact Explore Worldwide (☎ 01252-760 000, fax 760 001, W www.exploreworldwide.com).

Many operators organising cycling tours (see the preceding Cycling Tours section) also run walking tours to the same or nearby regions, notably Sherpa Expeditions, ATG Oxford, Headwater Holidays and Backroads. Ramblers Holidays (☎ 01707-331 133, fax 333276, W www.ramblersholidays.co.uk) organises easy one- or two-week walks in the valleys of the Lot (based at Puy l'Évèque) and Dordogne (based at Souillac). World Walks (☎ 01242-254353, fax 518888, W www.worldwalks.com) has self-led or self-led one-week trips from Figeac to Sarlat; and Inntravel (☎ 01653-629004, fax 628741, W www.inntravel.co.uk) offers flexible trips to the Basque, upper Dordogne and Albi areas.

Other Specialist Tours

For sampling wines in the Bordeaux region, contact UK-based Winetrails (☎ 01306-712111, fax 713504, W www.winetrails.co.uk) about escorted walking/cycling trips or tailor-made self-drive tours; or Arblaster & Clarke Wine Tours (☎ 01730-893344, fax 892888, W www.winetours.co.uk), which offers vineyard walks or coach tours. Walkers' France (☎ 020-7831 3125, fax 7831 3180, W www.walkersfrance.com) has wine-tasting trips at grape-harvest time from St-Émilion to the Médoc, while The Chain

Gang (see Cycling Tours) offers special Bordelais trips accompanied by a wine tutor.

Martin Randall Travel (☎ 020-8742 3355, fax 8742 7766, W www.martinrandall.com) arranges high-quality, four- to 14-day art and architecture tours in the Toulouse and Albi region.

Fancy trotting around the region on horseback? Contact Equitour (☎ 01865-511642, fax 512583, e eqtours@aol.com) for its programs in Périgord Noir, Quercy and the Médoc.

US-based International Kitchen (toll-free ☎ 1 800 945 8606, fax 312-803 1593, W www.theinternationalkitchen.com) runs a six-day, cycling-and-cooking tour of the Bordeaux area plus a week in Bordeaux wine country.

Family-Oriented Programs

Canvas Holidays (☎ 0870 902 2022, fax 01383-620075, W www.canvasholidays .com) and Eurocamp (☎ 01606-787878, W www.eurocamp.co.uk) offer kid-friendly camping holidays at deluxe camp sites all over Southwest France. Eurocamp affiliates can also help with sites and bookings for those with their own tents or caravans. A UK tour operator offering adventure packages aimed at families and children is Pyrenees Adventures (see under Walking Tours).

Self-Drive, Self-Catering & Short Breaks

Perhaps you would just like to chill out for a week or two in a rural farmhouse or a restored chateau. One of the first UK operators to arrange cottage holidays, VFB Holidays (☎ 01242-240340, fax 570340, W www .vfbholidays.co.uk) offers a huge choice of places plus travel services and escorted holidays. Other UK agencies specialising in quality villas as well as self-drive and guided trips are Chez Nous (☎ 0870 444 6600, fax 01282-445411, W www.cheznous.com), Inghams Just France (☎ 020-8780 4480, fax 8780 4405, W www.justfrance.co.uk), French Affair (☎ 020-7381 8519, fax 7381 5423, W www.frenchaffair.com) and The Magic of France (☎ 0990-462442, fax 020-8748 3731, W www.magictravelgroup.co .uk). Cresta (☎ 0870 161 0910, fax 0870 169 0792, W www.crestaholidays.co.uk) can arrange good chateau short breaks and flexible fly-drive deals. Select Site Reservations (☎ 01873-859876, fax 859444, W www .select-site.com) provides a comprehensive reservations service for campers and caravanners.

Several UK-France ferry operators have set up their own bargain-holiday agencies, including Brittany Ferries Holidays (☎ 0870 5360 360, W www.brittany-ferries.com) and SeaFrance's European Life (☎ 0870 242 4455, W www.seafrance.co.uk).

The France Holiday Store (W www.fr-holi daystore.co.uk) and Holiday France (W www .holidayfrance.org.uk) are one-stop online shops for holidays from the UK, with databases of tour operators, properties and also late deals.

Getting Around

This is not as easy as you might think, thanks to a national transport policy biased in favour of the state-owned rail system and to the compartmentalisation of bus transport by région (administrative region) and *département* (administrative department).

With the exception of a pricey Toulouse-Bordeaux service, there are no regular air links that run between the airports in Southwest France.

Domestic bus links between the Aquitaine and Midi-Pyrénées regions are scarce; from Toulouse, for example, it's easier to find a bus to Spain than to Bayonne. Bus routes within each region are department-centred, with inter-department services doled out to specific companies or associations. Eurolines and its privately owned long-haul competitors are limited to international routes.

The regional express train (TER) services of SNCF, the state-run railway company, are slower and less frequent than services on the main Paris-Bordeaux, Paris-Toulouse and Bordeaux-Toulouse lines, but the network runs just as efficiently. Trains are generally the way to go if you don't have the dosh for a car or the stamina for a bike.

Note that this chapter deals only with transport within Southwest France. For connections to other parts of France, see the Getting There & Away chapter.

AIR
The Portuguese airline Portugália (Bordeaux ☎ 05 56 34 58 40, Toulouse ☎ 05 34 60 55 44) flies three to four times weekly between Toulouse and Bordeaux (€102; 40 minutes). Taking airport transport into account, however, you could make the journey almost as quickly by TGV, for a quarter of the cost.

TRAIN
For details on SNCF services, tickets and discounts, see Train under Other Parts of France in the Getting There & Away chapter.

For those planning a lot of rail travel, SNCF publishes *Indicateur Horaires: Ville à Ville* (about €9), with point-to-point timetables for just about any major journey. The Aquitaine and Midi-Pyrénées regional governments each publish a free *Guide Régional des Transports,* with detailed SNCF bus and interregional rail schedules. They're available from larger tourist offices throughout the region.

Reservations are unnecessary on most regional trains, though if you plan to travel on

---

Little Trains

Several narrow-gauge trains ply short lines in Aquitaine in the warm months. A century-old locomotive pulls equally old carriages up to the Ecomusée de la Grande Lande (see under Parc Naturel Régional des Landes de Gascogne in the Bordeaux, the Atlantic Coast & the Landes chapter for more on timetables and fares).

From the vallée d'Ossau, a former dam-workers' train runs for 10km through the splendid mountains of Haut-Béarn (see under Le Petit Train d'Artouste in the Béarn chapter). A 4km-long cog-wheel railway ascends La Rhune mountain, south-east of St-Jean de Luz (see under Sare in the French Basque Country chapter).

JANE SMITH

Built to climb: a sturdy mountain railway

Rail Route Information

route	TGV time (hrs)	TGV fare (€)	non-TGV time (hrs)	non-TGV fare (€)
Bordeaux–Bayonne	1¾	22.55	2	21.05
Toulouse–Bayonne	n/a	n/a	3¾	30.50
Toulouse–Bordeaux	2¼	27.30	2½	25.75
Toulouse–Brive-la-Gaillarde	n/a	n/a	2½	22.25
Bordeaux–Brive-la-Gaillarde	n/a	n/a	2½	21.35

a main route like Toulouse-Bordeaux in the high season, it's wise to buy your ticket at least a few days in advance. Reservations can be made through travel agencies, by telephone (☎ 08 36 35 35 35 in French, ☎ 08 36 35 35 39 in English), online (at ⓦ www.sncf .com), at any SNCF ticketing office or at one of the automatic ticket vending machines in every station. Tickets are valid for two months from the date of purchase.

See the boxed text 'Rail Route Information' for some sample 2nd-class, one-way, full-price fares and journey times.

BUS

Buses are useful for short-distance travel within departments – especially in the Gers

and eastern Landes where there are no railway lines – and they're fairly frequent between main towns. Away from these towns, services can shrink to almost nothing, especially at the weekend and even more acutely when schools are on holiday (see the boxed text 'School Holidays'). Without a car you'll find it hard to visit more than one or two of those pretty perched villages in a day.

Autocars (regional buses) are operated by a muddle of different companies. One company may sell tickets for all the others operating from the same station. Many local tourist offices have surprisingly little information on bus services, except for those to the nearest market town. In small villages you may get the best information from the cafe or hotel nearest to the bus stop. You can always buy a ticket on the bus.

Over the years, SNCF has replaced certain unprofitable railway lines with its own bus services – and these are free if you happen to have a rail pass.

Every student of French learns that *une voiture* is a car, but did you know that *un car* is a long-distance bus? Another one to watch for – ask for *la gare* and you're directed to the train station, but say *la gare routière* and you'll end up at the bus station.

CAR & MOTORCYCLE

Unless you're cycling, a car or motorcycle is the key to discovering the many parts of Southwest France where public transport hardly ever goes. If you stay off the autoroutes, driving costs are lower than train fares (though of course this neglects added costs such as insurance, maintenance, and wear and tear). A car also gives you cheaper

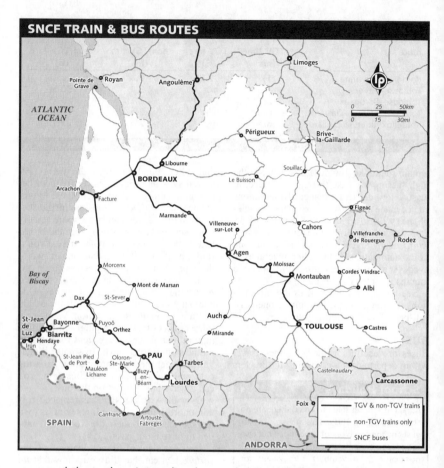

SNCF TRAIN & BUS ROUTES

accommodation options (camp sites, hostels and hotels on city outskirts) or at least more interesting ones (restored farmhouses and chateaux, for example). Renting a car for even a couple of days will change the way you see this region.

Drivers should refer to Other Parts of France/Car & Motorcycle in the Land section of the Getting There & Away chapter for information on getting to Southwest France from elsewhere in the country.

The fastest arteries across the region are the E72/A62 (the Autoroute des Deux Mers, alongside the Canal Latéral) between Bor-

deaux and Toulouse, and the E80/A64 between Bayonne and Toulouse. Plans are afoot to make the N89 into a major east-west route, from Bordeaux via Périgueux to Clermont-Ferrand. The E5-E70 (variously A10, N10 or A63) runs arrow-straight through the Landes from Bordeaux to Bayonne. When it's completed (don't hold your breath), the E9/A20 between Brive-la-Gaillarde and Toulouse will be another north-south axis; until then, drivers are shunted on and off the scenic but congested N20.

But you're here to see the place, not cross it. If you're not in a hurry, get off the autoroutes and even the lorry-choked N roads. Michelin and other road maps indicate many scenic routes (green shading), though of course everybody else has one of these maps too. Obscure, rambling D roads will show you more gentle landscapes and faraway places than we could possibly fit into this book.

Documents & Equipment

By French law, all drivers must carry a national ID card or passport; a valid *permis de conduire* (driving licence); car-ownership papers, known as *carte grise* (grey card); and proof of insurance, known as *carte verte* (green card). If you're stopped by the police and don't have one or more of these, you are liable for a €140 on-the-spot fine. Keep photocopies of all of them in a safe place. Never leave car-ownership or insurance papers in the vehicle.

A reflective warning triangle, to be used in the event of breakdown, must be carried in the car. Recommended accessories are a first-aid kit, a spare light-bulb kit and a fire extinguisher. A right-hand drive vehicle brought to France from the UK or Ireland must have deflectors fixed to the headlights to avoid dazzling oncoming traffic.

Road Rules

In France, as throughout Continental Europe, people drive on the right and overtake on the left. Note that, unless otherwise indicated, you must give way to cars coming from the right (see the boxed text *'Priorité*

Priorité à Droite

For overseas visitors, France's most confusing and dangerous traffic law is the 'priority to the right' rule, under which any car entering an intersection from a road on your right (including those entering main roads from smaller ones) has the right-of-way over you. French drivers tend to take full advantage of this, pulling boldly into intersections and onto main roads.

This is a recipe for pandemonium at roundabouts (traffic circles). Fortunately priorité à droite has been suspended at most roundabouts, so that cars already on the roundabout have right-of-way. This is indicated by signs on approach roads reading *vous n'avez pas la priorité* (you don't have the right-of-way) or *cédez le passage* (give way), or with a roundabout symbol (a circle of three curved arrows). But pay attention, because in a few places the old protocol still exists (eg, in the centre of Auch).

Priorité à droite is also suspended on major highways and other *routes à caractère prioritaire* (priority roads), marked by a yellow diamond with a black diamond in the middle. Such signs appear every few kilometres and at intersections. Priorité à droite is reinstated if you see the same sign with a diagonal bar through it.

à Droite'). North American drivers should also remember that turning right on a red light is illegal in France.

Unless otherwise signposted, there is a speed limit of 50km/h in all areas designated as built up, no matter how rural they may look. On intercity roads, you must slow to 50km/h the moment you pass a white sign with a red border bearing a place name in black or blue letters. This limit remains in force until you arrive at the other edge of town, where you'll pass an identical sign with a red diagonal bar across the name.

Outside built-up areas, speed limits are:

> 90km/h (80km/h if it's raining) on undivided N and D highways;

Bis

You will often see signs for autoroute exits marked 'Bis' on an orange panel. This indicates alternative routes that avoid areas prone to peak-period congestion. An annually updated, free map of Bis routes is published by the French government; contact your local motoring organisation or Maison de la France (see Tourist Offices in the Facts for the Visitor chapter) for a copy. Bis routes can also be viewed at Ⓦ www.bison-fute.equipement.gouv.fr.

110km/h (100km/h if it's raining) on dual
   carriageways (divided highways) or short
   sections of highway with a divider strip;
130km/h (110km/h in the rain, 60km/h in icy
   conditions) on autoroutes.

Speed limits are generally not posted unless
they deviate from these. If you keep to the
speed limit, count on having lots of cars ap-
proaching to within a few metres of your
rear bumper and overtaking at the first opportunity.

Oncoming drivers who flash their lights
at you are probably indicating that there are
gendarmes (police) ahead, and that you'd
better watch your speed. The police often
hang around in groups, watching for errant
drivers, and on-the-spot fines are common.
If you're clocked at 25km/h above the
speed limit your driving licence can be immediately confiscated.

Both the motorcycle riders and the passengers are required to wear crash helmets
in France.

Road Distances & Tolls The charts below
show the distances (in kilometres) for the
shortest/fastest routes between towns. The
fastest routes, which use motorways, can be
radically different from the shortest ones –
for example, the fastest Agen-Bayonne and
Auch-Périgueux routes are via Bordeaux!

Some routes include toll-roads (autoroutes; see Car & Motorcycle under Land in
the Getting There & Away chapter), and the
table also shows approximate car tolls; motorcycle tolls are about 40% less. Of course
if your budget's tight, you need never use a
toll-road at all.

For current tolls on major autoroute seg-
ments, visit W www.autoroutes.fr. A multilingual Web site with traffic reports and
forecasts is W www.bison-fute.equipement
.gouv.fr.

Road Signs On signs showing the way to
towns, parts of towns or highways, *toutes directions* (all directions) or *autres directions*

SHORTEST ROAD DISTANCES (KM) & TOLLS (€)

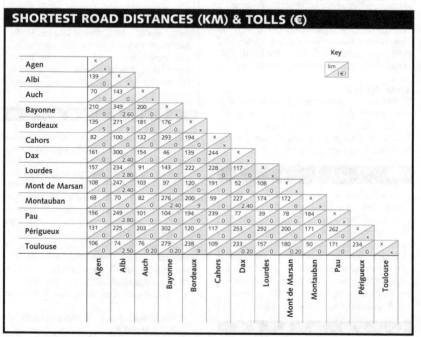

	Agen	Albi	Auch	Bayonne	Bordeaux	Cahors	Dax	Lourdes	Mont de Marsan	Montauban	Pau	Périgueux	Toulouse
Agen	x												
Albi	139 / 0	x											
Auch	70 / 0	143 / 0	x										
Bayonne	210 / 0	349 / 2.60	200 / 0	x									
Bordeaux	135 / 5	271 / 9	181 / 0	176 / 0	x								
Cahors	82 / 0	100 / 0	132 / 0	293 / 0	194 / 0	x							
Dax	161 / 0	300 / 2.40	154 / 0	46 / 0	139 / 0	244 / 0	x						
Lourdes	157 / 0	234 / 2.80	91 / 0	143 / 0	222 / 0	228 / 0	117 / 0	x					
Mont de Marsan	108 / 0	247 / 2.40	103 / 0	97 / 0	120 / 0	191 / 0	52 / 0	108 / 0	x				
Montauban	68 / 0	70 / 0	82 / 0	276 / 2.40	200 / 9	59 / 0	227 / 2.40	174 / 0	172 / 0	x			
Pau	156 / 0	249 / 2.80	101 / 0	104 / 0	194 / 0	239 / 0	77 / 0	39 / 0	78 / 0	184 / 0	x		
Périgueux	131 / 0	225 / 0	203 / 0	302 / 0	120 / 0	117 / 0	253 / 0	292 / 0	200 / 0	171 / 0	262 / 0	x	
Toulouse	106 / 0	74 / 2.50	76 / 0.20	279 / 0.20	238 / 9	109 / 0	233 / 0.20	157 / 0	180 / 0.20	50 / 0	171 / 0	234 / 0	x

Key

km
(€)

(other directions) indicates the route to anything not listed on the sign.

Sens unique means 'one way'. If you come to a *route barrée* (closed road), you'll usually also find a yellow panel with instructions for a *déviation* (detour). *Sauf riverains* on a no-entry sign means 'except residents'. *Verglas fréquent* means 'frequent road ice'. Road signs containing the word *rappel* (remember) mean you should already know what the sign is telling you (such as the speed limit).

Alcohol

French law is very tough on drunk drivers. To catch drivers whose blood-alcohol concentration is over 0.05%, the police sometimes conduct random breathalyser tests. Fines range from €75 to €1200, and licences can be suspended.

Petrol

At the time of writing, *essence* (petrol or gasoline), also called *carburant* (fuel), was a bit cheaper in France than in the UK, but a lot more expensive than in Australia or North America. In mid-2001, 95-octane *sans plomb* (unleaded) petrol cost around €1.10 per litre (US$3.75 per US gallon); for a medium-size car this works out to about €6 to €8 per 100km. *Gazole* (diesel fuel) was €0.85 per litre (US$2.90 per US gallon). Prices may fluctuate by as much as 20% depending on where you go; fuel is cheapest at petrol stations on city outskirts and those at supermarkets.

Petrol stations stay open 24 hours along motorways and other major roads. *Le plein, s'il vous plaît* means 'fill it up, please'.

Parking

Whether you're in a big city or a touristy village, parking may be your single biggest headache. In city centres, your best bet is to park the car and then walk or take public transport.

For street parking, the old *disque bleu*

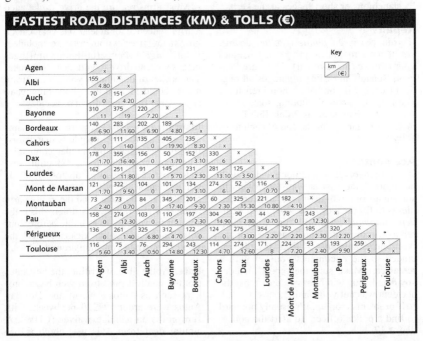

FASTEST ROAD DISTANCES (KM) & TOLLS (€)

Key: km (€)

	Agen	Albi	Auch	Bayonne	Bordeaux	Cahors	Dax	Lourdes	Mont de Marsan	Montauban	Pau	Périgueux	Toulouse
Agen	x												
Albi	155 (4.80)	x											
Auch	70 (0)	151 (4.20)	x										
Bayonne	310 (11)	375 (19)	220 (7.20)	x									
Bordeaux	140 (6.90)	283 (11.60)	202 (6.90)	189 (4.80)	x								
Cahors	85 (0)	111 (140)	135 (0)	405 (19.90)	235 (8.30)	x							
Dax	178 (1.70)	355 (16.40)	156 (0)	50 (1.70)	152 (3.10)	330 (6)	x						
Lourdes	162 (0)	251 (11.80)	91 (0)	145 (5.70)	231 (2.30)	281 (13.10)	125 (3.50)	x					
Mont de Marsan	121 (1.70)	322 (9.50)	104 (0)	101 (1.70)	134 (3.10)	274 (6)	52 (0)	116 (0)	x				
Montauban	73 (2.40)	73 (0.70)	84 (0)	345 (17.40)	201 (9.30)	60 (2.30)	325 (15.30)	221 (10.80)	182 (4.10)	x			
Pau	158 (0)	274 (12.30)	103 (0)	110 (5)	197 (2.30)	304 (14.90)	90 (2.80)	44 (0.70)	78 (0)	243 (12.30)	x		
Périgueux	136 (0)	261 (1.40)	325 (6.80)	312 (4.70)	122 (0)	124 (0)	275 (3.00)	252 (2.20)	185 (2.30)	354 (2.20)	320 (2.20)	x	
Toulouse	116 (5.60)	75 (3.40)	76 (0.50)	294 (14.80)	243 (12.30)	114 (4.70)	274 (12.60)	171 (8)	224 (7.20)	53 (2.40)	193 (9.90)	259 (5)	x

honour system is still in use in many towns: Where a time-limited space is outlined in blue, you set a small cardboard disk to your time of arrival and leave it on the dashboard. Should you come across such *zones bleu*, you can buy a disque bleu (which isn't necessarily blue) at any *tabac* (tobacconist). Increasingly, street parking is metered, as indicated by *payant* on a sign or painted on the road. You feed a meter or buy a ticket from the nearest *horodateur* (ticket machine) and leave that on the dashboard, at least at certain hours. Typical rates are €0.80 to €1.60 per hour.

Most big cities have public car parks (often underground), which are signposted with a white 'P' on a blue background. Many touristy hilltop villages keep cars out by requiring visitors to park in purpose-built car parks down below.

'No parking' is *defense de stationner*; 'parking this side only' is *côte de stationnement*. No-parking areas may be indicated by stanchions or short fences at the kerb.

Repairs

If your car is *en panne* (broken down), you'll have to find a garage that handles your *marque* (make of car). There are Peugeot, Renault and Citroën garages all over the place, but if you have a non-French car you may have trouble finding someone to service it in remote areas. Michelin's *Guide Rouge* lists garages at the end of each town entry.

Accidents

If you're involved in a minor accident with no injuries, the easiest way for drivers to sort things out with their insurance companies is to fill out a *Constat Aimable d'Accident Automobile* (jointly agreed accident report), known in English as a European Accident Statement. This is usually included in the documents you get with a rental car. Make sure the report includes any details that will help you prove that the accident was not your fault.

If problems crop up, it's usually not hard to find a police officer. To alert the police, dial ☎ 17.

Rental

Some of the best advance-booking rates available are offered by Internet-based brokers such as Autos Abroad (Hire for Lower; Ⓦ www.autosabroad.com) and Holiday Autos (Ⓦ www.holidayautos.com). Although multinational agencies such as Hertz, Avis, Budget and Europcar are absurdly expensive for on-the-spot rental, their prepaid promotional rates can be a fraction of walk-in rates. Fly-drive deals are also worth looking into. Book at least a few days ahead in summer.

For on-the-spot rental, domestic firms such as Rent-a-Car Système (Ⓦ www.rentacar.fr), Sixt (Ⓦ www.e-sixt.com) and Century (Ⓦ www.century-location.fr), and some youth travel agencies, have the best rates. The largest French car-hire company is ADA (☎ 08 36 68 40 02, Ⓦ www.ada.fr), with offices in many bigger towns. Companies are noted in the Getting There & Away sections for individual cities; major firms also have desks at Bordeaux and Toulouse airports.

Most firms require the driver to be aged over 21 (in some cases 23) and to have had a driving licence for at least one year. Check how many 'free' kilometres are included; *kilométrage illimité* (unlimited mileage) means you can drive to your heart's content. The packet of documents you get on hiring a car should include a 24-hour number to call in case of a breakdown or accident.

Insurance *Assurance* (insurance) for damage or injury to other people is mandatory, but policies offered by smaller companies may leave you liable for a deductible (excess) cost *(franchise)* of up to €1200. If you're in an accident where you're at fault, or if the car is damaged and the guilty party is unknown, or if the car is stolen, this is the amount for which you're liable before your collision-damage policy kicks in. Check the small print when you shop around.

Rates At the time of writing, the best rates (for the smallest cars) from Web-based brokers such as Autos Abroad and Holiday Autos were around €220 per week, with zero collision-damage waiver (CDW). A similar deal from Avis was about €265.

A Bordelais busker does his thing.

The River Garonne, Bordeaux

Start 'em young, Bordeaux

The Ponte de Pierre, elegantly spanning the Garonne River, Bordeaux

JULIA WILKINSON

All-weather traditional fishing near the confluence of the Rivers Garonne and Dordogne

GARETH McCORMACK

A couple of swells in world-class surfing territory, Hossegor

SALLY DILLON

Prime oystering grounds in the Bassin d'Arcachon

ADA was asking €230 per week, with an excess of about €300.

All the major rental companies accept payment by credit card. All insist on a *caution* (deposit); for this, some ask you to leave a signed credit card slip without a sum written in. If this makes you uncomfortable, ask them to make out separate slips for the rental and for the deposit, and see that the latter is destroyed when you return the car.

Motorcycle

Southwest France is gorgeous for motorcycle touring, with good roads and stunning scenery. Be sure your wet-weather gear is up to scratch in spring and autumn. Riders and passengers must wear helmets; those caught bareheaded can be fined and have their bikes confiscated. Bikes of over 125cc must have headlights on during the day. No special licence is required to ride a motorcycle of less than 50cc.

To rent a *scooter* or *moto* (motorcycle) you must leave a deposit of several hundred euros, which you forfeit – up to the value of the damage – if you're in an accident and it's your fault. Since insurance companies won't cover theft, you'll also lose the deposit if the bike is stolen. Most places accept deposits made by credit card or travellers cheque.

BICYCLE

If you've got the stamina, you couldn't ask for a better way to see Southwest France up close than by bicycle. The network of old inland D roads with relatively light traffic are the ideal vantage point for viewing its rural landscapes (one pitfall: they rarely have proper shoulders). Périgord in particular attracts legions of pedal-pushers. Probably because so many French people ride bikes themselves, you're also more likely to be treated with warmth (and admiration) if you roll up on a bicycle.

Beside the Canal du Midi and Canal Latéral runs one of Europe's longest unbroken bicycle paths – flat, cool, sheltered, unasphalted and scenic. For more on cycling beside the Canal du Midi, pick up Tony Roberts' *Cycling along the Waterways of France* (Bicycle Books).

By law your bicycle must have two functioning brakes, a bell, a red reflector on the back and yellow reflectors on the pedals. After sunset, and when visibility is poor, you must turn on a white light in front and a red one at the rear. When being overtaken by a car or truck, cyclists are required to ride in single file.

Never leave your bike locked up outside overnight if you want to see it again. You can leave bikes in train station left-luggage offices for around €5 a day.

Cycling Organisations

For its members, the Cyclists' Touring Club in the UK (CTC; ☎ 01483-417217, fax 426994, **e** cycling@ctc.org.uk, **w** www .ctc.org.uk) publishes a useful, free booklet on cycling in France, plus touring notes for some 70 routes around the country, including in the Dordogne and Vézère Valleys, the Bordeaux area, Gironde, the Landes, the Gers, Tarn gorges, Canal du Midi, the Pyrénées and the French Basque country. The CTC also offers tips on bikes, spares, insurance and other general information, and sells maps, topoguides and other publications by mail order.

European Bike Express (☎ 01642-251440, fax 232209, **w** www.bike-express .co.uk) facilitates independent cycling holidays by transporting cyclists and their bikes by bus and trailer from the UK to places all over France.

See Activities in the Facts for the Visitor chapter for more cycling information. Organised Tours in the Getting There & Away chapter contains information on bicycle tours.

Transporting a Bicycle

Bicycles can rarely be taken on local buses, but some intercity lines (eg, Cars Ouest Aquitaine and Citram Aquitaine) allow them for around €3 to €5.

You can take your bike aboard some trains at no extra charge. Services where this is permitted are indicated in timetables by a little bicycle symbol on the bottom row of the timetable. If you plan on doing a lot of train travel with your bike, pick up SNCF's free brochure, *Train + Vélo*, with everything you need to know, including all services that accept bikes.

You can also send a boxed bicycle as checked baggage between any two stations with a Sernam baggage agency for €30.20, or door to door for €45. It normally takes one day. Arrange it when you buy your ticket, or at a Sernam office, or book it with SNCF on ☎ 08 03 84 58 45 at least a day in advance. Stations in Southwest France with Sernam agencies are Agen, Bayonne, Bordeaux, Brive-la-Gaillarde, Pau, Périgueux and Toulouse.

To take your bike with you on an aircraft, you can either take it apart and pack it in a bike box, or wheel it to the check-in desk, where it will be treated as baggage. Check all this (and weight limits) with the airline well in advance.

See The UK, under Sea in the Getting There & Away chapter, for information about taking a bicycle on cross-channel ferries.

Rental

Most sizable towns and many resorts have at least one shop that hires out *vélos tout-terrains* (VTTs; mountain bikes) for €10 to €16 per day or €40 to €80 per week; some also have cheaper *vélos* (touring bikes). Most require a deposit of up to €300, which you forfeit if the bike is damaged or stolen. Deposits can usually be made in cash, with travellers cheques or by credit card (though a passport may suffice). Rental outlets are listed in the Getting Around sections of city and town listings.

HITCHING

Auto-stop (hitching) is never entirely safe in any country, and travellers who hitch should understand that they are taking a small but potentially serious risk. On the other hand, if you speak some French, thumbing affords opportunities to meet local people from all walks of life and pick up the occasional tip on what to see. So we offer the following advice.

The best (and safest) combination is a man and a woman. A woman hitching on her own faces a definite risk; two women hitching together are somewhat safer. Two men together may have a harder time getting picked up than a man travelling alone. *Never* get into a car with someone about whom you are the least bit uneasy. Always keep your belongings with you on the seat.

To maximise your chances of being picked up, stand where it's easy for drivers to stop, look cheerful, presentable and non-threatening, and make eye contact with drivers. It also helps to hold up a sign with your destination followed by the letters *s.v.p.* (*s'il vous plaît*, meaning 'please').

Paris-based Allostop (☎ 01 53 20 42 42 within Paris, ☎ 01 53 20 42 43 from outside Paris, ⓔ allostop@ecritel.fr, ⓦ www.ecritel .fr/allostop) puts people seeking rides in touch with drivers. Each passenger pays a per-kilometre fee to the driver, in addition to a subscription fee to Allostop that depends on the length of the journey. Allostop has branches in Bordeaux (☎ 05 57 95 91 11) and Toulouse (☎ 05 61 21 20 20). Toulouse's Centre Régional d'Information Jeunesse (CRIJ; see under Toulouse in the Toulouse, Tarn-et-Garonne & Tarn chapter) has a similar service, called J-Stop, costing €6.85 to advertise plus €2.45 per 100km.

Drivers and hitchhikers also advertise for one another under *Trajets* (Journeys) in the regional *Sud-Ouest* newspaper.

BOAT

A unique and relaxing way to see Southwest France is to rent a houseboat or cabin-cruiser and tootle along the region's many canals and rivers. You can tie up at a marina, a village or in the middle of nowhere, unload your bicycle and go exploring or shopping, and at the end of the day your boat is your hotel. Anyone aged over 18 can pilot a river boat without a licence. Learning the ropes and the rules of the river takes about half an hour.

With the completion – in 2007 by unofficial estimate – of locks and canals between Fumel and Luzech on the River Lot, a continuously navigable 350km network of canals and rivers will snake through the Gers, Lot, Lot-et-Garonne and Tarn-et-Garonne departments. These waterways include the Canal du Midi, the Canal Latéral à la Garonne

Les Canaux des Deux Mers

The Romans were the first to study the idea of a canal across southern France between the Mediterranean and the Atlantic, a low-anxiety alternative to the 5000km sea journey via the Straits of Gibraltar. The stumbling block was always the Seuil de Naurouze (Naurouze Sill) watershed, a 190m-high ridge along the boundary between today's Midi-Pyrénées and Languedoc-Rousillon regions: how to get a canal over it, and how to keep it filled with water?

The solution, suggested by a Languedoc tax collector and amateur scientist named Pierre-Paul Riquet (1604–80), was to collect water from the streams of the Montagne Noire, store it on the Seuil de Naurouze and spill it down both sides of the watershed. Riquet backed up his idea with calculations of feasibility and economic potential (eg, for the transport of grain from Toulouse to the markets of the Languedoc).

In 1666 Louis XIV gave official blessing to what would be the century's biggest-ever engineering project, 14 years in the building and stretching 241km from the Bassin de Thau to Toulouse. Riquet, who was granted hereditary control over the canal and sank his life savings into its construction, died exhausted and penniless with just 4km left to build. His two sons carried on, and the canal was inaugurated in May 1681.

The canal got off to a roaring start. Cargo and passenger traffic shot up in the following decades. Riquet's descendants did well from the canal's tolls and in return maintained a smoothly functioning system.

In 1776 the Brienne Canal bypassed the shallows at Toulouse, linking the Canal du Midi directly with the River Garonne. Even so, all goods going beyond Toulouse had to be shifted to river boats, and navigation down the Garonne was at the mercy of low summer flows and often-violent flooding.

The Marquis de Vauban, the king's commissioner for fortifications, was brought in to tackle residual design problems. He realised that the sea-to-sea crossing needed something better than the fickle Garonne, and urged the construction of a canal *latéral à la Garonne* (parallel to the Garonne), allowing canal boats to make the entire journey. Less inspired but equally amazing, the Canal Latéral was inaugurated in 1856 and linked to the Canal du Midi at Toulouse's Port de l'Embouchure, completing Riquet's dream.

With the arrival of the railway, however, canal traffic began to decline. Despite a state buy-out in 1898 and the abolition of tolls, the slide continued. Today, cargo traffic has vanished: the Canal du Midi's locks cannot accommodate boats longer than about 30m. Passenger traffic, on the other hand, has recovered with the advent of canal-boat tourism (see the main text), and the cool, tree-shaded canals are fine, hill-free venues for walking and cycling.

This is Europe's oldest functioning system of canals, strewn with little brick bridges, handsome aqueducts and cascades of locks to hoist the boats up and down the flanks of the Montagne Noire. It's an achievement of extraordinary harmony, imagination and breadth, and in 1996 the two canals were together designated a Unesco World Heritage Site.

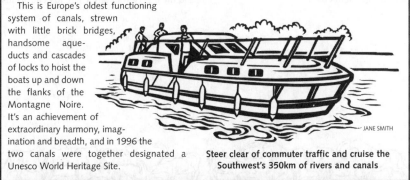

JANE SMITH

Steer clear of commuter traffic and cruise the Southwest's 350km of rivers and canals

(Castets-en-Dorthe to Toulouse), the Baïse (below Valence-sur-Baïse), the Lot (below St-Cirq-Lapopie) and the Tarn (below Montauban). Other major rivers with navigable stretches include the Garonne, Dordogne and Adour, and the Gironde Estuary.

The tourist cruising season lasts from Easter to November, but to get a boat in July and August you must reserve months ahead. Boats typically accommodate two to 12 passengers and are hired out on a weekly basis, though there are some short breaks on offer. Prices for a two-person boat in the low/high season start at around €690/1070 per week, with a security deposit of €500 to €900.

France's biggest river-tourism agency is Crown Blue Line (W www.crown-blueline .com), with offices for Aquitaine (☎ 05 53 89 50 80, fax 05 53 89 51 13) in Le Mas d'Agenais and for the Canal du Midi (☎ 04 68 94 52 72, fax 04 68 94 52 73) in Castelnaudary. Two other big houseboat-rental firms are Locaboat Plaisance (☎ 03 86 91 72 72, fax 03 86 62 42 41, e info@locaboat .com, W www.locaboat.com) and Aquitaine Navigation (☎ 05 53 84 72 50, fax 05 53 84 03 33, e aquinav@aquitaine-navigation .com, W www.aquitaine-navigation.com).

Many more local outfits hire boats by the hour, day or evening, and others offer short guided cruises – for examples, see under Cahors, Agen, Nérac and Bouziès in the Lot & Lot-et-Garonne chapter and under Condom in the Gers chapter.

Crown Blue also has an office in the UK (☎ 01603-630513, fax 664298, e boating@ crownblueline.co.uk). Locaboat Plaisance's UK agent is Andrew Brock Travel (☎ 01572-821330, fax 821072, e abrock3650@ aol.com).

LOCAL TRANSPORT

Getting around towns in Southwest France is straightforward, thanks to good public-transport systems. Toulouse is the only city with a metro. Details of routes, fares and tourist passes are available at tourist offices and local bus-company information counters; see the Getting Around sections for individual cities and towns.

Taxis tend to be expensive. Most towns have a taxi rank in front of the train station. Typical fares are about €1.70 flag fall plus €1.10 per kilometre for daytime travel and €1.50 per kilometre at night, on Sunday and public holidays (including the price of a return trip if you go somewhere where a return passenger is not assured). Sitting still or creeping along in traffic at less than about 20km/h is calculated by time (€20 per hour). There may be a €1.50 surcharge to get picked up at a train station or airport, and a fee of around €0.80 per item of luggage.

Some towns have pedestrian-only shopping zones, though more commonly they're *semi-piéton* (semi-pedestrian), meaning that cars can drive through slowly, cannot park and must give way anywhere to pedestrians.

Bordeaux, the Atlantic Coast & the Landes

Bordeaux, capital of the Aquitaine region, is the southwest's second-largest city after Toulouse, and the centre of a world-renowned wine-growing area. With an international airport and excellent transport links it's a natural jumping-off point for the region. But don't hurry away: Bordeaux itself has much to offer, as does the immediate area including the Médoc wine district and the 230km of Atlantic coastline – the so-called Côte d'Argent (Silver Coast) – which has some of Europe's greatest surfing spots. Inland are a million hectares of pine plantations, threaded with bike trails and dotted with lakes. Lazy, hedonistic options include taking time to relax in one of the southern Landes' many thermal spas, or else getting soaked in a tub of grape seeds (see the boxed text 'Get Soaked' later in this chapter).

Two *départements* (administrative departments) cover this area: Gironde (France's largest department) and the Landes. Their respective Comités Départemental du Tourisme (departmental tourism offices) are in Bordeaux and Mont de Marsan (see under those towns for contact details).

Bordeaux

postcode 33000 • pop 735,000 (city centre 215,000)
Bordeaux is known for its neoclassical architecture and wide avenues that give the city a certain 18th-century grandeur. It's traditionally been considered rather dowdy and reserved, but excellent museums and restaurants, ethnic diversity (including sizable Spanish, Portuguese and North African communities) and a lively university population actually make it a great place to hang out for a few days. In fact, the city is bubbling now as never before, thanks to extensive gentrifi-

---

Highlights

- Tour the Médoc and sample the finest wines in the world without going broke
- Feast on Bordeaux's excellent museums, lively nightlife and superb seafood
- Get sand in your shoes on the highest dune in Europe
- Follow the champions to Europe's best surfing beaches
- Marvel at some of France's finest modern sculpture in Mont de Marsan

Food Highlights

entrecôte a la Bordelaise – grilled steak in a thick wine sauce

canelé pastries from Bordeaux – small, soft-centred custard cakes

macaroons of St-Émilion – soft biscuits of egg white, almond powder and sugar

---

cation of the city centre and the long-awaited rehabilitation of the quays.

HISTORY

Inhabited from the 4th century BC, Bordeaux (then called Burdigala) was seized in 56 BC by the Romans, who made this

BORDEAUX

BORDEAUX, THE ATLANTIC COAST & THE LANDES

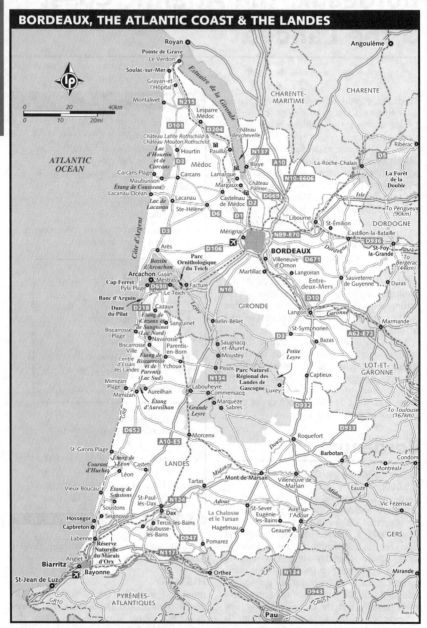

flourishing port the capital of Aquitainia. Pillaged by the Vikings in AD 848, it revived under a dynasty of dukes all named Guillaume, the most famous being Guillaume IX (1071–1127), early troubadour and grandfather of Eleanor of Aquitaine.

With Eleanor's 1152 marriage to Henry Plantagenet, Bordeaux became English 'territory' and remained so for 301 years. The city did well under the English, who grew so fond of the region's red wine (which they called claret) that they granted tax breaks and other privileges to the local wine-growers. It's no wonder the Bordelais resisted when the French retook the city in 1453. Commerce slumped with the loss of the English wine trade.

From 1648 to 1653 the city joined in the series of urban revolts known as Les Frondes, with Bordeaux's the last to be quelled. By the 18th century the city had found new wealth from the trade in slaves and sugar, and the centre was rebuilt by several enthusiastic royal governors, notably Claude Boucher and the Marquis de Tourny.

Bordeaux took a triple blow in the 19th century with the end of the slave trade in 1815, a slump in the sugar trade and the 1878 destruction of its vines by phylloxera. Shame and occupation arrived with WWII: Bordeaux was the scene of the 1940 armistice with Hitler.

The city served briefly as the capital of France on three occasions when the country was on the verge of defeat: during the Franco-Prussian War of 1870–71; at the beginning of WWI (1914); and for two weeks in 1940, just before the Vichy government was proclaimed.

In the last decade, thanks to a vigorous aeronautical industry and wine trade (the city's top economic activity is the marketing and export of fine wines), Bordeaux has started to revive. In 1995 ex-prime minister Alain Juppé took over as mayor from the ageing Jacques Chaban-Delmas, who had 'reigned' for 48 years. Juppé, who was re-elected in 2001, has injected new life into the city with a flurry of urban projects, notably 'Les Deux Rives' (one of only two EU-funded Urban Pilot Projects in France), aimed at transforming the landscape and amenities on both sides of the River Garonne.

ORIENTATION

The city centre lies between place Gambetta and the wide River Garonne. The train station, Gare St-Jean, is in a seedy area 3km south-east of the centre. The main shopping district is the 1.1km-long pedestrianised rue Ste-Catherine.

INFORMATION
Tourist Offices

The Bordeaux tourist office (☎ 05 56 00 66 00, fax 05 56 00 66 01, e otb@bordeaux -tourisme.com, w www.bordeaux-city.com), 12 cours du 30 Juillet, is open 9am to 7pm from Monday to Saturday, May to November (9.30am to 6.30pm on Sunday and bank holidays and 9am to 7.30pm daily during July and August); during the rest of the year it opens 9am to 6.30pm from Monday to Saturday (9.45am to 4.30pm on Sunday and bank holidays). Useful free publications available in this office are the bimonthly *Bordeaux Tourisme* magazine listing tours and current events; the excellent *Plan Guide du Patrimoine* with detailed historical descriptions and suggested walking routes, and the clubber's guide, *Clubs et Concerts*.

A branch tourist office at Gare St-Jean (☎/fax 05 56 91 64 70) is open 9am to noon and 1pm to 6pm daily from May to November (10am to noon and 1pm to 3pm on Sunday and bank holidays) and 9.30am to 12.30pm and 2pm to 6pm on weekdays only the rest of the year. There is no tourist office at the airport, but two information desks (☎ 05 56 34 50 50), open 5.30am to 11.30pm daily, can provide maps and assistance.

Offices covering a wider area include La Maison du Tourisme de la Gironde (☎ 05 56 52 61 40, fax 05 56 81 09 99, e tourisme@ gironde.com, w www.tourisme-gironde.cg33 .fr), 21 cours de l'Intendance, open Monday to Saturday (with several good walking and cycling booklets for sale); and La Maison des Pyrénées (☎ 05 56 44 05 65, fax 05 56 52 37 29), 6 rue Vital Carles, open weekdays only.

Useful weekly or bimonthly what's-on booklets that can be bought at newsagents include *Bordeaux Plus, Bordeaux Poche* and *L'Essentiel* (which also covers the Gironde). The English-language free quarterly, *Spirit of Bordeaux,* listing events, shops and restaurants, is often available at hotels.

La Maison du Vin de Bordeaux

For maps and information on the wine regions, the chateaux and wine-tasting courses, visit La Maison du Vin de Bordeaux (☎ 05 56 00 22 66, fax 05 56 00 22 82, e civb@vins-bordeaux.fr, w www.vins -bordeaux.fr), 3 cours du 30 Juillet, the headquarters of the Conseil Interprofessionel du Vin de Bordeaux, representing all the region's winegrowers and shippers. It opens 10am to 5.15pm weekdays (and 9am to 4pm on Saturday between June and mid-October).

CIJA

The Centre d'Information Jeunesse d'Aquitaine (☎ 05 56 56 00 56, fax 05 56 56 00 53, e cija@cija.net, w www.info-jeune.com), 5 rue Duffour Dubergier and around the corner at 125 cours d'Alsace et Lorraine, is Bordeaux's youth information centre. The latter branch includes a youth travel agency and Internet facility; at the other branch are noticeboards for jobs, accommodation and items for sale. Both are open 9.30am to 6pm on weekdays (to 5pm Friday).

Gay & Lesbian Centre

La Maison de l'Homosocialité (☎/fax 05 56 01 12 03, e m.homo@netcourrier.com) at 30 rue Paul Bert, is open 7pm to 11pm on Tuesday, Thursday and Friday and holds debates and social activities from 8.30pm. Thursday is girls' night. A local helpline for gays is Ligne Arc en Ciel (☎ 05 56 79 74 49).

Money

There are numerous banks on cours de l'Intendance (eg, Crédit Lyonnais at No 11) and allées de Tourny (eg, BNP at No 10). AmEx (☎ 05 56 00 63 33, fax 05 56 00 63 39), 14 cours de l'Intendance, is open 9am to 5pm, weekdays only.

Post

The main post office is at 52 rue Georges Bonnac. Branch offices include one on place St-Projet and another at 29 Allées de Tourny.

Email & Internet Access Free Internet access is offered at CIJA (see earlier in this section) for one hour maximum, with prior reservation. You can also surf for free at Fnac (see under Shopping), which operates a first-come-first-served system at a stand-only booth at the entrance to the store, 24-hours daily.

Other cyber outfits include Esp@ce Internet (☎ 08 00 35 23 19), located at the corner of rue Judaïque and rue du Château d'Eau. This France Telecom-run venue charges €4.55 per hour (students €3.05) and is open noon to 7pm Monday to Friday.

Cyberstation (☎ 05 56 01 15 15, e info@ cyberstation.fr), 23 cours Pasteur, charges €3.80/6.10 per 30/60 minutes (€4.55 per hour noon to 2pm and 7pm to 9pm). It's open 11am to 2am Monday to Saturday (2pm to midnight on Sunday). There's another Cyberstation (☎ 05 57 14 29 92) at 8 rue de la Devise, which is open noon to midnight, Monday to Saturday (3pm to 9pm on Sunday). Charges are the same as at the other Cyberstation. La Cybersalle (☎ 05 56 48 00 14), 28 rue Huguerie, charges €4.55 per hour (€2.30 per hour for guests of the Hôtel Studio chain). It's open 9am to 10pm Wednesday to Sunday (8am to 10pm Monday to Tuesday).

L'Heroique Cybercafé (☎ 05 56 52 76 63), 47 rue St-James, charges €3.05 per hour and is open 11am to 2am Monday to Saturday (3pm to 2am on Sunday). Nexus 2000 (☎ 05 56 44 20 20), 31 rue Montbazon, charges €3.80 per hour and is open 10am to 10pm Tuesday, Friday & Saturday (2pm to 10pm on Monday, Wednesday and Thursday). Netzone (☎ 05 57 59 01 25), 209 rue Ste Catherine, asks for €3.80/4.55 per 30/60 minutes and is open 9am to 10pm daily.

Travel Agencies

Two good outfits selling cheap fares and ISIC cards are usit Connections (☎ 05 56 33 89 90, fax 05 56 33 89 91, e usitconnect@ usit.ie), 284 rue Ste-Catherine, and Wasteels

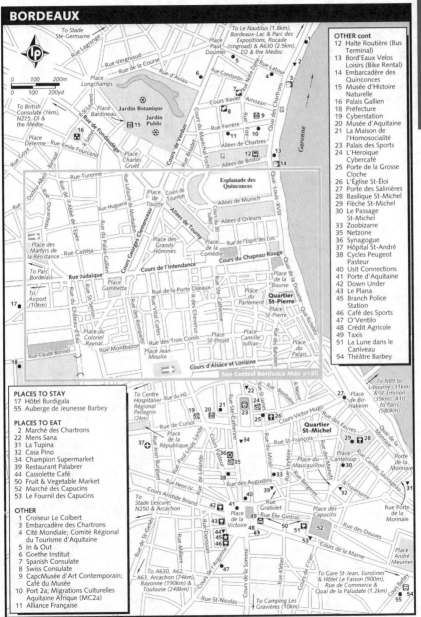

BORDEAUX

See Central Bordeaux Map p130

OTHER cont
12 Halte Routière (Bus Terminal)
13 Bord'Eaux Velos Loisiers (Bike Rental)
14 Embarcadère des Quinconces
15 Musée d'Histoire Naturelle
16 Palais Gallien
19 Préfecture
20 Musée d'Aquitaine
21 La Maison de l'Homosocialité
23 Palais des Sports
24 L'Heroique Cybercafé
25 Porte de la Grosse Cloche
26 L'Église St-Éloi
27 Porte des Salinières
28 Basilique St-Michel
29 Flèche St-Michel
30 Le Passage St-Michel
33 Zoobizarre
35 Netzone
36 Synagogue
37 Hôpital St-André
38 Cycles Peugeot Pasteur
40 Usit Connections
41 Porte d'Aquitaine
42 Down Under
43 Le Plana
45 Branch Police Station
46 Café des Sports
47 O'Ventilo
48 Crédit Agricole
49 Taxis
51 La Lune dans le Caniveau
54 Théâtre Barbey

PLACES TO STAY
17 Hôtel Burdigala
55 Auberge de Jeunesse Barbey

PLACES TO EAT
2 Marché des Chartrons
22 Mens Sana
31 La Tupina
32 Casa Pino
34 Champion Supermarket
39 Restaurant Palabrer
44 Cassolette Café
50 Fruit & Vegetable Market
52 Marché des Capucins
53 Le Fournil des Capucins

OTHER
1 Croiseur Le Colbert
3 Embarcadère des Chartrons
4 Cité Mondiale; Comité Régional du Tourisme d'Aquitaine
5 In & Out
6 Goethe Institut
7 Spanish Consulate
8 Swiss Consulate
9 CapcMusée d'Art Contemporain; Café du Musée
10 Port 2a; Migrations Culturelles Aquitaine Afrique (MC2a)
11 Alliance Française

BORDEAUX

CENTRAL BORDEAUX

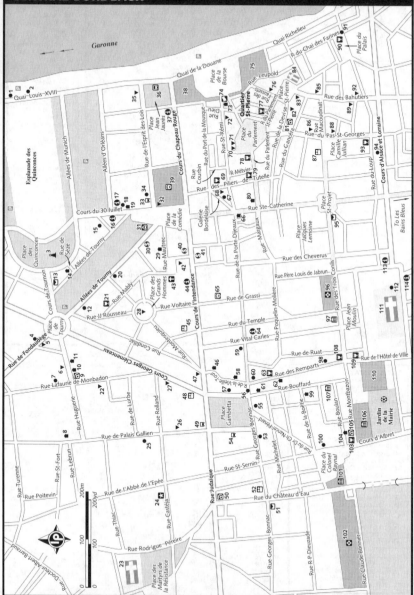

Garonne

Quai Louis-XVIII

Quai de la Douane

Place de la Bourse

Quai Richelieu

R. du Chai des Farines

Place du Palais

Quartier St-Pierre

Rue des Bahutiers

Esplanade des Quinconces

Place des Quinconces

Cours du 30 Juillet

Allées de Munich

Allées d'Orléans

Rue de l'Esprit des Lois

Cours du Chapeau Rouge

Place Jean Jaurès

Rue St-Rémi

Rue du Port de la Mousque

Rue Dieu

Place du Parlement

Rue du Parlement St-Pierre

Rue de la Devise

Rue du Cancéra

Rue Macoudinat

Rue du Pas-St-Georges

Place Camille Jullian

Rue du Loup

Cours d'Alsace et Lorraine

Place St-Projet

To Les Bains Bleus

Galerie Bordelaise

Rue Ste-Catherine

Place Jacques Lemoine

Rue des Piliers de Tutelle

Rue des Cheverus

Rue de la Porte Dijeaux

Rue Maréchal

Place de la Comédie

Rue Mautrec

Rue de Sèze

Rue de Tournay

Place des Grands Hommes

Rue Mably

Rue Père Louis de Jabrun

Rue des Trois Conils

Rue de Grassi

Place Jean Moulin

Place de Tourny

Allées de Tourny

Cours de Tournon

Rue J-J Rousseau

Rue Voltaire

Cours de l'Intendance

Rue Poquelin-Molière

Rue du Temple

Rue Vital-Carles

Place Pey-Berland

Rue de Ruat

Rue de l'Hôtel de Ville

Rue de Fondaudège

Cours Georges Clémenceau

Rue Condillac

Rue Montesquieu

Rue des Remparts

Rue Bouffard

Rue Montbazon

Rue Lafaurie de Monbadon

Rue Huguerie

Rue de la Vieille Tour

Rue de la Boëtie

Rue Boulan

Jardin de la Mairie

Rue de Lurbe

Rue Rolland

Place Gambetta

Cours d'Albret

Rue de Palais Gallien

Rue Georges-Bonnac

Rue du Dr Ch Nancel-Pénard

Rue Michelet

Place du Colonel Raynal

Rue Huguerie

Rue Lebrun

Rue St-Fort

Rue Turenne

Rue Poitevin

Rue Thiac

Rue de l'Abbé de l'Épée

Rue Castéja

Rue St-Sernin

Rue Judaïque

Rue du Château d'Eau

Rue Rodrigue-Péreire

Rue Docteur Albert Barraud

Place des Martyrs de la Résistance

Rue Georges-Bonnac

Rue R P-Dieuzaide

Rue Claude-Bonnier

200m
200yd
100
100
0
0

CENTRAL BORDEAUX

PLACES TO STAY
8 Hôtel Dauphin
10 Hôtel Studio
11 Hôtel Touring
14 Hôtel Royal Médoc
19 Hôtel des 4 Soeurs
29 Hôtel Blayais
46 Hôtel de la Tour Intendance
58 Hôtel d'Amboise
61 Hôtel Bristol
62 Hôtel de Lyon
66 Hôtel de la Presse
73 Hôtel Acanthe
80 Hôtel Quality Ste-Catherine
99 Hôtel La Boëtie
104 Hôtel Boulan

PLACES TO EAT
5 Fromagerie Antonin
6 Restaurant Baud et Millet
22 Le Flambeau
26 Restaurant Agadir
27 La Crêperie
28 Champion Supermarket;
Food shops (Marché des
Grands Hommes)
32 Café Louis
35 Jean Ramet
42 La Chanterelle
47 Le Grand Café
68 Chez Joël D.
70 Café de la Place
71 Chez Édouard
72 Seang-Thai
76 Le Petit Pavé
82 Saveur Latine
83 La Bonne Bouille
85 Amazonia
86 Didier Gélineau
88 Claret's
89 Au Clair de Lune
92 Le Médiéval

PUBS & BARS
21 La Factory

63 Le Moyen Age
69 Bodega Bodega
77 Milo's Café
78 XO Café
89 Calle Ocho
90 La Reine Carotte
93 L'Aztecal
103 Connemara
108 Le Kitsch
109 BHV

OTHER
1 Bord'Eaux Velos Loisirs
(Bike Rental)
2 Ville de Bordeaux; Alienor
ticket offices
3 Monument aux Girondins
4 Espace Laverie (Laundrette)
7 Bordeaux Language Studies
9 La Cybersalle
12 Air France
13 Post Office
15 Bordeaux Magnum
16 La Maison du Vin de
Bordeaux
17 Bordeaux Tourist Office
18 Vinothèque
20 Cadiot-Badie
23 Basilique St-Seurin
24 Hôtel de Police
25 Laverie Lincoln (Laundrette)
30 BNP
31 Taxis
33 Jet'Bus to Airport
34 Air France
36 Urban Bus Station
37 Espace Bus
38 Chambre de Commerce
et d'Industrie
39 Grand Théâtre
40 Crédit Lyonnais
41 American Express
43 Église Notre Dame
44 La Maison du Tourisme
de la Gironde

45 Centre Jean Vigo
48 Cinéma Gaumont
49 Jet'Bus to Airport
50 Esp@ce Internet
51 Main Post Office
52 UGC Ciné Cité
53 Espace Bus
54 Bus to Gare St-Jean
55 Virgin Megastore
56 Porte Dijeaux
57 Espace Tram
59 Librairie Mollat
60 Bouquets de Chocolats
de Bayonne
64 La Maison des Pyrénées
65 Théâtre Femina
67 Box Office
74 American Consulate
75 Hôtel des Douanes &
Musée National des
Douanes
81 Cyberstation
84 Église St-Pierre
87 Cinéma Utopia
91 Porte Cailhau
94 Wasteels
95 Post Office
96 Centre St-Christoly & FNAC
97 Centre National Jean Moulin
98 Occitanie
100 Bradley's Bookshop
101 Galerie des Beaux-Arts
102 Centre Commercial
Mériadeck; Auchan
Supermarket
105 Nexus 2000
106 Musée des Beaux-Arts
107 Musée des Arts Décoratifs
110 Hôtel de Ville (Town Hall)
111 Cathédrale St-André
112 Tour Pey-Berland
113 Centre d'Information
Jeunesse d'Aquitaine (CIJA)
114 Centre d'Information
Jeunesse d'Aquitaine (CIJA)

(☎ 05 56 44 51 04 or ☎ 08 03 88 70 31, e bordeauxalsace@wasteels.fr), 65 cours d'Alsace et Lorraine. CIJA (see earlier in this section) also has an efficient travel agency.

Bookshops
Bordeaux's biggest bookshop is Librairie Mollat (☎ 05 56 56 40 40, 15 rue Vital Carles), open 9.15am to 7pm Monday to Saturday. Bradley's Bookshop (☎ 05 56 52 10

57, 8 cours d'Albret) is open 9.30am to 12.30pm and 2pm to 7pm Tuesday to Saturday, and 2pm to 7pm Monday. It sells a wide selection of English-language books.

Cultural Centres
The library at the Goethe Institut (☎ 05 56 48 42 60, fax 05 56 48 42 66, e goetbxp@ easynet.fr), 35 cours de Verdun, is open 2pm to 6.30pm Monday and Friday and

9am to noon and 2pm to 8pm Tuesday to Thursday (to 6.30pm on Wednesday).

Laundry

Self-service laundrettes that open daily include Espace Laverie, 5 rue de Fondaudège (7am to 9pm) and Laverie Lincoln at 31 rue de Palais Gallien (8am to 9pm).

Medical Services & Emergency

Centre Hospitalier Régional Pellegrin (hospital; ☎ 05 56 79 56 79), at Place Amélie Raba-Léon (2km west), is the main hospital. More central is Hôpital St-André (☎ 05 56 79 56 79), 1 rue Jean Burguet. Both are open 24 hours. The tourist office has a list of private doctors and dentists speaking English or German. The Hôtel de Police (main police station; ☎ 05 56 99 77 77) is at 29 rue Castéja; branch police stations are at place de la Victoire (☎ 05 56 94 27 64) and Gare St-Jean (☎ 05 56 91 34 88).

MUSEUMS

The outstanding Musée d'Aquitaine (*Museum of Aquitaine; ☎ 05 56 01 51 00, 20 cours Pasteur; adult/child €3.80/2.30; open 11am-6pm Tues-Sun*) presents 25,000 years of history and ethnography. Exceptional artefacts include several prehistoric stone carvings of women and a collection of Gallo-Roman steles, statues and ceramics. A booklet (available in English for a €1.50 deposit) explains the exhibits; signs are minimal.

Monument aux Girondins

By far the most interesting thing in place des Quinconces is the exuberant 1902 Monument aux Girondins, dedicated to a group of National Assembly deputies executed for trying to moderate the French Revolution. The entire ensemble was dismantled by the Nazis for its 52 tonnes of bronze, but the Résistance bombed the train, carrying it away. It wasn't until 1983, when Bordeaux mayor Jacques Chaban-Delmas needed a few votes, that restoration was completed.

The collection of the Musée des Beaux-Arts (*Fine Arts Museum; ☎ 05 56 10 16 93, 20 cours d'Albret; adult/child €3.80/2.30; open 11am-6pm Wed-Mon*), in two wings of the 1770s Hôtel de Ville, includes 17th-century Flemish, Dutch and Italian paintings and 20th-century works by Matisse, Picasso and others. Around the block, an annexe called the Galerie des Beaux-Arts (*☎ 05 56 96 51 60, place du Colonel Raynal; adult/child €4.55/2.30; open 11am-8pm Wed & 11am-6pm Thur-Mon*) hosts short-term exhibitions. The nearby Musée des Arts Décoratifs (*Museum of Decorative Arts; ☎ 05 56 00 72 50, 39 rue Bouffard; adult/child €3.80/2.30; open 11am-6pm Mon, Wed-Fri & 2pm-6pm Sat-Sun*) specialises in faïence, porcelain, silverwork, glasswork, furniture and the like.

Entrepôts Lainé, built in 1824 as a warehouse for exotic imported products (eg, coffee, cocoa and peanuts) from France's colonies, now houses the CapcMusée d'Art Contemporain (*Museum of Contemporary Art; ☎ 05 56 00 81 50; 7 rue Ferrère; adult/child €3.80/2.30; €5.35/3.05 for temporary exhibitions; open 11am-6pm Tues, Thur-Sun & 11am-8pm Wed*). Works by a variety of internationally acclaimed artists are displayed. Opposite, Port 2a (*☎ 05 56 51 00 78, 16 rue Ferrère; admission free; open 2pm-6pm Tues-Sat*) is a focus of African culture, housing the Migrations Culturelles Aquitaine Afrique (MC2a) and displaying African arts as well as occasional 'mini' performances.

The Musée d'Histoire Naturelle (*Natural History Museum; ☎ 05 56 48 26 37, 5 place Bardineau; adult/child €3.80/2.30; open 11am-6pm Mon, Wed-Fri & 2pm-6pm Sat-Sun*) is on the south-western edge of the nearby Jardin Public. Founded at the time of the French Revolution, this museum has a huge collection of animal and plant specimens, particularly on the region's famous palaeontology.

The Centre National Jean Moulin (*Jean Moulin Documentation Centre; ☎ 05 56 79 66 00, place Jean Moulin; admission free; open 11am-6pm Mon-Fri & 2pm-6pm Sat-Sun*) has exhibits on France during WWII.

Croiseur Le Colbert (*☎ 05 56 44 96 11, quai des Chartrons; adult/those under 16 or student under 26 €7.15/5.65; open 10am-6pm Mon-Fri & 10am-7pm Sat-Sun Apr-May, Sept; 10am-8pm daily June-Aug; 1pm-6pm Mon-Fri & 10am-6pm Sat-Sun Jan-Mar, Oct-Dec; closed usually 1-12 Dec*) The French navy's last battle cruiser (decommissioned in 1991) is now permanently docked in this eye-catching location. Guided visits (in French) take place at 2.30pm every Saturday.

CATHÉDRALE ST-ANDRÉ
In 1137, the future King Louis VII married Eleanor of Aquitaine in this impressive and spacious cathedral *(admission free; open 10am-11.30am & 2pm-6.30pm Mon, 7.30am-11.30am & 2pm-6pm Tues-Sat, 8am-12.30pm Sun, but 2.30pm-5.30pm on 1st Sun of month)*. It's a Unesco World Heritage Site along with the Basiliques de St-Seurin and St-Michel, all important sites on the pilgrimage route to Santiago de Compostela (see the boxed text 'The Pilgrims of St-Jacques' under Religion in the Facts about Southwest France chapter). The exterior wall of the nave dates from 1096, and most of the rest from the 13th and 14th centuries. Renovation of the north portal is now uncovering fantastic carvings from the centuries-worth of grime.

The separate 15th-century belfry, the **Tour Pey-Berland** *(adult/under-26s €3.95/2.45; open 10am-6.30pm daily June-Sept; 10am-12.30pm & 2pm-5.30pm daily Oct-May)* has 184 narrow steps to reach its first storey, or a breath-taking 232 for the panoramic top level.

BASILIQUE ST-SEURIN
One of Bordeaux's oldest sacred sites, the place des Martyrs de la Résistance, where the Basilique St-Seurin now stands, was once the site of a Gallo-Roman cemetery and church. The basilica *(admission free; 7.45am-11.45am & 2.15pm-7.45pm Mon-Sat, 8.15am-12.45pm & 4.15pm-8.15pm Sun)* dates from the 11th century, with many later additions, notably from the 18th and 19th centuries. Look at the 11th- to 14th-

century carvings on and above the central door and the 7th-century sarcophagus (now the altar) in the chapel of St-Étienne. Under the crypt is a 4th-century **Paleo-Christian site** *(adult/child under 12 €2.30/free; 3pm-7pm daily June-Sept)*, which is the oldest-known evidence of civilisation in Bordeaux.

BASILIQUE & FLÈCHE ST-MICHEL
This Gothic basilica *(place Canteloup)*, finished in the mid-16th century, took 200 years to build. Check out the chapels for fine sculptures, paintings and carved altarpieces. The separate belfry, the 114m-high, late-15th-century **Flèche St-Michel**, is the tallest tower in the region. You can climb to a 47m-high look-out point *(adult/child under 12 €2.30/free; open 3pm-7pm daily June-Sept)*. Now at the heart of a vibrant Portuguese–North African quarter, it also overlooks a fantastic flea market (see Shopping later in this section).

PORTE DE LA GROSSE CLOCHE & PORTE CAILHAU
The 15th-century Grosse Cloche (Big Bell) clock-tower-cum-gateway spans the ancient road to Compostela, rue St-James. It was restored in the 19th century and has recently been spruced up again.

On the edge of the St-Pierre district, Porte Cailhau *(place du Palais; adult/child under 12 € 2.30/free; open 3pm-7pm daily June-Sept)* is the city's other ornate 15th-century gateway, built to commemorate a military victory by Charles VIII in 1495. The top floor has a great view.

PLACE DE LA BOURSE
This square boasts the city's finest ensemble of 18th-century architecture. On the northern side you can see the Palais de la Bourse, now housing the Chambre de Commerce et d'Industrie (Chamber of Commerce and Industry). To the south is the Hôtel des Douanes (customs house) and Musée National des Douanes. In the centre is La Fontaine des Trois Grâces, representing Queen Victoria, Empress Eugénie and the Queen of Spain.

SYNAGOGUE

The architecture of this synagogue (*☎ 05 56 91 79 39, rue du Grand Rabbin Joseph Cohen; open to visitors 9am-noon & 2-4pm Mon-Thur*) is a mix of Sephardic and Byzantine styles. Inaugurated in 1882, it was ripped apart and turned into a prison by the Nazis but painstakingly rebuilt after the war. To visit, ring the bell marked *gardien* at 213 rue Ste-Catherine.

GRAND THÉÂTRE

South of the Esplanade des Quinconces, one of Bordeaux's architectural highlights on the place de la Comédie is the neoclassical Grand Théâtre. It was designed by Parisian architect Victor Louis in the 1770s, and its imposing Corinthian colonnade is decorated with 12 figures of the Muses and Graces. There's some fantastic decor inside, too (accessible only on a tourist-office guided visit, see Organised Tours later in this section).

OTHER THINGS TO SEE

The landscaped **Jardin Public** along cours de Verdun, established in 1755, includes a meticulously catalogued **Jardin Botanique** (*☎ 05 56 52 18 77, cours de Verdun; admission free; open 8am-6pm daily*), founded in 1629. Nearby, off rue de Fondaudège, is the city's most impressive Roman site, the **Palais Gallien**, the ruins of a 3rd-century amphitheatre (*rue du Dr Albert Barraud; adult/children under 12 €1.50/free; 3pm-7pm daily June-Sept*).

The city centre's vast **Esplanade des Quinconces** was once the site of the fortress-like Chateau Trompette, built in 1691 but demolished less than a century later to create this dull square (see the boxed text 'Monument aux Girondins'). The nearby **riverside area** is the focus of an ambitious redevelopment scheme, which will eventually transform banks of the river into 30 hectares of parkland and promenades.

The **St-Pierre district** to the south, once a separate, walled quarter and later a medieval merchants' enclave, is now the heart of a lively ethnic restaurant district. It has some fine 18th-century *hôtels particuliers* (town houses), for example in place St-Pierre.

ACTIVITIES FOR CHILDREN

Ask for the free, quarterly *Clubs & Comptines* from the tourist office for details of kid-friendly events and facilities. You'll find decent playgrounds in place des Martyrs de la Résistance, the Jardin Public (take bus No 7 or 8 from place Gambetta) and Parc Bordelais (about 2km north-west of the centre; take bus No 17 or 18 from place Jean Jaurès); the latter also has pony riding. A small adventure-style playground and carousel are on the quai des Chartrons near Croiseur Le Colbert; a larger carousel is opposite the tourist office on cours du 30 Juillet.

WHAT'S FREE

All Musée de Bordeaux museums offer free admission to students; they're also free to everyone on the first Sunday of every month. On this day you can also rent bikes for free (see Bicycle under Getting Around later in this section).

Fnac (see under Shopping) has a program of free exhibitions, concerts and mini-performances in its forum. Pick up its monthly *agenda culturel* for details.

ORGANISED TOURS

The tourist office runs a wide range of guided tours, including good two-hour **walking tours** of the city centre with French and English commentary (adult/senior & student €6.10/5.35; 10am daily). From 15 April to 15 November the tours on Wednesday and Saturday are by bus.

River cruises run from Embarcadère des Quinconces: *Ville de Bordeaux* (*☎/fax 05 56 52 88 88, quai Louis XVIII*) runs daily 1½-hour daytime cruises (€7.60) and longer Sunday-only cruises (€28.95 with lunch; 12.30pm to 6pm). *Alienor* (*☎ 05 56 51 27 90, quai Louis XVIII*) offers different cruises at least four times weekly (€19.80 or €41.15 with lunch; 11.30am to 6.30pm); and dinner-dance cruises (€41.15; 9pm to midnight). Tickets and information are available at their adjacent prefab offices on Quai Louis XVIII (Hangar 7).

Various **bike tours** in the Médoc and Entre-deux-Mers regions are organised by *Bord'Eaux Velos Loisirs* (see under Getting *Around later in this section)* including a two-hour jaunt around Pauillac after a 2½-hour boat trip from Bordeaux (€22.85). Between June and September it also offers a trip to Langoiran by motorboat (€28.95 one-way) from where you can follow a bike trail back to Bordeaux.

SPECIAL EVENTS

A major event is the Foire Internationale de Bordeaux (☎ 08 36 69 61 62), an international trade fair in May featuring 10 days of music, drama and other events at the Parc des Expositions, Bordeaux-Lac.

During late June in even-numbered years, the Fête du Vin (Wine Fair; ☎ 05 56 00 66 00), a three-day event with stalls and wine-tasting, is held at place de la Bourse and elsewhere. In odd-numbered years, the Fête du Fleuve (River Celebration; ☎ 05 56 00 66 00) enlivens the city's quaysides. Also in early June, there's the Gay Pride festival (☎ 06 14 56 45 01).

In October, the Fête du Vin Nouveau et de la Brocante (☎ 05 56 81 50 25) celebrates *vin nouveau* (still-fermenting white wine, traditionally enjoyed with hot chestnuts). It's organised by *brocante* (bric-a-brac) shops on rue Notre Dame in the north of the city, where the festival takes place.

For exact dates, contact the tourist office.

PLACES TO STAY – BUDGET

The heart of Bordeaux has lots of reasonably priced hotels, so you're better off *not* staying in the seedy area around Gare St-Jean.

Camping & Hostels

A couple of good-value choices are the following.

Camping Les Gravières (☎ 05 56 87 00 36, fax 05 56 87 24 60, place de Courréjean) 2-person forfait with/without car €10.35/9.25. Open year round. This 150-site camping ground, 10km south-east of the city in Villenave d'Ornon, has a pleasant location and good amenities. Take bus B from place de la Victoire towards Courréjean and get off at the terminus.

Auberge de Jeunesse Barbey (☎ 05 56 33 00 70, fax 05 56 33 00 71, 22 cours Barbey) Dorm beds HI members/non-members €12/13.55. Open 24 hours. Recently reopened after major renovations, the hostel has a cafe-bar, kitchen, laundry and Internet facility, plus adapted rooms for the disabled. There's an annexe at 208 cours de l'Argonne.

Hotels

There are a number of budget hotels to choose from.

Hôtel de Lyon (☎ 05 56 81 34 38, fax 05 56 52 92 82, 31 rue des Remparts) Singles/doubles/twins/triples with WC & shower €18.30/20.60/24.40/27.45. This place is pretty scruffy and rundown, with flimsy shower units, although many rooms are spacious.

Hôtel Boulan (☎ 05 56 52 23 62, fax 05 56 44 91 65, 28 rue Boulan) Singles/doubles/triples €19.80/22.85/27.45. The quiet Boulan is old and fraying, but many rooms are recently renovated, include shower and WC, and offer excellent value.

Hôtel Studio (☎ 05 56 48 00 14, fax 05 56 81 25 71, 26 rue Huguerie) Singles €14.95-20.60, doubles/triples €24.40/27.45, 5-person room €38.10. This is the headquarters of Bordeaux's cheap-hotel empire: The family owns three other city-centre places. Rooms are small and charmless, but have a flimsy shower, WC, mini-fridge and cable TV. All Hôtel Studio guests get cheap Internet access at La Cybersalle (see Email & Internet Access earlier in this section).

Hôtel Dauphin (☎ 05 56 52 24 62, fax 05 56 01 10 91, 82 rue du Palais Gallien) Singles €21.20-27.30, doubles €24.25-30.35, triples €30.35-33.40. The tastefully decorated and quiet Dauphin is good value, with bright, high-ceilinged rooms complete with WC, shower, TV and a telephone (some cheaper rooms minus WC are available).

PLACES TO STAY – MID-RANGE

Mid-price hotels in Bordeaux include the following.

Hôtel Bristol (☎ 05 56 81 85 01, fax 05 56 51 24 06, ⓔ bristol@hotel-bordeaux.com, 2 rue Bouffard) Doubles/triples €32/45.75. The busy, central Bristol (part of the Hôtel

Studio chain) has cheerful, if somewhat noisy rooms.

Hôtel Blayais (☎ 05 56 48 17 87, fax 05 56 52 47 57, 17 rue Mautrec) Singles €30.50, doubles €35.05-44.20. The Blayais has big, simple rooms, plus some studios with kitchenette (€41.15-44.20 or €33.55-36.60 for periods longer than 16 nights).

Hôtel Touring (☎ 05 56 81 56 73, fax 05 56 81 24 55, 16 rue Huguerie) Doubles with WC & shower €28.95-35, without €24.40. This homely, quiet place, with its spotless rooms, is the best in this area. From Gare St-Jean, take bus No 7 or 8.

Hôtel Acanthe (☎ 05 56 81 66 58, fax 05 56 44 74 41, e info@acanthe-hotel -bordeaux.com, 12-14 rue St-Rémi) Singles €27.45-39.65, doubles €39.65-45.75. The professionally run Acanthe, right by place de la Bourse, has immaculate if somewhat thin-walled rooms in a quiet location. Advance booking is essential from June to September.

Hôtel Royal Médoc (☎ 05 56 81 72 42, fax 05 56 51 74 98, 3 rue de Sèze) Singles/doubles €41.15/45.75. The Royal Médoc has comfortable, soundproofed accommodation.

Hôtel de la Tour Intendance (☎ 05 56 81 46 27, fax 05 56 81 60 90, 14-16 rue de la Vieille Tour) Singles €33.55, doubles €39.65-50.30, triples €57.95. This is a friendly, well run hotel with good amenities.

Hôtel des 4 Soeurs (☎ 05 57 81 19 20, fax 05 56 01 04 28, 6 cours du 30 Juillet) Singles €50.30, doubles €60.95-76.20. By the tourist office, the 18th-century Hôtel des 4 Soeurs has attractive rooms, all with air-con, some overlooking an inner courtyard.

Hôtel de la Presse (☎ 05 56 48 53 88, fax 05 56 01 05 82, 68 rue de la Porte Dijeaux) Doubles/twins/triples with shower €60.20/69.35/75.45, with bath €67.05/76.20/82.30. This is a good central choice; rooms have air-con, TV, mini-bar and telephone.

Hôtel Le Faisan (☎ 05 56 91 54 52, fax 05 56 92 93 83, 28 rue Charles Domercq) Singles €36.60-50.30, doubles €45.75-53.35, triples €60.95. Opposite Gare St-Jean's departure terminal, Le Faisan has decent rooms with shower, WC and TV. There are several other choices nearby.

PLACES TO STAY – TOP END

If you can afford a little more luxury, your options include the following.

Hôtel Quality Ste-Catherine (☎ 05 56 81 95 12, fax 05 56 44 50 51, e quality .bordeaux@wanadoo.fr, 27 rue du Parlement Ste-Catherine) Singles €74.70-135.70, doubles €89.95-150.90. This modest chain hotel, in the heart of the pedestrianised shopping district, offers smallish rooms with TV and air-con.

Hôtel Burdigala (☎ 05 56 90 16 16, fax 05 56 93 15 06, e burdigala@burdigala .com, 115 rue Georges Bonnac) Doubles €150.90-228.65. This five-star property, in a renovated 18th-century building, provides all the frills (including Internet access in the rooms).

PLACES TO EAT

Those on a strict budget will find cheap *cafes* and *pizzerias*, *sandwich* and *kebab bars* at the southern ends of rue Ste-Catherine and rue du Palais Gallien, as well as in the St-Michel district. But on weekday lunchtimes you can eat much better, and for not much more, at many restaurants offering bargain *menus*.

Restaurants – Budget & Mid-Range French

These are some of the modestly priced eateries of Bordeaux.

Cassolette Café (☎ 05 56 92 94 96, 20 place de la Victoire) Midday/evening *menus* €7.90/9.90, small/large *cassolettes* (plates) €2.15/6.40. This kid-friendly cafe offers great value in French food.

Café de la Place (☎ 05 56 48 12 85, 13 place du Parlement) Lunch *menus* €9.25. This is an unpretentious choice for a coffee or lunch on the popular place du Parlement.

Chez Édouard (☎ 05 56 81 48 87, 16 place du Parlement) Midday *menus* €10.50, evening *menus* €15.10-21.10, dishes €11-15.25. The lively Chez Édouard offers French bistro-style fare.

Le Grand Café (☎ 05 56 52 61 10, 65 cours de l'Intendance) Lunch *formule* €9.90. A vibrant, popular cafe with a prime people-watching location and snappy service.

Le Petit Pavé (☎ *05 56 44 16 16, 16 rue des Faussets) Menus* €10.50-19.05, dishes €6.85-14.50. The gay-friendly, rustic-style Petit Pavé serves a variety of regional fare. This street is packed with other tempting restaurants, too.

La Chanterelle (☎ *05 56 81 75 43, 3 rue de Martignac)* Midday *menus* €11.45, evening *menus* €14.95-22.85, dishes €10-13.70. Open Mon-Sat, except Wed night. La Chan-terelle serves moderately priced traditional French and regional cuisine.

Chez Joël D. (☎ *05 56 52 68 31, 13 rue des Piliers de Tutelle)* Oysters €6.25-10.35 per half-dozen. This appealing oyster bistro serves the region's famous shellfish, plus other gourmet snacks.

Claret's (☎ *05 56 01 21 21, place Camille Jullian)* Midday/evening *menus* €9.90/15.10, dishes €16-27.45. Open midday & evening Mon-Fri & evening only Sat. Here's a chic little venue in a trendy, gentrified district that has several other attractive restaurants.

Café Louis (☎ *05 56 44 07 00, Grand Théâtre)* Dishes €11.45-13.70. Occupying a wing of the Grand Théâtre, this sumptuous cafe-restaurant has a simple menu but an opulent 18th-century-style decor of chandeliers and carved columns.

Café du Musée (☎ *05 56 44 71 61, 7 rue Ferrère)* Dishes €11.45-12.95. Open lunch only Tues-Sun. A stylish gem of a place (with furniture designed by Andrée Putman) on the CapcMusée d'Art Contemporain's rooftop terrace, with a sushi bar and delicious outdoor seating.

Restaurants – Top-End French
For a taste of Bordeaux's more ritzy restaurant culture, try one of the following.

Jean Ramet (☎ *05 56 44 12 51, 7 place Jean Jaurès)* Midday *menus* €25.90, evening *menus* €42.70-53.35. Open Tues-Sat. Classic French and Bordelais cuisine is served here amid mirrors, white tablecloths and sparkling tableware.

La Tupina (☎ *05 56 91 56 37, 6 rue porte de la Monnaie)* Midday/evening *menus* €15.25/44.20. The most famous bistro in Bordeaux, unpretentious La Tupina has lav-

ish *menus* of traditional southwest cuisine by renowned chef, Jean Pierre Xiradakis.

Didier Gélineau (☎ *05 56 52 84 25, 26 rue du Pas St-Georges)* Menus* €19.80-48.80. Open midday & evening Mon-Fri & evening only Sat. This eight-table, Michelin-starred eatery has a modern setting and cuisine, with seasonally changing *menus*. The desserts are out of this world.

Restaurants – Other
Bordeaux has a sumptuous supply of ethnic restaurants. The best haunts are rue du Hâ and rue des Augustins near place de la Victoire (especially for Vietnamese, Indian and Lebanese fare); rue St-Rémi near place de la Bourse (especially for Chinese and East-Asian cuisine); cours de l'Yser and the St-Michel district to the north (Spanish and Portuguese); and rue Bahutiers (African) and the nearby St-Pierre district for everything from Russian to Basque, Tex Mex to Turkish.

Seang-Thai (☎ *05 56 44 29 78, 26 rue St-Rémi)* Menus* €7.60-13.55, dishes €5.35-10.65. Open midday & evening Mon-Sat & evening only Sun. This is a plain, good-value Chinese restaurant, popular with families.

Restaurant Palabrer (☎ *05 56 92 77 32, 9 rue Gratiolet)* Dishes €6.85-8.40. Open Tues-Sat. The Palabrer serves a select menu of simple, tasty African food at great prices.

Restaurant Agadir (☎ *05 56 52 28 04, 14 rue du Palais Gallien)* Midday/evening *menus* €9.25/16.95. Moroccan couscous and *tagines* (spicy North-African stews) are on the menu here.

Le Médiéval (☎ *05 56 48 22 81, 42 rue des Bahutiers)* Menus* €13.55, grills (over a wood fire) €8.85, brochettes €10.65. Open Mon-Sat. Richly adorned Le Médiéval offers tasty Lebanese cuisine.

Saveur Latine (☎ *05 56 51 02 75, 3 rue de la Devise)* Menus* €10.50-13.70, dishes €7.60-11.40. Open evening only Tues-Sun. If you fancy Tex-Mex delights, head for this popular place.

La Bonne Bouille (☎ *05 56 79 13 12, 7 rue des Bahutiers)* Menus* €22.85-38.10, dishes €7.60-12.20. Open dinner only Tues-Sun. This attractive, cheery restaurant specialises in the cuisine of Madagascar, Réunion, Antilles and Seychelles. The vanilla-flavoured coffee is a treat.

***Amazonia** (☎ 05 56 81 72 38, 14 rue Bahutiers) Menus* €10.50-14.50, dishes €9.25-12.95. Open dinner only Mon-Sat. If you like wacky decor (eg, toy gorillas hanging from the ceiling) this exotic Brazilian-ambience place will fit the bill.

***Casa Pino** (☎ 05 56 92 82 88, 40 rue Traversanne) Menus* €9.25, dishes €6.85-10.65. This is the best-known (and best-value) Portuguese restaurant in town, its simple menu inevitably featuring plenty of codfish.

Restaurants – Vegetarian
As elsewhere in France, vegetarian restaurants are few and far between, but meat-haters should be happy at the following venues.

***Mens Sana** (☎ 05 56 51 00 03, 16 rue Ravez)* Midday/evening *menus* €9/11.45, dishes €5.35-9.90. Neat and bright, Mens Sana offers organic and vegetarian dishes.

***Restaurant Baud et Millet** (☎ 05 56 79 05 77, 19 rue Huguerie)* All-you-can-eat cheese buffet or *raclette* €17.55, four dishes plus dessert €26.70. Open Mon-Sat. This renowned restaurant serves cheese-based, mostly vegetarian cuisine.

***La Crêperie** (☎ 05 56 48 54 47, 23 cours Georges Clémenceau)* Pancakes €3.35-8.55, salads €5.50-6.10. La Crêperie serves delicious *galettes* (wheat pancakes, with plenty of vegetarian choices), crepes and cider by the mug or jug. It also has a no-smoking area.

Self-Catering
Fending for yourself can be a tasty experience in Bordeaux if you take advantage of the local markets.

***Marché des Capucins** (place des Capucins)* This huge covered market opens every morning except Monday. West of here, along rue Élie-Gintrac, a lively, super-cheap *fruit and veg market* operates every Thursday, Friday and Saturday morning.

***Marché des Chartrons** (quai des Chartrons)* This superb Sunday-only market (beside Croiseur Le Colbert), sells

seafood and prepared dishes (with places to sit and eat them) as well as general produce. It may be disrupted from 2002 to 2003, however, due to tram and quayside works.

There's a ***Champion supermarket*** and several upmarket *food shops (place des Grands Hommes)*, open 7am to 8pm Monday to Saturday, in the basement of the Marché des Grands Hommes, a modern, glassed shopping centre.

Other big supermarkets open Monday to Saturday include ***Auchan** (☎ 05 56 99 59 00, Centre Commercial Mériadeck off rue du Château d'Eau)*, open 8.30am to 10pm; and ***Champion** (☎ 05 56 92 47 47, 190 rue Ste-Catherine)*, open 8.30am to 8pm.

***Fromagerie Antonin** (☎ 05 56 81 61 74, 6 rue de Fondaudège)* Open 9am-12.45pm, 4pm-7.30pm; Open Tues-Sat & Mon afternoon; Open Tues-Fri, Sat morning & Mon afternoon July-Aug and from 5-20 Aug. This is the city's best cheese shop.

***Le Fournil des Capucins** (☎ 05 57 95 85 65, 62-64 cours de la Marne)* This is a 24-hour boulangerie.

ENTERTAINMENT
Bordeaux has a really hopping nightlife scene; details on events appear in the what's-on periodicals (see Information earlier in this section). Student nightlife centres on place de la Victoire.

Buy tickets for gigs, shows, concerts and sporting events at the ***Virgin Megastore Billetterie** (☎ 05 56 56 05 55)* or ***Fnac Billetterie** (☎ 08 03 80 38 03)*. See under Shopping for details. You can also check Fnac's Web site, ⓦ www.fnac.com. Clubs et Concerts (see under Information) has its own (French-only) Web site for clubbing news, ⓦ www.clubsetconcerts.com.

***Box Office** (☎ 05 56 48 26 26, 24 Galerie Bordelaise)* is another ticket outlet, mainly for shows at Théâtre Fémina and other major venues.

Cinemas
Bordeaux has several major cinema chains, plus some more specialised places.

***Centre Jean Vigo** (☎ 05 56 44 35 17, 6 rue Franklin, ⓔ centre@jeanvigo.com)*

Tickets €4.55, €3.80 Mon & Wed (and daily for students). This veteran venue screens nondubbed films and also hosts various events, including Le Printemps des Ciné-concerts (usually late March), showing a dozen international golden oldies with musical accompaniment.

Cinéma Utopia (☎ *05 56 52 00 03, 3 place Camille Jullian)* In a fashionably renovated former church, the popular five-screen Utopia screens nondubbed films and publishes its own gazette of film reviews.

UGC Ciné Cité (☎ *05 55 48 43 43, 13 rue Georges Bonnac)* This cinema also shows VO *(version originale)* films.

Cinéma Gaumont (☎ *05 56 52 03 54, 9 cours Georges Clémenceau)* Tickets €5.50 (€4.40 Wed & first showings every weekday), €3.80 students & seniors on weekdays. The Gaumont likes international blockbusters.

Concert Halls, Theatres & Gig Venues

From rough rock venues to neoclassical grand theatres, Bordeaux has it all.

Grand Théâtre (☎ *05 56 48 58 54, place de la Comédie)* Ticket office open 11am-6pm Tues-Sat. This 18th-century theatre stages operas, ballets and concerts. It also handles tickets for some smaller events at *Théâtre Femina (10 rue de Grassi).* This theatre is the venue for plays, dance performances and operettas.

Théâtre Barbey (also called Rock School Barbey; ☎ *05 56 33 66 00, cours Barbey)* This is one of the city's major venues for rock shows and other music events.

Palais des Sports (☎ *05 56 52 76 03, Place de la Ferme de Richemont)* This often hosts big classical concerts.

Zoobizarre and *Le Nautilus (see under Clubs & Live Music)* mainly host underground and avant-garde musical events.

Bars

Whether you want a wild night out or a cosy taste of home, Bordeaux has bars to suit.

Calle Ocho (☎ *05 56 48 08 68, 24 rue des Piliers de Tutelle)* Open 7pm-2am Mon-Sat. Calle Ocho is one of the hottest bars in town, attracting a colourful crowd and serving seductive mixed drinks; try its house speciality, *mojito* (€3.80), a mint, lemon and rum concoction.

Down Under (☎ *05 56 94 52 48, 104 cours Aristide Briand)* Open 7pm-2am daily. This bar, run by an ex-Aucklander, is a favourite among Aussie and Kiwi rugby players and other Anglophones.

Bodega Bodega (☎ *05 56 01 24 24, 4 rue des Piliers de Tutelle)* Open noon-3.15pm, 7pm-2am Mon-Sat, 7pm-2am Sun; closed bank holidays. This is a hugely popular tapas bar where the beautiful crowd like to hang out.

Connemara (☎ *05 56 52 82 57, 18 cours d'Albret)* Open noon-2am Mon-Sat, 6pm-2am Sun. The recently expanded Connemara has big-screen football, darts, pool, regular live Irish music and a restaurant serving Irish and English grub.

Milo's Café (☎ *05 56 44 69 11, 21 rue du Parlement St-Pierre)* Open 2pm-2am daily. This is a friendly, pleasantly scruffy bar near place du Parlement.

Café des Sports (5 cours de l'Argonne) Open 11am-2am Mon-Sat. This popular bar serves nonstop sport on cable TV; there's also a brasserie upstairs.

Clubs & Live Music

For zoning reasons, many of the city's late-late dance venues are a few blocks northeast of Gare St-Jean along the river, on quai de Paludate (just south of the railway bridge) and perpendicular rue du Commerce. Most places are bars with dancing and have deafening, pulsating music. There are bouncers but invariably no cover charge. They can get incredibly crowded, especially just after 2am, the statutory closing time for most of the city's regular bars.

La Plage (☎ *05 56 49 02 46, 40 quai de la Paludate)* Open midnight-5am Wed-Sat. Among the best of the dancing bars, tropical beach-themed La Plage attracts those aged between 24 and 35.

Quai Sud (☎ *05 56 85 53 83, 37 quai de la Paludate)* Open midnight-5am Wed-Sat. This club attracts an older crowd, especially those aged between 25 and 35.

Le Duplex (☎ *05 56 85 71 85, 18 rue du Commerce*) Open midnight-5am Thur-Sat. Thur €3.05, Fri free, Sat €7.60 (free for women and students). Le Duplex can pack in a thousand boogying bodies on two dance floors and is a particular favourite with those aged between 18 and 25.

Le Living Room (*14 rue du Commerce*) Open midnight-5am Thur-Sat. This dancing bar attracts a slightly older set. There's a relatively quiet Oriental-style corner at the back, complete with rugs and couches.

Spirit Club (☎ *05 56 49 10 00, 88 quai de Paludate*) Open noon-5am Wed-Sat, to 6am Sun. Electronic beats are Spirit Club's speciality.

Le Plana (☎ *05 56 91 73 23, 22 place de la Victoire*) Open 7am-2am Mon-Sat, 2pm-2am Sun. Le Plana is one of the most lively student venues in place de la Victoire. It has live jazz on Sunday (except in July and August) at about 10.30pm and sometimes has funk and soul concerts – or jam sessions – on Monday, Tuesday and Wednesday at 10.30pm.

O'Ventilo (☎ *05 56 92 33 98, 34 cours de l'Argonne*) Open 9pm-2am Tues-Fri, 9pm-6am Sat-Sun. This house and techno club gets going late, hosting rave parties for a mainly student clientele.

La Lune dans le Caniveau (☎ *05 56 31 95 92, 39 place des Capucins*) Open midnight or 1am-5am Wed-Sat. Admission charge for some gigs. La Lune is a hardcore club with down-and-out surroundings and a nonpop soundtrack (punk rock, reggae, ska) attracting some of the grungiest members of the counter-culture scene.

XO Café (☎ *05 56 01 12 43, 11 rue du Parlement Ste-Catherine*) Open 6pm-2am Tues-Sat. This is a DJ bar featuring everything from 70s to hip hop and soul.

L'Aztecal (☎ *05 56 44 50 18, 61 rue du Pas-St-Georges*) Open 11pm-5am Tues-Sat. L'Aztecal plays salsa, Latino, soul and motown.

Zoobizarre (☎ *05 56 91 14 40, 58 rue du Mirail*) Bar open 9pm-2am Thur-Sat, plus other days when gigs take place. This leading bar-disco-cum-theatre is a showcase for international avant-garde musical events.

Check its Web site, Ⓦ www.zoobizarre.free .fr, or published program in the regular events publications (see under Information).

Le Nautilus (☎ *05 56 50 55 96, 122 quai de Bacalan*) Open midnight-5am Sat-Sun. Le Nautilus, along the river 2.4km north of esplanade des Quinconces, hosts live bands playing reggae, pop and rock (plus electronic music later in the evening) in a cavernous old warehouse, converted into a vast house and techno dance floor.

Gay & Lesbian Venues

Bordeaux has one of the largest gay and lesbian communities in Southwest France, and, as such, has a fair number of venues.

Le Moyen Age (☎ *05 56 44 12 87, 8 rue des Remparts*) Open 10pm-2am Wed-Mon. This mellow spot is one of France's oldest gay bars.

BHV (☎ *05 56 44 05 08, 4 rue de l'Hôtel de Ville*) Open 6pm-2am daily. This lively, 95% gay bar usually has a transvestites' night at 11pm on Sunday.

La Factory (☎ *05 56 01 10 11, 28 rue Mably*) Cover charge €7.60 Fri & Sat. Open midnight-5am daily. This is a mainly gay club.

Le Kitsch (☎ *05 56 48 13 79, 73 rue des Trois Conils*) Cafe open 6pm-2am daily, disco 5am-noon or 1pm Sat & Sun. The basement dance floor gets going on Saturday and Sunday morning after La Factory closes.

La Reine Carotte (☎ *05 56 01 26 68, 32 rue du Chai des Farines*) Open 7pm-2am Tues-Sat. This is a mainly lesbian bar.

In & Out (☎ *05 56 48 22 13, 32 rue Cornac*) Cover charge €7.60. Open 10pm-5am Thur-Sun. This disco is mainly geared to the guys.

SPECTATOR SPORTS

The city's football team, Girondins de Bordeaux (☎ 05 56 16 11 11, fax 05 56 57 54 46), is the region's best, with (almost) championship-quality playing. Catch them at Stade Lescure on place Johnston, 2km south-west of town. Rugby enthusiasts will find Stade Bordelais UC playing at Stade Ste-Germaine, rue Ferdinand de Lesseps.

SHOPPING

Le Triangle, the large area bordered by cours de l'Intendance, allées de Tourny and cours Georges Clémenceau, is the most prestigious shopping district (favoured by Cartier, Hermes, Dior, etc). Pedestrianised rue de la Porte Dijeaux and rue Ste-Catherine (once major Gallo-Roman thoroughfares) are more mainstream, chock-a-block with department stores and cafes. Where they meet is Galerie Bordelaise, an ornate and charming 19th-century shopping arcade.

Bordeaux wine is obviously top of many shoppers' lists: It's on sale at several specialist stores near the tourist office, including *Bordeaux Magnum* (☎ 05 56 48 00 06, 3 rue Gobineau) and *Vinothèque* (☎ 05 56 52 32 05, 8 cours du 30 Juillet).

Occitanie (☎ 05 56 44 88 63, 68 rue des Remparts) Occitanie sells deluxe Périgord groceries, regional souvenirs and handicrafts.

Bouquets de Chocolats de Bayonne (☎ 05 56 44 55 72, 6 rue des Remparts) Chocolates from their famous south-west Basque heartland, Bayonne, are the speciality at this shop.

Cadiot-Badie (☎ 05 56 44 24 22, 26 allées de Tourny) This prestigious *artisan chocolatier* has been in business since 1826, serving delicacies such as chocolate wine bottles stuffed with chocolate truffles (€31.25).

For low-brow antiques and junk, go to the *flea market* by Basilique St-Michel, active 8am to 5pm Tuesday to Friday and 8am to 1pm on Sunday – especially the second Sunday of March, June, September and December.

Le Passage St-Michel (☎ 05 56 92 14 76, 14 place Canteloup) Open 9.30am-6pm Mon-Sat & 9.30-noon Sun. Some 45 antique dealers operate from this former banana-ripening warehouse near the flea market. Most items are 20th century. More upmarket antique shops can be found along city-centre rue Bouffard and rue Notre Dame (near Cité Mondial).

Fnac (☎ 05 56 00 21 30, Centre St-Christoly, 17 rue Père Louis de Jabrun) Open 10am-7pm Mon-Sat. Fnac has plenty of CDs, DVDs and cassettes as well as books and computer gear.

Virgin Megastore (☎ 05 56 56 05 56, 15 place Gambetta) Open 10am-10pm Mon-Thur, 10am-midnight Fri-Sat, 11am-7pm Sun. The Virgin Megastore stocks a huge range of CDs, DVDs and cassettes.

GETTING THERE & AWAY
Air
Bordeaux's international airport (☎ 05 56 34 50 50) is 10km west of the centre at Mérignac.

Air France operates multiple daily flights to Bordeaux from Paris (mainly Orly). There are also daily or almost-daily flights from at least 17 other French cities, and from Barcelona, Basel, Brussels, Geneva, Madrid, Munich and Rome. British Airways flies to Bordeaux daily from London Gatwick while Buzz flies daily from London Stansted.

Air France (☎ 05 56 00 40 40 or toll-free ☎ 0 802 802 802) has offices at 29 rue de l'Esprit des Lois and 44 allées de Tourny. Other airlines are represented only at the airport. See the Getting There & Away chapter for details, and for booking numbers.

Bus
The Halte Routière (bus terminal) is on Esplanade des Quinconces. Citram Aquitaine (☎ 05 56 43 68 43) runs most buses to destinations in the Gironde (eg, Libourne, Pauillac, Soulac, Pointe de Grave) and a few other places farther afield (eg, Auch, Condom). The information kiosk in the terminal (☎ 05 56 43 68 43) is open 7am to 8.30am and 1pm to 8.15pm weekdays, 9am to 12.30pm and 5pm to 8.15pm on Saturday, and 8.30am to 10.30am and 5pm to 8.30pm on Sunday.

Various other bus companies run infrequent services to the Landes and Côte d'Argent destinations from Gare St-Jean: RDTL (☎ 05 58 56 80 80) serves Mont de Marsan; Rapides de la Côte d'Argent (☎ 05 58 09 10 89) goes to Biscarrosse and Cars Ouest Aquitaine (☎ 05 56 70 12 13) runs to Lacanau and Carcans. For details of all these services, refer to the relevant towns in this or subsequent chapters.

Eurolines (☎ 05 56 92 50 42), facing

Gare St-Jean at 32 rue Charles Domercq, is open 9am to noon and 2pm to 7pm Monday to Saturday. You can also buy Eurolines tickets at CIJA (see Information earlier in this section).

Train

The train station, Gare St-Jean (☎ 08 36 35 35 35), is about 3km south-east of the city centre, and is served by bus Nos 7 and 8. The SNCF information office at Gate 14 is open 9am to 7pm Monday to Saturday, closed on bank holidays. An 'Accueil' (Reception) help desk at Gate 36 is open 24 hours. The left-luggage office at Gate 54 is open 8am to 12.15pm and 1.30pm to 8pm daily, and lockers (€2.30-4.55 per 72 hours, depending on size) are available 7am to 10.30pm weekdays (to 8.30pm Saturday; from 9am to 11pm Sunday). Bikes can also be left here.

Some of the regional destinations that are served by multiple daily direct trains include Sarlat (€18.45), Bergerac (€12.20), Bayonne (€20.90), Brive-la-Gaillarde (€21.35, most changing at Périgueux), Arcachon (€8.25), and Toulouse (€25.25). The non-TGV fare to Paris is €47.55 (five hours, Gare d'Austerlitz); by TGV it's €54.75 (3½ hours, Gare Montparnasse).

Car

Major car-rental agencies, represented at the airport and Gare St-Jean, include Europcar (☎ 05 56 34 05 79), Budget (☎ 05 56 47 84 22), Hertz (☎ 05 56 34 59 59) and the cheaper French company ADA (☎ 05 56 31 21 11).

To reach the motorway ringroad (A630) follow sings for 'Rocade'.

GETTING AROUND
To the Airport

Jet'Bus (☎ 05 56 34 50 50) shuttles between Gare St-Jean, bus stops opposite the Grand Théâtre (29 rue de l'Esprit des Lois) and place Gambetta, and the airport every 30/45 minutes on weekdays/weekends from 5.30am until 9.30pm (last departure from the airport at 10.45pm and from Gare St-Jean at 9.30pm or 10pm Friday to Sunday).

The trip takes around 30 minutes and costs €5.65 one way (those aged under 26 and seniors €4.10). Inbound, the bus stops wherever you want. No announcements are made, so get a city map from the airport's information office. Taxis charge around €22.85 to the city centre.

Bus

Bordeaux's urban bus network, Compagnie Génerale Français des Transports d'Enterprise (CGFTE, nicknamed Allo Bus; ☎ 05 57 57 88 88), has information and ticket offices ('Espace Bus') at Gare St-Jean, place Gambetta (4 rue Georges Bonnac) and place Jean Jaurès. They, the tourist office and sometimes *tabacs* (tobacconists), can provide an easy-to-use, free *Plan Poche* (pocket route map).

Single tickets sold on board cost €1.15 and no transfers are allowed. With tickets from a prepaid carnet of 10 (€8.40), available at tabacs and CGFTE offices, you can transfer up to three times; you must time-stamp the ticket each time you board.

A Bordeaux Découverte card, sold at CGFTE offices and the tourist office, allows unlimited bus travel for one/three/six days (€3.60/8.30/11.80). Time-stamp it only the first time you use it.

Tram

Some time in early 2003, the first three lines (22km) of a new tramway system is due to open, serving the city centre and suburban area and linking both sides of the River Garonne. Espace Tram, at 9 place Gambetta, can fill you in on the details.

Car

Street parking is scarce in the centre of town and invariably metered. If you're lucky you may find an unmetered space in the back streets east or west of the Jardin Public. A new scheme may allow free street parking during August only: enquire at the tourist office. Most mid-range and up-market hotels can provide parking space for around €6.10 per night (or per 24 hours: always ask).

The cheapest car parks are the northern

edge of esplanade des Quinconces (€3.05 per day, 6am to 6pm) and opposite place de la Bourse (€1.20 per hour, €6.25 per 12 hours, free overnight). Pricier, shadier car parks are north of allées d'Orléans and allées de Bristol. Sogeparc underground car parks (eg, at allées de Tourny) charge €1.65 per hour or €10.65 per day, 8am to 8pm (€0.75/1.50 per night, 8pm to 8am).

Taxi
Useful *bornes* (taxi ranks) are at Gare St-Jean (☎ 05 56 91 48 11), allées de Tourny (☎ 05 56 81 99 15) and place de la Victoire (☎ 05 56 91 47 05). Among taxis operating 24 hours are Allo Taxis Girondins (☎ 05 56 99 28 41). The tourist office can arrange a one or two-hour sightseeing trip by air-con taxi for €27.45/54.90.

Bicycle
Bordeaux has some 15km of *pistes cyclables* (bike lanes) running north along the riverside from quai Louis XVIII to Bordeaux-Lac.

Bord'Eaux Velos Loisirs (☎ 06 81 83 23 03, fax 05 56 44 77 31, quai Louis XVIII) is open 9.30am to 9pm daily (2.30pm to 6.30pm daily except Tuesday and Thursday between November and April). The company rents bikes and rollerblades at €3 per hour. They also have *voiturettes* for children (€5 per hour); four-person *rosalies* (€16) and *vélos électriques* (€11). This outfit also has a summer-only branch under Place Gambetta (☎ 05 56 51 20 24).

The multilingual *vélos parlants* (talking bikes) available here and the tourist office feature a two-hour recorded tour (€15), an evening tour or one based on the city's wine history.

Cycles Peugeot Pasteur (☎ 05 56 92 68 20, 42 cours Pasteur) is open Monday afternoon to Saturday (Monday afternoon to Friday evening during July and August). This place rents mountain bikes for €10.65/38.10 per day/week.

On the first Sunday of every month, city bikes are available for free. Pick them up by the Monument aux Girondins, and take them down to a traffic-free zone running to the quais.

Around Bordeaux

ST-ÉMILION
postcode 33330 • pop 2500
• elevation 106m

This medieval village, 39km east of Bordeaux, first found fame when Émilion, a miracle-working Benedictine monk from Brittany, lived in a cave here from 750 to 767. A monastery founded on the site became a stop on one of the medieval pilgrimage routes to Santiago de Compostela.

Today St-Émilion is best known for its full-bodied, deep-red wines and its gorgeous, golden-hued medieval houses and monuments – recognised (together with seven surrounding communes or districts) as a Unesco World Heritage Site. The wines and the town's picturesque location above the River Dordogne attract vast numbers of tourists. Try to visit early in the morning or late in the afternoon to see the place at its best.

Orientation & Information
Rue Guadet (the D122) is the main commercial street. From place du Marché a steep lane climbs to the tourist office (☎ 05 57 55 28 28, fax 05 57 55 28 29, e st -emilion.tourisme@wanadoo.fr) at place des Créneaux. It opens 9.30am to 7pm daily (to 8pm in July and August and 9.30am to 12.30pm and 1.45pm to 6.30pm from 1 April to 15 June and 16 September to 31 October; closing at 6pm the rest of the year).

Banks include Crédit Agricole at 6 rue Madame Bouquey. The post office, on rue Guadet, can also exchange foreign currency.

La Maison du Vin
La Maison du Vin (☎ 05 57 55 50 55), on place Pierre Meyrat, has a permanent exhibition on the local wines and a variety of publications (some in English) as well as loads of wine from the 250 local chateaux whose produce it sells. It opens 9.30am to 12.30pm and 2pm to 6pm Monday to Saturday (from 10am between November and March) and 10am to 12.30pm and 2.30pm to 6.30pm on Sunday (9.30am to 7pm daily in August).

BORDEAUX

Wine-tasting sessions (€16.75 per person) take place daily between 16 July and 16 September. The tourist office also organises two-hour bilingual **wine tours** *(adult/child €7.75/4.75; 3.30pm Mon-Sat May, June & Sept; 2pm & 4.15pm July & Aug)* to nearby wine chateaux.

Town Tour

The most interesting sites can be visited only on the 45-minute **guided tours** (in French, with printed English text) operated by the tourist office (adult/student/child aged between 12 and 18 €5.05/3.05/2.45; every 45 minutes 10am-11.30am, 2pm-5.45pm). In the high season, two or three a day are in English.

The 13th-century **Chapelle de la Trinité**, with original frescoes, is just above **Grotte de l'Ermitage**, the saint's famous cave. The **Catacombs**, first used for burials in the 9th century, came to light in the 1950s when a villager attempted to enlarge his wine cellar. In fact, the town sits atop some 200 caves but archaeologists can't excavate them for fear the buildings above might collapse.

The astounding **Église Monolithe**, carved out of solid limestone over the 9th to the

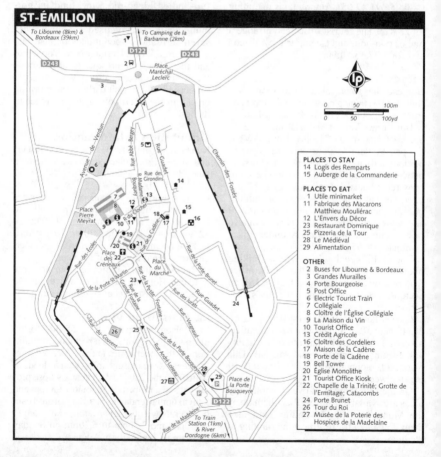

ST-ÉMILION

To Libourne (8km) & Bordeaux (39km)

To Camping de la Barbanne (2km)

D122
D243
D243

Place Maréchal Leclerc

Avenue de Verdun
Rue Abbé-Bergey
Rue Guadet
Chemin-des-Fossés
Rue des Girondins
Rue Madame
R. du Clocher
Rue de la Cadène
Rue de la Porte-Brunet
Rue Guadet
Place Pierre Meyrat
Place des Créneaux
Place du Marché
Rue des Écoles
Rue de la Porte St-Martin
Grande Fontaine
Rue de la Porte-Fontaine
Rue des Jurats
Rue Vergnaud
Rue de la Madeleine
Rue du Couvent
Rue André-Loiseau
Rue de la Porte Bouqueyre
Place de la Porte Bouqueyre
D122

To Train Station (1km) & River Dordogne (6km)

PLACES TO STAY
14 Logis des Remparts
15 Auberge de la Commanderie

PLACES TO EAT
1 Utile minimarket
11 Fabrique des Macarons Matthieu Mouliérac
12 L'Envers du Décor
23 Restaurant Dominique
25 Pizzeria de la Tour
28 Le Médiéval
29 Alimentation

OTHER
2 Buses for Libourne & Bordeaux
3 Grandes Murailles
4 Porte Bourgeoise
5 Post Office
6 Electric Tourist Train
7 Collégiale
8 Cloître de l'Église Collégiale
9 La Maison du Vin
10 Tourist Office
13 Crédit Agricole
16 Cloître des Cordeliers
17 Maison de la Cadène
18 Porte de la Cadène
19 Bell Tower
20 Église Monolithe
21 Tourist Office Kiosk
22 Chapelle de la Trinité; Grotte de l'Ermitage; Catacombs
24 Porte Brunet
26 Tour du Roi
27 Musée de la Poterie des Hospices de la Madelaine

0   50   100m
0   50   100yd

12th centuries, measures 20m by 38m with an 11m-high ceiling. None of the original frescoes have survived but a few hauntingly simple bas-reliefs remain. Scaffolding has been erected in the middle of the church to keep the roof from collapsing due to the weight of the **bell tower** directly above.

The tower *(☎ 05 57 55 28 28, entrance on place des Créneaux; admission €0.90; open same hours as the tourist office)*, a Gothic spire on a Romanesque base, dating from the 12th to 15th centuries, offers a grand view of the village.

Other Things to See
The former **Collégiale** (collegiate church), now a parish church, has a narrow Romanesque nave (12th century) and a spacious, almost square, choir (14th to 16th centuries). The church's 14th-century cloister, **Cloître de l'Église Collégiale**, is accessible via the tourist office.

The **Cloître des Cordeliers** *(rue de la Porte Brunet; admission free; open 8.30am-6.30pm Mon-Fri & 10am-7pm Sat-Sun)* is a ruined monastery with a pleasant garden where you can snack on macaroons or ices bought from the eponymous winery *(☎ 05 57 24 72 07; open 8.30am-6.30pm Mon-Fri & 10am-7pm Sat-Sun)* that has shared the site for over a century. It gives free tours of its cellars of sparkling wine at 3pm, 4pm, 5pm and 6pm daily between April and November (4pm and 5pm other times).

Spectacular views are available from the 13th-century donjon known as the **Tour du Roi** *(King's Tower; ☎ 05 57 24 61 07; admission €0.90; open 10.30am-12.45pm & 2.15pm-at least 6.45pm daily May-Oct; mainly afternoons only Nov-Apr)*.

The **Musée de la Poterie des Hospices de la Madelaine** *(☎ 05 57 55 51 65, 21 rue André Loiseau; adult/student €3.80/1.50; open 10am-7pm daily)* has an attractive display of ancient iron and ceramic pots and jugs.

Several of the city's medieval gates survive, including **Porte de la Cadène** (Gate of the Chain), just off rue Guadet. Next door is **Maison de la Cadène**, a half-timbered house from the early 16th century.

Places to Stay
The tourist office has a list of nearby *chambres d'hôtes* (B&Bs); doubles cost around €45.75-60.95. Cheaper hotel accommodation can be found in Libourne, 8km to the west.

Camping The following is a well equipped camp site close to St-Émilion.

Camping de la Barbanne (☎ 05 57 24 75 80, fax 05 57 24 69 68, ⓔ camping.dom aine.de.la.barbanne@wanadoo.fr, route de Montagne) 2-person forfait €12.20 (€16.45 July-Aug). Open Apr-Sept. This three-star camping ground is on the D122 about 2km north of St-Émilion and boasts two swimming pools, tennis, mini-golf and other activities.

Hotels Hotel options in St-Émilion include the following.

Auberge de la Commanderie (☎ 05 57 24 70 19, fax 05 57 74 44 53, ⓔ contact@ aubergedelacommanderie.com, rue des Cordeliers) Doubles €53.35-83.85 high season, family quads €83.85-111.30. Closed mid-Jan–mid-Feb. The Auberge has a variety of 18 rooms, including six family rooms in a separate annexe.

Logis des Remparts (☎ 05 57 24 70 43, fax 05 57 74 47 44, ⓔ logis-des-remparts@ wanadoo.fr, 18 rue Guadet) Doubles €70.10-85.35 high season. Open Jan-Nov. Logis des Remparts has pleasant rooms (including pricier ones with bath) plus a 12m-long pool.

Places to Eat – Restaurants
There are some good spots to enjoy some good food in St-Émilion.

Restaurant Dominique (☎ 05 57 24 71 00, rue de la Petite Fontaine) Midday *menus* €10.65, evening *menus* €13.55-20.60, dishes €7-10.65. Open Tues-Sat midday and evening & midday only Sun, Sept–mid-Dec & Mar-June; Mon-Sat midday & evening & midday only Sun, July-Aug). Dominique serves excellent regional specialities (eg, *magret de canard*, sliced duck breast in a Sauternes wine sauce, €10.65).

L'Envers du Décor (☎ 05 57 74 48 31, 11 rue du Clocher) Menus €14.95-22.55.

Open midday & evening Mon-Sat, midday only Sun. This popular, attractive bistro offers excellent plats du jour (€9.90), vintage wine by the glass and a delightful garden.

Le Médiéval (☎ *05 57 24 72 37, place de la Porte Bouqueyre) Menus* €13.55-22.85. Generous lunchtime dishes (€7.30) make Le Médiéval a favourite with locals.

Pizzeria de la Tour (☎ *05 57 24 68 91, 19 rue de la Grande Fontaine*) Pizzas & pastas €7.45-11.90. This pizzeria is one of the cheaper places in town to eat.

Places to Eat – Self-Catering

The *Utile* minimarket (☎ *05 57 24 70 08, rue de Montagne*) 150m north of town on the D122, is open 8am to 7pm daily, June to mid-September (to 1pm Sunday and closing for lunch from mid-September to June). The smaller *Alimentation* (☎ *05 57 24 71 77, place de la Porte Bouqueyre)* at the southern entrance to town, operates similar hours.

Fabrique des Marcarons Matthieu Mouliérac (☎ *05 57 74 41 84, rue Tertre de la Tente)* This is the best place to pick up some of St-Émilion's famous macaroons (€4.55 per two dozen), soft biscuits made from egg whites, almond powder and sugar, a recipe brought here in the 17th century by Ursuline nuns.

Getting There & Away

Trains to Bordeaux (€6.85, 40 minutes) run two or three times daily. The last one back usually leaves at 6.27pm. St-Émilion's train station is just over 1km south of town.

Citram Aquitaine buses (☎ 05 56 43 68 43) run from Bordeaux to Libourne (€5.35; 45 minutes; one to three daily except Sunday October to April), where you change to a Marchesseau (☎ 05 57 40 60 79) bus for St-Émilion (€1.80; 15 minutes; two to three daily). The last bus back to Libourne leaves at 5.10pm. The bus stop is on place Maréchal Leclerc at the northern edge of town.

Getting Around

The tourist office rents bicycles for €13.70 per day. An electric tourist train does a 35-minute circuit around the town and nearby vineyards 10 times daily from mid-April to mid-November (adult/child €4.55/3.35). It leaves from av de Verdun.

THE MÉDOC

North-west of Bordeaux, along the shore of the Estuaire de la Gironde (Gironde Estuary), lie some of Bordeaux's most celebrated vineyards, those of Haut Médoc, Margaux and neighbouring *appellations* (wine-producing areas).

Information

The Médoc's central tourist information centre, the Maison du Tourisme et du Vin (☎ 05 56 59 03 08, fax 05 56 29 23 38, e tourismeetvindepauillac@wanadoo.fr) is in Pauillac. It opens 9am to 7pm daily from July to mid-September, 9.30am to 12.30pm and 2pm to 6.30pm daily in June and mid-September to November; 9.30am to 12.30pm and 2pm to 6pm Monday to Saturday, 10am to 12.30pm and 2.30pm to 6pm Sunday in other months. It offers wine-tasting courses, sells some 300 different wines at chateaux prices and can make appointments (for €3.80) to visit specific *chais* (wine cellars). The annual *Médoc Guide Découverte* map-brochure, available here and at other tourist offices, has details on chateaux that welcome visitors. See the Organised Tours section in the Getting There & Away chapter for details of tours through the region.

Vineyards & Chateaux

The gravelly soil of the Médoc's rolling hills nurtures meticulously tended grapevines (mainly Cabernet Sauvignon) that produce

---

Wine-Tasting à Pied

An unusual way to see the Médoc is by running in the Marathon des Châteaux du Médoc (☎ 05 56 59 17 20, fax 05 56 59 62 38, e medoc@vins-medoc.com, w www.marathondumedoc.com). Held in early September (you must book in January), it's limited to 7500 participants, most of whom are in costume and invariably fall for the charms of the wines en route.

some of the world's most sought-after red wines. The most beautiful part of the wine-growing area is along the D2 and D204 north of Pauillac.

Dozens of chateaux are open for visits but it's advisable to telephone ahead even for those where advance reservations are officially unnecessary. Illustrious growers in the Pauillac appellation – famed for their *premier grand cru classé* (the most prestigious classification for excellent wine) – that welcome visitors by appointment only (at least several days in advance in the high season) include the beautifully landscaped **Château Lafite Rothschild** (☎ *01 53 89 78 00, fax 01 53 89 78 01,* e *pm@DBR-Paris.com, 33250 Pauillac; admission free; open 1.30pm-3.30pm Mon-Thur & 1.30pm-2.30pm Fri, Nov-July)*; and **Château Mouton Rothschild** (☎ *05 56 73 21 29, fax 0556 73 21 28, 33250 Pauillac; admission €4.55; open 9.30am-11am & 2pm-4pm Mon-Thur, 9.30am-11am & 2pm-3pm Fri Jan-Dec; 9.30am-11am &*

Get Soaked

If the idea of squishing grapes under your feet has a certain hedonistic appeal, you're going to love *vinothérapie*. This is the latest, most-indulgent beauty treatment, and the world's first spa dedicated to it is at Les Sources de Caudalie (☎ 05 57 83 83 83, e sources@sources-caudalie.com, chemin de Smith Haut Lafitte, 33650 Martillac), in the Graves wine district just south of Bordeaux.

The owners of Château Smith Haut Lafitte estate have turned their leftover grape seeds – packed with anti-ageing polyphenols – not only into a range of beauty products but, since 1999, into the basis for some amazing revitalising treatments. Take your pick from a red-wine bath or wine-and-honey wrap (to improve circulation), a crushed Cabernet-grape-seed scrub or an underwater massage with grape-seed oil. It's delicious, and dear: an introductory day with four treatments costs €122.95. If you fancy an overnight stay at the deluxe spa hotel it'll cost at least €195.15 (minus any vintage wine consumed, of course).

❋ ❋ ❋ ❋ ❋ ❋ ❋ ❋ ❋ ❋ ❋ ❋

2pm-3pm Sat-Sun Apr-Nov) whose wine museum has a fabulous collection of post-war art.

Nearby in the St-Julien appellation, **Château Beychevelle** (☎ *05 56 73 20 70, fax 05 56 73 20 71,* e *beychevelle@beychevelle .com, 33250 St-Julien Beychevelle; admission free; open 10am-noon & 1.30pm-5pm Mon-Fri Apr-June, Sept-Oct; 10am-5pm Mon-Sat July-Aug)* produces *4e grand cru classé* (the 4th-highest classification of excellent wine). About 20km to the south, in Margaux, you can visit the handsome fortified castle and vast, grandiose cellars of **Château Margaux** (☎ *05 57 88 83 83, fax 05 57 88 31 32,* e *chateau-margaux@chateau -margaux.com, 33460 Margaux; admission free; open 10am-noon & 2pm-4pm Mon-Fri all year except Aug & during grape harvest)*. Nearby, 3km south of Margaux, is **Château Palmer** (☎ *05 57 88 72 72, fax 05 57 88 37 16, 33460 Cantenac; admission €4.55 including tasting; open 9am-11.30am & 2pm-5pm daily)* whose wines were classified as *grand cru classé* in 1855.

For more information on Medoc wines, check out the official Web site, w www .medoc-wines.com.

Getting There & Away

From Bordeaux you can reach Pauillac by train (€8.25, one hour, six daily on weekdays, two to four at weekends) or Citram Aquitaine bus (€7.30, one hour, at least seven daily). The Maison du Tourisme et du Vin rents bikes for €10.65 per day. The bike trails are currently in poor condition, however.

A car-ferry service (☎ 05 57 42 04 49) crosses the estuary between Lamarque and Blaye (17km south). The trip costs €2.90/1.35/2.90/11.10 per person/bicycle/motorcycle/car.

The Atlantic Coast

The fine-sand beaches of the Côte d'Argent, backed by dunes, lagoons and the vast pine forest of the Landes, stretch for 230km from Pointe de Grave to Biarritz. This is the perfect family destination, with 200km of easy bicycle trails, quiet lakes (including 16km-long Lac d'Hourtin et de Carcans, France's longest lake), well equipped camp sites and holiday villages. It's ultra-sporty, too, thanks to some of Europe's finest surfing beaches and to the scores of places to sail, kayak, ride a horse or play golf.

SOULAC-SUR-MER
postcode 33780 • pop 2800

This lively summer resort, 9km south of Pointe de Grave, seems an unlikely religious site nowadays but its Romanesque basilica – twice buried by the sands – was once the first stop for English pilgrims heading to Santiago de Compostela (see the boxed text 'The Pilgrims of St-Jacques' in the Facts about Southwest France chapter). The place curls up and hibernates in winter, but you can always take a stroll through the backstreets to view some of the town's 500 Art-Deco or neocolonial villas built in the late 19th century by Bordelais holiday-makers and still presenting a weather-beaten charm.

Orientation & Information
The commercial axis is pedestrianised rue de la Plage, perpendicular to the beach. The tourist office (☎ 05 56 09 86 61, fax 05 56 73 63 76) at No 68 is open 9am to 12.30pm and 2pm to 5.30pm weekdays and 10am to noon, 3pm to 5pm weekends (9am to 7pm daily in July and August; 9am to 7pm weekdays and 9am to noon weekends October to April). It has Internet access, bus and ferry timetables and a booklet (*Circuit découverte des villas anciennes,* €3.05) on the most picturesque old villas. Nearby, at 60 rue de la Plage, there's a Crédit Agricole bank. The post office, which also exchanges currency, is one street north on rue du Maréchal d'Ornano.

Most of the holiday villages and watersports activities are at Plage Sud in L'Amélie, 3km south.

Basilique de Notre Dame de la Fin des Terres
One of many Santiago de Compostela sites on the Unesco World Heritage list is this Romanesque Benedictine abbey *(Esplanade Alienor d'Aquitaine; admission free; open 9am-6pm daily)* with a dramatic name (Our Lady at the End of the Earth). Inside are some finely carved capitals, including one dedicated to Ste Veronica, said to have brought Christianity to the region.

Activities
The swells and the wide, safe beach here are good for bodyboarders and novice surfers. For courses or equipment hire, contact **CAP 33** or **Soulac Surf School** *(both ☎ 05 56 09 82 99, fax 05 56 09 99 78, Centre Municipal Culturel et Sportif, rue du RP Brottier; €56.40/104.40 per 2-day novice/pro course, €15.25 per day surfboard rental).* CAP 33 operates from July to August only (giving free introductory courses to youngsters), Soulac Surf School operates from April to October (for those aged six and over) from Plage Sud.

Places to Stay
Soulac is a popular holiday haunt for Bordelais. Lots of furnished flats or villas are available (€228.65-762.20 per week): The tourist office has a list. Prior reservation is essential for everything in July and August.

Camping Of nearly a dozen nearby sites, four are close to the beach and in shady pine forests at L'Amélie.

Camping des Pins (☎ 05 56 09 85 52, fax 05 56 73 65 58, **e** *campingdespins@ lemel.fr; passe de Formose)* 2-person forfait €12.20. Open June-Oct. This two-star site is set back from the beach a bit but has reasonable facilities.

Camping Les Sables d'Argent (☎ 05 56 09 82 87, fax 05 56 09 94 82, **e** *camping .sables.d.argent@wanadoo.fr,* **w** *www.sables -d-argent.com, blvd de l'Amélie)* 2-person forfait €13.10 (€16.30 July-Sept). Open April-Oct. Les Sables is a well equipped three-star site of 2.6 acres, right on the beach.

Euronat (☎ 05 56 73 24 52, fax 05 56 09 39 73, **e** *info@euronat.fr; 33590 Grayan et L'Hôpital)* 2-person forfait €19.05, 4-person 'ready-to-live-in' tent €36.60, 4-person studio €59.45 (July-Aug prices). Euronat, 10km south, is one of two huge, well equipped naturist camp sites in the area, with 1.5km of beachfront, indoor heated pool and free activities (eg, archery, jazz, arts and crafts) in the high season. For more on naturism in the region, see Activities in the Facts for the Visitor chapter.

Hotels Among the few hotels in the town itself are the following.

Hôtel La Dame de Coeur (☎ *05 56 09 80 80, fax 05 56 09 97 47, 103 rue de la Plage)* Singles/doubles/triples €30.50/38.10/45.75. This run-down, unstarred hotel has the cheapest, plainest rooms in town. Reception only opens at 6pm in the low season.

Hôtel Lescorce (☎ *05 56 09 84 13, 36 rue Trouche)* Singles €35.80, doubles €48.80-54.85 including breakfast. Open Apr-Oct. The Lescorce, a lovely villa 300m southwest of the church, has been run by the same family for over a century and has a pleasant garden and conservatory.

Hôtel L'Hacienda (☎ *05 56 09 81 34, fax 05 56 73 65 57, 4 av Perier de Larsan)* Singles €41.15-56.40, doubles €39.65-54.85. Half-board (€51.85) may be obligatory in August. The Logis de France L'Hacienda, 150m south of the church, offers comfortable, well equipped rooms.

Places to Eat & Drink

Spots to eat or drink in Soulac-sur-Mer include the following.

Le Nautilus (☎ *05 56 09 90 38, 2 rue de la Plage)* Pizzas €7.45-9.30. Beachfront Le Nautilus is a relaxing, low-key venue popular with all ages.

Le California (☎ *05 56 73 65 43, 2 esplanade des Girondins)* Menus €10.65-14.50, dishes €9.25-13.70. Open mid-April to Oct. Friendly, seafront California serves generous portions of Tex-Mex food and paellas, but watch the drinks bill.

Le Pavillon de la Mer (☎ *05 56 09 80 82, 19 rue de la Plage)* Midday *menus* €10.65, evening *menus* €13.70-36.60, seafood platter €18.30. This is an upmarket option, with pleasant outdoor seating.

Café le Rallye (☎ *05 56 09 71 49, 70 rue de la Plage)* This cafe-bar not only has a huge sports video screen but also an artisan

barman, Jean-Claude Debourg, who makes fantastic scale models of Soulac's old villas in between serving customers.

Opposite the tourist office is a *covered food market*, open until 1pm daily.

Getting There & Away

Bus & Train Soulac is linked to Bordeaux by train (€12.50, two hours, change at Lesparre, four daily), SNCF bus (€12.50, two hours, two to five daily) or Citram Aquitaine bus (€12.35, two hours, three to five daily). From Pointe de Grave there are two to four buses daily (€1.80, 15 minutes). Soulac's bus stand is near the basilica, and the train station is 700m south of town.

Ferry Soulac is linked with Royan, across the estuary, by a car-ferry service (☎ 05 56 73 37 73; 25 minutes, six to 17 daily) from Le Verdon, 2km south of Pointe de Grave. Fares are €2.90/1.35/2.90/19.80 per person/bicycle/motorcycle/car. The service runs from 7am (6.30am July and August; 8am winter weekends) to 8.30pm (9.30pm from Royan), or until 6.30pm (7.15pm from Royan) outside July and August.

Getting Around

There are excellent bike trails from Soulac along the coast to Pointe de Grave (9km), or through the pine forests to Montalivet (18km); the tourist office can supply a map.

Cyclo Star (☎ 05 56 09 71 38, 9 rue Fernand Laffargue) Open 9.30am-noon, 2pm-7pm daily Apr-Sept (to at least 8pm in summer). One block west of the post office, Cyclo Star rents all kinds of bikes (VTTs €11.45 per day).

A little tourist train, called PGVS or Le Petit Train (☎ 05 56 09 61 78), does a one-hour, Pointe de Grave–Le Verdon–Soulac circuit five times daily in July and August (twice daily on weekends in May and June and daily during the Easter holidays) for €3.80 return (child €1.50).

CARCANS-MAUBUISSON

postcode 33121 • pop 1580

If you're more into get-fit than get-a-tan, this is the place for you. With both the ocean and a huge lake on its doorstep, plus excellent biking trails, the adjacent holiday hubs of Carcans-Maubuisson can offer everything from cycling, land yachting or tennis to every kind of water sport, especially surfing. Dozens of camp sites, holiday villages and chalets are tucked away in the pine forests. With an official 'Kid Station' (ie, kid-friendly) accreditation, it's perfect for families.

Orientation

As with several other towns along this stretch of coast, Carcans has both an inland town (Carcans-Ville) and, 12km to the west, a coastal one (Carcans-Océan). Between the two there's a lake – Lac d'Hourtin et de Carcans – France's longest. There's also a sizable midway town, Maubuisson (7km west of Carcans-Ville) and a special sports and activities area, Domaine de Bombannes (4km north of Maubuisson) on the shores of the lake. Most of the activity is centred in Maubuisson.

Information

The tourist office (☎ 05 56 03 34 94, fax 05 56 03 43 76, e tourisme@carcans-maubuisson.com, w www.carcans-maubuisson.com) is at Maison de la Station, 127 av de Maubuisson, in Maubuisson. It opens 9am to 12.30pm and 2pm to 6.30pm Monday to Saturday, 10am to 12.30pm and 2.30pm to 6pm Sunday (7am to 7pm daily in July and August; 9am to 12.30pm and 1.30pm to 6pm Monday to Friday and 9am to 12.30pm Saturday from October to April).

It has an Internet facility and masses of documentation on the area's activities, including a free map *Plan des Pistes Cyclables,* showing the local bike trails. A post office and bank are in the same building.

Réserve Naturelle de l'Étang de Cousseau

This protected lake, between Lac d'Hourtin et de Carcans and Lac de Lacanau, is a haven for birds and other wildlife. There are free guided visits (usually daily, in French only) from July to September. The tourist office has details.

Activities

UCPA (☎ 05 56 03 38 00, fax 05 56 03 43 07, e upca.bombannes@ucpa.asso.fr) in Bombannes is the biggest operator, renting windsurfs, catamarans, canoes, etc, and running all kinds of watersport courses (including for those aged five and over); two-hour windsurfing courses cost €76.20/60.95 adult/child.

Sailing is also provided at Bombannes by **Cercle de la Voile de Bordeaux** (☎ 05 56 03 30 19, fax 05 56 03 45 01, e jegric@aol .com, w www.asso.ffv.fr/cvbordeaux), costing €25.90/22.85 adult/child for two-hour *séances,* plus various longer courses.

Right on the beach at Carcans-Océan, **Surf Club** (☎ 05 56 03 41 81, fax 05 57 70 16 82, w www.carcans.surfclub.free.fr, *Maison de la Glisse*) offers a two-hour 'initiation' course for €27.45.

Char à voile (land yachting) and speed sailing are organised by **Sail-Wheeling-Club** (☎ 05 57 70 14 60, fax 05 56 03 37 40, e s.w .c.carcans@free.fr, av du Pouch, Carcans-Océan). Introductory one-hour courses by the lake at Maubuisson cost €10.65/7.60 adult/child.

Places to Stay & Eat

There are over a dozen camp sites clustered around Carcans-Ville, plus holiday villages and *locations meublés* (furnished accommodation) galore. The tourist office has all the details. Other options include the following.

Camping de Maubuisson (☎ 05 56 03 30 12, fax 05 56 03 47 93, e camping .maubuisson@wanadoo.fr, 81 av de Maubuisson) 1-2 people & tent €12.60-16.75, car €2. Open Mar-Dec. Near the lake in Maubuisson, this large, two-star site is one of the best equipped in the area.

Camping Municipal (☎/fax 05 56 03 41 44, Carcans-Océan) 1-2 people & tent €10.50-13.05, car €1.15. Open Apr-Oct. This is the only site near the beach, simple but shady. Over a dozen other camp sites are clustered around Carcans-Ville.

Chez Heidi (☎ 05 56 03 42 92, av des Dunes, Carcans-Océan) Grilled ham €9.90. Right by the beach, this well known restaurant (famous for its grilled ham) also serves other simple dishes.

Getting There & Away
Cars Ouest Aquitaine (☎ 05 56 70 17 27) runs buses from Bordeaux's Gare St-Jean to Carcans-Ville and Maubuisson at least once daily (€10.65, 1½ hours), and on to Carcans-Océan (€10.65, 1¾ hours, one to three daily). Services are fewer on Sunday and in the low season (September to July).

Getting Around
Bikes are a perfect way to get around this area, and you can hire them from Locations de Velos (☎ 05 57 70 16 92, Carrefour des Mimosas, Maubuisson), located 200m west of the tourist office. This rental company charges €9.25/47.25 per day/week for a VTT. It opens from April to November.

LACANAU
postcode 33680 • pop 2800
This little resort, with some of the finest surfing in the southwest, hosts 120,000 World Surfing Championship spectators at the Lacanau Pro in late August. Even in July you'll share Lacanau with about 80,000 visitors, so you'll need to book accommodation well in advance.

Orientation
Inland Lacanau Ville (also known as Lacanau Médoc or just Lacanau), on Lac de Lacanau, is 13km east of the livelier, coastal Lacanau Océan. There are four main beaches, from plage Nord, 800m north of the centre, to plage Super Sud, 1km south.

Information
Lacanau Océan's tourist office (☎ 05 56 03 21 01, fax 05 56 03 11 89, e lacanau@ lacanau.com, w www.lacanau.com, Place de l'Europe) is 400m east of the seafront blvd de la Plage. It opens 9am to 7pm daily in July and August; 9am to noon and 1pm to 6.30pm daily in September, May and June; 9am to noon and 1pm to 5.30pm October and April; 9am to noon and 1pm to 6.30pm Monday to Saturday and 9am to noon Sunday November to March. It has

an Internet facility, but only from June to September.

You can exchange money at the post office (opposite the tourist office) and at Crédit Agricole on av Garnung (from the tourist office head seaward and turn left).

Surfing, Bodyboarding & Windsurfing
Lacanau's surf clubs offer lessons (typically from €25.90 for two hours), courses (€229 five days) and surf camps with cheap accommodation. Many cater for kids. July and August rates are about 10% higher.

Lacanau Surf Club (☎ 05 56 26 38 84, fax 05 56 26 38 85, e courrier_l@lacanausurf .com, Maison de la Glisse, w www.lacanau surf.com) At the far northern end of blvd de la Plage, this surf club is the official organiser of the Lacanau Pro, offering everything from kids' courses (for those aged five and over) to 20-hour 'perfectionist' adult courses.

Surf Sans Frontiers (☎ 05 56 26 22 80, fax 05 56 03 02 19, e contact@ssf.fr, Villa Margalex, blvd de la Plage, w www.ssf.fr) This outfit has a range of weekend to 12-day courses.

Les Dauphins (☎ 05 56 26 33 55, fax 05 56 03 19 66, e lesdauphins@multimania .com, 23 rue des Ecureuils, plage Sud) This club caters especially for youngsters.

Bo & Co (☎ 05 56 26 33 99, fax 05 57 70 09 61, e olivier-beudou@bosurf.com, 5 av Poincaré) This is a small outfit that offers surfing and bodyboarding as well as longboard courses.

Voile Lacanau Guyenne (☎ 05 56 03 05 11, fax 05 56 26 23 34, e V.L.G@wanadoo .fr, Club House de la Grande Escoure) On the western shore of Lac de Lacanau, this club provides both sailing and catamaran courses, plus surfing and windsurfing.

Places to Stay
Lacanau has tons of accommodation options (ask the tourist office about the many *villas* and *apartments* for rent), including camp sites and hotels on the seafront.

Les Grands Pins (☎ 05 56 03 20 77, fax 05 57 70 03 89, e grands.pins@wanadoo.fr) 2-person forfait €25. Open May–mid-Sept.

Of eight camp sites around Lacanau, this one, 350m from plage Nord, is the closest to the sea.

Wave Trotters (☎ 05 56 03 13 01, fax 05 56 03 19 87, av Sylvain Marian) Dorm beds €12.95-18.30, doubles €24.40-33.55. Wave Trotters, 300m west of the tourist office, is a dinky villa popular with surfers. It has two kitchens. For information, go to Mata Hari surf shop at 2 rue Jules Ferry (next to Le Summertime bar on blvd de la Plage).

Villa Zénith (☎ 05 56 26 36 49, fax 05 56 03 23 77, e lacanau-z@ifrance.com, 16 av Adjudant Guittard) Dorm beds €15.25, chalet bed €12.95. Open Apr-Nov. This lovely old villa, 200m north-west of the tourist office, has a kitchen and BBQ facility. Washing facilities are in a separate block.

Hôtel-Restaurant Le Marian (☎ 05 56 03 21 02, fax 05 56 03 16 47, 19 allée Pierre Ortal) Doubles €38.10-79.25 including breakfast. Le Marian, on the main road to the beach, has decent rooms all with shower, WC, TV and telephone.

Hotel L'Oyat (☎ 05 56 03 11 11, fax 05 56 03 12 29, Front de Mer) Doubles €60.95-94.50. Open Apr-Nov. The modern two-star Hotel L'Oyat is right on the seafront.

Places to Eat
Among the many pizzerias and cafes in Lacanau are a few more interesting venues, including the following.

Chez L'Australien (☎ 05 56 03 21 02, fax 05 56 03 16 47, 19 allée Pierre Ortal) Dishes €5.80-11.45 in bar-brasserie, *menus* €22.10-28.20 in restaurant. Part of the Hôtel-Restaurant Le Marian (see Places to Stay) this has both a casual bar-brasserie and an adjoining, spiffy restaurant, open evenings only and Sunday lunchtime.

Casa Lolita (☎ 05 56 26 39 94, blvd de la Plage) Tapas €3.05-3.80, dishes €9.90-12.20. This cosy spot right on the seafront serves delicious tapas and other Spanish specialities.

La Taverne de Neptune (☎ 05 56 03 21 33, place de l'Europe) Midday/evening *menus* €11.90/19.65, fish dishes €14.95-21.35. The Neptune, opposite the tourist office, has a good range of dishes and relaxing ambience.

Nearby is a *Spar supermarket*, open 8am to 8pm Monday to Saturday and 8am to 1pm Sunday in high season.

Getting There & Away
Cars Ouest Aquitaine (☎ 05 56 70 17 27) run a number of buses to Bordeaux via Lacanau Ville (€10.65, 1¼ hours, three to five daily).

Getting Around
Bike rental outfits include Locacycle (☎ 05 56 26 30 99), near the tourist office, where VTTs and *vélos tous chemins* (VTCs; bikes suitable for all paths) cost €9.90/53.35 per day/week. It opens 9am to 9pm daily April to October.

ARCACHON
postcode 33120 • pop 11,400 (50,000 in summer)

Arcachon became popular with bourgeois Bordelais at the end of the 19th century, thanks to a casino, luxury seaside hotels and a new railway line. Today the attractions are seafood – especially *huîtres* (oysters) – a broad beach, and the extraordinary Dune du Pilat (see Around Arcachon later in this section). The resort is well served by trains and makes an easy day trip from Bordeaux.

Orientation
Arcachon is on the southern shore of the Bassin d'Arcachon (Arcachon Basin), linked to the Atlantic by a 3km-wide channel west of town. Across the channel is the peninsula of Cap Ferret, Aquitaine's mini-St-Tropez, buzzing with beautiful folk all summer.

The town has two distinct quarters: the summertime, bayfront Ville d'Été and the sheltered, inland Ville d'Hiver to the south.

Information
The tourist office (☎ 05 57 52 97 97, fax 05 57 52 97 77, e tourisme@arcachon.com), on place Président Roosevelt, is open 9am to 12.30pm and 2pm to 6pm Monday to Saturday and 10am to 1pm Sunday (9am to 7pm Monday to Saturday and 9am to 1pm Sunday during July and August). Between October and April it closes at 5pm weekdays and all-day Sunday.

Banks include Crédit Agricole, 252 blvd de la Plage. The main post office, at place Président Roosevelt, has an Internet facility.

The laundrette, at the corner of blvd Général Leclerc and rue Molière, is open 7am to 10pm daily.

Central Arcachon
The liveliest part of the Ville d'Été is around the **Jetée Thiers** (Thiers Pier).

The **Ville d'Hiver** dates from the start of the 20th century, when rich Bordelais came to amuse themselves or recover from tuberculosis. A lift near the southern end of rue du Maréchal de Lattre de Tassigny climbs to **Parc Mauresque**, where you can see a model of the ornate 19th-century Casino Mauresque, burned to a cinder in 1977.

A verdant promenade runs west and south from plage d'Arcachon to **plage Péreire**, **plage des Abatilles** and **Pyla-sur-Mer**. Cycle paths link Arcachon with Biscarrosse, 30km to the south, and towns around the bay.

Casino
The casino (☎ 05 56 83 41 44, e arcachon@ europe-casinos.com, 163 blvd de la Plage) in the fairy-tale former Château Deganne, is

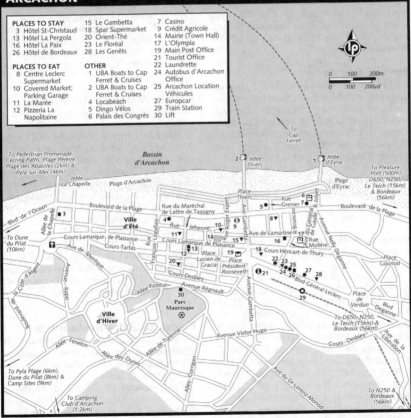

ARCACHON

PLACES TO STAY		
3	Hôtel St-Christaud	
13	Hôtel La Pergola	
16	Hôtel La Paix	
26	Hôtel de Bordeaux	

PLACES TO EAT		
8	Centre Leclerc Supermarket	
10	Covered Market; Parking Garage	
11	La Marée	
12	Pizzeria La Napolitaine	

15	Le Gambetta	
18	Spar Supermarket	
20	Orient-Thé	
23	Le Floréal	
28	Les Genêts	

OTHER		
1	UBA Boats to Cap Ferret & Cruises	
2	UBA Boats to Cap Ferret & Cruises	
4	Locabeach	
5	Dingo Vélos	
6	Palais des Congrès	

7	Casino	
9	Crédit Agricole	
14	Mairie (Town Hall)	
17	L'Olympia	
19	Main Post Office	
21	Tourist Office	
22	Laundrette	
24	Autobus d'Arcachon Office	
25	Arcachon Location Véhicules	
27	Europcar	
29	Train Station	
30	Lift	

worth a look even if you don't toss a coin into one of its 80 machines. The machines are open 10am to 4am daily (blackjack and roulette open from 9.30am). 'Appropriate attire' is requested but there's no strict policy.

Boat Excursions
Union des Bateliers Arcachonnais *(UBA;* ☎ *05 57 72 28 28, fax 05 56 83 21 50)* runs daily cruises around Île aux Oiseaux (Bird Island) in the bay (adult/child €12.20/9.25) twice daily April-June and five times daily in July and August, from both piers. Once daily (usually 11am) in July and August, and at weekends and by request in June, UBA goes to Banc d'Arguin (€12.20), a sandbank off the Dune du Pilat. At very high tide, UBA boats also sail up the River Leyre. A variety of other tours and fishing excursions are also offered: Pick up a UBA brochure for details.

Special Events
For a week in late September, Arcachon hosts the Festival de Cinéma au Féminin, an international women's film festival, which awards hotly contested prizes. Films are shown in L'Olympia on av du Général de Gaulle and the Palais des Congrès, blvd Veyrier Montagnères (behind the casino).

Places to Stay
In July and August, accommodation is scarce and many hotels require that you take half board.

Camping & Hostel Camping and budget hostel accommodation is provided in and around Arcachon.

Camping Club d'Arcachon (☎ *05 56 83 24 15, fax 05 57 52 28 51, 1 allée de la Galaxie)* 1-3 people forfait €9.15-22.85. This shady camp site, 1.2km south of town, is the nearest. See Around Arcachon later in this section for details of other options.

Auberge de Jeunesse (☎ *05 56 60 64 62, 87 av de Bordeaux)* Dorm beds €6.85. Open July & Aug only. Reception open 7.30am-1pm, 6pm-9pm. This small, idyllic hostel, across the bay in Cap Ferret, fills up fast. There's no restaurant or kitchen.

Hotels – Budget The following prices are all high season.

Hôtel La Paix (☎*/fax 05 56 83 05 65, 8 av de Lamartine)* Singles/doubles/triples without shower €31.25/33.55/43.15; singles/doubles/quads with shower & WC €41.30/43.60/66.45, all including breakfast. Half-board singles/doubles €50.30/61.90. Studio apartments €487.85 per week. Open late-Apr–Nov (apartments Apr-Oct). This charming, family-run hotel is a particular favourite. From June to September, half board is obligatory.

Hôtel St-Christaud (☎*/fax 05 56 83 38 53, 8 allée de la Chapelle)* Singles/doubles without shower €30.50/33.55, with shower €33.55/38.10, doubles with WC & shower €45.75. Reception opens 4pm in the low season. It's seen better days but the hotel's spacious rooms (some with additional bunk beds) overlooking a tiny courtyard have a certain charm. New owners are gradually improving facilities.

Hotels – Mid-Range For those after a little more luxury, Arcachon has some pricier hotels.

Hôtel La Pergola (☎ *05 56 83 07 89, fax 05 56 83 14 21, 40 cours Lamarque de Plaisance)* Doubles with/without shower & WC €63.55/42.70, studios €396.35 per week. Considering its central location, the old-fashioned Pergola offers reasonable rates. There are no hall showers available for the two double rooms without shower.

Hôtel de Bordeaux (☎ *05 56 83 80 30, fax 05 56 83 69 02, 39 blvd Général Leclerc)* Singles/doubles with shower & WC €38.10/53.35-64. Half board (€68.60) encouraged July-Aug. This traditional hotel, opposite the train station, has plain rooms but a good bar-brasserie.

Places to Eat – Restaurants
In summer, the cheapest places are the *pizzerias* and *creperies* along the seafront. Many places also offer mounds of mussels for a bargain €7.60.

Le Gambetta (☎ *05 57 52 29 69, 25 av Gambetta)* Plat du jour €9.25, *menus* €12.95-16. Central Le Gambetta has a huge range of dishes and a great people-watching location.

Le Floréal (☎ 05 56 83 48 44, 49 blvd Général Leclerc) Plat du jour €6.10, *menus* €11.45. Easy-going Le Floréal attracts lots of locals.

Pizzeria La Napolitaine (☎ 05 57 52 20 50, 28 rue du Maréchal de Lattre de Tassigny) 3-course *menus* €7.30. Great prices at this tiny, simple place; on the same road are other Italian, Chinese and Indian restaurants.

Orient-Thé (☎ 05 57 52 29 11, 39 rue du Maréchal de Lattre de Tassigny) Menus €12.05, dishes €6.40-13.70. Open lunch only Tues-Sat (lunch & dinner daily July & Aug). The vegetarian Orient-Thé has an enticingly large choice of dishes.

La Marée (☎ 05 56 83 24 05, 21 rue du Maréchal de Lattre de Tassigny) Seafood *menus* €15.10-22.10, dishes €10.65-15.25. Open midday & evening Wed-Sun, & midday only Mon. The attractive Marée is highly regarded for its excellent fresh seafood at reasonable prices.

Les Genêts (☎ 05 56 83 40 28, 25 blvd Général Leclerc) Seafood *menus* €15.55-22.85, dishes €7.60-18.30. Open midday & evening Tues-Sat, & midday only Sun. You can be sure of a fine dinner at this posh place.

Self-Catering

The *covered market* (rue Roger Expert), beneath a car park, is open 8am to 1pm daily. Supermarkets include *Spar* (57 blvd Général Leclerc) and *Centre Leclerc* (☎ 05 56 83 25 21, 224 blvd de la Plage), both open daily except Sunday afternoon.

Getting There & Away

Arcachon is best reached from Bordeaux by train (€8.25, 45 minutes, nine to 17 daily). The last one back to Bordeaux leaves at 8pm (9.50pm on Sunday and holidays, 9pm on other nights in July and August).

From June to September, UBA runs hourly ferries from Jetée Thiers and Jetée d'Eyrac to Cap Ferret (€5.35/9.25 one way/return). Off season, there is at least one run (four in April, May and October) each on Monday, Wednesday, Friday and Sunday from Jetée Thiers.

Getting Around

Car & Motorcycle There's unmetered parking at the train station, south of the casino on av de Gaulle and at the western end of blvd de la Plage.

Car-rental firms include Europcar (☎ 05 56 83 48 00), at 35 blvd Général Leclerc, and a cheaper local outfit, Arcachon Location Véhicules (☎ 05 57 72 40 40), at No 43. Locabeach (☎ 05 56 83 39 64), 326 blvd de la Plage, rents mopeds/scooters from €18.30/32 per day.

Bicycle You can rent VTTs and VTCs at Locabeach (see Car & Motorcycle) for €12.20 per day. Dingo Vélos (☎ 05 56 83 44 09, rue Grenier), open 9.30am to 7pm daily (to midnight in July and August), has similar rates but a bigger (crazier) variety of bikes, including *dos à dos* (push-me-pull-yous).

AROUND ARCACHON
Dune du Pilat

The remarkable Dune du Pilat (or Dune de Pyla) is Europe's highest sand dune, some 114m high. It begins 8km south of Arcachon along the D218 and stretches for almost 3km. While the sea-facing side is gentle and dotted with grass, the inland side is steep enough to ski down. At the bottom, dead trees smothered by the dune as it moves relentlessly eastwards – at about 4.5m each year – poke out of the sand.

The view from the top is magnificent. To the west are the shoals at the mouth of the Bassin d'Arcachon and Cap Ferret. Eastwards, almost as far as the eye can see, stretch the dense pine forests of the Landes. The GR8 passes nearby.

Be careful while swimming in this area as powerful currents can swirl around the small sandy bays, especially when the sea is rough.

Places to Stay On the inland side of the dune are five pine-shaded, pricey camp sites, including this one.

La Forêt (☎ 05 56 22 73 28, fax 05 56 22 70 50, e camping.foret@hol.fr, route de Biscarrosse) 2-person forfait €22.85. This place is open from Easter to October.

Getting There & Away Autobus d'Arcachon (☎ 05 56 83 07 60) runs between Arcachon train station and the camp sites (€2.90, 23 minutes, two to four daily), and every 45 minutes to the Dune du Pilat car park (€2.60). From September to June, buses go only to Pyla Plage (Haïtza), 1km from the dune (€1.80, five to seven times daily). Pick up timetables from Autobus d'Arcachon, 47 blvd du Général Leclerc or the tourist office.

Gujan-Mestras

The Arcachon Basin is renowned for its oysters and Gujan-Mestras is the basin's oyster-farming capital. Along some 9km of the inland sea, east of Arcachon, is a string of seven oyster-fishing ports, home to dozens of *producteurs* and their flat-bottomed *pinasses* (oyster boats). La Barbotière is the busiest port, but Port de Larros is where you'll find the **Maison de l'Huître** (☎ 05 56 66 23 71; adult/child €2.45/1.50; open 10am-noon & 2.30pm-6.30pm daily Mar-Oct; Mon-Sat Oct-Mar), a small museum beside a row of the fishermen's *cabanes* (wooden shacks), with displays on the history and method of oyster farming.

Orientation & Information Consisting of four districts in all, Gujan-Mestras is strung out along the D650. From west to east, the districts are: La Hume, Meyran, Gujan and Mestras. The tourist office (☎ 05 56 66 12 65, fax 05 56 66 94 44), 16 av de Lattre de Tassigny, is in La Hume (on the D650, 100m east of La Hume train station). It opens 8.30am to 12.30pm and 2.30pm to 7.30pm Monday to Saturday (9am to noon on Sunday from mid-June to September); 8.30am to noon and 2pm to 6pm Monday to Saturday from mid-September to June. Pick up the free brochure, *La Route de l'Huître*, which lists oyster-related activities and oyster sellers.

From La Hume it's 4.5km east to Gujan and the Maison de l'Huître (400m west of Gujan-Mestras train station).

The major oyster event of the year is La Foire aux Huîtres, a four-day celebration in mid-August with special restaurant menus, music and sporting events, and naturally *dégustation des huîtres* (oyster tasting).

Places to Eat In Port de Larros, several producteurs offer oyster tastings from their simple cabanes.

Cabane 117 (☎ 06 85 23 59 76) Dozen oysters €2.60-3.50, €6.10-9.25 including bread & glass of wine. Open around 11am-6pm. This is one of many cabanes overlooking the harbour, where you can sit and savour the finest Banc d'Arguin oysters.

Les Pavois (☎ 05 56 66 38 71) Midday *menu pecheur* €12.95, six large oysters €6.70. Open daily April-Oct. Next to the Maison de l'Huître, this pleasant restaurant has an outdoor terrace overlooking the harbour.

Getting There & Away Trains from Arcachon to La Hume (€1.35, seven minutes) or Gujan-Mestras (€1.80, ten minutes) run every one to two hours.

Parc de Loisirs

Some 3km south of La Hume, on the Route des Lacs (just off the N250) is a cluster of family-geared attractions including: **Aqualand** (☎ 08 92 68 66 13; adult/child under 12 €15.55/13.70; open 10am-6pm daily June, 10am-7pm or 8pm daily July-Aug), an aquatic funfair; **La Coccinelle** (☎ 05 56 66 30 41; adult/child under 14 €7.15/5.65; open 10am-6.30pm daily 24 May-June; 10.30am-7.30pm daily July & Aug), an amusement park and petting zoo; **Kid Parc** (☎ 05 56 66 06 90; adult/child aged 2-12 €5.35/10.50; open 11am-6.30pm Sat-Sun 28 Apr-May; 11am-6.30pm daily June; 10.30am-7pm daily July-Sept), a vast playground including fairground attractions, water rides, trampolines and clown performances.

Parc Ornithologique du Teich

The Parc Ornithologique du Teich (W www .parc-ornithologique-du-teich.com), within the Parc Naturel Régional des Landes de Gascogne, is an important centre for the preservation of endangered species and a fine place to see some of Europe's rarest, most beautiful birds (also see the main section on the Parc later in this chapter).

The Parc Ornithologique is 15km east of Arcachon on the D650. Le Teich's train station, 1.2km south of the park, is on the line linking Bordeaux (€6.85, 35 minutes) with Arcachon (€2.45, 15 minutes), with at least ten connections daily.

BISCARROSSE
postcode 40600 • pop 10,000

Biscarrosse, 30km south of Arcachon, is one of the Landes department's most popular resorts, thanks partly to its proximity to two lakes, étang de Cazaux et de Sanguinet (Lac Nord for short) and étang de Biscarrosse et de Parentis (or Lac Sud). Not so well publicised is the large oilfield at Parentis-en-Born and the strictly off-limits Centre d'Essais des Landes missile range between Biscarrosse and Mimizan, but you're unlikely to notice them once you get seduced by Biscarrosse's aquatic charms.

Orientation & Information

The tourist office (☎ 05 58 78 20 96, fax 05 58 78 23 65, ℮ biscarrosse@biscarrosse .com, ⓦ www.biscarrosse.com, place de la Fontaine) is in Biscarrosse Plage, on the coast 10km west of Biscarrosse Ville (or Biscarrosse Bourg). It opens 9am to 12.30pm and 2pm to 6.30pm on weekdays, and 10am to 12.30pm and 3pm to 6pm on weekends (9am to 7pm daily in July and August, closing at 10pm 7 July to 19 August). It has a good descriptive regional map (€0.75) showing bike trails.

The main post office is in Biscarrosse Ville, at 102 rue de la Poste. Cybercafe L'Estrela (☎ 05 58 78 74 86), 93 av de la République, 700m north of the church, is open 10am to 12.30pm and 4pm to 1am daily Monday to Wednesday, Friday and Saturday (4pm to 1am on Sunday). Internet access costs €4.55/7.60 per 30/60 minutes.

Musée Historique de l'Hydraviation

This little museum (☎ 05 58 78 00 65, 332 av Louis Bréguet; adult/child aged 6-12 €3.80/0.75; open 3pm-7pm daily Apr-June, Sept-Oct; 10am-7pm daily July-Aug; 2pm-6pm daily Nov-Apr) in Biscarrosse Ville exhibits full-size seaplanes and lots of aviation paraphernalia. Biscarrosse's big, sheltered lakes made it a centre of interwar seaplane development, with St-Exupéry and other pioneers flying from here.

Activities

Biscarrosse Plage has several companies offering surf or bodyboard courses, including **La Vigie Maison du Surf** (☎ 05 58 78 37 79, fax 05 58 78 37 79, ℮ lavigie-surf@wanadoo .fr, 31 rue Grand Vivier; €13.70 introductory hour, €3.15 per hour board rental).

Sailing and scuba-diving outfits use Lac Nord, especially Port Maguide, on the western shore and Navarrosse on the south. **B Plongée** (☎ 06 03 17 47 19, fax 05 56 66 59 34, ℮ b.plongee@wanadoo.fr, La Vigie, rue Grand Vivier, Biscarrosse Plage, €30.50-38.10 introductory scuba-diving course, daily from July-Aug); **Centre Nautique Biscarrosse Olympique** (☎ 05 58 78 10 51, fax 05 58 78 73 49, ℮ cnbiscarrosse@aol.com, Port de Navarrosse, €53.95 per hour private sailing or windsurfing lesson, (105.20/76.25 5-day sailing course adult/child, (6.30/8.10 per hour kayak/canoe).

For hikers and horse-riders, the GR8 meanders past both lakes.

Places to Stay

The area has both camp sites and hotels to choose from.

Camping Lou Galip (☎ 05 58 09 81 81, fax 05 58 09 86 03, 710 chemin de Navarrosse) 2-person forfait €12.35. There are nine shady lakeside camp sites including this simple one at Navarrosse, which has a swimming pool.

Campéole Le Vivier (☎ 05 58 78 25 76, fax 05 58 78 35 23, ℮ cpllevivier@ ATCIAT.com, 681 rue du Tit) 2-person forfait €16.95. Open May–mid-Sept. This site is 800m from the beach (plus it has a pool) and organises summertime activities.

Hôtel Les Fermes d'En Chon (☎/fax 05 58 78 13 52, 346 chemin d'En Chon) Doubles €32-38.10. This is a good-value hotel in a forest location near Lac Sud.

Les Jardins de L'Océan (☎ 05 58 83 98 98, fax 05 58 78 32 03, 1068 av de la Plage) Doubles €45.75-76.20. Just 800m from the beach, Les Jardins has a relaxing ambience (and a pool).

Places to Eat

There's not a huge choice of restaurants around but these two are worthwhile.

Restaumer (☎ 05 58 78 20 26, rue Pietonnée, 210 av de la Plage, Biscarrosse Plage) Menu de la mer €15.25, fish dishes €9.25-19.50. If you fancy a seafood splurge, this big, smart restaurant near the beach could fit the bill nicely.

Uncle Sam's Saloon (☎ 05 58 78 80 80, 236 av Latécoère, Biscarrosse Ville) Enchiladas €10.65, T-Bone steak €19.05. Open 7pm-2am daily. Texan and Mexican fun and fare is on the menu at this cowboy-style outfit 400m south-west of the church (en route to the Musée de l'Hydraviation). Expect live music on Friday or Saturday night.

Getting There & Away

Les Rapides Côte d'Argent buses (☎ 05 58 09 10 89) connect Bordeaux Gare St-Jean with Biscarrosse Ville (€9, 1¾ hours, one to three daily). In July and August only a *navette* minibus shuttles visitors between the Ville and Plage (€2, 20 minutes, five daily); Autobus d'Arcachon (☎ 05 56 83 07 60) runs to Arcachon (€5.95, one hour, three to four daily); and a bus links Biscarrosse (Plage and Ville) with Ychoux train station, on the Bordeaux–Dax line, 17km east of Biscarrosse Ville (€4.85, 20 minutes, two daily).

Getting Around

Bike-rental outfits include Cycles Evasion (☎ 05 58 78 33 63, Loisirs Boulevard), opposite the tourist office in Biscarrosse Plage, where VTTs cost €12.95/44.20 per day/week.

The Landes

The Landes (literally 'moors') is France's second-largest department and one of its emptiest – a 14,000-sq-km plain, over 40% of it densely forested, with a flat Atlantic coastline running straight as an arrow for over 100km from Biscarrosse to Bayonne. Backing up the almost nonstop beaches is the longest, highest band of dunes in Europe, a wall of sand that once marched inland at up

to 27m a year. In the 19th century, Napoleon III had the first maritime pine and oak, shrubs and grasses planted, and since then the Landes have turned from moors into Europe's largest cultivated forest.

The coastline is punctuated with resorts, and the surf is some of Europe's best. Sheltering behind the coastal dunes is a string of lakes and lagoons beloved by birds and holiday-makers alike. The forests are threaded with practically hill-free bike trails (see the boxed text). In the middle of it all is the vast Parc Naturel Régional des Landes de Gascogne, which you can explore by foot (eg, on 220km of the GR8), bike, horse and even canoe. Wild broom turns the forest landscape yellow in March and April, and heather turns it mauve in October.

South of Mont de Marsan, beyond the fish-rich River Adour, the forests give way to the fertile Chalosse et Tursan area, famous for its foie gras, wines and thermal spas, and to the foothills of the Pyrénées.

PARC NATUREL RÉGIONAL DES LANDES DE GASCOGNE

This 2900-sq-km regional park, established in 1970, stretches from the Bassin d'Arcachon to just north of Mont de Marsan and encompasses the valleys of the Leyre, Petite Leyre and Grand Leyre Rivers, and almost half the pine forests of the interior. Its prime attractions are a fine ornithological reserve, a first-rate *ecomusée* (open-air museum) and abundant opportunities for hiking, biking, canoeing and kayaking.

Information

The park's head office (☎ 05 56 88 06 06, tourist information ☎ 05 58 07 52 70, fax 05 56 88 12 72, e info@parc-landes-de-gascogne.fr, w www.parc-landes-de-gascogne.fr) is at 22 av d'Aliénor, 33830 Belin-Béliet, though you'll find park information (mostly in French) at the Ecomusée de la Grande Lande, the Maison de la Nature du Bassin d'Arcachon at the Parc Ornithologique du Teich, and in local tourist offices.

Useful park publications include *Carteguide des Découvertes,* showing bike trails and listing activity centres; *Le Parc Vous*

Biking the Coast

There are 200km of *pistes cyclables* – paved bike trails – along the Landes coast, most of them conveniently pine-shaded. Once sandy tracks used by resin tappers, they were paved by the Germans in WWII. Dozens of bike-hire companies make it easy to go exploring. Pick up maps, complete with suggested circuits and bike outlets, from most Gironde and Landes tourist offices.

Guide, with details on where bikes, horses, boats and gear may be hired; and *Weekends & Séjours au Naturel,* with details on weekend discovery tours (on foot, bike, canoe, horse or donkey) and week-long hikes.

Parc Ornithologique du Teich

The Bassin d'Arcachon is a 250-sq-km tidal bay at the mouth of the River Leyre (or L'Eyre). So shallow that just 20% of it is submerged at low tide, it's prime bird habitat, boasting some 260 resident and migratory species. The Parc Ornithologique du Teich, at the eastern end of the bay, is a fine place to see some of Europe's rarest and most beautiful birds, including spoonbill, little egret, bluethroat and black kite. The park is also home to two dozen nesting pairs of storks.

The park entrance and visitor centre, the **Maison de la Nature du Bassin d'Arcachon** (*☎ 05 56 22 80 93, fax 05 56 22 69 43, rue du Port; adult/child aged 5-14 €5.65/3.95; open 10am-7pm daily, except to 6pm mid-Sept–mid-Apr*), is 600m north of Le Teich town centre. Binoculars can be hired here for €3.05 per visit. In Le Teich, opposite the post office, is a tourist office (*☎ 05 56 22 80 46, fax 05 57 70 31 70*), open 10.30am to 12.30pm and 2pm to 4pm Monday to Friday (10am to 1pm and 2.30pm to 7pm daily in July and August).

May is a good time to observe species rarely seen farther north (eg, in the UK). From August to October, waders and other migratory birds from Scandinavia and Greenland pass through. From late summer and throughout the winter, it's easiest to ob-

serve the birds at high tide when they're close to shore. Walking circuits of 2.5km and 6km take you to a series of 13 camouflaged observation points.

The **Sentier du Littoral** footpath passes the park, running 5km south-east to Lamothe along the forested banks of the Leyre, and 5km west to the oyster-fishing port of Gujan-Mestras. The visitor centre organises guided sea-kayak tours of the Leyre delta (€18.30, three hours) and of the Bassin d'Arcachon (€38.10, all day) up to five times monthly (almost daily in July and August) and, from June to September, unguided canoe trips on the Leyre (€24.40 per 2½-hour trip, €32 per five-hour trip). These trips must be booked at least a few days ahead.

The Parc Ornithologique is most conveniently reached from Arcachon (see Around Arcachon earlier in this section).

Ecomusée de la Grande Lande

The park operates a three-part open-air museum that is devoted to life in the unique 'Landes-scape'. There's an old resin products workshop at Luxey, a museum of popular beliefs at Moustey and, best of all, a reconstructed 19th-century settlement at Marquèze (*☎ 05 58 08 31 31, fax 05 58 07 56 85,* e *ecomusee-marqueze@parc-landes -de-gascogne.fr; admission €7.30/6.55/ 5.35 for those aged over 25/19-25/6-18; open daily Apr-Oct*) that illustrates the finely balanced web of interdependence between humans, animals and a fairly barren land 'before the trees came', as well as its descent into feudal monoculture afterwards.

You can walk through the houses of shepherds, labourers and the resin-tappers who displaced them, and through fields, mills and kitchens where their work is again carried on in traditional ways. The museum holds a series of special events, including sheep shearing in mid-May and a week of traditional cooking in mid-October.

Adding to the atmosphere is the fact that you can only get there on a century-old, narrow-gauge railway line from the village of Sabres – the only surviving segment of a line laid in 1880 to Labouheyre in the days of the pine-resin trade. The train ticket

THE LANDES

On Your Stilts

Before the marshland of the Landes was tamed by Napoleon III, local farmers and shepherds had a hard time moving around their fever-swamp. Someone in the 16th century discovered that on stilts (*tchanques* in Gascon, *échasses* in French) they could navigate the bogs and keep track of their flocks on this flat landscape. People even learned to dance with the things on.

Stilt-walking died out once the forest took hold, but some 20 folk groups keep the dancing alive at local festivals and summer tourist events, for example at Seignosse (at 9.30pm on Tuesday during July and August) and Hossegor (at 9pm on Monday from June to September).

If you'd like to try it yourself, contact Nouvelles Échasses (☎ 05 56 88 80 58) at Belin-Béliet, which organises stilt-walking courses and even stilt-rambles.

NICKY CAVEN

Stilts: once the height of fashion

is also your ticket to the ecomusée, good for a guided visit (in French) and an excellent guidebook (with text in other languages).

Trains depart from Sabres every 40 minutes: from 2pm to 4pm in April, May and from mid-September to October (with two to three additional services at weekends), and 10.10am to 12.10pm and 2pm to 5.20pm from June to mid-September. The last train back down allows plenty of time for a visit in any case. A small tourist office (☎ 05 58 08 31 31) at the station is open 10.30am to 6.30pm daily from mid-June to mid-September.

Limited accommodation options in Sabres include the following.

Camping du Peyricat *(☎ 05 58 07 51 88, fax 05 58 07 51 86)* Forfait €13.70. Open mid-June–mid-Sep. This comfortable camp site is about 400m south of the town centre on the D327.

Auberge des Pins *(☎ 05 58 07 50 47, fax 05 58 07 56 74)* Doubles €46-107. This Logis de France hotel-restaurant is close to the camp site.

Sabres is 35km north-west of Mont de Marsan on the N134. There's no public transport to speak of.

Activities

The Parc Naturel's big year-round activity centres – for canoeing, sea and river kayaking, nature rambles, bird-watching, cycling, orienteering, rock-climbing, archery and multiactivity courses – are the **Maison de la Nature du Bassin d'Arcachon** *(see Parc Ornithologique du Teich earlier in this section)*, the **Centre du Graoux** *(☎ 05 57 71 99 29, fax 05 57 71 99 20, Belin-Béliet)* and **Atelier-Gîte de Saugnac-et-Muret** *(☎ 05 58 07 73 01, fax 05 58 07 72 71, Saugnac)*.

Canoes and kayaks can be hired at various places along the Grande Leyre, including the Centre de Graoux and the Atelier-Gîte de Saugnac-et-Muret. Two specific companies are the **Base Nautique de Mexico** *(☎ 05 58 07 05 15, fax 05 58 07 19 50, Commensacq; open May-Oct)* and the **Base de Testarrouman** *(☎ 05 58 08 91 58, fax 05 58 08 92 93, Pissos; open year round)*.

HOSSEGOR & CAPBRETON
postcodes Hossegor 40150, Capbreton 40130
• pop 5000

These two villages astride a small pleasure port form a single resort, the busiest seaside destination between Arcachon and Biarritz. Several kilometres offshore is a 3km-deep undersea canyon, the Gouf de Capbreton, probably instrumental in producing the huge swells that have made the area a surfers' paradise.

Capbreton was a medieval whaling port when, for a time, the River Adour emptied into the sea here. In the early 20th century, environmentally conscious artists, writers and architects founded a lively community in what is now Hossegor. The 1930s saw the start of a property boom and the slow demise of the area's charm. Capbreton still has a fishing harbour, but little beyond its tiny square has survived the bulldozer.

Orientation & Information
The two towns are separated – Hossegor north and Capbreton south – by the canal du Bourret and the marina. Just north of Hossegor is another popular resort and surfing centre at Seignosse.

The Hossegor tourist office (☎ 05 58 41 79 00, fax 05 58 41 79 09, e hossegor.tourisme@wanadoo.fr), on av de Paris, is open 9am to 7pm daily in July and August, and 9am to noon and 2pm to 6pm Monday to Saturday the rest of the year. Just about everything useful is within a few blocks – including the post office, at least three banks, several bike-rental outfits (see Getting Around later in this section), surf shops and cheap eateries.

English-run Powder Monkey (☎ 05 58 43 54 76), 288 av Touring Club de France, about 200m south of the tourist office, offers Internet access from 2pm to 11pm daily.

From the tourist office, walk west on av Paul Lahary and av de la Grande Dune for 1.3km to place des Landais, the plaza facing Hossegor's splendid plage Central (Central beach).

Surfing
Capbreton's swells tend to be smaller (and more polluted) than those at Hossegor and Seignosse. The best spots are to the north: Épi Nord and Gravière, within 500m of place des Landais; Culs Nuls, a farther 1km up; and the Seignosse beaches of Estagnots, Bourdaines, Penon and Casernes. These include several regular World Championship venues.

Local surf schools include **Hossegor Surf Club** (☎ 05 58 43 80 52, fax 05 58 43 91 17, e hossegor.surf.club@wanadoo.fr, impasse de la Digue Nord, place des Landais) and **Surf Trip** (☎ 05 58 41 91 06, fax 05 58 41 91 11, 555 quai de la Pêcherie, Capbreton), about 1km south of the tourist office, across the Canal du Bourret. Five days of instruction (two/four hours per day) in the high season at Hossegor Surf Club starts at about €135/245.

Lac Marin d'Hossegor
This 2km-long tidal lake, parallel to the seafront, has several beaches, warm salt water and tiny waves, making it ideal for children. You can rent windsurfs and sailing gear or take lessons at plage du Rey.

Ecomusée de la Mer
This little museum (☎ 05 58 72 40 50, av Georges Pompidou, Capbreton; adult/child €4.25/2.75; open 9.30am-noon & 2pm-6.30pm daily July-Aug; 2pm-6pm daily Apr–June & Sept; 2pm-6pm Sun & holidays Oct-Mar), in Capbreton's municipal casino, presents a history of fishing along the Landes coast, with model ships, aquaria and marine fossils.

Étang Blanc & Étang Noir
These two lakes, just north of Hossegor, are home to over 400 plant species and a veritable encyclopaedia of fish and migratory birds. Elevated walkways allow you to get a proper look. The smaller Étang Noir (Black Lake) is classified as a Réserve Naturelle (reserve office ☎/fax 05 58 72 85 76, av du Parc des Sports, Seignosse; admission free; guided visits €2.30, child aged 1-5 free, reservation only, at 10.30am, 3pm & 5pm Mon-Fri, July-Aug).

Special Events
The tourist office organises **street events** almost daily, from children's shows to dance

THE LANDES

and music concerts. You can see weekly **pélote Basque** at Sporting Casino (just over the canal from the tourist office): *Grand chistéra* at the outdoor court at 9pm Monday and *cesta punta* indoors at 9pm Thursday. **Courses landaises** (see Spectator Sports in the Facts for the Visitor chapter) take place on Wednesday at 9.30pm in the arena five blocks north-east of the tourist office.

Among big annual events here are a weekend kite festival at the end of April and the big Hossegor Rip Curl Pro World Surfing Championships at the end of August.

Places to Stay

Camping There's plenty of choice if you're looking to camp near Hossegor or Capbreton.

Camping La Forêt (☎ 05 58 43 75 92, 116 av de Bordeaux, Hossegor) Adult/pitch/car €3.65/3.65/1.05. Open Apr-Oct. Hossegor's modest municipal camping ground is crowded but shady.

Camping du Lac (☎ 05 58 43 53 14, fax 05 58 43 55 83, e hossegorlac@free.fr, 480 rte des Lacs, Hossegor) adult/pitch (with car) €4.40/4.90. Open Apr-Sept. This spacious, shady camping ground is closer to the lake.

Camping Bel Air (☎ 05 58 72 12 04, av du Bourret, Capbreton) 2-person forfait €14.20. Open year round. About 1km south of the tourist office is Capbreton's tiny, squashed but shady municipal camping ground.

Camp-o-Land La Civelle (☎ 05 58 72 15 11, fax 05 58 72 31 22, rue des Bishes, Capbreton) 2-person forfait €14.80. Open June-Sept. This 600-pitch place, south of the centre of Capbreton, has a pool, shop, bar and restaurant.

Several more camp sites are northward at Seignosse.

Camping Municipal Hourn-Naou (☎ 05 58 43 30 30, fax 05 58 41 64 21, av des Tucs, Seignosse) 2-person forfait €7.80. Open Apr-Sept. Seignosse's good-value municipal site is close to plage des Estagnots.

Near plage des Casernes are shady *Campeole Les Oyats (☎ 05 58 43 37 94, fax 05 58 43 23 29)* and *Les Chevreuils (☎ 05 58 43 32 80, fax 05 58 90 10 49)*, each with swimming pools, open from June to mid-September and charging about €16 forfait.

Hotels The hotels in the area include these three.

Hôtel Le Rond Point (☎ 05 58 43 53 11, fax 05 58 43 85 85, 866 av du Touring Club de France, Hossegor) Rooms €35-55. Breakfast €5.50. The Rond Point, 300m north of the tourist office, rates one Logis de France chimney; its rooms are uninspiring but quite comfortable.

Les Hélianthes (☎ 05 58 43 52 19, fax 05 58 43 95 19, e hotel.helianthes@wanadoo .fr, 156 av Côte d'Argent, Hossegor) Rooms mid-season €43-72, high season €49-77 with buffet breakfast for two, obligatory July-Aug; €28-49 (breakfast separate & optional) otherwise. Open Apr–mid-Oct. This good-value, Logis de France place is about 600m west of the tourist office.

Hôtel Le Pavillon Bleu (☎ 05 58 43 49 48, fax 05 58 43 49 49, e pavillon.bleu@ wanadoo.fr, 1053 av du Touring Club de France, Hossegor) Rooms with WC, bath, Jacuzzi and air-con €106 (€69 outside July-Aug). The lakeside Pavillon Bleu has big rooms with balconies (none facing the road), and a sunny terrace-restaurant (open lunch and dinner Tuesday to Saturday, and lunch only Sunday). It's 500m north of the tourist office.

Places to Eat

Place des Landais is wall-to-wall with pizzerias and bar-cafes, open all day and evening. If you've busted your budget, this is the place to eat.

Rock Food (☎ 05 58 43 43 27, place des Landais) Dishes €5.80-7.70. Open 24 hours. This bar-restaurant and surfers' haunt dispenses cheap and tasty summertime fare, including generous salads, fried chicken and hamburgers, and is one of the best choices on this strip.

Dégustation du Lac (☎ 05 58 43 54 95, 1830 av du TCF) Fish dishes €9-15, seafood platters €8.50-32. Open daily July-Aug; Wed-Mon Apr-June & Sept. If you're in an indulgent mood, this venerable place on the eastern side of Lac Marin d'Hossegor (and 1.4km north of the town centre) offers spectacular seafood platters.

And don't forget the *market*, just north of

the tourist office: inside every morning and outside on Monday, Wednesday, Friday and Sunday mornings.

Getting There & Away
RDTL's Dax-Bayonne bus service runs two or three times daily, Monday to Saturday, via Capbreton, Hossegor and Seignosse; Dax-Hossegor costs €5.95 (extra services are laid on in July and August at a 'go-to-the-beach' price of €7.15 return). RDTL's once-a-day, Monday to Saturday, coastal service to Bayonne stops at Capbreton and Hossegor about every 1½ hours.

Getting Around
At least three outfits near the tourist office rent bikes (€9-11/42-50 per day/week) and scooters: Lannemajou (☎ 05 58 43 54 45, 619 av du Touring Club de France); Locavelo (☎ 05 58 43 73 54, 60 av Paul Lahary); and VTT Loisirs (☎ 05 58 41 91 81, allée des Pins Tranquilles). The Sunrise Bike Shop (☎ 05 58 43 92 90) is at Point d'Or, just south of place des Landais.

RÉSERVE NATURELLE DU MARAIS D'ORX
Just inland of another surfing haven, at Labenne, is the Orx Marsh, for centuries a major nesting site for migratory birds. Napoleon III had it drained, but over the years nature has reclaimed it and the birds have returned. In 1989, the Worldwide Fund for Nature and the private Conservatoire du Littoral bought 800 hectares of marshland and adjacent meadows and farmland, and established a nature reserve.

The most dramatic months are October and November, when birds in their thousands stop on their way south. Around a thousand greylag geese and 1500 common teal stay for the winter, along with rare white-fronted geese. During the spring you can see breeding spoonbill, heron and little egret. Among the four-legged denizens are some of Europe's last remaining mink.

Six hectares of the reserve are open to the public via a network of walkways, accessible through a visitor centre, the Maison du Marais (☎ 05 59 45 42 46, fax 05 59 45 81 75, Domain du Marais d'Orx, Labenne; admission free; open 10am-noon & 2pm-6pm Mon-Fri, 2pm-6pm Sun Apr-June; 10am-1pm & 2pm-7pm daily July-Sept; 9am-noon & 2pm-5pm Mon-Fri, 2pm-5pm Sun Oct-Mar). Guided tours, at 10am daily from July to September, cost €3.05 (children aged 6-16 years €2.30).

Places to Stay & Eat
Between Labenne and the coast are at least eight camp sites, including four with forfait rates under about €17: *La Saveane* (☎ 05 59 45 41 13, [e] la-saveane@ville-labenne.fr, Labenne Océan; open Apr-Sept), *Marina* (☎ 05 59 45 45 49, Labenne Océan; open May-Sept), *Oceanic* (☎ 05 59 45 46 22, Labenne Océan; open Apr-Oct) and *La Mer* (☎ 05 59 45 42 09, fax 05 59 45 43 07, Labenne Océan; open mid-Apr–Sept). La Mer has a pool, and all also have chalets or bungalows available by the week.

Hotel-restaurants in Labenne include *Chez Léonie* (☎ 05 59 45 41 64, fax 05 59 45 78 30, av Charles de Gaulle) and *L'Européen* (☎ 05 59 45 41 49, fax 05 59 45 72 91, av Charles de Gaulle); both offer good food and doubles at €28-37.

Getting There & Away
The visitor centre is just east of the A63 and N10 at Labenne. See Getting There & Away in the preceding Hossegor & Capbreton section for details of buses from there and from Dax and Bayonne.

DAX
postcode 40100 • pop 20,900
Dax is France's biggest thermal spa, in terms of both visitor count and the sheer volume of hot water bubbling from the ground. These waters have been known since Roman times for their relief of rheumatic ailments, and Dax has also become a centre for special mud treatments (see the boxed text overleaf). The town has avoided the twee, cloying atmosphere of many smaller spas.

Dax's train station is on the TGV Atlantique line where it branches to Bayonne and to Pau. It's therefore a transport hub and gateway – west to the resorts of Hossegor,

Capbreton and Seignosse, as well as east into Gascony.

Orientation & Information

The neighbouring train and bus stations are nearer the satellite spa town of St-Paul-lès-Dax than to Dax (though many bus services also stop at place St-Pierre). From the station, climb up av de la Gare and turn left (south) for 1km along av St-Vincent de Paul, across the River Adour to place Thiers.

Here is the tourist office (☎ 05 58 56 86 86, fax 05 58 56 86 80, e tourisme.dax@ wanadoo.fr), open 9.30am to 12.30pm and

2pm to 6pm weekdays (to 6.30pm from April to October, and daily without a lunch break in July and August). Its useful, French-language booklet, *Dax en poche!*, has details of activities, museums and food, plus other highlights around the Landes.

Internet access is available at €1.50/6.10 per 15 minutes/one hour in Le Grand Siècle, a cafe-bar on place St-Pierre. The post office also has a Cyberposte terminal. The police station (☎ 17 or ☎ 05 58 56 58 58) is on rue des Fusillés, behind the post office. The municipal hospital (☎ 05 58 91 48 48) is east out of blvd Yves du Manoir.

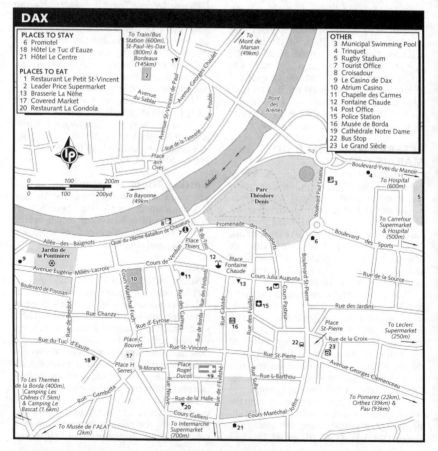

DAX

PLACES TO STAY
6 Promotel
18 Hôtel Le Tuc d'Eauze
21 Hôtel Le Centre

PLACES TO EAT
1 Restaurant Le Petit St-Vincent
2 Leader Price Supermarket
13 Brasserie La Nèhe
17 Covered Market
20 Restaurant La Gondola

OTHER
3 Municipal Swimming Pool
4 Trinquet
5 Rugby Stadium
7 Tourist Office
8 Croisadour
9 Le Casino de Dax
10 Atrium Casino
11 Chapelle des Carmes
12 Fontaine Chaude
14 Post Office
15 Police Station
16 Musée de Borda
19 Cathédrale Notre Dame
22 Bus Stop
23 Le Grand Siècle

Fontaine Chaude

This is the perfect symbol for the town: a perpetually steaming pool on place Fontaine Chaude, built in 1818 and overflowing with 64°C water (through lion-headed spigots) from the biggest of the town's wells. It's fenced off, presumably to keep enthusiastic visitors from boiling themselves alive.

Cathédrale Notre Dame

This cross-breed cathedral (*☎ 05 58 74 05 66, place Roger Ducos; admission free; open 9am-noon & 2pm-5pm Mon-Sat, 8.45am-noon & 4pm-7pm Sun*) is all flying buttresses and towers outside, gloomy baroque and classical inside. The interior portal in the north transept, depicting the Last Judgement, is an amazing 13th-century southern Gothic wonder that somehow escaped the revolutionaries and renovators.

Musée de Borda

This museum (*☎ 05 58 74 12 91, 27 rue Cazade; adult/child €15/free; open 2pm-6pm Mon, Wed-Sat; closed bank holidays*), housed in a 17th-century townhouse, has a fine collection of Stone-Age and Gallo-Roman artefacts, medieval sculpture, 18th- and 19th-century paintings, and also the personal treasures of a local physician, scholar and maritime inventor named Jean-Charles Borda (1733–99).

The museum ticket also admits you to the remains of a 2nd-century **Roman temple** (*across the street; guided visits from the museum at 4pm*), and to the museum's exhibition centre in the **Chapelle des Carmes** (*11 bis rue des Carmes*).

Musée de l'ALAT

Here's one for the kids: the French Army Air Corps' Musée de l'Aviation Légère de l'Armée de Terre et de l'Hélicoptère (*☎ 05 58 74 66 19, 58 av de l'Aerodrome; southbound bus No 1 from place St-Pierre 1.30pm only; admission €4.55; open 2pm-6pm Mon-Sat mid-Feb–Nov*), with over 25 old aircraft dating back to WWII.

Walk-in Spas

Two resorts are open to the casual visitor,

with pools, Jacuzzis, hot and cold fountains, saunas and more.

Les Thermes de la Borda (*☎ 05 58 74 86 13, 30 rue des Lazaristes; bus No 4 from place St-Pierre to Lazaristes stop; 1 hour/day €6.10/12.20; open 3pm-8pm Mon-Sat*) is 1.5km west of the centre.

Calicéo (*☎ 05 58 90 66 66, Lad de Christus; bus No 1 north from place St-Pierre to Frison stop; 2 hours/day €9.20/21.35; open 10am-10pm Sun-Thur & 10am-11pm Fri-Sat July-Aug; 10am-9pm Mon-Thur & 10am-10pm Fri-Sat & 10am-8pm Sun Sept-June*) is in St-Paul-lès-Dax.

River Trips

From the quay near the tourist office, **Croisadour** (*☎ 05 58 74 87 07, fax 05 58 56 14 25, quai du 28ème Bataillon de Chasseurs*) runs half-day cruises along the Adour. Boats depart 9am and 2.30pm, Monday to Saturday, and 2pm on Sunday, March to November. Tickets for adults/children aged 3 to 12 cost €11.45/6.10 (€6.85/3.80 on Sunday).

Special Events

The **Feria de Dax**, which is held annually for a week around 15 August, features bullfights, courses landaises, pélote Basque, brass bands and much more. Bullfights and lots of Latin music are part of the three-day **Toros y Salsa** festival in the second week of September.

Places to Stay

Two well equipped camp sites, both with restaurants and open from mid-March to October, are about 2km west of the centre.

Les Chênes *(☎ 05 58 90 05 53, fax 05 58 56 18 77, Bois de Boulogne)* Forfaits (tent/caravan) €9.45/14.65-17.05. Four-star Les Chênes is the bigger, shadier site, also offering a swimming pool. Take bus No 4 from the covered market to the Bascat stop.

Le Bascat *(☎ 05 58 56 16 68, fax 05 58 56 20 56, rue de Jouandin)* Adult/pitch €2.75/5.20. Le Bascat is a bit more laid-back and somewhat remoter from the town. Take bus No 4 from covered market to the Jouandin stop.

St-Paul-lès-Dax also has several camp sites. On the other hand, Dax brims with top-end hotels for spa patients (the tourist office has a list of these and half a dozen chambres d'hôte). There are three modest, nonspa hotels within 500km of the tourist office.

Hôtel Le Centre *(☎ 05 58 74 07 02, 6 cours Maréchal Joffre)* Rooms with/without WC & shower €22.85/18.30. It's dreary and street-noisy but it's the cheapest place in town. Pay up front.

Promotel *(☎ 05 58 74 18 11, fax 05 58 56 97 63, 1 blvd St-Pierre)* Rooms €27.45. Breakfast €4.25. Open mid-Feb–Dec. Superior value in this range is the no-frills, blindingly clean hotel with a buffet breakfast. All rooms have a WC and either shower or bath.

Hôtel Le Tuc d'Eauze *(☎ 05 58 90 90 60, 9 rue du Tuc d'Eauze)* Rooms €30.50-35.06. Open Feb-Dec. The Tuc d'Eauze beats the others for character, with well kept rooms and a good restaurant (see Places to Eat). Rooms come with a WC and either a shower or bath.

Places to Eat
Dax has a good choice of places to eat.

Restaurant Le Petit St-Vincent *(☎ 05 58 56 97 92, 63 av St-Vincent de Paul)* Menus €8.40-21.20. Open Mon-Sat. This restaurant, 300m north of the river, is good value at the lower end of the price range.

Restaurant Le Tuc d'Eauze *(see Places to Stay)* Menus €18.30-30.50. Open Feb-Dec. Come here for a mix of good Landaise and Basque specialities, plus a sizable fish and seafood list.

Restaurant Le Borda *(see Walk-In Spas earlier in this section)* Menus €22.10. The Thermes de la Borda spa's restaurant is one of Dax's best. Its wide range of *formules* (€6.85-14.65) also means you needn't go broke eating here.

Brasserie La Nèhe *(☎ 05 58 74 14 69, cours Julia Augusta)* Midday *formules* €10.65-12.20. Have a salad and sit in the sun at this cheerful, always-crowded brasserie.

Restaurant La Gondola *(☎ 05 58 90 89 01, 6 rue de la Halle)* Pizzas & pasta €6-9. Open lunch & dinner Fri-Sat & Mon-Tues, lunch only Wed. The Gondola is one of many adequate pizzerias in Dax.

For do-it-yourselfers there's a big ***food market*** on Saturday morning (and a smaller one Sunday morning) at the covered market. There are four ***supermarkets*** near the centre.

Entertainment
Nightlife in Dax centres on the casino.

Le Casino de Dax *(☎ 05 58 58 77 77, 8 av Eugène Miliès-Lacroix)* Open 11am-3am Sun-Thur, 11am-4am Fri-Sat. This casino has roulette, blackjack and floorshows.

The Art-Deco Atrium Casino (1928), on cours de Verdun, is not for gambling but for conventions.

Spectator Sports
From June to September you can watch pelote Basque every Wednesday evening at 8.30pm in the main trinquet near the rugby stadium on blvd Yves du Manoir. For scheduled rugby matches, ask at the tourist office.

Shopping
The Landes' biggest foie gras market is on Monday and Wednesday at Pomarez, 22km south-east of Dax, though it's busiest in November and December. Get there by 6am to see it at its best.

Getting There & Away
Daily train connections to Dax include eight from Bayonne (€7.30, 40 minutes) and five from Bordeaux (€16.75, 1½ hours). SNCF buses come from Mont de Marsan (€10.05, 1¼ hours, four to five daily).

Most RDTL buses stop at place St-Pierre as well as the train station, including from Mont de Marsan (€7.95, one to 1½ hours, one to three daily) and Bayonne (€7.40, 1½ to 2½ hours, two to three daily) – though Bayonne is a tedious trip by bus compared with the train.

Getting Around
All Urbus local buses pass through place St-Pierre, timed to permit transfers. Most only run every hour or two. For a local taxi, call ☎ 05 58 74 71 53.

Bike-rental companies include Localoisirs (☎ 05 58 90 80 81) who will deliver the bike to you.

MONT DE MARSAN
postcode 40000 • pop 32,000
• elevation 27m

Mont de Marsan, prefecture of the Landes department, is best known as a base for visiting the fine Romanesque monastery-church of St-Sever (see St-Sever later in this chapter). Its own pride and joy is France's only museum of modern figurative sculpture, the Musée Despiau-Wlérick, and the compact town centre is dotted with arresting, life-size bronze nudes by two favourite sons, Charles Despiau and Robert Wlérick. The place has more spirit than charm, but nevertheless has a welcoming feel.

Orientation
Old Mont de Marsan straddles the confluence of the Rivers Douze and Midou that form the Midouze. From the train station, the centre is a 10-minute walk north via place Jean Jaurès, av Sadi-Carnot and rue Léon Gambetta, and less than that from the various bus stands.

Information
The tourist office (☎ 05 58 05 87 37, fax 05 58 05 87 36, e tourisme@mont-de-marsan .org), 6 place du Général Leclerc, is open 9am to 12.30pm and 1.30pm to 6pm Monday to Saturday (all day and to 6.30pm from mid-June to August). For information about the Landes in general, visit the Comité Départemental du Tourisme (☎ 05 58 06 89 89, fax 05 58 06 90 90, e cdt.landes@wanadoo.fr, w www.tourismelandes.com), upstairs at 4 av Aristide Briand.

There are three banks with ATMs and exchange facilities around place du Général Leclerc, and others on rue Léon Gambetta and av Sadi-Carnot. The post office faces place du Général Leclerc. Internet access is available for €0.15/6.10 per minute/hour at Difintel (☎ 05 58 06 44 79, 79 rue Léon Gambetta) on Tuesday to Saturday and Monday morning.

Two good bookshops are Maison de la Presse (☎ 05 58 75 01 27) at 3 rue Laubaner, with guidebooks, maps and foreign newspapers, and Librairie Plein Ciel Lacoste (☎ 05 58 75 01 75), 65 rue Augustin Lesbazeilles.

Musée Despiau-Wlérick
This museum (☎ 05 58 75 00 45, 1 place Marguerite de Navarre; admission €3.05, free for students, free Mon; open 10am-noon & 2pm-6pm Wed-Mon; closed bank holidays), in the 14th-century Donjon Lacataye, is the only one in France dedicated exclusively to early-20th-century sculpture. Some 100 artists are represented, with the Art-Deco period of the 1930s figuring strongly. Prominent are the works of two locals, Charles Despiau (1874–1946) and Robert Wlérick (1882–1944).

Despiau's life-size bronze, marble and plaster figures look still and vulnerable, as if the models themselves were sitting there without their clothes. Upstairs, Wlérick's figures have more dash and muscle. Many works by contemporaries and followers are more statue than sculpture.

Parc des Nahuques
Take the children to this open-air wildlife park and walk among llamas, wallabies, flamingos, emus and black swans. The park (☎ 05 58 75 94 38; admission free; open 9am-noon & 2pm-8pm daily June-mid–Sept; 9am-noon & 2pm-6pm Mon-Fri, 3pm-8pm Sat, Sun & holidays mid-Sept–May) is about 2km east of the town centre; take bus No 1 to the Nahuques stop. There are also tennis courts and a riding school nearby.

Other Things to See & Do
An old mill, now partly converted to an art gallery, sits picturesquely at the confluence

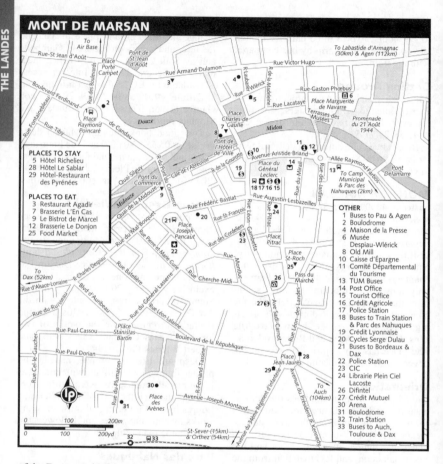

MONT DE MARSAN

PLACES TO STAY
5 Hôtel Richelieu
28 Hôtel Le Sablar
29 Hôtel-Restaurant
     des Pyrénées

PLACES TO EAT
3 Restaurant Agadir
7 Brasserie L'En Cas
9 Le Bistrot de Marcel
12 Brasserie Le Donjon
25 Food Market

OTHER
1 Buses to Pau & Agen
2 Boulodrome
4 Maison de la Presse
6 Musée
   Despiau-Wlérick
8 Old Mill
10 Caisse d'Épargne
11 Comité Départemental
     du Tourisme
13 TUM Buses
14 Post Office
15 Tourist Office
16 Crédit Agricole
17 Police Station
18 Buses to Train Station
     & Parc des Nahuques
19 Crédit Lyonnaise
20 Cycles Serge Dulau
21 Buses to Bordeaux &
     Dax
22 Police Station
23 CIC
24 Librairie Plein Ciel
     Lacoste
26 Difintel
27 Crédit Mutuel
30 Arena
31 Boulodrome
32 Train Station
33 Buses to Auch,
     Toulouse & Dax

of the Douze and Midou, but nobody seems to know a thing about it. **Boulodromes**, where you can watch boules and pétanque being played, include a covered one near the train station and an open-air one by place Raymond Poincaré.

Special Events
For a week following the first Monday in July, Monte de Marsan echoes to stamping feet during its **Fête de Flamenco**. The townspeople take centre stage from the Saturday after 14 July (Bastille Day) for the six-day **Fête de la Madeleine**, with parades, fire-

works, concerts and sports events (including bullfights and courses landaises in the arena), and an airshow at the air base north of town.

Places to Stay
There is a variety of accommodation in the area.

Camp Municipal (☎ 05 58 75 04 73, *341 route de Villeneuve*) Bus No 1 to Nahuques stop. 2-person forfait €7.15. Open year round. This plain, shady camp site is beside Parc des Nahuques, about 2km out of town (see the earlier Parc des Nahuques section).

Hôtel-Restaurant des Pyrénées (☎ 05 58

46 49 49, fax 05 58 06 43 57, 4 av du 34ème Régiment d'Infanterie) Doubles with WC & shower €36.60, without €19.80-33.55. The well run Pyrénées, a five-minute walk from both the town centre and the train station, has comfortable, spacious rooms (but no hall showers). Its good restaurant (see Places to Eat) has earned it a two-chimney Logis de France rating.

Hôtel Le Sablar (☎ 05 58 75 21 11, fax 05 58 75 67 13, 3 place Jean Jaurès) Doubles €32, with WC & shower/bath €38.10/42.70. Try for a quiet room facing the garden at the Sablar, midway between town and the train station.

Hôtel Richelieu (☎ 05 58 06 10 20, fax 05 58 06 00 68, rue Wlérick) Rooms with WC & shower/bath €44.20/45.75. The Richelieu is cheerless but polite, posh and spotless.

Places to Eat
As well as two brasseries for midday noshing, there are several restaurants.

Brasserie l'En Cas (☎ 05 58 75 17 58, 2 place Charles de Gaulle) Midday *formules* €5-9, salads €5-8. This place, by the Midou bridge, offers generous savoury plates and big salads.

Brasserie le Donjon (☎ 05 58 46 09 09, 2 av Aristide Briand) Plat du jour €7, salads €7-11. Open daily. The Donjon has gourmet salads, omelettes and light meals.

Hôtel-Restaurant des Pyrénées (see Places to Stay earlier in this section) Menus €11-30, meat & fish dishes €8-10. This smartly run hotel restaurant dresses up in black tie, though the food is not terribly expensive. The €8.40 salade landaise, full of ham and gizzards, makes a delicious and interesting carnivore's lunch.

Le Bistrot de Marcel (☎ 05 58 75 09 71, 1 rue du Pont du Commerce) Dishes €7.90-13.55. Open lunch & dinner Tues-Sat & dinner only Mon. Bistrot de Marcel has the town's best take on Landaise cooking, with a few choice fish dishes and a long list of meaty specials, as well as an outdoor terrace above the Midouze.

Restaurant Agadir (☎ 05 58 06 22 33, 19 rue Armand Dulamon) Couscous & tagine €9.15-12.20, grills €7.60-12.20. Open Tues-Sun. For a change, try the Moroccan dishes at this little restaurant.

Self-caterers will like the *food market* on Saturday and Tuesday mornings in place St-Roch.

Getting There & Away
Bus Long-distance operators include RDTL (☎ 05 58 05 66 00; place Joseph Pancaut), Rivière (Auch ☎ 05 62 05 46 24; train station), SNCF (☎ 05 58 75 22 89; train station), Serag (☎ 05 58 75 22 89; train station) and Citram Pyrénées (Pau ☎ 05 59 27 22 22; place Raymond Poincaré).

For Dax, RDTL has one to three services daily (€7.95, 1½ hours); SNCF has four to five daily (€10.05, 1¼ hours). For Bayonne, change at Dax. Citram Pyrénées runs once-a-day, Monday to Saturday, services to Pau (€12.65, two hours). Rivière goes to Auch (€10.35, 1¾ hours) once a day from Sunday to Friday. RDTL has one service per weekday to Bordeaux (€17.25, two hours). Buy tickets on board.

Train Direct trains link Mont de Marsan with Bordeaux (€16.75, 1½ hours, two daily) and with Dax (€8.70, 1¼ hours, two to three daily). For Bayonne, change either at Dax or Morcenx.

Getting Around
From allées Raymond Farbos, useful Transport Urbain Montois buses (TUM; ☎ 05 58 05 66 00; €0.90) include No 1 to the camp site and Parc des Nahuques and No 2 to the train station.

Cycles Serge Dulau (☎ 05 58 75 28 60), 25 rue Frédéric Bastiat, rents VTTs for €9.15 per day (summer only).

ST-SEVER
**postcode 40500 • pop 5000
• elevation 100m**
One of southern France's finest Romanesque buildings is the Benedictine abbey-church in this otherwise uninspiring town 15km south of Mont de Marsan, on the edge of the hilly Chalosse et Tursan region. Dedicated to St-Severus, who in the 5th century managed to convert the Roman governor

himself to Christianity, this was the Landes' most important monastery in medieval times.

Orientation & Information
The bus drops you at place de la République, from where it's 400m north-west to the abbey-church on place du Tour du Sol. Opposite the church is the tourist office (☎ 05 58 76 34 64, fax 05 58 76 43 70), open 9.30am to 1pm and 2.30pm to 6.30pm Monday to Saturday from June to August, and 9.30am to noon and 1.30pm to 5.30pm Monday to Friday (to 4.30pm Saturday) from September to May.

Abbaye-Église St-Sever
The abbey-church *(place Tour du Sol; admission free; open 8am-noon & 2pm-6pm daily)* was founded in 988 as part of an effort by Guillaume Sanche, Count of Gascony, to stake a political claim in the region. A major reconstruction under the abbacy of Grégoire de Montaner (1028–72) set a tone of artistic exuberance, and not only in its multichapel floor plan.

Let your eye climb the interior columns for a parade of carved stone capitals, high enough or subtle enough to have escaped the ravages of Huguenots, Revolutionaries and 19th-century restorers. The earliest look like foliage, with animals grinning out at you. Later highlights include The Feast of Herod, complete with dancing Salome, just inside the west door; a quartet of phoenix birds and a tiny, realistic human figure, across the nave from The Feast of Herod; and Daniel holding two lions by their tongues, between the middle and inner sidechapels on the southern side. Outside, the (otherwise 19th-century) northern portal bears a crumbling Romanesque tympanum.

Musée des Jacobins
Upstairs in the remnants of a 13th-century Dominican cloister is the dusty little Musée des Jacobins *(same ☎ as tourist office, rue de Général Lamarque; admission free; open 3pm-6.30pm daily June-Aug; 3pm-6.30pm Wed Sept-May)*, with old postcards, artefacts from an excavated Roman villa, and... the Hall of the Apocalypse! Here is a series of reproductions of the *Apocalypse of St-Sever*, an illuminated manuscript produced under Grégoire de Montaner and now in the Bibliothèque National in Paris. The museum is near the bus stop.

Morlanne
From the abbey-church, walk north-east down rue Lafayette, across the main road and left up av de Morlanne to a park on the site of the original Roman governor's palace. It's easy to see what attracted the Romans, and later the Counts of Gascony: St-Sever sits on a cornice of land historically known as the Cap de Gascogne (Cape of Gascony), with an impressive view north over the Adour to the forests of the Landes.

Places to Stay & Eat
The tourist office has details of several *campings à la ferme*, *chambres d'hôte* and *gîtes* in the area. Otherwise, local accommodation options include the following.

Camping Les Rives d'Adour (same ☎/fax as tourist office, rue Renée Crobos) Adult/pitch/car €1.50/0.75/0.75. Open June-Aug. This simple municipal camping ground is on the Adour, 2km north-east of the centre.

Hôtel Lauqué (☎ 05 58 76 00 25, 2 rue du Bellocq) Rooms €16.75-19.80. Open year round. This old hotel, on the main road beside the Musée des Jacobins, has a few plain doubles with shared shower and WC.

Restaurant Le Touron (☎ 05 58 76 03 04, rue de Touron) Menus €9.15-22.85. The modest Touron is 200m north-west of the tourist office.

Getting There & Away
SNCF has daily buses from Mont de Marsan (€2.90, 15 minutes); useful departures are at 7.30am (8.50am weekends) and 2.20pm; with 11.39am and 5.12pm departures from St-Sever. You can also catch a SNCF bus from Dax at 10.50am daily. Check current times with the tourist office.

The Dordogne

The Dordogne *département* (administrative department), an area historically and still locally known as Périgord (after the name of the region's pre-Roman tribe, Petrocorii), is one of the cradles of human civilisation. The prehistoric remains of Neanderthal and Cro-Magnon people have been discovered throughout the region, and quite a number of local caves – including the world-famous Lascaux – are adorned with extraordinary works of prehistoric art (see the Arts section in Facts about Southwest France). In addition, Périgord's numerous hilltop chateaux and defensive *bastides* (fortified villages) testify to the bloody battles that were once waged here during the Hundred Years' War when much of the area was in English hands (see the Bastides & Chateaux Special Section).

For promotional purposes, Périgord has been divided into four areas and assigned colours according to their most prominent features. The fields and forests to the north are known as Périgord Vert (green). In the centre, the limestone area surrounding the capital, Périgueux, is known as Périgord Blanc (white). The wine-growing area of Périgord Pourpre (purple) lies to the south around Bergerac. Périgord Noir (black) encompasses the Vézère Valley and the Dordogne Valley to the south, an area known for its dark oak and pine forests.

Thanks to all its natural and cultural attractions, the Dordogne attracts some two million tourists a year. During the summer you may well encounter mammoth coaches navigating back roads barely wide enough for a couple of bikes. In winter, however, the region goes into a deep hibernation and many hotels, restaurants and tourist sites close for the season.

Included in this chapter are several places officially belonging to the neighbouring Corrèze department: Brive-la-Gaillarde (an important transport hub), and Collonges-la-Rouge and Beaulieu-sur-Dordogne, both major attractions nearby.

Highlights

- Marvel at Lascaux II, the replica of one of the world's most famous prehistoric painted caves; then see real 12,000-year-old paintings, still in situ, at Font de Gaume in Les Eyzies de Tayac
- Canoe or kayak down the grand River Dordogne
- Meander through the beautifully preserved medieval and Renaissance town of Sarlat-la-Canéda
- Shop for home-made pâté and preserves and the freshest produce at local markets

DORDOGNE

Périgueux ● p182

Brive-la-Gaillarde ● p216

Vézère & Dordogne Valleys p195

Sarlat-la-Canéda p206 ●

Bergerac ● p174

Medieval Town p207

Food & Wine Highlights

pâté de foie gras – pâté made with rich goose or duck liver

omelette aux truffes – an omelette made with the prized subterranean tubers

pommes de terre sarladaises – fried potatoes with truffles

gâteau aux noix – walnut cake

fruity **Bergerac** and little-known **Pécharmant** red wines, and sweet **Monbazillac** whites

Information

The department's main tourist office is in Périgueux (see Tourist Offices under Information in the Périgueux section). It includes the Service de Reservation Loisirs Accueil

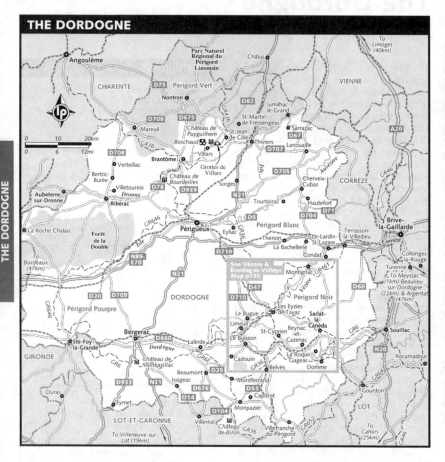

THE DORDOGNE

whose *Dordogne* brochure details accommodation, activity holidays, organised tours (everything from a gastronomic weekend to a week's trundle in a deluxe gypsy caravan) and courses in the region. Other useful publications, available at most tourist offices, are *La Fête en Périgord*, giving festival dates and opening times of everything from caves to chateaux; and *Bienvenue à la Ferme*, which lists rural places to stay, eat or buy farm produce. Sarlat's *Guide Touristique* is packed with information (including courses and organised activities) in Périgord Noir. The department's Web site at **W** www

.perigord.tm.fr is also worth checking, as is **W** www.arachnis.asso.fr/Dordogne, a multilingual site on the culture, history, gastronomy and tourist facilities of the area.

Activities
Walking Useful Topoguides for exploring the GR6 and GR36 are Nos 41 and 321. *Sentiers d'Emilie en Périgord Noir* is recommended for gentler family strolls. The UK-published *Holiday Walks in the Dordogne*, by Norman Buckley, covers 25 walks and maps. Or why not walk through the hills the easy way, with a donkey to carry

the load? **Association Arcâne Anes de Ran-
donneés** (☎ *05 53 59 63 79,* e *arc.ane@
wanadoo.fr,* w *www.bourricot.com, Le
Moulin Peyrié, 24250 Daglan)* can arrange
an accommodating animal for the price of
about €38.10 per person per day.

Horse Riding There are dozens of horse-
riding outfits (most with ponies for kids
too), usually charging around €15.25 per
hour. Details are available from local tourist
offices.

Canoeing & Kayaking Most canoe and
kayak operators are based near the River
Dordogne's La Roque Gageac and Cénac,
or near Montignac or Le Bugue on the
River Vézère. Costs per person per day are
about €18.30/21.35 for a canoe/kayak.
Two- to seven-day trips (or longer) are also
possible (roughly €35.05 to €111.30 per
person, including tent). Remember to check
whether the operator includes free transport
and life-jackets. The following are mostly
open from June to September and accept
reservations during the rest of the year.

Canoë Copeyre (☎ 05 53 28 95 01, Beynac-et-
Cazenac) This company has a dozen centres in
the area, including ones in Beynac-et-Cazenac
and Beaulieu-sur-Dordogne (☎ 05 55 91 27 25)
Canoës des Courrèges (☎ 05 53 08 75 37, fax 05
53 03 98 02) This outfit, 2km south of Le Bugue,
offers trips on both the Vézère and Dordogne.
Canoë Dordogne (☎ 05 53 29 58 50, fax 05 53
29 38 92, La Roque Gageac) This company offers good rates for four-person canoes.
Canoë-Kayak (☎ 05 53 50 19 26, Montignac) A
leading company for trips along the Vézère (eg,
to La Roque St-Christophe).
Randonnée Dordogne/Canoë Cénac (☎ 05 53
28 22 01, fax 05 53 28 53 00, e randodor
dogne@wanadoo.fr, Cénac) This big, professional outfit, headquartered 500m east of Cénac,
also has bases in Vézac and Carsac.
Randonnée Vézère (☎ 05 53 51 27 50) This
company has three bases: Condat, Thonac and
St-Léon-sur-Vézère.
Safaraid (☎ 05 65 30 74 47, fax 05 65 30 74 48,
w www.canoe-france.com) This is part of a
major chain of canoe-kayak centres that can
arrange trips on the Dordogne (one to 14 days)
plus organise camp-site reservations and luggage transport.

Rock-Climbing & Potholing A couple of
canoe operators (eg, Canoë Dordogne and
Randonnée Dordogne; see the preceding
section) can also arrange *escalade* (rock-
climbing) for around €16.90 per person per
half-day.

Based at Vézac, **Couleurs Périgord**
(☎/fax *05 53 30 37 61,* e *couleurs.peri
gord@wanadoo.fr,* w *www.perso.wanadoo
.fr/couleurs.perigord)* organises both rock-
climbing in the Castelnaud region and
speleologie (potholing) in the Les Eyzies/
Groléjac areas for around €45.75 per person per half-day (less if you join a group).

Périgord Pourpre

'Purple' Périgord, stretching both sides of
the River Dordogne, is famous for its vineyards (especially around Bergerac) and its
medieval bastides (notably Monpazier).

BERGERAC
**postcode 24100 • pop 27,500
• elevation 60m**
The town of Bergerac, on the right bank of
the Dordogne, makes a convenient stopover
on the way from Bordeaux (93km to the
west) to Périgueux (47km to the north-east).
In addition to its vines, Bergerac is also an
important tobacco-growing centre and has a
fascinating tobacco museum.

The old town and harbour quarter near
the museum are well worth exploring; as a
Protestant stronghold in the 16th century,
much of the rest of the town sustained
heavy damage during the Wars of Religion.

Information
Tourist Offices The east-west rue de la Résistance is the modern town's main shopping
street. The old town is south of here, towards
the river, with place du Dr Cayla at its heart.

The tourist office (☎ 05 53 57 03 11, fax
05 53 61 11 04, e tourisme-bergerac@
aquinet.tm.fr) at 97 rue Neuve d'Argenson
is open 9.30am to 1pm and 2pm to 7pm
daily except Sunday and holidays. From
mid-June to mid-September it opens 9.30am
to 7pm daily. It has an Internet facility.

THE DORDOGNE

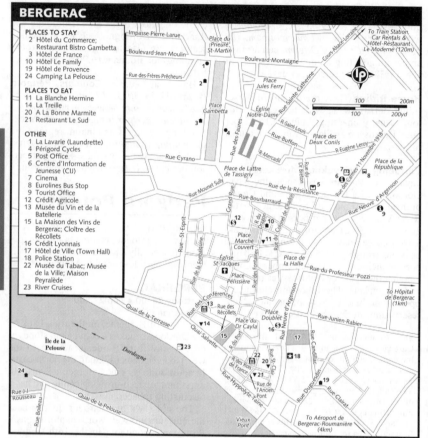

BERGERAC

PLACES TO STAY
2 Hôtel du Commerce;
   Restaurant Bistro Gambetta
3 Hôtel de France
10 Hôtel Le Family
19 Hôtel de Provence
24 Camping La Pelouse

PLACES TO EAT
11 La Blanche Hermine
14 La Treille
20 A La Bonne Marmite
21 Restaurant Le Sud

OTHER
1 La Lavarie (Laundrette)
4 Périgord Cycles
5 Post Office
6 Centre d'Information de
   Jeunesse (CIJ)
7 Cinema
8 Eurolines Bus Stop
9 Tourist Office
12 Crédit Agricole
13 Musée du Vin et de la
   Batellerie
15 La Maison des Vins de
   Bergerac; Cloître des
   Récollets
16 Crédit Lyonnais
17 Hôtel de Ville (Town Hall)
18 Police Station
22 Musée du Tabac; Musée
   de la Ville; Maison
   Peyralède
23 River Cruises

A Centre d'Information de Jeunesse (CIJ,
☎ 05 53 58 11 77, fax 05 53 61 78 88), in the
Galerie du Tortoni shopping arcade, 6 rue des
Carmes, provides information on jobs and
youth-geared events. It opens 8.30am to noon
and 1.30pm to 5.30pm Tuesday to Saturday.

Money Banks include Crédit Agricole at
place Marché Couvert and Crédit Lyonnais
at 8 place Doublet.

Post & Communications The post office
on rue de la Résistance offers currency exchange and Internet facilities.

Laundry The self-service laundrette, La
Lavarie, at 44 place Gambetta, is open 7am
to 10pm daily.

Medical Services & Emergency Hôpital
de Bergerac (☎ 05 53 63 88 88) is at 9 ave
de Prof Albert Calmette, about 1km east of
town. The municipal police station (☎ 05 53
74 66 22) is at 19 rue Neuve d'Argenson.

Musée du Tabac & Musée de la Ville

The Tobacco Museum (☎ 05 53 63 04 13,
10 rue de l'Ancien Pont; adult/child €2.75/

2.75, student free; open 10am-noon & 2pm-6pm Tues-Fri, 10am-noon & 2pm-5pm Sat, 2.30pm-6.30pm Sun), housed in the elegant, early 17th-century Maison Peyralède, has fascinating details of the origins and uses of tobacco (eg, for rituals and medicine) and all varieties of smoking utensils including some incredibly ornate 19th-century pipes. Several other rooms in this well restored old building are devoted to Bergerac's past, with various prehistoric, Neolithic and Gallo-Roman remains.

Musée du Vin et de la Batellerie

This little museum (☎ 05 53 57 80 92, 5 rue des Conférences; adult/child/student €1/0.70/free; open 10am-noon & 2pm-5.30pm Tues-Fri, 10am-noon Sat, 2.30pm-6.30pm Sun; closed Sun 15 Nov-15 Mar), also known as the Musée Régional, mainly records the traditions and modes of transport along the River Dordogne, with models of the gabarres (flat-bottomed boats) once used to transport wine down to Bordeaux and the sabliers for carrying sand. There's also a small display about the traditional methods of batallerie (making wine-barrels).

La Maison des Vins de Bergerac

Housed in a former 17th-century monastery and cloisters (Le Cloître des Récollets), this imposing riverside building is now the headquarters of the Conseil Interprofessionel des Vins de la Région de Bergerac (CIVRB – a promotional organisation for Bergerac wines) known as La Maison des Vins (☎ 05 53 63 57 55, fax 05 53 63 01 30, e vin.civrb@wanadoo.fr, 2 place du Dr Cayla or quai Salvette; admission free). You can wander through the former cloisters or pick up information about the surrounding vineyards and wine chateaux open to the public. From May to September free wine-tasting is on offer in the shop, where you can also buy wines.

The museum is open 10am to 7pm daily 15 June to August; 10am to 12.30pm and 2pm to 6pm Monday to Friday, 10am to noon and 2pm to 5pm on Saturday, 2.30pm to 6.30pm on Sunday March to 15 June and September to October.

Sweet, Mouldy Monbazillac

There's nothing so delicious as a sweet, golden and icy-cold Monbazillac to drink with your foie gras or walnut gateau. Like other sweet, rich wines, this famous vin liquoreux from south of Bergerac depends on a particular mould (Botrytis cinereaor, literally 'noble rot') growing on the grape skins to achieve its superb sweetness and fragrance.

You can have a free tasting after a tour of the Monbazillac Cooperative's beautiful headquarters, the Château de Monbazillac (☎ 05 53 61 52 52, Monbazillac; €5.33) 6km south of Bergerac. Built in 1550, it has scarcely changed, still displaying its machicolations and round towers, its Renaissance decorations and defensive moat. Inside are 17th-century furnishings and tapestries, old documents and rustic Périgord items.

The chateau opens 10am to noon and 2pm to 6pm daily, April to May and in October; 10am to 7pm daily, June and September; 10am to 7.30pm daily, July and August; 10am to noon and 2pm to 5pm Tuesday to Sunday, November to December and February to March.

A taxi from Bergerac (☎ 05 53 57 20 70) will cost around €13.72 plus €12.20 an hour waiting and drinking time.

❋ ❋ ❋ ❋ ❋ ❋ ❋ ❋ ❋ ❋ ❋ ❋ ❋

Organised Tours

At 11am daily in July and August the tourist office runs bilingual, one-hour guided tours of the old town (adult/child aged six to 12 years €3.80/2.30). At noon daily, 8 July to 25 August, an Autorail Esperance tourist trip leaves for Sarlat (adult/child €10.95/3.95 return) with local specialities to taste on board.

Special Events

On the first Sunday morning of every month, a Marché aux Puces (Flea Market) is held in place du Dr Cayla and surrounding streets.

During July and August, free jazz performances take place at 6pm every Wednesday in the Cloître des Récollets and again at 9pm in a nearby square (usually place Pélissière).

Les Tables de Cyrano, held between 12 and 15 July, is a gastronomic celebration of the region's fare, with restaurants offering special *menus*. There's some musical fare on offer, too.

Places to Stay

Bergerac has plenty of accommodation options, including the following.

Camping La Pelouse (☎/fax 05 53 57 06 67, 8 bis, off quai de la Pelouse) Adult/pitch €2.50/1. This simple, municipal camp site is on the southern bank of the river, with 87 shady plots.

Cyrano de... Where?

You'd be forgiven for thinking that Cyrano de Bergerac – sad, big-nosed romantic hero of Edmond Rostand's 1897 play – was born, bred and died in Bergerac town, so well have the locals adopted him (they've even erected a statue in his honour) and used his name and image in all kinds of promotions (including Bergerac wine and a food festival). But the truth is that the real-life dramatist, swordsman and satirist, Savinien Cyrano de Bergerac (1619–55), on whom Rostand based his play, has an extremely tenuous connection, if any, with his namesake town; it is said that he actually came from another town called Bergerac near Paris, or at most stayed here just a few nights en route elsewhere.

JANE SMITH

Hôtel de Provence (☎ 05 53 57 12 88, fax 05 53 24 14 99, 2 rue Clairat) Doubles €22.95-27.45, triples €35.05. The friendly, old-fashioned Provence has bargain rooms with shower (pricier ones with TV).

Hôtel-Restaurant Le Moderne (☎ 05 53 57 19 62, fax 05 53 61 80 50, 19 ave du 108ème RI) Doubles with/without shower & WC €35.05/24.40, triples €41.15/32. Le Moderne is the best of the hotels opposite the train station, with spacious (though thin-walled) modern rooms (those without shower have TV and telephone). Hall showers are clean and free. There is also a very good-value restaurant (see Places to Eat).

Hôtel Le Family (☎ 05 53 57 80 90, fax 05 53 57 08 00, 3 rue du Dragon) Doubles/triples with shower, WC & telephone €34.30/35.85. Midday *menus* (set menus) €6.85, evening *menus* €13.40-25.75. This family-run place is popular with tourists; book ahead in the high season.

Hôtel de France (☎ 05 53 57 11 61, fax 05 53 61 25 70, 18 place Gambetta) Doubles €44.95-51.85. This upmarket, modern hotel boasts a swimming pool; some rooms have balconies overlooking the square.

Hôtel du Commerce (☎ 05 53 27 30 50, fax 05 53 58 23 82, Ⓦ www.hotel-du-commerce24.fr, 36 place Gambetta) Doubles €30.50-48.80. This modern Logis de France hotel has 35 comfortable rooms (the cheaper ones minus TV). It also has a spiffy restaurant (see Places to Eat).

Places to Eat

In addition to several good hotel-restaurants, there are several venues in the old town worth a visit. For snacks, drinks and people-watching, the cafe-bars along pedestrianised rue du Colonel de Chadois are also fun.

A La Bonne Marmite (☎ 05 53 61 96 76, 14 rue St-Clair) Fondues €12.95-16, pastas €7.30-11.90. Open midday & evening Tues-Sat, evening only Mon. This atmospheric nook specialises in fondues, but also serves regional cuisine including a €15.25 *menu Cyrano*.

Restaurant Le Sud (☎ 05 53 27 26 87, 19 rue de l'Ancient Pont) Couscous €11.45, *tajines* €10.95. Open Tues-Sat & 1st Sun of month (midday only). This beautifully decorated venue in the old town provides excellent Moroccan fare.

La Treille (☎ *05 53 57 60 11, 12 quai Salvette)* Midday *menus* €12.95, evening *menus* €18.30-30.20. Bagging a prime riverside location, the Treille has classy *menus* of regional specialities.

La Blanche Hermine (☎ *05 53 57 63 42, place Marché Couvert)* Crepes & salads €3.65-7.45, evening-only *curiosités* (eg, stuffed pineapple) €6.10. Open Tues-Sat. This is a refreshingly stylish venue by the market.

Hôtel-Restaurant Le Moderne *(see Places to Stay)* Midday *menus* €9.90, evening *menus* €14.50-24.40, dishes €10.65-16.95. Open Sat-Thurs. The amazingly generous five-course *menu du jour* is available until 9pm.

Restaurant Bistro Gambetta *(see Places to Stay) Menus* €14.95-21.35. This smart restaurant, situated in Hôtel du Commerce serves traditional fare.

Getting There & Away
Air The Aéroport de Bergerac-Roumanière (☎ 05 53 22 25 25), 4km south-east of town, has one to three flights daily, Monday to Friday to Paris (Orly Sud) with Air France (☎ 0 820 820 820).

Bus Limited bus services leave from outside the train station: SAB (☎ 05 53 40 23 30) runs to Villeneuve-sur-Lot (€8.40, 1¼ hours, twice daily in term-time, once at other times); and CFTA (☎ 05 53 08 43 13) runs to Périgueux (€6.25, 1½ hours, three to four daily).

Eurolines' international services stop on place de la République (opposite the cinema) but only by prior request.

Train Bergerac is on the tertiary rail line that links Bordeaux (€12.20, 1½ hours, four to six daily) with Sarlat-la-Canéda (€9.30, 1¼ hours, two to four daily) via St-Émilion (€10.80, 50 minutes, two daily) and Le Buisson (€5.65, 45 minutes, three to four daily). The station's information and ticket office

(☎ 05 53 63 53 81) is open 5.50am to 7.45pm daily (8.30am to 10.30pm on Sunday).

Getting Around
A taxi (☎ 05 53 57 20 70) from the airport to the town centre will cost around €12.20.

On ave du 108ème RI near the train station are Europcar (☎ 05 53 58 97 97, fax 05 53 27 13 00) at No 3, and Budget (☎ 05 53 74 20 00, fax 05 53 74 20 01) at No 14. AVIS (☎ 05 53 57 69 83, fax 05 53 61 80 52) is at nearby 26 cours Alsace Lorraine. All are open Monday to Saturday.

Périgord Cycles (☎ 05 53 57 07 19) at 11 place Gambetta rents mountain bikes for €15.25/64 per day/week. It opens 9am to noon and 2pm to 7pm Tuesday to Saturday.

One-hour trips along the Dordogne in a *gabarre* (adult/child €6.10/4.25) take place at least three times daily in summer from quai Salvette.

MONPAZIER
postcode 24540 • pop 530
• elevation 180m
Of all the bastides in Southwest France, Monpazier, 45km south-east of Bergerac, is considered the best model. Its buildings and *carreyrous* (narrow alleyways) are breathtakingly well preserved. But what makes Monpazier particularly appealing is the fact that it's still very much alive as a village and market centre, catering as efficiently to its residents as to its summertime visitors.

Perfectly laid out in rectangular grid-style, most of its buildings date from the 13th century. Over 30 are classified as historic monuments. Of particular note are the wonderful main square **place des Cornières** with its covered arcades, the covered market with its set of 15th-century measures, and the town's three fortified gateways.

Established in 1285 by King Edward I, Monpazier had a tough life, assaulted during the Hundred Years' War, taken over by the Huguenots during the Wars of Religion, and the hub of peasant uprisings in the 17th century. Today, it thrives on the region's produce of tobacco, chestnuts, mushrooms and strawberries. If you've got your own wheels, the **Château de Biron** or bastide town of

THE DORDOGNE

Beaumont make excellent day-trips from here (one reader recommends a great two-day bike circuit to Beaumont, Cadouin and Belvès).

Information
The tourist office (☎ 05 53 22 68 59, fax 05 53 74 30 08, e o.t.monpazier@perigord.tm.fr) in the main square is open from 9.30am to 12.30pm and 2pm to 6.30pm Monday to Friday, and 10am to 12.30pm and 3pm to 6.30pm at weekends (10am to 7pm daily in July and August, and to 6pm during October to May).

The post office is on the northern edge of town, near the Foirail Nord (northern parking lot), and there's a Crédit Agricole bank at 17 rue notre Dame, just south of the main square.

Organised Tours & Activities
The tourist office runs guided visits of the bastide on request for €3.05/1.50 per adult/child. During July and August these include evening *visites flambeaux* (medieval-style torch-lit tours), usually 9pm on Friday.

During the summer it also offers guided *circuits randonnées* (walking tours) in the nearby forested countryside for €2.30 per person, usually on Wednesday and Thursday, with advance reservation.

Horse-riders can head for the Centre Équestre de Marsalès (☎/fax 05 53 22 63 14, Marsalès, €14.50/65.55 per hour/day), 2km north, off the D660.

Places to Stay
In addition to the following, the tourist office has details of *chambres d'hôtes* (B&Bs) in the region.

Le Moulin de David (☎ 05 53 22 65 25, fax 05 53 23 99 76, e courrier@moulin-de-david.com, 24540 Gaugeac) 2-person *forfait* (package rate) €10.65. Open mid-May–Sept. This is a tranquil, shady camp site 3.2km west, off the D104.

Hôtel-Restaurant Le Londres (☎ 05 53 22 60 64, fax 05 53 22 61 98, Foirail Nord) Singles €24.40, doubles €33.55-36.60. Le Londres, on the northern edge of town by the parking lot, offers pleasant rooms.

Hôtel-Restaurant de France (☎ 05 53 22 60 06, fax 05 53 22 07 27, 21 rue St-Jacques) Doubles with shower €33.55-44.95. This hotel is right by the main square, with prime-position outdoor seating. Its pricier rooms have TV.

Hôtel Edward 1er (☎ 05 53 22 44 00, fax 05 53 22 57 99, 5 rue St-Pierre) Singles €56.40-102.15, doubles €76.20-137.20. Open Apr-Nov. If you fancy a turreted mini-chateau (plus pool) for a deluxe stay right within the old village, here it is. Go royal and take the King Edward room (€152.45), complete with Jacuzzi and steam bath.

Places to Eat
As well as several restaurants on place des Cornières, others along rue St-Jacques (the north-south road west of place des Comières) include the following.

Le Croquant (☎ 05 53 22 62 63, 28 rue St-Jacques) Midday *menus* €9.25, evening *menus* €12.95-28.95. This is a relaxing, simple venue with generous *menus*.

La Bastide (☎ 05 53 22 60 59, 52 rue St-Jacques) *Menus* €12.20-38.10. Open Tues-Sun. This is a large, fairly stylish place serving excellent regional fare.

Two hotel-restaurants (see Places to Stay) in town are also worth a try. *Hôtel-Restaurant Le Londres* serves good Périgord fare. It has *menus* for €14.50 to €33.55 and dishes for €6.10 to €18.30. *Hôtel-Restaurant de France* has midday *menus* for €10.35, evening *menus* for €14.30 to €25.90 and dishes for €6.85 to €13.70.

Getting There & Away
The nearest train station is at Belvès, 19km to the north-east (see Getting There & Away under Belvès later in this chapter). The closest major bus service (from Villeneuve-sur-Lot) goes to Villeréal, 15km to the west (€3.60, one hour, one daily during term-time, one weekly otherwise). For a taxi, call ☎ 05 53 22 07 15. A taxi from Villeréal to town will cost you about €17.

Getting Around
Bikes can be rented from Monsieur Mouret (☎ 05 53 22 63 46) at 17 rue St-Jacques for

€9.25/38.10 per day/week. He opens Tuesday to Saturday, plus Sunday morning in July and August.

AROUND MONPAZIER
Château de Biron
This grand chateau (☎ 05 53 35 50 10, Biron; adult/child aged 6-12 €4.55/2.30), 8km south of Monpazier, dominates the peaceful land around it.

It wasn't always so tranquil: first established in the 11th century, the chateau was razed by Simon de Montfort and fought over bitterly by the English and French during the Hundred Years' War. And all the time, various generations of the Gontaut-Biron family (who owned it for 800 years) rebuilt, altered and fiddled with it. New additions included a Renaissance chapel and colonnaded arcade, a great state hall and a redesigned keep.

Today owned by the department, many of its rambling basement rooms have been converted to display medieval activities (eg, a tannery, pottery, bakery and a particularly gruesome torture chamber) with moody candlelit lighting.

The chateau opens 10am to 12.30pm and 2pm to 6.30pm daily, May, June and September; 10am to 7pm daily, July and August; 10am to 12.30pm and 2pm to 5.30pm Tuesday to Sunday, 6 February to April, October to December; closed January to 6 February. Visits are sometimes guided (in French), but you can also pick up an English text.

VILLEFRANCHE-DU-PÉRIGORD
postcode 24550 • pop 850 • elevation 153m
This big lively bastide town, founded in 1261 by Alphonse de Poitiers, has unfortunately lost most of its central square layout (a rather ugly church is now the dominant feature), but there's still an eye-catching covered market with stout pillars. This is the focus for the town's most famous attraction, its Marché aux Cèpes (Mushroom Market), which is held around 4pm daily between September and October and attracting mushroom-lovers from all over the region.

Information
The tourist office (☎ 05 53 29 98 37, fax 05 53 30 40 12, e o.t.villefranchepgd@perigord.tm.fr) is about 100m east of the main Place de la Halle, on rue Notre Dame, the town's shopping street. It opens 9.30am to noon and 3pm to 6pm Monday and Tuesday, Thursday to Saturday and Monday morning (closed all day Monday and Sunday afternoon June to October).

Accessible from the tourist office is the **Maison du Châtaignier, Marrons et Champignons** (open same hours as tourist office; adult/child €3.05/1.50), which tells you everything you'll ever need to know (in French only, sadly) about chestnuts, mushrooms and their harvesting.

Places to Stay & Eat
There's not a lot of choice in town, but you should find something reasonable at the following places.

Camping La Bastide (☎ 05 53 28 94 57, fax 05 53 29 47 95, e campingbastide@aol.com, route de Cahors) 1-2 person forfait €9.90. Open June–mid-Sept. This small, friendly camp site, 400m south-east of town, has a small swimming pool and bar.

Café de la Bastide (☎ 05 53 30 22 67, route de Cahors) Singles €30.50, doubles 35.05-38.10, triples €39.65. Pizzas & other dishes €4.55-8.40. Restaurant open midday & evening Fri-Sat, Mon-Wed & evening only Sun. The low-key, ten-room Bastide, en route to the camp site, also sports a swimming pool.

Hôtel du Commerce (☎ 05 53 29 90 08, fax 05 53 29 79 95, Place de la Halle) Doubles €30.50-33.55, triples/quads €42.70/54.85. Open Mar-Dec. Midday menus €9.25, evening menus €12.20-32, dishes €6.85-16.95. This imposing Logis de France hotel, opposite the market, has a friendly reception and good restaurant.

Getting There & Away
Villefranche's train station, 3km west of town, is on the Paris-Agen line. Services include Périgueux (€11.60, 1¼ hours, twice daily) and Agen (€8.70, one hour, twice daily), both once only on Sunday.

BEAUMONT
postcode 24440 • pop 1200
• elevation 160m

Another substantial English bastide town, 16km north-west of Monpazier, Beaumont was founded in 1272 in the name of King Edward I. Traffic on the D660 now rushes past its spacious, unguarded square, **place Jean Moulin**, and the only major fortification left is a 13th-century gateway, **porte de Luzier**, on the western edge of town. But grabbing the limelight still is a huge fortified 13th-century church, **Église de St-Front**, overlooking place Jean Moulin with four fortress-like towers and an incongruously ornate western doorway.

Dolmen fans might like to head 3km to the south to see the **Dolmen du Blanc** (just off the D676), a Neolithic burial chamber of three huge stones.

Orientation & Information
Facing the main square is the well stocked tourist office (☎ 05 53 22 39 12, fax 05 53 22 05 35, **e** ot.beaumont@perigord.tm.fr, **w** www.paysdesbastides.com), open 10am to 6.30pm daily, July to mid-September; 10am to noon and 2pm to 5pm Tuesday, Thursday and Friday, 2pm to 5pm Wednesday, 10am to noon Saturday mid-September to October and April to June (also closed Monday, Wednesday and weekends from November to March).

Places to Stay & Eat
This town has limited options for an overnight stay.

Camping Les Remparts (☎/fax 05 53 22 40 86, route de Villeréal) Adult/pitch €3.80/4.55. Open May-Sept. This friendly, pine-shaded, 60-site camping ground, 800m south-west (off the D676), has a pool and adjacent municipal tennis courts.

Hôtel-Restaurant Le Beaumontois (☎ 05 53 22 30 11, fax 05 53 22 38 99, rue Romieu) Singles €16.95, doubles €22.85-42.70, triples €45.75. Midday *menus* €9.25, evening *menus* €14.50-45.75. By the church, on the main road, this welcoming place has fraying but perfectly adequate rooms (cheaper ones without WC but with the bonus of a bath). The restaurant (whose buffet of hors d'oeuvres is overseen by a stuffed goose wearing a tie) is rather pricey, but worth the splurge.

Getting There & Away
The nearest train station, Lalinde, 10km to the north, is on the Bordeaux (€14.20, 1¾ hours) to Sarlat (€7.15, one hour) line, with three services a day Monday to Saturday. For a taxi call ☎ 05 53 22 98 52.

ISSIGEAC
postcode 24560 • pop 638 • elevation 105m
This picturesque, laid-back, medieval village, 19km south-east of Bergerac, is delightful for an afternoon's stroll. Its **late-Gothic church**, which suffered during the Wars of Religion but was rebuilt, is very impressive, as is the 17th-century former **bishop's palace** nearby. But just as captivating is **La Maison des Têtes**, a humble 15th-century abode in the central Grand'Rue, decorated with carved grinning faces. Many other photogenic half-timbered houses are nearby. Most days, the loudest sounds in Issigeac are from the doves and pigeons that hang out in the lofts of these old buildings. On Sunday morning, the place comes alive with a vibrant market.

Information
The tourist office (☎/fax 05 53 58 79 62, **e** si.issigeac@perigord.tm.fr, **w** www .perso.libertysurf.fr/Issigeac), place du 8 mai, is housed in the former bishop's palace (on the north edge of town by the D14 to Bergerac). It opens 9.30am to noon and 2pm to 6.30pm daily in July and August; and 10am to noon and 2pm to 6pm Tuesday to Sunday other months (closing at 5pm and on Saturday and Sunday afternoons, mid-November to April).

It runs guided one-hour tours (text available in English and German) twice-daily on Tuesday and once on Friday between June and September (adult/child €1.80/0.90).

Places to Stay & Eat
Try the tourist office for a list of *chambres d'hôte* in the area, including two in the town itself.

Camping Municipal (☎ mairie 05 53 58 70 32 or ☎ 05 53 58 79 62, fax 05 53 61 39 65, route de Bergerac) Adult/pitch/car €2.60/0.90/1.30. Open mid-May–Sept. This small riverside site, 150m north of town, is simple but shady and grassy.

Auberge du Café de France (☎ 05 53 58 76 43, Grand'Rue) Doubles with shower & WC €30.50-38.10. Midday *menus* €10.35, evening *menus* €14.95-18.30. This well worn auberge has four newly renovated rooms and a genial proprietor. Its cheerfully decorated restaurant serves a generous midday *menu* including wine.

Getting There & Around
From Bergerac, SARL Cars Bleus (☎ 05 53 23 81 92) buses pass Issigeac (€3.30, 30 mins, once a day Monday to Friday) on their Marmande run. For taxis, call ☎ 05 53 61 76 74. Ets Beau (☎ 05 53 73 51 51), an agricultural equipment retailer 1km north (off the D14), rents bikes for €10.65/53.35 per day/week.

Périgord Blanc

At the heart of the Dordogne, the focus of 'White' Périgord is the departmental capital, Périgueux, while its cultural highlight is the Château de Hautefort.

PÉRIGUEUX
postcode 24000 • pop 43,000
• elevation 106m

Périgueux, capital of Périgord and prefecture of the Dordogne department, is a busy university and commercial city with one of the largest 'safeguarded' historic urban areas in France: The well restored medieval and Renaissance quarter of Puy St-Front. Although not very exciting otherwise, it does have one of France's best museums of prehistory, the Musée du Périgord. With its plentiful supply of accommodation and excellent restaurants it makes a decent base for a few days.

Founded over 2000 years ago on a hill bounded by a curve in the gentle River Isle, Périgueux (originally called Vesunna) flourished under Roman rule, only to be deci-

mated by post-Roman invaders. It became the modest capital of Périgord in the 10th century but was soon eclipsed by its neighbour, the sanctuary and market town of Puy St-Front. The two finally united under the name of Périgueux in the 13th century.

Today the town is at its most appealing on the Wednesday and Saturday market days (from November to March truffles and foie gras are the market's main attractions).

Orientation
Puy St-Front, the old medieval and Renaissance city, is on the hillside between the River Isle (to the east) and blvd Michel Montaigne and place Bugeaud (to the west). On the other side of place Bugeaud is the largely residential Cité, centred around the ruins of a Roman amphitheatre. The train station is about 1km west of Puy St-Front.

Information
Tourist Offices The town's tourist office (☎ 05 53 53 10 63, fax 05 53 09 02 50, ⓔ tour isme.perigueux@perigord.tm.fr, ⓦ www .ville-perigueux.fr) at 26 place Francheville, next to Tour Mataguerre, is open 9am to 12.30pm and 2pm to 6pm Monday to Saturday (9am to 7pm daily during July and August). An extra information kiosk opens up on place André Maurois 9am to 9pm daily between 15 June and 15 September. They have an excellent (multilingual) free map describing the Renaissance and Gallo-Roman sights in the city.

For general information about the Dordogne department (and the Service de Reservation Loisirs Accueil), head for the Comité Départemental du Tourisme's Espace Tourisme Périgord (☎ 05 53 35 50 24, fax 05 53 09 51 41, ⓔ dordogne.perigord .tourisme@wanadoo.fr, ⓦ www.perigord .tm.fr) at 25 rue du Président Wilson. It opens 9am to noon and 2pm to 5pm on Monday to Thursday (and to 4.45pm on Friday).

The Centre d'Information Jeunesse (CIJ; ☎ 05 53 53 52 81, ⓔ contact@ville-peri gueux.fr) is beside the Nouveau Théâtre de Périgueux at 1 ave d'Aquitaine, and has information on jobs, long-term lodging and

THE DORDOGNE

PÉRIGUEUX

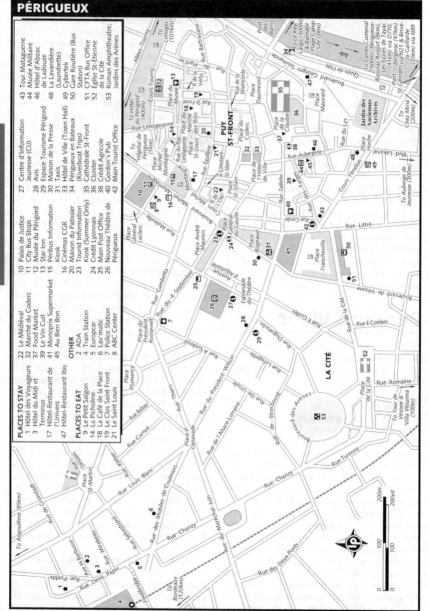

PLACES TO STAY
1 Hôtel des Voyageurs
3 Hôtel du Midi et Terminus
17 Hôtel-Restaurant de l'Univers
47 Hôtel-Restaurant Ibis

PLACES TO EAT
9 Le Petit Saïgon
14 La Picholine
18 La Café de la Place
19 Le Clos Saint Front
21 Le Saint Louis

22 Le Médiéval
32 Marché du Coderc
37 Food Market
39 Le Vin Cuit
41 Monoprix Supermarket
45 Au Bien Bon

OTHER
2 ADA
4 Train Station
5 Europcar
6 Lav'matic
7 Le Clos Saint Front
8 ABC Center

10 Palais de Justice
11 City Bus Stops
12 Food Market
13 Star Inn
15 Péribus Information Kiosk
16 Cinémas CGR
20 Maison du Patissier
23 Tourist Information Kiosk (Summer Only)
24 Crédit Lyonnais
25 Main Post Office
26 Nouveau Théâtre de Périgueux

27 Centre d'Information Jeunesse (CIJ)
28 Avis
29 Espace Tourisme Périgord
30 Maison de la Presse
31 Taxis
33 Hôtel de Ville (Town Hall)
34 Périgueux en Bateaux (Riverboat Trips)
35 Cathédrale St-Front
36 Cloister
38 Crédit Agricole
40 Gordon's Pub
42 Main Tourist Office

43 Tour Mataguerre
44 Musée Militaire
46 Hôtel d'Abzac
48 La Lavandière (Laundrette)
49 Cybertek
50 Gare Routière (Bus Station)
51 CFTA Bus Office
52 Église St-Étienne de la Cité
53 Roman Amphitheatre; Jardins des Arènes

Ecomusée de la Truffe

To unravel the mysteries of truffles, pay a visit to **La Musée de la Truffe** (☎ 05 53 05 90 11, fax 05 53 46 71 43, e si.sorges@perigord.tm .fr; adult/student/child aged 10-15 €4/3/2) in Sorges, 20km north-east of Périgueux. This village calls itself the capital of truffles (as do several other Dordogne towns!), thanks largely to its major truffle market held on the Sunday nearest 20 January.

The museum makes a heroic attempt at explaining why and where truffles grow (signs in English and French) and then encourages you to take a 3km walk in fields across the road to see typical truffle terrain. The adjacent tourist office (open same hours) organises guided visits at 3.30pm every Tuesday and Thursday in July and August (€4), plus the chance to taste truffle-flavoured toast (€2).

The museum opens 9.30am to 12.30pm and 2.30pm to 6.30pm daily, 17 June to 6 October; 10am to noon and 2pm to 5pm Tuesday to Sunday, 7 October to 10 November, 16 to 22 December, 4 February to 3 March and 1 April to 16 June; 2pm to 5pm Tuesday to Sunday the rest of year.

If the museum visit whets your appetite you can taste more of the real thing at nearby **Auberge de la Truffe** (☎ 05 53 05 02 05, fax 05 53 05 39 27, e contact@auberge-de-la-truffe.com), where award-winning chef, Pierre Core, can whip up an omelette aux truffes for €18.30.

❈ ❈ ❈ ❈ ❈ ❈ ❈ ❈ ❈ ❈ ❈ ❈

youth-related activities. It opens 8.30am to noon and 2pm to 6pm Monday to Friday.

Bookshops Regional guides and maps are available at the Maison de la Presse bookshop, 11 place Bugeaud.

Money Central banks include Crédit Lyonnais at 1 place Général de Gaulle and Crédit Agricole at 40 rue Taillefer.

Post & Communication The main post office, at 1 rue du 4 Septembre, has exchange and Internet facilities. You can also

connect to the Internet for €4.60 per hour at Cybertek, 14 cours Fénelon (open 10am to 12.30pm, 2pm to 7pm Tuesday to Saturday), or for €1.50 per 15 minutes at ABC Center, a photocopying shop at 1 place du Général Leclerc, (open 8am to 7.15pm Monday to Friday, 8am to 6pm on Saturday).

Laundry La Lavandière, on place Hoche, opens 8am to 8pm daily. Lav'matic, at 18 rue des Mobiles de Coulmiers, stays open an hour later.

Medical Services & Emergency The Hôpital de Périgueux (hospital; ☎ 05 53 07 70 00) is at 80 ave Georges Pompidou, 1km north-east of the city centre. The Hôtel de Police (police station; ☎ 05 53 01 17 67) is at 17 rue du 4 Septembre.

Left Luggage You can leave luggage at the train station (see Getting There & Away later) ticket counter (open 5am or 6am to 8pm Monday to Thursday, 6am to 10.15pm Friday to Sunday) for €4.60 per bag per 24 hours.

Puy St-Front

Established around the abbey of St-Front in the 6th century, Puy St-Front is Périgueux's most appealing neighbourhood. On the site of the abbey stands the eye-catching **Cathédrale St-Front**, (rue St-Front; open 8am-12.30pm & 2.30pm-7.30pm daily), topped with five domes studded with bumps and many equally bumpy smaller domes. When seen against the evening sky it looks like something you might come across in Istanbul. But by day, the sprawling structure, controversially 'restored' in the late 19th century by Abadie (who used similar designs in his later creation of Paris' Sacré Cœur), looks contrived and overwrought in the finest pseudo-Byzantine tradition. The best views of the cathedral (and the town) are from pont des Barris.

The unadorned interior of the cathedral, whose entrance faces the south end of rue St-Front, is shaped like a Greek cross. It is noteworthy only for the spectacularly carved 17th-century baroque **retable** in the choir. The eclectic cloister, next to place de la Clautre, is equally unexceptional.

The ancient narrow streets north of the cathedral include **rue du Plantier** and the area's main thoroughfare, **rue du Puy Limogeanne**, which has graceful Renaissance buildings at Nos 3 and 12. Nearby, **rue Éguillerie** and **rue de la Miséricorde** have more such structures. Particularly attractive is the **Maison du Patissier**, a turreted mansion, built in 1518, at the corner of rue Éguillerie and place St-Louis. The 15th- and 16th-century houses along rue Aubergerie include **Hôtel d'Abzac de Ladouze**, across from No 19, with its two octagonal towers.

The **Musée du Périgord** (☎ 05 53 06 40 70, 22 cours Tourny; adult/student/those under 18 years €3.05/1.50/free; open 11am-6pm Mon & Wed-Fri, 1pm-6pm Sat-Sun Apr-Sept; 10am-5pm Mon & Wed-Fri, 1pm-6pm Sat & Sun Oct-Mar) is renowned for its rich collection of prehistoric tools and implements. It also has a wealth of Gallo-Roman artefacts from ancient Vesunna.

The **Musée Militaire** (☎ 05 53 53 47 36, 32 rue des Farges; adult/child €3.05/free; open 10am-noon & 2pm-6pm Mon-Sat Apr-Sept; 2pm-6pm Mon-Sat Oct-Dec; 2pm-6pm Wed & Sat Jan-Mar), founded right after WWI, has a particularly varied collection of swords, weapons, uniforms and insignia from the Napoleonic wars and the two world wars.

Of the 28 towers that once made up Puy St-Front's medieval fortifications, only **Tour Mataguerre**, a stout, round bastion on place Francheville (next to the tourist office) remains. It was given its present form in the late 15th century. Entry to the tower is only granted as part of the tourist office's Medieval Renaissance tour.

La Cité

One of the few remains of Vesunna – later known simply as La Cité – are the crumbling stones and arches of Périgueux's 1st-century **Roman amphitheatre**, now an almost-forgotten part of a pleasant little public garden, the **Jardins des Arènes** (blvd des Arènes; admission free; open 7.30am-6pm daily Oct-Mar; 7.30am-9pm daily Apr-

Sept). The rest of the massive structure, designed to hold 30,000 spectators, was disassembled and carried off in the 3rd century to construct the city walls.

Some 300m to the south is the 20m-high **Tour de Vésone**. Shaped like a gargantuan anklet, it's the only remaining section of a Gallo-Roman temple thought to have been dedicated to the Goddess Vesunna, protector of the town. The nearby remains of the **Villa Vesunna**, a 1st- to 4th-century Roman villa, is planned to be the centrepiece of a new **Musée Gallo-Roman**, due to open late 2002.

Église St-Étienne de la Cité, 50m southeast of the amphitheatre on place de la Cité, is an 11th- and 12th-century church that served as Périgueux's cathedral until 1669. Only two cupolas and two bays survived the devastation wrought by the Huguenots during the Wars of Religion (1562–98), which also destroyed a neighbouring episcopal palace.

Organised Tours

The tourist office organises guided 90-minute tours of the city (adult/child €4.60/3.50; in French but with guides who speak some English). Between mid-June and mid-September they take place at 10.30am (Gallo-Roman tour), 2.30pm and 4pm (both Medieval Renaissance tours) Monday to Saturday. The rest of the year, a Medieval-Renaissance tour takes place at 2.30pm Monday to Saturday.

Fifty-minute river trips (with commentary) are operated by the **Périgueux en Bateaux** (☎ 05 53 24 58 80, Quai de L'Isle). The boats leave 10am to 6pm daily, May to September, from near pont des Barris, east of the cathedral. Adult/child tickets cost €6.10/3.80.

Special Events

Périgueux's most dynamic cultural event is its Festival Internationale Mime Actuel (☎ 05 53 53 18 71, ℮ contact@ville-perigueux.fr), held for a week in early August, with stage as well as free street performances (usually on place St-Louis or Esplanade du Théâtre). The Festival Sinfonia en Périgord (☎ 05 53 53 32 95, fax 05 53 03 78 77, ℮ sinfonia@perigord.tm.fr) features highbrow classical concerts in the cathedral and nearby chateaux

Périgord Market Days

Périgord's open-air markets are the ideal places to find home-made or home-grown produce such as honey, goat's cheese, jam and cakes, wine, fruit and *confits* (preserves of duck or goose). In winter look for specialities such as foie gras, truffles, walnuts and *cèpes* (ceps or wild mushrooms). During September, ceps get their own special fair every Thursday afternoon in Montpazier's place des Cornières and daily at Villefranche-du-Périgord. Truffles are available in the markets every Wednesday and Saturday in Périgueux between about mid-November and March; and walnuts every Wednesday from October to December in Montignac and Ribérac, and every Friday in Brantôme.

Here are when the regular markets take place year-round:

Monday Les Eyzies de Tayac
Tuesday Le Bugue
Wednesday Périgueux, Hautefort, Montignac, Bergerac, Sarlat-la-Canéda
Thursday Monpazier, Domme
Friday Brantôme, Ribérac
Saturday Bergerac, Belvès, Beaumont, Le Bugue, Monpazier, Montignac, Périgueux, Sarlat-la-Canéda, Thiviers
Sunday St-Cyprien

(eg, Château de Bourdeilles) for two weeks from late August to early September.

Places to Stay

Camping & Hostels Those who are on a budget could try the following.

Barnabé Plage (☎ 05 53 53 41 45, 05 53 54 16 62, Boulazac) Open year round. Adult/pitch/car €2.75/2.60/3.05. This 56-pitch riverside camp site has mini-golf, ping pong and other games. Take the hourly bus No 8 from Palais de Justice (opposite place Michel Montaigne) to the rue des Bains stop (last bus at 7.27pm; no service on Sunday).

Auberge de Jeunesse (☎ 05 53 06 81 40, fax 05 53 06 81 49, rue des Thermes Prolongés, e fjt24@perigord.tm.fr) Dorm bed €11.10 with breakfast. Reception 4pm-9am;

open year round. Bus No 6 from Palais de Justice to Lakanal stop (last bus at 6.42pm). This auberge, in the Foyer de Jeunes Travailleurs complex, is just off blvd Lakanal, 600m south of the cathedral, and has a kitchen and canteen.

Hotels Some good-value options can be found to the west of town.

Hôtel des Voyageurs (☎/fax 05 53 53 17 44, 26 rue Denis Papin) Singles €12.20-13.70, doubles €13.70-16.95. The cheapest of the bunch of budget hotels near the train station, the old but friendly Voyageurs has linoleum-cracked but clean rooms, most without shower or WC (hall showers free).

Hôtel du Midi et Terminus (☎ 05 53 53 41 06, fax 05 53 08 19 32, 18 rue Denis Papin) Singles with shower €26.70, without €21.35; doubles with shower €26.70-32.75, without €22.10; singles with shower & WC €32.75, doubles €32.75-38.85. Hall showers free. This is an amiable two-star hotel with good-value rooms. Reception is closed until 6pm on Sunday.

Hôtel-Restaurant de l'Univers (☎ 05 53 53 34 79, fax 05 53 06 70 76, 18 cours Michel Montaigne) Attic doubles €27.43, other doubles €38.10-48.80. This modest, very central hotel has two small attic doubles without shower, and ten others with shower and WC.

Hôtel du Périgord (☎ 05 53 53 33 63, fax 05 53 08 19 74, 74 rue Victor Hugo) Singles €32-38.10, doubles €35.05-45.75, all with shower and WC. Several notches higher is this pleasant 20-room hotel north of town. It's on a busy main road so try to get a room facing the back garden.

Hôtel-Restaurant Ibis (☎ 05 53 53 64 58, fax 05 53 07 51 79, w www.ibishotel.com, 8 blvd Georges Saumande) Doubles €53.35. This modern hotel has all the comforts (if not much character) you'd expect of the Ibis chain and a great riverside position right below the cathedral.

Places to Eat

Restaurants There's a fantastic choice of restaurants in Puy St-Front, especially in the streets below the Musée Militaire and

THE DORDOGNE

around pedestrianised place St-Louis and place St-Silain.

Au Bien Bon (☎ *05 53 09 69 91, 15 rue des Places)* Midday *formules* €9.15-12.95, dishes €8-10.65. Open midday & evening Tues-Sat, midday only Mon. This popular place serves regional fare in a cheery setting.

Le Vin Cuit (☎ *05 53 09 48 90, 7 rue des Farges)* Open Mon-Sat. Midday *plat du jour* (dish of the day) €6.10, *menus* €7.60-11.45. This unpretentious seven-table restaurant is a homely place serving traditional, good-value food.

Le Médiéval (☎ *05 53 53 63 35, 9 place St-Silain)* Open Tues-Sun. Midday *menus* €9.90, evening *menus* €16.95-25.90, dishes €12.95-14.50. A reader recommends this 'dinky' restaurant, which serves both mainstream dishes and lighter meals.

La Picholine (☎ *05 53 53 86 91, 6 rue du Puy Limogeanne)* *Menus* €13.55-17.55, dishes €9.90-11.30. The Picholine, tucked away in a quiet alley, specialises in Provençale cuisine and has a tempting midday €9.90 *menu*.

Le Saint Louis (☎ *05 53 53 53 90, 26 rue Éguillerie)* Pastas & salads €4.90-7.75, *menus* €10.50-14.95. Open daily (except Sun off-season). This friendly bar-brasserie has great outdoor seating in the attractive, spacious square.

La Café de la Place (☎ *05 53 08 21 11, 7 place du Marché du Bois)* Midday *menus* €7.75, dishes €9-12.80. This is a very pleasant, relaxing venue, with Charlie Chaplin-era decor inside and timeless ambience outside.

Le Petit Saïgon (☎ *05 53 09 51 99, 1 place Général Leclerc)* *Menus* €11.45-14.95, dishes €5.35-10.35. Open Mon-Sat. There's a huge range of good-value Chinese-Vietnamese dishes here.

Chez Mina (☎ *05 53 09 73 68, 7 place due 8 Mai)* Couscous €9.90-18.15, midday *menus* €9.90 including ¼L of wine. Open Mon-Sat. This locally popular lunchtime riverside eatery offers a refreshing change from foie-gras fare.

Le Clos Saint Front (☎ *05 53 46 78 58, 5 rue de la Vertu, entrance on rue St-Front)* Midday *menus* €15.25, evening €19.05-22.85. Open daily (except Sun & Mon off-season, and Mon-Wed evenings July & Aug). For 'serious regional cooking' a reader recommends this renowned restaurant, which serves market-fresh traditional cuisine in a refined setting (plus outdoor seating in a cosy courtyard).

Self-Catering Near the cathedral, a lively *food market* *(place de la Clautre)* is held on Wednesday and Saturday mornings. From mid-November to March an additional speciality market, *marché de gras* (literally 'market of fatty livers'), takes place on the same days in nearby place St-Louis, selling not only foie gras but also truffles, wild mushrooms, walnuts, *confits* (conserves, typically of duck or goose) and other delicacies.

Marché du Coderc *(place du Coderc)* is open daily until about 1.30pm. On the first floor of ***Monoprix*** *(place Bugeaud)* there's a supermarket open 9am to noon and 2pm to 7pm Monday to Saturday.

Entertainment

If you're still wide awake in the evening, you may want to have a look into the following.

Gordon's Pub (☎ *05 53 35 03 74, 12 rue Conde)* Open 11am-2am, Mon-Sat. You'll find Murphy's on tap and good vibes at this centrally located bar.

Star Inn (☎ *05 53 08 56 83, place du Musée)* Open 8pm-1am or 2am. This welcoming Anglo-Irish pub has a happy hour from 8pm to 9pm Monday to Thursday and a stack of English-language books available.

Le Key Largo (☎ *05 53 53 01 58, 51 rue Aubarède)* Open 11pm-5am Fri & Sat. This is a gay-friendly bar, about 300m north-east of Pont des Barris.

Cinémas CGR (☎ *05 53 09 40 99, 19 blvd Michel Montaigne)* This screens nondubbed films, except during school holidays.

Getting There & Away

Air The Périgueux-Bassilac airport (☎ 05 53 02 79 70) is 8km east of the city. Air France (☎ 0 820 820 820) flies to Paris (Orly Sud) one to three times daily. Taxis to town cost around €10.65.

Bus The Gare Routière, or bus station, is on the southern side of place Francheville. Timetables are posted on the platforms (and are also available at the tourist office). The major carrier, CFTA (☎ 05 53 08 43 13), has an office (open 8am to noon and 2pm to 6pm Monday to Friday; to 5pm on Friday) at the terminal's western end. Non-CFTA timetables are hard to find: You'll need to telephone Rey (☎ 05 53 07 27 21) for details of services to Le Bugue; Auvezere Tourisme (☎ 05 53 05 30 07) for Hautefort; and Cournil (☎ 05 53 55 02 77) for Thiviers and Sorge.

Except on Sunday and holidays, destinations served include Bergerac (€6.25, 1½ hours, three daily), Brantôme (€7.40, 40 minutes, one or two daily), Le Bugue (€7, one hour, one daily during term-time), Ribérac (€4.70, one hour, four daily) and Sarlat-la-Canéda (€7.60, 1½ hours, one or two daily; only on Wednesday and Saturday in July and August) via the Vézère Valley town of Montignac (€5.35, one hour).

Train The train station (☎ 08 36 35 35 35), on rue Denis Papin, is connected to place Michel Montaigne and the bus station by bus Nos 4 and 5, and also to place Bugeaud by bus No 1.

Destinations with direct services include Agen (€17.70, 2½ hours, five daily); Bordeaux (€15.40, 1½ hours, six to nine daily), Brive-la-Gaillarde (€10.05, one hour, four daily) and Les Eyzies de Tayac (€6.25, 30 minutes, two to four daily).

Services to Paris' Gare d'Austerlitz (€43.15, 4½ hours, 12 daily) are mostly via Limoges; to Toulouse (€27.45, four hours, up to 16 daily from Agen) they're via Agen. To get to Sarlat (€11.75), change at Le Buisson (€7.45, 44 minutes, two daily).

Car Rental firms include Europcar (☎ 05 53 08 15 72), at 7 rue Denis Papin, ADA (☎ 05 53 53 17 70) at 6 ave H Barbusse and Avis (☎ 05 53 53 39 02, fax 05 53 03 45 88) at 18 rue du Président Wilson.

Getting Around

Péribus, the local bus company, has an information kiosk (☎ 05 53 53 30 37) on place Michel Montaigne, the main bus hub, open 9am to 12.15pm and 2pm to 5.45pm Monday to Friday.

Free car-parking is available at Parking des Quais. The central underground car parks at place Michel Montaigne and place Francheville cost €2.45 up to nine hours. For a taxi call ☎ 05 53 09 09 09 or 05 53 53 70 47.

Cycles Cumenal (☎ 05 53 53 31 56), about 500m east of the city at 41 bis cours St-Georges, rents town/mountain bikes for €7.60/12.20 per day or €25.90/38.10 per week. It opens 9.30am to noon and 2pm to 7pm Tuesday to Saturday.

HAUTEFORT
postcode 24390 • pop 1100
• elevation 200m

This small hilltop village, 40km east of Périgueux, is dominated by one of the Dordogne's grandest chateau. There are also some tempting walks in the nearby Auvézère Valley.

Information

The tourist office (☎ 05 53 50 40 27, e ot .hautefort@perigord.tm.fr) has a splendid location in part of the 17th-century Ancien Hospice de Hautefort, on place de l'Église, at the top (eastern end) of the village. It opens 10am to noon and 2pm to 6pm daily (10am to 7pm daily June to September). Also in the building is the **Musée de la Médecine** *(open same hours as tourist office; €3.80/1.50 adult/child aged under 12)* with a small, intriguing display on the history of medicine.

Available from the tourist office is *Promenades et Randonnées Canton de Hautefort* (€2.30), indicating 120km of signposted trails for walkers, horse-riders and mountain-bikers.

Château de Hautefort

Visible for miles around, the strategically placed hilltop chateau *(☎ 05 53 50 51 23; admission on 50-minute guided visits only, adult/child aged 5-13 €6.10/3.20; gardens only €3.80/2.30)*, with its eye-catching domed towers, had several predecessors to its present 17th-century-style reincarnation by

THE DORDOGNE

Jacques-François de Hautefort (whose sister, Marie, was Louis XIII's secret mistress). Its 12th-century version was the birthplace of the famously pugnacious troubadour, Bertrand de Born; in 1836, Eugène Le Roy (author of *Jacquou le Croquant*) was also born here, to a family working on the estate.

In the 20th century, the chateau was meticulously restored over a period of 39 years by the Bastard family but in 1968, the year it was finished, the whole thing went up in flames, thanks to a smouldering cigarette. Undeterred, the indomitable (and, fortuitously, extremely wealthy) Madame Durosoy set to work all over again. Most of the interior features, then, are new but extremely fine replicas; especially outstanding are the parquet floors and carved chestnut timberwork. Other highlights include 17th-century paintings and tapestries and the original 15th-century round tower. The chateau is surrounded by gorgeous gardens: immaculate topiary on one side and a rambling English-style park on the other.

The chateau's opening hours vary throughout the year. It opens 10am to noon and 2pm to 6pm daily, 1 April to 12 July and 26 August to 7 October; 9.30am to 7pm daily, 12 July to 26 August (last visit 6.15pm); 2pm to 6pm daily, 8 October to 4 November (last visit 5pm); 2pm to 6pm on Sunday only, 8 October to 2 December; 2pm to 6pm, 3 to 25 February; 2pm to 6pm on Sunday only in March; closed 3 December to 2 February. Smoking everywhere is, of course, strictly forbidden.

Places to Stay & Eat
Though small, this village has a handful of decent places to eat and sleep.

Le Moulin des Loisirs (℡/fax 05 53 50 46 55, Étang de Coucou) 2-person forfait €8.85. Open May-Oct. This camp site, 3km to the south (off the D704), is beside Étang de Coucou, a large lake with a bar-restaurant, *Le Moulin de Nicette* (℡/fax 05 53 50 46 55), open July to August, at one end. The site has bikes, canoes and horses – and fearsome guard dogs!

Les Tourterelles (℡ 05 53 51 11 17, fax 05 53 50 53 44, Tourtoirac) Adult/pitch/car

€3.60/8.55/1.50. Some 10km west of Hautefort (1km north of Tourtoirac, off the D73), this upmarket camp site has a pool and tennis court plus horses to ride.

Hôtel-Restaurant Le Médiéval (℡ 05 53 50 40 47, place de l'Église) Doubles with/without shower €21.35/18.30. Midday *menus* €9.90, evening *menus* €12.20-15.25. Le Médiéval is an unfussy place near the tourist office with basic rooms and honest fare, for example, *magret, frites et salade* (duck breast, chips and salad) for €9.90.

Hôtel Auberge du Parc (℡ 05 53 50 88 98, fax 05 53 51 61 72, place René Lavaud) Doubles/triples €30.50/38.10. *Menus* €14.50-18.30. Restaurant open midday & evening Mon-Tues, Thur-Sat, midday only Sun. The Parc, at the bottom of the main shopping street, rue du Bertrand de Born, is very good value. All rooms have shower, WC, TV and telephone. The menu has some surprises – how about kangaroo meat with roquefort sauce? (€12.95).

Getting There & Away
There's only one bus daily on weekdays from Périgueux (€5.50), departing at 5.25pm, returning at 7.30am the next day (1.10pm on Wednesday). The bus stop is on place de l'Église, by the tourist office.

The nearest train station is at La Bachellerie (15km to the south), with connections to Brive-la-Gaillarde (€5.20, 30 minutes) and Périgueux (€6.55, 40 minutes) twice daily. A taxi (℡ 05 53 50 44 64) between the train station and Hautefort costs around €12.95.

Périgord Vert

Stretching in a crescent shape across the north of the Dordogne department, 'Green' Périgord receives less of the limelight than areas to the south, though it has a generous sprinkling of chateaux and attractive towns. Useful bases include Ribérac and Brantôme.

RIBÉRAC
postcode 24600 • pop 4450 • elevation 68m
There's not much to see in this drowsy little town in the heart of the Dronne Valley,

32km west of Périgueux, unless you come on a Friday when the biggest market in Périgord makes the place really buzz. But it's a relaxing base for exploring the lovely surrounding countryside by bike, or on foot or horseback. Two major attractions are the 50,000-hectare Forêt de la Double (once notorious for harbouring brigands and disease, now a haven for wildlife), which stretches to the south and west of town, and the dozens of Romanesque churches in the area, several within easy walking and cycling distance.

Orientation & Information
Place National, and the rue du 26 mars (D709) that runs through it, are the commercial focus of town. The Friday market encompasses both this area and, to its west, the spacious twin squares, place Debonnière and place du Général de Gaulle. On their western side, near Café du Palais, is the Maison du Pays, displaying and selling local products and also housing the tourist office (☎ 05 53 90 03 10, fax 05 53 91 35 13, e ot .riberac@perigord.tm.fr). It opens 9am to noon and 2pm to 6.30pm Monday to Saturday (to 5pm November to May). In July and August it opens 9am to 12.30pm and 1.30pm to 7pm Monday to Saturday (9am to 7pm on Friday) and 10am to 1pm on Sunday and holidays.

An SNCF train ticket service (☎ 05 53 90 26 82) operates from the tourist office from 9am to noon and 2pm to 5pm Monday, Tuesday, Thursday and Friday, and 9am to noon on Wednesday and Saturday (also open Wednesday afternoon in July and August).

The post office, at 20 rue du 26 mars, has currency exchange and Internet facilities. Nearby banks include Crédit Agricole on place National.

Activities
Walkers on the Romanesque churches' trail can find *Le circuit des églises à coupoles du Ribéracois* brochure at the tourist office, as well as *Sentiers du Périgord* (€10.65), a pack of *petits randonnées* (small walks from two to 20km). From mid-June to mid-September (usually on Wednesday or Thursday), the tourist office runs free multilingual guided

Église Monolithe de St-Jean
Some 17km west of Ribérac (just over the border in the Charente *département*, or administrative department), the delightful little village of Aubeterre-sur-Dronne boasts an astonishing sight – the largest monolithic church in France, the **Église Monolithe** (☎ 05 45 98 50 33; adult/child aged 7-16 €3.35/0.90; open 9.30am-12.30pm & 2pm-7pm daily mid-June–mid-Oct; 9.30am-12.30pm & 2pm-6pm daily mid-Oct–mid-June).

This formidable structure was hewn from the rockface high above the River Dronne by Benedictine followers of St-Maur in the 12th century. The vast 20m-high semi-circular vaults were probably carved out from much earlier grottoes – a crypt that came to light in 1961 may even have been used during the Roman period to celebrate the bloody cult of Mithras.

Most spooky of all are the many stone sarcophagi – 80 in one chamber alone (possibly pre-Christian) – where the dead were interred one above another. The main chamber of the church was also used as a vast cemetery (now covered over). A €0.90 English leaflet, available at the entrance, explains what you're seeing (and stepping on!).

tours of Romanesque churches in and around Ribérac.

The nearest horse-riding centre is **Madrix** (☎ 05 53 90 03 53, Villetoureix; around €15.25 per hour), 2km north.

Canoes can be rented from **Camping de la Dronne** (see Places to Stay & Eat; €6.10 per person per hour, mid-June to mid-September).

Special Events
The Festival Musiques et Paroles en Ribéracois is the biggest annual event, celebrating world music, classical and jazz, from mid-July to mid-August. Contact the tourist office for details.

Places to Stay & Eat
Ribérac's accommodation and restaurants include the following.

A Ton of Snails

For most of the year, nothing very exciting happens in the little village of Bertric Burée, 7km north of Ribérac. But every May for the last 50 years – always on the first Monday following the first Sunday in May – a unique event has taken place: Bertric Burée holds a gigantic feast of snails.

A ton of 80,000 large wild snails (locally called *cagouilles*) are on the menu to cater for the thousands of gourmets who turn up for the lunch and dinner (Bertric Burée itself has only 400 inhabitants). It takes 70 people three days to clean and prepare the chosen molluscs and then cook them *à la Bertricoise* – with garlic, sausage meat, parsley, 15L of wine, and other secret liquid ingredients known only to the local blacksmith, Michel Burguet, who's the mastermind behind the event. Advance bookings aren't possible, so just turn up and be prepared to have the snail feast of your life!

✳ ✳ ✳ ✳ ✳ ✳ ✳ ✳ ✳ ✳ ✳ ✳

Camping de la Dronne (☎ 05 53 90 50 08, fax 05 53 91 35 13) Adult/pitch €1.75/1.85. Open June–mid-Sept. The friendly municipal camp site is a couple of kilometres to the north (off the D708) on the banks of the River Dronne, with a municipal pool and tennis courts nearby.

Hôtel-Restaurant Le Commerce (☎ 05 53 91 28 59, 8 rue Gambetta) Doubles €24.40-27.45 with shower, €30.50 with shower & WC. Midday *menus* €8.40, evening *menus* €9.90-17.55. Restaurant open daily (except Sat & Sun eve off season). This modest seven-room hostelry has huge rooms and a pretty restaurant; try its unusual €20.60 *menu Antillaises* (Antilles cuisine).

Hôtel de France (☎ 05 53 90 00 61, fax 05 53 91 06 05, ℮ hdfr@club-internet.fr, 3 rue Marc-Dufraisse) Singles €32-41.15, doubles €38.90-46.50, triples €43.45-44.95, quads €47.25-49.55. Midday *menus* €12.95, evening *menus* €15.25-35.05, dishes €13.70-21.35. Restaurant open daily (except Sat & Tues midday, & Mon all day

off-season). This very appealing 20-room Logis de France hotel has an excellent restaurant; it even offers a vegetarian *menu* (€15.25).

Getting There & Away
The nearest train station is at Périgueux, connected to Ribérac by four CFTA (☎ 05 53 08 43 13) buses daily Monday to Friday, two on Saturday (€4.70; one hour). The bus stop is by Café du Palais (Place Debonnière on timetables).

Getting Around
Opposite the post office at 35 rue du 26 mars, Cycles Cumenal (☎ 05 53 90 33 23) rents VTTs (*vélos touts terrain*; mountain bikes) for €13.70/38.10 per day/week. You can drop the bike off at Cumenal's other shops in Périgueux or Sarlat. It opens 9am to noon and 2pm to 7pm on Tuesday, Wednesday, Friday and Saturday.

For taxis call ☎ 05 53 90 11 99.

BRANTÔME
postcode 24310 • pop 2000
• elevation 105m
One of the most attractive towns in Périgord Vert, Brantôme lies 22km north of Périgueux in a crook of the River Dronne. Famous for its extraordinary 11th-century abbey and picturesque setting on an island in the river, Brantôme has long been popular with middle-aged Brits. Off-season, avoid Tuesdays, when the abbey, tourist office and many restaurants are closed.

Orientation & Information
The abbey is built into a cliff-face on the north-western side of the river, connected to the island-town by several bridges, including an attractive zig-zag one. At the far end of this bridge is Jardin des Moines, site of the May Fair (see Special Events later).

The tourist office (☎/fax 05 53 05 80 52) is located inside the abbey and open the same hours.

L'Abbaye
The abbey (☎ 05 53 05 80 63; adult/child aged 7-18 €3.05/2.30; open 10am-12.30pm

& *2pm-6pm Wed-Mon, Apr-June & Sept; 10am-7pm daily July-Aug; 10am-noon & 2pm-5pm Wed-Mon Feb-Mar, Oct-Dec),* founded in the 8th century by Charlemagne to house the relics of St Sicaire, was rebuilt in the 11th century and became a major pilgrimage site. But the natural spring and surrounding caves of the cliff-site had attracted pagan worship long before. The monks initially lived in the caves and later used them as refuges at times of attack. They're still the most atmospheric and extraordinary part of the complex, especially the one decorated with a haunting 15th-century carving of the Last Judgement. The oldest and most interesting part of the abbey building – largely rebuilt in the 18th and 19th centuries and now housing the town hall – is the detached 11th-century gabled belltower.

An English text is available to supplement fascinating explanatory boards at each cave.

Musée Rêve et Miniatures

This quaint little museum (☎ *05 53 35 29 00, 8 rue Puyjoli de Meyjounissas; adult/child €5.80/3.05; open 2pm-6pm Sat-Thur Apr-June; 11am-6pm daily July-Aug; 2pm-5pm Sat-Thur Sept-11 Nov)* on the island-town opposite the abbey entrance, displays a collection of miniature interiors from different eras; not your trivial doll's house affair but a haven for serious miniaturists.

Activities

Boat trips with commentary (in French) run around Brantôme five to eight times daily (adult/child €5.30/3.05), leaving from the zig-zag bridge.

For trips along the River Dronne, contact **Allo Canoës** (☎ *05 53 06 31 85, blvd Coligny; canoe/kayak €21.35/13.70; open daily mid-Apr–mid-Sept),* 300m east of the abbey.

Special Events

Huge trade fairs have been held here every 1 May since the medieval pilgrimages of St-Sicaire; the fair is currently held at the Jardin des Moines. Every Friday from November to mid-December there's also a special market devoted to the walnut harvest.

Brantôme's Saucy Abbot

The most notorious abbot in the history of Brantôme – and one of French literature's wittiest storytellers – was Pierre de Bourdeilles (1540–1614), who became the abbey's 'lay' or commendatory abbot in 1562. Hardly pious, he spent most of his life racing round Europe on various military or romantic adventures – though he did save his abbey from the Huguenots during the Wars of Religion after a tête-a-tête with their leader, a former military buddy. Finally grounded after a fall from his horse, Brantôme (as he came to be known) spent the rest of his life at the abbey writing saucy, spicy tales culled from his roving days (notably *Les Vies des Dames Galantes,* Lives of Court Mistresses), which made his posthumous fame.

Places to Stay

There are some excellent hotels in this popular town.

Camping Municipal de Peyrelevade (☎ *05 53 05 75 24, ave André Maurois)* Adult/pitch €2.30/2.30. Open May-Sept. This friendly riverside camp site is off the D78, 1.2km east of town, and next to the municipal tennis courts.

Camping de Puynadal (☎ *05 53 06 19 66, route de Périgueux)* Adult/pitch/car €2.30/2.45/1.35; chalets €243.90 per week in the high season. Open Apr-Sept. This smaller, hilltop site is off the D939, 2.3km to the south. It has an assortment of dogs, a small swimming pool and horses for hire.

Maison Fleurie (☎ *05 53 35 17 04, fax 05 53 05 16 58,* e *holsfrance@aol.com, 54 rue Gambetta)* Doubles €38.10-76.20 including breakfast. This English-run chambre d'hôte, on the main street, has five handsome bedrooms (all non-smoking) and a swimming pool.

Restaurant-Hôtel Bar Brasserie Versaveau Frères (☎/*fax 05 53 05 71 42, 8 place Charles de Gaulle)* Doubles with shower/WC €22.85/30.50, with shower & WC €38.10. This excellent place, east of the abbey, has vast rooms (most overlooking the river). It also serves good food (see Places to Eat).

Hostellerie du Périgord Vert (☎ *05 53 05 70 58, fax 05 53 46 71 18, route de Thiviers)* Doubles with shower & WC €41.15, €48.80 with bath. Midday *menus* €10.65, evening *menus* €14.50-32.75, dishes €11.45-24.40. This nearby ivy-clad Logis de France hostelry is one of several more upmarket places to stay in Brantôme and also has a decent restaurant.

Places to Eat

You won't go hungry in Brantôme, which has a wide choice of restaurants.

La Petite Venise (☎ *05 53 05 74 16, Impasse Puyjoli de Meyjounissas, off 24 rue Puyjoli) Galettes* (wholemeal pancakes) & crepes €2.30-6.10, salads €3.05-7.60. Open Wed-Mon. The chic Petite Venise, tucked down an alley, has a charming outdoor dining area.

Au Fil de L'Eau (☎ *05 53 05 73 65, 21 quai Bertin)* Midday *menus* €14.50, evening *menus* €16.95-27.45. Open midday & evening Wed-Sun, midday only Mon. This place has an irresistible location by the side of the river, and opposite the Jardin des Moines. It also serves some excellent regional fare.

Restaurant-Hôtel Bar Brasserie Versaveau Frères (see Places to Stay) Menu du jour (set menu of the day) €9.90, dishes €7.60-9.25. The restaurant at this hotel dishes up simple fare, served with smiles: try the *cassoulet perigourdin* (€7.60).

Le Vieux Four (☎ *05 53 05 73 65, 7 rue Pierre de Mareuil)* Pizzas & pastas €3.80-10.35. Le Vieux Four, around the corner from the Versaveau Frères (see Places to Stay), is tucked into the rockface, giving it an ambience that it calls *typique troglodyte* (literally 'typical cave-dweller'). Their pizzas, which are cooked in a traditional oven, are the best in town, but the service can be a bit on the slow side.

Getting There & Away

Brantôme is connected with Périgueux by CFTA buses (€7.40, 35 minutes, two to four daily, one on Sunday).

AROUND BRANTÔME
Château de Bourdeilles

The tiny village of Bourdeilles, about 10km south-west of Brantôme, was once the seat of Périgord's oldest barony (the others are Mareuil, Beynac and Biron) and is still completely overshadowed by its chateau (☎ *05 53 03 73 36, place de la Halle; adult/child aged 6-12 €4.55/2.30).* There are two parts: a medieval section with a huge octagonal keep (built to keep the English out during the Hundred Years' War and still affording great views); and a 16th-century addition next door that was designed by Jacquette de Montbron (sister-in-law to Pierre de Bourdeilles; see the boxed text 'Brantôme's Saucy Abbot' earlier in this chapter) to impress the visiting Catherine de Medici (who, ironically, never turned up). The Renaissance features and furnishings are outstanding, notably the *salon doré* (gilded room), with its painted ceiling.

The chateau is open 10am to 12.30pm and 2pm to 5.30pm Wednesday to Monday, 7 February to April and October to December; 10am to 12.30pm and 2pm to 6.30pm Wednesday to Monday, May to June and in September; 10am to 7pm daily July and August; closed January to 7 February. Visits may be guided if there are enough people; otherwise a detailed text in English, French or German is available.

Places to Stay & Eat There's just one place to stay in Bourdeilles.

Hôtel-Restaurant Les Tilleuls (☎ *05 53 03 76 40, place de la Halle)* Doubles with shower €22.86, with shower & WC €27.45. *Menus* €13.55-22.85, dishes €9.90-22.85. This dinky place makes up for its simple rooms with some ambitious restaurant *menus* and a very nice outdoor dining area.

Grottes de Villars

Situated 4km north-east of Villars (16km north-east of Brantôme), these grottoes (☎ *05 53 54 82 36, Le Cluzeau, Villars; adult/child €5.80/3.80; open 2pm-6.30pm daily Apr, Oct; 10am-noon & 2pm-7pm daily May, June, Sept; 10am-7pm daily July-Aug; closed Nov-Apr)* are more impressive for

The cloistered Abbaye de Cadouin, Périgord

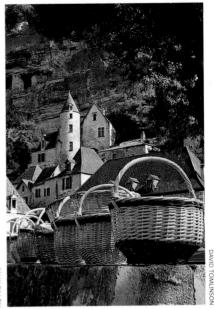

Baskets for sale in La Roque Gageac, Dordogne

SEMITOUR PÉRIGORD

The Hall of the Bulls – often called the Sistine Chapel of prehistory – is reproduced in Lascaux II.

Fruit and vegetable market, Sarlat-la-Canéda

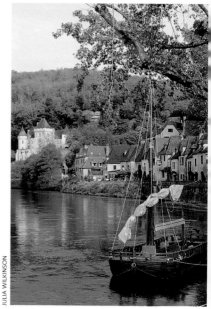

Beynac-et-Cazenac by the River Dordogne

Free-range foie gras, Dordogne

Vivid sunflowers are grown as a cash crop.

their stalactites and stalagmites than their cave art, but the 18,000-year-old blue horses and the dusky image of a bison and a so-called wizard (a rare painting of a human) are noteworthy.

Château de Puyguilhem

Set in dreamy countryside 1km north-west of Villars, this 16th-century chateau *(☎ 05 53 35 50 10 or ☎ 05 53 54 82 18, Villars; adult/child aged 6-12 €4.55/2.30)* is famous for its ornate stone carvings, both inside and out (more were lost during 18th-century renovations); a stone chimney carved with the Labours of Hercules is the *pièce de résistance*.

The chateau is open for 90-minute guided tours 10am to 7pm daily, July and August; 10am to 12.30pm and 2pm to 6.30pm daily, May and June; 10am to 12.30pm and 2pm to 6.30pm Tuesday to Sunday in September; 10am to 12.30pm and 2pm to 5.30pm Tuesday to Sunday, October to December and February to April; closed from 1 January to 8 February.

Places to Stay & Eat There's not a lot of choice within Villars itself but you can find some tempting *chambres d'hôtes* in the countryside.

Le Relais de L'Archerie (☎ 05 53 54 88 64, fax 05 53 54 21 92) Doubles €28.95-39.65. *Menus* €12.20-28.95. This charming little 19th-century chateau on the western D3 side of Villars has smallish but immaculate rooms, set in lovely grounds.

Chambres et Table d'Hôtes (☎ 05 53 54 82 86, Les Vergnes, Villars) Doubles €27.45 with breakfast. *Menus* €13.70. This friendly and fabulously quiet *ferme de séjour* (farm offering accommodation and meals), 4km east of Villars en route to St-Jean de Côle, has three homely rooms, full of frills and soft toys, and the house is generously adorned with gourds and baskets of walnuts.

St-Jean de Côle

This picturesque and amazingly unspoilt village, 8km north-east of Villars beside the Côle River, was once a busy base for the Knights Templar crusaders, its main street by the church broad enough for an army of galloping knights. The 15th-century **Château de la Marthonie** *(☎ 05 53 62 14 15; adult/child €3.05/1.50; open 10.15am-noon & 2pm-7pm daily July-Aug)* is in the village centre. The tourist office *(☎/fax 05 53 62 14 15, ⓔ info@ville-saint-jean-de-cole.fr)*, by the chateau, is open 10am to 12.30pm and 2.30pm to 6pm Thursday, Friday and Monday (also from 10.30am on Tuesday), and 2.30pm to 6pm Saturday and Sunday. During July and August it also opens on Wednesday.

Places to Stay & Eat The few options in St-Jean de Côle include the following.

Hôtel St-Jean (☎ 05 53 52 23 20, rue principale) Doubles with shower & WC €30.50-38.10. Midday *menus* €10.65, evening *menus* €14.50-19.05. Situated on the main road through St-Jean, this pleasant, wysteria-clad hotel has neat, simple rooms and a shady terrace where you can enjoy its good food.

Restaurant Les Templiers (☎ 05 53 62 31 75, place de l'Église) Menu du jour €9.25; *menus* €11.90-22.10. The Templiers, by the tourist office, has all the usual regional specialities and a good-value €15.25 *menu Templiers*.

Getting There & Away Thiviers train station is 7km east of St-Jean de Côle (see Getting There & Away under Thiviers later for services). A taxi *(☎ 05 53 55 16 54)* from Thiviers to St-Jean de Côle costs around €9.90.

CFTA buses connect Périgueux with Villars (€5.35; 70 minutes) once or twice daily, Monday to Friday, in term-time only.

THIVIERS

postcode 24800 • pop 3620
• elevation 270m

This small, busy market town 34km northeast of Périgueux calls itself the foie-gras capital of Périgord. Its winter foie-gras markets (held every Saturday from mid-November to mid-March) are the oldest and most famous in the region, and it even boasts a museum on the subject. Rather dull otherwise (Jean-Paul Sartre recalled horrible childhood holidays here, at his grandparents' house), it does have useful train connections, making it a handy base for exploring the hinterland.

Orientation & Information

The tourist office (☎/fax 05 53 55 12 50) is in the town centre on place du Maréchal Foch, 600m north of the train station. It opens 10am to noon and 2pm to 6pm on Monday, 9am to 12.30pm and 2.30pm to 6pm on Tuesday, 9am to 7pm Wednesday to Friday, 9am to 1pm and 2pm to 7pm on Saturday, 10am to 1pm and 2pm to 6pm on Sunday. The **Musée du Foie Gras**, in the same building and open the same hours (adult/child €1.50/1.05), diligently describes the production and history of foie gras.

See the special section 'Food & Wine of the Southwest' earlier in the book for more information about foie gras.

Places to Stay & Eat

If you fancy an overnight stay, you could try the following.

Municipal Le Repaire (☎/fax 05 53 52 69 75, route de Lanouaille) Adult/pitch €3.80/5.35. Open May-Sept. This spacious camp site, 2.3km east, off the D707, has a swimming pool, small fishing lake and tennis court.

Hôtel-Bar Restaurant des Voyageurs (☎ 05 53 55 09 66, rue Pierre-Sémard) Doubles with shower €28.95, without €21.35-25.90. Midday *menus* €9.45, evening *menus* €14.50-25.15. Opposite the station, the Voyageurs is rather run-down, but locals like its good-value restaurant.

Hôtel de France et de Russie (☎ 05 53 55 17 80, fax 05 53 52 59 60, 51 rue du Général Lamy) Doubles with shower & WC €41.15-48.80. This pleasant little hotel, about 400m north of the centre, has attractive, bright-white rooms.

Getting There & Away

Thiviers station (☎ 05 53 55 00 21) is on the Bordeaux-Limoges line, with connections to Périgueux (€5.80, 20–35 minutes) and Bordeaux (€18.30, 2¼ hours, a few change at Périgueux), both at least 12 times daily.

Périgord Noir

This very popular region, encompassing the Vézère and Dordogne Valleys, is dense with attractions dating from prehistoric to Renaissance times. Of the Vézère Valley's 175 known prehistoric sites, the most famous ones (including the world-renowned cave paintings in Lascaux) are situated between Le Bugue (near where the Vézère joins the Dordogne) and Montignac, 25km to the north-east. Most are closed in winter, so the best time to come is in spring or autumn, when things are open but the crowds not overwhelming.

Public transport is very limited; if you don't have your own car, biking through the area is a pleasant alternative. Good bases include Le Bugue, Montignac or the capital of Périgord Noir, Sarlat-la-Canéda (between the two valleys).

LE BUGUE

postcode 24260 • pop 2800
• elevation 63km

This small market town, 10km west of Les Eyzies de Tayac, has managed to retain something of its own character despite being surrounded by tourist sites and theme parks. As a base, it makes a pleasant alternative to staying in dull Les Eyzies.

Orientation & Information

The centre of town is place de la Volaille, where the market takes place (on Tuesday and Saturday) and where the D710 from Périgueux crosses the Vézère. North of the square is the main shopping street, rue de Paris. Some 200m west of the square is the tourist office (☎ 05 53 07 20 48, fax 05 53 54 92 30, e bugue@perigord.com, w www.perigord.com/bugue). It opens 9.30am to 12.30pm and 2.30pm to 6.30pm Monday to Saturday, and 10am to 1pm on Sunday (closed Sunday and Monday from December to April). In July and August it opens 9am to 1pm and 3pm to 7pm daily. Pick up its *Livret de chemins de randonées* (€2.30) for suggested walks in the area.

There's an SNCF train-ticketing service

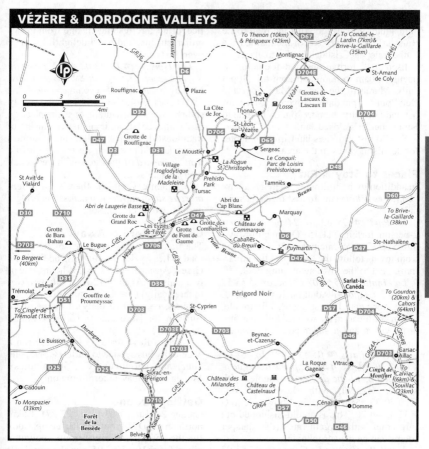

VÉZÈRE & DORDOGNE VALLEYS

here (☎ 05 53 53 41 45, open daily July
and August; closed Sunday morning other
months) plus a pay-by-card Internet facility.
Another such facility is available at the
Maison de la Presse, 8 rue de Paris.

The post office is 80m north of the tourist
office, on rue de la Boétie.

Things to See

Some 600m east of the town centre, just off
the D703 Les Eyzies road, the **Aquarium du
Périgord Noir** (☎ 05 53 07 10 74; adult/
child €7.30/5.50; open 10am-7pm daily
May-Oct; 10am-5pm daily Oct–mid-Nov,

mid-Feb–May; closed mid-Nov–mid-Feb)
makes a change from prehistoric attractions.
It is the largest privately owned aquarium in
Europe.

The adjacent **Village du Bournat** (☎ 05
53 08 41 99; adult/child €7.60/4.55; open
10am-7pm daily May-Oct; 10am-5pm Oct-
Dec & Feb-May; closed Jan) is a Périgordian theme park where you can watch
bakers, carpenters and other artisans at
work on traditional local crafts. There are
funfair rides and restaurants, too.

The **Gouffre de Proumeyssac** (☎ 05 53
07 27 47, Route du Buisson; 45-minute

guided tours only, adult/child €7/4.55), 3km south of Le Bugue (off the road to Le Buisson), is a huge cavern nicknamed the Cathédrale de Cristale thanks to its crystallised rock formations and fountains. It opens 9.30am to noon and 2pm to 5.30pm daily, March to the end of May, Sept and Oct; 2pm to 5pm daily, November, December and February; 9am to 7pm daily June to September; it's closed Jan.

See Prehistoric Sites later in this chapter for details of caves in the area.

Places to Stay & Eat

In addition to the following, there are many *chambres d'hôte* (the tourist office has details).

Le Port (☎ 05 53 07 24 60, Le Port) 2-person forfait €11.15. Open mid-May–mid-Sept. This municipal camp site is 1km from town (follow the track past the aquarium), next to the town swimming pool.

La Linotte (☎ 05 53 07 17 61, fax 05 53 54 16 96, La Linotte) Adult/pitch €4.90/6.40. Open Apr-Sept. This spacious, hilltop site, 3.4km north-east in the wooded hills, has fantastic views and a super pool with waterslides.

Hôtel de Paris (☎ 05 53 07 28 16, fax 05 53 04 20 89, ☒ hotel.de.paris.le.bugue@wanadoo.fr, 14 rue de Paris) Doubles with shower €25.90, with shower & WC €29.70-33.55; triples with shower & WC €33.55-44.20. This is an old-fashioned but tidy hotel with bargain rates (the cheaper rooms can be claustrophobic).

Hôtel-Restaurant Le Cygne (☎ 05 53 07 17 77, fax 05 53 03 93 74, rue du Cingle) Doubles with shower & WC €39.65-45.75. Lunch *menus* €13.40, evening *menus* €17.55-25.60, dishes €7.90-12.50. Open year round except 14-31 Oct and end-Dec–end-Jan; restaurant open Tues-Sat, midday only Sun Sept-June, midday & evening daily July-Aug. More upmarket is the pleasant Logis de France Cynge, a few steps from the tourist office, whose rooms all have a minibar and TV.

Le Phà (☎ 05 53 08 96 96, 25 rue du Jardin Public) Menus €12.95-18.30, dishes €4.55-10.65. This fragrant Vietnamese-Chinese restaurant, next to the tourist office, offers a refreshing change from Périgordian cuisine, and has a delightful terrace over the river.

Les Trois As (☎ 05 53 08 41 57, place du Royal Vézère, Oct-Apr at 89 rue de Paris) Midday *menus* €16.75, evening *menus* €25-48. Dishes €14.05-38.55. This extremely stylish riverside restaurant, opposite place de la Volaille, boasts an imaginative cuisine of traditional delicacies: Millionaire gourmets might fancy the *ragout de truffes au foie frais de canard* (truffle stew with fresh duck liver), a snip at €58.70.

For picnic supplies, there's an *Intermarché supermarket* just across the bridge, on the road to Le Buisson.

Getting There & Away

The train station is 1km east of town, off road to Les Eyzies. Le Bugue is on the Paris Gare d'Austerlitz (€45.45, 5¾ hours, one or two daily) to Agen (€12.65, 1¼ hours, two to three daily) line via Périgueux (€7.15, 37 minutes, one or two daily). Change at Le Buisson for Bordeaux (€16.45, 2 hours, three daily).

Voyages Rey (☎ 05 53 07 27 22) run a once-daily bus service to Sarlat (€5.95, one hour) and Périgueux (€7, 50 minutes), Monday to Friday in term-time only.

Getting Around

Garage Perusin (☎ 05 53 07 22 27), 1.5km north on the D710 route de Périgueux (look for the Avia petrol sign), rents mountain bikes for €10.65/57.95 per day/week. It opens daily except Saturday afternoon and Sunday.

AROUND LE BUGUE
Limeuil

This charming little village, 6km down-river from Le Bugue, and where the Rivers Vézère and Dordogne meet, is surprisingly unspoilt despite its picturesque location. Climb up its steep streets to the **Jardin-Musée Limeuil** (☎ 05 53 63 32 06; place des Fosses; adult/child €3.80/1.50; open 10am-noon, 2.30pm-7pm July–mid-Sept), an 'ethno-botanic' attraction in six themed gardens, created from a rambling arboretum originally planted in 1891 and featuring unusual varieties of exotic or medicinal plants.

Places to Stay & Eat Tiny Limeuil has just one place to stay.

Hôtel-Restaurant Au Bon Accueil (☎ 05 53 63 30 97, fax 05 53 73 33 85, Le Bourg) Doubles with shower €27.45-32, without €24.40. *Menus* €12.95-25.90. Open midday & evening Sat-Thur, midday only Fri. This hotel-restaurant has a delightful wysteria-covered terrace and serves imaginative versions of Périgordian fare.

Getting There & Away The nearest train stations are at Le Bugue or Le Buisson (5km to the south, see Getting There & Away in the following Cadouin section). For a taxi call ☎ 05 53 22 06 51.

Cadouin
postcode 24480 • pop 380
• elevation about 60m
This tiny, sleepy village 9km to the south of Limeuil is entirely dominated by the astonishingly grand Cistercian **L'Abbaye de Cadouin**, a Unesco World Heritage Site. Built in 1117 to house what was thought to be the cloth used to wrap the head of Christ (and which was later revealed to be of 11th-century Egyptian origin), it became a major pilgrimage site. It consists of a sturdy Romanesque church *(admission free)* and a gorgeous Gothic cloister *(☎ 05 53 63 36 28, place de l'Abbaye; adult/child aged 6-12 €4.55/2.30)* where carved stone faces peep out at every corner and the doorways are intricately carved. The cloister is open 10am to 12.30pm and 2pm to 5.30pm Wednesday to Monday, February to April and from October to December; 10am to 12.30pm and 2pm to 6.30pm Wednesday to Monday, May to June and Sept; 10am to 7pm daily, July and August; closed in January. Opposite is a fine old **covered market**.

The other attraction in Cadouin is the **Musée du Vélocipède** *(☎ 05 53 63 46 60, rue de la República; adult/child €4.55/3.05; open 10am-6pm daily)*, which houses

the world's largest collection of vintage bicycles including Penny Farthings.

Places to Stay & Eat Cadouin can boast two fine places to stay for both budget and mid-range travellers.

Auberge de Jeunesse (☎ 05 53 73 28 78, fax 05 53 73 28 79, place de l'Abbaye). Dorm beds with/without breakfast €10.65/8.10. Reception open 9am-noon, 5pm-9pm. Open Mar–mid-Dec. This is one of the region's most spectacularly located hostels, right inside the abbey complex.

Hôtel-Restaurant d'Abbaye (☎ 05 53 63 40 93, fax 05 53 61 72 08, place de l'Abbaye) Doubles with bath & WC €32. Midday *menus* €10.65, evening *menus* €12.95-16.95, dishes €7.60-12.20. Restaurant open Mon-Sat. This charming place, opposite the abbey, serves good regional fare.

Getting There & Away The nearest train station is at Le Buisson, 5km to the northeast, where you can pick up connections to Les Eyzies and Périgueux.

For a taxi call ☎ 05 53 22 06 51.

LES EYZIES DE TAYAC
postcode 24620 • pop 930 • elevation 74m
Completely devoted to tourism, this dull town but immensely important prehistoric centre shelters under a huge cliff and an eye-catching (and misleadingly brutish) model of Cro-Magnon man (Cro-Magnon, the place that gave its name to this line of *Homo sapiens sapiens*, after a discovery of three of their skeletons in 1868, is just north of town). Les Eyzies' two museums are an excellent place to bone up on prehistory before visiting the valley's other sites.

Information
The tourist office (☎ 05 53 06 97 05, fax 05 53 06 90 79, @ ot.les.eyzies@perigord.tm.fr) is on Les Eyzies' main street, Grand'Rue (the D47), right below the most prominent part of the cliff. It opens 9am to noon and 2pm to 6pm Monday to Saturday, and 10am to noon and 2pm to 5pm on Sunday (closed on Sunday from October to March). From June to September it opens 9am to 7pm Monday to

Saturday (to 8pm in July and August), and 10am to noon and 2pm to 6pm on Sunday. There's Internet access available here.

IGN maps and topoguides are on sale here and at the Librairie de la Préhistoire, opposite the tourist office.

Currency exchange is available at both the tourist office and post office (200m to the south).

Musée National de la Préhistoire

This absorbing and recently expanded National Museum of Prehistory (☎ 05 53 06 45 45, e mnp.eyzies@culture.gouv.fr; adult €3.35, youth & senior & all on Sun €2.30), built into the cliff above the tourist office, provides a great introduction to the area's prehistoric human habitation. Its collection of artefacts is well presented.

The museum opens 9.30am to noon and 2pm to 5pm Wednesday to Monday, mid-November to mid-March; 9.30am to noon and 2pm to 6pm Wednesday to Monday, mid-March to June and September to mid-November; 9.30am to 7pm daily, July and August.

Abri Pataud

About 250m north of the Musée National de la Préhistoire along the cliff face, this Cro-Magnon shelter, now a private museum (☎ 05 53 06 92 46; adult/child aged 6-12 €4.55/2.30) was inhabited over a period of 15,000 years starting some 37,000 years ago. The ibex carved into the ceiling is from about 19,000 BC. The museum opens 10am to 12.30pm and 1.30pm to 7pm Tuesday to Sunday, April, June, September and October; 10am to 12.30pm and 1.30pm to 5.30pm Tuesday to Sunday, November, December, February and March; 10am to 7pm daily, July and August; closed 3 to 25 January.

Places to Stay & Eat

It's not the most exciting place to stay overnight but Les Eyzies has plenty of accommodation if you're stuck.

Camping à la Ferme Le Queylou (☎ 05 53 06 94 71, Le Queylou) Pitch including person €4.55. Open Apr-Oct. Cottages €305 per week high season (available year round).

This simple, gloriously quiet hilltop camp site is in a tiny, remote-feeling hamlet 2.5km west, off the D706 (3.1km from the train station; pick-up is possible). Rates include use of a fridge.

Hôtel des Falaises (☎ 05 53 06 97 35, Grand'Rue) Doubles €27.45-30.50, triples €38.10. This modest hotel, opposite the Abri Pataud, has decent rooms with shower and WC, the pricier ones overlooking a garden at the back.

Auberge La Grignotière (☎ 05 53 06 91 67, place de la Mairie) Doubles €30.50, triples €35. Midday *menus* €9.25, evening *menus* €10.35-21.35. Open Apr-Nov. This simple four-room inn, located across the square from the tourist office, serves traditional *menus*.

Hôtel du Centre (☎ 05 53 06 97 13, fax 05 53 06 91 63, place de la Mairie) Doubles €48.05-83.85, triples €64. *Menus* €20.60-34.30, dishes €14.35-23.65. Open Mar-Oct. Next to La Grignotière is this more upmarket Logis de France riverside establishment, which has an extensive menu.

Getting There & Away

Les Eyzies is on the Paris' Gare d'Austerlitz (€44.80, 5½ hours, three to five daily, one direct) to Agen (€13.40, 1¾ hours, two daily) line via Périgueux (€6.25, 30 minutes) and Le Buisson (€3.05, 15 minutes, both two to four daily). Change at Le Buisson for Bordeaux (€16.90, two to three hours, four daily) and Sarlat-la-Canéda (€7.15, 50 minutes, three daily).

The train station (☎ 05 53 06 97 22) is 600m north of the tourist office.

Getting Around

Classic/mountain bikes can be rented from the tourist office for €9.25/13.70 a day or €45.75/74.70 a week.

PREHISTORIC SITES

The following are the most important sites in the Vézère Valley, listed here roughly from south-west to north-east. For details of Lascaux, see Montignac later in this chapter. Note that guided tours are obligatory at all the sights and that many of the French-language ones (eg, Font de Gaume, Les Combarelles) can be extremely detailed and unsuitable for young children.

Grotte de Bara-Bahau

Some 2km south-west of Le Bugue, this 100m-long cave (☎ 05 53 07 44 58, Le Bugue; adult/child aged 5-16 €4.55/2.75) displays eerie claw-scratchings made by bears some 150,000 years ago, as well as outlines of various animals drawn on the rock around 115,000 years later.

It opens 10am to noon and 2pm to 5.30pm daily, February to June; 9.30am to 7pm daily, July and August; 10am to noon and 2pm to 5pm September to December; closed January; last visits 35 minutes before closing time.

Grotte de Font de Gaume

This cave (☎ 05 53 06 86 00, fax 05 53 35 26 18, Route de Sarlat; adult/those aged 12-25 €5.50/3.50), just over 1km east of Les Eyzies on the D47, has one of the most astounding collections of prehistoric paintings still open to the public. About two dozen of its 230 remarkably sophisticated polychrome figures of bison, reindeer, horses, bears, mammoths and other creatures, created by Cro-Magnon people 14,000 years ago, can be seen. A number of the animals, engraved and/or painted in red and black, are depicted in movement or in three dimensions.

The cave is open 9am to noon and 2pm to 6pm Thursday to Tuesday, April to September; 10am to noon and 2pm to 5pm Thursday to Tuesday, November to February; 9.30am to noon and 2pm to 5.30pm Thursday to Tuesday, October and March; it's closed on public holidays.

To protect the cave, discovered in 1901, the number of visitors is limited to 200 a day, and the 40-minute group tours (twice-daily in English at 10.30am and 2.15pm, plus explanatory sheets in English available) are limited to 20 participants. To make reservations, stop at the cave or call on the above number. From April to October, reserve a place several days ahead; in July and August do so at least a week in advance. The last visit is one hour before closing time.

Grotte des Combarelles

The long and very narrow Combarelles Cave (telephone, opening hours and admission fees identical to Font de Gaume), 3km east of Les Eyzies and 1.6km east of Font de Gaume, averages only 80cm in width (worth noting if you get claustrophobic). Discovered in 1894, it is renowned for its 600 often-superimposed engravings of animals, especially reindeer, bison and horses; there are also some rarely seen human and anthropomorphic figures and equally rare engravings of bears, lions and wolves. Practically every part of the inner cave is covered with the engravings, some overlaid with black colouring, some so tiny it's amazing they've even been noticed. The works date from 12,000 to 14,000 years ago.

The number of visitors is limited to 70 a day. To reserve a place in a six-person group (the French-only tours last around one hour), stop by the Grotte de Font de Gaume or call their number.

Abri du Cap Blanc

When archaeologists started probing the pre-historically rich area of the River Beune in 1909, they stumbled upon one of the most exciting archaeological finds of the century – an extraordinary frieze of sculpted images carved some 15,000 years ago into the rock, including life-size, high-relief representations of Przewalski horses, reindeer and bison, some overlapping one another to create remarkable images of perspective. By the time the shelter had been cleared of its protective rubble and undergrowth, part of the frieze had been destroyed, and in a subsequent cleaning process (and as a result of its contact with the air), the ochre and black colouring was also lost. But the sculptures – the only such prehistoric frieze open to the public – are still hugely impressive and were recently added to Unesco's World Heritage list.

The small shelter (☎ 05 53 59 21 74, Cap Blanc; adult/child €5.20/3.05; open 10am-noon & 2pm-6pm daily April-June, Sept-Oct; 9.30am-7pm daily July-Aug) is situated on a pristine, forested hillside 9km east of Les Eyzies and has now been enclosed within a modern gallery, which

THE DORDOGNE

displays (with English and German translations) how the carvings were probably made and provides a good background to the prehistory of the area. The 10-minute tour is in French but multilingual text is available.

Grotte du Grand Roc

Grand Roc Cave (☎ 05 53 06 92 70, Les Eyzies; adult/child aged 6-12 €6.10/3.20; open 9.30am-6pm daily Apr-June, Sept-Oct; 9.30am-7pm daily July-Aug; 10am-5pm Feb, Mar, Nov-Dec; closed Jan), known for its masses of delicate, translucent stalactites and stalagmites, is a few kilometres northwest of Les Eyzies along the D47. The regular bilingual tours last 30 minutes.

Nearby is a still-inhabited troglodytic hamlet and the prehistoric **Abri de Laugerie Basse** (adult/child aged 6-12 €4.55/2.30), which is accessible to wheelchair-users. The telephone number and opening times are the same as for Grand Roc.

Grotte de Rouffignac

The cave at Rouffignac (☎ 05 53 05 41 71, Rouffignac; adult/child 6-12 years €5.65/ 3.35; open 10am-11.30am & 2pm-5pm daily 1 Apr-June, Sept-1 Nov; 9am-11.30am & 2pm-6pm daily July-Aug), the largest in the area (it has some 10km of galleries), is 10km north of Les Eyzies along the D47 and the D3. It is known for its 100 engravings and paintings of mammoths (many sadly disfigured by graffiti), which you reach by an electric train. It's accessible to wheelchair-users.

Village Troglodytique de la Madeleine

This cave-dwelling village (☎ 05 53 06 92 49, Tursac; adult/child aged 5-12 €4.55/2.60; open 9.30am-7pm daily July-Sept; 10am-6pm daily Oct-June), 8km north of Les Eyzies along the D706, is in the middle of a delightfully lush forest overlooking a hairpin curve in the River Vézère. The site has two levels – a prehistoric site (closed to the public) by the riverbank, dating back 10,000 to 14,000 years, and a former medieval fortified village – now in ruins – halfway up the cliff

---

Rambles Through the Past

The Abri du Cap Blanc, 8km east of Les Eyzies along the beautiful D48, is a fine place to begin a day hike. When the path – actually the GR6 from Les Eyzies – isn't impossibly muddy, you can walk about 1km south-east from the Abri to the eerie ruins of the fortified 12th-century **Château de Commarque** (☎ 05 53 59 00 25; adult/child €4.55/2.30; open 10am-6pm daily Apr; 10am-7pm daily May-Sept) on the other side of the River Beune. Facing it is the **Château de Laussel** (not open to the public), a much-restored 14th-century fairytale of a chateau.

A few kilometres farther south-east on the GR6 you'll reach the **Cabanes du Breuil** (☎ 05 53 29 67 15; adult/child €3.05/1.50; open 10am-noon & 2pm-7pm daily Mar-May, Oct-Nov; 10am-7pm daily June-Sept; by reservation only Dec-Feb), a charming hamlet of traditional dry-stone huts, now a historical monument.

---

face. The village's chapel, dedicated to St Madeleine, gave its name to the site, and to the entire Magdalenian era. On the plateau above the cliff are the ruins of a 14th-century castle (closed to the public). Many of the artefacts discovered here are in the prehistory museum in Les Eyzies.

Guided tours (45 minutes) are in French (English brochure available).

La Roque St-Christophe

This 900m-long series of terraces and caves (☎ 05 53 50 70 45, Peyzac Le Moustier; adult/student/child aged 5-13 €5.50/4.25/ 2.90; open 10am-6pm daily Mar-June & Sept-15 Nov; 11am-5pm daily 15 Nov-Feb; 10am-7pm daily July-Aug), on a sheer cliff-face 30m above the River Vézère, has had an extraordinary history as a natural bastion, serving Mousterian (Neanderthal) people some 50,000 years ago, enemies of the Normans in the 10th century, the English from 1401 to 1416 and Protestants in the late 16th century.

La Roque St-Christophe is on the D706,

overlooking the River Vézère 9km north-east of Les Eyzies, 1km south-east from the village of Le Moustier (finds here gave the Mousterian era its name). The informative brochure in English, which can be borrowed from the ticket kiosk, makes a valiant effort to bring the now-empty caverns alive.

Just 3km south of here (off the road to Les Eyzies) the themed **Prehisto Parc** (☎ 05 53 50 73 19, Tursac; adult/student/child aged under 5 €4.75/3.20/2.30; open 10am-6pm daily Mar-June, Sept-mid-Nov; 9.30am-7.30pm daily July-Aug) is just the kind of thing to make serious anthropologists shiver but it's fun for the kids nonetheless, with its figures of cavemen throwing arrows at hairy mammoths (some with sound effects).

Le Conquil: Parc de Loisirs Prehistorique

Across the river from St-Léon-sur-Vézère is a densely wooded area, pitted with intriguing rock shelters. As with La Roque St-Christophe, the limestone shelters (one housing an extraordinary dovecote – or, some believe, a place of worship) were popular medieval refuges and even served as an occasional hideout for the Resistance in WWII. They are now one of the main attractions of Le Conquil (☎ 05 53 51 29 03, St-Léon-sur-Vézère; adult/child €7.60/6.40; open 10am-6pm daily Apr & Sept; 10am-7pm daily May-Aug), which includes fantastic adventure-style playgrounds deep in the woods, and various displays of 'prehistoric' activities (flint-making, cave painting, etc). A delightful forested path leads to a panoramic viewpoint over the valley. You'll need about two hours to see it all. Explanatory signs (including botanical ones) are in French but multilingual texts are available at the entrance.

ST-LÉON-SUR-VÉZÈRE

postcode 24290 • pop 430 • elevation 70m

This atmospheric village, 9km south-west of Montignac, lies in a picturesque loop of the River Vézère. Once an island, encircled by the river, and a Roman centre of agriculture, crafts and port activity, its main attraction today is its well preserved stone houses and one of Périgord's finest **Romanesque churches**. Once part of a Benedictine priory, it was built on the ruins of a Roman villa, part of whose walls can still be seen between the church and the river. Making up the picturesque ensemble are two chateaux (not open to the public) – the squat 14th-century **Manoir de la Salle** with a magnificent donjon, and the more refined, Renaissance-turreted **Château de Clérans**.

Across the bridge (and believed to be linked to the Château by a secret underground passage!) are various rock shelters, now within the delightful **Le Conquil: Parc de Loisirs Prehistorique** (see the previous Prehistoric Sites section).

Places to Stay & Eat

Camping The village has only a tiny camp site but you'll find several others nearby.

Camping Municipal (☎ town hall 05 53 50 73 16, or ☎ 06 73 05 33 60). Adult/pitch €1.35/1.85. Open 15 June-Sept. This very simple, riverside site in the village has just 27 pitches and a basic shower/WC block.

Le Paradis (☎ 05 53 50 72 64, fax 05 53 50 75 90, e le-paradis@perigord.com, St-Léon-sur-Vézère) Adult/pitch €6.15/9.60. Open Apr–late-Oct. Off the Les Eyzies road, 3km west of St Léon, is this deluxe riverside camp site. It has swimming pools, tennis courts, bike and canoe rental and Internet facilities.

Hotels & Restaurants Tempting choices for food and accommodation include the following.

L'Auberge du Pont ☎ 05 53 50 73 07, St Léon) Menus €11.45-15.25. This cafe-restaurant serves regional fare and yummy 'artisan' ices.

Hôtel le Relais de la Côte de Jor (☎ 05 53 50 73 07, fax 05 53 51 16 22, e relaisjor@free.fr, Côte de Jor) Doubles €35.05-42.70, triples €42.70-57.95. Open Apr-Nov. Run by the same people as L'Auberge du Pont, this 22-room hotel has a lovely, quiet position 2.5km above the village.

L'Auberge de la Poste (☎ 05 53 50 73 08, St Léon) Menus €13.70-22.85. Open midday & evening Tues-Thur, Sat & Sun, midday only Fri. Opposite L'Auberge du Pont, this renowned restaurant serves up excellent local cuisine and some fantastic desserts.

Auberge de Castel-Merle (☎ 05 53 50 70 08, fax 05 53 50 76 25, Sergeac) Doubles €33.55-39.65. *Menus* €15-29.75. Open Mar-Nov; closed 23-30 Sept. Near the ancient hamlet of Sergeac, across the river, the ridgetop Logis de France Castel-Merle has four charming rooms and a great shady outdoor dining area with spectacular views. Veggies can enjoy a €13.25 vegetarian *menu.*

Hôtel La Roque St-Christophe (☎ 05 53 50 70 61, fax 05 53 50 81 29, Le Moustier) Doubles €27.45-33.55. Open Mar-Nov. This quiet, seven-room hotel has the bonus of a swimming pool.

Auberge du Vimont (☎ 05 53 50 75 17, fax 05 53 50 46 06, Le Moustier) Singles/doubles with WC €28.95/35.05, without €24.40/

Meditation on the Côte de Jor

High above the Vézère Valley, on the hilltop ridge of La Côte de Jor a kilometre above Le Moustier, flutter the incongruous prayer flags of a Tibetan Buddhist centre, the **Dhagpo Kagyu-Ling** (☎ 05 53 50 70 75, fax 05 53 50 80 54, [e] acceuil@dhagpo-kagyu.org, [w] www .dhagpo-kagyu.org; workshops & courses day/ weekend €9.15/15.25).

Established in 1975, this is now one of the largest Tibetan Buddhist centres in France and is in the process of establishing a European Institute, including a library of sacred texts, to preserve the Buddhist tradition.

Accommodation is available but must be pre-booked (dorm bed/double room for a student €2.30/12.20; dorm bed €3.80–4.55, single €10.65–12.20, double or twin €12.20–16.75 for an income-earner, depending on your means). Cheap and simple meals are offered. The temple is open 7am to 10pm daily, with meditation sessions taking place several times daily (usually at 7am, 6pm and 8pm).

To reach the centre, take a taxi (☎ 05 53 06 93 06) from Les Eyzies or Montignac (☎ 05 53 51 97 20), the nearest public-transport hubs.

28.95. Midday *menus* €8.40, evening *menus* €10.95-22.85, dishes €5.35-14.50. Around the corner from the St-Christophe, the Vimont has a good-value restaurant.

Getting There & Away

The nearest you can get by bus is Montignac (see the following section), 9km north-east of St-Léon. A taxi from Montignac costs around €15.25.

The nearest train stations are at Les Eyzies (14km south-west) or Condat-le-Lardin (9km north-east of Montignac; see Montignac for details).

Getting Around

Bikes are available from Le Paradis (see Places to Stay & Eat) for €11.45/45.75 per day/week. Canoes are also available here, or from Aventure Plein Air (APA, ☎ 05 53 50 67 71), by the river in St-Léon.

MONTIGNAC
postcode 24290 • pop 3100
• elevation 300m

The relaxing and very picturesque town of Montignac, on the River Vézère, achieved sudden fame after the discovery of the nearby Grotte de Lascaux. It has an attractive old town on the river's right bank, and a vibrant local market every Wednesday and Saturday.

Orientation & Information

The town straddles both sides of the river. On the left bank is the tourist office (☎ 05 53 51 82 60), 150m west of place Tourny at 22 rue du 4 Septembre, next to the 14th-century Église St-Georges le Prieuré. It opens 9am to noon and 2pm to 6pm Monday to Saturday (until 7pm with no midday closure during July and August).

IGN maps are sold at the Maison de la Presse across the street. Banks include the nearby Crédit Agricole at place Bertrand de Born. A self-service laundrette is at 42 rue du 4 septembre.

Post & Communication

The post office on place Tourny also has currency-exchange facilities. There's a pay-by-card Internet facility in the Intermarché supermarket (☎ 05 53 51 85 60), 1km south-west, on the D706 Route de Thonac. It opens 9am to noon and 2.30pm to 7pm Monday to Thursday, and 9am to 7pm Friday and Saturday.

Grotte de Lascaux & Lascaux II

Lascaux Cave, hidden in the wooded hills 2.5km south of Montignac off the D704E, has some of the most extraordinary prehistoric paintings in the world, dating back 15,000 to 17,000 years and depicting wild oxen, deer, horses, reindeer and other creatures in vivid reds, blacks, yellows and browns.

The cave, discovered by chance in 1940 by four teenage boys, was opened to the public in 1948 but closed 15 years later when it became clear that human breath and the resulting carbon dioxide and condensation were causing a green fungus and even tiny stalactites to grow over the paintings, and their colours to fade.

To respond to massive public curiosity about the prehistoric art, a precise replica of the most famous section of the original was meticulously recreated a few hundred metres away. The idea of Lascaux II sounds kitschy, but the reproductions are surprisingly evocative and well worth a look.

The 40m-long **Lascaux II** (☎ 05 53 35 50 10, Regourdou, Montignac; adult/child aged 6-12 €7.60/3.80) can handle 2000 visitors a day (in groups of 40). It opens 10am to 12.30pm and 2pm to 6pm daily except from Monday 6 February to March; 9.30am to 6.30pm daily, April to June; 9am to 8pm daily, July and August; 9.30am to 6.30pm daily in September; 10am to 12.30pm and 2pm to 6pm daily, October to 4 November; 10am to noon and 2pm to 5.30pm daily except from Mon 5 November to December; closed January. The last visits take place 50 minutes before these closing times.

Note that in the high season, tickets are sold *only* in Montignac, at the ticket booth next to the tourist office (get there early as queues are long). During the low season, tickets are sold at Lascaux II itself. For an extra €1.05/0.75 you get admission to Le Thot (see Around Montignac later in this chapter). The ticket office is open 9am to 6pm daily, April to June and September; 9am to 7pm daily in July and August; and 10am to noon and 2pm to 5.30pm Tuesday to Sunday from November to March. No telephone or written bookings can be made.

Musée Eugène Le Roy

Above the tourist-office (last visit 45 minutes before office-closing times), this small museum shows typical farming implements and local crafts, and a figure scene representing the 19th-century peasant household of Jacquou le Croquant, hero of Eugène Le Roy's novel (see Literature in the Facts about Southwest France chapter). Admission costs €1.50/0.90 per adult/child.

Special Events

The Festival du Périgord Noir (☎ 05 53 51 61 61) is the region's premier cultural event of the year, with classical concerts by French and international musicians taking place in abbeys (especially Abbaye Ste-Claire in Sarlat) and churches (especially in St-Léon-sur-Vézère) for three weeks in August. Tickets are available at the Montignac tourist office.

Much more flamboyant and fun is the Festival du Folklore de Montignac (☎ 05 53 51 86 88), held in late July for five days, with groups from all over the world parading in the streets here and in nearby towns.

Places to Stay

Lascaux's fame has ensured that Montignac has a reasonable supply of accommodation.

Le Moulin de Bleufond (☎ 05 53 51 83 95, fax 05 53 51 19 92, [e] le.moulin.du .bleufond@wanadoo.fr) Adult/pitch €3.20/ 3.50 (€4.55/4.10 July-Aug). Open Apr-Nov. This camp site, 700m downriver (from the tourist office turn left at the bridge), has been completely revamped and now boasts a swimming pool, snack-bar, bungalows, and canoe/kayak (€24.40/13.70 per day) as well as bike rental (€11.45 per day).

Hôtel de la Grotte (☎ 05 53 51 80 48, fax 05 53 51 05 96, 63 rue du 4 Septembre) Doubles with shower & WC €38.10-46.50, without €25.15-29.70. Midday *menus* €10.35,

THE DORDOGNE

evening *menus* €15.10-35.80. This pleasant, low-key hotel serves good-value Périgord-style *menus*.

Auberge Le Lascaux (☎ *05 53 51 82 81, fax 05 53 50 04 73, route de Sarlat)* Doubles/triples/quads €33.55/39.65/44.20. Midday *menus* €10.65, evening €13.40-27.15. Some 400m farther down the road (past the gendarmarie), this Logis de France property offers charming rooms.

Le Relais du Soleil d'Or (☎ *05 53 51 80 22, fax 05 53 50 27 54,* e *lesoleildor@ le-soleil-dor.com, 16 rue du 4 Septembre)* Doubles €48.80-68.60, half-board (€57.95-74.70) obligatory July-Aug. Midday *menus* €9.90 evening *menus* €18.30-43.45. Belonging to the Inter Hotel chain, the long-established, traditional Soleil d'Or has up-market rooms and a swimming pool.

Hostellerie La Roseraie (☎ *05 53 50 53 92, fax 05 53 51 02 23, place d'Armes)* Doubles €68.60-99.10, half-board (€67.85, minimum 3 nights) obligatory July-Aug. Open April-Nov. *Menus* €19.80-28.20. Across the bridge, in a picturesque riverside square, the attractive La Roseraie has a swimming pool and beautiful rose garden, plus a smart restaurant.

Places to Eat

In addition to the hotel-restaurants mentioned above, there are several more casual places.

Restaurant Pizzeria Les Pilotis (☎ *05 53 50 88 15, 6 rue Laffitte)* Menus €9.90-16, pizzas €5.35-6.40. Open mid-Feb–Oct. Open daily, except Mon & Thur off-season. This is a great little restaurant, with delightful riverside or balcony dining.

Le Bellevue (☎ *05 53 51 81 29, Le Regourdou)* Menus €9.25-21.05. Open lunch only. Le Bellevue, which has a fantastic panorama over Montignac, is popular with locals as well as Lascaux-visitors – it's just 500m up the hill from Lascaux II.

There's a good *Casino* supermarket, on place Tourny next to the post office, open daily except Sunday afternoon.

Entertainment

Montignac doesn't exactly have a buzzing nightlife scene, but you can try the following.

Bar Le Tourny (☎ *05 53 51 59 95, 38 rue du 4 Septembre)* Open 8am-2am daily in season. Near the post office, this popular bar-brasserie has light meals, a happy hour (6pm to 8pm, at the bar only) and live music most Friday or Saturday nights (from 10.30pm to 4am).

The Flanagan's Pub-Brasserie (☎ *05 65 24 30 75, place des Omnibus)* Open 10am-2am daily. Need a tot of Irish whisky or a draught of Murphy's? Try this new venue, near Les Pilotis; it also serves food and has great riverside seating.

Getting There & Away

The nearest train station, 9km north-east, is at Condat-le-Lardin (between Condat and Le Lardin-St-Lazare) on the Périgueux (€7.15, 40 minutes) to Brive-la-Gaillarde (€4.25, 20 minutes) line, with two to three services daily.

Buses run (except on Sunday) to Sarlat-la-Canéda (€3.60, 30 minutes, two daily), Brive-la-Gaillarde (€4.40, 1½ hours, one daily) and Périgueux (€5.20, one hour, two daily). The bus stops are at place Tourny and place de l'Église. The tourist office has timetables.

Getting Around

Bike rental is available at Le Moulin de Bleufond camp site (see Places to Stay earlier). Taxis (☎ 05 53 51 97 20 or ☎ 05 53 51 82 20) usually charge about €4.55 to Lascaux, €12.20 to Condat-le-Lardin train station.

AROUND MONTIGNAC
Le Thot

This museum and animal park, 5km south-west of Montignac (1.5km off the D706), is known as Le Thot – Espace Cro-Magnon (☎ *05 53 50 70 44, Thonac; adult/child aged 6-12 €4.55/2.30; open 10am-12.30pm & 1.30pm-7pm Tues-Sun Feb-June, Sept-Dec; 10am-7pm daily July-Aug).* Intended as an introduction to the world of prehistoric people, it has models of animals that appear in prehistoric art, live specimens of similar animals and fascinating exhibits on the creation of Lascaux II. In July and August, tickets must be purchased in Montignac below the tourist office.

St-Amand de Coly

Ten kilometres east of Montignac, in a verdant valley resonant with birdsong, the old slate-tiled houses of St-Amand de Coly are dominated by the village's outrageously tall, yellow-limestone **abbey-church** with high defensive walls – a splendid example of the region's fortified churches. At one time there were 400 monks here, but following the Hundred Years' War only two remained. Now the abbey is a perfect venue for classical concerts.

If you fancy staying overnight, you could try the following.

Hôtel-Restaurant Gardette (☎ 05 53 51 68 50, fax 05 53 51 04 25, Le Bourg) Doubles €26.70-32.80, triples €38.10-38.65, quads 45.75-47.25. Midday & evening *menus* €11.45-19.80. Open Apr-Oct. This charming place is in a converted village house next to the abbey.

SARLAT-LA-CANÉDA

postcode 24200 • pop 10,423
• elevation 173m

The beautiful, well restored town of Sarlat, administratively twinned with nearby La Canéda, is the capital of Périgord Noir. Established around a Benedictine abbey founded in the late 8th century, the town became prosperous in the Middle Ages but was ravaged during the Hundred Years' War (when it was on the border between French and English territory) and the Wars of Religion. These days, Sarlat's medieval and Renaissance old town – much of it built of tan sandstone in the 16th and 17th centuries – attracts large numbers of tourists, especially for the year-round Saturday market.

Sarlat is an excellent base for car trips to the prehistoric sites of the Vézère Valley and the fortresses and chateaux of the Dordogne Valley, but you'd need to book accommodation way ahead in the high season.

Orientation

Sarlat's heart-shaped medieval town *(cité médiévale)*, centred around place de la

Liberté, is bisected by the main commercial street, rue de la République, laid out during the last century. See Getting Around later for details of car restrictions.

Information

Tourist Offices The main tourist office (☎ 05 53 31 45 45, fax 05 53 59 19 44, ℮ ot24.sarlat@perigord.tm.fr), on place de la Liberté, occupies the beautiful Hôtel de Maleville, made up of three 15th- and 16th-century Gothic houses. It opens 9am to 7pm Monday to Saturday (10am to noon and 2pm to 6pm on Sunday) from April to October (9am to noon and 2pm to 7pm Monday to Saturday, from November to April). During July and August, it has an annexe (☎ 05 53 59 18 87) on ave du Général de Gaulle, open 10am to noon and 2pm to 7pm Monday to Saturday. Pick up its excellent free *Guide Pratique*, detailing a walking tour round the old town, and its *Guide Touristique* comprehensively listing nearby sites, suggested tours and activities.

From April to October the tourist office runs 90-minute guided walking tours of the old town (usually in French only, €3.80/2.30 adult/child) at least twice daily (plus one at 10pm in June, July and August, 9.30pm in September).

There's a Bureau d'Information Jeunesse (☎ 05 53 31 56 36, fax 05 53 31 56 34), at the Espace Economie Emploi (place Marc Buisson), where you can get information about temporary jobs. It opens 8.30am to 5.30pm Monday to Friday.

On rue de la République, at No 34, there's a Maison de la Presse, stocking guides and maps.

Money There are several banks, including Crédit Lyonnais at No 15, that line the rue de la République.

Post & Communication The main post office on place du 14 Juillet has currency exchange and Internet facilities.

You can also connect to the Internet at Cyber Espace (☎ 05 53 31 22 37), 13 ave Gambetta, for €1.50 per 15 minutes. It opens 5pm to 8pm Tuesday and Thursday,

THE DORDOGNE

9am to noon and 1.30pm to 8pm on Wednesday, 1.30pm to 9.30pm on Friday, and 9am to 1pm and 2.30pm to 8.30pm on Saturday. A pay-by-card Internet facility is also available at Le Central Café (☎ 05 53 31 67 04), 19 rue de la République, open 9am to around 2am daily.

Laundry La Lavarie laundrette, at 74 ave de Selves, is open 7am to 9pm daily.

Medical Services & Emergency Centre Hospitalier Jean Leclaire (☎ 05 53 31 75 75, rue Jean Leclaire), off the ave de Selvès (D704) is about 1.2km north-east of the centre. The gendarmerie (police station, ☎ 05 53 31 71 10) is at place Salvador Allende.

Medieval Town

The **Cathédrale St-Sacerdos**, once part of Sarlat's Cluniac abbey, is a hotchpotch of styles. The wide, airy nave and its chapels date from the 17th century; the cruciform chevet (at the far end) is from the 14th century; and the western entrance and much of the belfry above it are 12th-century Romanesque. The organ dates from 1752.

Behind the cathedral is the **Jardin des Enfeus**, Sarlat's first cemetery, and the 12th-century **Lanterne des Morts** (Lantern of the Dead), which looks like the top of a missile. It may have been built to commemorate St Bernard, who visited Sarlat in 1147 and whose relics were given to the abbey.

Across the square from the front of the cathedral is the ornate facade of the Renaissance **Maison de la Boétie**, birthplace of the 16th-century writer Étienne de la Boétie (see under Literature in the Facts about Southwest France chapter).

The quiet, largely residential area to the west of rue de la République is also worth exploring. Rue Jean-Jacques Rousseau makes a good starting point.

Special Events

The biggest event on the cultural calendar is the Festival des Jeux du Théâtre (☎ 05 53 31 10 83), with events in churches and on place de la Liberté over a fortnight at the

THE DORDOGNE

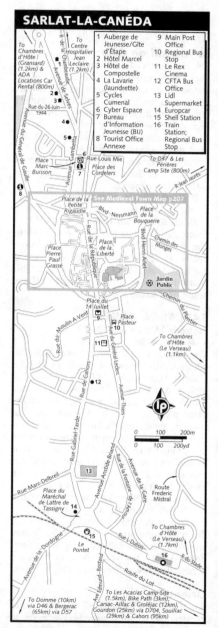

SARLAT-LA-CANÉDA

1 Auberge de Jeunesse/Gîte d'Étape	9 Main Post Office
2 Hôtel Marcel	10 Regional Bus Stop
3 Hôtel de Compostelle	11 Le Rex Cinema
4 La Lavarie (laundrette)	12 CFTA Bus Office
5 Cycles Cumenal	13 Lidl Supermarket
6 Cyber Espace	14 Europcar
7 Bureau d'Information Jeunesse (BIJ)	15 Shell Station
8 Tourist Office Annexe	16 Train Station; Regional Bus Stop

end of July. The Festival du Cinéma, in early November at Le Rex cinema complex (☎ 08 36 68 69 24), ave Thiers, features a week's worth of good French movies.

Places to Stay

Camping & Hostels There are several decent camp sites nearby.

Auberge de Jeunesse/Gîte d'Etape (☎ 05 53 59 47 59 or ☎ 05 53 30 21 27, 77 ave de Selves) Pitch & person €5.35 (€4.55 successive nights), dorm beds €9.25 (€8.40). Open 15 Apr-15 Nov. Reception opens 6pm. This hostel (not in the Hostelling Federation) has a tiny back garden where tents can be pitched; call ahead to see if there's space. From the train station, walk down to Le Pontet roundabout to catch a local bus (Ligne A; six times daily) to the Cimetière stop. The Auberge is hard to spot – look for the Leader store opposite.

Les Acacias (☎ 05 53 31 08 50, fax 05 53 59 29 30, route de Souillac) 2-person forfait €11.45. Open Apr-Oct. This pleasant site 1.5km south-east of the train station, 300m south of the village of La Canéda (and 1km from the *piste cyclable* or bicycle path), has a pool and snack-bar. Local bus Ligne A runs to town six times daily.

Les Périères (☎ 05 53 59 05 84, fax 05 53 28 57 51, @ lesperieres@wanadoo.fr, Route Ste-Nathalène) 2-person forfait €23. Open Apr-Sept. This swanky camp site, 800m north-east along the D47 towards Ste-Nathalène, has a pool, tennis courts and lots of other ball-game facilities.

Chambres d'Hôtes There are dozens of *chambres d'hôtes* in and around Sarlat; ask at the tourist office.

Madame Gransard chambres d'hôte (☎ 05 53 59 35 20, La Colline de Péchauriol) Doubles/triples with shower & WC €30.50/36.60. Open Apr-Nov. This chambre d'hôte, about 1.2km north of town, has three comfy doubles, and a pleasant covered

THE DORDOGNE

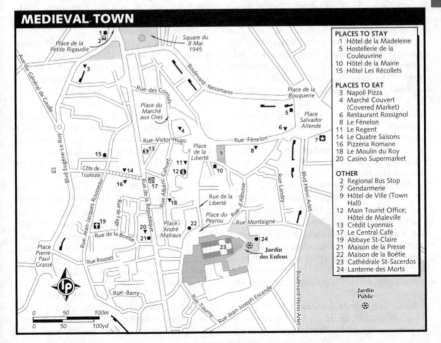

MEDIEVAL TOWN

PLACES TO STAY
1 Hôtel de la Madeleine
5 Hostellerie de la Couleuvrine
10 Hôtel de la Mairie
15 Hôtel Les Récollets

PLACES TO EAT
3 Napoli Pizza
4 Marché Couvert (Covered Market)
6 Restaurant Rossignol
8 Le Fénelon
11 Le Regent
14 Le Quatre Saisons
16 Pizzeria Romane
18 Le Moulin du Roy
20 Casino Supermarket

OTHER
2 Regional Bus Stop
7 Gendarmerie
9 Hôtel de Ville (Town Hall)
12 Main Tourist Office; Hôtel de Maleville
13 Crédit Lyonnais
17 Le Central Café
19 Abbaye St-Claire
21 Maison de la Presse
22 Maison de la Boétie
23 Cathédrale St-Sacerdos
24 Lanterne des Morts

terrace. Follow the northbound D704 past the Intermarché supermarket, turn right just before the entrance to the Mazda garage and follow the 'chambres' signs.

Le Verseau (☎ *05 53 31 02 63,* e *verseau-sarlat@ifrance.com, 49 route des Pechs)* Singles €15.25, doubles €19.80-30.50, quads €33.55. The six rooms here (three with shower & WC) are complemented by a lovely garden. From the train station, it's a 1.7km uphill walk along rue de Stade then first left onto route Frédéric Mistral (Les Pechs). There's a shorter (1.1km) route from the town centre via chemin du Plantier.

Hotels The following prices are all high-season rates.

Hôtel Marcel (☎ *05 53 59 21 98, fax 05 53 30 27 77, 50 ave de Selves)* Doubles €38.10-48.80. Open mid-Feb–mid-Nov. The two-star Hôtel Marcel has 12 decent, bargain rooms.

Hôtel de Compostelle (☎ *05 53 59 08 53, fax 05 53 30 31 65,* e *hotel.compostelle@wanadoo.fr, 64 ave de Selves)* Doubles €44.20-50.30. Open Easter–mid-Nov. The modern, 23-room Compostelle has bland but spacious rooms (some with glassed-in balconies). The two-/three-room combinations (€65.55-83.85) would suit families.

Hôtel Les Récollets (☎ *05 53 31 36 00, fax 05 53 30 32 62,* e *contact@hotel-recollet-sarlat.com, 4 rue Jean-Jacques Rousseau)* Doubles €38.10-59.45, triples €53.55, quads €68.60. The friendly Récollets is up a narrow old alleyway (nearest parking is on blvd Eugène Le Roy). It has quiet, tastefully decorated rooms.

Hôtel de la Mairie (☎/fax *05 53 59 05 71, 13 place de la Liberté)* Doubles €39.65-51.85, triples €54.85, quads €73.15. This cheerful hotel (with a busy bar downstairs) has a variety of spacious, often timbered rooms with loads of medieval character. Some overlook the market square and several are so huge (eg, Nos 1 and 8) they'd be perfect for families (though not all have showers and WC).

Hostellerie de la Couleuvrine (☎ *05 53 59 27 80, fax 05 53 31 26 83, 1 place de la Bouquerie)* Doubles €40.40-51.85, half-

board (€85.35-96.95, minimum 2 nights) obligatory July-Aug. This large fortress-like Logis de France hotel, parts of which belong to the medieval defences of the town, has rather sombre decor but comfy rooms (three with balconies).

Hôtel de la Madeleine (☎ *05 53 59 10 41, fax 05 53 31 03 62,* e *hotel.madeleine@wanadoo.fr, 1 place de la Petite Rigaudie)* Singles €54.85-66.30, doubles €62.50-75.45, triples €86.10. Open Mar-Dec. The elegant Madeleine has luxurious rooms and an excellent restaurant (see Places to Eat)

Places to Eat

Restaurants & Bar-Brasseries In addition to the town's hotel-restaurants, there are dozens of chic little restaurants in the old town offering traditional Périgordian cuisine or cheaper fare.

Napoli Pizza (☎ *05 53 31 26 93, 2 blvd Eugène Le Roy)* Pizzas & pastas €5.30-10.70. Open midday & evening Mon-Sat, evening only Sun. This spacious, rustic venue has an enticingly long menu.

Pizzeria Romane (☎ *05 53 59 23 88, 3 côte de Toulouse)* Pizzas €5.80-8.85, other dishes €8.55-10.95. Open midday & evening Tues-Sat, evening only Sun. In addition to pizzas, the Romane also has a Périgordian *menu* (€13.75) that includes *confit de canard* (duck preserved in its own fat).

Le Regent (☎ *05 53 31 06 36, place de la Liberté)* Midday *menus* €10.55. This lively brasserie, with outdoor seating at the heart of the old town, offers a tempting *menu du terroir* (€16.95) including foie gras, confit de canard and *gateau aux noix* (walnut cake).

Le Fénelon (☎ *05 53 29 47 80, 10 rue Fénelon)* Menus €12.95-19.05. Open midday & evening daily June-Sept, midday only Oct-May. This popular bar-brasserie (its walls covered with photos of visiting film stars) serves traditional fare in a casual setting. Try its *omelette aux cèpes* (wild-mushroom omelette), a bargain at €8.40.

Le Moulin du Roy (☎ *05 53 31 11 94, 7 rue Albéric Cahuet)* Menus €9.90-13.70. Closed mid-Nov–Feb. The small, unpretentious Moulin du Roy offers good-value regional cuisine in an intimate setting.

More upmarket establishments offering deluxe French cuisine include:

Restaurant Rossignol (☎ 05 53 31 02 30, 15 rue Fénelon) Midday *menus* €13.40, evening *menus* €16.95-44.20. Open Fri-Wed. At this posh place you can try delicacies such as *cuisses de grenouilles aux cèpes* (frogs' legs with cep mushrooms, €22.85).

Le Quatre Saisons (☎ 05 53 29 48 59, côte de Toulouse) Midday *menus* €14.50, evening *menus* €17.55-34.30. The reliable Quatre Saisons has a select *menu* of traditional fare.

Hôtel de la Madeleine (see Places to Stay) *Menus* €20.60-35.85, dishes €16.75-30.20. The classy Madeleine has a very stylish restaurant for that once-in-a-lifetime splurge.

Self-Catering Long a driving force in the town's economy, Sarlat's Saturday *market* offers edibles in the morning (on place de la Liberté) and durables (such as clothing and handicrafts) all day long (especially on rue de la République). Depending on the season, Périgord delicacies on offer include truffles, foie gras, mushrooms and walnuts and their various products. A smaller *fruit and vegetable market* is held on place de la Liberté on Wednesday morning. A new *marché couvert* (covered market) housed in the vast former Église Ste-Marie, off place de la Liberté, opens 8.30am to 1pm Tuesday to Sunday, May to mid-October (9am to 12.30pm on Tuesday, Wednesday, Friday and Saturday other months).

The *Casino supermarket* at 32 rue de la République is open 8am to 12.15pm and 2.30pm to 7.15pm Tuesday to Saturday and 8.30am to 12.15pm on Sunday (open longer during July and August). The *Lidl* supermarket, between rue Gabriel Tarde and ave Aristide Briand, is open 9am to 12.30pm and 2.30pm to 7.30pm Monday to Friday (9am to 7pm on Saturday).

Getting There & Away
Sarlat has very poor bus and train links to the rest of the region.

Bus There's no bus station – departures are from the train station, place Pasteur or place de la Petite Rigaudie, depending on your destination. The tourist office has timetables, or visit the CFTA office (☎ 05 53 59 01 48) at 31 rue de Cahors. It's usually open 10am to noon and 2pm to 4pm Monday to Friday.

CFTA run services to Périgueux (€7.70, 1½ hours) via Montignac (€3.60, 30 minutes), the town nearest Lascaux II, from place Pasteur, twice-daily; and to Brive (€6.10, 1½ hours via back roads) once-daily in term-time (three times weekly in holidays) from place de la Petite Rigaudie (called 'Madeleine' on timetables).

A trans-Périgord bus (run by the Conseil Général de la Dordogne) runs from the train station and place Pasteur to Souillac via the Dordogne Valley (€4.55, 50 minutes, three to four daily).

Train The train station (☎ 05 53 59 00 21) is 1.3km south of the old town; the ticket windows are staffed until 7.25pm daily (closed at lunchtimes).

Sarlat is directly linked to Bordeaux (€18.45, 2½ hours, three or four daily) via Bergerac (€9.30, 1½ hours). Change at Le Buisson (€5.20, 40 minutes, three daily) to reach Périgueux (€11.75) and Les Eyzies de Tayac (€7.15). To get to Paris' Gare d'Austerlitz (€46.50) change at Souillac, linked to Sarlat by bus (see Bus earlier in this section).

Car & Taxi Europcar (☎ 05 53 30 30 40, fax 05 53 31 10 39) has an office near the train station. Cheaper ADA Locations (☎ 05 53 29 97 95, fax 05 53 30 25 38) is on the route de Brive. For a taxi call ☎ 05 53 59 02 43.

Getting Around
Cycles Cumenal (☎ 05 53 31 28 40) at 8 ave Gambetta has VTTs for €12.20/38.10 per day/week. It opens Tuesday to Saturday. You can drop off the bike at its branches in Périgueux or Ribérac.

There's a *piste cyclable* that begins about 3km south-east of town (near the junction of the D704 and D704A) and continues to Carsac-Aillac (12km from Sarlat) and, across the river, to Groléjac.

For details of walking/biking circuits in and around town, pick up *Promenades et*

THE DORDOGNE

Randonnées (€1.20 for one or €11.45 for all 29) from the tourist office.

The Cité Médiéval is a no-go area for cars. Free parking is most easily available along blvd Eugène Le Roy (a five-minute walk above town). Cars are also banned along rue de la République on Saturday and every day during July and August.

DOMME
postcode 24250 • pop 1010
• elevation 150m

Set on a dramatically steep promontory high above the River Dordogne, the unusual trapezium-shaped walled village of Domme is one of the most famous bastides in the region. It's one of the few to have retained most of its 13th-century ramparts, including three fortified gates: porte del Bos, porte des Tours and porte de la Combe. A one-time base for the Knights Templars (whose religious graffiti can still be seen in the towers by porte des Tours, where they were imprisoned in 1307), it was fought over and besieged frequently during the Hundred Years' War and Wars of Religion.

The village is so picturesque it has become very touristy and commercialised, but you can't beat its stunning panoramas of the River Dordogne and its valley.

Orientation & Information

There are two main entrances – southern porte del Bos (the D46/D50 approach from Cénac) or eastern porte des Tours (D46E from Sarlat). At the top of the village's main street, Grand'Rue, is the central market place, place de la Halle, and the tourist office (☎ 05 53 31 71 00, fax 05 53 31 71 09). It opens 10am to noon and 2pm to 6pm daily (10am to 7pm daily in July and August). It's closed during January.

Car parking inside the walls is metered. There's a free parking lot just outside porte des Tours.

Things to See & Do

The best views are a few steps from place de la Halle, from the cliff-side **Esplanade du Belvédère** and the adjacent **Promenade de la Barre**, which stretches west along the

forested slope to the Jardin Public. The precipitous bluff below was, amazingly, scaled by Huguenot besiegers during the Wars of Religion, one of the few times the bastide was captured.

Across from the tourist office, the 19th-century reconstruction of the 16th-century *halle*s (covered market) houses the entrance to the **grottes** *(caves; ☎ 05 53 31 71 00, place de la Halle; adult/student/child €5.35/4.55/3.05)*, 450m of stalactite-filled galleries underneath the village that gave the inhabitants a handy refuge during times of attack; a lift whisks you back up at the end of the 30-minute tour. Visits are only at specific tour times (three times daily in winter, eight times daily April to June and every 15 to 20 minutes during July and August). Tickets are sold at the tourist office (at the cave entrance during July and August). The caves open 11am to 5pm daily, 4 February to March, October and 1 to 11 November; 10.30am to 6pm daily, April to June and September; 10.15am to 6.40pm daily, July and August; closed 11 November to February except Christmas school holidays.

On the far side of the square from the tourist office, the **Musée d'Arts et de Traditions Populaires** *(☎ 05 53 31 71 00, place de la Halle; adult/child €2.75/1.85; open 10am-12.30pm & 2.30pm-6pm daily Apr-June, Sept-Oct; 10.30am-7pm July-Aug)* has nine rooms of clothing, toys, tools and other memorabilia from the past (especially the 19th century).

Several **canoe operators** are based in Cénac, including Randonnée Dordogne. See activities at the start of this chapter for details. For **bike rental**, see the following La Roque Gageac section.

Places to Stay & Eat

The tourist office has details of many other camp sites, *chambres d'hôte* and *locations meublés* (self-catering places) nearby.

Camping Municipal *(☎ 05 53 28 31 91)* Adult/pitch €3.05/3.80. Open June–mid-Sept. This simple, grassy camp site, 1.5km down the D46 in Cénac, is a few steps from the river.

Nadine & Daniel Delpech chambres d'hôte (☎ 05 53 28 58 55, La porte del

Bos) Doubles €35.05-50.30. This attractive house, just outside the porte del Bos, has four beautifully furnished rooms, a garden and swimming pool.

Nouvel Hôtel (☎ 05 53 28 38 67, fax 05 53 28 27 13, place de la Halle) Doubles with WC €33.55-38.10, without WC €27.45. Midday menus €10.65, evening menus €15.10-28.95, dishes €7.60-15.25. Open mid-Apr–Dec. The Nouvel, close to the tourist office, has reasonable rooms, all with shower, and a decent midday menu.

Les Quatre Vents (☎ 05 53 28 20 33, fax 05 53 31 57 59, 24250 Domme) Doubles €47.25-73.15. This quiet, beautifully situated hotel, on a verdant sloping hillside 1.5km north-east (follow the D46E from porte des Tours) has 20 rooms in traditional-style stone houses, plus a restaurant and two swimming pools.

La Poivrière (☎ 05 53 28 32 52, place de la Halle) Midday menus €10.65, evening menus €12.95-30.20. This is a great-value restaurant with a small, shady terrace for watching people disappear into the caves.

Getting There & Away
Taxis (☎ 05 53 28 35 71) charge around €15.25 one way to Sarlat, the nearest train and bus hub (see Getting There & Away under Sarlat).

LA ROQUE GAGEAC
postcode 24250 • pop 360 • elevation 80m
This outrageously picturesque hamlet of tan stone houses, nestled under a cliff on the right bank of the Dordogne, entices visitors up steep, residential lanes with delightful river views. There's a tiny tourist office (☎ 05 53 29 17 01) in the riverside car park, officially open (but often not) 11am to noon and 4pm to 6pm daily, June to September.

Things to See & Do
The **Fort Troglodytique** (☎ 05 53 31 61 94; adult/child €4.10/1.50; open 10am-noon & 2pm-6pm daily Apr-Nov), halfway up the cliff-face, are fortified cave dwellings originally built in their incredible position during the 12th century. They resisted all attacks

during the Hundred Years' War, but were finally captured by the unstoppable Huguenots during the Wars of Religion. The fortifications were rebuilt during the 17th century but gradually dismantled and their stones used elsewhere.

Les Caminades (☎ 05 53 29 40 95) and **Les Gabares Norbert** (☎ 05 53 29 40 44) both offer one-hour river trips (French commentary with English/Dutch audio translations) on board replicas of wine-carrying gabarres (adult/child €7.15/4.10). Between April and November they operate regularly from 10am to 5pm or 6pm (every 30 minutes in July and August).

Canoë Dordogne has canoes and kayaks for rent from the riverside at the back of the car park and also offers rock-climbing and potholing through a separate company, **Couleurs Périgord** (see Activities at the start of this chapter).

Places to Stay & Eat
There's a string of places along the riverside D703.

Bar-Hôtel (☎ 05 53 29 51 63) Doubles with shower €28.95. Open Easter-Oct. This modest, old-fashioned place has unpretentious rooms (none with private WCs).

Hôtel-Restaurant Gardette (☎ 05 53 29 51 58, fax 05 53 31 19 32, ⓔ egardette@aol.com) Doubles with shower or bath & WC €27.45-42.70. Menus €18.30-37.35. The 12-room Gardette is rather quaint, with some rooms definitely dowdy but others delightful. Adventurous gourmets may fancy the restaurant's specialities, for example, cassolette d'escargots aux cèpes (snail stew with cep mushrooms; €14.50).

Hôtel La Belle Étoile (☎ 05 53 29 51 44, fax 05 53 29 45 63) Doubles with shower €30.50, with shower & WC €42.70-68.60. Menus €19.05-30.50. Open Apr–mid-Oct. The Belle Étoile is a smartish Logis de France property with most rooms overlooking the river.

L'Ancre d'Or (☎ 05 53 29 53 45) Midday menus €10.35, evening menus €18.30-35.05. This welcoming place, at the western end of the road, has a nice covered terrace and an extensive menu of reasonably priced

The River Dordogne

The mighty Dordogne rises on the Puy de Sancy high in the Massif Central, flowing south-westwards and then due west for 472km – through five dams – to a point about 20km north of Bordeaux, where it joins the River Garonne to form the Gironde Estuary. The river, though fast and temperamental, was once a vital economic byway, with *gabarres* (flat-bottomed boats) taking wine and oak to Bordeaux, and *saliers* returning with salt from Libourne. Today, it's been harnessed and generates huge quantities of hydroelectric power.

Périgord Noir boasts some of the most scenic and famous stretches of the river, particularly the two huge loops known as Cingle de Trémolat (west of Limeuil) and Cingle de Montfort (east of Domme), and the stretch between Limeuil and Domme, with its fairy-tale chateaux and fortresses, and meadows of tobacco, maize, walnut and poplars.

dishes. Try the *tourrain blanchi* (traditional garlic soup; €3.80).

Near here is a small **grocery store**, **bakery** and a **Pizzeria Saladerie** (☎ 05 53 29 20 74) offering pizzas and yummy salads (€3.05-11.45).

Getting There & Around
Sarlat, 13km north, has the nearest train and bus stations (see Getting There & Away in that section). For a taxi call ☎ 05 53 59 39 65 or mobile ☎ 06 08 57 30 10.

The ELF garage (☎ 05 53 28 30 79) about 3km north on the Route de Sarlat, rents bikes for €13.70/68.60.

BEYNAC-ET-CAZENAC
postcode 24220 • pop 460 • elevation 80m
For centuries Beynac and Cazenac, 3km to the west, were arch enemies; today, ironically, their names remain inextricably linked for administrative convenience. Beynac's dramatic fortress, rising from the cliff face, was once one of the greatest Périgord strongholds, dominating a strategic bend in the Dordogne and rivalling the English-held fortress of Castelnaud on the other bank of the river. Today, it's in the full glare of the tourist traffic, while neighbouring Cazenac – still worth a visit for its Gothic church and exceptional views – is little more than a sleepy hamlet.

Information
The tourist office (☎/fax 05 53 29 43 08, e ot.beynac@perigord.tm.fr), in the car park between the river and the busy D703 (which passes right through the lower village), is open 10am to 12.30pm and 2.15pm to 6pm daily (to 5.45pm Saturday and Sunday; closed Sunday during winter). It opens 9.30am to 12.30pm and 2pm to 7pm daily during July and August.

Château de Beynac
The heavily fortified chateau (☎ 05 53 29 50 40; adult/child €6.10/2.60) has a wild and colourful past. During the Middle Ages it was the seat of one of Périgord's four baronies (the others were at Biron, Mareuil and Bourdeilles); during the Albigensian Crusade it was seized and sacked by Simon de Montfort; and during the Hundred Years' War it was continually tussled over by the French and English. Not surprisingly, it has been rebuilt many times and retains features from all ages (notably some rare 15th-century frescoes) as well as a timeless view over the river.

The chateau opens 10am to noon and 2pm to 4.30pm daily in November; noon to 5pm daily, December to February; 10am to noon and 2pm to 6pm daily, March to May, June and October; 10am to noon and 2pm to 6.30pm daily, July to September. One-hour guided tours (French only) take place every half-hour within the above opening hours from mid-March to mid-November.

Behind the chateau is an open-air **Parc Archaeologique** (☎ 05 53 29 51 28; adult/child aged 6-16 €4.55/3.05; open 10am-7pm Sun-Mon July-Aug), containing a series of reconstructed Neolithic dwellings and tools.

Château de Castelnaud
This 12th- to 16th-century chateau (☎ 05 53 31 30 00, Castelnaud La Chapelle; adult/child aged 10-17 €5.80/2.90), about 4km

across the river from Beynac (along the D57), has everything you'd expect from a cliff-top castle – walls up to 2m thick (as you can see from peering through the loopholes, some designed for crossbows, others for small cannon); a superb panorama of the meandering Dordogne; and fine views of the fortified chateaux that dot the nearby hilltops.

The interior rooms are occupied by a **museum of medieval warfare**, whose displays range from daggers and spiked halberds to huge catapults. The houses of the medieval village of Castelnaud cling to the steep slopes below the fortress.

The chateau opens 10am to 6pm daily March, April and October to mid-November; 10am to 7pm daily May, June and September; 9am to 8pm daily July and August; 2pm to 5pm daily the rest of year. A comprehensive English-language guidebook can be borrowed at the ticket counter.

Places to Stay & Eat
Beynac's best camp sites are by the river, and its hotels and restaurants are mostly squeezed along the D703.

Camping Le Capeyrou (☎ 05 53 29 54 95, fax 05 53 28 36 27) Adult/pitch €3.95/5.50. Open mid-May–early-Sept. This grassy riverside camp site, 600m east of Beynac off the D703, is a popular spot with a pool and various sports facilities.

Camping La Cabane (☎ 05 53 29 52 28, fax 05 53 59 09 15, e camping.la.cab ane@wanadoo.fr, Vézac) Adult/pitch/car €2.60/2.60/2.60; farmhouse room with/without shower €19.80/18.30. The spacious, riverside La Cabane, 5km south-east of Beynac, also offers *chambres d'hôte* in an old-fashioned farmhouse.

Hôtel-Restaurant du Château (☎ 05 53 29 50 13, fax 05 53 28 53 05, e hotel_du_Chateau@perigord.com) Doubles with shower €42.70. Menus €12.95-21.35. This central, flashy place has a popular restaurant and a swimming pool.

Café de la Rivière (☎ 05 53 28 35 49, e hamish.xanthe@wanadoo.fr, Le Bourg) Doubles €44.95, half-board (€53.35) obligatory July-Aug. Dishes €5.80-10.95. This new, British-run, kid-friendly spot has

The Rainbow Tribe's Home
The claim to fame of the smallish, late-15th-century **Château des Milandes** (☎ 05 53 59 31 21; Castelnaud La Chapelle; adult/child €7.30/5.35; open 10am-6pm daily Apr-June; 9.30am-7pm daily July-Aug; 10am-6pm daily Sept; 10am-5pm Oct) is its post-war role as the home of the African-American dancer and music-hall star Josephine Baker (1906–75), who helped bring black American culture to Paris in the 1920s with her *Revue Nègre* and created a sensation by appearing on stage wearing nothing but a skirt of bananas.

Awarded the Croix de Guerre (Military Cross) and the Légion d'Honneur (Legion of Honour) for her very active work with the French Résistance during WWII, and later participating in the US civil-rights movement, Baker established her Rainbow Tribe here in 1949, adopting 12 children from around the world as 'an experiment in brotherhood'. But by 1964 she was broke and had to sell the chateau and retire to Monaco.

Today, the totally renovated chateau has changing exhibitions (visits guided by laser-disk commentary) and somewhat incongruous but captivating displays of the medieval art of falconry (the present owner is a falconry fan). The displays take place four times daily between May and August, and once daily, at 3.30pm, in September and October.

just two bright rooms and a lovely terraced garden for charming light meals.

Hôtel-Restaurant Bonnet (☎ 05 53 29 50 45, fax 05 53 28 29 58) Singles €22.85-41.15, doubles €53.35-58. Menus €14.50-27.45. The Bonnet, at the far-eastern end of the road, has rather old-fashioned rooms but a lovely sun-dappled terrace overlooking the river.

Getting There & Away
Voyages Rey (☎ 05 53 07 27 21) run a once-daily Monday to Friday service via Beynac between Le Bugue (€5.80, 55 minutes) and Sarlat (€4.25, 30 minutes), but only in term-time.

Sarlat, 11km north-east, is the nearest train and bus hub (see Getting There & Away under Sarlat earlier in the chapter). For a taxi call ☎ 05 53 29 87 89.

BELVÈS
postcode 24170 • pop 1600
• elevation 190m

Perched high above the River Nauze, this lively, ancient market town, 22km to the south-west of Beynac-et-Cazenac, has a well preserved old bastide core with some attractive Gothic and Renaissance houses. Bell towers are its speciality (its nickname is the City of Seven Bell Towers) but it also has a timeless ambience and makes a pleasant base for a couple of days. Horse-riders and hikers may be particularly happy, with several horse-riding outfits in the area and the GR36 passing close by, via the dense Fôret de la Bessède to the west.

Orientation & Information

The old town is between the busy D710, 2km below, and the D53 to its west. At its heart is the place d'Armes; overlooking this, in the old Maison des Consuls, is the tourist office (☎/fax 05 53 29 10 20, e belves@peri gord.com, w www.perigord.com/belves), open 10am to 1pm and 3pm to 7pm daily, mid-June to mid-September, and 10am to 12.30pm and 3pm to 6.30pm Monday to Friday at other times. It has a pay-by-card Internet facility.

Things to See

On place d'Armes there is an imposing 15th-century **covered market** with stone and wooden pillars. Spot the pillory chain in a glass case on one of them, once used for tying up criminals.

From the tourist office, you can get tickets for the nearby **Abris Troglodytiques** (place d'Armes; adult/child €3.05/1.50; open 10.30am-12.30pm & 3pm-7pm daily Apr-Nov), an underground series of rooms where people lived from the 13th to 18th centuries. Guided visits (lasting 45 minutes) are at 11am, 3pm and 5.30pm daily except Sunday (eight times daily during mid-June to mid-September, including three in English).

Places to Stay & Eat

The gîte d'étape *Relais de St-Paradoux*, on the GR36, 3km south-west of Belvès, charges €9.25 a bed; bookings must be made through the tourist office (see Orientation & Information earlier in this section).

Les Nauves (☎/fax 05 53 29 12 64, Le Bos-Rouge) Adult/pitch €3.95/5.65. One of several nearby camp sites, this place, 4km south-west off the D53, has a pool, tennis courts and horses to ride (€16.95 per hour, unaccompanied).

Le Bugou (☎ 05 53 29 01 08, Le Bugou) Singles/doubles €24.40/36.60 including breakfast. Half-board €30.50 per person. Some 1.5km east of the D710 (3.8km from Belvès), is this hilltop *ferme de séjour* (farm accommodation) on a working farm complete with horses (€12.20 per hour to ride), ducks and rabbits: a great place for kids. The six rooms, all with shower and WC are in a converted barn, and are plain but perfectly adequate.

Hôtel Le Home (☎ 05 53 29 01 65, fax 05 53 59 46 99, place de la Croix-des-Frères) Doubles with shower €28.20-35.05, without €20.60. Midday *menus* €9, evening *menus* €15.10-23.15, dishes €8.05-17.05. This hotel, on the D53's western edge of town, is a decent little place with bargain rates.

Belvédère de Belvès (☎ 05 53 31 51 41, fax 05 53 31 51 42, 1 ave Paul-Crampel) Doubles €38.10-50.30, triples €55.65. Midday *menus* €11.90, evening *menus* €18.30-38.10. Open Mar-Dec. Nearby is this considerably classier 20-room Logis de France property.

Café Brasserie Le Madelon (☎ 05 53 31 15 70, place de la Croix-des-Frères) Dishes €4.55-9.90. Open Tues-Sun (open daily July-Aug). Opposite Le Home is this attractive, laid-back venue.

Getting There & Away

Belvès is on the Agen (€10.65, 1¼ hours) to Périgueux (€9.75, 1¼ hours) train line, via Le Buisson (€2.45, 25 minutes) and Les Eyzies (€4.85, 45 minutes). Services to all these destinations run two to three times daily. The train station (☎ 05 53 29 00 22) is 2km east (downhill), just off the D710.

Getting Around
Monsieur Baconnier, who works at the train station, rents out mountain bikes for €15.25 per day. The office is open 5.45am to 6.30pm on Monday, 7.30am to 3pm Tuesday to Saturday and 3pm to 11pm on Sunday.

East of Périgord Noir

One of the best jumping-off points to Périgord Noir if you are relying on public transport is Brive-la-Gaillarde in the neighbouring Corréze department, which also has several other worthwhile sights on or near the River Dordogne.

BRIVE-LA-GAILLARDE
postcode 19100 • pop 50,000
• elevation 142m
Sprawling, commercial Brive, a major rail junction 73km east of Périgueux, has little going for it apart from one outstanding museum and a small, largely pedestrianised historic centre. But it's a major transport hub and with its plentiful cheap accommodation serves as a useful base.

Situated on the left bank of the River Corrèze, it earned the moniker *la gaillarde* (the bold one) in 1356 as a reward for its martial gallantry. Nowadays, its prowess is directed largely to rugby, with its local team, Club Athlétique Brive Corrèze, scoring regional successes.

Orientation
Brive's old town is centred around the heavily restored Église St-Martin on place Charles de Gaulle. The train station is some 900m to the south-west, and the tourist office and bus hub 400m north, on place du 14 Juillet.

Information
Tourist Offices Housed in a 19th-century water tower in place du 14 Juillet, the tourist office (☎ 05 55 24 08 80; fax 05 55 24 58 24, e tourisme.brive@wanadoo.fr) is open 9am to noon and 2pm to 6pm Monday to Saturday

(9am to 7pm in July and August, when it's also open 10am to 1pm on Sunday).

The Service Information Jeunesse (SIJ; ☎ 05 55 23 43 80, fax 05 55 17 07 66), at 12 place Jean-Marie Dauzier, has information on lodgings and youth-oriented events (including sports). It opens 9am to noon and 1.30pm to 6pm Monday to Friday.

Bookshops There's a Maison de la Presse bookshop at 2 place des Patrioles Martyrs.

Money Crédit Agricole banks can be found at place de la Halle and 22 rue de l'Hôtel de Ville.

Post & Communication The main post office, near place Thiers, has currency exchange and Internet facilities. A branch office is at 28 blvd Anatole France. Internet connections are also available at Ax'ion (☎ 05 55 23 44 22), 33 blvd Géneral Koenig, which charges €2 per 15 minutes (€7.60 per hour). It opens 11am to 7pm on Monday, 9am to 7pm Tuesday to Saturday.

Laundry La Lavarie laundrette at 39 rue Dubois is open 6.30am to 9.30pm daily.

Medical Services & Emergency The Centre Hospitalier (hospital; ☎ 05 55 92 60 00) is at blvd Dr Verlhac about 1km north of the town centre. The main police station, Hôtel de Police (☎ 05 55 17 46 00), is at 4 blvd Anatole France.

Église St-Martin
This former monastery, dating from the 12th century but with 14th- to 19th-century additions and restorations, is at the very heart of the old town.

Built over the 5th-century tomb of St-Martin (a Spaniard who brought Christianity to ungrateful inhabitants who promptly massacred him), it has a Romanesque apse and choir, and tall, cylindrical pillars of exceptional slenderness.

Musée Labenche
This fantastic museum (☎ 05 55 24 19 05, 26 bis blvd Jules Ferry; adult €4.10, child &

BRIVE-LA-GAILLARDE

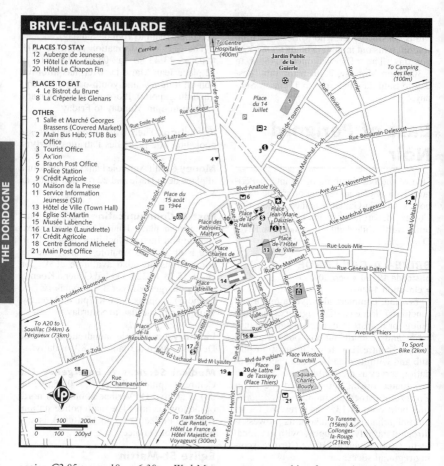

PLACES TO STAY
12 Auberge de Jeunesse
19 Hôtel Le Montauban
20 Hôtel Le Chapon Fin

PLACES TO EAT
4 Le Bistrot du Brune
8 La Crêperie les Glenans

OTHER
1 Salle et Marché Georges
  Brassens (Covered Market)
2 Main Bus Hub; STUB Bus
  Office
3 Tourist Office
5 Ax'ion
6 Branch Post Office
7 Police Station
9 Crédit Agricole
10 Maison de la Presse
11 Service Information
  Jeunesse (SIJ)
13 Hôtel de Ville (Town Hall)
14 Église St-Martin
15 Musée Labenche
16 La Lavarie (Laundrette)
17 Crédit Agricole
18 Centre Édmond Michelet
21 Main Post Office

senior €2.05; open 10am-6.30pm Wed-Mon Apr-Oct; 1.30pm-6pm Wed-Mon Nov-Mar), housed in the most outstanding of Brive's Renaissance mansions (its facade adorned with various busts peering down, including a coquettish lady with handkerchief poised), is worth the visit to Brive alone. Its highlight is France's largest collection of huge, 17th-century English Mortlake tapestries, collected between 1982 and 2000 – three of the finest, looking as good as new, came from the Château de Cosnac near Brive. The other five were subsequently bought from Paris sales.

The museum's other 15 exhibition rooms

cover everything from archaeology to local historic heroes, and a very fine ethnological exhibition including a great display of accordions made by François Dedenis from the late 1890s to 1930 (accordion-playing continues to be a famous Corrèze tradition).

Centre Édmond Michelet

Housed in the family home of Édmond Michelet, a former minister under General de Gaulle who was interned at Dachau during WWII, this Centre National de la Résistance et de la Déportation (*☎ 05 55 74 06 08, 4 rue Champanatier; admission free;*

open 10am-noon & 2pm-6pm Mon-Sat; closed bank holidays) has exhibits on the French Resistance during WWII and the deportations to Nazi concentration camps.

Places to Stay

Several nondescript cheap hotels are located near the train station. Better options, including several Logis de France establishments are town.

Camping les Iles (☎ 05 55 24 34 74, fax 05 55 17 62 42, 13 blvd Michelet) Adult/ pitch €2.75/2.45. This riverside municipal facility, about 400m north-east of the town centre, has 80 sites and is close to the municipal swimming pool and tennis courts.

Auberge de Jeunesse (☎ 05 55 24 34 00, fax 05 55 84 82 80, e brive@fuaj.org, 56 ave du Maréchal Bugeaud) Dorm beds €7.60. This modern hostel is in a pleasant little park about 700m east of town. Bus Nos 2 and 4 run this way from place du 14 Juillet.

Hôtel Majestic et Voyageurs (☎ 05 55 24 10 20, 67 ave Jean Jaurès) Singles/doubles €12.20/15.25, doubles with shower €18.30-24.40. This cheap, undistinguished place is close to the train station.

Hôtel Le France (☎ 05 55 74 08 13, fax 05 55 17 04 32, 60 ave Jean Jaurès) Doubles €22.85-27.45. This is a modern Logis de France without much character but with a decent restaurant (see Places to Eat).

Hôtel Le Montauban (☎ 05 55 24 00 38, fax 05 55 84 80 30, 6 ave Édouard Herriot) Singles €27.45-31.25, doubles €30.50-38.10, triples €41.15. This rather dowdy Logis de France hotel has a good-value range of spacious rooms, all with shower (the cheaper ones without WC).

Hôtel Le Chapon Fin (☎ 05 55 74 23 40, fax 05 55 23 42 52, e lechaponfin@ yahoo.fr, 1 place de Lattre de Tassigny) Singles €35.80-38.85, doubles €41.90-53.35, triple €45.75. Definitely a notch up, friendly Le Chapon Fin has bright, welcoming rooms.

Places to Eat

The three following eateries are particularly good.

Hôtel le France (see Places to Stay) Midday *menus* €8.40, evening *menus* €12.95-

19.80. This is one of several brasserie-type restaurants near the train station, serving honest fare (accompanied by sports TV).

Le Bistrot du Brune (☎ 05 55 24 00 91, 13 ave de Paris) Dishes €5.35-14.65. Open midday & evening Mon-Sat, midday only Sun. In another popular dining area, Le Bistrot is more stylish than most, with a simple but tempting plat du jour (€6.85).

La Crêperie les Glenans (☎ 05 55 24 56 66, 12 place de la Halle) Menus €8.40-12.95, galettes & salads €4.55-7. Open daily. The big draw to this creperie is its outdoor dining area in a quiet corner of the old town.

Getting There & Away

Bus The town centre's bus hub is on place du 14 Juillet, though many services also stop at the train station. The urban bus service (STUB; ☎ 05 55 74 20 13) has an information kiosk on place du 14 Juillet that may be able to answer queries concerning regional services. Otherwise call the main bus company, CFTA (☎ 05 55 86 07 07 or ☎ 05 55 17 91 19). Destinations served include Collonges-la-Rouge (€2.60, 30 minutes, four daily); Montignac (€4.40, 1½ hours, one daily); and Sarlat-la-Canéda (€6.10, 1¾ hours, one daily), Monday to Saturday.

Train Brive is on the north–south Paris' Gare d'Austerlitz (€42.25, four hours) to Toulouse (€22.25, 2¼ hours) line via Limoges (€12.50, one hour 10 minutes) and Cahors (€12.35, 1¼ hours). It's also on the east-west line linking Bordeaux (€21.35, 2½ hours) with Clermont-Ferrand (€20.90, 3¾ hours), via Périgueux (€10.05, one hour). The station's information office (☎ 05 55 18 41 16) is open 9am to 7pm Monday to Friday (to 6.30pm on Saturday, closed bank holidays).

If you're feeling rich and lazy you can take your car on the train all the way to Calais (see Train in the Getting There & Away chapter for details).

Getting Around

Opposite the train station on ave Jean Jaurès, Europcar (☎ 05 55 74 14 41), Hertz (☎ 05

THE DORDOGNE

55 24 26 75) and Avis (☎ 05 55 24 51 00) are at Nos 52, 54 and 56 respectively. The easiest car parking is the well signed, underground car park (€0.75/2 per hour/ 3 hours) at place Thiers, officially called place de Lattre de Tassigny.

Sport Bike (☎ 05 55 17 00 84) at 142 ave Georges Pompidou (about 2km east of town) rents VTTs for €12.20/52.60 per day/week. It opens Tuesday to Saturday.

For taxis call ☎ 05 55 24 24 24.

AROUND BRIVE-LA-GAILLARDE
Turenne
postcode 19500 • pop 740 • elevation 480m

Dubbed 'the small town with a great past', Turenne takes its name from the powerful family of viscounts who held sway here for centuries, independent of the French Crown. But in the 18th century, when they finally ran out of money, they sold out to Louis XV, who taxed the place so ferociously the monied class fled and the village sank into decline.

Today, the pretty village, 15km south of Brive, is dominated by its ruined hilltop chateau (☎ 05 55 85 90 66, adult/child aged 7-18 €2.75/1.80; open 10am-noon & 2-6pm daily Apr-June, Sept-Oct; 10am-7pm daily July-Aug; 2pm-5pm Sun only Nov-Mar), perched on a rocky promontory. All that remains is **Caesar's Tower**, with stunning views, and a 13th-century red-stone **clock tower**.

The large 16th-century **Collègiale** (collegiate church) below the chateau is in the form of a Greek cross. The rest of the village has steep, narrow streets and attractive, cream-coloured, stone houses with slate turrets, including the imposing **Maison Tournadour**, near the church, once a salt warehouse.

Orientation & Information The tourist office (☎ 05 55 85 94 38) is just off the D8, at the entry to town, the steep rue du Commandant-Charollais. It opens 10am to 12.30pm and 3pm to 6pm daily, 15 June and 15 September (weekends and public holidays only from 15 April to 15 June).

Places to Stay & Eat There are several cheap restaurants at Turenne-Gare, the new

town 2.8km south (down the D8). For more salubrious and expensive places in Turenne itself, try the following.

Restaurant-Hôtel Maison des Chanoines (☎ 05 55 85 93 43) Doubles €56.40-65.55. Midday *menus* €15.25, evening *menus* €25.90-48.80, dishes €12.20-28.20. Open Mar–mid-Nov. Restaurant open midday & evening Fri-Mon, evening only Tues-Thur; midday & evening daily July-Aug. This small, attractive place has just three stylish doubles and a popular restaurant with a shady terrace.

La Vicomte (☎ 05 55 85 91 32) *Menus* €18.30, dishes €9.25-12.20. Open midday only. Opposite des Chanoines, this jovial, eye-catching place (with a model of a viscount at the window) serves deluxe regional fare.

Getting There & Away Cars Quercy Corrèze (☎ 05 65 39 71 90) and CFTA Centre Ouest Brive (☎ 05 55 86 07 07) both run buses from Brive (€2.80, 30 minutes, one to three daily). These companies also connect Turenne-Gare with Turenne. Trains to Turenne-Gare (€2.75, 15 minutes) run once or twice daily.

Collonges-la-Rouge
postcode 19500 • pop 380 • elevation 280m

On a gently angled slope situated above a tributary of the River Dordogne, 18km south-east of Brive, the quaint narrow lanes of 'Collonges the Red' (built entirely of bright red sandstone) squeeze between old, wysteria-covered houses topped with round turrets. The tiny hamlet is entirely devoted to tourism, with souvenir shops and craft displays on every corner. But it can be a delightful place for a stroll, and there are some tempting walks out into the lush green countryside.

Information The tourist office (☎ 05 55 25 47 57), called Collonges Accueil, is in the car park alongside the D38. It opens 10am to noon and 2pm to 6pm daily, April to mid-November (9.30am to 12.30pm and 2.30pm to 7pm daily during July and August). Out of season, the *mairie* (city or town hall; ☎ 05 55 25 41 09) can provide tourist information during weekday office hours.

The tourist office has a comprehensive booklet (€3.05, in English) on the village, published by a local group, Les Amis de Collonges, which also organises one-hour guided tours (€2.30, including admission to the Maison de la Sirène) twice daily in summer, leaving from the tourist office (see the following section).

Maison de la Sirène This charming 16th-century house (named after the decoration on the outside of a mermaid) has been converted into a tiny two-room museum *(☎ 05 55 84 08 03, adult/child under 12 €1.50/ free; open 10.30am-12.30pm & 3pm-6pm usually daily April-Nov, definitely daily July-Aug)* showing old agricultural tools and household furnishings from the 19th-century.

Church The partly Romanesque church, built between the 11th and 15th century on the foundations of an 8th-century Benedictine priory, was once an important resting place on the pilgrimage route to Santiago de Compostela. In the late 16th century, local Protestants held prayers in the south nave and their Catholic neighbours prayed in the north nave, where a gilded wood retable erected in the 17th century still stands. Nearby, the ancient wood-and-slate roof of the **old covered market**, held up by stone columns, shelters an ancient baker's oven.

Castel de Vassinhac and Castel de Maussac These are the two most impressive manor houses in the village, the first (follow the lane east of the church) adorned with a mighty array of towers and turrets (its owner was a captain); and the second, to the north, a smaller, more homely affair with an elegant turret over its doorway. Neither are open to the public.

Nearby, the **Musée vivant de l'oie** *(☎ 05 55 25 31 40; admission free; open 10am-noon & 2pm-7pm daily except Wed in term-time)* reveals the secrets of foie gras

(including a demonstration of *gavage*, or force-feeding, at 2.30pm daily).

Places to Stay & Eat In addition to the following, the tourist office has details of several good *chambres d'hôte* in the area.

Le Moulin de la Valane (☎ 05 55 25 41 59, fax 05 55 84 07 28, route de Meyssac) 2-person forfait €10.05. Open May-Oct. This 120-site camp site, 700m south of Collonges off the D38, has a swimming pool and reasonable facilities.

Le Relais de Saint Jacques de Compostelle (☎ 05 55 25 41 02, fax 05 55 84 08 51) Doubles with shower & WC €47.25 (one double without shower €25.90). Midday *menus* €11.45, evening *menus* €13.40-38.10, dishes €12.20-25.15. Open mid-Mar –mid-Nov. Le Relais, in a partly medieval building, is the village's only hotel, serving Périgord- and Quercy-style fare in its restaurant.

Auberge Le Prieuré (☎ 05 55 25 41 00, place de L'Église) Double/triple apartment €45.75/76.20. *Menus* €12.95-19.80, dishes €11.45-13.70. Open daily, except Wed Sept-June. Le Prieuré has a delightful outdoor dining area by the church, and a romantic upstairs apartment, including a fridge and dining area (no kitchen).

Le Tourtou (☎ 05 55 25 34 15) Midday/evening *menus* €9.90/14, *tourtous* (a kind of wheat pancake) €3.05-7. Open daily Apr-Sept, closed Thur off-season. A 100m downhill stroll from Le Prieuré, this restaurant specialises in tourtous, but also offers other regional fare.

Relais du Quercy (☎ 05 55 25 40 31, fax 05 55 25 36 22) Doubles with shower €45.75-48.80, without €33.55-39.65. Midday *menus* €10.65, evening *menus* €16-24.40. In busy, untouristy Meyssac, 1.7km south, you'll find this pleasant Logis de France property, which has a swimming pool and brightly decorated rooms.

Getting There & Away
Buses to Brive run three to four times daily Monday to Friday, with one or two on Saturday (€2.50, 25 minutes). The bus stop is near the tourist office.

THE DORDOGNE

BEAULIEU-SUR-DORDOGNE
postcode 19120 • pop 1300
• elevation 140m

The verdant, aptly named town of Beaulieu (literally 'beautiful place'), 44km south-east of Brive, is one of the most attractive medieval villages along the upper Dordogne, famed for its majestic abbey-church and surrounding strawberry farms. Nearby streets have picturesque houses that date from the 14th and 15th centuries.

With its plentiful accommodation and restaurants, Beaulieu makes a good stopover, especially for walkers – there are some lovely spots for a stroll nearby, and the GR480, a spur of the GR46, passes close by. A multilingual brochure of suggested walking trails (€1.50) is available at the tourist office.

Orientation & Information

Beaulieu has two main squares – place Marbot and place du Champ de Mars, on the south-west side of rue du Général de Gaulle (as the D940 is known in the town centre).

The tourist office (☎ 05 55 91 09 94, fax 05 55 91 10 97), on place Marbot, is open 9.30am to 12.30pm and 2pm to 7pm daily from April to June and in September, and 9am to 7pm daily in July and August. Other months it opens 10am to noon and 2.30pm to 6pm daily except Sunday. At the time of research it was expected to install an Internet facility for visitors.

It runs one-hour guided visits (€2.30) at 9.45am on Tuesday from mid-June to mid-September and during Easter holidays. At 9am on Thursday during the same period, it also runs free guided walks of five to 12km (depending on the group's stamina!) in the surrounding countryside.

Abbatiale

The Abbatiale is a 12th-century Romanesque abbey-church that was once a stop on the way to Santiago de Compostela. The southern portal's brilliant tympanum (circa 1130) illustrates the Last Judgement with vivid medieval scenes. Based on prophecies from the books of Daniel and The Apocalypse, the graphic figures include monsters devouring the heads and arms of the condemned, and a seven-headed dragon from hell.

The treasury, displayed in a glass case by the Sacristy, includes a gorgeous 12th-century gilded Virgin and several reliquaries from the 11th to 13th centuries (including a 13th-century enamel one).

Places to Stay & Eat

Beaulieu-sur-Dordogne has a wide selection of restaurants and accommodation to choose from.

Camping des Iles (☎ 05 55 91 02 65, fax 05 55 91 05 19, e jycastanet@aol.com) 2-person forfait €11.30. Open mid-April–mid-Oct. This lovely, shaded camp site is on an island sandwiched between two branches of the Dordogne.

Auberge de Jeunesse de la Riviera Limousine (☎ 05 55 91 13 82, fax 05 55 91 26 06, e beaulieu@fuaj.org, place du Monturu) Dorm bunks €6.85. Breakfast €2.90. Open Apr-Nov. Reception open 8am-10am and 6pm-10.30pm. This delightful 28-bed hostel, along the river by the Romanesque Chapelle des Penitents, occupies a partly 14th-century building. It has a kitchen.

Hôtel L'Étape Fleurie (☎ 05 55 91 11 04, 17 place du Champ de Mars) Doubles with shower & WC €33.55-35.05, without €25.90-28.95. Midday *menus* €9.90, evening *menus* €11.90-29.70, dishes €7.60-14. L'Étape Fleurie is the best of the budget hotels, with modern rooms and a decent restaurant.

Auberge des Charmilles (☎ 05 55 91 29 29, fax 05 55 91 29 30, 20 blvd Rodolphe de Turenne) Doubles/triples/quads €47.25/56.40/67.05. Midday *menus* €10.35, evening *menus* €14.95-34.75, dishes €7.60-20.60. Open Dec-Oct. Restaurant open daily, except Tues & Wed off-season. This delightful hotel, right by the river, has just eight rooms, each with shower and WC, and a lovely garden terrace for open-air dining.

Central Hôtel Fournie (☎ 05 55 91 01 34, fax 05 55 91 23 57, 4 place du Champ de Mars) Singles €39.65, doubles €39.65-45.75, triples €45.75, all with shower & WC. *Menus* €21.35-36.60, dishes €11.45-

22.85. Open mid-Mar–mid-Nov. Restaurant open Wed-Mon. This 23-room Logis de France property is a popular mid-range choice, with a smart restaurant.

Au Beau Lieu Breton (☎ *05 55 91 20 46, rue du Presbytère*) Galettes & salads €2.30-8.40, *menus* €11.90-17.55. Open daily except Mon-Wed off-season & Dec. This chic little creperie, tucked in an alley behind the church, serves savoury galettes and other delicious fare.

Le Vieux Logis (☎ *05 55 91 01 43, place de la Bridolle*) Pizzas €5.95-9.15, other dishes €8.40-12.20. The casual Vieux Logis is a family-friendly place, right by the church, is the best bet for simple fare (eg, steak and chips €8.40).

On Wednesday and Saturday mornings, there's an open-air *market* next to the Abbatiale. There are two *grocery stores* on place Marbot, open all day Monday to Saturday and Sunday morning. In early May you can feast for free on strawberries galore during the town's Fête de la Fraise, which usually features a 800kg strawberry cake!

Getting There & Away
One to three buses daily (except Sunday and holidays) run to Brive (€5.25, 70 minutes). Timetables are posted at the bus shelter on place du Champ de Mars and outside the tourist office.

The nearest train station, Bretenoux-Biars (8km to the south), is on the Brive-Aurillac line, with twice-daily connections to Brive (€6.40, 40 minutes).

Getting Around
To rent mountain bikes, try Beaulieu Sports (☎ 05 55 91 13 87), at 21 rue du Général de Gaulle. It charges €12.20/68.60 per day/week, and opens all day Monday to Friday and Sunday morning.

From May to September, gabarres run 90-minute trips along the river (from near the Auberge de Jeunesse) for €4.55/3.05 per adult/child.

THE DORDOGNE

Lot & Lot-et-Garonne

South-east of the Dordogne lies the Lot *département* (administrative department), a warm, distinctively southern region where many residents still speak Occitan. The Lot still tends to be known by its pre-Revolution name, Quercy (recalling the tough Celtic tribe, Cadurcii), which once included most of present-day Tarn-et-Garonne.

Dry limestone *causses* (plateaus) are a feature of the area. The plateau in the north, known as Haut Quercy, is covered with oak trees and cut by dramatic canyons created by the serpentine River Lot and its tributaries. Here are two of Southwest France's most famous and popular destinations – the rock-clinging pilgrims' haven of Rocamadour and the deep cavern of Gouffre de Padirac. South of here, the departmental capital, Cahors, is surrounded by fine vineyards; to its east is one of the prettiest stretches of the River Lot and the dreamy Célé Valley, home to some of the finest prehistoric cave paintings in Southwest France, at the Grotte du Pech Merle.

To the west of Cahors lies the agricultural and fruit-rich Lot-et-Garonne department, whose southern region still considers itself part of proud Gascony. There are a scattering of impressive *bastides* (fortified villages) and some great boat trips on the Rivers Lot, Baïse and Garonne and Canal Latéral.

This chapter lists the towns of the Lot in roughly north to south order before heading west to Lot-et-Garonne.

Information
The Comité Départemental du Tourisme du Lot (see Tourist Offices in the Cahors section for contact details) is notably efficient. Among its many useful free publications in English (available at most tourist offices) is *Key to the Lot,* which details transport, activities, accommodation and much more; and *Countryside Sports in the Lot* with contacts for horse-riding, walking, cycling and canoeing. The *Guide Horaire des Transports*

Highlights

• Follow in pilgrims' footsteps at cliff-hugging Rocamadour

• Relax in low-key Cahors with great wines, markets and restaurants

• Meander along the delightful Célé Valley with its once-grand hamlets

• Marvel at the cave paintings of Cougnac, and prehistoric footprints at Pech Merle

• Navigate a houseboat down the Canal Latéral or the Garonne, Baïse or Lot Rivers

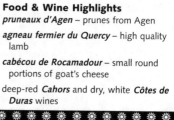

Food & Wine Highlights
pruneaux d'Agen – prunes from Agen

agneau fermier du Quercy – high quality lamb

cabécou de Rocamadour – small round portions of goat's cheese

deep-red *Cahors* and dry, white *Côtes de Duras* wines

makes a valiant effort at listing the department's confusing bus services. Don't rely on the Lot-et-Garonne's version, *Trans47*, which is hopelessly incomplete.

Boating & Canoeing
One of the most relaxing ways to see the region is by renting a houseboat on one of its many waterways. The River Lot runs

across the Lot department for 170km, 65km of which is navigable, between St-Cirq Lapopie and Luzech (and by 2007 or so, all the way to Villeneuve-sur-Lot). There are also around 200km of navigable waterways in the Lot-et-Garonne, on the Rivers Lot, Garonne and Baïse and Canal Latéral. The main boat-hire bases are Agen, Le Mas d'Agenais, Buzet-sur-Baïse, Nérac, Luzech and Bouziès. For general information see Boat in the Getting Around chapter; for specific information see Cahors, Agen, Nérac, Bouziès and West of Cahors in this chapter. For an all-organised boating trip, contact Les Services Loisirs Accueil in Agen or Cahors (for contact details see Organised Tours later in this section).

Canoeing and kayaking are popular on these waterways, as well as on the 60km-stretch of the Dordogne between Souillac and Bretenoux. The Comité Départemental du Lot de Canoë-Kayak (☎/fax 05 65 35 91 59), at Bureau 218, Palais des Sports, place Bessières, Cahors, can provide lists of canoeing clubs and a program of activities. Canoe-hire outlets are mentioned under individual towns and the West of Cahors section. The River Célé region is particularly popular (see the East of Cahors section for contacts).

Walking & Cycling
This is great walking and biking country – the Lot alone has 2950km of signposted paths. *Grandes Randonnées* (long-distance trails) that cross the Lot and Lot-et-Garonne include the GR36 and GR65 (both passing through Cahors), GR6, GR46, GR64, GR652 and GR636.

Details on day hikes in the area between Bouziès and Figeac appear in *Entre Lot et Célé* (€5.65), a French-language topoguide in the Promenades et Randonnées series published by the Comité Départemental du Tourisme du Lot and available at most tourist offices. Other useful French topoguides (available from bookshops and some tourist offices) include *Vallées du Lot et de la Garonne* (€7.90) and *Le Pays du Dropt et Le Pays d'Albret* (€7.90/7.45) for the area around Duras/Nérac. The English-language *Walking, Riding & Mountain-Biking in the*

Lot (€6.10) describes 28 circuits. Gentle hikes are covered by *Les Sentiers d'Émilie en Lot-et-Garonne* (€12.20).

Backroads and off-road options for cyclists are detailed in the French-language topoguides *Cyclotourisme en Quercy* (€6.10), *Guide du Cyclotourisme dans le Lot* (€6.10) and *VTT 36 Circuits – Le Lot en Quercy* (€7.60).

Organised Tours
For organised outdoor activities, excursions, cookery courses or special camps for kids, contact *Les Services Loisirs Accueil* (☎ 05 65 53 20 90, fax 05 65 53 20 94, e loisirs.accueil.lot@wanadoo.fr, Maison du Tourisme, place François Mitterand, 46000 Cahors), or the same outfit in Agen (☎ 05 53 66 14 14, fax 05 53 68 25 42, e c.d.t@wanadoo.fr, 4 rue André Chénier, 47008 Agen) – this office is sometimes promoted under the name ACTOUR 47.

Lot

GOURDON
postcode 46300 • pop 4900 • elevation 264m
On the northern fringe of Quercy and eastern edge of Périgord, Gourdon is the capital of a lush rural area known as La Bouriane. Its high hilltop position has made it a prominent place since the 10th century: it once had four monasteries and a mighty castle. Ransacked in 1189 by Richard the Lion-Heart, the town suffered even worse during the Wars of Religion. But though the monasteries were largely wiped out, the central old town is still packed with picturesque, well restored medieval houses.

Well situated between Sarlat (26km) and Cahors (44km), Gourdon makes a very pleasant stop-over, with the nearby caves of Cougnac (see the boxed text 'Prehistoric Fingerprints & Mysterious Men' later in this chapter) an added incentive to visit.

Orientation & Information
Gourdon's old town is encircled by a modern ring-road where you'll find hotels, restaurants, banks and shops. Place de la

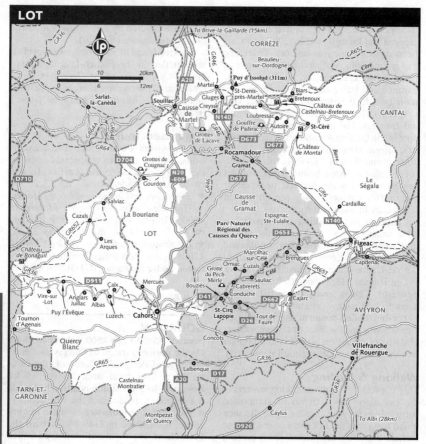

Liberation, on the south-western side, is the main entry point into the old town and to the tourist office (☎ 05 65 27 52 50, fax 05 65 27 52 52, ⓔ gourdon@wanadoo.fr), at 24 rue du Majou. It opens 10am to noon, 2pm to 6pm Monday to Saturday (to 5pm November to February) and 10am to 7pm Monday to Saturday during July and August (plus 10am to noon on Sunday between June and September).

It runs guided tours of the old town (adult/child €2.30/1.20) at 5pm on Tuesday and Thursday and 9pm on Wednesday during July and August.

Post & Communications

The post office is on place du Général de Gaulle; money exchange is available.

You can access the Internet at Hôtel de la Promenade (see Places to Stay) for €6.85 per hour, or at Internet 46 (☎ 05 65 41 34 26), 16 rue du Majou, for €4.55 per hour; it opens 10am to noon, 3pm to 8pm Monday to Saturday.

La Cité Médiéval

At the very top of town, the site of the former castle has been transformed into an **Esplanade** with superb views over the

Lot is full of picturesque villages and towns nestled in lush green valleys. Three outstanding examples are Autoire (top, and centre left), St-Céré (centre right) and Carennac (bottom).

SALLY DILLON

The village vehicle of choice, St-Céré

SALLY DILLON

JULIA WILKINSON

Colourful open-air market, Cahors

The old marketplace, St-Céré

SALLY DILLON

A prime side of beef from the lively cattle market, St-Céré

Prehistoric Fingerprints & Mysterious Men

The **Grottes de Cougnac** (☎ 05 65 41 22 25, guided visits adult/child (5.35/3.35; open 9.30am-11am and 2pm-5pm daily between Easter and November; 9.30am-6pm July & Aug), 32km south of Souillac and 3km north of Gourdon, contain some of the most amazing prehistoric cave paintings in Southwest France: 20,000-year-old ochre and black images of mountain goats and humpbacked deer, a flurry of fingerprints and some mysterious half-human, half-animal 'wounded men', with misformed heads and pierced with spears. There's another cave, 200m away, with delicate stalactites and stalagmites.

surrounding countryside. Just below is the huge **Église St-Pierre**, a 14th-century creation with 17th-century additions. The nearby **Hôtel de Ville**, a former 13th-century consulate, overlooks a handsome square (site of the Tuesday and Saturday market). It's at the top end of **rue du Majou**, once the town's high street and still lined with fine old houses (check out the mullioned windows of Maison d'Anglars, at No 17, and the ancient, delightfully named rue Zig-Zag opposite No 24).

Places to Stay & Eat
Gourdon has an agreeable choice of hotels and restaurants.

Camping Municipal Écoute S'il Pleut (☎ 05 65 41 06 19) Adult/pitch €3.05/3.35. Located 1.2km north of town (off the N704 to Sarlat), this site is in a dedicated leisure zone, with plenty of sports facilities nearby.

Le Nouvel Hôtel (☎ 05 65 41 00 23, fax 05 65 41 39 09, blvd de la Madeleine) Doubles €30.50. Menus €10.65-18.30. Just 300m from the train station, on the busy D673, Le Nouvel is a simple hostelry with a decent restaurant.

Hôtel de la Promenade (☎ 05 65 41 41 44, fax 05 65 41 41 22, e lapromenade gourdon@.fr, 48 blvd Galiot de Genouillac) Doubles €35.05-39.65. Menu du jour €10.80, grills €7.30-10.50. This Logis de France hotel, on the north-western side of town, has 10 very stylish rooms and some noticeable British trappings (red telephone box, Guinness on tap, plaid decor) thanks to the owner's Scottish wife.

Le Grand Café Divan (place de la Libération) is a great central spot for people-watching; its proprietor sports surely the grandest handlebar moustache in the southwest!

Getting There & Away
Gourdon is on the main Paris-Toulouse line, with connections to Cahors (€6.25, 25 minutes) and Brive-la-Gaillarde (€8.25, 40 minutes), both at least four times daily. The train station (☎ 05 65 41 02 19) is about 800m north-east of town.

For taxis, call ☎ 05 65 41 36 31.

SOUILLAC
postcode 46200 • pop 3700 • elevation 80m
This small town, squeezed between the Rivers Dordogne and Borrèze and the N20, with its traffic hurtling between Brive-la-Gaillarde (34km north) and Cahors (69km south), isn't worth an overnight stay but does have two good reasons for a few hours' diversion: a superb Romanesque abbey and a fascinating museum. The nearby Grottes de Lacave also make a worthwhile excursion.

Orientation & Information
The tourist office (☎ 05 65 37 81 56, fax 05 65 27 11 45, e souillac@wanadoo.fr), on blvd Louis-Jean Malvy (the N20), is open 10am to noon and 2pm to 6pm Monday to Saturday (9.30am to 12.30pm and 2pm to 7pm daily in July and August). The abbey and adjacent museum are five minutes' walk downhill (to the west) from the tourist office.

Abbaye Ste-Marie
The former Benedictine abbey *(place de l'Abbaye; admission free; open 9am-7pm daily)* dates from the 12th century but the

The Gauls' Last Stand

Some still say it's at Capdenac, others favour Luzech, but in May 2001 archaeologists announced new findings to confirm that the Puy d'Issolud, a 311m-high plateau 14km east of Martel, is almost certainly the site of Uxellodunum, where the Gauls lost their last bastion to the Romans. Heavily defended with earthworks, ditches and dry-stone defences, Uxellodunum fell only after the canny Romans cut off the water supply; the Cadurcii tribe inside believed their gods had deserted them and gave up the fight.

Hundred Years' War and Wars of Religion, plus fires and over-enthusiastic 'restorers', have given it a hard time. Still outstanding, however, are its three huge Islamic-like domes, its sparsely decorated single nave and the extraordinary carved doorway, which was turned to face the inside after damage caused during the Wars of Religion. The carvings show how St-Theophilus made a pact with the devil and was rescued by the Virgin Mary and feature an amazingly lifelike bas-relief of the so-called 'dancing' Isaiah (on the right side).

Musée de l'Automate

Around the corner from the abbey, this fascinating museum *(☎ 05 65 37 07 07, place de l'Abbaye; adult/student/child €4.60/3.05/2.30; open 10am-noon & 3pm-6pm Tues-Sun Apr, May, Oct; 10am-noon & 3pm-6pm daily June, Sept; 10am-7pm daily July-Aug; 2pm-5pm Wed-Sun Nov-Mar)* has a beguiling collection of some 3000 automata, many dating from the late 19th and early 20th centuries.

Grottes de Lacave

In one of the most picturesque loops of the Dordogne, 11km south-east of Souillac, the vast caverns of Lacave *(☎ 05 65 37 87 03, Lacave; adult/child €6.70/4.55; open 10am-noon & 2pm-5pm daily Mar, Oct-11 Nov; 9.30am-noon & 2pm-6pm daily Apr-14 July; 9.30am-6.30pm daily 15 July-25 Aug; 9.30am-noon & 2pm-5.30pm daily 26 Aug-15 Sept; 10am-noon & 2pm-5.30pm 16 Sept-30 Sept; closed 12 Nov-Feb)*, accessible by train and lift, are famous for their unusual rock formations and fantastic lighting effects, reflected in numerous lakes.

Getting There & Away

Souillac train station is 1.1km north of town. It's on the main Paris-Toulouse line with regular connections to Brive (€5.80, 25 minutes) and Cahors (€8.70, 40 minutes). Bus services include Sarlat-la-Canéda (€4.55, 50 minutes, four to seven daily) and Martel (€2.30, 20 minutes, twice daily).

MARTEL

postcode 46600 • pop 1470 • elevation 270m

Twelfth-century Martel, the 'Town of the Seven Towers', 24km north of Rocamadour, 15km east of Souillac, is an attractive, historic town which has long been the centre of the regional walnut trade – the ancient weighing measures can still be seen at the covered wooden marketplace in the square.

The town is reputedly named after the Frankish conqueror Charles Martel (whose son founded the Carolingian dynasty); he built an abbey here after his victory over the Moors in 732. It later became the capital of the viscounts of Turenne, its strong fortifications bearing witness to its violent past – even the church is comprised of battlements and buttresses.

Orientation & Information

The best entrance to the old town is from the N140 which runs along the northern, modern edge of town: The post office is here and banks and cafe-restaurants are on nearby place Gambetta. At the heart of the old town, on place des Consuls, is the tourist office (☎ 05 65 37 43 44, fax 05 65 37 37 27, ⓔ martel2@wanadoo.fr), open 9am to noon and 3pm to 6pm Monday to Friday, 9am to noon Saturday (9am to 7pm Monday to Saturday, 9am to 1pm and 2pm to 7pm Sunday in July and August).

Things to See & Do

The **place des Consuls**, with its 18th-century **covered market**, is surrounded by picturesque medieval buildings and decorated towers including the striking 14th-century **Hôtel (or Palais) de la Raymondie**, which houses the town hall, tourist office and a small **Musée d'Uxellodunum** (☎ *05 65 37 30 03, place des Consuls; adult/child €1.05/1.05; open 10am-noon & 2pm-6pm Mon-Sat July-Aug)* with a display of Gallo-Roman remains (see the boxed text 'The Gauls' Last Stand').

The **Maison Fabri**, sited in the square's south-eastern corner, is where Henry 'Short Coat' died of fever-ridden guilt in 1183 after ransacking Rocamadour's shrines to pay for his fight against his father, King Henry II. You can follow **rue Droite** south of here to find more Gothic and Renaissance townhouses.

Offering a charming 90-minute round trip, the **Chemin de Fer Touristique de Haut Quercy** (☎ *05 65 37 35 81, route de Creysse, steam engine trip adult/child €7.60/4.55 return; 2.30pm & 4pm Sun Apr-Oct, Wed mid-July–mid-Aug; diesel engine trip €5.35/3.05; 2.30pm Thur Apr-June & Sept, 2.30pm & 4pm Tues-Sun July-Aug)* runs 11km from Martel to St-Denis-près-Martel. Extra services are common – ask at the tourist office. The station (for this train only) is 500m south-east of town, off the D23 to Creysse.

Activities

On the Dordogne, Gluges (5km south) and Creysse (a further 4km south) both have canoe and bike rental outfits, for example, **Port-Loisirs** (☎ *05 65 32 27 59, fax 05 65 32 20 40; canoe/kayak €12.20/12.20 per person; VTT €13.70 per day)*, which operates both from Camping Les Falaises (see Places to Stay) and Camping du Port at Creysse. It also runs potholing trips (€14.50 half-day).

Special Events

The Festival du Haut Quercy is a three-week festival of sacred music and instrumental works performed here and in Rocamadour.

Places to Stay & Eat

There are several decent options to choose from here.

Camping Municipal La Callopie (☎ *05 65 37 30 03, or* ☎ *06 89 42 21 39, fax 05 65 37 37 27, av de Turenne)* Adult/pitch €1.50/1.50. This basic, shady site is off the D23, opposite the Auberge des 7 Tours (see later in this section).

Camping Les Falaises (☎ *05 65 37 37 78, fax 05 65 32 20 40, Gluges)* 2-person *forfait* (package deal) €15.25. Open May-Oct. Camping Les Falaises, 5km south, has a spectacular location by the Dordogne, under towering cliffs.

La Mère Michèle (☎ *05 65 37 35 66, rue de la Remise) Gîte d'étape* (hikers' accommodation) dorm beds €8.40 (€10.65 with linen), doubles €33.55-35.05. Midday *menus* €6.10-9.90, evening *menus* €14.95-21.05. This delightful place, 50m down rue Montpezat opposite Le Quercy-Turenne (follow the cat drawings), has just two rooms opening onto a garden, and restaurant tables in the old lane outside.

Auberge des 7 Tours (☎ *05 65 37 30 16, fax 05 65 37 41 69,* [e] *auberge7tours@ wanadoo.fr, av de Turenne)* Doubles/triples with shower €28.95-35.05/50.30. This recently revamped *auberge* has brightly decorated rooms (pricier ones include WC) and English/Dutch-speaking owners. At the time of research, the restaurant was also undergoing a complete renovation.

Hôtel-Restaurant Le Quercy-Turenne (☎ *05 65 37 30 30, av Lavayssière)* Doubles with shower €29.70-38.55, with shower & WC €37.35-48.45. Midday *menus* €11.45, evening *menus* €16.95-39.65. On the south-western edge of town this Logis de France property has reasonable rooms and bargain bar *menus* (€6.10).

Getting There & Away

St-Denis-près-Martel, the nearest train station (☎ *05 65 32 42 08)* is 8km to the east, and has connections to Brive about six times daily (€4.40, 25 minutes). A bus from the station goes to Martel (€2.30, and on to Souillac: €3.80, 20 minutes) twice daily.

CARENNAC

postcode 46110 • pop 370 • elevation 180m
This charming little village tucked beside the Dordogne, 33km east of Souillac, is famous for its typical Quercy houses and turrets, its

finely decorated Romanesque priory-church and its association with the renowned 17th-century bishop, writer and philosopher, François de Salignac de la Mothe-Fénelon who was abbot at the priory for 15 years (see the Arts section in the Facts about Southwest France chapter for more about Fénelon).

Orientation & Information
The village clusters by the river between the D20 and the river-hugging D43. The main sites are inside Le Prieuré (the former priory), accessible through a stone archway. The tourist office (☎/fax 05 65 10 97 01, e ot.intercom.carennac@wanadoo.fr), also here, is open 10am to noon, 1.30pm to 6pm daily April to May and mid-September to October; 10am to 7pm daily June to mid-September; 10am to noon and 2pm to 5pm weekdays (2pm to 5.30pm weekends) November to February; 10am to noon, 1.30pm to 6pm weekdays (2pm to 6.30pm weekends) in March.

Things to See
The most notable part that remains of the priory – founded in the 10th century, rebuilt and fortified in the 16th century, and ruined during the Revolution – is the Romanesque **Église St-Pierre**. Its highlight is a magnificent carved tympanum over the porch, with doe-eyed, light-of-foot apostles and a frieze of animals. The **cloisters** (access adjacent to the tourist office and open the same hours; adult/child €1.50/0.75) boast a fine 15th-century **Mise au Tombeau** Entombment scene, with expressive, life-size figures.

Next to the church, the 16th-century Château du Doyen houses the **Maison de la Dordogne Quercynoise** (☎ 05 65 32 59 19, Le Château, adult/child & student €4.55/3.05; open usually 10.30am-12.30pm & 1.30pm-6.30pm Mon-Fri, 1.30pm-6.30pm Sun Apr-June, Sept-Oct; 9am-7pm Sun-Fri, afternoon only Sat July-Aug), which has audio-visual displays (French only) on the Dordogne, its geology, culture, flora and fauna. The square tower with round turret above (best seen from outside the priory, across the road) is believed to be the **Tour de Télémaque**, named after the hero of

Fénelon's *Les Aventures de Télémaque,* written here in 1699.

Places to Stay & Eat
Carennac is a popular stopover for walkers and bicyclists so book ahead in summer.

Camping L'Eau Vive (☎ 05 65 10 97 39, fax 05 55 28 12 12, e info@dordogne-soleil.com) Adult/pitch €3.80/3.50. Open Apr-Nov. This riverside site, 1.1km southeast, off the D30, has a swimming pool plus canoes/kayaks (June to September) for €11.45/14.50 per day.

Hôtel-Restaurant des Touristes (☎ 05 65 10 94 31, fax 05 65 39 79 85, postal address 46110 Carennac) Doubles with/without €36.60/28.95. Menus €16.95, dishes €5-11. Near the D20 entrance to town, this friendly, family-run place has it all: attractive rooms (No 4 has its own patio overlooking the garden), quiet location and decent restaurant serving honest fare.

There are two Logis de France inns (both with swimming pools).

Hostellerie Fénelon (☎ 05 65 10 96 46, fax 05 65 10 94 86, postal address 46110 Carennac) Singles €41.15-44.20, doubles €47.25-53.35. Midday menus €12.95, evening menus €16-44.20. The welcoming Fénelon, near Hôtel-Restaurant des Touristes, has well kept rooms (pricier ones overlook the garden and river).

Auberge du Vieux Quercy (☎ 05 65 10 96 59, fax 05 65 10 94 05, postal address 46110 Carennac) Doubles €42.70-54.85. Midday menus €12.95, evening menus €14.95-34.30. The ivy-clad Auberge du Vieux Quercy, on the D20 above town, is not as attractively located as the other hotels but has slightly superior facilities.

Getting There & Around
The nearest train station is Bétaille (4.5km to the north) with around six services daily to Brive-la-Gaillarde (€4.25, 25 minutes). For a taxi, call ☎ 05 65 32 40 32.

Cars Quercy Corrèze (☎ 05 65 39 71 90) pass Carennac on their Brive-Gramat run only once-daily during term-time (€5.35, one hour 10 minutes). The bus stop is on the D20 above the village.

Auberge du Vieux Quercy (see Places to Stay) rents mountain bikes for €12.20 per day.

ROCAMADOUR

postcode 46500 • pop 600 • elevation 250m

This famous pilgrimage centre, 59km north of Cahors, is one of the most dramatic sites in France, spectacularly situated on a vertical, 150m-high cliff-face above the River Alzou. It was founded in the 12th century, on the site of a shrine to a Black Virgin (or Madonna) and a hermit's rocky cave (*roc amator* means 'he who likes the rock' in Occitan). The hermit was supposedly the tax-gatherer Zaccheus, disciple of Jesus, who was believed to have fled with his wife, Veronica, to this remote corner of France. The shrine rapidly became famous for its miraculous powers and hosted tens of thousands of pilgrims and a stream of VIPs.

For 200 years, the expanding village of shrines – called the Cité – was an important stop on the pilgrimage route to Santiago de Compostela, but its riches also attracted a succession of pillagers. Desecrated during the Wars of Religion and the Revolution, Rocamadour was restored in the 19th century

NICKY CAVEN

Rocamadour attracts many a pious pilgrim

and has once again become a major pilgrimage site. Now crammed with souvenir shops and tourists it's frequently a high-season nightmare. Come here at dusk or dawn if you want a glimmer of its uncommercial precipitous attractions.

Orientation

Rocamadour is on three levels: the medieval Cité, full of shops, hotels and restaurants; the level above this featuring the chapels; and the plateau, 500m above the Alzou River valley, with the remains of a 14th-century chateau and ramparts.

Some 900m to the east of the plateau is L'Hospitalet (1.7km via the D32 from the Cité). This busy village (once the site of an 11th-century pilgrims' hospital) is centred on the place de l'Europe crossroads. Near here is the main tourist office, a few hotels and restaurants and various nonpilgrimage tourist attractions.

Information

The tourist office (☎ 05 65 33 22 00, fax 05 65 33 22 01; ℮ rocamadour@wanadoo.fr), in a big modern glass-fronted building just off L'Hospitalet's place de l'Europe, is open 10am to 12.30pm, 2pm to 6.30pm daily May to mid-September (10am to 7.30pm daily mid-July to 25 August); it closes Saturday morning in April, weekend mornings mid-September to mid-November and at 5.30pm daily mid-November to April. There's an SNCF ticket office here. A smaller tourist office (☎ 05 65 33 62 59) in the Cité's main street, rue de la Couronnerie, is open 10am to 12.30pm and 1.30pm to 6pm daily (to 6.30pm May to mid-September and 9.30am to 7.30pm daily mid-July to 25 August). It closes at 5.30pm mid-September to mid-November and all mornings mid-November to April.

There's a post office in the Cité and banks both here and in L'Hospitalet; currency exchange is also available at the post office and tourist offices.

In the Cité

Coach tourists with glazed eyes obediently plod through a number of over-restored

Gothic chapels, notably **Chapelle Notre Dame**, home to the renowned, smoke-blackened Black Virgin. Other sights in the Cité to refresh less pious visitors include the **Musée du Jouet Ancien Automobile** (*☎ 05 65 33 60 75, place Ventadour; adult/child €3.80/1.50; open 10am-noon & 2pm-6pm daily Apr-Oct*), at the top (north-eastern) entrance to the Cité, which has over a hundred early-20th-century model and kiddie cars.

The Cité's main street is connected to the chapels and to the plateau above by the **Grand Escalier** (Great Staircase, or Via Sancta) – the 223 steps were once climbed by the pious on their knees – and a path whose switchbacks are marked with graphic stations of the Cross.

L'Hospitalet

One of the best attractions here is simply the view of the Cité below from the ramparts of the **chateau** (*☎ 05 65 33 23 23, L'Hospitalet; adult/child €2.60/2; open 8am-8pm daily*). The **Grotte des Merveilles** (*☎ 05 65 33 67 92, L'Hospitalet; adult/child €4.55/2.75; open 10am-noon & 2pm-6pm daily Apr-June, Sept-Nov; 9am-7pm daily July-Aug*), a small cave next to the tourist office, has some mediocre stalactites and prehistoric cave paintings. The bizarre **La Feerie du Rail** (*☎ 05 65 33 71 06, L'Hospitalet; adult/child €6.10/3.80; open Apr-mid-Nov, only for shows at specific times, 3 to 8 times daily depending on the season*) is an animated and illuminated miniature fantasyland. At the other end of the spectrum, the engrossing natural attraction of **Le Rocher des Aigles** (*☎ 05 65 33 65 45, route du Château, L'Hospitalet; adult/child €6.10/3.80; open 1pm-5pm daily Apr-June & Sept; 1pm-6pm July-Aug; 2pm-4pm Oct-Nov*), near the chateau, has demonstrations by various birds of prey three to four times daily during the high season.

Places to Stay & Eat

You'll need to book accommodation well ahead in the high season.

Relais du Campeur (*☎ 05 65 33 73 50, fax 05 65 10 68 21, L'Hospitalet*) 2-person forfait €9.90. Open Apr-Oct. This grassy site in L'Hospitalet is pretty basic but does have a swimming pool.

Comp'Hostel (*☎ 05 65 33 73 50, fax 05 65 33 69 60, place de l'Europe, L'Hospitalet*) Doubles/triples/quads €44.20/50.30/56.40. Open Apr-Oct. Close by, the gaudy Comp'Hostel has plain, modern rooms.

Hôtel le Globe (*☎ 05 65 33 67 73, fax 05 65 38 81 72, rue de la Couronnerie, Cité*) Doubles/triples with shower & WC €32/41.15. Open mid-Feb–mid-Nov. *Menus* €13.55-20.60. This cosy and old-fashioned hotel is near the tourist office in the Cité. Its small restaurant serves a decent plat du jour (€9.90) plus pizzas and salads.

Hôtel-Restaurant du Lion D'Or (*☎ 05 65 33 62 04, fax 05 65 33 72 54, e contact@ liondor-rocamadour.com, rue de la Couronnerie, Cité*) Doubles €28.95-41.15. Midday *menus* €10.20, evening *menus* €13.70-32. Open Apr-Nov. The Lion D'Or is a respectable Logis de France hostelry at the top (north-eastern) end of the Cité's main street.

Hôtel-Restaurant Le Terminus des Pélerins (*☎ 05 65 33 62 14, fax 05 65 33 72 10, place de la Carreta, Cité*) Doubles €41.15-53.35, triples €56.40. Open Apr-Nov. Midday *menus* €10.95, evening *menus* €13.55-19.05. For more frills, head to this Logis de France property (opposite the Grand Escalier), which has a great terrace overlooking the valley (the pricier rooms have balcony views).

Getting There & Away

Rocamadour is 4km south-west of the Rocamadour-Padirac train station (*☎ 05 65 33 63 05*), which is on the Toulouse to Brive-la-Gaillarde (€6.55, 37 minutes, three to five daily) line. At the time of research, there were plans to start a *navette* shuttle bus to town. For a taxi, call ☎ 05 65 33 72 72.

Getting Around

Car drivers are advised to park in L'Hospitalet near the chateau and take the lift down to the Cité (see later in this section) or head for the parking lot in the valley and walk or take the tourist train (Le Petit Train) up. It runs every 15 minutes 10am to 7.30pm daily between Easter and September (adult/child €3.05/1.85).

The Ascenseur Incline Solveroc links the chateau in L'Hospitalet with the shrines below for €2.30/3.50 one way/return. The Ascenseur de Rocamadour lift runs between the Cité and the shrines for €1.65/2.30. Both run between 8am and 8pm daily in the high season (to 10pm during July and August) and less frequently in the low season.

ST-CÉRÉ
postcode 46400 • pop 3500 • elevation 137m
The old market town of St-Céré, 30km east of Rocamadour in the valley of the River Bave, is a picturesque, prosperous place, renowned for its strawberries and plums and for being the adopted home town of the tapestry designer, Jean Lurçat (see the boxed text 'Tapestries & Cockerels'). It makes a pleasant base for touring the area – traditional Quercy hamlets such as Autoire to the west or the emptier, rye lands of Le Ségala to the east.

Orientation & Information
The huge place de la République forms the hub of town. The old town comprises the area on either side of the main shopping street, rue de la République, which runs for 300m north-west of the square; turn right (to the north) off rue de la République to reach place du Mercadial, the old market square.

The tourist office (☎ 05 65 38 11 85, fax 05 65 38 38 71, e saint-cere@wanadoo.fr), on place de la République, is open 10am to noon and 2pm to 6pm Monday to Saturday (9am to 12.30pm and 2.30pm to 7pm in July and August, when it is also open on Sunday morning). It has comprehensive information on the surrounding Pays de St-Céré and Haut Quercy region. Its Randonnées au pays de Saint-Céré features a choice of trail leaflets (€2.30-5.35 each).

Banks include Crédit Lyonnais at 11 rue de la République.

Post & Communications
The post office is 300m west of place de la République, on rue Faidherbe. A pay-by-card Internet facility is available at Grand Café (☎ 05 65 38 11 60), 9 place de la République, open Tuesday to Sunday.

Tapestries & Cockerels

The artist Jean Lurçat (1892–1966), who specialised in bright, inventive paintings, mosaics and ceramics, first won fame for reviving the flagging, 500-year-old tapestry industry of Aubusson where he was appointed chief designer in 1939. During WWII Lurçat joined the Resistance in the Lot and once the war was over he settled in St-Céré, establishing a studio in the hilltop Tours de St-Laurent. It was here that he produced some of his most famous designs, characterised by enormous cockerels – a rallying cry to restore French pride in the post-war days.

Place du Mercadial & Old Town
This attractive old heart of the town is surrounded by picturesque half-timbered houses; one at the corner of rue Pasteur still has the *taouilé* (stone bench) where fishermen once displayed their catch. Nearby, the glass-fronted **Maison des Consuls** now holds temporary art exhibitions. South-east off place du Mercadial, rue St-Cyr and rue du Mazel have attractive medieval and Renaissance houses. Across the other side of rue de la République is the 17th-century **Église Ste-Spérie** and more turreted houses.

Galerie d'Art du Casino & Atelier-Musée Jean Lurçat
Some 200m north-east of the tourist office, the **Galerie d'Art le Casino** (☎ 05 65 38 19 60, admission free; open 9am-noon & 2pm-6.30pm daily July-Sept; Wed-Mon Oct-July), off blvd Jean Lurçat, has a permanent display of some of Lurçat's brilliantly coloured tapestries (as well as temporary exhibitions of other artwork).

Just behind the gallery, a footpath leads to the medieval **Tours St-Laurent** on a hill overlooking the town, worth the climb for the great views alone. The tower, once Lurçat's studio, is now the **Atelier-Musée Jean-Lurçat**, a museum of his work (☎ 05 65 38 28 21; adult/child & student €2.30/1.50; open 9.30am-noon & 2.30pm-6.30pm 14 July-Sept; also 2 weeks around Easter).

Places to Stay

St-Céré has a fair range of accommodation options.

Camping Le Soulhol (*☎/fax 05 65 38 12 37, quai Auguste-Sallesses*) Adult/pitch €3.35/3.70. Open Apr-Oct. This pleasantly shady site is 700m south across the Bave near the municipal sports grounds.

Grand Hôtel Maury (*☎ 05 65 38 29 99, fax 05 65 38 22 75, 9 place de la République*) Doubles €38.10-42.70. This imposing, old-fashioned establishment in the town centre has undistinguished but adequate rooms.

Hôtel-Bar-Restaurant Victor Hugo (*☎ 05 65 38 16 15, fax 05 65 38 39 91, 7 av des Maquis*) Doubles/triples with shower, WC & TV €38.10-45.75/48. Midday *menus* €9.90, evening *menus* €13.70-33.55. The attractive, Irish-run Victor Hugo is a Logis de France establishment nearby, overlooking the Bave, and has a decent restaurant.

Places to Eat

In addition to the hotel-restaurants (see Places to Stay for details), there are the following possibilities.

Restaurant Pizzeria du Mercadial (*☎ 05 65 38 35 77, 4 place du Mercadial*) Pizzas & salads €3.05-7.60. Open Tues-Sat & Mon evening. Not just a pizzeria, this restaurant, in the picturesque old centre, also serves standard meat-chips-and-salad dishes for under €9.25.

Le Puymule (*☎ 05 65 10 59 10, 1 place de l'Eglise*) Midday *formules* (set menu with choice of courses) €6.40-9.60, dishes €7.90-11.45. Open Tues-Sun. Another attractively located restaurant, by the church, offering bargain fare.

Getting There & Away

St-Céré is 8km south of Bretenoux-Biars' train station, with connections to Brive (€6.40, 45 minutes) three to four times daily. There's an occasional shuttle bus to town. For a taxi call ☎ 05 65 10 80 80.

Buses (☎ 05 65 38 08 28) run infrequently to Figeac (€5.80, one hour, four times weekly or twice out of term-time) and Cahors (€7.60, 1¾ hours, twice weekly). The bus stop is on place de la République.

Getting Around

Peugeot Cycles (☎ 05 65 38 03 23), at 43 rue Faidherbe (opposite the post office), rents mountain bikes for €9.25/53.35 per day/week. It opens Monday to Saturday.

AROUND ST-CÉRÉ
Gouffre de Padirac

The spectacular Padirac Cave (*☎ 05 65 33 64 56, Padirac; adult/child €7.30/4.10; open 9am-noon & 2pm-6pm daily Apr-June, Sept-10 Oct; 8.30am-noon & 2pm-6.30pm daily 1-9 July; 8.30am-6.30pm daily 10-31 July; 8am-7pm daily Aug*), 15km north-east of Rocamadour and 18km west of St-Céré, offers the closest thing to a cruise to Hades across the River Styx. Discovered in 1889, the cave's navigable river – 103m below ground level – is reached through a 75m-deep, 33m-wide chasm (and three lifts and 300 steps!). Boat pilots ferry visitors along a 500m stretch of the subterranean waterway, guiding them up and down a series of stairways to otherworldly pools and vast, floodlit caverns. The whole operation is unashamedly mass-market, but it retains an innocence and style reminiscent of the 1930s, when the first lifts were installed. Tours take 45 minutes.

Château de Castelnau-Bretenoux

This imposing red-stone chateau (*☎ 05 65 10 98 00, Prudhomat; adult/those under 23/child €5.50/3.50/free; open 9.30am-12.15pm & 2pm-6.15pm daily Apr-June, Sept; 9.30am-6.45pm daily July-Aug; 10am-12.15pm & 2pm-5.15pm Wed-Mon Oct-Mar*), 9km north-west of St-Céré, by the village of Prudhomat, towers over the surrounding countryside. Its amazing medieval fortifications, built during the Hundred Years' War and among the best of its era, include a huge keep and six round towers, fortified curtain walls and ramparts.

It belonged to the Castelnau-Bretenoux family for centuries, but after the family line died out in 1715 it changed hands continually and by 1896, when it was already in ruins, it was rescued and restored by Jean Mouliérat, a tenor in the Parisian Comic Opera. He filled it with his eclectic collection of furnishings, tapestries and objets d'art, mostly from the 16th to 18th centuries and donated the castle and its contents to the state in 1932.

You can wander round the grounds freely (the views alone are spectacular), but the interior rooms are accessible only on the 45-minute guided tours (French only, with multilingual printed summaries available).

Château de Montal

Three kilometres west of St-Céré, off the D673, this delightful chateau (☎ 05 65 38 13 72, St-Jean Lespinasse; adult/student/child €4.55/3.80/1.85; open 9.30am-noon & 2.30pm-6pm Sun-Fri 8 Apr-31 Oct) was built in 1523 by Jeanne de Balsac for her eldest son, Robert, who was away fighting in Italy. No expense was spared to create the beautiful Renaissance facade with finely sculpted portrait busts and the staircase of golden Carennac stone with individually different carvings. But after Robert was killed in battle, his mother had the words plus d'espoir ('no more hope') carved on a stone scroll at one of the windows.

Badly damaged during the Revolution, the chateau was bought in the 19th century by a wheeler-dealer who sold off its treasures. In 1908, a new owner, oil magnate Maurice Fénaille, came to the rescue and spent years (and a small fortune) retrieving almost everything.

The one-hour visits are with a (French-speaking) guide – the latest morning one starts at 11.15am, and the latest afternoon one at 5.15pm.

AUTOIRE

postcode 46400 • pop 270 • elevation 300m
No other village in Quercy boasts as many towers and turrets as Autoire, one of the most beautiful villages in France, 7km west of St-Céré in what was once an important wine-growing area. The village has many grand Renaissance manor houses built by wealthy vignerons (wine merchants). At the top of the surrounding high cliffs, you can just see the ruins of a folly-like fortress dating from the Hundred Years' War, called the Château des Anglais (a name given to many ancient ruins of uncertain history in the

region) which became a hideout for brigands, finally abandoned in 1588. On the top of the ridge (5km by road), Loubressac is another stunningly pretty village, boasting more noble houses and spectacular views.

Places to Stay & Eat

Among several chambres d'hôtes (B&Bs) in the area, Madame Gauzin's modest, homely La Plantade (☎ 05 65 38 15 61, La Plantade), 1.5km north-east of Autoire, off the D38, has doubles/triples/quads for €27.45/38.10/42/68 (including breakfast).

Auberge de la Fontaine (☎ 05 65 10 85 40, fax 05 65 10 12 70, Le Bourg) Doubles €38.10-44.95. Midday menus €9.90, evening menus €14.95-23.65. Open midday & evening Tues-Sat, midday only Sun & Mon. This nine-room Logis de France property at the heart of Autoire has a locally popular restaurant that serves some imaginative dishes (including kangaroo steaks!).

Hôtel-Restaurant Lou Cantou (☎ 05 65 38 20 58, fax 05 65 38 25 37, Loubressac) Doubles €42.70-53.35. Midday menus €10.50, evening menus €16.75-28.20. This Logis de France place, in Loubressac, has a fantastic view.

CAHORS

postcode 46000 • pop 20,000
• elevation 128m
Cahors, the departmental capital of the Lot (and former capital of the Quercy region), is a low-key city with a relaxed atmosphere. Surrounded on three sides by a bend in the Lot and circled by a ring of hills, it is endowed with a couple of minor Roman sites, a famous medieval bridge and a large medieval quarter.

Cahors was founded by the Romans, who called it Divona Cadurcorum and, like their Celtic predecessors, the Cadurcii, worshipped Divona the goddess of a sacred riverside spring, now known as the Fontaine des Chartreux. During the Middle Ages, Cahors became a prosperous commercial and financial centre, thanks to steady rule by powerful Catholic bishops and to the famously usurious Italian Lombard merchants who had fled here from the Albigensian Crusade. Pope

234 Lot – Cahors

John XXII, a native of Cahors and the second of the Avignon popes, established a university here in 1331.

Cahors kept the English at bay during the Hundred Years' War, but the Wars of Religion led the fiercely Catholic city right into the fray: After massacring its Protestants in 1560, it was besieged by the Huguenots 20 years later and thoroughly sacked.

Orientation
The main commercial thoroughfare, blvd Léon Gambetta, divides Vieux Cahors (Old Cahors), to the east, from the new quarters to the west. At its northern end is place Général de Gaulle, a giant car park surrounded by bar-brasseries catering to students; 500m to the south is place François Mitterrand, central Cahors' lively main square. The famous pont Valentré is 600m to the west.

Information
Tourist Offices The town's tourist office is in the Maison du Tourisme (☎ 05 65 53 20 65; fax 05 65 53 20 74, e cahors@wanadoo .fr), on place François Mitterrand. It opens 9am to 12.30pm and 1.30pm to 6.30pm Monday to Saturday (to 6pm on Saturday). It opens 9am to 6.30pm Monday to Saturday and 10am to noon Sunday during July and August. Ask for its *Itineraires à Travers la Ville* leaflet showing a suggested walking route round the historic centre. In the same building is Les Services Loisirs Accueil (see under Organised Tours earlier).

For further information contact the Comité Départemental du Tourisme du Lot (☎ 05 65 35 07 09, fax 05 65 23 92 76, e le-lot@ wanadoo.fr, W www.tourisme-lot.com) at 107 quai Eugène Cavaignac, open 8am to 12.30pm and 1.30pm to 5.30pm Monday to Friday (to 4.30pm on Friday).

There's a Bureau Information Jeunesse (BIJ; ☎ 05 65 23 95 90, fax 05 65 22 60 66, e bij.cahors@caramail.com) in the same building as the Auberge de Jeunesse (see Places to Stay) where you can find information on temporary jobs, lodgings and courses. It opens 9am to noon and 1pm to 6pm on weekdays and until 5pm on Saturday.

Money Banks along blvd Léon Gambetta include Société Générale at No 85 and Crédit Agricole at No 22 (the latter is open Monday).

Post & Communications The main post office, at 257 rue du Président Wilson, has exchange services and an Internet facility.

You can also access the Internet at the BIJ (see under Tourist Offices) for €3.05 per hour (free on Wednesday and Saturday by prior reservation) and at Les Docks (see Entertainment) for €1.50 per hour 2pm to 6pm Monday to Saturday plus 8pm to 10pm Thursday and Friday.

Bookshops There are maps and topo-guides available from Maison de la Presse (73 blvd Léon Gambetta). It opens Monday to Saturday and Sunday morning.

Laundry Laverie GTI, at 208 rue Georges Clémenceau, is open 7am to 9pm daily.

Honourable Statesman or Raving-Mad Dictator?

Cahors' most famous son, Léon Gambetta (1838–82), came from humble beginnings (his father was a grocer) to become an outstanding lawyer and politician. After Napoléon's downfall, Gambetta became Minister of the Interior. When Paris fell to the Prussians soon afterwards, he escaped to Tours in a hot-air balloon and organised the fight against the enemy with dictatorial skill (though not always with military success).

In 1879 he became head of the Republican Union, promoting liberty of the press, separation of Church and State and other radical ideas (radical enough that even fellow Republicans thought he was raving mad). He became Prime Minister in November 1881, resigning only three months later when his bill to reform the electoral process was defeated.

LOT & LOT-ET-GARONNE

CAHORS

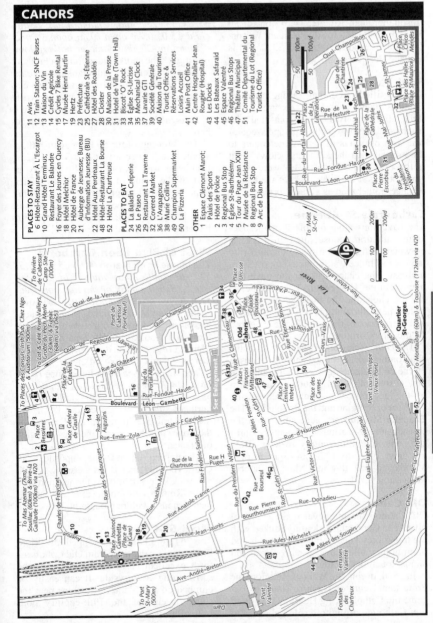

PLACES TO STAY
6 Hôtel-Restaurant À L'Escargot
10 Grand Hôtel Terminus;
   Restaurant Le Balandre
16 Foyer des Jeunes en Quercy
18 Hôtel Melchior
20 Hôtel de France
21 Auberge de Jeunesse; Bureau
   d'Information Jeunesse (BIJ)
22 Hôtel Aux Perdreaux
48 Hôtel-Restaurant La Bourse
52 Hôtel La Chartreuse

PLACES TO EAT
24 La Baladin Crêperie
26 Le Paseo
29 Restaurant La Taverne
32 Covered Market
36 L'Arapagus
38 Marie Colline
49 Champion Supermarket
50 La Pizzeria

OTHER
1 Espace Clément Marot;
   Palais des Sports
2 Hôtel de Police
3 Regional Bus Stop
4 Église St-Barthélémy
5 Tour du Pape Jean XXII
7 Musée de la Résistance
8 Regional Bus Stop
9 Arc de Diane
11 Avis
12 Train Station; SNCF Buses
13 Maison du Vin
14 Crédit Agricole
15 Cycles 7 Bike Rental
17 Musée Henri Martin
19 Hertz
23 Préfecture
25 Cathédrale St-Étienne
27 Hôtel des Roaldés
28 Cloister
30 Maison de la Presse
31 Hôtel de Ville (Town Hall)
33 Biscot 'O' Rock
34 Église St-Urcisse
35 Mechanical Clock
37 Lavarie GTI
39 Société Générale
40 Maison du Tourisme;
   Tourist Office &
   Réservations Services
   Loisirs Accueil
41 Main Post Office
42 Centre Hospitalier Jean
   Rouger (Hospital)
43 Les Docks
44 Les Bateaux Safaraïd
45 Espace Valentré
46 Regional Bus Stops
47 Théâtre Municipal
51 Comité Départemental du
   Tourisme du Lot (Regional
   Tourist Office)

LOT & LOT-ET-GARONNE

Medical Services & Emergency Centre Hospitalier Jean Rougier (☎ 05 65 20 50 50) is opposite 428 rue du Président Wilson. The Hôtel de Police (☎ 05 65 23 17 17) is at place Bessières.

Pont Valentré

This fortified medieval bridge, one of France's finest, consists of six arches and three tall towers, two of them outfitted with machicolations (projecting parapets equipped with openings that allow defenders to drop missiles on the attackers below). Built in the 14th century (the towers were added later), it was designed as part of the town's defences rather than as a traffic bridge.

Cathédrale St-Étienne

The cavernous nave of this Romanesque-style cathedral, consecrated in 1119, is crowned with two 18m-wide cupolas (the largest in France), an obvious import from the east. The chapels along the nave (repainted in the 19th century) are Gothic, as are the choir and the massive western facade. The wall paintings between the organ and the interior of the west facade are early-14th-century originals.

The *cloître* (**cloister**), accessible from the choir or through the arched entrance opposite 59 rue de la Chanterie, is in the Flamboyant Gothic style of the early 16th century. Most of the decoration was mutilated during the Wars of Religion and the Revolution. The **Chapelle St-Gausbert**, accessible from the cloister, houses various liturgical treasures and some fine 15th-century frescoes. Both are open 10am to 12.30pm, 3pm to 6pm Monday to Saturday mid-May to October (admission €2.30).

Old Cahors

Old Cahors, the medieval quarter east of blvd Léon Gambetta, is densely packed with old four-storey houses, linked by streets and often grungy alleyways so narrow you can almost touch both walls.

In 1580, during the Wars of Religion, the Protestant Henri of Navarre (later to become the Catholic King Henri IV) captured the Catholic stronghold of Cahors and

stayed in the **Hôtel des Roaldès** (☎ 05 65 35 04 35, 271 quai Champollion; adult/child €3.05/0.75; open 10am-noon & 2pm-4.30pm Apr-20 Sept & major holidays) for one night. The short guided tour (in French) of the privately owned mansion reveals richly furnished, fusty rooms and some extravagant stone doorways carved with roses. Nearby, at place St-Urcisse, there's an eye-catching **mechanical clock**, placed here in 1997.

The 34m-high **Tour du Pape Jean XXII**, a square, crenellated tower at 1-3 blvd Léon Gambetta, was built in the 14th century as part of the home of Jacques Duèse, later Pope John XXII (reigned 1316–34). The interior is closed to the public. Next door is the 14th-century **Église St-Barthélémy**, with its massive brick and stone belfry.

West of Blvd Léon Gambetta

The **Musée Henri Martin** (☎ 05 65 30 15 13, 792 rue Émile Zola; adult/child €3/1.50, free 1st Sun of month; open 11am-6pm Wed-Mon & 2pm-6pm Sun Apr-Sept), also known as the Musée Municipal, has some archaeological artefacts and a collection of works by the Cahors-born pointillist painter Henri Martin (1893–1972). It is open only when there are temporary exhibitions.

The small **Musée de la Résistance** (☎ 05 65 22 14 25, place Général de Gaulle; admission free; open 2pm-6pm daily), on the northern side of place Général de Gaulle, has illustrated exhibits on the Résistance, the concentration camps and the liberation of France.

The unsung **Arc de Diane**, opposite 24 av Charles de Freycinet, is a stone archway with red-brick stripes that once formed part of a Gallo-Roman bath-house and now stands incongruously before modern houses.

Mont St-Cyr

The 264m-high, antenna-topped hill, Mont St-Cyr, across the river from Old Cahors affords excellent views of the town and the surrounding countryside. It can easily be climbed on foot – the trail begins near the southern end of the 19th-century pont Louis-Philippe.

Boating

To rent a houseboat or motorboat for jaunts along the Lot, contact **Baboumarine** (☎ 05 65 30 08 99, fax 05 65 23 92 59, e babou .marine@wanadoo.fr, w www.baboulene -jean.fr, Port St-Mary, 46000 Cahors; 2-4 person houseboat €815-1120 per week) at Port St-Mary.

Organised Tours

The tourist office organises guided visits of Cahors on specific themes (such as the old city or pont Valentré) throughout the year, usually at 3pm on Saturday and/or Monday and at 5pm daily during July and August, except on Sunday (adult/student €5.35/3.80).

Les Bateaux Safaraid (☎ 05 65 35 98 88) Adult/child €8.40/4.55. Three to four times daily Apr-Oct. Tours leave from Terrasses Valentré, just south of pont Valentré, for 90-minute river cruises with commentary in French and English.

An enjoyable day-trip excursion is on the *Train Touristique Quercyrail* (☎/fax 05 65 23 94 72, place de la Gare). Adult/child €22.85/7.60. This restored 1950s Micheline train trundles as far as Cajarc (about 40km). The trip (9am to 6pm) runs on Sunday May to October (plus on Saturday in July and August). Shorter Quercyrail trips include a train ride plus a 4.5km riverside walk below St-Cirq Lapopie on Wednesday in July and August (adult/child €15.25/7.60).

Special Events

Le Printemps de Cahors, a three-week exhibition of photography and the visual arts, begins in mid-June. The week-long Festival de Blues attracts jazz fans and stars in mid-July.

Places to Stay – Budget

Cahors has surprisingly poor budget accommodation, though there are a couple of hostels. Note that the two hotels mentioned here are closed on Sunday and public holidays.

Rivière de Cabessut (☎ 05 65 30 06 30, fax 05 65 23 99 46, rue de la Rivière) Adult/pitch €2.30/7.60. Open Apr-Nov. This large, 3-star site, on the other side of the river, is very pleasant, with river swimming and canoes available for rent.

Auberge de Jeunesse (☎ 05 65 35 64 71, fax 05 65 35 95 92, 20 rue Frédéric Suisse) Dorm beds with/without breakfast €10.65/ 8.10. This hostel is in a complex known as Espace Frédéric Suisse, with a cheap restaurant downstairs. It opens 24 hours (but you'll need to ring the bell for entry if you arrive after 8pm).

Foyer des Jeunes en Quercy (☎ 05 65 35 29 32, fax 05 65 53 69 68, 129 rue Fondue Haute) Bed in 1- or 3-bed room €8.85. This antiquated but friendly place, run by nuns, provides accommodation for students during the academic year but welcomes travellers of all religions, sexes and ages whenever there's space (usually from late May to early September). There's no curfew.

Hôtel-Restaurant La Bourse (☎/fax 05 65 35 17 78, 7 place Claude Rousseau) Singles with/without shower €30.50/24.40, doubles €30.50/24.40, triples €38.10/28.95. This popular, laid-back place in Old Cahors has large rooms in a medieval house down a nearby grungy alley. Hall showers are free.

Hôtel Aux Perdreaux (☎ 05 65 35 03 50, 137 rue du Portail Alban) Singles €22.85, doubles with shower €25.90-28.95. The friendlier Perdreaux, on place de la Libération, has smallish, nondescript rooms.

Places to Stay – Mid-Range & Top End

There are a number of pricier hotels in Cahors.

Hôtel Melchior (☎ 05 65 35 03 38, fax 05 65 23 92 75, place Jouinot Gambetta) Singles €26.70-36.60, doubles €33.55-39.65, triples €44.20. The Melchior has adequate, nothing-special rooms. Reception is closed on Sunday (except in July and August when it opens at 5.30pm).

Hôtel de France (☎ 05 65 35 16 76, fax 05 65 22 01 08, 252 av Jean Jaurès) Doubles €36.60-56.40. This plain modern hotel in the Inter-Hotel chain, has predictable, comfortable rooms with TV, telephone and mini-bar.

Hôtel-Restaurant À L'Escargot (☎ 05 65 35 07 66, fax 05 65 53 92 38, 5 blvd Léon Gambetta) Singles/doubles/triples €35.05/43.60/54.85. Efficient, comfortable L'Escargot is near several lively brasseries.

Hôtel La Chartreuse (☎ 05 65 35 17 37, fax 05 65 22 30 03, chemin de la Chartreuse, St Georges) Singles €39.65-54.85, doubles €44.20-57.15. At this modern riverside hotel some rooms have balconies overlooking the river.

Grand Hôtel Terminus (☎ 05 65 53 32 00, fax 05 65 53 32 26, e terminus .balandre@wanadoo.fr, 5 av Charles de Freycinet) Doubles with shower €48.80-56.40, with bath €59.45-121.95. The elegant and discreetly located 1920s Terminus offers all the frills (plus period stained-glass decor).

Places to Eat

Self-Catering Regional specialities, such as deep-red Cahors wine, foie gras, truffles and *cabécou* (a small, round goat's cheese) – plus the freshest of fruits and vegetables and take-away dishes – can be found in the *marché couvert (covered market)*, also known as Les Halles, on place des Halles. It opens 8am to noon and 3pm to 7pm Tuesday to Saturday and 9am to noon on Sunday and holidays. There's a fantastic *open-air market* in place de la Cathédrale on Wednesday and Saturday morning (or the previous day if it clashes with holidays).

Close to the tourist office, the *Champion supermarket*, across from 109 blvd Léon Gambetta, is open Monday to Saturday.

Budget & Mid-Range There is a good range of reasonably priced places to eat out.

La Pizzeria (☎ 05 65 35 12 18, 58 blvd Léon Gambetta) Pizzas & pasta €3.70-8.85, *menus* €9.90-13.55. Open Mon-Sat, evening only Sun May-Oct; Mon & Tues midday only and Wed-Sat Nov-Apr. This is a popular pizzeria, with brisk service and good-value fare.

Marie Colline (☎ 05 65 35 59 96, 173 rue Georges Clémenceau) Plats du jour €6.40, desserts €2-3.35. Open midday only Tues-Sat Sept-July. Attractive Marie Colline serves home-cooked vegetarian plats du jour (two only per day) and fantastic desserts.

Le Paseo (☎ 05 65 53 15 16, 24 place Champollion) Tapas €2.75-3.05, midday/evening *menus* €10.35/13.70. One of several atmospheric restaurants in this area, Le Paseo specialises in *grillades au bois* (charcoal-grilled dishes, €8.40-15.25).

La Baladin Crêperie (☎ 05 65 22 36 52, 57 rue Clément Marot) Pancakes & crepes €2.30-6.85, plat du jour €5.35. Chic and popular, La Baladin has some unusual crepes (including a *crepe savoyard* featuring wild boar ham, €6.70).

L'Arapagous (☎ 05 65 35 07 66, 134 rue St-Urcisse) Midday *menus* €9.90, evening *menus* €12.20-28.95, dishes €10.65-13.70. This restaurant serves tempting *menus* featuring regional specialities.

Chez Ngo (☎ 05 65 22 17 30, place des Consuls) Dishes €5.50-10.65. Come to Chez Ngo for a wide variety of Oriental dishes.

Places to Eat

Top End Gourmets can enjoy a couple of top-notch restaurants in Cahors.

Restaurant La Taverne (☎ 05 65 35 28 66, place Pierre Escorbiac) Midday *menus* €11.45-14.50, evening *menus* €18.15-22.70. Open daily July-Aug; Mon-Fri Sept-June. Renowned La Taverne specialises in French and regional cuisine. Reservations are recommended on Friday and Saturday nights.

Restaurant Le Balandre (☎ 05 65 30 01 97, 5 av Charles de Freycinet) Midday bar/restaurant *menus* €13.70/30.45, evening restaurant *menus* €30.50-73.15, dishes €14.95-27.45. Open daily July-Aug; Tues-Sat, Sun midday only Sept-June. The elegant Balandre, attached to the Grand Hôtel Terminus (see Places to Stay – Top End), serves creative cuisine based on traditional regional ingredients.

Entertainment

For late-night drinks with a rock-music backing, head for *Biscot 'O' Rock* (☎ 05 65 35 99 63, 10 rue St-James) open till 2am; or *Irish Pub* (☎ 05 65 53 15 15, place des Consuls), hidden at the side of a car park, which has regular live music and is open 6pm to 2am. Both are open Monday to Saturday.

Espace Valentré (☎ 05 65 20 37 37, allées des Soupirs) Concerts, plays and other events happen at this venue or in the *Auditorium*

(☎ 05 65 30 18 16, place des Consuls). Tickets are available at the tourist office.

***Les Docks** (☎ 05 65 22 36 38, fax 05 65 23 13 89, 430 allées des Soupirs)* Office open 9am-noon & 2pm-6pm Mon-Fri. Skate park open 2pm-6pm daily plus 8pm-10pm Tues, Thur & Fri. Music workshops €1.50 per hour for instrument loan. This former warehouse is Cahors' latest youth venue, offering everything from rooms for young musicians to practise to a Cyber Cafe (see Post & Communications).

Getting There & Away

Bus SNCF buses leave from the train station for Fumel (€7.15, one hour 10 minutes, five times daily) via Puy l'Évêque (€5.15, 45 minutes, eight times daily); Capdenac (€10.35, two hours, once daily Tuesday to Sunday) via Bouziès (€4.25, 27 minutes), Cajarc (€6.70, 50 minutes) and Figeac (€9.75, 1¾ hours); and Montauban (€8.55, one hour 15 minutes, once daily). Some of these services also stop in town, for example, on or near place Général de Gaulle or along rue St-Géry, just west of allées Fénelon (Terres Rouges on Cahors bus timetables refers to a suburb north-east of town).

Train The train station (☎ 08 36 35 35 35) is on place Jouinot Gambetta (place de la Gare). The information office is open from 6.20am to 9.30pm daily (7.30am to 11.20pm on Sunday).

Cahors is on the main SNCF line that links Paris' Gare d'Austerlitz (€48.75, 5½ hours, five daily) with Brive-la-Gaillarde (€12.35, around one hour 10 minutes), Souillac (€8.70, 45 minutes), Montauban (€8.55, 45 minutes) and Toulouse (€13.55, one hour 10 minutes, five to seven times daily). To get to Bordeaux (€26.55), you should change at Montauban.

Car Avis (☎ 05 65 30 13 10) is at 512 av Jean Jaurès and Hertz (☎ 05 65 35 34 69) at 385 rue Anatole France. Both are open Monday to Friday and Saturday morning.

Free car parking is possible at place Charles de Gaulle and along the riverside.

Getting Around

Cycles 7 (☎ 05 65 22 66 60), at 417 Quai de Regourd, rents mountain bikes for €12.20/53.35 per day/week. It's open 9am to noon and 2pm to 7pm Tuesday to Saturday.

EAST OF CAHORS

The limestone hills between Cahors and Figeac are cut by the dramatic, cliff-flanked Rivers Lot and Célé. The narrow, winding and supremely scenic D662 (signposted 'Vallée du Lot') follows the Lot, while the even narrower and more spectacular D41 (signposted 'Vallée du Célé') follows the tortuous route of the Célé, as does the GR651. The invaluable *Lot-Célé Guide Pratique*, available from tourist offices, lists accommodation, sights, and canoe and bike rental outlets.

Activities

Canoeing/kayaking is particularly popular here as well as rock-climbing or spelunking in the region's rugged cliffs and *causses* (limestone plateaus). The following outfits all operate June to September or by special arrangement at other times.

Bureau Sports et Nature *(☎ 05 65 24 21 01, fax 05 65 24 21 03, e bureau-sports-nature@wanadoo.fr, w http://perso.wanadoo.fr/bureau-sports-nature, 46330 Conduché, canoe/kayak/biking trips €22.85 per person per day, rock-climbing/spelunking €30.50, canyoning €35.05; open 9am-7pm daily July-Aug; 9am-noon & 1.30pm-6.30pm Mon-Fri Sept-June)* This bureau promotes several operators (such as Kalapca, see below) as well as arranging its own activities in July and August. Arrangements can be made off-season, too, but a minimum of six is required. The bureau is at Conduché, 4km south of Cabrerets at the junction of the D662 and D41.

Kalapca *(☎ 05 65 30 29 51, fax 05 65 30 23 33, e kalapca@wanadoo.fr, La Plage, St-Cirq Lapopie; canoes/kayaks €35.05/19.80 per day, mountain bikes €15.25 per day).* Kalapca is another multi-activity operator, and arranges weekend or week-long walking, biking, rock-climbing, canyoning or spelunking packages. In July and August different activities take place daily (€15.25-25.90 per person).

Nature & Loisirs Base d'Anglanat *(☎ 05 65 30 25 69, 46330 Orniac; canoes/kayaks/ VTTs €13.70/15.25/14.50 per person per day)*. Based 4.5km north-east (upriver) from Cabrerets, (opposite the turning to the Musée en Plein Air du Quercy) Nature & Loisirs have pick-up points at Bouziès and Sauliac.

Les Amis du Célé *(☎ 05 65 31 26 73, fax 05 65 30 26 10, Le Liauzu, 46330 Orniac; W www.amisducele.com; canoes/kayaks €30.50/19.80 per canoe/kayak, half-day/ full-day rock-climbing €18.30/27.45 per person, spelunking €19.80/28.95)* Based 3.5km upriver from Cabrerets (signs point to Base Nautique), off the D41, Les Amis organises a range of activities.

Bouziès
postcode 46330 • pop 80
• elevation approx 115m

The quiet hamlet of Bouziès, near the confluence of the Rivers Lot and Célé, 28km east of Cahors, has an impressive location opposite the **Défilé des Anglais**, the remains of a Hundred Years' War fortress carved into the rockface.

Boating & Canoeing From the riverbank below the Hôtel les Falaises (see Places to Stay & Eat), **Safaraid** *(☎ 05 65 35 98 88, Les Falaises, Bouzièes)* runs 90-minute riverboat trips (with bilingual commentary) four times daily April to November (adult/ child €8.40/4.55). Also operating from here is **Nature & Loisirs** (see Activities at the start of this section).

To rent a houseboat, contact **Nicols** *(☎ 05 65 30 24 41, fax 05 65 31 72 25, Bouziès)*; a 2-4 person houseboat costs €950-1245 per week.

Places to Stay & Eat Bouziès is tiny but there's a couple of highly recommended places to stay.

Chambres Chez l'Habitant Pech Larive *(☎ 05 65 30 20 93)* Doubles with/without shower €36.60/30.50, with kitchen/dining area €51.85, all including breakfast. The

remote and beautifully situated home of Monsieur Girma, in the hills 1.6km to the south, has a fabulous view over the valley and neat rooms in a converted barn. The owners produce delicious honey.

Hôtel Les Falaises *(☎ 05 65 31 26 83, fax 05 65 30 23 87, e falaises@crdi.fr, W www.crdi.fr/falaises, 46330 Bouziès)* Doubles €40-55.70. Midday *menus* €12.05, evening *menus* €14.50-17.55. Open May-Oct. This splendid riverside hotel has a pool and tennis courts, plus bike and canoe rental (€13.70 per day) and organised outings. Check its Web site for special *rando pédestre* walking/biking packages. The restaurant, which has a lovely terrace, serves good regional cuisine.

Getting There & Away The SNCF bus that links Cahors (€4.25, 25 minutes, five to seven daily) with Figeac (€6.85, one hour) stops on the D662 across the narrow suspension bridge from Bouziès.

Cabrerets
postcode 46330 • pop 200 • elevation 130m

The hamlet of Cabrerets, on the River Célé 5km upriver from Bouziès, is a dozy place en route to the famous Grotte du Pech Merle. It's dramatised only by the restored 14th-century **Château de Gontaut-Biron** on a clifftop overlooking the road, illuminated at night.

There's a tourist office (☎ 05 65 31 27 12, fax 05 65 30 27 17) in what little there is of a village centre, the place de la Mairie (just off the D41, the turning to the grotte), open 2pm to 5.30pm Wednesday to Saturday, and 10am to 12.30pm, 2pm to 5.30pm Sunday.

Around Cabrerets

Grotte du Pech Merle This spectacular, 1200m-long cave *(☎ 05 65 31 27 05, Cabrerets; adult/child €7/4.55; open 9.30am-noon & 1.30pm-5pm daily Apr-Nov)*, 30km east of Cahors and 3km from Cabrerets, is not only a natural wonder, with thousands of stalactites and stalagmites of all varieties and shapes, but also a prehistoric art gallery with dozens of paintings of mammoths, horses and 'negative' human handprints, drawn by Cro-Magnon people 16,000 to

20,000 years ago. Prehistoric artefacts that have been found in the area are on display in an adjacent museum.

One-hour guided tours (English text available) begin every 45 minutes (every 15 minutes in summer). During the high season, get there early as only 700 people daily are allowed to visit. Reservations are accepted.

On foot, the cave is about 3km from Bouziès via the GR651 and 1km from Cabrerets (follow the path behind the tourist office).

Le Petit Musée de l'Insolite You can't miss this bizarre private museum (☎ 05 65 30 21 01, route de Cabrerets; admission free but contributions welcome; open 9am-1pm & 2pm-7pm daily June-Sept), on the D41 3.3km north-east of Cabrerets, with its sculptures and model figures hanging from the rock-face (photos strictly forbidden!). Inside are more curiosities including paintings, sculptures and surreal compositions.

Musée en Plein Air du Quercy This appealing open-air museum (☎ 05 65 22 58 63, Cuzals; adult/those aged 10-21 €7.60/3.80; open 2pm-6pm Sun-Fri Apr, May, Sept, Oct; 9.30am-6.30pm Sun-Fri June; 10am-7pm Sun-Fri July-Aug) at Cuzals, 7km north-east of Cabrerets, off the D41, is an ethnological museum recreating farm life from the 1900s. Admission is 20% less if you have a ticket to Grotte du Pech Merle.

Places to Stay & Eat Surprisingly, there isn't a huge choice of places to stay or eat in the Cabrerets area.

Camping Familial Cantal (☎ 05 65 31 26 61, fax 05 65 31 20 47, Cabrerets) Adult/pitch €2.20/2.20. Open Apr-Nov. If you're keen to camp try this simple municipal site in a shady, grassy area on the riverside, 700m north-east of Cabrerets.

Gîte d'étape & Chambres d'hôte (☎ 05 65 31 27 04, place de la Mairie) Dorm beds with/without linen €10.65/7.60; doubles €33.55 with breakfast. Opposite the Cabrerets tourist office is the home of Madame Bessac who offers camp beds for walkers in the converted loft (which also has a kitchen). The comfortable doubles are downstairs.

Hôtel des Grottes (☎ 05 65 31 27 02, fax 05 65 31 20 15, Cabrerets) Doubles with WC €35.05-40.15, without €28.95, triples €54.85-57.95. Midday menus €10.50, evening menus €13.55, dishes €7.95-14.50. Open Apr-Nov. This riverside hotel is on the D41, its pricier rooms sporting river views and balconies.

Auberge de la Sagne (☎ 05 65 31 26 62, fax 05 65 30 27 43, route de la Grotte) Doubles €42.70-48.80, half-board (€42.70) recommended July-Aug. Open mid-May–mid-Sept. This spiffier option is 2km up the road towards the Grotte du Pech Merle. It has a swimming pool and a pleasant garden.

O'Louise Restaurant (☎ 05 65 30 25 56, place de la Mairie) Menus €9.90. Open Mon-Sat. Next to Madame Bessac's gîte d'étape is this cosy restaurant, which serves an excellent-value menu as well as snacks.

Getting There & Away SNCF buses (☎ 08 36 35 35 35) on the Cahors (€4.70, 30 minutes, four to five daily) to Figeac (€6.85, one hour, three to four daily) route stop at Conduché, just under 4km south of Cabrerets at the intersection of the D662 and the D41.

Marcilhac-sur-Célé
postcode 46160 • pop 200 • elevation 200m

One of the most striking sights along this languid stretch of the Célé is the **ruined abbey** of this once-important hamlet, with the towering cliff-face of the limestone plateau opposite. Marcilhac, 16km upstream of Cabrerets, might have been a good deal more important today had the abbots of its 12th-century Benedictine abbey kept their hands on Rocamadour, which it originally controlled (the canny abbots of Tulle took over instead). After bouts of devastation during the Hundred Years' War and the Wars of Religion, the abbey gradually sunk into ruin but you can still glimpse its grandeur from the carved lintel and Romanesque chapterhouse.

There's a tourist office (☎ 05 65 40 68 44) within the grounds of the abbey. It opens 10am to noon, 2pm to 5pm Wednesday to Saturday, 2pm to 5pm Sunday. Guided visits of the abbey's interior are available here for €2.30.

Places to Stay & Eat The *gîte d'étape* (☎ 05 65 40 61 43 or ☎ 05 65 40 64 51 after 8pm), in the abbey grounds, charges €6.10 per person.

Camping Municipal le Pré du Monsieur (☎ 05 65 40 77 88, route de Brengues) Adult/pitch €3.05/3.35. Open May-Oct. This pleasant, grassy riverside site, 200m north of town off the D41, has a tennis court (and canoes, kayaks and bikes available during the high season).

There are several *chambres d'hôtes*. Contact the tourist office or the *Café des Touristes* (☎ 05 65 40 65 61, place de la Mairie) on the main road through the village; the latter also serves up hearty *menus* (€12.20-15.25) on request.

Espagnac Ste-Eulalie
postcode 46320 • pop 70 • elevation 250m
Some 12km upstream of Marcilhac-sur-Célé, on the southern bank of the Célé, this handsome hamlet is dominated by an ornately topped 16th-century bell tower, once part of a 12th-century convent, Notre Dame du Val Paradis. Walk through the ancient gateway, past an incongruously modern wooden statue of a pilgrim, to find Madame Bonzani (first house on the right) who provides guided tours of the church.

Places to Stay & Eat Remote Marcilhac offers only a few choices of places to stay and eat.

Gîte d'étape d'Espagnac (☎/fax 05 65 40 06 34, e danielesenac@minitel.net, Le Prieuré) €10.65/6.85 per person in 3/8 bed dorm. This excellent walkers' hostel is in a well restored mansion right inside the convent grounds.

Camping du Moulin Vieux (☎ 05 65 40 00 41, route de Brengues) Adult/pitch €3.65/3.80. Open May-Oct. This spacious, grassy, riverside site, 1.5km south-west, has a pool plus canoes/kayaks for rent (€7.60/4.55 per hour).

Les Jardins Café (☎ 05 65 40 08 34, Le Prieuré) Crepes €1.80-3.80. Open 11am-1pm & 3pm-7pm Mon-Sat; Tues, Fri-Sun Sept-Mar. Under the arches of the convent, this cafe offers *bio-dynamique* sorbets, fruit juices and crepes and (summer only) a *table paysanne menu* (country menu).

Restaurant-Hôtel de la Vallée (☎ 05 65 40 05 24, fax 05 65 40 38 90, Brengues) Doubles €32-36.60. Midday *menus* €7.30-9.90, evening *menus* €12.20. This hotel-restaurant, 3.2km south-west, also operates *Le Romantic Bar* (☎ 05 65 40 04 00, route d'Espagnac) where you can rent kayaks/canoes (€15.25/24.40 per day) from June to October.

Getting There & Away There are no regular buses to Espagnac Ste-Eulalie or Marcilhac-sur-Célé. For a taxi, call ☎ 05 65 31 26 15.

ST-CIRQ LAPOPIE
postcode 46330 • pop 200 • elevation 147m
St-Cirq Lapopie, 25km east of Cahors, is perched on a clifftop 100m above the Lot. It's named after St Cirq, a child martyred in Asia Minor under Diocletian; his relics, it is believed, later found their way here. Lapopie, a word of Celtic origin that refers to an elevated place, was the family name of the local lords during the Middle Ages.

Although swamped with tourists in summer, the spectacular views and the area's natural beauty make up for the village's overstated charm. Lovers of arts and crafts will like it here – there is an artisan's workshop or gallery in every other house.

Information
The tourist office (☎/fax 05 65 31 29 06, e saint-cirq-lapopie@wanadoo.fr), in the town hall, is open 10am to 1pm, 2pm to 6pm Monday to Saturday and 11am to 1pm, 2pm to 6pm Sunday. During June it opens 10am to 7pm daily (till 7.30pm July and August). It's well stocked with maps and guides and rents laser disks (€3.05 per 24 hours; in French only), from a collection called *Les Chemins Qui Parlent,* of 19 different walks around the countryside. The guides that accompany the disks can be bought separately (€0.75) or as a pack (€11.45).

At 3pm on Friday, Saturday and Sunday mid-June to mid-September it runs guided tours of the town (adult/child €3.35/2.45).

Things to See

The fortified **Gothic church** dating from the early 16th-century is of no special interest but for its stunning location. The ruins of the 13th-century **chateau** topping the hill also afford a fine panorama. Along the narrow alleyways below, the restored stone and half-timbered houses, with steep, red-tile roofs, shelter **artisans' studios** offering leather goods, pottery, jewellery and wooden items.

The **Musée Rignault** (☎ 05 65 31 23 22, adult/child €1.50/free; open 10am-12.30pm & 2.30pm-6pm Wed-Mon mid-Apr–Nov; closing at 7pm in July-Aug), perched on the edge of a cliff, has a delightful garden (with panoramic valley views) and an eclectic collection of French furniture and art from Africa and China, plus changing modern art or sculpture exhibitions.

The **Musée de la Fourdonne** (☎/fax 05 65 31 21 51, adult/child €1.50/free; open 10am-1pm & 2pm-6pm daily to 7pm May-Sept), housed in a grand, restored Renaissance mansion at the lower end of the village, has a small local history display.

Places to Stay & Eat

There's a fair range to choose from here.

Gîte d'étape (☎/fax 05 65 31 21 51) Dorm bed €9.90. This walkers' hostel is in the Maison de la Fourdonne, which also houses the Musée de la Fourdonne (see Things to See). There are two kitchens and a communal hall.

Camping de la Plage (☎ 05 65 30 29 51, fax 05 65 30 23 33, Tour de Faure) Adult/pitch €4.55/3. This 120-pitch, shady riverside camping ground, 2km below St-Cirq, is by the bridge linking St-Cirq with Tour de Faure and the D662. Kalapca (see Activities in the East of Cahors section) organises all kinds of activities here.

Hôtel-Restaurant du Causse (☎ 05 65 31 24 16, fax 05 65 30 26 48, route de Concots) Doubles/triples €36.60/51.05. This hilltop hotel, 2.8km south (off the D26 to Concots), is great for a quiet get-away.

Auberge du Sombral (☎ 05 65 31 26 08, fax 05 65 30 26 37, place de la Mairie) Doubles €39.65-68.60. Midday menus €11.90, evening menus €16-33.55. Open Apr–mid-Nov. Restaurant & reception closed Wed Oct-June. This rather spiffy place is directly across the square from the tourist office.

Café-Restaurant Lou Bolat (☎ 05 65 30 29 04) Midday menus €9.90, evening menus €16.75-26.70. The Lou Bolat is less pretentious than most of the chic cafes and restaurants in the village; it's just below the post office, and has a pleasant terrace overlooking the village.

Auberge du Roucayrol (☎/fax 05 65 31 29 99, Tour de Faure) Midday menus €8.85-9.90, evening menus €12.20-16.95. Convenient for La Plage campers, this restaurant on the D662 is 200m north of the Tour de Faure bridge and has a pleasant terrace.

Getting There & Away

St-Cirq Lapopie is 2km across the river and up a very steep hill from Tour de Faure and the D662; the bus stop on the D662 is 300m south-east of the bridge. Buses run to Cahors (€4.70, 35 minutes) and Figeac (€6.85, 50 minutes) around four times daily.

Car parking in St-Cirq is restricted to a free car park at the very top (western) end of the village, or a pay car park mid-way: The €1.85 fee gives you free entry to the two museums.

CAJARC

postcode 46160 • pop 1100 • elevation 160m
This low-key town, 22km east of St-Cirq Lapopie and about the same south-west of Figeac, boasts no great sights but makes a pleasant midway stop. Its one unusual attraction is the **Maison des Arts Georges Pompidou** (☎ 05 65 40 63 97, route de Gréalou; adult/child €3.05/free; open 2pm-6pm Wed-Mon Feb-June, Sept-Nov; 10.30am-12.30pm & 3pm-7pm daily July-Aug; 2pm-6pm Thur-Sun Dec-Jan), a modern art gallery donated by Pompidou who was once a town councillor here. It is situated 100m north of the town's central place du Foirail and hosts changing exhibitions.

The tourist office (☎ 05 65 40 72 89, fax 05 65 40 39 05), on place du Foirail, is open 3.30pm to 6.30pm Monday to Saturday and 10am to 12.30pm on Sunday mid-June to end-June and during September, and 10am to 1pm and 3.30pm to 7pm daily during July and August.

Places to Stay & Eat
Options include the following.

Camping Municipal du Terriol (☎ 05 65 40 72 74) Adult/pitch €2/2.90. Open mid-May–Oct. This is in a pleasant shady spot by the municipal swimming pool 400m south of place du Foirail (on the GR65).

Hôtel-Restaurant La Promenade (☎ 05 65 40 61 21, fax 05 65 40 79 12, place du Foirail) Doubles €3.50. Menus €12.20-18.30. Restaurant open Mon-Sat. This is a decent central hotel with plain but adequate rooms and a reasonable restaurant.

Getting There & Away
Cajarc is on the Cahors (€6.70, one hour, four daily) to Figeac (€4.55, 50 minutes, four daily) SNCF bus route. See Organised Tours in the Cahors section for details about an excursion here by Micheline train on summer weekends.

Getting Around
Garage Citroen (☎ 05 65 40 66 48), on place du Foirail, rents bikes for €10.65/45.75 per day/week. It opens Monday to Saturday and Sunday afternoon.

FIGEAC
postcode 46100 • pop 9600 • elevation 250m
The town of Figeac, on the River Célé 68km north-east of Cahors, has a picturesque old quarter, with many houses dating from the 12th to 18th centuries, and a traffic-clogged surrounding new town. Founded in the 9th century by Benedictine monks, it became a prosperous medieval market town, an important stopping place for pilgrims travelling to Santiago de Compostela and, later, a Protestant stronghold (1576–1623). Figeac's most illustrious son is the brilliant linguist and founder of the science of Egyptology, Jean-François Champollion (see the boxed text 'Champollion the Egyptologist').

Orientation
The town spreads on either side of the River Célé. The old quarter, on the north-ern side, is characterised by narrow streets and several intimate squares, notably place Carnot. The train station is 600m south of town.

Information
The tourist office (☎ 05 65 34 06 25, fax 05 65 50 04 58, e figeac@wanadoo.fr) is in Hôtel de la Monnaie on place Vival. It opens 10am to noon and 2.30pm to 6pm Monday to Saturday; it also opens 10am to 1pm on Sunday in May and June. It opens 10am to 1pm and 2pm to 7.30pm daily July to mid-September. Worthwhile free publications are its *Pays de Figeac et Cajarc* booklet and a *Ville d'Art et d'Histoire* leaflet (available in English) with a suggested walking route round the old town.

The office organises guided visits (adult/child €3.80/2.30) at 4.30pm almost every Wednesday and Saturday from April to September (at 5pm daily except on Saturday in July and August).

Maps and topoguides are available at the Maison de la Presse, 2 rue Gambetta, open Monday to Saturday and Sunday morning.

Allo Laverie laundry at 23 rue Orthabadial (behind the tourist office) is open 6am to 10pm daily.

Champollion the Egyptologist
Jean-François Champollion (1790-1832), a brilliant academic and linguist from Figeac, became a history professor at the age of 19 and went on to unravel the mysteries of Egyptian hieroglyphics – considered until then to be just decorative pictures. The breakthrough came in 1822 when Champollion deciphered the Greek and Egyptian inscriptions on a basalt tablet dubbed the Rosetta Stone, discovered in Egypt in 1799. After deciphering many more ancient texts in Egypt to prove his theory worked – that hieroglyphics were simultaneously 'figurative, symbolic and phonetic' – he became the first curator of the Egyptology Museum he founded at the Louvre, working and lecturing on the language of the pharaohs until his early death.

Medical Services & Emergency

The Centre Hospitalier (☎ 05 65 50 65 50) is at 33 rue des Maquisards. The main police station (☎ 05 65 34 17 17) is on rue de la Pintre, 4km west of the town centre; there's a more central post (☎ 05 65 50 73 73) at the Cité Administrative, av Casimir.

Post & Communications

The post office, at 6 av Fernand Pezet, offers currency exchange and Internet facilities. Banks include Crédit Agricole, at No 9 on the same street and Crédit Lyonnais, at 33 rue Gambetta.

You can also access the Internet at Bar Musical L'Expérience (☎ 05 65 34 00 57), 10 av Emile Bouyssou, for €3.05 per half-hour. It opens 10am to 2am Monday to Saturday.

Things to See

The name of the handsome 13th-century building that houses the tourist office, **Hôtel de la Monnaie** (*Oustal de la Mounédo* in Occitan) refers to the Royal Mint that Figeac was granted by Philippe IV, though money was only exchanged here, not minted. It is one of the finest Gothic secular buildings in

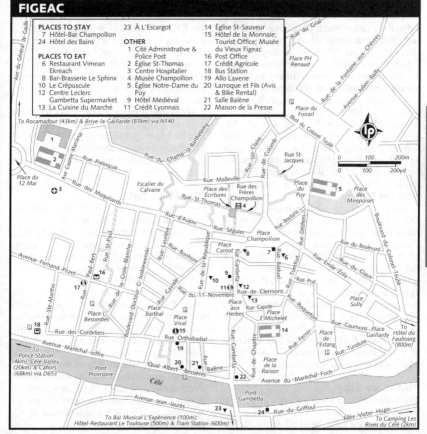

FIGEAC

PLACES TO STAY
7   Hôtel-Bar Champollion
24 Hôtel des Bains

PLACES TO EAT
6   Restaurant Vimean Ekreach
8   Bar-Brasserie Le Sphinx
10 Le Crêpuscule
12 Centre Leclerc Gambetta Supermarket
13 La Cuisine du Marché

23 À L'Escargot

OTHER
1   Cité Administrative & Police Post
2   Église St-Thomas
3   Centre Hospitalier
4   Musée Champollion
5   Église Notre-Dame du Puy
9   Hôtel Médiéval
11 Crédit Lyonnais

14 Église St-Sauveur
15 Hôtel de la Monnaie; Tourist Office; Musée du Vieux Figeac
16 Post Office
17 Crédit Agricole
18 Bus Station
19 Allo Laverie
20 Larroque et Fils (Avis & Bike Rental)
21 Salle Balène
22 Maison de la Presse

LOT & LOT-ET-GARONNE

Quercy with its arcade of arches and traditional *soleilho* (covered rooftop terrace used for drying clothes and food). Upstairs is the **Musée du Vieux Figeac** (☎ *05 65 34 06 25; adult/child €1.50/0.75*) which has a varied collection of antique clocks, coins, minerals and a propeller blade made by a local aerospace firm. It is open the same hours as the tourist office.

The privately owned **Hôtel Médiéval** (☎ *05 65 50 15 47, 41 rue Gambetta; adult/student/child €4.25/3.35/2.30; open variable times July-Oct, Dec & school holidays*) is a former Knights Templar commandery with a fine Gothic facade. Guided visits are given five times daily during opening hours (call for exact times). Nearby is the picturesque old market square **place Carnot** and the adjacent **place Champollion**, once hosting major chestnut markets. Off here, on tiny rue des Frères Champollion, is the childhood home of Jean-François Champollion, now the **Musée Champollion** (☎ *05 65 50 31 08, rue des Frères Champollion; adult/senior/student & child €3.05/2.60/1.85; open 10am-noon, 2.30pm-6.30pm Tues-Sun Mar-June & Sept-Oct; 10am-noon, 2.30pm-6.30pm daily July-Aug; 2pm-6pm Tues-Sun Nov-Feb*), with a small collection of Egyptian antiquities. An enlarged copy of the Rosetta Stone fills the ground of the adjacent ancient courtyard of **place des Écritures**.

North of place Champollion, **rue de Colomb** is lined with centuries-old mansions in sandstone, half-timber and brick. Continue up rue St-Jacques for good views of the town from **Église Notre Dame du Puy**, a Romanesque church with many 17th-century additions. Near the river, the musty **Église St-Sauveur**, on rue du Chapitre, a Benedictine abbey church built between the 12th and the 14th centuries, still has many of its original features. The nearby 14th-century **Salle Balène** (or **Hôtel de Balène**), at 8 rue Balène, a fortress-like building, now hosts plays and exhibitions.

Places to Stay
The following are some decent choices for the area.

Les Rives du Célé (☎ *05 65 34 59 00, fax 05 65 34 20 80, Le Domaine du Surgié*) 2-person forfait €10.20-14.50. This riverside place, at the far end of a huge leisure park 2km east of town, has a swimming pool and tennis courts.

Hôtel du Faubourg (☎ *05 65 34 21 82, fax 05 65 34 24 19, 59 Faubourg du Pin*) Doubles with shower €27.45-32, without €22.85. This hotel, on the noisy N122, has clean, fragrant rooms.

Hôtel-Restaurant Le Toulouse (☎/fax *05 65 34 22 95, 4 av de Toulouse*) Doubles with shower €32, without €27.45. The Toulouse, on the busy D922, 500m south of town, has nothing-special but adequate rooms.

Hôtel des Bains (☎ *05 65 34 10 89, fax 05 65 14 00 45,* e *hotel-des-bains@ wanadoo.fr, 1 rue du Griffoul*) Doubles with shower €36.60-57.95, without €25.90, triples €51.85-74.70. This efficient and welcoming 21-room hotel is the best bargain in town, with brightly decorated rooms overlooking the river.

Hôtel-Bar Champollion (☎ *05 65 34 04 37, fax 05 65 34 61 69, 3 place Champollion*) Double/triples with shower €41.15/44.20. The chic, 10-room Champollion, in the heart of the old city, has tastefully decorated rooms and a popular cafe-bar.

Places to Eat
For good meals or snacks, try the following.

Bar-Brasserie Le Sphinx (☎ *05 65 50 07 36, 7 place Carnot*) Dishes €6.70-9.25. This casual cafe-brasserie serves bargain fare in a surprisingly smart restaurant; for regional specialities, try the *assiette du terroir* (local dish) (€13.70).

Le Crépuscule (☎ *05 65 34 28 53, 4 rue de la République*) Pizzas & pastas €4.75-8.40. Open midday & evening Mon-Sat, evening only Sun. Modest diners may like this eatery, which serves fresh pasta dishes, salads and pancakes.

Restaurant Vimean Ekreach (☎ *05 65 34 79 65, 10 rue Baduel*) Midday menus €8.40, evening menus €12.95-19.05, dishes €5.35-7.30. Open Tues-Sun. Choose from a great selection of bargain Chinese dishes at this popular restaurant.

À l'Escargot (☎ *05 65 34 23 84, 2 Av Jean Jaurès) Menus* €13.40-25.90, dishes €8.70-13.70. Open midday & evening Tues-Sun, midday only Mon. This smart restaurant, which has been run by the same family since 1950, not only specialises in dishes featuring *escargots* (snails) but also serves family-style Quercy cuisine.

La Cuisine du Marché (☎ *05 65 50 18 55, 15 rue de Clermont)* Midday *menus* €13.70, evening *menus* €20.60-28.95. Open Mon-Sat. This is one of the town's best restaurants where you can splurge on a gourmand *menu*.

The *Centre Leclerc Gambetta* supermarket (open Mon-Sat) is at 32 rue Gambetta. There's a Saturday morning *food market* on place Carnot.

Getting There & Away
The SNCF (☎ 08 36 35 35 35) bus from Cahors (€9.75, 1¼ hours, four or five times daily) via Tour de Faure (St-Cirq Lapopie) stops at Figeac's train and bus stations.

The train station (☎ 05 65 80 29 06, staffed from 4am to midnight), is on two major rail lines: the one that links Toulouse (€17.70, 2¼ hours, five daily) with Clermont-Ferrand (€23.80, four hours, three to five daily); and the one from Paris' Gare d'Austerlitz (€48, about six hours, five daily, two of them direct) to Rodez via Brive-la-Gaillarde (€11.25, 1½ hours, five daily) and Rocamadour-Padirac (€6.40, about 30 minutes).

Getting Around
The Larroque et Fils garage, at 10 quai Albert Bessières, has an Avis car-rental office (☎ 05 65 34 10 28) where you can also rent mountain bikes for €13.70/68.60 per day/week. It opens Monday to Friday and Saturday morning.

WEST OF CAHORS
West of Cahors, the River Lot loops and wriggles all the way to Fumel past rich AOC Cahors vineyard estates. A free map with contact details for visiting chateaux and wine-tasting is available from local, or Cahors, tourist offices, or the Maison du

Vin (☎ 05 65 23 22 24, fax 05 65 23 22 27), at 430 av Jean Jaurès, Cahors.

You can hire houseboats on this stretch of the river from **Locaboat Plaisance** (☎ *05 65 30 71 11, fax 05 65 30 53 17)* at their base in Luzech (see the Agen section for sample rates). For canoes and kayaks, contact **Le Lot Canoe-Kayak** (☎ *05 65 36 27 39, fax 05 65 21 41 00,* ⓔ *campingfloiras@aol.com),* at nearby Anglars Juillac.

Puy L'Évêque
postcode 46700 • pop 2160 • elevation 85m
One of the most picturesque spots between Cahors and Fumel, tiny Puy l'Évêque clusters high above the Lot. Cahors *évêques* (bishops) seized the town in the 13th century, building a castle; the **keep** is the only bit left, but the sturdy 14th- to 15th-century **Église St-Sauveur** and the medieval houses in the steep narrow lanes are worth a look.

The tourist office (☎ 05 65 21 37 63, fax 05 65 36 40 40), on the ground floor of the attractive Mairie (town hall), in place de la Truffière at the top end of town, is open 9am to 12.30pm Monday and Saturday, and 8.30am to 12.30pm, 2pm to 5.30pm Tuesday to Friday (9am to 12.30pm, 2pm to 6.30pm Monday to Saturday in July and August).

Places to Stay & Eat Here are some options for an overnight stay.

Camping de la Plage (☎ *05 65 30 81 72, fax 05 65 30 85 89)* Adult/pitch €3.80/4.10. Open Apr-Oct. This site is set among vineyards by the river 4km west of town.

Hôtel-Restaurant La Truffière (☎ *05 65 21 34 54, fax 05 65 30 84 47, route de Fumel)* Doubles €28.20-38.10. Midday *menus* in brasserie/restaurant €9.90/11.45, evening *menus* €15.25-23.65. Just 100m west of the Mairie, the Truffière offers bargain fare in its brasserie and Quercy specialities in its restaurant, such as *salade quercynois*, salad with duck gizzards; €6.40.

Hôtel Bellevue (☎ *05 65 36 06 60, fax 05 65 36 06 61, place de la Truffière)* Doubles €56.40-79.25. *Menus* €29.70-39.65, dishes €11.45-28.20. This classy new place by the Mairie boasts deluxe rooms and a great view over the valley from its restaurant.

LOT & LOT-ET-GARONNE

Restaurant Le Fournil (☎ 05 65 36 45 15, 24 Grand'Rue) Midday *menus* €11.45, evening *menus* €15.10-19.65. Open daily (except Tues out of season). Le Fournil is a chic little place on the main street offering some particularly imaginative salads.

Getting There & Away The SNCF Cahors (€5.20, 45 minutes) to Fumel (€3.35, 25 minutes) bus stops here around eight times daily.

Château de Bonaguil

This ruined but still imposing fortress-chateau *(☎ 05 53 49 59 76, St-Front-sur-Lémance, Fumel, adult/those aged 7-16 €4.55/3.05; open 10.30am-noon & 2.30pm-6.30pm daily May, Sept-Nov; 10.30am-noon & 2.30pm-5pm daily Feb-Apr; 10am-noon & 2pm-5pm daily June; 10am-5.45pm daily July-Aug)* is set in dreamy countryside on the path of the GR36, about 18km north-west of Puy l'Évêque and 8km north-east of Fumel. Built in the 13th century, in the mid-15th century it fell into the hands of the cruel, megalomaniac Bérenger de Rocquefeuil who transformed it into an impregnable fortress against his many imagined enemies. Even designed to deflect modern cannon fire, it wasn't touched until the Revolution. A vast moat, an enormous barbican, huge towers and a towering, vessel-shaped keep still seem haunted by their owner's paranoia.

There are English-language guided visits at 11am, 2pm and 4pm daily Sunday to Friday and night-time illuminations until midnight daily during July and August.

Lot-et-Garonne

VILLENEUVE-SUR-LOT
postcode 47300 • pop 24,100
• elevation 150m

Dominated by its red-brick church tower, this old bastide, founded in 1253 and once one of the most powerful in the region, is now surrounded by a busy modern commercial town, with a thriving trade in *primeurs* (early vegetables) and fruit (especially plums). There's not a lot to see or do in the town itself, but it makes a useful base for visiting the hamlets and bastides of the Haut Pays des Serres to the south and several pretty villages along the Lot to the east.

Orientation

The old town fits snugly between the Lot to the south and a strip of broad boulevards (with three different names) to the north. Two ancient gateways still stand: porte de Paris in the middle of the boulevards to the north-east and porte de Pujols across the river to the south-west. Rue de Paris and parallel rue des Cieutat are the main pedestrianised shopping streets.

Information

The tourist office (☎ 05 53 36 17 30, fax 05 53 49 42 98 **e** tourisme@ville-villeneuve -sur-lot.fr), on blvd Georges Leygues (opposite the grandiose Théâtre Georges Leygues), is open 9am to noon and 2pm to 6pm Monday to Friday (to 5pm on Saturday). It opens 9am to 7pm Monday to Saturday and 10am to noon Sunday during July and August.

There's a Bureau d'Information Jeunesse (☎ 05 53 41 84 60), at 29 rue des Cieutat, open 9am to noon, 2pm to 5pm Monday to Friday. Banks include Crédit Agricole, at 31 rue de Paris.

A self-service laundry, open 7am to 9pm daily, is at 35 rue Arnaud Daubasse (off rue des Cieutat).

Post & Communication

The main post office, by pont Neuf (also called pont de la Libération), has currency exchange and Internet facilities.

Internet access is also available at Difintel Micro (☎ 05 53 36 15 44), 25 rue des Cieutat, for €3.05 per half-hour. It opens 10am to noon, 2pm to 7pm Tuesday to Saturday.

Pont Vieux & Old Town

The town's central bridge over the Lot, **pont Vieux**, was originally built by the English in the 13th century and is reminiscent of the famous pont Valentré at Cahors; it was a major thoroughfare across the Lot on the route to Santiago de Compostela. At the

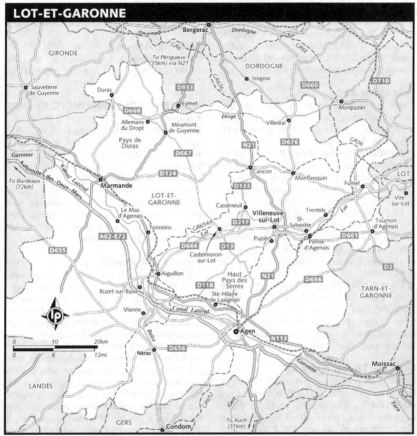

LOT-ET-GARONNE

heart of the old town, **place La Fayette** is a busy square surrounded by attractive arched arcades. Markets are held here on Tuesday and Saturday mornings. Towering over the square is the red-brick **Église Ste-Catherine** built in the 1930s on the site of an earlier Gothic church whose restored 14th- and 15th-century stained glass can still be seen inside.

Special Events
In mid-July, the town hosts a renowned five-day Festival de Jazz (☎ 05 53 36 17 30, W www.jazz.en.villeneuvois@free.fr).

Places to Stay
Your choices for accommodation include the following.

Camping Municipal Le Rooy (☎ 05 53 70 24 18, rue du Rooy) Adult/pitch €2.15/1.50. Open mid-Apr–Oct. This simple, shady site is 1km to the south, off the D661.

Hôtel les Platanes (☎ 05 53 40 11 40, fax 05 53 70 71 95, 40 blvd de la Marine) Singles €24.40-27.45, doubles €27.45-33.55, all with shower. This hotel, near the tourist office, has plain, road-noisy rooms (the pricier ones include WC).

La Résidence (☎ 05 53 40 17 03, fax 05

53 01 57 34, 17 av Lazare-Carnot) Doubles with shower & WC €33.55-39.65, without €22.10, triples with shower & WC €45.75. This immaculate, friendly hotel, 400m south of pont Neuf (near the defunct train station) is an excellent bargain.

Places to Eat

There are several bar-brasseries with decent *menus* from around €12.20 along the boulevards. You can find more atmospheric venues in the old town.

Bar-Brasserie La Mine (☎ 05 53 01 46 61, place La Fayette) Midday *menus* €7.45, evening *menus* €12.20-14.95. Open evening only weekends. La Mine is a popular central rendezvous, serving bargain fare.

Le Parmentier (☎ 05 53 70 35 02, 13 rue Parmentier) Midday *menus* €9.25, evening *menus* €14-24.40, dishes €11.45-30.50. Open Mon-Sat. This smartish restaurant has outdoor tables and an extensive choice of meat dishes.

Chez Caline (☎ 05 53 70 42 08, 2 rue Notre Dame) Menus €11.45-17.55. Bagging the best riverside location is cosy Chez Caline, popular with tourists for its regional fare. It costs 10% more to sit on the terrace.

Getting There & Away

Public transport is very limited. It's often easiest to go first to Agen: SNCF buses run there (€4.90, 45 minutes, up to 10 daily) from the defunct train station 500m south of town (where you can buy SNCF tickets; the office is open 8.30am to 6pm Monday to Friday, 9.30am to 5pm Saturday).

Also leaving from here (and/or the Théâtre opposite the tourist office) are Cars Loiseau (☎ 05 53 40 23 30) buses to Bergerac (€8.40, 1¼ hours, twice daily in term-time, once at other times) and Monflanquin (€2.65, 20 minutes, once daily in term-time only). The company's information office, at 1 place du 4 Septembre (near the post office), is open 9am to noon and 3pm to 7pm Monday to Friday (6.30am to noon Saturday).

Cars Evasion (☎ 05 53 40 88 20) run a twice-daily service to Fumel (€3.80, 40 minutes) except in July or August. The stop

is opposite the hospital on blvd Bernard Palissy (just north of place du 4 Septembre).

Getting Around

The tourist office rents VTTs for €13.70/67.05 per day/week. For a taxi call ☎ 05 53 70 43 31.

AROUND VILLENEUVE-SUR-LOT
Pujols

On a hilltop with fabulous views, 2km south-west of Villeneuve-sur-Lot (a pleasant walk from porte de Pujols), this pretty medieval village is a honey-trap for tourists and antique-lovers, with many art and antique shops in its lovingly restored half-timbered houses. Check out the **St-Nicholas bell tower** whose archway serves as the main entrance, and the faded 15th-century frescoes in **Église Ste-Foy-la-Jeune**.

Penne d'Agenais

Eight kilometres upriver from Villeneuve-sur-Lot, this is another picturesque *village perché* (hilltop village), its steep lanes of brick and half-timbered cottages kept immaculately tidy all year and dripping with honeysuckle and roses in summer. It was once the site of a fortress founded by Richard the Lion-Heart and a Cathar stronghold, both affiliations attracting savage attacks, repeated during the Wars of Religion. You can see the huge basilica of its church, **Notre Dame de Peyragude**, from miles around. Close up, it's a bit of a disappointment, a 19th-century neo-Byzantine affair to replace its predecessor, once an important pilgrimage stop on the route to Compostela, and destroyed during the Revolution.

The tourist office (☎ 05 53 41 37 80, fax 05 53 41 40 86), at rue du 14 Juillet, just inside the main gateway, is open 9am to 12.30pm and 3pm to 6pm Monday to Saturday and 3pm to 6pm on Sunday (2pm to 6pm daily in low season).

Tournon d'Agenais

This imposing 13th-century hilltop bastide, 26km east of Villeneuve-sur-Lot, is better from the outside than in, thanks to its towering white ramparts, now turned into houses. There are grand views from the **Chemin de Ronde** (around the ramparts) of the surrounding Haut Pays des Serres. In the village itself, the most famous thing to try is *tourtière,* a round flaky apple or prune pie (often sold at markets throughout the region). There's even a fete in its honour in mid-August.

The tourist office (☎ 05 53 40 75 82, fax 05 53 40 76 98), right in the village centre, operates 8am to noon and 1.30pm to 5.30pm weekdays only (to 5pm on Friday). Shops are more plentiful in the new town development on the D656 below.

Places to Stay & Eat There are a couple of hotel-restaurant choices in the area.

Hôtel-Restaurant Les Voyageurs (☎ 05 53 40 70 28, fax 05 53 70 28 85, route de Cahors) Doubles with/without bath €32/21.35. *Menus* €9.90-12.95. This busy little place is in the newer part of Tournon d'Agenais, down at the junction of the D656 and D661, and has simple rooms and a decent restaurant.

Hôtel-Restaurant Le Compostelle (☎ 05 53 41 12 41, fax 05 53 41 00 20, rue Jean Moulin) Doubles €44.20-53.35, triples €57.95-68.60. This spick-and-span modern hotel has an incongruous location in a modern residential district 800m below Penne d'Agenais.

Getting There & Away The Villeneuve-sur-Lot to Fumel bus (☎ 05 53 40 88 20) stops at St-Sylvestre, 2km across the river from Penne d'Agenais (€2.30, 10 minutes, one daily). No buses go to Tournon d'Agenais (but it's on the GR652).

MONFLANQUIN
postcode 47150 • pop 2340 • elevation 181m
This beautifully preserved hilltop bastide, 17km north-east of Villeneuve-sur-Lot, is one of the finest examples of its kind. It was founded in 1256 by the indefatigable brother of King Louis IX, Alphonse de Poitiers, who strengthened the French hold on the region by also establishing Villeréal, Villeneuve-sur-Lot as well as a dozen other bastides.

Information
The Maison du Tourisme office (☎ 05 53 36 40 19, fax 05 53 36 42 91, ⓔ office .de.tourisme.monflanquin@wanadoo.fr), on place des Arcades, is open 10am to noon and 2pm to 6pm Monday to Friday, 10am to noon and 3pm to 5pm on Saturday and 3pm to 5pm on Sunday (closed Monday morning and by 5pm weekdays between November and March). It opens 10am to 12.30pm and 2.30pm to 7pm daily during July and August.

In summer, the office organises group visits of the bastide at 6pm (€2.30) and/or 9.30pm (€3.05) Monday to Thursday, led by a costumed guide.

Things to See & Do
At the heart of Monflanquin is the unspoiled **place des Arcades**, surrounded by *cornières* (arched arcades) and dominated by a fortified 15th-century **church**. Every Thursday morning, a lively market takes place here, supplemented in summer with a smaller farmers' market on Wednesday and Saturday.

Upstairs from the tourist office is the excellent **Musée des Bastides** *(same ☎ and opening hours as the tourist office; adult/child under 12 €3.05/free)*, with interactive displays (listen to troubadour songs or the medieval chants of pilgrims) and explanations (including in English) on all aspects of bastide life.

Places to Stay & Eat
Monflanquin has just a few places to offer.

Camping de Coulon (☎ 05 53 36 47 35, fax 05 53 36 47 36, route de Cancon) 2-person forfait €7.60-9.45. Open June-Oct. This 120-pitch grassy camping ground, 2.2km west of Monflanquin, is part of the Site Touristique de Coulon (see below). You get free use of the Site's pool in July and August and two free entries per adult per week to the Espace Forme (fitness centre) facilities.

Site Touristique de Coulon (☎ 05 53 36 47 35, fax 05 53 36 40 29, www.espace -forme-47.com, route de Cancon) Doubles/triples €39.65/48.80. The Site offers plain, modern rooms, but guests can use the Espace Forme facilities for €6.10 extra.

Hôtel L'Entrecôte (☎ 05 53 36 40 01,

fax 05 53 01 75 17, av de la Libération) Doubles €27.45. Midday *menus* €9.90, evening *menus* €11.45-25, pizzas €5.35-9.30. L'Entrecôte, 200m to the south, on the D676, has road-noisy rooms but a good-value restaurant (the midday *menu* includes wine and coffee).

Le Bistrot du Prince Noir (☎ 05 53 36 63 00, place des Arcades) Midday *menus* €9.25, evening *menus* €13.70-21.35. This long-popular *bistrot* serves excellent regional specialities in a prime central location.

Getting There & Away
On weekdays in term-time only, there's a once-daily Villeneuve-sur-Lot to Monflanquin bus (☎ 05 53 40 23 30; €2.65, 20 minutes), which stops 400m south of place des Arcades by a car park. In holidays it runs on Thursday only. For a taxi, call ☎ 05 53 36 31 08.

VILLERÉAL
postcode 47210 • pop 1250 • elevation 120m
This untouristy bastide market town is 13km north of Monflanquin by the River Dropt. Its spacious central square, place de la Halle, has a picturesque 14th-century timbered **covered market**, overlooked by an impressive fortified twin-towered 13th-century **church**. The tourist office (☎ 05 53 36 09 65, fax 05 53 36 00 37, e ot.villereal@ wanadoo.fr, w www.aavie.com/villereal), on place de la Halle, is open 10am to noon and 2pm to 9pm daily between mid-June and mid-September (9am to noon and 2pm to 6pm daily Tuesday to Saturday and afternoon only Monday at other times).

Places to Stay & Eat
Villéreal makes a pleasant overnight stop. Try one of the following.

Camping du Pesquie-Bas (☎ 05 53 36 05 63, fax 05 53 36 09 55, route d'Issigeac) Adult/pitch/car €3.20/4.70/1.85. Open May-Oct. This 53-pitch camp site, 600m west of Villéreal, is part of a Complexe Touristique, with a small lake and tennis courts.

Hôtel-Restaurant de L'Europe (☎ 05 53 36 00 35, place Jean Moulin) Doubles with shower & WC €27.45-33.55, without

€24.40. Midday *menus* €10, evening *menus* €16.95-27.45, dishes €6.85-16.95. This excellent-value hotel-restaurant, next to the church, has well kept, spacious rooms and friendly service.

Getting There & Away
One bus daily in term-time (once weekly at other times; ☎ 05 53 40 23 30) connects Villéreal with Villeneuve-sur-Lot (€3.60, one hour). For taxis, call ☎ 05 53 36 62 97.

Getting Around
Bikes can be rented (☎ 05 53 36 01 21) from a garage-workshop 500m north of town on the D207 (route d'Issigeac) for €10.65/38.10 per day/week. It opens Tuesday to Saturday.

DURAS
postcode 47120 • pop 1240 • elevation 120m
Set in the drowsy valley of the River Dropt, this little hilltop town makes a pleasant base for a couple of days' exploration in the surrounding Pays de Duras – a region famed for its wines, bastides and Romanesque churches. There's nothing much to see or do in the town itself after you've delved into the depths of the Château des Ducs de Duras so try and time your visit for a Monday when at least the market makes the place buzz a bit.

Orientation & Information
The chateau dominates the western edge of town, with the tourist office (☎ 05 53 83 63 06, fax 05 53 83 65 45), on blvd Jean Brisseau, on the northern side (near Hostellerie des Ducs). It opens 9am to 12.30pm and 1.30pm to 6pm Monday to Saturday (daily until 7pm between mid-June and mid-September). The office promotes the area's fine Côtes de Duras wines with a pamphlet detailing all the *caves particulières* (wineries); it also offers free tastings. Among useful publications available here is *Châteaux et Bastides en Haut-Agenais* (€6.10).

Château des Ducs de Duras
This imposing chateau (☎ 05 53 83 77 32, *blvd Jean Brisseau; adult/student/child*

€4.25/3.35/2.30; open 10am-7pm daily June-Sept; 10am-noon & 2pm-6pm Oct; 10am-noon & 2pm-7pm Apr & May; 2pm-6pm Nov-Mar) dates from the 12th century but was in ruins by the 20th. Taken over and restored by the town, its rambling halls now host exhibitions, musical events and displays (including one on the novelist Marguerite de Duras whose memories of a happy childhood here inspired her to take Duras as a pen-name). The ethnological museum in the basement is more engaging, with its huge grape presses, threshers, ploughs and prune harvesting implements.

Allemans du Dropt
One of the best excursions from Duras is to this charming little village 9km to the east, famous for the extraordinary 15th-century frescoes in its church depicting lively devils and gruesome goings-on. It opens 9am to noon, 2pm to 6.30pm daily (€0.75 for lighting), closed to visitors during mass on Saturday (10am to noon) and Sunday (6pm). The tourist office (☎/fax 05 53 20 25 59), on adjacent place de la Liberté, is open 10am-noon (variable afternoon hours) Tuesday to Saturday (9.30am to noon, 3pm to 6pm Tuesday to Saturday in July and August).

Places to Stay & Eat
Choices here include the following.

Camping Municipal Le Château (☎ 05 53 83 70 18, fax 05 53 83 65 20, blvd Jean Brisseau) Adult/pitch €2.35/1.50. Open July-Aug only; other times on request. This basic, 20-pitch site is right at the foot of the castle.

Auberge du Château (☎ 05 53 83 70 58, fax 05 53 93 95 64, place Jean Bousquet) Doubles/quads €25.90/39.65. Midday *menus* €10.65, evening *menus* €13.70-19. Restaurant open Thur-Tues. The Auberge, opposite the Château, has plain rooms but a locally popular restaurant.

Hostellerie des Ducs (☎ 05 53 83 74 58, fax 05 53 83 75 03, 20 blvd Jean Brisseau) Doubles €33.40-61.75 (€55.35-73.95 with air-conditioning). Midday *menus* €13.40, evening *menus* €19.50-45.40. Restaurant open midday & evening Tues-Fri, evening only Sat, midday only Sun. Near the tourist office is this posh Logis de France property which boasts a swimming pool and pleasant garden.

Don Camillo (☎ 05 53 83 76 00, 4 rue Paul Persil) Pizzas & pastas €5.95-11.75. Open Wed-Mon. Opposite the MBK bike shop, Don Camillo is small and simple but serves decent, cheap fare.

Getting There & Away
The nearest train station is Marmande, 23km to the south, on the Agen (€7.95, 30 minutes, 12 daily) to Bordeaux (€10.35, 45 minutes, 15 daily) line. A taxi (☎ 05 53 83 07 87) from Marmande to Duras should cost around €27.45.

SARL Cars Bleus (☎ 05 53 23 81 92) run once-daily between Marmande and Bergerac via Allemans du Dropt (€5.55, 30 minutes).

Getting Around
MBK bike shop (☎ 05 53 83 72 05), on rue Paul Persil (100m south of the tourist office), rents mountain bikes for €12.20/53.35 per day/week. It's open Monday to Friday and Saturday morning.

AGEN
postcode 47000 • pop 32,200
• elevation 50m
To the French, Agen means one thing: prunes. This lively university capital of the Lot-et-Garonne department, on the banks of the River Garonne and Canal Latéral, is the centre of the famous *pruneaux d'Agen* trade (see the boxed text 'Prunes Galore'), a busy commercial town with horrid outskirts. There's little left of its history as a Roman oppidum (defensive town) and Hundred Years' War target (it changed hands between the French and English 11 times), but it's got a good supply of accommodation and restaurants and a renowned rugby team, the Sporting Union Agénais (SUA). It has one big cultural gem: the Musée des Beaux-Arts. Or to amuse the kids, try Walibi Parc d'Attractions, the region's biggest amusement park.

Orientation
The principal shopping street, blvd de la République, runs for 1.1km from place

Jasmin to place du 14 Juillet (also called place du Pin). The Garonne is crossed by pont de Pierre (600m south of town) while the handsome 23-arched, 19th-century Pont Canal aqueduct carries the Canal Latéral over the river 1.5km north-west of place Jasmin. There are pleasant paths (good for biking) beside the river and canal, especially by the peristyle du Gravier and the port de Plaisance (riverboat base).

Information

Tourist Offices The tourist office (☎ 05 53 47 36 09, fax 05 53 47 29 98, **e** otsi .agen@wanadoo.fr), at 107 blvd du Président Carnot, is open 9am to 12.30pm and 2pm to 6.30pm Monday to Saturday (9am to 7pm between July and September) and 10am to noon on Sunday. At 9pm on Thursday and at 6pm on Monday mid-July to September it organises free one-hour tours of the town.

The regional Comité Départemental du Tourisme du Lot-et-Garonne (☎ 05 53 66 14 14, fax 05 53 68 25 42, **e** cdt47@ wanadoo.fr), at 4 rue André Chénier, is only useful if you need specific information on the department. It opens 9am to noon and 2pm to 5pm Monday to Friday. Maison de la Presse is at 65 blvd de la République.

Money Banks include Crédit Lyonnais, at 58 blvd de la République and Crédit Agricole, at 108 blvd du Président Carnot.

Post & Communications The main post office, on blvd du Président Carnot, has currency exchange and Internet facilities. Internet access is also available for €1.52 per hour at Le Florida community hall (☎ 05 53 47 59 54), at 167 blvd du Président Carnot, open 9am to 7pm Tuesday to Saturday. At the time of research, Internity (☎ 05 53 66 93 99), at 90 blvd de la République, was soon to open a cybercafe.

Laundry Lavarie Speed Wash, in the covered market complex, is open 7am to 10pm daily.

Medical Services & Emergency Centre Hospitalier Agen (hospital; ☎ 05 53 69 70

71), at 21 route Villeneuve, is 3km north-east of the town centre, off the N21. The main police station (☎ 05 53 69 30 00) is 2km to the south, at 15 rue Valence.

Musée des Beaux-Arts

Next to the over-the-top Théâtre Municipal on place Dr Esquirol, this is one of the finest provincial museums in the country, housed in 16th- and 17th-century mansions (☎ 05 53 69 47 23, place Dr Esquirol; adult/students & those under 18 €3.05/free; open 10am-6pm Wed-Mon, closing at 5pm Nov-Apr). The collection includes some outstanding Gallo-Roman remains (notably the 1st century BC Vénus de Mas marble statue) and a treasure-trove of 17th- and 18th-century paintings, including five by Goya. Don't miss the upstairs collection of Impressionists, including some memorable scenes by Eugène Boudin.

Activities

From Port de Plaisance, 90-minute trips along the Canal Latéral on the **L'Agenais tourist boat** (☎ 05 53 87 51 95, port de Plaisance; adult/child aged 5-13 €5.95/ 3.50) take place twice daily except Monday (2.30pm and 5pm; plus 11am on Saturday

---

Prunes Galore

Prunes are big business in the Lot-et-Garonne, especially around Agen, which has given its name to the famous dried *pruneaux d'Agen* – despite the fact that they mostly come from just north of the River Lot, 40km away. Originally introduced from the Middle East by crusaders, the area's *prunier d'ente* plum trees produce some 30,000 tonnes of plums a year, 65% of France's total output.

You can try them served as *galette aux pruneaux* (pancakes), *pruneaux fourrés* (stuffed with almond paste or chocolate), soaked in Armagnac, or distilled into an *eau de vie* (brandy). For more temptations, trawl the speciality shops in Agen. Several offer free *dégustation* (tasting) – including La Confiserie P Boisson, at 20 rue Grande Horloge, which has been making prune delicacies since 1835.

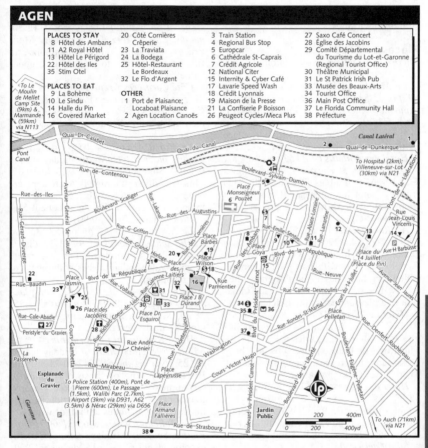

AGEN

PLACES TO STAY
8 Hôtel des Ambans
11 A2 Royal Hôtel
13 Hôtel Le Périgord
22 Hôtel des Iles
35 Stim Otel

PLACES TO EAT
9 La Bohème
10 Le Sindu
14 Halle du Pin
16 Covered Market

20 Côté Cornières
    Crêperie
23 La Traviata
24 La Bodega
25 Hôtel-Restaurant
    Le Bordeaux
32 Le Flo d'Argent

OTHER
1 Port de Plaisance;
    Locaboat Plaisance
2 Agen Location Canoës

3 Train Station
4 Regional Bus Stop
5 Europcar
6 Cathédrale St-Caprais
7 Crédit Agricole
12 National Citer
15 Internity & Cyber Café
17 Lavarie Speed Wash
18 Crédit Lyonnais
19 Maison de la Presse
21 La Confiserie P Boisson
26 Peugeot Cycles/Meca Plus

27 Saxo Café Concert
28 Église des Jacobins
29 Comité Départemental
    du Tourisme du Lot-et-Garonne
    (Regional Tourist Office)
30 Théâtre Municipal
31 Le St Patrick Irish Pub
33 Musée des Beaux-Arts
34 Tourist Office
36 Main Post Office
37 Le Florida Community Hall
38 Préfecture

and Sunday) during July and August, twice-daily (2.30pm and 4.30pm) on Wednesday and Sunday in June and September, and Sunday only (2.30pm and 4.30pm) during April, May and October. There are also special 'Croisières Musicales' musical cruises, with live music, one or two Sundays a month from April to August (€13.55/9.60 per adult/child).

If you want to cruise the waters yourself, contact **Agen Location Canoës** (☎ 05 53 66 18 49, Quai de Dunkerque; canoes/kayaks €9.25/7.60 per hour daily July-Aug; Sat & Sun Sept) or **Locaboat Plaisance** (☎ 05 53 66

00 74, port de Plaisance; reservations ☎ 03 86 91 72 72, fax 03 86 62 42 41, ⓔ info@locaboat.com, ⓦ www.locaboat.com; Pénichettes 2-person houseboat €546/1211 per weekend/week in the high season.

Walibi Parc d'Attractions This huge amusement park (☎ 05 53 96 58 32, route de Nérac; adult/child 1m-1.4m high €20.60/10.20; open 10am-6pm Sat & Sun & occasional Wed late-Apr, May & Sept; generally 10am-9pm daily July-Aug, closed 1-13 July), 2.7km south-west of town, has water rides, seal performances, train rides

LOT & LOT-ET-GARONNE

and other entertainment. Call ahead to confirm opening times.

Places to Stay

There's an excellent cross-section of hotels here.

Le Moulin de Mellet (☎ 05 53 87 50 89, fax 05 53 47 13 41, *e* moulin.mellet@ wanadoo.fr; Ste-Hilaire de Lusignan) Adult/ pitch €3.20/3.80. The nearest camp site, 9km west, is a pleasant, kid-friendly place by the Garonne, shady and calm.

Hôtel des Ambans (☎ 05 53 66 28 60, fax 05 53 87 94 01, 59 rue des Ambans) Singles €22.10-26.70, doubles €24.40-28.95. This friendly hotel has nine small, but decent rooms, all with shower (the pricier ones also have WC).

A2 Royal Hôtel (☎ 05 53 47 28 84, fax 05 53 47 79 04, 129 blvd de la République) Doubles with shower & WC €32, without €25.90 (€36.60 with bath). This central, welcoming hotel has 17 brightly decorated rooms. The pricier ones at the back (adjacent to a pleasant patio) are quieter.

Hôtel Le Périgord (☎ 05 53 77 55 77, fax 05 53 77 55 70, 42 cours du 14 Juillet) Singles €24.40-38.10, doubles €27.45-38.10. This Logis de France property is on a busy crossroads, but rooms are double-glazed. There's free parking nearby.

Hôtel des Iles (☎ 05 53 47 11 33, fax 05 53 66 19 25, 25 rue Baudin) Singles/ doubles/triples €28.95/32/39.65. The quiet Hôtel des Iles is an excellent deal, offering rooms with shower, TV, WC and telephone.

Stim Otel (☎ 05 53 47 31 23, fax 05 53 47 48 70, 105 blvd du Président Carnot) Singles/doubles €47.25/49.55. The Stim hasn't much character but is a reliable, chain hotel. Similar chain hotels are in the Le Passage district, across the river.

Places to Eat

The modern *covered market*, just off place Wilson, is the best place to pick up fresh produce daily. There's also an open-air *market* on Wednesday and on Sunday morning in Halle du Pin (off place du 14 Juillet) and on Saturday morning on the esplanade du Gravier.

La Traviata (☎ 05 53 47 46 79, 39 av du Général de Gaulle) Pizzas €5.35-12.20, menus €8.40-12.95. Open midday Mon-Fri, evening daily. This popular pizzeria fills up fast, thanks to its generous, good-value fare.

Côté Cornières Crêperie (☎ 05 53 66 52 37, 5 rue des Cornières) Pancakes & salads €2.45-7.30. This is a smarter creperie than most, with pleasant seating under the arcades.

Le Flo d'Argent (☎ 05 53 47 23 00, 24 bis, place JB Durand) Midday menus €8.40-9.60, evening menus €13.70-19.05. This friendly restaurant is a great place, open even on Sunday when almost everything else is closed. Try the excellent *brochettes* (kebabs; €6.85-9.90).

Le Sindu (☎ 05 53 66 60 52, 36 rue Emilie Sentini) Menus €9.90-21.20, dishes €4.10-12.20. Le Sindu offers a wide range of good-value Indian dishes with plenty of veggie options.

La Bodega (☎ 05 53 48 26 83, 7 bis place Jasmin) Tapas €3.80-9.25, menus €13.55-18.30. Jovial La Bodega serves tapas and other Spanish specialities.

Hôtel-Restaurant Le Bordeaux (☎ 05 53 68 46 46, 8 place Jasmin) Midday menus €9.25, evening menus €12.20-21.35. The Bordeaux is one of those old-fashioned restaurants where you can expect hearty, traditional fare without fuss or flourish. The midday *menu* includes 250mL of wine.

La Bohème (☎ 05 53 68 31 00, 14 rue Emilie Sentini) Midday menus €10.50, evening menus €15-25.15, dishes €12.20-23.65. Open midday & evening Mon-Tues, Thur-Fri, midday only Wed, evening only Sat. A chic, minimalist place, La Bohème serves excellent regional fare.

Entertainment

For a bit of night-time cheer, check out the following.

Saxo Café Concert (☎ 05 53 48 02 47, 55 peristyle du Gravier) This place offers live music and cheap beer as well as food.

Le St Patrick Irish Pub (☎ 05 53 66 60 61, 6 rue Garonne) Open 3pm to at least 1am Mon-Sat. This is a lively central pub.

Getting There & Away

Air There are one to three flights daily to Paris with Air France/Regional. The tiny airport (☎ 05 53 96 22 50) is 3.5km to the south-west; a taxi to the town centre will cost around €7.60.

Bus SNCF bus services (all leaving from the train station) include Auch (€9.45, 1½ hours, six daily) and Villeneuve-sur-Lot (€4.85, 45 minutes, up to 10 daily). Citram buses run to Nérac (€4.85, 40 minutes, four to five daily Monday to Saturday, fewer during school holidays).

Train Agen is on the Bordeaux (€15.70, 1¼ hours) to Toulouse (€14.35, one hour 10 minutes) line via Montauban (€9.45, 45 minutes) with around a dozen services daily Monday to Saturday. For Cahors, change at Montauban. There are two to three services daily to Périgueux (€17.70, two hours 20 minutes) via Le Buisson (€11.90, one hour 40 minutes). The train station office is open 9am to 7.30pm Monday to Saturday.

Getting Around

For car hire try Europcar (☎ 05 53 47 37 40, 120 blvd du Président Carnot), opposite the train station, or National Citer (☎ 05 53 48 11 04, 100 blvd Sylvain Dumon).

For bike hire try Peugeot Cycles/Meca Plus (☎ 05 53 47 76 76, fax 05 53 47 75 97, 18 av du Général de Gaulle; VTTs for €13.70/67.85 per day/week; open 9am-7pm Monday to Saturday). For a taxi, call ☎ 05 53 98 32 33.

NÉRAC

postcode 47600 • pop 7450
• elevation approx 50m

A pleasant day trip from Agen or a brief stopover, this small town, 27km to the south-west, draws the tourists today mainly for its boat trips along the pretty River Baïse. Its chateau is today a low-key attraction, but it was once the seat of the powerful d'Albret family who turned the tide of French history during the 15th and 16th centuries: Henri d'Albret married the sister of King François I, Marguerite d'Angoulême,

who welcomed poets and Protestant preachers to Nérac. Their daughter, the Protestant bigot Jeanne d'Albret, was to fan the flames of the Wars of Religion while her son, Henri of Navarre, the future King Henri IV, finally had the sense to stop the conflict (for more information see the History section of the Facts about Southwest France chapter).

Orientation & Information

The wide and busy allées d'Albret (D930) runs above (to the west of) town, lined with shops, banks and bar-brasseries. But the heart of town, 100m downhill, is place de l'Hôtel de Ville with its jovial modern clocktower. Just below this, at 9 av Mondenard, is the tourist office (☎ 05 53 65 27 75), open 9am to noon and 2pm to 6pm Tuesday to Sunday (closed Sunday in the low season). The chateau is opposite, overlooking the river.

Things to See & Do

The **Château Henri IV** *(rue Henri IV)* is a shadow of its former self, thanks to 17th-century destruction; only one wing with a loggia of columns is left. Inside is a museum *(☎ 05 53 65 21 11; adult/child €3.05/1.50; open 10am-noon & 2pm-6pm Tues-Sun, 10am-noon & 2pm-7pm Tues-Sun July-Sept)* about the town's history.

The loveliest part of the **old town**, called Petit Nérac, is in the lanes across the river where former tanneries have been restored. By the bridge below the chateau, the extensive royal hunting grounds, **La Garenne**, are now a delightful park.

Activities

To cruise along the Baïse you've got several options, all starting at the quai de la Baïse below the chateau: The **Croisière du Prince Henry** *gabarre (flat-bottomed boat; ☎ 05 53 65 66 66, quai de la Baïse)* does one-hour trips (with commentary) at least twice daily June to September, Sundays only in April, May and October (adult/child aged 4-12 €6.85/4.25). You can also rent your own two-to-four-person gabarre (€68.60/83.85 per half/full day), heading downriver to where the Baïse meets the Canal Latéral at Buzet-sur-Baïse.

If you've got your own transport, an excursion to **Vianne** 10km north, is well worthwhile. Within this 13th-century walled bastide (which has retained its four magnificent towered gateways) are several artisans including a crystal-engraver and glass-blower.

Places to Stay & Eat

Accommodation and restaurants include the following.

Hôtel-Restaurant Le Château (☎ 05 53 65 09 05, fax 05 53 65 89 78, 7 av Mondenard) Singles/doubles €30.50/33.55. *Menus* €15.25-36.60. This traditional Logis de France property, next to the tourist office, has comfortable doubles and a decent, if rather stuffy restaurant.

Les Terraces du Petit Nérac (☎ 05 53 97 02 91, fax 05 53 65 65 98, 7 rue Séderie) Doubles €42.70-53.35. Midday *menus* €10.65, evening *menus* €15.25-38.10. This attractive riverside venue has beautifully decorated rooms.

Au Bon Moulin (☎ 05 53 97 52 41, quai de la Baïse, Vianne) Menus €12.05, daily specials €6.85-12.95. Open daily Apr-Oct, weekends only other times. Whether you arrive by boat or car, this huge, half-ruined former mill by the Baïse in Vianne is a great place to stop for lunch.

Getting There & Away

The bus to Agen runs around four times daily Monday to Saturday (€4.90, 40 minutes); the bus stop is by the clocktower.

Toulouse, Tarn-et-Garonne & Tarn

Toulouse, much of Tarn-et-Garonne and Tarn belong to a part of France that for centuries tried to go its own way: spiritually under the influence of Catharism, politically with the counts of Toulouse and economically on the Canal du Midi.

One side of its persona is Toulouse, the high-tech capital of the Midi-Pyrénées, the Southwest's biggest city and a mainstay of Europe's aerospace industry.

The other side is the 'country' side: a generous landscape of oak forests, limestone plateaus, sunny vineyards and the peaks of the Montagne Noir. The Tarn-et-Garonne *département* (administrative department) alone grows 80% of the region's fruit – melons, plums, table grapes, peaches, nectarines, kiwi fruit, cherries and apples – making it also one of the best places for temporary summer work. For those with an itch to be outdoors – on foot, bicycle, horse or boat – there's the beautiful Parc Naturel Régional du Haute-Languedoc and the gorges and limestone plateaus of the Aveyron River.

Walking is a burgeoning pastime and the GR36, GR46 and GR653 walking trails – the last following a branch of the pilgrim route to Santiago de Compostela – make it easy. Without strong feet or a bike you'll probably need a car since public transport is limited, with bus connections to smaller villages sometimes petering out to nothing.

Note that some small towns on the western borders of Tarn-et-Garonne, which belong temperamentally to Gascony, have been included in the Gers chapter.

Highlights

- Go interplanetary at Cité de l'Espace, Toulouse's amazing space museum and planetarium complex
- Wonder at the Romanesque statuary of Abbaye St-Pierre at Moissac
- Choose between kayaking, walking or cycling through the limestone landscape of the Averyon Gorges
- Explore Le Sidobre's landscape of fantastic granite shapes and gravestone factories
- Stroll beside, or float upon, Europe's oldest operating canal system, the Canal du Midi, now with Unesco World Heritage status

Food Highlights

cassoulet – a rich stew of confit de canard, sausages and haricot beans

sanglier – wild boar from the Forêt de Grésigne

Chasselas – sweet white dessert grape of the Bas-Quercy

Toulouse

postcode 31000 • pop 741,000
• elevation 147m
Toulouse – capital of the Midi-Pyrénées region and *préfecture* (prefecture, capital) of the Haute-Garonne department – is the southwest's largest city. It's renowned for its high-tech industries, including some of Europe's most advanced aerospace facilities.

TOULOUSE

TOULOUSE, TARN-ET-GARONNE & TARN

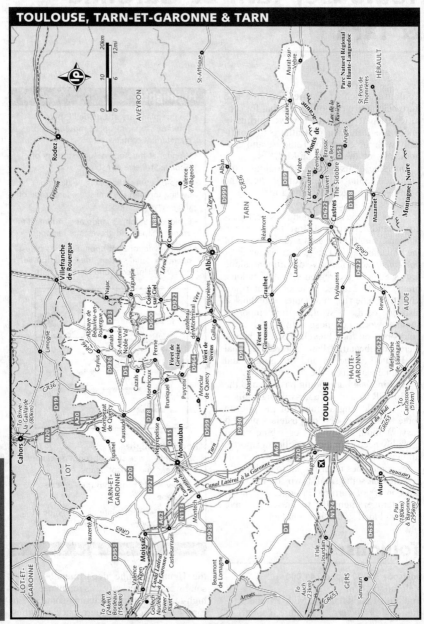

Since the anti-Cathar movement of the 13th century, this has also been a major centre of higher education, with a student population second in size only to Paris.

This sunny, go-getting city has some of the friendliest people you'll meet in France. The telephone book is full of Spanish names (descendants of refugees from the Spanish Civil War) and Toulousains are proud of this ingredient in their collective civic personality, along with a large North African community. This, and the huge student population, provides a nice buzz – and an abundance of *bodegas* (Spanish-style wine bars), North African restaurants and laid-back cafes. Nationwide magazine polls identify Toulouse as most French people's favourite city.

With no quarries nearby, all the older buildings in the centre were built of red brick. Many were smothered in stucco in the 19th century, but it's gradually being stripped away, restoring the city's staid elegance, a certain monotony of colour, and its old nickname, *la ville rose* (the pink city).

HISTORY

The city was born in ancient times at an easy ford of the River Garonne. Known as Tolosa in Roman times, it was the Visigoth capital from AD 418 until it fell to the Merovingians in 508.

In 778 it became the seat of the counts of Toulouse, southern France's greatest feudal dynasty. Even then this was a tolerant city, but the counts' patronage of the Albigensian or Cathar heresy in the 12th and 13th centuries cost them their power base in the Languedoc (see the boxed text 'The Albigensian Crusade' in the Albi section later in this chapter). The Toulouse *parlement* (local court of law) ruled the Languedoc from 1420 until the 1789 Revolution.

During WWI the French government chose Toulouse as a centre for arms and aircraft manufacture. In the 1920s, Antoine de St-Exupéry – best known as the author of *Le Petit Prince* (The Little Prince) – and other daring pilots pioneered mail flights from Toulouse to north-western Africa, the south Atlantic and South America. The government built on this aeronautical base by

making Toulouse the centre of the country's post-WWII aerospace industry.

ORIENTATION

Toulouse's administrative heart is place du Capitole ('place du Cap'). Its human heart is probably place du Président Wilson (or just place Wilson), ringed with cafes and shops. Northwards from place du Capitole to the Basilique St-Sernin runs the student haunt of rue du Taur. To the south is the regional transport hub of place Esquirol.

The main bus station and Gare Matabiau, the train station, are about 1km north-east of place Wilson via allées Jean Jaurès, and the airport is 7km north-west of the city centre. Beneath the centre runs a one-line metro system; to get from the train station to the city centre, take the metro for two stops (direction Basso Cambo) to Capitole.

INFORMATION
Tourist Offices

The tourist office (☎ 05 61 11 02 22, fax 05 61 22 03 63, e ottoulouse@mipnet.fr, w www.ot-toulouse.fr) is in square Charles de Gaulle, in the 16th-century Donjon du Capitole. It opens from 9am to 7pm Monday to Saturday and 10am to noon and 1pm to 6.15pm Sunday June to September; 9am to 6pm Monday to Friday, 9am to 12.30pm and 2pm to 6pm Saturday and 10am to 12.30pm and 2pm to 5pm Sunday October to May.

CRIJ

The Midi-Pyrénées region's Centre Régional d'Information Jeunesse (CRIJ; ☎ 05 62 21 20 20, fax 05 61 27 28 29, e crij-tlse@crij.org), 17 rue de Metz, has a library full of work contacts, information on events, discounts and accommodation, and its own travel agency (selling ISIC student cards and SNCF rail discount cards). The CRIJ is open 10am to 1pm and 2pm to 7pm Monday to Saturday (10am to noon and 2pm to 6pm weekdays only, July to mid-September).

Money

There are banks with exchange facilities and ATMs all over the city centre, including on place du Capitole, square Charles de Gaulle

TOULOUSE

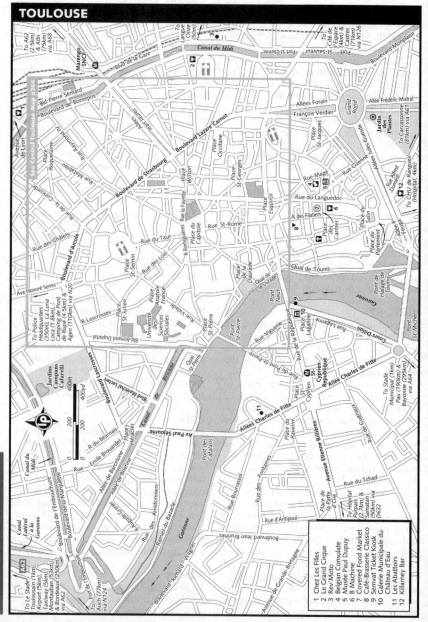

TOULOUSE

1 Chez Les Filles
2 Le Grand Cirque
3 Rev'Moto
4 Belgian Consulate
5 Musée Paul Dupuy
6 B Machine
7 Covered Food Market
8 Café-Brasserie Classico
9 Semvat Ticket Kiosk
10 Galerie Municipale du
   Château d'Eau
11 Les Abattoirs
12 Killarney Bar

TOULOUSE

and rue d'Alsace-Lorraine. A handy one is Crédit Agricole at 3 place du Capitole, open from 9am to 5pm on weekdays. The post office also exchanges foreign currency.

Post & Communication

The main post office is opposite the tourist office at 9 rue La Fayette.

Internet access is free at the CRIJ (see earlier in this section), though you must book hours ahead and there's a one-hour-a-week limit. There are also several cybercafes in town. Blod Station (☎ 05 61 22 54 15), 54 rue Peyrolières, provides Internet access for €0.15/5.34 per minute/hour (€3.80 per hour, 8pm to midnight). It's open noon to midnight Monday to Saturday, 2pm to 8pm on Sunday. Cyber Média-Net (☎ 05 61 23 71 45), 19 rue des Lois, costs €1.50 per 15 minutes (€1.15 students). It's open 9am to 11.30pm weekdays, 10am to midnight on Saturday. Cybermedia (☎ 05 62 73 40 37), 10 rue de la Colombette, costs €1.50/4.55 per 10 minutes/hour and opens 9am to 8pm Monday to Saturday. Résomania (☎ 05 62 30 25 64), 85 rue Pargaminières, costs €4.50 per hour and opens 10am until at least midnight Monday to Saturday.

The main post office has Cyberposte terminals. On allées du Président Roosevelt there's a 24-hour pay-by-card kiosk with Internet access.

Travel Agencies

A France-based student travel agency is OTU Voyages (☎ 05 61 12 18 88), 60 rue du Taur, open to 6.30pm on weekdays. Voyages Wasteels (☎ 08 03 88 70 63), 1 blvd Bonrepos, is open until 7pm Monday to Saturday. Usit Connections (☎ 05 61 11 52 42) is at 5 rue des Lois (open Monday to Saturday). The CRIJ (see earlier in this section) has its own youth travel service.

Bookshops

Toulouse has scores of bookshops, concentrated west and north of place du Capitole. Most open weekdays and Saturday. Two good places for English-language books are The Bookshop (☎ 05 61 22 99 92), 17 rue Lakanal), and Librairie Étrangère (☎ 05 61 21 67 21, 16 rue des Lois). Just off place du Capitole at 50 rue Gambetta, Ombres Blanches (☎ 05 34 45 53 33) specialises in travel guides and maps.

A fine place to sell books or browse second-hand volumes is Books & Mermaides (☎ 05 61 12 14 29, 3 rue Mirepoix). There are other used-book shops along rue du Taur; one specialising in Occitania and Catharism is Librairie Occitania (☎ 05 61 21 49 00, 46 rue du Taur).

Universities

The city's three universities, 14 *grandes écoles* and other institutes have some 111,000 students. Most are based at least 5km from the centre, although the Université des Sciences Sociales, place Anatole France, brings a student atmosphere into the city centre.

Cultural Centre

The Goethe Institut (☎ 05 61 23 08 34) is at 6 bis rue Clémence Isaure.

Laundry

Central, self-service laundrettes include those at 10 rue Stalingrad, 29 rue Pargaminières, 7 rue Mirepoix, 20 rue Cujas and 67 rue Pierre-Paul Riquet. All are open at least 7.30am to 8.30pm daily.

Toilets

A handy public toilet is in the underground car park at the corner of place du Capitole.

Medical Services & Emergency

Two regional hospitals are Hôpital Purpan (☎ 05 61 77 22 33), 4km west of the city centre at place du Dr Baylac (westbound bus No 14 from place Esquirol); and CHU Rangueil (☎ 05 61 32 25 33), 5.5km south of the centre on av Jean-Poulhes (southbound bus No 2 from place Esquirol).

Police headquarters (☎ 17 or ☎ 05 61 12 77 77) are north of the city centre at 23 blvd de l'Embouchure. Toulouse also has a cadre of unarmed young men and women in baseball caps and blue jumpsuits who walk or cycle round the city in twos and threes, dealing with 'social' problems such as domestic arguments and unruly street people.

TOULOUSE

CENTRAL TOULOUSE

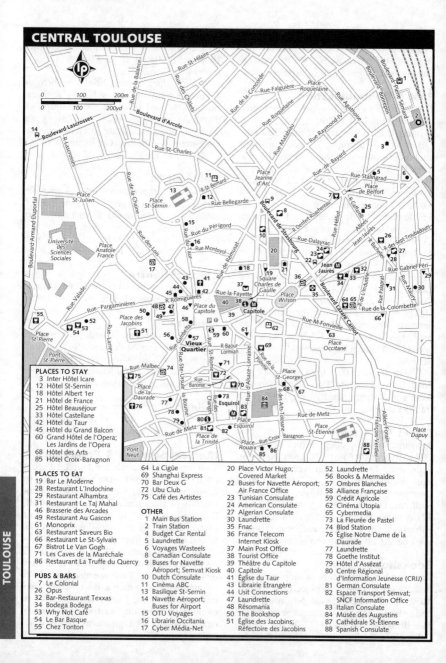

PLACES TO STAY
3 Inter Hôtel Icare
12 Hôtel St-Sernin
18 Hôtel Albert 1er
21 Hôtel de France
25 Hôtel Beauséjour
33 Hôtel Castellane
42 Hôtel du Taur
45 Hôtel du Grand Balcon
60 Grand Hôtel de l'Opera;
   Les Jardins de l'Opera
68 Hôtel des Arts
85 Hôtel Croix-Baragnon

PLACES TO EAT
19 Bar Le Moderne
28 Restaurant L'Indochine
29 Restaurant Alhambra
31 Restaurant Le Taj Mahal
46 Brasserie des Arcades
49 Restaurant Au Gascon
61 Monoprix
63 Restaurant Saveurs Bio
66 Restaurant Le St-Sylvain
71 Les Caves de la Maréchale
86 Restaurant La Truffe du Quercy

PUBS & BARS
7 Le Colonial
26 Opus
32 Bar-Restaurant Texxas
34 Bodega Bodega
53 Why Not Café
54 Le Bar Basque
55 Chez Tonton

64 La Cigüe
69 Shanghai Express
70 Bar Deux G
72 Ubu Club
75 Café des Artistes

OTHER
1 Main Bus Station
2 Train Station
4 Budget Car Rental
5 Laundrette
6 Voyages Wasteels
8 Canadian Consulate
9 Buses for Navette
   Aéroport; Semvat Kiosk
10 Dutch Consulate
11 Cinéma ABC
13 Basilique St-Sernin
14 Navette Aéroport;
   Buses for Airport
15 OTU Voyages
16 Librairie Occitania
17 Cyber Média-Net

20 Place Victor Hugo;
   Covered Market
22 Buses for Navette Aéroport;
   Air France Office
23 Tunisian Consulate
24 American Consulate
27 Algerian Consulate
30 Laundrette
35 Fnac
36 France Telecom
   Internet Kiosk
37 Main Post Office
38 Tourist Office
39 Théâtre du Capitole
40 Capitole
41 Église du Taur
43 Librairie Étrangère
44 Usit Connections
47 Laundrette
48 Résomania
50 The Bookshop
51 Église des Jacobins;
   Réfectoire des Jacobins

52 Laundrette
56 Books & Mermaides
57 Ombres Blanches
58 Alliance Française
59 Crédit Agricole
62 Cinéma Utopia
65 Cybermedia
73 La Fleurée de Pastel
74 Blod Station
76 Église Notre Dame de la
   Daurade
77 Laundrette
78 Goethe Institut
79 Hôtel d'Assézat
80 Centre Régional
   d'Information Jeunesse (CRIJ)
81 German Consulate
82 Espace Transport Semvat;
   SNCF Information Office
83 Italian Consulate
84 Musée des Augustins
87 Cathédrale St-Etienne
88 Spanish Consulate

TOULOUSE

PLACE DU CAPITOLE

Pedestrianised 'place du Cap' is the city's main plaza, the past symbolised by an inlaid bronze cross of Languedoc and the present by a grid of blue 'runway lights'. On the ceiling of the arcades on the western side are 29 vivid serigraphs by contemporary artist Raymond Moretti, illustrating the city's history.

Along the eastern side runs Toulouse's city hall, the **Capitole**, a name deriving from the ancient city council (*capitol* in Occitan) whose eight *capitouls* (councillors) enjoyed considerable autonomy and prestige in the centuries after the Albigensian Crusade. Completed in 1760, the brick and marble structure is a focus of civic pride. Under the same roof is the Théâtre du Capitole, a prestigious opera venue (not open to the public).

On the eastern side of the Capitole is the square's green alter ego, square Charles de Gaulle or Jardin du Capitole.

SQUARES

Place Wilson appealingly combines the genteel and the weathered, both architectural and human.

The Old Quarter, hardly changed since the 18th century, is a web of narrow lanes and pocket-size plazas south of place du Capitole and place Wilson. With buskers in summer, place St-Georges has some of the feel of a small-town square.

Place de la Daurade is the city's 'beach' on the Garonne, peaceful and sun-drenched by day and romantic by night, looking out on the floodlit Pont Neuf.

BASILIQUE ST-SERNIN

Architecturally speaking, St-Sernin Basilica (☎ 05 61 21 80 45, place St-Sernin; admission to basilica free, crypt €1.50, those under 15 years admission free; basilica open 9am-6.30pm Mon-Sat, 9am-7.30pm Sun July-Sept; 8am-noon & 2pm-6pm Mon-Sat, 2pm-7pm Sun Oct-June; crypt open 10am-6pm Mon-Sat, 12.30pm-6pm Sun July-Sept; 10am-11.30am & 2.30pm-5pm Mon-Sat, 2.30pm-5pm Sun Oct-June) is Toulouse's finest attraction – and at 115m long it's one of Europe's largest, most complete Romanesque buildings. This was an

St Sernin

Sernin, or Saturninus, was a local evangelist who annoyed the Romans with his teachings. He was martyred in 257 by being dragged behind a *taureau* (wild bull). This is the origin of the name of the Église Notre Dame du Taur, and of rue du Taur.

important stop on the way to Santiago de Compostela (whose own cathedral, begun at about the same time, is almost identical in design), and is on Unesco's list of Compostela-related World Heritage Sites.

The chancel was built between 1075 and 1096 and the nave added in the 12th century. It's topped by a magnificent eight-sided **tower** dating from the early 13th century. No significant changes have been made since then, save the 15th-century spire. Over the porte Miègeville, the nave's southern entrance, is a deeply carved tympanum depicting the Ascension, witnessed by 12 cringing disciples.

Inside are ambulatory chapels full of gilded 17th-century reliquaries. The two-level **crypt**, rebuilt in the 13th and 14th centuries, contains several medieval tombs; the lower crypt is part of an older church, dating from 402. Directly above the crypt is the sculpted, mid-18th-century **tomb of St-Sernin** (see the boxed text 'St Sernin'). The northern transept bears a **12th-century fresco** of Christ's Resurrection.

ÉGLISE DES JACOBINS

The Dominican, or Jacobin, order was founded by St Dominic in 1215 to preach Church doctrine to the Cathars. The order's mother church, the Church of the Jacobins (☎ 05 61 22 21 92, parvis des Jacobins; admission to church free; cloister €2.15, those under 15 years charge; open 10am-7pm daily year round) was completed in 1385.

Inside the imposing Gothic structure a single row of seven columns – topped with fan vaulting that makes them look like gigantic palm trees – runs down the middle of the nave. The remains of St Thomas Aquinas

TOULOUSE

(1225–74), Italian theologian-philosopher and an early leader of the Dominican order, are interred below the grey marble altar on the northern side. After midday the sun through the lovely nave windows fills the place with a fiery light.

All that remains of the ancient monastery are the sacristy, the chapterhouse, a chapel decorated with 14th-century murals and the serene **cloister**.

Also within the complex is the **Réfectoire des Jacobins**, a 14th-century Dominican refectory which now serves as a gallery for changing art exhibitions.

ÉGLISE DU TAUR

The Église du Taur (☎ 05 61 23 11 50, 12 rue du Taur; open 10am-noon & 2pm-7.15pm Mon-Sat; admission free) was built in Southern Gothic style in the 14th century, an extra honour for St Sernin. At the end of the nave are three chapels; the middle contains a 16th-century Black Madonna called Notre Dame du Rempart (Our Lady of the Rampart).

CATHÉDRALE ST-ÉTIENNE

One of Toulouse's most striking churches, for its unnerving hotch-potch of styles (it took five centuries to complete), is the Cathedral of St Étienne (☎ 05 61 52 03 82, place St-Étienne; admission free; open 8am-7pm Mon-Sat & 9am-7pm Sun). The nave, begun around 1100, is out of line with the vast choir, built in northern French Gothic style as part of an ambitious (and unfinished) late 13th-century plan to enlarge and realign the whole building; note the improvised Gothic vaulting linking the two sections.

The rose window facing the square dates from 1230, the organ case above the nave portal from four centuries later. The belfry has Romanesque foundations, a Gothic middle and a 16th-century top. The western portal was added about 1450, the northern portal not until 1929.

HÔTEL D'ASSÉZAT & TOULOUSE'S HÔTELS PARTICULIERS

Toulouse boasts some 50 handsome *hôtels particuliers* – grand private townhouses,

---

Le Pastel

A number of Toulouse merchant families grew rich in the 16th century – as testified by the city's line-up of fine Renaissance *hôtels particuliers* (mansions) – from the trade in dyer's woad (*le pastel; Isatis tinctoria*), a member of the mustard family whose leaves, wetted and fermented, produce a distinctive blue dye.

Woad blue was originally a royal colour, its production a royal secret. With sun to grow it and the river to ship it, Toulouse was its natural home. The woad bubble burst after the Portuguese discovered indigo in India and the Spanish began farming it cheaply, with the help of slave labour, in South America. Indigo came to be known as 'people's blue' during the French Revolution. That old American standby, blue denim, is a descendant of European indigo-dyed work clothing.

When Napoleon I's blockade cut off his own supplies of indigo (for uniforms), he arranged for intensive production of woad in Southwest France, based on techniques known since at least Roman times, and probably before. Today research is again underway to recover the lost art of making high-quality dye from woad (eg, see under Lectoure in the Gers chapter).

---

mostly built in the 16th century by merchants enriched by the trade in dyer's woad (see the boxed text *'Le Pastel'*). Together they form a unique body of fine civil Renaissance architecture. Many have towers, a privilege granted only to capitouls of the time.

The Hôtel d'Assézat, at 18 rue de Metz, is one of the finest, built in the 1550s for councillor Pierre Assézat, with Greek-style columns and an elegant arcaded portico. It now houses the paintings, bronzes and *objets d'art* of the Fondation Bemberg (☎ 05 61 12 06 89, ⓦ www.fondation-bemberg.fr; €4.57; open 10am-6pm Tues, Wed, Fri-Sun, 10am-9pm Thur), founded by Austrian collector Georges Bemberg.

One-hour guided tours of the building and Bemberg collection are offered at 3.30pm on weekdays and 2.30pm and 4pm Saturday and Sunday for an additional €2.75.

MUSÉE DES AUGUSTINS

The Musée des Augustins (☎ 05 61 22 21 82, 21 rue de Metz; €2.15, admission free for students and those under 18 years, admission free 1st Sun of month; open 10am-6pm Thur-Mon, 10am-9pm Wed) displays paintings and stone artefacts from Roman times to the late 19th century, including a fine collection of Romanesque sculpture. Among the stone carvings are religious statuary, sarcophagi, gargoyles, tombstones and inscriptions, some in Hebrew.

The museum occupies an Augustinian monastery whose two fine **cloisters** date from the 14th century. The lovely cloisters' medieval-style **gardens** are among the prettiest in southern France.

LES ABATTOIRS

The Espace d'Art Moderne et Contemporain (☎ 05 62 48 58 00, w www.lesabattoirs.org, 76 allées Charles de Fitte; permanent collection €3.05, admission free 1st Sun of month, special exhibitions €3.05-7.60; open noon-8pm Tues-Sun) is the city's brand-new gallery of modern art, opened in 1998 on the site of the city's old slaughterhouse (hence its common name). The focus is on the second half of the 20th century, with some 2000 works by nearly 700 artists, predominantly from Mediterranean countries. Most of the influential painters of this period are represented.

Pride of place goes to a work slightly in advance of this time-slot, Picasso's 14m by 20m La Dépouille du Minotaure en Costume d'Arlequin (The Hide of the Minotaur in the Costume of Harlequin).

MUSÉE PAUL DUPUY

In one of the city's elegant townhouses is the Musée Paul Dupuy (☎ 05 61 14 65 50, 13 rue de la Pleau; €2.15, admission free for students and those under 18 years, admission free 1st Sun of month; open 10am-6pm Wed-Mon June-Sept; 10am-5pm Wed-Mon Oct-May), an engrossing collection of 'applied art' from medieval times to the 18th century. A section on drawings and prints includes minor works by Ingres, Toulouse-Lautrec and lesser-known artists of the Languedoc, plus engravings, posters, photographs and postage stamps. The section on objets d'art is dominated by a fine clockwork collection, including an Arabic astrolabe and a 16th-century astronomical clock.

GALERIE MUNICIPALE DU CHÂTEAU D'EAU

This municipal photography museum (☎ 05 61 77 09 40, e www.galeriechateaudeau.com, 1 place Laganne; adults/students/child under 12 €2.30/1.50/free; open 1pm-7pm Wed-Mon; closed holidays), founded in 1974, is Toulouse's most visited museum and Europe's oldest photography gallery. Here you'll find thought-provoking exhibitions by the world's finest photographers, with a new show in one of the three galleries each month. It's in a 19th-century château d'eau (water-pumping station), and its shop has a fine collection of postcards and posters.

CITÉ DE L'ESPACE

The amazing Space Park museum and planetarium complex (☎ 05 62 71 48 71, w www.cite-espace.com, av Jean Gonord; adult/child €10.50/7.45; open 9.30am-7pm daily July-Aug; 9.30am-6pm Sept-June), on the eastern outskirts, is marked by a full-size Ariane 5 rocket. The museum – a must for kids of all ages – includes interactive exhibits and fascinating displays on satellites and future life aboard space stations. The newest exhibit, the Terr@dome, takes you right through the earth's 4.5-billion-year history. The only drawback – most of it's in French.

Bus No 19 goes to Cité de l'Espace every 1¼ hours from place Marengo, near the train station.

TAXIWAY

Aérospatiale runs impressive, 1½-hour tours (☎ 05 61 18 06 01, fax 05 62 74 08 68, e taxiway@afatvoyages.fr; adult €8.90, child aged 8-18/under 8 €7.40/free; 9am-12.30pm & 2pm-6pm Mon-Sat) of its huge Clément Ader facility – probably the world's most modern aircraft production unit, where Airbus A330s and A340s are assembled – on av Jean Monnet in Colomiers, about 7km west of the city centre. Book at least 10 days in advance; in July and August you can do so through the tourist office. Bring along a passport or national ID card.

THE GARONNE & THE CANALS
The city's many canalside paths are very peaceful places to walk, run or cycle. Port de l'Embouchure is the junction of the Canal du Midi (completed in 1681) to the Mediterranean, the Canal de Brienne (1776), which bypasses the river shallows below Pont St-Pierre, and the Canal Latéral à la Garonne (1856) to the Atlantic.

Several operators do short passenger trips along the river and canals. Garonne trips are run from quai de la Daurade by **Toulouse Crosières** (☎ *05 65 30 55 33; adult €7.60, child aged 3-12/under 3 €4.55/free; 1½ hours, departing 10.30am, 3pm, 4.30pm & 6pm daily)* and **Baladine** (☎ *05 61 80 22 26; adult/child under 12 €6.10/3.80; 1¼-hour trips departing 2.30pm, 4pm & 5.30pm Wed, Sat & Sun, Easter-Oct)*. Buy tickets at the quayside or from the tourist office.

L'Occitania (☎ *05 61 63 06 06)* tootles along the Canal du Midi from opposite the train station, and **Cap d'Ambre** (☎ *05 61 71 45 95)* runs along the Canal de Brienne, through a lock to the Garonne and back. These two only go if there are enough passengers.

For more on the history of the canals and on self-navigated canal holidays, see under Boat in the Getting Around chapter.

GUIDED TOUR
A two-hour, English-language tour of the Capitole, Basilique St-Sernin, Église des Jacobins and other attractions (adult €7.60, child aged 10-16/under 10 €6.40/free) departs from the tourist office at 3pm Saturday from July to September.

LANGUAGE COURSES
You can study French at a number of places here. **Alliance Française** (☎ *05 34 45 26 10, fax 05 34 45 26 11,* e *af.toulouse@wanadoo .fr, 9 place du Capitole)* offers an array of French courses for foreigners. Among other, smaller schools is **Langue Onze Sud-Ouest** (☎ *05 61 54 11 69, fax 05 63 58 41 30,* e *sudouest@langue-onze.asso.fr, 10 rue*

Dardenne), recommended by one reader for its smaller classes and laid-back atmosphere. These schools will also arrange budget accommodation for the course period. For details see under Courses in the Facts for the Visitor chapter.

SPECIAL EVENTS
Toulouse's biggest annual events include the following:

Festival International de Théâtre d'Enfants Kids' theatre (in French, but does it matter?); four days in June
Garonariége Boat races down the rivers Ariége and Garonne to Toulouse; June
Festival Garonne Riverside celebration of music, dance and theatre; two weeks in early July
Musique d'Été Festival of jazz, classical, choral and other music, 9pm Tuesday and Thursday evenings in churches and other venues; July and August
Jazz sur Son 31 International jazz festival ('31' refers to the Haute-Garonne department); October
Journées de la Danse Traditionelle en Midi-Pyrénées Concerts and courses on the theme of Occitan traditional dance; 3rd week of November in odd-numbered years

PLACES TO STAY
Many of Toulouse's hotels cater for business people, so rooms are easiest to find on the weekend and – surprisingly – for most of July and August. Many mid-range places offer much better value for money than the budget ones.

PLACES TO STAY – BUDGET
Camping You can camp reasonably close to the centre of Toulouse.

Camping de Pont de Rupé (☎ *05 61 70 07 35, fax 05 61 70 93 17, 21 chemin du Pont de Rupé)* 2-person *forfait* (package deal) with tent €9.15/11 with bicycle/car. Open year round. Bus No 59 from place Jeanne d'Arc to Rupé stop; last bus 7.25pm daily. This well equipped, three-star camp site is 6km north-west of the train station, by Lac des Sesquières.

Hostels Toulouse has no official youth hostel, although there are several inexpensive *foyers de jeunes* (student dormitories).

Some student accommodation agencies may also have spaces in the summer. The best place to ask about all of these is the CRIJ (see Information earlier in this chapter).

Hotels Most cheap hotels near Gare Matabiau and the red-light district of place de Belfort are dirty, noisy and unpleasant. If you arrive by train, head towards allées Jean Jaurès or take the metro into town.

Hôtel Beauséjour (☎/fax 05 61 62 77 59, 4 rue Caffarelli) Rooms €17.55, or with shower/shower & WC€21.35/23.65; hall showers about €2. The polite, tidy Beauséjour has plain, soundproofed rooms facing the street or a rear courtyard.

Hôtel des Arts (☎ 05 61 23 36 21, fax 05 61 12 22 37, 1 bis rue Cantegril) Doubles €24.40-25.90, with shower €25.15-28.20, shower & WC €26.70-29.70. Hall showers cost about €2. Breakfast €3.80. This central hotel offers plain, adequate doubles (some noisy).

Hôtel du Grand Balcon (☎ 05 61 21 48 08, fax 05 61 21 59 98, 8 rue Romiguières) Rooms €24.40-32, or with shower €32-35.05, shower & WC €35.05-41.15. Hall showers about €2. Breakfast €3.80. The faded and genteel Grand Balcon is where aviator-author Antoine de St-Exupéry first stayed (room 32) between his 1920s flights, and the lobby is a veritable shrine to him. Spacious doubles are pretty good value.

PLACES TO STAY – MID-RANGE
Hotels There are several mid-range hotels in the city centre and one convenient to the station.

Hôtel Castellane (☎ 05 61 62 18 82, fax 05 61 62 58 04, 17 rue Castellane) Rooms with WC & shower or bath €46-54, family rooms €58-74. Off-street parking €7 per day. The Castellane is good value, convenient and surprisingly quiet. All the rooms have TV and air-conditioning, and breakfast (€6) is available all morning. English is spoken.

Hôtel Croix-Baragnon (☎ 05 61 52 60 10, fax 05 61 52 08 60, 17 rue Croix Baragnon) Singles €24.40-29.75, doubles €26.70-31.75, quads €34.30 with WC & shower. Peaceful Croix-Baragnon offers good mid-range value in the city centre. With more than the usual number of dedicated single rooms, it's a good bet for solo travellers.

Hôtel de France (☎ 05 61 21 88 24, fax 05 61 21 99 77, 5 rue d'Austerlitz & 4 rue Victor Hugo) Doubles with WC & shower €29.75-42.70, with WC & bath €48.80-57.95. The Hôtel de France is one of the better-run of many two-star hotels around the covered market. It has spotless, air-conditioned rooms.

Hôtel du Taur (☎ 05 61 21 17 54, fax 05 61 13 78 41, 2 rue du Taur) Doubles with WC & shower/bath €39.65/48. Breakfast €5.35-6.10. Most of the plain, spacious rooms here face an interior courtyard. St-Exupéry stayed here too, perhaps to escape the noise at the Grand Balcon.

Hôtel St-Sernin (☎ 05 61 21 73 08, fax 05 61 22 49 61, 2 rue St-Bernard) Doubles with shower €42.70-61, with bath €57.95-64.05. Off-street parking about €7. The well kept St-Sernin has fully equipped, quiet rooms.

Hôtel Albert 1er (☎ 05 61 21 17 91, fax 05 61 21 09 64, e hotel.albert.1er@wanadoo .fr, 8 rue Rivals) Singles €36.60, doubles with WC & shower or bath €48.80-54.90. Breakfast €7.45. Attractive, spick-and-span rooms, polite staff and a buffet breakfast make this a good bet in the centre.

Inter Hôtel Icare (☎ 05 61 63 66 55, fax 05 61 63 00 53, e hotelicare@wanadoo.fr, 11 blvd de Bonrepos) Singles/doubles with WC & shower €32/41.15. Breakfast €5.35. The two-star Inter Hôtel Icare, opposite the train station, has uninspiring but spacious, soundproofed and air-conditioned rooms.

PLACES TO STAY – TOP END
Stay here when you've made your first hundred thousand.

Grand Hôtel de l'Opera (☎ 05 61 21 82 66, fax 05 61 23 41 04, w www.grand-hotel -opera.com, 1 place du Capitole) Rooms €106.70-213.45. Breakfast €16.75. A sumptuous, professionally run hotel in a converted 17th-century convent, with rooms full of felt and wood and marble. Downstairs is a superb restaurant (see Places to Eat).

PLACES TO EAT

Toulouse has it all. You can get by on €8 per meal, or go to town with superb regional cuisine at €30 and up. Like the Spanish, whose blood runs in their veins, Toulousains•like to eat late and linger.

Quick & Cheap

Some of Toulouse's best value for money can be found at six more or less identical, madly crowded *restaurants*, in a row on the mezzanine of Les Halles, the covered market (stairway at the market's south-east corner). Filling *menus* cost €12 to €15. They're only open at midday, Tuesday to Saturday.

Almost every square in the Vieux Quartier has a cafe-brasserie or two. In good weather, place St-Georges is a sea of heads bent over lunch, and at night it's one of the town's liveliest outdoor spots. Brasseries around place Wilson tend to be brusque and overpriced. Pizzerias, *sandwicheries* and cafe-bars – most closed Sunday – line the streets radiating north and south from place du Capitole.

Bar Le Moderne (☎ *05 61 21 87 72, 5 rue du Rempart Villeneuve*) Midday specials around €7. Open midday on weekdays only. The modest Moderne, opposite the market, has lots of salads and a daily hot dish or two.

Café-Brasserie Classico (☎ *05 61 53 53 60, 37 rue des Filatiers*) Salads €6.70-10.35, *formules* (set menus with a choice of courses) €9.90-12.20. Open Mon-Sat. The Classico is a worthy choice among sunny lunch-time eateries along this trendy street, and carries on until 2am as a good bar (see Entertainment).

Brasserie des Arcades (☎ *05 61 21 57 04, 14 place du Capitole*) Salads €10-15, midday dishes €10, evening *menus* €11-13. Open daily. This is the snappiest of several places under the arcades, opposite the Capitole. You pay for the location, but the food is good too.

Bistrot Le Van Gogh (☎ *05 61 21 03 15, 21 place St-Georges*) Midday formules €10, evening *menus* €10-19. Open daily. The best of several eateries vying for space on the square, the Van Gogh offers good re-

gional specialities such as *cassoulet* (meat and bean casserole).

Restaurants – French

It isn't all couscous and tapas here; Toulouse has plenty of first-rate French restaurants, including the following.

Restaurant La Truffe du Quercy (☎ *05 61 53 34 24, 17 rue Croix Baragnon*) Midday *menus* €8.40, evening *menus* €11.90-19.50. Open Mon-Sat. Choose from fine French and Spanish dishes at this small restaurant beside the Hôtel Croix-Baragnon.

Restaurant Au Gascon (☎ *05 61 21 67 16, 9 rue des Jacobins*) *Menus* €12.95-19.50. Open daily. The intimate Au Gascon is an excellent place for duck, duck and more duck; *menus* are generous.

Restaurant Le St-Sylvain (☎ *05 61 62 31 44, 17 rue de la Colombette*) Evening *menus* €10-15. Open midday & evening Wed-Fri, evening only Sat, midday only Mon-Tues. The St-Sylvain presents delicious, good-value regional specialities in a quiet setting.

Les Caves de la Maréchale (☎ *05 61 23 89 88, 3 rue Jules Chalande*) Midday *menus* €12.95, evening *menus* €19.05-22.70. Open Tues-Sat, morning only Mon. Enjoy first-rate regional cuisine in the vaulted brick cellar of an old convent (enter through a courtyard). The €10.65 midday *formule rapide* is one way to eat within your budget. Book ahead for dinner.

Les Jardins de l'Opera (*Hôtel de l'Opera;* ☎ *05 61 23 07 76*) Midday *menus* €35, evening *menus* €46-84. Owned by home-grown (and now famous) chef Dominique Toulousy, the Michelin-starred Jardins de l'Opera is certainly Toulouse's best, with imaginative variations on cuisine of the Languedoc. Budget gourmets can nibble the €21.35 *dégustation de legumes*, a vegetable sampler.

Restaurants – Vegetarian

Meatless places are rare and generally uninspiring, though vegetarians won't starve here.

Restaurant Saveurs Bio (☎ *05 61 12 15 15, 22 rue Maurice Fonvieille*) *Menus* €14.50-19.05. Open midday & evening Mon-Sat. No hippie cafe this, but a restaurant with a serious interest in health. Offerings include a €7.60 lunchtime *assiette* (assorted plate) and €7.60 evening buffet.

Restaurant Le Taj Mahal (☎ 05 61 99 26 80, 24 rue Palaprat) The Taj Mahal has some vegetarian offerings, including a €12 *menu*.

Restaurants – Other
For something a little 'outlandish' try the following:

Restaurant L'Indochine (☎ 05 61 62 17 46, 46 place Bachelier) Midday *menus* €7.15-7.95, evening *menus* €8.55-15.10. Open daily. Indochine offers lots of tasty Chinese and Vietnamese dishes, and big portions.

Restaurant Alhambra (☎ 05 61 62 56 49, 58 rue Pierre-Paul Riquet) Midday *menus* €12.20-24.40, evening *menus* €16.75-24.40. Open daily. Alhambra's delicious, filling North African *menus* could easily feed two, and the desserts are a knockout.

Restaurant Le Taj Mahal (see Restaurants – Vegetarian) Menus €12.05-17.55. Open evenings daily. This curry house has a huge list of dishes, mostly €7.50-13.50, and a good-value midday formule for €5.

Self-Catering
See the boxed text 'The Markets of Toulouse' later in this section for details of food markets. The *Monoprix* supermarket, at 39 rue d'Alsace-Lorraine, is open until 9pm Monday to Saturday.

ENTERTAINMENT
For up-to-date information on Toulouse's vibrant cultural life, visit the tourist office or pick up one of the several weekly or monthly French-language 'what's-on' guides (eg, *Toulouse Hebdo*) sold at bigger newsagents.

Bars
The city has enough laid-back bars to keep you busy for months, most of them open until 2am. Several cluster around riverside place St-Pierre: *Le Bar Basque (☎ 05 61 21 55 64, 7 place St-Pierre)*, a popular, dyed-in-the-wool sports bar; *Chez Tonton (☎ 05 61 21 89 54, 16 place St-Pierre)*, with bizarre decor and a cheerful atmosphere; and the

Why Not Café (☎ 05 61 21 89 08, 5 rue Pargaminières), with a soothing interior courtyard garden.

A popular spot with a Spanish flavour is *Bodega Bodega (☎ 05 61 63 03 63, 1 rue Gabriel Péri)*, with live music at the weekend.

Bar-Restaurant Texxas (☎ 05 61 99 01 94, 26 rue Castellane) Open nightly 7pm-2am. The south-of-the-border music is the main thing, but the Tex-Mex food (chilli, tacos, Mexican and American wines) is pretty good too.

Killarney Bar (☎ 05 62 26 52 04, 14 rue Alfred Duméril) Bus No 1 from blvd Lazare Carnot, or No 52, 53, 54, 56 or 62 from place Esquirol to St-Michel. The Killarney, 1.5km south of the city centre, has live Irish music on Saturday night.

Café des Artistes (☎ 05 61 12 06 00, 13 place de la Daurade) This is an art-student hangout, easygoing and cerebral.

Café-Brasserie Classico (see Places to Eat) With modern art on the walls and rock on the box, the Classico mutates daily from a pavement brasserie to a bar.

Opus (☎ 05 61 62 09 83, 24 rue Bachelier) Offering food until 1.30am and dancing all night, Opus has live bands on some summer evenings.

Discos & Clubs
Toulouse has lots of discos, most of them several kilometres from the centre. A hot one near the centre, open until dawn Monday to Saturday, is the *Ubu Club (☎ 05 61 23 26 75, 16 rue St-Rome)*.

Gay & Lesbian Venues Toulouse is a very gay city – it ain't called *la ville rose* just for those pink bricks – with some of the best clubs this side of the Marais in Paris. The following bars have a young, mixed gay-straight crowd.

Bar Deux G (2G; ☎ 05 61 23 16 10, 5 rue Baronie) Open 6pm-2am Tues-Sun. Gays and lesbians mingle here.

La Cigüe (☎ 05 61 99 61 87, 6 rue de la Colombette) Open 6pm-2am Mon-Thur, 6pm-dawn Fri-Sun. Young gays in particular are drawn to this tiny club.

TOULOUSE

Shanghai Express (Le Shanghai; ☎ *05 61 23 37 80, 12 rue de la Pomme)* Open midnight-dawn daily. One of the oldest and best-known gay and lesbian clubs in Toulouse.

B Machine (☎ *05 61 55 57 59, 37 place des Carmes)* Open 6pm-2am. This place is frequented almost exclusively by gays.

Le Colonial (☎ *05 61 63 64 11, 8 place de Belfort)* Open noon-1am. Another gay hot spot with a predominantly male clientele.

Le Grand Cirque (☎ *05 61 62 84 14, 14 blvd Riquet)* Open 4pm-2am daily. Le Grande Cirque is a large and exclusively gay club.

Le Pharaon (☎ *05 61 20 70 90, 43 av de la Gloire)* Open noon-2am daily. This is an Egyptian-style cruising bar.

La Luna Loca (☎ *05 62 72 03 46,* Ⓔ *luna loca@libertysurf.fr, 15 rue Pierre Rubens)* Women only Thur, Sat & Sun, mixed crowd Wed & Fri. This is a welcoming and cultural place for gay women.

Chez Les Filles (mobile ☎ *06 03 60 04 45, 71 blvd Pierre Sémard)* This women-only bar near the train station is open Friday and Saturday evenings.

Cinemas

Two cinemas with nondubbed foreign films are the triplex *Cinéma Utopia (*☎ *05 61 21 22 11, 24 rue Montardy;* €5*)* and *Cinéma ABC (*☎ *05 61 29 81 00, 13 rue St-Bernard;* €6.40*, students* €4.90*)*. The ABC is closed for most of August.

SPECTATOR SPORTS

Toulouse's rugby league team, frequent national champions, is called Stade Toulousain or 'Le Stade', after the stadium (☎ 05 62 72 47 47) where they usually play, at 114 rue des Troènes, near the airport. Toulouse Football Club or TFC, teetering at the edge of the first division, plays at Stade Municipal (☎ 05 61 55 11 11), on allée Gabriel Biénès in Parc Toulousain, south of the city centre.

SHOPPING

Toulouse's main shopping districts are rue de la Pomme, place St-Georges, rue des

---

The Markets of Toulouse

The following covered food markets are open 6am to 1pm (Tuesday to Sunday), selling deli meats, fish, cheeses, bread, wine and sometimes prepared foods:

Place Victor Hugo The city's biggest covered market
Place des Carmes Includes lots of hawkers in adjacent rue des Filatiers
Place St-Cyprien Across the river, the best source of fresh *cèpe* (cep) mushrooms and other seasonal items

Toulouse also has several good open-air markets (but beware of pickpockets):

Place du Capitole Small food market 6am to 1pm daily except Monday; organic produce market 6am to 1pm Tuesday and Saturday; flea market (including books) 8am to 6pm Wednesday
Place St-Sernin Flea market 6am into the evening Saturday and Sunday
Place St-Georges Fruit, flowers and veggies, daily except Monday
Blvd du Strasbourg Fruit and vegetables only
Place St-Étienne Antiquarian book market, 9am to 6pm Saturday

---

Arts and place St-Étienne for fashionable boutiques; rue St-Rome, rue des Changes and rue des Filatiers for trendy clothes and small curiosity shops; and rue d'Alsace-Lorraine for upmarket international brands.

La Fleurée de Pastel (☎ *05 61 12 05 94, 20 rue de la Bourse)* This is one of Toulouse's loveliest shops, with articles coloured by genuine dyer's woad *(le pastel)*, source of the city's fortune in the 15th and 16th centuries (see the boxed text, *'Le Pastel'*, earlier in this section).

Two giant department stores are *Fnac (16 allée Président Roosevelt, ticket desk blvd Lazare Carnot)*, which is open Monday to Saturday and is also a good source for concert tickets; and *Monoprix (39 rue d'Alsace-Lorraine)*, open Monday to Saturday.

See the boxed text 'The Markets of Toulouse' for a list of good food markets.

GETTING THERE & AWAY
Air
Toulouse's international airport (☎ 05 61 42 44 00) is 7km north-west of the city centre in the suburb of Blagnac.

Air France and Air Liberté between them have several dozen flights a day to Toulouse from Paris (mainly Orly). Buzz has weekend-only flights in July and August from London Stansted. There are also daily or almost-daily flights from many other cities in France and Europe. See the Getting There & Away chapter for details.

Bus
Toulouse's modern bus station (☎ 05 61 61 67 67) is on blvd Pierre Sémard. The information lobby is open 7am to 7pm daily (from 8am on Sunday).

Among destinations served by various bus lines from here, with multiple daily departures, are Agen (€10.65, two hours), Albi (€10.80, 1½ hours), Auch (€9.30, 1½ hours), Castres (€9.15, 1½ hours) and Montauban (€6.10, 1¼ hours).

Buses to southern and Central Europe are handled by Intercars (☎ 05 61 58 14 53). Those to Brussels, Amsterdam, Morocco and parts of Spain are handled by Eurolines (☎ 05 61 26 40 04). For details, see the Getting There & Away chapter.

Train
Toulouse's train station, Gare Matabiau (☎ 08 36 35 35 35), is on blvd Pierre Sémard. The information office is open 5.30am to 10.30pm daily (6am to midnight Friday and Sunday).

Regional destinations served by multiple daily direct trains include Albi (€9.90, 1¼ hours), Auch (€11.30, 1¼ hours), Bayonne (€30.50, 3¾ hours), Bordeaux (€25.75, 2½ hours), Carcassonne (€11.45, 50 minutes), Castres (€11, 1¼ hours), Montauban (€7.15, 30 minutes) and Pau (€22.55, 2¾ hours). The non-TGV fare to Paris is €55.35 (6½ hours, Gare d'Austerlitz); by TGV it's €71.05 (5½ hours, Gare Montparnasse).

SNCF has a city centre information and ticketing office, open 2pm to 6pm on weekdays, in Espace Transport Semvat (for details

see Bus & Metro under Getting Around later in this section), 7 place Esquirol.

Car
Car-rental firms are concentrated around the train station and at the airport. Those with offices in the north end of the train station include ADA (☎ 05 61 63 68 63), Citer/National (☎ 05 61 62 02 96), Budget (☎ 05 61 62 09 34), Avis (☎ 05 61 62 50 40) and Hertz (☎ 05 62 73 39 47). Budget has another office (☎ 05 61 63 18 18) nearby at 49 rue Bayard. These and others also have desks at the airport.

GETTING AROUND
To the Airport
The Navette Aéroport bus service (☎ 05 34 60 64 00) links the city centre with the airport. Buses run about every 20 minutes from 5.20am to 9pm (every 30 minutes from 6am at the weekend) and take about 20 minutes. Get on/off at the bus station, or on allées Jean-Jaurès, at place Jeanne d'Arc or at Compans Caffarelli on blvd Lascrosses (see the maps). The adult/youth fare is €3.50/2.75 (€5.50/4.10 return; tickets valid two months).

A taxi from the airport costs about €16.

Bus & Metro
City buses and the 15-station metro line are run by Semvat (☎ 05 61 41 70 70). Most bus lines run until 8pm or 9pm daily; seven night bus lines, all terminating at Gare Matabiau, run from 10pm to just after midnight. Marengo and Esquirol metro stations are major metro-bus interchanges. The metro logo is a white 'M' on a grey background.

The system's magnetic tickets can be used on both bus and metro. For travel in central Toulouse, one/10 *tickets rouge* (red tickets) cost €1.20/9.75. Tickets are valid for one hour and up to three transfers after they've been time-stamped. Multiday and multitrip tickets are available, but of marginal value to visitors.

Single tickets are available from bus drivers. These and carnets of 10 are also available from *tabacs* (tobacconists); from machines at each metro station; from bus

TOULOUSE

stops at place Jeanne d'Arc and place Laganne; from Semvat kiosks at Marengo and Jean Jaurès metro stations (6.30am to 7.30pm weekdays, 12.30pm to 7pm Saturday, 4.30pm to 10pm Sunday); and from the Espace Transport Semvat kiosk (ticket sales 6.30am to 7.30pm weekdays, 6.45am to 7pm Saturday) at 7 place Esquirol. Route maps are also available from kiosks.

Car
Parking is tight in the city centre. There's a huge car park beneath place du Capitole, and a multistorey car park above the covered market at place Victor Hugo. Parking meters cost about €1.80 per hour.

Taxi
There are 24-hour taxi stands at gare Matabiau, place Wilson, place Esquirol and elsewhere. Two radio taxi companies are Toulousain (☎ 05 61 42 38 38) and Capitole (☎ 05 34 25 02 50). A typical cross-town fare is about €9.

Bicycle
Rev'Moto (☎ 05 62 47 07 08), 14 blvd de la Gare, rents bicycles (€15.25/64.05 per day/week), scooters and motorcycles; payment is in advance. Semvat (see Bus & Metro) also rents bicycles at Basso Cambo metro station, for €4.55/7.95 per half/full day, and for longer periods.

Tarn-et-Garonne

MONTAUBAN
postcode 82000 • pop 53,800
• elevation 80m

Montauban, prefecture of the Tarn-et-Garonne department, was founded in 1144 by Count Alphonse Jourdain of Toulouse who, legend says, was so charmed by its willow trees (*alba* in Occitan) that he named the place Mont Alba. The town was the prototype for what came to be known as *bastides* (fortified settlements on a rectangular grid plan around a central arcaded square).

Montauban took a beating during the Albigensian Crusade, after which the Church put its stamp on it by creating a bishopric here in 1317. The Pont Vieux (old bridge) was built soon afterwards, to better link rebellious Toulouse with the rest of France.

Montauban was a Huguenot (French Protestant) stronghold during the Wars of Religion. It later held out against several sieges by Louis XIII but finally fell, on the heels of the 1628 capture of La Rochelle. After the Edict of Nantes was repealed by Louis XIV in 1685, the town's beleaguered Protestants suffered badly. Montauban's many classical townhouses date from the prosperous decades following the Catholic reconquest.

Orientation
Place Nationale, lined with arcaded 17th-century brick buildings, is the town's ancient heart. It's the mercantile heart of today's Montauban too, surrounded by a grid of semi-pedestrianised lanes full of trendy shops.

Most buses from Auch and Toulouse stop in place Prax-Paris, near the tourist office. Those from Agen stop at place Maréchal Foch. SNCF buses from Albi stop at the train station. Eurolines coaches (see the Getting There & Away chapter) stop on rue du Châteauvieux, from where it's a 10-minute walk south to the town centre.

The train station is in the district called Ville Bourbon, west across the Tarn, about 1km from place Nationale.

Information
The tourist office (☎ 05 63 63 60 60, fax 05 63 63 65 12) on place Prax-Paris is open 9.30am to 12.30pm and 2pm to 6.30pm Monday to Saturday (9am to 7pm Monday to Saturday, and 10am to noon and 3pm to 6pm on Sunday, in July and August).

The post office is at 4 blvd Midi-Pyrénées. Montauban's BIJ (☎ 05 63 66 32 12, fax 05 63 66 32 62, [e] bij82@bij82.org), at Espace Jeunes on square Piquard, offers free Internet access (book ahead). It opens 1pm to 8pm Monday, 10am to 6pm Tuesday, Thursday and Friday, 10am to 8pm Wednesday and 1pm to 7pm Saturday.

The Centre Hospitalier (hospital; ☎ 05 63 92 82 82) is at 100 rue Léon Cladel. The

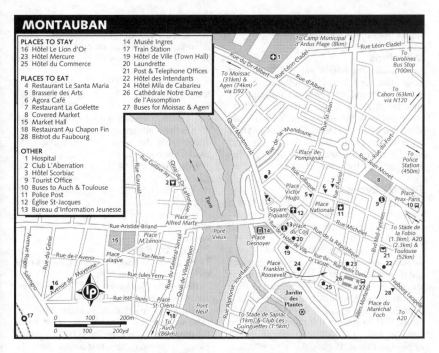

MONTAUBAN

PLACES TO STAY
16 Hôtel Le Lion d'Or
23 Hôtel Mercure
25 Hôtel du Commerce

PLACES TO EAT
4 Restaurant Le Santa Maria
5 Brasserie des Arts
6 Agora Café
7 Restaurant La Goélette
8 Covered Market
15 Market Hall
18 Restaurant Au Chapon Fin
28 Bistrot du Faubourg

OTHER
1 Hospital
2 Club L'Aberration
3 Hôtel Scorbiac
9 Tourist Office
10 Buses to Auch & Toulouse
11 Police Post
12 Église St-Jacques
13 Bureau d'Information Jeunesse

14 Musée Ingres
17 Train Station
19 Hôtel de Ville (Town Hall)
20 Laundrette
21 Post & Telephone Offices
22 Hôtel des Intendants
24 Hôtel Mila de Cabarieu
26 Cathédrale Notre Dame
de l'Assomption
27 Buses for Moissac & Agen

police station (☎ 05 63 21 54 00) is at 50 blvd
d'Alsace-Lorraine, and a small police post is
open Tuesday to Saturday on place Nationale.

There's a laundrette at 26 rue de l'Hôtel
de Ville, open daily.

Place Nationale
This not-quite-square square, all in red brick,
is the heart of the old bastide. Two sides were
destroyed by fire in 1614 and the others by
another fire in 1649, although everything
was rebuilt to the original plans. In the middle of the northern side is a sundial with the
inscription *una tibi* (Occitan for 'your time
will come'). In warm weather the square
sprouts cafe tables and a daily market.

Musée Ingres
Many of the detailed, splendidly sensual
portraits of the neoclassical painter Jean
Auguste Dominique Ingres (1780–1867), a
Montauban native, are exhibited in the
Musée Ingres *(☎ 05 63 22 12 92, 19 rue de*

*l'Hôtel de Ville; adult €3.80, admission
free students & those under 18; admission
free 3rd Sunday of month; open 10.30am-
noon & 2pm-6pm Tues-Sat, 2pm-6pm Sun
Sept-June; 9.30am-noon & 1.30pm-6pm
daily July-Aug)*, in the former episcopal
palace. For more about Ingres, see Arts in
the Facts about Southwest France chapter.

The museum is also home to many sculptures by another famous Montalbanais, Antoine Bourdelle.

Churches
The 18th-century **Cathédrale Notre Dame
de l'Assomption**, on place Franklin Roosevelt, contains Ingres' 1824 masterpiece *Le
Vœu de Louis XIII,* in which the king pledges
France to the Virgin. The building's other attraction is its boastful classical exterior.

Up the hill from the Pont Vieux is **Église
St-Jacques**, begun in 1230 with revenue
from, among other things, fines levied on
citizens thought to be dressed too finely.

Its hexagonal belfry still bears cannonball marks from the Wars of Religion.

Mansions
Among elegant hôtels particuliers dating from after the Catholic resurgence are the **Hôtel des Intendants** (18th to 19th century), once home to the king's *intendant* or governor and now the prefecture, on place du Maréchal Foch; the **Hôtel Mila de Cabarieu** (17th to 18th century) at 24 rue des Carmes; and the **Hôtel Scorbiac** (17th to 18th century) just off place Léon Bourjade.

Special Events
Montauban's biggest annual show is Jazz à Montauban, in the second half of July. Tickets, available from the tourist office or BIJ, cost €15 to €30.

Quatre-cent Coups (400 Blows) is a weekend street festival with parades, rides and music. It's held at the end of September, though the date is only decided a few months ahead. Local lore says that during a siege in 1621 a Spanish fortune-teller told Louis XIII to set up 400 cannons and fire them at the town all at once. It didn't work – so this is, if you like, a celebration of the town's independent spirit.

Alors Chante is a festival of traditional French songs, held during the week before Easter.

Montauban has an ancient royal charter for four annual fairs, which fill the streets from place Nationale to blvd Midi-Pyrénées and from place Prax-Paris to the cathedral, on 19 March, 26 July, 13 October and 20 December.

Places to Stay
The tourist office can recommend some good *chambres d'hôte* (B&Bs) in the area.

Camp Municipal d'Ardus Plage (☎ 05 63 31 89 20, fax 05 63 31 36 07, Lamothe-Capdeville) Adult/pitch €1.50/1.50. Open July-Aug. This plain, riverside facility is the nearest camp site to Montauban – 8km north, just off the D959.

Hôtel du Commerce (☎ 05 63 66 31 32, fax 05 63 03 18 46, 9 place Franklin Roosevelt) Doubles €19.80, with WC €22.10,

with WC & shower €26.68-39.64, with WC & bath €32.01-47.26. Generous €4.55 breakfast. Service can be curt, but this old hotel is well kept, well run, central and cheap.

Hôtel Le Lion d'Or (☎ 05 63 20 04 04, fax 05 63 66 77 39, 22 av de Mayenne) Doubles with shower €28.95-38.10. Breakfast €5.35. *Menus* €8.85-19.80. The Lion d'Or's main advantage is that it's clean and 100m from the train station, though the food's not bad either.

Hôtel Mercure (☎ 05 63 63 17 23, fax 05 63 66 43 66, 12 rue Notre Dame) Singles/doubles €71.65/82.30. Breakfast €8.40. Identikit, posh rooms make this the choice if you want to be pampered and be in the centre.

Places to Eat
There are a few good-value restaurants near the centre of Montauban.

Bistrot du Faubourg (☎ 05 63 63 49 89, 111 Faubourg Lacapelle) Menus €15.25-22.10. Open midday & evening Mon-Fri, midday only Sat. Montauban's best value for money may well be the €10.35 midday *menu* at this smokey restaurant, and the dessert list will melt your heart.

Bar Le Santa Maria (☎ 05 63 91 99 09, 8 quai Montmurat) Open evenings Mon-Sat. Salsa music and Tex-Mex food rule here.

Restaurant Au Chapon Fin (☎ 05 63 63 12 10, 1 place St-Orens) Menus €14.50-27.45. Open midday & evening Mon-Thur, midday only Fri, evening only Sun. Here's another place for pretty good French food at modest prices; their midday-only €13.40 formule is based around a suggested dish of the week.

Brasserie des Arts (☎ 05 63 20 20 90, 4 place Nationale) Menus €12.95-19.05. Open midday & evening daily. Brasserie des Arts occupies half the square in good weather, with the fixed mealtimes and wide choice typical of a French restaurant. Light eaters will like the €7.30 plat du jour.

Agora Café (☎ 05 63 63 05 74, 9 place Nationale) Open midday only Mon-Sat. Salads & other snacks €4.55-6.85. Tables spill onto the pavement from this cheerful bar. The €6.85 Salade Ingres is full of foie gras, *confit* and other countryside treats.

Restaurant La Goélette (☎ 05 63 91 49 42, 12 rue d'Auriol) Menus €8.40-10.05, crepes €2.45-13.70, omelettes €3.95-5.65. Open midday Mon, midday & evening Tues-Sat. This Breton restaurant and creperie is a good refuge from heavy mainstream French meals.

If you're self-catering, there are open-air *farmers markets* on Saturday in place Prax-Paris and Wednesday in place Lalaque, and a small daily one in place Nationale.

Entertainment
If you're not ready for bed just yet, try the following.

Club L'Aberration (☎ 05 63 63 26 69, 12 quai du Dr Lafforgue, 2nd floor) Open 11pm-1am Thur-Sun night (admission free) and a members' club for over-25s (€22.90 to join) 1am-5am Fri-Sat night. This is a lively pub and the closest disco to the town centre.

Club Les Guinguettes (☎ 05 63 91 47 46, 993 rue de l'Abbaye, Sapiac) The retro Club Les Guinguettes, about 1.5km south, packs them in on Friday and Saturday evenings.

Spectator Sports
Rugby matches are held at Stade de Sapiac, 1km south of the centre on rue Léo Lagrange; for match information call ☎ 05 63 66 28 18. The main football venue is Stade de la Fobio (☎ 05 63 66 36 90), rue du Général d'Amade.

Getting There & Away
Bus Local bus operators include Jardel (☎ 05 63 22 55 00) for Toulouse and Auch, and Autocar Barrière (☎ 05 63 93 34 34) and Société Moissagaise de Transports (☎ 05 63 04 92 30) for Moissac and Agen. Buses depart from place Prax-Paris several times daily for Auch (about €11.30, 1¾ hours) and Toulouse (€6.10, 1¼ hours). Buses to Moissac (€3.80, 45 minutes) and Agen (about €9, two hours) go from place Maréchal Foch twice daily Monday to Saturday. Two or three SCNF buses run to Albi (€9.45, 1¼ hours) from the train station, daily Sunday to Friday.

Train Direct daily train services include Toulouse (€7.15, 30 minutes), Cahors (€8.40, 40 minutes), Moissac (€4.40, 20 minutes) and Agen (€9.45, 45 minutes), all several times daily.

Getting Around
Local buses of Transports Montalbanais (☎ 05 63 63 52 52) run daily Monday to Saturday; No 3 connects the train station with blvd Midi-Pyrénées two to four times hourly (€0.85).

MOISSAC
postcode 82200 • pop 12,000 • elevation 2m
Moissac was a major stop for pilgrims on the way to Santiago de Compostela, and today it's a major stop for connoisseurs of the Romanesque. Here in this quiet artists' colony is France's most beautiful ensemble of Romanesque art and the oldest surviving collection of carved Romanesque capitals anywhere. Here also is a major marketplace for the glorious fruit of the Bas-Quercy, most famously a sweet white dessert grape called Golden Chasselas, with its own *appellation d'origine contrôlée* (AOC; a system of strict definition and control of quality wines, spirits and a few other products).

Day-trip access from Montauban, Agen and Toulouse couldn't be easier, by car, train, bus, canal or even on foot. The GR65, which follows one ancient route to Compostela, runs right through the town.

One of Southwest France's two nuclear power stations – at Golfech, 20km west of Moissac – takes cooling water from the Garonne and produces towers of steam visible for miles (Electricité de France will give you a free tour on weekdays; call ☎ 05 63 29 39 06).

Orientation & Information
Moissac sits on the northern bank of the Tarn, 5km from where it empties into the Garonne. The Canal Latéral à la Garonne runs picturesquely alongside.

The busy tourist office (☎ 05 63 04 01 85, fax 05 63 04 27 10, ⓔ office.moissac@wanadoo.fr, Ⓦ www.frenchcom.com/moissac), 6 place Durand de Bredon, is a three-minute walk from the intercity bus stop (called Tribunal), west through the place des

Récollets market and north up rue de la République; or a five-minute walk northeast from the train station along av Pierre Chabrié. The office is open 9am to noon and 2pm to 5pm daily (to 6pm mid-March to mid-October; to 7pm in July and August).

Abbaye St-Pierre

A Benedictine monastery here was on the skids when St Odilon, abbot of Cluny, took it under his wing in the early 11th century. Under Durand de Bredon and successive abbots it was reborn – with a new church in 1063 and cloister in 1100 – as one of southern France's most influential monasteries, spiritually and artistically.

It has taken a beating over the centuries – besieged during the Albigensian Crusade, occupied by the English, trashed in the Wars of Religion, nationalised and defaced during the Revolution. In 1856, already designated a historic monument, it was nearly demolished to make way for the Bordeaux-Sète railway. Today it's part of the Unesco-protected inventory of *chemin de St-Jacques* pilgrim sites. TGVs thunder past just beyond the cloister wall and everything rattles; what the railway line didn't wreck initially, it will surely shake to pieces eventually.

The church's **southern portal**, dating from 1130, is a panorama of biblical stories in stone, with little moral tales enacted around the edges. Over the door is an extraordinary **tympanum** depicting St John's Vision of the Apocalypse, with Christ surrounded by symbols of the four evangelists, two angels and 24 awestruck elders. After this the interior is a letdown, a muddle of Romanesque stone and Gothic brick, the latter from its reconstruction after the Hundred Years' War.

What you mustn't miss is the **cloister**, with 116 delicate marble columns topped by robust, deeply carved capitals, every one different and each a little masterpiece of foliage, earthy figures or biblical scenes. The Revolution's toll is sickening, with nearly every face smashed.

The cloister is entered through the tourist office and has the same opening hours. The tourist office will show you a free video (in French, English or Spanish), and a detailed visitors guide is on sale. A single €4.55 ticket (children aged 12-18 and students half-price) admits you to the cloister, an exhibition on Compostela pilgrimages, a museum of folk art in the former abbot's residence, and a picture library containing replicas of the monastery's beautiful illuminated manuscripts.

Moissac Town

Take a 10-minute stroll south past the cafes on rue de la République to the market square, place des Récollets, and via rue Jean Moura to the canal. Head west along the canal to the Pont St-Jacques, one of France's last remaining swivel bridges. A 15-minute walk along the canal in the other direction takes you to an aqueduct that vaults the canal right over the river.

Moissac has a large community of artists and in the lanes south of the abbey are many small workshops. The tourist office can tell you more about them.

Special Events

The Fête des Arts, a festival featuring the work of regional artists, takes over the streets in late April.

Moissac's biggest bash is the Grande Fête de Pentecôte, on the seventh weekend after Easter, with street and boat parades, music, fairs and food.

The Fête des Fruits et des Légumes celebrates the region's fine produce on the third weekend in September of odd-numbered years.

Places to Stay & Eat

The tourist office keeps a list of *chambres d'hôte* (B&Bs) in town. Contact them for details.

Camping l'Île du Bidounet (☎ 05 63 32 52 52, fax 05 63 32 52 82, [e] *camping .bidounet@wanadoo.fr, St Benoit)* Adult/pitch €3.35/3.35. Open Apr-Sept. Moissac's riverside camp site, 2km south of the town centre on the N113, also offers canoe rental and kids' activities.

Le Carmel (☎ 05 63 04 62 21, fax 05 63 04 62 22, [e] *accueil.cafmoissac@wanadoo .fr, 5 Sente du Calvaire)* Bed €12.20, breakfast €3.80, kitchen use €1.90. Within this former convent, two minutes' walk west of the tourist office, is Moissac's *gîte-d'étape* (simple accommodation for hikers or pilgrims), with basic facilities for walkers and pilgrims.

Hôtel-Restaurant Le Luxembourg (☎ 05 63 04 00 27, fax 05 63 04 19 73, 2 av Pierre Chabrié) Doubles with/without shower & WC €24.40/36.60. Breakfast €4.90. *Menus* €10.35-24.40. The Luxembourg, on the way to the train station, is bland but convenient and pretty good value, and has its own restaurant.

Hôtel Le Chapon Fin (☎ 05 63 04 04 22, fax 05 63 04 58 44, 3 place des Récollets) Doubles with shower €25.90-33.55, or with WC & shower €43.45-47.25, with WC & bath €43.45-51.85. *Menus* €16.75-27.45. This Logis de France hotel offers well kept rooms and good food in its range.

Place Roger Delthil and rue de la République are full of *restaurants* and summertime *cafes*. At place des Récollets is a small indoor *market* selling cheese, bread and the region's superb fruit (Tuesday to Sunday), and a big outdoor food and clothes market (on Saturday and Sunday mornings).

Getting There & Away

By train there are useful departures from Montauban (€4.55, 20 minutes) at about 8.15am and 1.30pm daily, returning about 1pm and 6.25pm. Useful trains from Agen (€6.40, 30 minutes) depart about 10am and 12.30pm daily, returning about 1.50pm, 7.10pm and 8pm. From Toulouse (€10.35, 50 minutes) there are two trains daily, though you'd probably have to spend the night in Moissac.

The only useful bus service departs from the train station at Agen (€5.20, 1½ hours) at 6.40am, or from place Maréchal Foch in Montauban (€3.80, 45 minutes) at 12.10pm, daily Monday to Saturday. There are return buses to both at 5pm. For current times contact the tourist office.

Moissac is on the Toulouse-Agen N113 road. There is parking just behind the tourist office and at place des Récollets.

Getting Around

If there are at least 30 passengers, Moissac Navigation Plaisance (☎ 05 63 04 48 28, fax 05 63 04 26 70), quai Charles de Gaulle, runs two-hour canal cruises for €9.15 (kids aged 3 to 10 €5.35), plus longer trips with meals.

CAYLUS
postcode 82160 • pop 1300
• elevation 600m

With its Gothic market hall in an arcaded square, Caylus would be a bastide if the streets were more perpendicular. But this town, in a cirque beside the Bonnette, a tributary of the River Aveyron, has some of the bastides' appeal and importance. Historically Caylus belongs more to Quercy (see the Lot & Lot-et-Garonne chapter) than to Tarn.

In 1176 the Seigneur de Montpezat acquired Caylus from the count of Toulouse, built a castle – and promptly lost it in the Albigensian Crusade. The new overlord, Alphonse de Poitiers, third son of Louis VIII, fortified the town massively. Nevertheless it fell to the English in 1362, and was sacked by the Huguenots in 1562. The walls were torn down in the 18th century.

Orientation & Information

The tourist office (☎ 05 63 67 00 28, fax 05 63 24 02 91, e ot.caylus@wanadoo.fr), on rue Droite, is open 9am to noon and 2pm to 5.30pm Tuesday to Wednesday, Friday to Saturday, and Thursday morning; to 6pm May; to 6.30pm June and September; and 9am to noon and 2pm to 7pm daily in July and August.

West up rue Droite is the market square, place du Marché. Market days are Tuesday (food and bric-a-brac, all day) and Saturday (food, morning only).

Town Centre

Medieval houses line rue Droite and its extension, rue du Long. Spookiest of the lot, opposite the tourist office, is the late-13th-century **Maison des Loups** (not open to the public), bristling with wolf gargoyles and reliefs. Beside the tourist office is the 14th-century **Église St-Jean Baptiste**, with a striking crucifixion carved from an elm tree in 1954 by the Polish sculptor Ossip Zadkine (1890–1967).

The basin in the ledge around the 14th-century **covered market** is an ancient grain measure – an indication of the traditional importance of this market.

South of the market, is the **Château de Caylus** *(closed to the public)*, built about 1900 in 15th-century style; and a square tower, the only survivor of the Seigneur de Montpezat's 12th-century **Château Royal**.

Some 400m south of the tourist office on the D19 is the **Maison du Patrimoine** *(☎ 05 63 24 06 26; €2.30/1.50 adult/those aged 6–18; open 2pm-6pm Tues-Sun, Mar–mid-June & mid-Sep–Oct; 10am-12.30pm & 2pm-6.30pm daily mid-June–mid-Sept)*, an interactive museum of natural and cultural heritage; and a tiny **reservoir** *(admission free; open year round for swimming)*.

Abbaye de Beaulieu-en-Rouerge

In truth, many Caylus visitors are on their way to a monastery in a wooded vale 12km to the south-east. Founded in 1144, this rather in-austere Cistercian abbey was trashed in the Wars of Religion and rebuilt in the 17th century. In 1963 it was bought, restored, donated to the state and opened as a centre for contemporary art *(☎ 05 63 24 50 10, Ginals; adult/those under 18 years €5.50/free; open 10am-noon & 2pm-6pm daily July-Aug; 10am-noon & 2pm-6pm Wed-Mon Sept-June)*. The serene Gothic church has a fine rose window.

The only way to get here is by car, bicycle or on foot.

Places to Stay

With the GR46 running through it, Caylus has its fair share of *chambres d'hôte* and *gîtes*; the tourist office has details.

Camping La Bonnette (☎/fax 05 63 65 70 20, Les Condamines) Adult/pitch & bicycle/pitch & car €2.90/2.75/3.50. Open Mar-Oct. The town's well kept riverside camp site, 800m south of the tourist office on the D19, has a small pool.

Hôtel-Restaurant La Renaissance (☎ 05 63 67 07 26, fax 05 63 24 03 57, cnr av du Père Huc & rue de l'Hôtel) Doubles with

WC & shower/bath €33.60/39.65. Midday *menus* €10.65, evening *menus* €16.80-30.50. This Logis de France place offers comfortable rooms and good Quercy cuisine.

Hôtel de la Vallée (☎ 05 63 67 06 80, fax 05 63 24 03 24, Cornusson) Doubles with shower & WC €30.50. This plain, cheerful hotel, in a tiny village 10km south of Caylus, has a small pool.

Getting There & Around

Caylus is 43km north-east of Montauban on the D926. Jardel (☎ 05 63 91 01 91) runs two or three buses daily Monday to Saturday to Montauban (€3.95, 35-55 minutes). There are additional buses from Caussade (€3.05), where frequent Toulouse-Montauban-Paris trains stop.

The closest bicycle rental is Ça Roule à Puylaroque (Mme Brousses; ☎ 05 63 64 92 55), open Tuesday to Saturday in Puylaroque, 14km west on the D20; VTTs go for €12.20/45.75 per day/week.

GORGES OF THE AVEYRON

In its lower reaches the River Aveyron, tributary to the River Tarn, has cut a gorge through the limestone plateau, snaking along the boundary between the Tarn and Tarn-et-Garonne departments. Pretty, medieval towns dot the landscape, perched on their own hills or at the edges of the gorge. The GR36 and GR46 run north to south.

By car or bicycle, the area is equally accessible from Montauban (by the D115, running along the Aveyron) and from Albi (on the D600 via Cordes-sur-Ciel). Few buses reach the area.

Activities

This is the kingdom of the walker, cyclist, climber, caver and boater. Floating down the Aveyron costs about €23 per half-day in a two-person canoe, or €16 in a one-person kayak. You can rent VTTs for around €16 per day at many places. Following are some major outdoor-adventure outfits:

Association pour l'Animation des Gorges de l'Aveyron et des Causses (AAGAC) (☎ 05 65 29 73 94, fax 05 65 29 77 33) Open July-Aug.

Camping Municipal, Najac. Canoes & kayak trips, VTT rental.

Aventure 82 (☎/fax 05 63 24 11 58, ⓔ r82aven@ aol.com) place de la Porte Haute, Montricoux. VTT, canoe & kayak, climbing, caving & hiking trips.

Découverte (☎/fax 05 63 68 22 46) 15 blvd des Thermes, St-Antonin Noble Val. VTT, canoe, kayak, climbing, caving & hiking trips.

Nature et Loisirs (☎ 05 63 30 66 24) 16 blvd de la Condamine, St-Antonin Noble Val. Canoe & kayak trips.

Variation (☎ 05 63 68 25 25) La Plage, St-Antonin Noble Val. Canoe, kayak, climbing & caving trips.

Almost every tourist office has a list of local places offering horse riding. Topoguides and IGN maps are to be found in even the smallest newsagents.

Getting Around
GAU Autocars (☎ 05 63 30 44 45) buses to Montauban (except Sunday) serve Montricoux (35 minutes) and Bruniquel (40 minutes) three to four times daily during school term and twice daily during school holidays, and Penne (45 minutes) and St-Antonin Noble Val (one hour) once daily in school term and on Tuesday, Thursday and Saturday during school holidays.

Montricoux
postcode 82800 • pop 800 • elevation 125m
Here the Aveyron gorge begins in earnest. Montricoux is a small, pretty town with many elegant 15th- and 16th-century **half-timbered houses** as well as a late-13th-century church with a 16th-century belfry, and fragments of ancient **ramparts**.

The town's chateau (beside the church) is home to the **Musée Marcel Lenoir** (☎ 05 63 67 26 48, place Marcel-Lenoir; €3.80, child under 12 free; open 10am-noon & 2.30pm-7pm daily May-Sept), dedicated to a local artist – real name Jules Oury (1872–1931) – who made good in Paris. There's a fresco by him in the church.

Montricoux's market day is Friday.

Places to Stay & Eat Montricoux's limited options include the following.

Camping Le Clos Lalande (☎/fax 05 63 24 18 89, ⓔ lecloslalande@multimania .com, route de Bioule) 2-person forfait €11.30. Open year round. This shady riverside facility, 600m north-west of the village, has a pool and also rents bungalows.

Aventure 82 (see Activities earlier in this section) Dorm beds €8.25. This adventure centre, 150m north-east of place de la Mairie, has a modern gîte d'étape for its groups and – subject to space – anyone else. Meals are by arrangement, or you can use the kitchen. Call ahead as it fills up in summer.

Le Relais du Postillon (☎ 05 63 67 23 58, fax 05 63 67 27 68, D115 route de Montauban) Rooms with/without shower €16.75/ 19.80. Menus €14.50-27.45. Restaurant open midday & evening Sun-Thur, midday only Fri, daily July-Aug. Just across the Aveyron, this restaurant has a few unexceptional rooms but great food (including a good-value €9.15 lunchtime menu express), popular with locals and lorry drivers.

Bruniquel
postcode 82800 • pop 500 • elevation 130m
Snug, cobbled Bruniquel, perched atop a sheer 100m drop to the river, is the stuff of legends. One says it was founded in the 6th century by Brunehaut, queen of the Visigoths, though its chateau dates from the 12th century. It's full of 15th- and 16th-century houses and still has two of its seven medieval gates.

Orientation & Information Park below the village and walk up. The tourist office (☎/fax 05 63 67 29 84), opposite the car park, is stocked with maps and pamphlets on regional hiking and biking. It opens 10.30am to noon and 2pm to 6pm daily (except 10 am to 6pm in July and August).

Les Châteaux de Bruniquel Why plural? Around 1500 the property was split between two branches of the family and a second castle was built. It's now a hotchpotch of styles from the 13th to the 19th centuries. You can snoop around the original keep and the Gothic Salle des Chevaliers (Knights' Room) yourself, or take a tour (☎ 05 63 67

*27 67, rue de Château; adult/child €2.30/
1.50, with guide €3.05/1.85; open 2pm-6pm
Mon-Sat, 10am-12.30pm & 2pm-6pm Sun
in Apr, June & Sept; 10am-12.30pm & 2pm-
6pm Sun May & Oct; 10am-12.30pm &
2pm-7pm daily July-Aug).*

Maison des Comtes de Payrol This
severe 13th-century mansion, richly decorated in Gothic and Renaissance style inside
(with original murals), houses a **museum**
*(☎ 05 63 67 26 42; place des Monges; €2.30,
child under 12 free; open 10am-noon &
2pm-5pm Sat-Sun Mar; 10am-noon & 2pm-
5pm daily Apr-June; 10am-noon & 2pm-7pm
daily July-Aug; 10am-noon & 2pm-6pm
daily Sept-Oct)* about Bruniquel and the
Aveyron Valley.

Penne
Perched on a boat-shaped ridge, this unrestored village (which actually falls within
the Tarn department) is topped at one end by
the impossible, teetering ruins of a castle
dating back at least to the 13th century. The
villagers of that time, loyal to Toulouse, took
a thrashing during the Albigensian Crusade.
There is an unfenced, decidedly dangerous
but well worn path up to the ruins, with
sheer drops on both sides.

A small tourist office *(☎ 05 63 56 14 80)*
at the village's only intersection is open
10am to noon and 3pm to 6pm mid-June to
mid-September (to 7pm in July and August), 2.30pm to 5.30pm May to mid-June
and in late September, and 2pm to 5pm the
rest of the year. Here you can also find out
about several village *chambres-d'hôte*.

*Bar-Restaurant La Terrasse (☎ 05 63 56
35 03, opposite the tourist office)* Menus
€15.10-22.10. This place stumps up a very
hearty €9.90 *menu du jour*.

St-Antonin Noble Val
postcode 82140 • pop 1920 • elevation 130m
This flinty old town boasts France's oldest
civic building and a splendidly unrestored
medieval centre. A Cathar town, it was captured by Simon de Montfort in 1212, and
was occupied by the English in the Hundred
Years' War. Louis XIII took it in 1622 after

his siege of Montauban flopped (celebrated
at the Quatre-Cent Coups, see Special Events
under Montauban earlier in this chapter).

Orientation & Information The town sits
on the northern bank of the Aveyron, fronted
by blvd des Thermes.

The tourist office (☎ 05 63 30 63 47, fax
05 63 30 66 33, ⓔ tourisme@saint-antonin
-noble-val.com, ⓌW www.saint-antonin-noble
-val.com) is in a former convent two blocks
north from the bridge, up rue du Pont de
l'Aveyron. It opens 9.30am to 12.30pm and
2pm to 6.30pm daily in July and August, and
afternoons only during the rest of the year.

From the tourist office the ancient marketplace and town centre, place de la Halle,
is one block east and one block north. North
from here on rue de la Pélisserie is an English bookshop called... the English Bookshop. A Crédit Agricole bank is on av Paul
Benet, the thoroughfare one block north of
the bookshop.

St-Antonin's market day (food and bric-a-
brac) is Sunday. The town also hosts a district
fair on the third Wednesday of each month.

Things to See & Do The handsome early
12th-century **Romanesque mansion** on
place de la Halle became the town hall in
1313. The 19th-century architect-restorer
Viollet-le-Duc mutilated it with its present
curious tower. Today it houses the **Musée
Municipal** *(☎ 05 63 68 23 52; adult/child
aged 6-16 €2.30/0.75; open 10am-1pm &
3pm-6.30pm Wed-Mon)*, an ethnology and
archaeology museum including old fragments of the building itself.

In the middle of the shady square is a fine
Gothic **market hall**. The surrounding streets
are full of **half-timbered houses** testifying
to St-Antonin's medieval prosperity.

For a splendid view you can climb 660m
up the **Roc d'Anglars** across the river. The
shortest trip (6km) takes about two hours.
The tourist office sells a booklet outlining
this and other local walks.

About 3km north-east is **Grotte du Bosc**
*(☎ 05 63 30 60 03, D75 route d'Espasse;
adult/child aged 10-16 years/4-9 years
€4.25/3.35/2.75; open 2pm-6pm Sun Easter-*

June & Sept; 10am-noon & 2pm-6pm daily July-Aug), a cave formed by an underground river; take a warm jumper for the 35-minute guided tour.

Places to Stay & Eat St-Antonin food and accommodation are on the spartan side.

Camping Le Ponget (☎/fax 05 63 68 21 13, ⓔ camping-leponget@wanadoo.fr, D19 route de Caylus) Adult/pitch/tent €2.45/ 1.50/2.30. Open Apr-Oct. This functional municipal site is 800m north of town.

Camping Les 3 Cantons (☎ 05 63 31 98 57, fax 05 63 31 25 93, ⓔ info@3cantons.fr, route de Vivens) Adult/pitch €4.90/6.10. Open mid-Apr–Sept. Les 3 Cantons is fairly remote (7.5km north of town) but has a shop, a large pool and tennis courts.

Camping d'Anglars (☎ 05 63 30 69 76, fax 05 63 30 67 61, D115 route de Laguépie) Adult/pitch €3.20/4.25. Open mid-Apr–mid-Sep. This pleasant, shady site, 1.6km east of town, with a bar and snack bar, is 300m from the river.

Variation (see Activities earlier in this section) has a camp site and a small cafe at its La Plage site, east of the town centre.

Hôtel des Thermes (☎ 05 63 30 61 08, fax 05 63 68 26 23, ⓔ hotel.des.thermes@ wanadoo.fr, 1 promenade des Moines) Doubles with bath €28.95-33.55, twins €35.05-39.65. Menus €13.60-27.45. Rooms at this Logis de France hotel overlook the river or locals at *pétanque* (boules; a game, not unlike lawn bowls, played with heavy metal balls on a sandy pitch) in place des Moines. The terrace restaurant is strong on river fish and local produce; there's a good €9 weekday midday *menu*.

The tourist office has a list of half-a-dozen *chambres d'hôte*.

Tarn

ALBI
postcode 81000 • pop 64,500
• elevation 174m
The earliest written references to Albi date back to the 4th century AD, by which time it was a sizable provincial market town. This is the 'Albi' of the 12th- and 13th-century Albigensian heresy (see the boxed text 'The Albigensian Crusade'). Albi's massive Gothic cathedral was begun less than four decades after the Cathar movement was violently crushed.

Heavily influenced by Toulouse and the Languedoc, Albi has a southern feel, laid-back and not overrun with tourists. Most of the inner town, including the cathedral, is built of reddish brick made from the clay of the River Tarn.

One of Albi's most famous sons was Henri de Toulouse-Lautrec (1864–1901), famous for his posters and lithographs of the bars, brothels and music halls of Montmartre in *belle époque* Paris. Although he spent little time in Albi after an unhappy childhood, the town's Musée Toulouse-Lautrec is the most important collection of his work anywhere.

Orientation
Albi is about 80km north-east of Toulouse, on the Tarn's southern bank. Looming over the city centre – and a landmark from almost anywhere – is the Cathédrale Ste-Cécile. A web of narrow streets stretches south-east to place du Vigan, Albi's commercial hub. The train station lies about 1km south-west of the city centre.

Information
Tourist Office The tourist office (☎ 05 63 49 48 80, fax 05 63 49 48 98, ⓔ otsi.albi@ wanadoo.fr), on place Ste-Cécile, is open 9am to 12.30pm and 2pm to 6pm Monday to Saturday, and 10.30am to 12.30pm and 2.30pm to 5.30pm Sunday. Hours during July and August are 9am to 7.30pm Monday to Saturday and 10.30am to 1pm and 2.30pm to 6.30pm Sunday.

Money Because they're open late Saturday (Albi's market day), banks here close Monday. There are at least two each on place Ste-Cécile and place du Vigan. You can change money on Sunday at the tourist office and on Monday at the main post office.

Post & Communications The main post office on place du Vigan has a Cyberposte

The Albigensian Crusade

The dualistic doctrine of Catharism was based on the belief that the kingdom of God is locked in battle with an intrinsically evil material world created by Satan. Among other things, Cathars (or Albigenses as they were also known, after the town of Albi) believed that anything concerned with the physical body – eating, sex, materialism, indeed life itself – was ultimately to be renounced. In their struggle to free the spirit from the flesh, Cathars took inspiration from an ascetic, chaste and vegetarian clergy caste.

Catharism had spread from the Balkans to the region around Carcassonne, Toulouse and Albi in the 11th to 13th centuries, partly in response to the materialism of the Church in Rome, and found wide favour with common people and aristocrats alike. Preaching was in the old Occitan tongue (langue d'Oc).

A crusade against the Cathars instigated by Pope Innocent III in 1208 – after a papal representative was murdered by a vassal of the count of Toulouse – provided a perfect opportunity for the French kings to wage a war of conquest against the nobility of the south.

Some of the cruellest anti-Cathar campaigns were led by an Englishman, Simon de Montfort. He quickly took Béziers and Carcassonne, earning a reputation for merciless sieges and slaughter. In 1213 at Muret, near Toulouse, he defeated Raymond VI, count of Toulouse, and after the Church declared that Montfort should get Raymond's lands, he began styling himself count of Toulouse.

Four years later, Raymond's son stirred up an uprising in Provence and, while Montfort was tending to that, Raymond VI retook Toulouse. In his subsequent siege of Toulouse, Montfort was killed by a rock – lobbed, it's said, by a local woman.

The sons of Raymond and Montfort continued the struggle for another 16 years before the younger Montfort ceded his claim to the southern lands to Louis VIII, who then embarked on a more blatant 'crusade'. In 1229, with all of Languedoc's Cathar centres crushed and thousands of Cathars slaughtered or burned at the stake, Raymond VII finally surrendered. By 1321 Catharism in southern France had been destroyed.

---

terminal. There's a branch post office on av du Général de Gaulle near the university.

Albi's BIJ (☎/fax 05 63 47 19 55, e bij .albi@wanadoo.fr), 19 place Ste-Cécile, offers Internet access at €3.05 per hour (or free for finding summer work, for example); book ahead. It opens 10am to noon and 1.30pm to 6pm weekdays (no lunch break Wednesday). Mediathèque (☎ 05 63 38 56 20, e mediatheque@mairie-albi.fr), av du Général de Gaulle, charges €3.80 per hour and opens 1pm to 6pm on Monday, 1pm to 7pm on Tuesday, 10am to noon and 1pm to 6pm Wednesday to Saturday, and 10am to 6pm on Friday. Ludi.com (☎ 05 63 43 34 24, e ludi .com@ludimedia.com), 62 rue Séré de Rivière, charges €4.55 per hour and opens 11am to midnight Monday to Saturday.

Bookshops For walking and cycling guides and regional history books (in French). Siloë (33 rue de l'Hôtel de Ville) is good for walking and cycling guides and regional history books (in French). Transparence (9 rue Timbal) is a stationer with a hit-or-miss map selection. Maison de la Presse (place du Vigan) sells international newspapers and some guidebooks; it opens Monday to Saturday and Sunday morning.

University The Centre Universitaire Lapérouse, a branch of the Université de Toulouse with some 2000 students in humanities, social sciences and law, is 1km south-west of the city centre near the train station.

Laundry Two laundrettes that are open daily, are Lavomatique, 10 rue Émile Grand, and Lavotop, 96 av du Général de Gaulle. Someone else will do the washing for you at 5 à Sec, on place Lapérouse.

Medical Services & Emergency The city's Centre Hospitalier (hospital; ☎ 05 63

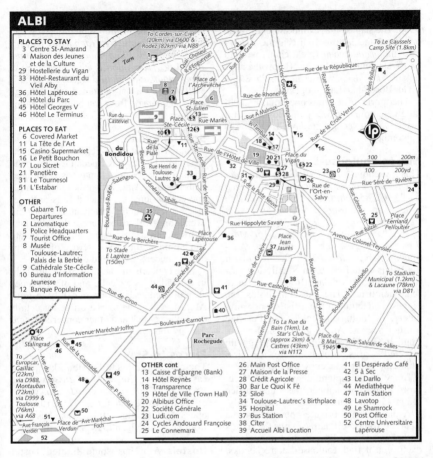

ALBI

PLACES TO STAY
3 Centre St-Amarand
4 Maison des Jeunes et de la Culture
29 Hostellerie du Vigan
33 Hôtel-Restaurant du Vieil Alby
36 Hôtel Lapérouse
40 Hôtel du Parc
45 Hôtel Georges V
46 Hôtel Le Terminus

PLACES TO EAT
6 Covered Market
11 La Tête de l'Art
15 Casino Supermarket
16 Le Petit Bouchon
17 Lou Sicret
21 Panetière
31 Le Tournesol
51 L'Estabar

OTHER
1 Gabarre Trip Departures
2 Lavomatique
5 Police Headquarters
7 Tourist Office
8 Musée Toulouse-Lautrec; Palais de la Berbie
9 Cathédrale Ste-Cécile
10 Bureau d'Information Jeunesse
12 Banque Populaire

OTHER cont
13 Caisse d'Épargne (Bank)
14 Hôtel Reynès
18 Transparence
19 Hôtel de Ville (Town Hall)
20 Albibus Office
22 Société Générale
23 Ludi.com
24 Cycles Andouard Françoise
25 Le Connemara
26 Main Post Office
27 Maison de la Presse
28 Crédit Agricole
30 Bar Le Quoi K Fé
32 Siloë
34 Toulouse-Lautrec's Birthplace
35 Hôpital
37 Bus Station
38 Citer
39 Accueil Albi Location
41 El Despérado Café
42 5 à Sec
43 Le Darllo
44 Mediathèque
47 Train Station
48 Lavotop
49 Le Shamrock
50 Post Office
52 Centre Universitaire Lapérouse

47 47 47) faces place Lapérouse. The police headquarters (☎ 05 63 49 22 81) is at 6 lices Georges Pompidou.

Dangers & Annoyances The area called du Bondidou, a big car park south-west of the cathedral, is dodgy after dark. So are the footpaths around the Palais de la Berbie.

Cathédrale Ste-Cécile
This mighty cathedral (☎ 05 63 43 23 43, 5 blvd Sybille; admission to nave free; admission to choir adult/child under 14 €0.80/free, admission to treasury adult/ those aged 12-25/child under 12 €3.05/ 1.85/free; open 8.30am-8.45pm daily June-Sept; 8am-noon & 2.30pm-6.30pm Oct-May) in Southern Gothic style took two centuries to build (1282–1480). It's quite outsized – big enough to hold the town's entire population of around 6000 at the time of construction – and it would be hard to describe it as attractive. Illuminated on a summer night, though, it's impressive.

In contrast to the plain, sunburned exterior, not one interior surface was left untouched by the Italian artists who painted it between 1509 and 1512. Spanning the sanctuary is an intricately carved rood screen from around 1500. The stained-glass windows in the apse date from the 14th to 16th centuries. Don't miss the *grand chœur* (great choir) with 30 Old Testament stone figures. Below the huge organ is *Le Jugement Dernier* (1475–84), a vivid, Bosch-like Last Judgement.

The tourist office runs one-hour, French-language tours (€5.20) of the cathedral twice daily (except Saturday) from June to September.

Musée Toulouse-Lautrec

This museum (☎ *05 63 49 48 70, place Ste-Cécile; adult €3.65, student and those aged 14-25 €1.85, child under 14 admission free; open 10am-noon & 2pm-5pm Nov-Feb; 10am-noon & 2pm-5.30pm Mar & Oct; 10am-noon & 2pm-6pm Apr-May; 9am-noon & 2pm-6pm June & Sept; 9am-6pm July-Aug; closed Tues Oct-May*) is in the Palais de la Berbie, an equally fortress-like archbishop's palace from the 13th to 15th centuries. The museum holds the biggest collection of the artist's work anywhere, including his celebrated Parisian brothel scenes. Audio-guides in French, English, German and Spanish, dealing with selected works, are available for hire. Changing exhibits occupy the top floor.

Entry to the splendid gardens is free. From June to September, the tourist office offers 45-minute tours (€6.70) twice daily.

A plaque on a private house at 14 rue Henri de Toulouse-Lautrec marks the artist's birthplace. If you haven't had enough already you'll find Toulouse-Lautrec books, photos, postcards, wines, recipes and pastries everywhere you look.

Hôtel Reynès

Albi – and particularly the Reynès merchant family – prospered from the woad trade (see the boxed text '*Le Pastel*' earlier in this chapter), even before Toulouse got wind of it. The family mansion, the Hôtel Reynès on rue Timbal, is now occupied by the chamber of commerce (and closed to the public). With its ornate window mullions and galleried courtyard, this is a fine example of civil Renaissance architecture.

River Trips

From mid-June to mid-September you can take a 35-minute trip (*departures every 35 minutes, 10.30am-noon & 2pm-6.30pm July-Aug, 11am-noon & 2pm-6pm June & Sept; adult/student/child aged 2-8 €3.95/ 3.20/0.75*) on a flat-bottomed sailing barge called a *gabarre*, from just below the Palais de la Berbie.

Special Events

Carnaval (about six weeks before Easter; see Public Holidays & Special Events in the Facts for the Visitor chapter) is celebrated with gusto in Albi, with folk music, bands and processions; the exact date is only decided a few months in advance. Other big events on Albi's calendar are the Albi Jazz Festival, in various squares and cafes in late June; and a three-day series of ancient music concerts at the end of July.

Free concerts of classical music are held in Cathédrale Ste-Cécile and other venues at 5pm Wednesday from mid-July to mid-August. Ask at the tourist office for details of free jazz, rock and other concerts around the city too.

Places to Stay

The closest camp site to Albi, 2km northeast of place du Vigan, is *Le Caussels* (☎/fax *05 63 60 37 06, route de Millau*), which offers a two-person forfait for €10.05. It opens April to mid-October. Take bus No 5 from place du Vigan to the end of the line.

Hostels Albi has some limited hostel options.

Maison des Jeunes et de la Culture (MJC; ☎ *05 63 54 53 65, fax 05 63 54 61 55,* e *fjt-aj-mjcalbi@wanadoo.fr, 13 rue de la République*) Bus No 1 from train station to République stop. Dorm beds €5.35. Breakfast €2.45, other meals weekdays & Sat morning €6.40. Reception 7pm-9pm Mon-Fri, 8pm-9pm Sat-Sun, year round. Accommodation here is spartan. A sign on rue Jules Rolland indicates whether it's *complet* (full).

Centre St-Amarand (☎ *05 63 48 18 29, fax 05 63 48 18 21, 16 rue de la République*)

The centre is meant for groups but may have a monastic room or two for travellers. The entrance is down adjacent impasse du Grand Séminaire.

Hotels The best hotels are largely in the centre or just south of town.

Hôtel Lapérouse (☎ 05 63 54 69 22, fax 05 63 38 03 69, 21 place Lapérouse) Doubles/twins €34.75-50.00/40.85-50.00. Breakfast €5.35. Nicely furnished rooms at the rear of this small hotel look downhill to a swimming pool in a garden straight out of the countryside.

Hôtel-Restaurant du Vieil Alby (☎ 05 63 54 14 69, fax 05 63 54 96 75, 25 rue Henri de Toulouse-Lautrec) Doubles with bath €39.65-41.15. Closed late Jan & early July. Rooms are simple and well furnished, but it's the food that makes the Vieil Alby worthwhile (see Places to Eat).

Hostellerie du Vigan (☎ 05 63 43 31 31, fax 05 63 47 05 42, 16 place du Vigan) Doubles with/without WC & bath €51.85/47.25. Breakfast €6.10. Parking €3.80. The best features of this Logis de France place are its big rooms and its position on place du Vigan.

Hotel Le Terminus (☎/fax 05 63 47 09 76, 33 av Maréchal Joffre) Rooms with WC & shower €32-36.60, without €27.45. Breakfast €4.25. This cheery, no-frills place opposite the train station has functional, newly renovated rooms.

Hôtel du Parc (☎ 05 63 54 12 80, fax 05 63 54 69 59, 3 av du Parc) Doubles with WC & shower €30.50-35.05. Breakfast €5.35. This budget choice has big rooms but no restaurant. Food in the neighbourhood (near the bus station) is limited.

Hôtel Georges V (☎ 05 63 54 24 16, fax 05 63 49 90 78, [e] hotel.georgesv@ilink.fr, 29 av Maréchal Joffre) Doubles with shower/bath €36.60/39.60. Breakfast €4.90-5.50. This small, family-run place near the train station has big, quiet rooms and attentive service.

Places to Eat
Albi has lots to offer foodies whatever their budgets.

Le Petit Bouchon (☎ 05 63 54 11 75, 77 rue de la Croix Verte) Menus €7.30-19.50. Open midday & evening Mon-Fri, midday only Sat. Just a cafe-bar with a few tables, this is the perfect choice for simple fare at reasonable prices (eg, €10 for crudités, plat du jour, dessert and a glass of wine).

Hostellerie du Vigan (see Places to Stay) Menus €16-22.10, salads €5.35-7.60. This hotel has a sunny brasserie facing place du Vigan, and a cafe spilling onto the square, with salads, sandwiches and grills.

Restaurant La Tête de l'Art (☎ 05 63 38 44 75, 7 rue de la Piale) Menus €12.95-22.85, entrées €7.60-13.70. La Tête de l'Art offers carefully prepared local cuisine in a traditional half-timbered house.

Hôtel-Restaurant du Vieil Alby (see Places to Stay) Menus €8.40-22.85. Here you'll find some of the best food in Albi. The cheapest *menu des petites gastronomes* lets you sample it without popping your buttons; the top *menu* is a rollcall of local specialities.

Restaurant Lou Sicret (☎ 05 63 38 26 40, 1 rue Timbal) Plat du jour €6.85, regional dishes €10.35-13.70, salads €6.40-10.35. Open midday & evening daily. Lou Sicret is the place to sample traditional Albigeoise cuisine, on rough wooden tables in a secluded courtyard.

L'Estabar (☎ 05 63 38 29 03, 12 av François Verdier) Main dishes €8.40-10.65, grills €6.40-6.85. Open midday & evening Mon-Fri, evening only Sat. This big, cheerful bar opposite the university specialises in Tex-Mex food.

Le Tournesol (☎ 05 63 38 38 14, 11 rue de l'Ort-en-Salvy) Entrées €4.25-5.35, hot dishes €7.30, salads €3.05. Open midday Tues-Sat, evening Fri. Albi's only vegetarian restaurant would be good value even if it weren't vegetarian. The simple menu also includes several fresh vegetable *assiettes* (platters).

Self-Catering Fresh fare can be picked up from the *covered market (place du Marché)* Tuesday to Sunday. *Panetière (place du Vigan)* sells bread and other baked goods until 8pm daily. The *Casino supermarket (lices Georges Pompidou)* stays open until 7.30pm Monday to Saturday.

TARN

On Saturday morning a *food market* fills place Ste-Cécile, with everything from bulging stalls to farmers with their three radishes.

Entertainment

Bars Three bars near the centre with occasional live music are *Le Darllo* (☎ 05 63 38 93 09, 10 av du Général de Gaulle), *Le Connemara* (☎ 05 63 54 92 42, 6 rue Balzac) and *Le Shamrock* (☎ 05 63 43 08 50, 57 av du Général de Gaulle).

L'Estabar (see Places to Eat) L'Estabar offers up a recorded Latin beat until 2am nightly except Sunday.

El Despérado Café (☎ 05 63 54 52 39, 25 place Edmond Canet) This place serves Tex-Mex food during the day (midday Monday to Friday, evening Friday to Saturday, €12.20 *menu*), and plays music to match until late, Friday to Saturday.

Bar Le Quoi K Fé (☎ 05 63 43 47 84, 10 rue de l'Ort-en-Salvy) Music here runs mainly to rock and disco.

Most bars in Albi stay open until 2am and are closed on Monday.

Discos Albi discos include *Le Star's Club* (☎ 05 63 56 61 11, N112 route des Castres) Open 11pm-dawn Thur-Sat. Albi's most popular disco is about 2.5km south of the centre; and *La Rue du Bain* (☎ 05 63 54 75 66, rue Lavazière, Côte de Lavazière) Open 11pm-5am Mon-Sat. This hot spot is 1.5km south of the centre near the N88.

Spectator Sports

The main rugby venue is Stadium Municipal, 1.5km south-east of the city centre on av Col Teyssier (D81; southbound bus No 5 from place du Vigan to Somme stop). Football matches are also played here and at the smaller Stade E Lagrèze (southbound bus No 2 or 4 from place du Vigan to Lagrèze stop).

Getting There & Away

Bus The bus station is on place Jean Jaurès, but there's no office; for timetables, ask at the tourist office. Destinations with multiple daily departures (except Sunday) include Castres (€5.05, 50 minutes), Montauban (€9.45, 1¼ hours) and Toulouse (€10.80, 1½ hours). Montauban buses and some Toulouse buses are run by SNCF, and also stop at the train station.

Train The train station is on place Stalingrad. Albi is on the Toulouse-Rodez line, with services about hourly during the week and less often Saturday (none Sunday). For Pau or other southern destinations, change at Toulouse (€9.90, 1¼ hours).

Car National car rental firms include Citer (☎ 05 63 38 45 33, 78 av Gambetta), and Accueil Albi Location (☎ 05 63 47 20 40, 17 blvd du Lude). Europcar (☎ 05 63 54 66 56) is just west of place de Verdun on av François Verdier. Others include ADA (☎ 05 63 38 96 48), Avis (☎ 05 63 54 76 54) and Hertz (☎ 05 63 54 17 34).

Getting Around

Bus Local buses are run by Albibus (☎ 05 63 38 43 43). Single tickets are available for €0.75 (€0.30 on the central shoppers' shuttle) from tabacs, drivers or Albibus, 14 rue de l'Hôtel de Ville. Bus No 1 goes from the train station to the bus station and place du Vigan. Buses don't run on Sunday.

Bicycle Cycles Andouard Françoise (☎ 05 63 38 44 47, 7 rue Séré de Rivière) rents VTTs per half-day/day/week €12.20/15.25/76.20).

AROUND ALBI
Cordes-sur-Ciel

This proud bastide, chartered in 1222 by Raymond VI, count of Toulouse, lords it grandly over the surrounding countryside about 20km north-west of Albi. Tourist literature gushes about the 'pearl of the bastides' and indeed it's extraordinarily picturesque, crowned with a cluster of very handsome Gothic residences. The atmosphere is being milked for all it's worth and the town – full of workshops, galleries and antique shops – has an aura of twee artiness. Try to visit early or late in the day to avoid the crowds.

Orientation The town has four layers of walls: two original inner ones, with old

14th-century Pont Vieux, Montauban

The lofty nave of Église des Jacobins, Toulouse

The apse, Basilique St-Sernin, Toulouse

The mighty Gothic tower of Cathédrale Ste-Cécile stands proud above Albi.

A 16th-century dovecote, L'Isle Bouzon

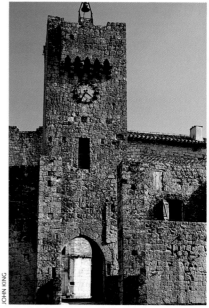

The fortified village of Larressingle's West Gate

A Séviac vineyard, all set to produce the famous Armagnac brandy

gates; another added in the early 14th century and the last in the 16th century as the population grew. The modern town has spread down to the D600 and beyond. From the D600 the principal access is from place de la Boutellerie at the eastern end of the hill.

Information The tourist office (☎ 05 63 56 00 52, fax 05 63 56 19 52, e officedu tourisme.cordes@wanadoo.fr), on Grand Rue, is open 10am to 1pm and 2pm to 7pm daily, year round. Pick up a free map or the excruciatingly detailed *Walking Guide* (€4.55) here.

Things to See The star attractions are the facades of four Gothic mansions, with filigree windows and extravagantly sculpted sandstone exteriors, built on Grand Rue by wealthy merchants or noble families: **Maison du Grand Fauconnier** (House of the Grand Falconer), the finest of the lot; **Maison du Grand Veneur** (Huntsman), with the most playful decorations; **Maison du Grand Ecuyer** (Equerry); and **Maison Prunet**. All date from the early 14th century. The names are 19th-century inventions. None are open to the public.

Stairways and passages climb between the town's layers, past stables, watchtowers, chapels and the workshops of artisans of the past. Near the central **Halle** or marketplace, originally 13th century, is place de la Bride, with fine views north across the land.

Special Events Two big annual events are Les Fêtes du Grand Fauconnier, a medieval festival in mid-July; and Musique sur Ciel, a music festival at the end of July.

Places to Stay The tourist office has a list of *chambres d'hôte*, most open year round and costing €45 and up for a double with breakfast.

Camp-Redon (☎ 05 63 56 14 64, Livers-Cazelles) Forfait €11.45. Open Apr-Oct. This small, shaded, Dutch-run camp site has a swimming pool; the turning is 5.5km east of Cordes.

Le Moulin de Julien (☎ 05 63 56 01 42, fax 05 63 56 11 10, route de Gaillac) For-

fait €13.70. Open Apr-Sept. This comfortable site is 1.5km south down the D922.

Hôtel-Restaurant de la Bride (☎/fax 05 63 56 04 02, place de la Bride) Doubles with shower €33.55, or with WC & shower/bath €38.10/42.70. Breakfast €5.80. Cordes' only lower-price hotel is unexpectedly modest and friendly. Big old rooms overlook the marketplace or the countryside. Parking is available. This is one way to see Cordes after hours, but book ahead in July and August.

Hôtel Chez Babar (☎ 05 63 56 02 51, fax 05 63 56 02 51, Les Cabannes) Doubles €22.87; €25.90/28.95/32 with shower/ shower & WC/bath & WC. This very plain village hotel is 2km west of Cordes on the D600.

Places to Eat Try *La Canaille*, in place de la Bride, for salads, crepes and snacks. The town has a wide choice of sometimes excellent but very expensive restaurants and cafes. Eat down on the D600 instead: try *Brasserie G&G (☎ 05 63 56 00 09, 11 place de la Boutellerie)*, open daily with adequate local dishes for €6.10-10.65, *menus* for €11.45-14.50 and a terrace with a view.

There are some fine *fermes auberges* in the area, too – the tourist office has details.

Getting There & Away Buses stop just south-east of place de la Boutellerie. During school term buses of Cars Coulom (☎ 05 63 54 18 39) depart Albi (€4.55, one hour) at 7.45am and 6.10pm weekdays and 12.15pm Wednesday and Saturday, returning at 6.45am daily Monday to Saturday, 1pm Wednesday and 4.50pm weekdays except Wednesday.

Cordes' train station at Vindrac, 3km to the west, has a daily direct connection from Albi (€5.65, 50 minutes), leaving Albi about 9.20pm or Cordes about 6.40am; and at least four daily direct services from Toulouse (€10.05, 55 minutes).

Getting Around Parking is heavily regulated, with large free car parks across the D600. Those who can't face the slog uphill can catch a shuttle bus (€1.05 adult/child aged 4 to 12; every 10 minutes) from place de la Boutellerie to the western end of the old town. Parking in the old town is prohibited from 15 March to 15 November.

You can rent a VTT or bicycle from Joël Guibert (☎ 05 63 56 08 68), Les Cabannes, for €9.15/12.20 per half/full day).

Castelnau de Montmiral
postcode 81140 • pop 1200 • elevation 286m
About 25km east of Albi, this pocket-size bastide, founded in 1222 by Raymond VI, remains appealingly unrestored, if a bit lifeless. In the lanes surrounding place des Arcades, the central square, are many cantilevered, **half-timbered houses**. *Montmiral* means 'hilltop with a view' in Occitan. Its long-gone chateau was granted in the 14th century to the last survivor of the Armagnac barony (see the introduction to the Gers chapter).

Base de Loisirs Vére-Grésigne (*☎ 05 63 33 16 00, D964 route de Bruniquel; adult/child aged 3-10 €2.15/1.50 plus activities charges; open 10.30am-8pm daily July-Aug)*, a small leisure park 3km to the west, has swimming, boating, fishing and a small cafe.

Within the Castelnau district is the deep **Forêt de Grésigne**, 35 sq km of oak forest laced with footpaths. Alongside the forest runs the GR46.

Information The tourist office (☎ 05 63 33 15 11, fax 05 63 33 17 60), on place des Arcades, publishes a free English-language walking tour of the village. The office is open 10am to 12.30pm and 2.30pm to 7pm daily in August and September, and 2pm to 5.30pm daily the rest of the year.

Places to Stay & Eat For information on the village's many *Gîtes de France*, ask at the tourist office.

Camping Le Rieutort (*☎ 05 63 33 16 10, fax 05 63 33 20 80, D67 route de Penne)* Adult/pitch €3.05/3.80. Open June-Sept. This small, plain camp site 3.5km west of Castelnau also has bungalows.

Auberge des Arcades (*☎ 05 63 33 20 88, place des Arcades)* Doubles/twins €27.45/30.50. This dour, traditional place has comfortable rooms and the village's favourite cafe-bar.

Hôtel de Consul (*☎ 05 63 33 17 44, place des Arcades)* Rooms €38.10. Breakfast €4.55. Under construction at the time of writing in a townhouse on the square, this will be a grand mix of old, wood-beamed rooms and sunny new ones in traditional style.

CASTRES
postcode 81100 • pop 45,400
• elevation 172m
Castres began life as a Roman settlement or *castrum*. It grew rapidly when a monastery was founded here in the 9th century, and later made its name as a textile centre. This is the birthplace of Jean Jaurès, considered the father of French Socialism (see the boxed text 'Jean Jaurès' later in this section).

While it may not warrant a special trip, this cheerful town is worth a detour en route between Albi and Toulouse, and is a natural springboard to the Parc Naturel Régional du Haut-Languedoc.

Orientation
Castres straddles the Agoût, a tributary of the Tarn. The centre of town, place Jean Jaurès, is a few blocks north-west of the bus station on place Soult and about 1km north-east of the train station on av Albert 1er. The airport is 8km to the south-east.

Information
The tourist office (☎ 05 63 62 63 62, fax 05 63 62 63 60, ⓔ otcastres@mediacastres .com), 3 rue Milhau Ducommun, is open 9am to 12.30pm and 2pm to 6.30pm Monday to Saturday, and 3pm to 5pm Sunday (with Sunday morning hours and no lunch breaks in July and August).

Castres' Bureau d'Information Jeunesse (BIJ; ☎ 05 63 72 67 40, fax 05 63 72 67 41, ⓔ bij.castres@wanadoo.fr), at 3 rue de la Platé, has free Internet access (book ahead). It opens 1.30pm to 5.30pm Monday, Tuesday and Thursday, 8am to 5.30pm Wednesday and 1.30pm to 5pm Friday.

Banks on place Jean Jaurès with ATMs and currency exchanges include Banque Populaire at No 7 and Crédit Agricole at No 17.

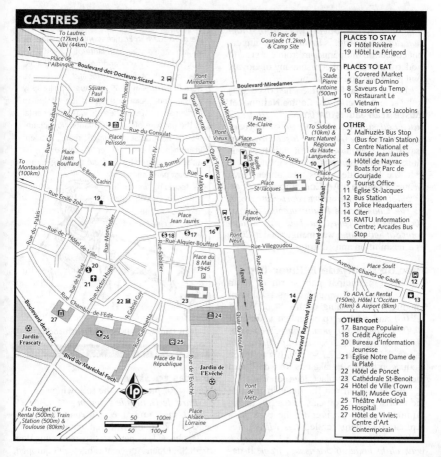

CASTRES

PLACES TO STAY
6 Hôtel Rivière
19 Hôtel Le Périgord

PLACES TO EAT
1 Covered Market
5 Bar au Domino
8 Saveurs du Temp
10 Restaurant Le Vietnam
16 Brasserie Les Jacobins

OTHER
2 Malhuziès Bus Stop (Bus for Train Station)
3 Centre National et Musée Jean Jaurès
4 Hôtel de Nayrac
7 Boats for Parc de Gourjade
9 Tourist Office
11 Église St-Jacques
12 Bus Station
13 Police Headquarters
14 Citer
15 RMTU Information Centre; Arcades Bus Stop

OTHER cont
17 Banque Populaire
18 Crédit Agricole
20 Bureau d'Information Jeunesse
21 Église Notre Dame de la Platé
22 Hôtel de Poncet
23 Cathédrale St-Benoit
24 Hôtel de Ville (Town Hall); Musée Goya
25 Théâtre Municipal
26 Hospital
27 Hôtel de Viviès; Centre d'Art Contemporain

The police headquarters (☎ 05 63 35 40 10) is at 2 av Charles de Gaulle. The hospital (☎ 05 63 71 63 71) is at 20 blvd du Maréchal Foch.

Town Centre
The Tour Romane (Roman Tower) on the 17th-century **Cathédrale St-Benoit** is a remnant of the original abbey. Opposite is the **Hôtel de Ville** (town hall) in the contemporaneous former Bishop's Palace, with the splendid Jardin de l'Evêché stretching out behind.

Castres' **houses** are a window on its history. Old ones along the Agoût, with cellars opening onto the river, began as the homes of 14th-century tanners, dyers and weavers. Among the handsome Renaissance **mansions** of 16th- and 17th-century merchants are Hôtel de Nayrac on rue Frédéric Thomas, Hôtel de Poncet on rue Gabriel Guy and Hôtel de Viviès on rue Chambre de l'Edit.

Museums & Galleries
Musée Goya (☎ 05 63 71 59 30, Hôtel de Ville, rue de l'Hôtel de Ville; €3.05 Apr–mid-Sept, €2.30 mid-Sep–Mar, those under 18 years admission free, admission free 1st Sun of month; open 9am-noon & 2pm-6pm

TARN

Tues-Sun Apr–mid-Sept; 9am-noon & 2pm-5pm Tues-Sun mid-Sept–Mar; from 10am Sun; daily July-Aug) is France's most important collection of Spanish art from classical to modern, including of course many of Goya's own paintings and engravings.

Local son Jean Jaurès (see the boxed text) is the sole subject of the **Centre National et Musée Jean Jaurès** (*☎ 05 63 72 01 01, 2 place Pelisson; €1.50, those under 18 years half-price; same hours as Musée Goya)*, an important, well mounted but rather tedious museum, with captions only in French.

In the Hôtel de Viviès (see under Town Centre) a **Centre d'Art Contemporain** (*☎ 05 63 59 30 20*, **W** *www.centredart-castres.org, 25 rue Chambre de l'Edit; admission free; 10am-noon & 2pm-6pm Tues-Fri, 10am-noon Sat Sept-June)* was inaugurated in 2001 as an exhibition and educational space.

Parc de Gourjade & River Trip

This vast municipal park north of town includes a camp site, golf course, 15km of jogging trails, a **riding centre** (*☎ 05 63 35 02 08)* and a water park called **L'Archipel** (*☎ 05 63 62 54 00; pool adult €3.05-3.65, child €2.45-3.05, ice-skating rink adult €2.45-3.35, child €2.15-2.75)*. It's on av de Roquecourbe (D89); take bus No 6 or 7 from the Arcades stop on place Jean Jaurès.

Alternatively, from the quay in front of the tourist office you can take a 30- to 50-minute journey upriver to the park in a replica river barge called *Les Miredames (adult/child aged 6-13 €3.80/1.50 each way, child under 6 admission free)*. It departs at 2pm, 3.20pm and 4.40pm daily from May to October (plus 6pm from May to September and 10.30am in July and August). For more information contact the tourist office or call ☎ 05 63 59 72 30.

Special Events

Festival Goya (*☎ 05 63 71 56 58)* has nothing to do with Goya but is an annual festival of Latin and North African music, held in the Art-Nouveau Théâtre Municipal from July to mid-August. The city also sponsors open-air jazz and folk concerts and other events throughout August.

Jean Jaurès

Hardly a town in France is without a street or square named after Jean Jaurès, a powerful orator, articulate writer and politician considered the founder of France's socialist movement. Born in Castres in 1859, he taught philosophy at Albi and Toulouse before being elected to Parliament in 1893. There he was instrumental in the passage of social legislation, and championed such causes as miners' rights, accident insurance and pensions for workers and peasants. He became head of the fledgling French Socialist party soon after its founding in 1905, but was assassinated in Paris on the eve of the declaration of WWI.

JANE SMITH

Jean Jaurès: the father of French socialism

Places to Stay

Take your pick from the following.

Parc de Gourjade Camping (*☎ 05 63 59 72 30, fax 05 63 50 88 91, route de Roquecourbe)* 2 adults with tent/caravan €4.10/5.35 plus €1.45 per car; 4-person bungalow €38.85. Open Apr-Sept. This well equipped, kid-friendly municipal camp site is in the middle of the city's leisure complex.

Hôtel Rivière (*☎ 05 63 59 04 53, fax 05 63 59 61 97, 10 quai Tourcaudière)* Doubles with WC & shower €38.80, without €18.20-22.80. Breakfast €5.35. Off-street parking €5.35. The central, good-value Rivière has plain, well kept rooms, though walls are thin. English is spoken.

Hôtel-Restaurant Le Périgord (*☎ 05 63 59 04 74, 22 rue Émile Zola)* Doubles/twins with WC & shower €21.35/27.45. This modest, briskly run place is also blessed with a good restaurant.

Hôtel L'Occitan (☎ *05 63 35 34 20, fax 05 63 35 70 32,* e *hotel-occitan@wanadoo .fr, 201 av Charles de Gaulle)* Doubles with shower/bath €54.90/64.05. Breakfast €6.85. Like most Logis de France places, this hotel 1km east on the airport road is well run, comfortable and quiet, and has a good restaurant.

Places to Eat

The *covered market*, on place de l'Albinque, is open 7am to 1pm (to noon Sun) Tues-Sun. You'll find *food stalls* on place Jean Jaurès on Tuesday, Thursday, Friday and Saturday.

Bar au Domino (☎ *05 63 59 31 00, 4 quai Tourcaudière)* Salads, *tartes salées* (savoury pies), light meals €6.50-7. Open 8am-6pm Thur-Tues. Le Domino's food is plain but well prepared, and there's outdoor seating facing the river.

Brasserie Les Jacobins (☎ *05 63 59 01 44, 1 place Jean Jaurès)* Salads & combination plates €6.50. Open daily. Generous salads, regional dishes and fine desserts make this central spot good value for money.

Restaurant Le Vietnam (☎ *05 63 35 56 39, 41 rue Fuziès)* Midday/evening *menus* €7.60/15.25. Open Tues-Sun. Le Vietnam offers Vietnamese and Chinese dishes (€5.35-7.60), with tasty sauces and an immense menu (shrimps are the house speciality).

Saveurs du Temp (☎ *05 63 35 39 32, 4 rue Fuziès)* Coffees €1.85-3.35. Open Tues-Sun. Stop in for a good-value breakfast (€6.55) or an elegant hit of coffee and pastry.

Spectator Sports

Castres' rugby union squad, Olympique, were French champions in 1993 and are the region's best after Toulouse. Most matches are held at Stade Pierre Antoine, just northeast of the centre.

Getting There & Away

Air France flies to Castres six days a week from Paris; see the Getting There & Away chapter for details.

Buses run from Castres bus station (☎ 05 63 35 37 31) to Albi (€5.05, 50 minutes) at least five times daily Monday to Saturday,

and Toulouse (€9.15, 1½ hours) at least seven times daily and twice Sunday. The only direct train line is from Toulouse (€11, 1¼ hours), with eight trains per weekday, fewer on weekends.

A central car hire agency is Citer (☎ 05 63 51 28 20), 16 blvd Raymond Vittoz. Farther away are ADA (☎ 05 63 51 10 26), 32 av Charles de Gaulle, and Budget (☎ 05 63 71 31 28), 98 av Albert 1er.

Getting Around

There's no bus service to the airport; a taxi costs around €12. From the train station, take bus No 7 to the Arcades stop (€0.90, once to twice hourly) on place Jean Jaurès; going to the station, catch it at the Malhuziès stop off blvd des Docteurs Sicard. The local bus company, RMTU, has an information centre (☎ 05 63 71 80 00) on place Jean Jaurès.

LAUTREC

postcode 81440 • population 1600
• elevation 328m

The region around this hilltop village, 16km north-west of Castres and 29km south of Albi, produces a tenth of all the garlic consumed in garlic-loving France, and is the centre of a region that produces *ail rose*, a special, pink-hued variety, boasting its own appellation contrôlée.

But there's considerably more to the place than garlic. Lautrec is a handsome medieval village in its own right, with a collection of photogenic old houses and a working windmill, among other things. The only hitch is that there's no way to get here by public transport.

Orientation & Information

The tourist office (☎ 05 63 75 31 40, fax 05 63 75 32 90, e ot.lautrec@free.fr, w lautrec .free.fr) occupies part of a 17th-century Benedictine convent on cour de Mairie, at the northern end of the old town. It opens 9am to 12.30pm and 2pm to 6.30pm Tuesday to Sunday from May to September, and only in the afternoon for the rest of the year (closed January). The post office is southeastwards along cour de Mairie.

Things to See & Do

The handsome village centre has a collection of unrestored but well kept 16th- and 17th-century half-timbered **houses**; fragments of ancient town **walls** and one old gate; and a listed 14th–16th-century church, the **Collègiale St-Rémy**.

Around the corner from the post office is **place des Halles**, a 15th-century market square. From here, walk two blocks south on rue de Leugouzy and two blocks east on rue du St-Esprit to place de l'Ayral. Nearby is a reconstructed turn-of-the-last-century **clogmaker's workshop** (*☎ 05 63 75 31 40, same as tourist office, rue du St-Esprit; admission free; open 10am-6.30 daily July-Aug*); if it's closed, ask at the tourist office.

From place de l'Ayral, climb steps to a restored and working 17th-century **windmill** (*☎ 05 63 75 31 40; admission €1.50; open 3pm-7pm daily July-Aug, 3pm-6pm Sun Sept-June*). From a **shrine** at the summit of the hill you, on a clear day, the Montagne Noir.

South-west of the village is **Aquaval water park** (*☎ 05 63 70 51 74, route de Vielmur; adult/child €2.30/1.50; open 10am-8pm daily mid-June–Aug, except 10am-5pm June*), with three pools, water slides and fishing lakes.

Garlic

During the garlic season – mid-July to March – you can buy the local pink-hued variety at a Friday morning market at Le Promenade, an open area on the southern side of the windmill hill. Naturally there's a **Fête de l'Ail Rose** (Pink Garlic Festival), a cheerful, colourful affair held in Lautrec on the first Friday of August.

Places to Stay

The tourist office has details of several *chambres d'hôte* in and around Lautrec, mostly €40-45 per person.

Camping Les Bories (*☎ 05 63 75 90 52, route de Roquecourbe*) €3.05 per person. Open May-Sept. This *camping à la ferme* (camping on the farm), 2km east of Lautrec, has a farm-products shop, fishing lake and horse riding.

Relais de Brametourte (*☎ 05 63 75 30 31, fax 05 63 75 31 54, D92 route de Vielmur*) €3 per person. Open year round. This small leisure complex 4km south of Lautrec has camping, a restaurant (open daily), a pool, horse riding (€7.60 per hour) and VTT rental (€4.60/38.10 per hour/week).

Places to Eat

There are several small *groceries* southwards from place des Halles on rue de Leugouzy.

Restaurant Le Moulin Gourmande (*☎ 05 63 75 30 13, route de Castres*) Midday *menus* €9.90, evening *menus* €12.95-29.75. Open midday daily, evening Wed-Sun (Thur-Sun Oct-Apr). The Moulin Gourmande, at the south-western end of rue de Leugouzy, specialises in local meat dishes prepared with garlic; the midday *menu* is good value.

Restaurant Le Champ d'Allium (*☎ 05 63 70 52 41, 4 route de Castres*) Menus €20-45. Open daily July-Aug; Mon, midday only Tues, evening only Sun Sept-June. This small place near the tourist office offers carefully prepared regional specialities, and other options including seafood, in a rustic setting.

Le Garde Pile (*☎ 05 63 75 34 58, Combelasse*) *menus* €16.75. Open evening Fri-Sun, reservation only. This *ferme auberge* (farm restaurant), 4km south-east of Lautrec, offers excellent local dishes prepared from fresh farm produce.

LE SIDOBRE

The Sidobre is a roughly 100 sq km, 650m-high granite plateau north-east of Castres, a geological oddity in the limestone-dominated south-west. It's an arresting landscape, full of weird extrusions and immense balanced boulders as well as oak forests, cascading streams and tiny villages.

It's also France's main source of granite, and *les granitiers* rule. Some 2500 people in the Sidobre depend directly on the rock for their livelihood, and tourist attractions sit side-by-side with quarries, workshops and rubble heaps. The narrow roads are always clogged with lorries loaded with everything from knick-knacks to gravestones.

Orientation & Information

The centre of the granite works, and the Sido-bre's main commercial town, is Lacrouzette.

Six *communes* (districts) – Boissezon, Le Bez, Burlats, Ferrières, Lacrouzette and St-Salvy de la Balme – have established the Maison du Sidobre (☎ 05 63 74 63 38, fax 05 63 73 04 57), just off the D622 near Vialavert. It opens 10am to 6pm daily June to September, and 10am to noon and 2pm to 5pm the rest of the year, with information on the granite industry as well as the land-scape.

Things to See & Do

The names are as dramatic as the **rocks**: Peyro Clabado ('keystone' in Occitan), Rocher Tremblant de Sept Faux (Trembling Rock of the Seven Scythes), Trois Fro-mages (Three Cheeses). If you've spent time in granite mountains elsewhere, these may not dazzle you, but it's an agreeable land to walk or cycle through in any case. The GR36 crosses the area and the Maison du Sidobre sells a packet of hiking cards, colour-coded to over a dozen **trails** from 3km to 25km long.

Burlats boasts some distinguished old buildings, remnants of a 12th-century castle of the lords of Trencavel, vassals of the counts of Toulouse. One of these, the **Pavillon d'Adélaïde** (☎ 05 63 51 09 86; admission free; open 2pm-6pm July-Aug), a rare French example of Romanesque civil architecture, was a meeting-place for the Occitan poet-musicians known as troubadours (see Arts in the Facts about Southwest France chapter).

You can take a **river trip** down the Agoût in July or August with **Burlats Canoë-Kayak** (☎ 05 63 35 70 77; kayak €12.20/ 22.85, canoe €22.85/38.10 per half/full day).

At Ferrières, on the D53 between Brassac and Vabre, is the small **Musée du Protes-tantisme en Haute-Languedoc** (☎ 05 63 74 05 49, Maison du Luthier; €1.50; open 11am-1pm & 2pm-7pm daily July-Aug; 2pm-7pm Sun Apr-Nov). A modest collec-tion of artefacts and documents charts the vicious ups and downs of Protestantism in the region since the 16th century.

Places to Stay & Eat

The Maison du Sidobre's free *Guide Pra-tique* has hotel and restaurant listings, in-cluding *chambres d'hote* and lots of *gîtes* throughout the Sidobre.

Camping Among half-a-dozen camp sites within the Sidobre are the following.

Camping de Vialavert en Sidobre (Camp-ing Club de France; ☎ 05 63 74 01 13, fax 05 63 73 04 57, Vialavert) 2-person forfait €6.10. Open mid-June–mid-Sept. This func-tional 33-pitch camp site is about 1km from (and run by) the Maison du Sidobre.

Camping Le Plô (☎/fax 05 63 74 00 82, e info@leplo.com, w www.leplo.com, Le Bez) 2-person forfait €12.70. Open July-Aug. This spacious, Dutch-run camp site, a 10-minute drive from the Maison du Sido-bre, also has a small shop and bicycle hire.

Camping Municipal La Landes (☎ 05 63 74 09 11, Brassac) Pitch/person about €1.50/1.50. Open Apr-Oct.

Sidobre's only gîte d'étape is *Gîte Le St-Jacques* (☎ 05 63 50 52 59, fax 05 63 50 74 15, Boissezon) Beds €10.65. Open year round. This is run by the town hall with basic accommodation and kitchen facilities for walkers.

Au Relais du Sidobre (☎/fax 05 63 50 60 06, 8 route de Vabre, Lacrouzette) Double with shower & WC €38.10. Breakfast €6.10. Restaurant *menus* €15.25-22.85, reservation only; brasserie *menus* €7.45-9.60. Open daily. This family-run Logis de France hotel-restaurant is recommended for good local cuisine (the English-speaking *patronne* cooks it all) and comfortable rooms.

Auberge de Crémaussel (☎/fax 05 63 50 61 33, Crémaussel) Rooms €30.50. Break-fast €3.80. *Menus* €13.70-17.55. Rooms Mar-Nov; restaurant open daily (except Sun evening & Wed Feb-Dec, & 1st week in Sept). The Sidobre's best food – local dishes using local ingredients – is at this isolated auberge by the GR36, 5km east of Lac-rouzette; it also has five plain, pretty rooms with WC and bath.

Le Castel de Burlats (☎ 05 63 35 29 20, fax 05 63 51 14 69, 8 place du 8 Mai 1945)

Doubles/twins €53.35/60. Ten deluxe rooms are part of the 16th-century Château de Trencavel in Burlats.

Getting There & Away
Vialavert is 15km east of Castres on the D622. Cars Balent (☎ 05 63 35 74 77) runs from Castres bus station at 4.15pm to Burlats (€1.85, 10 minutes), Lacrouzette (€2.30, 20 minutes) and Brassac (€3.20, 45 minutes), and returns starting at Brassac at 8.30am, daily Monday to Saturday, with additional services during school term.

PARC NATUREL RÉGIONAL DU HAUT-LANGUEDOC
This park *(information from Siège du Parc, ☎ 04 67 97 38 22, fax 04 67 97 38 18, 13 rue du Cloître, 34220 St Pons de Thomières, Hérault department; open year round)* was founded in 1973 with the aim of preserving the natural wealth and economic health of the region – an isolated, 2606 sq km zone straddling the divide between the Tarn and Hérault departments and between southern France's Atlantic and Mediterranean watersheds.

Within the park – jointly administered by the Languedoc-Roussillon and the Midi-Pyrénées regions – are 93 districts, 47 of them in Tarn. Major geological features on the Tarn side are the **Monts de Lacaune**, an ancient refuge for Cathars and Protestants, with some of France's best fishing and one of its largest collections of Stone Age menhirs; a section of the oak- and beech-forested **Montagne Noir**, source of the water that feeds the Canal du Midi (see the boxed text 'Les Canaux des Deux Mers' in the Getting Around chapter); and the **Sidobre** (see the preceding section).

Public transport is scarce but if travelling by car doesn't appeal to you, you can walk, cycle or ride (the GR653 spans the park from west to east and the GR36 crosses its western limb), canoe the Agoût River, or sail on Lac de la Raviège or Lac de Sts-Peyres.

The Gers

The region historically known as Gascony (French Gascogne) – roughly speaking, the area west of the River Garonne – first had a separate life under the Romans, as Novempopulana. The name, meaning 'nine tribes', refers to the separate branches of a people later called the Vascones, forebears of both Gascons and Basques. In 602 the Frankish kings created a Duchy of Vasconia, which by the 10th century controlled almost everything from the Garonne to the Atlantic and the Pyrénées.

Gascony was largely English from the 1259 Treaty of Paris until the end of the Hundred Years' War, after which it fell into three major domains – Armagnac, Foix-Béarn and Albret. During much of the 15th century the counts of Armagnac, based at Lectoure, were the most powerful baronial family in France, until being crushed by Louis XI in 1472. By the 16th century all of Gascony belonged to the House of Albret – first to Jeanne d'Albret and then to her son Henri of Navarre, the future Henri IV of France.

In 1789 Gascony ceased to exist politically, shrivelling on the post-Revolutionary map to 'The Gers' (locally, the 's' is pronounced), a sparsely populated agricultural hinterland in the Midi-Pyrénées region.

But don't assume there's nothing to see. Here you'll find a peaceful, undulating landscape of vineyards, orchards and fields of grain, etched by a score of rivers fanning north from the High Pyrénées. Through here runs the main artery of the medieval pilgrimage route, the *chemin de St-Jacques* to Santiago de Compostela, with five St-Jacques-related Unesco World Heritage Sites in the Gers alone. Here too is some fine medieval and Renaissance architecture, including a disproportionate number of 12th- to 14th-century *bastides* (fortified new towns).

And here is the soul of the southwest's hearty cuisine, a land of garlic and goose fat, sausages and beans, chestnuts and plums – and France's biggest foie gras market. Even run-of-the-mill eateries serve their Gascon

Highlights

- Ponder esoteric 14th-century frescoes in La Romieu's Collégiale St-Pierre church, then gaze across Gascon farmland from its Belvedere Tower
- Catch your breath at the astonishing carved-oak choir stalls and Renaissance stained glass of the Cathédrale Ste-Marie in Auch
- Imagine how life was for a 4th-century Gallo-Roman aristocratic family as you explore the remains of their state-of-the-art villa in Séviac
- Soak up the light in the austere Église Notre-Dame in Abbaye de Flaran, a medieval Cistercian monastery

Food & Wine Highlights

magret de canard – lightly roasted duck breast

pastisse Gascogne – a lightly flambéed tart of Armagnac-soaked apples and tissue-thin pastry

floc de Gascogne – a velvety fortified wine made from grape juice and the region's famous Armagnac

preparations with pride. Many of the Gers' attractions are farm-oriented – tastings and meals, rural accommodation, camping *à la ferme* (on the farm). This is also the heartland

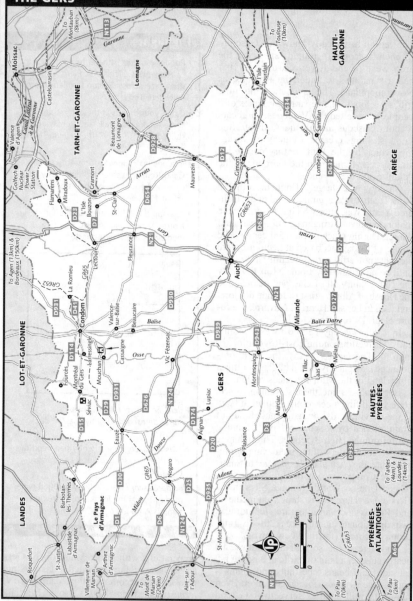

of farmer militancy against globalisation and the EU's Common Agricultural Policy.

One thing that stands out in the history of Southwest France is its self-confidence. In this it owes much to Gascony, a state of mind as much as a patch on the map. The swashbuckling Gascon is indeed a French icon, a defining component of the national temperament: The French often refer to boastfulness as *gasconnade*. The name D'Artagnan is everywhere – after the Gascon hero immortalised by novelist Alexandre Dumas in *Les Trois Mousquetaires* (The Three Musketeers; see the boxed text later in this chapter).

Accommodation is top-heavy, with budget places scarce. It's tight at any price in July and August, when the Gers overflows with Compostela pilgrims. And without a car or bike, or the stout shoes and energy of a pilgrim, getting around is harder than anywhere else in the southwest. The only useful train service is Toulouse-Auch, and bus connections into the Gers tend to terminate at Auch.

Auch

postcode 32000 • pop 25,000
• elevation 166m

Of all the prefectures in the southwest, Auch (rhymes with gauche) is the least dressed-up and self-important. But scratch the surface and you'll find a gorgeous cathedral with Unesco World Heritage status (look inside to see why), arguably the southwest's best provincial museum, a unique neighbourhood of medieval stepped streets, and a good place to enjoy genuine Gascon cuisine. Bang in the middle of the Gers, with roads radiating from it like the spokes of a wheel, Auch is also a good base to explore the lovely, underrated countryside of the Gers.

HISTORY

The first known settlers on this big hill by the River Gers were a Celtic tribe called the Auscii. The Romans who conquered them in 56 BC built their town, Augusta Auscorum, on the flats across the river, and that grew into a major trade crossroads. By the 9th century the hill was again the centre –

of a busy fortified town jointly run by the counts of Armagnac, the archbishops of Auch and the now-gone Priory of St Orens.

In 1473, after his soldiers had dispatched the Armagnacs at Lectoure, Louis XI installed the first in a series of *intendants* or governors here. When Gascony's lord, Henri of Navarre, became Henri IV of France in 1589, Auch became the province's administrative centre. Its golden era was the late 18th century, following the building of new roads to Toulouse and the Pyrénées by Intendant Antoine Mégret d'Étigny. A slide into rural obscurity followed the Revolution in 1789.

ORIENTATION

Hilltop Auch, centred on place de la Libération, contains most of the sights, restaurants and shops. Pedestrianised rue Dessoles is the main shopping street. The medieval town, falling away to the south, is a web of lanes, steps and little courtyards.

Across the river is 'new' Auch, and the train station. At the time of writing, the bus station, stranded in temporary quarters on place de l'Ancien Foirail, was due to move down beside the train station in 2002.

INFORMATION
Tourist Offices

The tourist office (☎ 05 62 05 22 89, fax 05 62 05 92 04, ℮ ot.auch@wanadoo.fr) is at 1 rue Dessoles in the restored 15th-century Maison Fedel. It opens 9.15am to 7pm daily in July and August; 9.15am to noon and 2pm to 6.15pm Monday to Saturday September to May (plus 10am to noon Sunday from Easter to June, September to 1 Nov).

For information about the Gers, go to the Comité Départemental du Tourisme du Gers (☎ 05 62 05 95 95, fax 05 62 05 02 16, ℮ cdtdugers@wanadoo.fr), at 7 rue Diderot.

Post & Communications

The main post office, at 12 rue Gambetta, has a Cyberposte terminal.

Internet access is available at Auch's Bureau d'Information Jeunesse (BIJ; ☎ 05 62 60 21 21, ℮ bij.auch@crij.org), 17 rue Rouget de Lisle, open 11am to 1pm and 2pm to 6.30pm Monday to Saturday. The rate is

THE GERS

€3.05 per hour, but it's free all day Wednesday and on Saturday afternoon (book ahead).

At Difintel (☎ 05 62 61 28 20), 1 bis place de la République, by the tourist office, Internet access costs €3.80 per hour.

Money

Most banks here open Saturday and close Monday. They include Crédit Agricole (7 bis rue Gambetta; av d'Alsace), Banque Populaire (rue Aragon), Caisse d'Épargne (place de la Libération) and Banque Courtois (opposite Cathédrale Ste-Marie). On Monday you can change money at the post office.

Medical Services & Emergency

The Centre Hospitalier (hospital; ☎ 05 62 61 32 32) is south of the town centre. The Commissariat de Police (☎ 05 62 61 54 54) is in the 18th-century episcopal palace, by Cathédrale Ste-Marie.

CATHÉDRALE STE-MARIE

This splendid church (☎ 05 62 05 04 64, place de la République; admission to cathedral free, to Grand Chœur adult/child aged under 13 €1.50/free; open 8.30am-6.30pm daily mid-July–Aug; 8.30am-noon & 2pm-6pm daily Apr–mid-July & Sept; 9.30am-

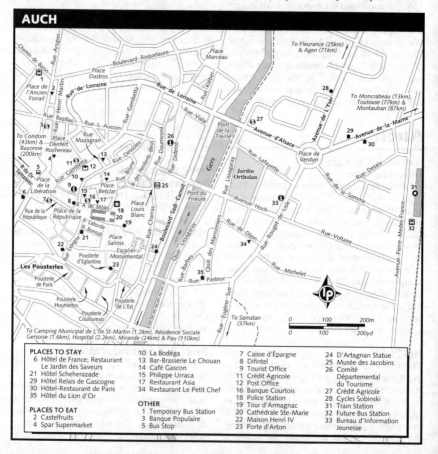

AUCH

To Fleurance (25km) & Agen (71km)

To Moncrabeau (13km), Toulouse (77km) & Montauban (87km)

To Condom (43km) & Bayonne (200km)

To Camping Municipal de L'Île St-Martin (1.2km), Résidence Sociale Gersoise (1.6km), Hospital (2.2km), Mirande (24km) & Pau (110km)

To Samatan (37km)

0   100   200m
0   100   200yd

PLACES TO STAY
6 Hôtel de France; Restaurant Le Jardin des Saveurs
21 Hôtel Scheherazade
29 Hôtel Relais de Gascogne
30 Hôtel-Restaurant de Paris
35 Hôtel du Lion d'Or

PLACES TO EAT
2 Castelfruits
4 Spar Supermarket

10 La Bodéga
13 Bar-Brasserie Le Chouan
14 Café Gascon
15 Philippe Urraca
17 Restaurant Asia
34 Restaurant Le Petit Chef

OTHER
1 Temporary Bus Station
3 Banque Populaire
5 Bus Stop

7 Caisse d'Épargne
8 Difintel
9 Tourist Office
11 Crédit Agricole
12 Post Office
16 Banque Courtois
18 Police Station
19 Tour d'Armagnac
20 Cathédrale Ste-Marie
22 Maison Henri IV
23 Porte d'Arton

24 D'Artagnan Statue
25 Musée des Jacobins
26 Comité Départemental du Tourisme
27 Crédit Agricole
28 Cycles Sobinski
31 Train Station
32 Future Bus Station
33 Bureau d'Information Jeunesse

noon & 2pm-5pm daily Oct-Mar), built by
the counts of Armagnac between 1489 and
1680, moved Napoleon III to say, 'A cathedral like this should be put in a museum!'
Gothic in plan but largely Italian Renaissance in execution, it was one of the last
cathedrals to be completed in France.

Though the heavy western face looks
rather grand illuminated at night, what people
come to see is inside: 18 vivid Renaissance
stained-glass windows, created between
1507 and 1513 by the celebrated Arnaud de
Môles; and the astonishing **Grand Chœur**
(Great Choir), completed in the 1550s by
Dominic Bertin of Toulouse and others, featuring over 1500 individual carvings of biblical scenes and mythological creatures in 113
choir stalls. A French-language audioguide
about the windows can be hired for €1.50.

The cathedral is a Unesco World Heritage
Site, jointly with other Compostela sites – a
good thing too, for its exterior is now under
badly needed restoration.

A ticket to the Grand Chœur also entitles
you to discounted admission to the Musée des
Jacobins.

The 40m-high **Tour d'Armagnac** behind
the cathedral, dating from the 14th-century,
served the medieval archbishops of Auch
(and Revolutionaries later) as a prison. It's
closed to the public.

MUSÉE DES JACOBINS
This eclectic art and archaeology collection
(☎ 05 62 05 74 79, 4 place Louis Blanc;
*adult/student & child €3.05/1.50; open
10am-noon & 2pm-6pm daily July-Aug;
10am-noon & 2pm-6pm Tues-Sun May-
June & Sept; 10am-noon & 2pm-5pm
Tues-Sun Oct-Apr)* is one of France's best
provincial museums, and would be reason
enough to visit Auch.

The museum, founded in 1793, is housed
in a 15th-century Dominican monastery.
Highlights include frescoes and other artefacts from a 1st- or 2nd-century Gallo-
Roman villa near Auch (including an epi-
taph for a pet dog); landscapes by locally
born Jean-Louis Rouméguère (1863–1925),
who was fascinated with sunsets; and one of
France's finest collections on the ethnogra-

phy of the Americas, from pre-Colombian
pottery to 18th-century religious art.

ESCALIER MONUMENTAL
Descending to the river from place Salinis
is the 370-step Monumental Stairway, completed in 1863. Bronze letters embedded in
the first landing, telling the story of the Biblical flood in Latin, are the work of a Catalan artist, Jaume Plensa, inspired by a flood
here in 1977.

Near the bottom of the stairway is a **statue
of D'Artagnan**, the famous Gascon hero immortalised by novelist Alexandre Dumas in
Les Trois Mousquetaires (see the boxed text
later in this chapter).

LES POUSTERLES
Plunging to the river from south of place
Salinis is a series of narrow, stepped alleyways, collectively called Les Pousterles.
Though unrestored, and in places dank and
graffiti-stained, this is the face of old Auch.
The layout allowed medieval citizens to
reach the river without leaving the town's
fortifications. One town gate, the **porte
d'Arton**, is on Pousterle d'Eglantine.

In 1578 the future Henry IV stayed in the
fine house at 22 rue Espagne (now called
Maison Henri IV), with a narrow, lofty
courtyard and a handsome wood and stone
stairway.

PLACES TO STAY
Camping & Hostels
There's one camp site and one hostel here.

Camping Municipal de l'Île St-Martin
(☎ 05 62 05 00 22, Île St-Martin, route de
Tarbes) Bus No 5 from place de la Libération
to Mouzon stop. €2.30 per adult plus
€1.15/2.30 per pitch with tent/caravan. Open
mid-Apr–mid-Nov. This spartan, riverside
camp site is 1.4km south of the town centre.

Résidence Sociale Gersoise (☎ 05 62 05
34 80, fax 05 62 60 00 44, 36 rue des Ca-
naris)* Bus No 1 or 2 from place de la
Libération to Grand Carros stop. Dorm/
private room €10.65/12.20. This youth and
workers' hostel (no curfew) is in a residential complex 1.8km south of the centre;
there's a small cafeteria.

Hotels – Old Town

The old town has the extremes.

Hôtel de France (☎ 05 62 61 71 71, fax 05 62 61 71 81, 2 place de la Libération) Singles €54.90-70.15, doubles €70.15-115.85. Buffet breakfast €9.15. This is top of the line, with splendid rooms in a 19th-century townhouse lording it over the old town, and one of the Gers' best restaurants (see Places to Eat).

Hôtel Scheherazade (Hôtel Les Trois Mousquetaires; ☎ 05 62 05 13 25, 7 rue Espagne) Doubles with shower €32/25.90 with/without WC. The Scheherazade is both cheap and convenient but decidedly downmarket – a last resort.

Hotels – New Town

Choices are more realistic down below, but it's a long climb to the cathedral.

Hôtel-Restaurant de Paris (☎ 05 62 63 26 22, fax 05 62 60 04 27, 38 av de la Marne) Doubles with/without shower €32/25.90, €39.65 with bath & WC. Breakfast €4.55. Menus (set menus) €9.75-19.80. Open Dec-Oct. This looks like Auch's best value for money, with well kept, nicely furnished old rooms, and a good restaurant. Front rooms get street noise.

Hôtel du Lion d'Or (☎/fax 05 62 63 66 00, 7 rue Pasteur) Rooms with WC & mini-bath €30.50-45.75. This rambling old place has rooms of every shape and size and a garden full of birdsong, but it's underilluminated, understaffed and a bit overpriced.

Hôtel Relais de Gascogne (☎ 05 62 05 26 81, fax 05 62 63 30 22, 5 av de la Marne) Doubles with bath €44.80-60.85. Breakfast €5.80. Open mid-Jan–mid-Dec. This Logis de France place offers unexceptional but comfortable, well tended rooms.

PLACES TO EAT

Auch's spectrum of eateries runs from humdrum to gastronomic, with a few good bargains in traditional Gascon cuisine.

Philippe Urraca (☎ 05 62 05 26 93, 6 rue Dessoles) Plat du jour (daily special) & salads €6. Open Tues-Sat. This sweetshop opposite the tourist office is open when others aren't, with welcome light meals.

Bar-Brasserie Le Chouan (☎ 05 62 05 08 47, 1 rue Mazagran) Menus €9.90-18.30. Open Mon-Sat. Main dishes are uninspiring but the €6.85 buffet des entrées – a glorified salad bar – is great value.

Café Gascon (☎ 05 62 61 88 08, 5 rue Lamartine, 1st floor) Menus €15.25-21.35. Open Tues-Sat (Tues-Sun July-Aug). Here's an original: family-run, cheerful and maddeningly slow, with good Gascon cooking that's almost too cheap. Have a taste with the midday €11.45 menu.

Restaurant Asia (☎ 05 62 05 93 17, 3 rue Arnaud de Môles) Open Tues-Sun. Dishes €6-8, menus €7.95-11.90. The Asia has good Chinese and Vietnamese dishes, and lots of them.

La Bodéga (☎ 05 62 05 69 17, 7 rue Dessoles) Midday formules (set menu with a choice of courses) €6.40-7.95, evening menus €16.75, tapas €2.25-6.85. Open midday & evening Mon-Sat, evening only Sun. La Bodéga has tapas, full meals and occasional live Latin music.

Restaurant Le Petit Chef (☎ 05 62 63 36 57, 6 rue de Dijon) Midday menus €6.10-9.15, evening menus €11.45-27.45. Open Tues-Sat & eve Sun. The Little Chef stakes his claim as a fondue specialist; other items are unexciting.

Restaurant Le Jardin des Saveurs (☎ 05 62 61 71 84, Hôtel de France – see Places to Stay) Menus €18.30-59.45. You'll never be able to afford it, but you can sample some of the region's best and most original Gascon cooking here.

For self-caterers there's a big fruit and vegetable shop called **Castelfruits** (14 rue Arago), open Tuesday to Saturday. A **Spar** supermarket (4 place Denfert Rochereau) is open 8.30am to 8.15pm daily (9am to 1pm Sunday). Auch's **weekly markets** (food, clothes and bric-a-brac) are held on Thursday around Jardin Ortholan and on Saturday in front of the cathedral.

GETTING THERE & AWAY

Useful bus connections from Auch include Condom (€5.35, 40 minutes, one to four daily), Mont de Marsan (€10.35, 1¾ hours, one daily) and Toulouse (€9.30, 1½ hours, one or two daily). SNCF buses run to Agen (€9.45, 1½ hours, up to eight daily).

SNCF has one useful direct train connection, to Toulouse (€11.30, 1¼ hours, three to six daily).

GETTING AROUND

Drivers should note that old right-of-way rules still apply at the place du Libération roundabout (ie, entering drivers have priority).

Cycles Sobinski (☎ 05 62 63 60 56, 35 av de l'Yser), rents touring bikes and VTTs. Try riding yours on the town's 4km foot/cycle path along the southern side of the river.

The Lomagne

Between the Rivers Gers and Garonne, reaching east into the Tarn-et-Garonne department, stretches the Lomagne, a postcard-pretty landscape of rolling green hills and aimless rivers, punctuated by limestone farmsteads, chateaux and ruined towers. This is the Gers' best farmland, and if the air has a certain tang about it, it's because a good third of France's garlic is grown here.

LECTOURE

postcode 32700 • pop 4500 • elevation 180m

Lectoure, old capital of the Lomagne, is a handsome, stoic place, with a turbulent past that seems to have left it enervated behind its neoclassical facades. It sits on a boat-shaped rock above the Gers that was already occupied by a tribe called the Lactoratii when the Romans moved in. The Romans built in the valley below, leaving the rock for temples to Jupiter and to Cybele, the ancient mother-goddess of Asia Minor.

Over time the high ground was reoccupied and the powerful counts of Armagnac made this their capital. In 1472 Louis XI's army, admitted to the town on the strength of false promises, trashed it and murdered the last count.

Protestant Lectoure was occupied by Catholic troops during the Wars of Religion. When Auch was made the Gers' capital after the Revolution, Lectoure faded away.

Orientation & Information

From the bus stand on rue Alsace-Lorraine, walk three blocks west to the tourist office (☎ 05 62 68 76 98, fax 05 62 68 79 30, e ot.lectoure@wanadoo.fr), on rue Nationale just beyond Cathédrale St-Gervais et St-Protais. The office is open 9am to noon and 2pm to 6pm daily, except Saturday afternoon and Sunday, and 9am to 12.30pm and 2.30pm to 7pm daily in July and August.

Most places of interest are clustered here at the eastern end of the old town. Three blocks west down rue Nationale are Caisse d'Épargne and Crédit Agricole banks.

Cathédrale St-Gervais et St-Protais

Most of this cathedral dates from a 15th-century rebuild after its predecessor was destroyed by Louis XI's soldiers. With its curious ornate tower, it's more interesting outside than in, though there's a display of **religious art** *(€1.20; same hours as the tourist office)* in the baptistry. The tower, alas, is closed.

Musée de Lectoure

Lectoure has an excellent museum *(☎ 05 62 68 70 22, place du Général de Gaulle; adult/child aged under 12 €2.30/1.50; open 10am-noon & 2pm-6pm daily March-Sept; 10am-noon & 2pm-6pm Wed-Mon Oct-Feb)* in the cellars of the 17th-century episcopal palace, now the town hall, beside the cathedral. 20 Gallo-Roman altars are decorated with bulls' or rams' heads (sacrificial animals used during ceremonies to Cybele). Other highlights include huge wine amphorae, early-Christian funeral monuments and an ominous mosaic portrait of the god Oceanus.

Other Things to See

The 14th-century **Tour du Bourreau** was once a defensive tower and the town executioner's home; from the cathedral walk two blocks north on rue Subervie and turn right. The **Tour d'Albinhac**, 1½ blocks west of the tourist office down rue Nationale, was part of a 16th-century fortified house.

Among several 18th-century **hôtels particuliers** (private townhouses) are the Hôtel de Trois Boules (still the cathedral's pastoral residence), across rue Nationale from the cathedral, and the Hôtel de Castaing (now the Hôtel-Restaurant de Bastard), north of the tourist office off rue St-Gervais.

All these buildings are closed to the public.

Bleu de Lectoure

Housed in an old tannery, Bleu de Lectoure (☎ 05 62 68 78 30, e *bleupastel@aol.com*, W *www.bleu-de-lectoure.com; open 9.30am–12.30pm & 2pm-6.30pm Mon-Sat, also Sun during school holidays)*, down by the former train station, is a shop full of everything blue, and not just any blue. At the back, in a laboratory full of vats and retorts, the mostly lost art of coaxing blue dye from the leaves of *le pastel* (woad; see the boxed text, *'Le Pastel'*, in the Toulouse, Tarn-et-Garonne & Tarn chapter) is being meticulously rediscovered and applied in novel ways, from *haute couture* to car finishes.

Walk-in visitors are welcome and can take an eye-opening free tour (in French or English). It's about 2.5km from the town centre.

Cycle Trails

The tourist office sells map-booklets covering 10 graded cycle trails in the hills around Lectoure and two around La Romieu (see Around Lectoure). You can also hire a VTT at the tourist office, for €6.10/8.40/11.45 per morning/afternoon/day, or for longer periods.

Places to Stay & Eat

The tourist office keeps a list of nearby *chambres d'hôte* (B&Bs), with double rates from €27.45 to €73.20.

Lac des Trois Vallées (☎ 05 62 68 82 33, fax 05 62 68 88 82, e lac.des.trois.vallees@ wanadoo.fr, N21 route d'Auch) €8.40 per person (walker or cyclist with tent), otherwise forfait €34.30. Open May–mid-Sept. This camp site is part of a vast leisure complex 4km south of town, with pool, open-air cinema, windsurfing and boating.

Relais de St-Jacques (☎ 05 62 68 83 79, av de la Gare) Rooms €19.80-23.65. Breakfast €3.50. This unexceptional but inexpensive place is down on the Fleurance-Agen bypass, 2km from the old centre.

Hôtel-Restaurant Le Bastard (☎ 05 62 68 82 44, fax 05 62 68 76 81, rue Lagrange) Doubles €41.15-60.20. Breakfast €7.60. *Menus* €14-55.35. Open Feb-Dec. Anyone, bastard or not, with the dosh can enjoy this splendid place in a former 18th-century townhouse. Rooms are simple but elegant, meals are served in a vaulted dining room and the pool is big.

Restaurant Rose du Chat (☎ 05 62 68 90 99, rue Ste-Claire) Menu du jour (set menu of the day) €9.15. Open midday Fri-midday Wed. Here's an exception to the rule, a small, unpretentious place with good Gascony dishes at modest prices. It's a block west and two blocks north of the tourist office.

On rue Nationale and rue Alsace-Lorraine, east of the town centre, are a *cafe* and several *pizzerias*.

Getting There & Away

Lectoure is 36km north of Auch. SNCF's (☎ 08 36 35 35 35) Auch-Agen buses stop here eight times daily Monday to Friday, less often at the weekend (Auch €5.50, 40 minutes; Agen €5.65, 50 minutes).

EAST OF LECTOURE
St-Clar

A fortified chateau and a Benedictine priory established here in the 10th century served as the nucleus of a little *castelnau* (a village around the chateau of a local lord) run by the viscount of Lomagne and the bishop of Lectoure. A separate English bastide was founded in 1274 by agreement between the then bishop and Edward I, duke of Aquitaine.

St-Clar's clearest landmark is its big **parish church**. Just to the south is ancient St-Clar, a tangle of alleys around place Dastros. Eastwards is **place de la République**, arcaded on three sides. The heart of 'English' St-Clar is two blocks north of the church in **place de la Mairie** (or place de la Halle), with the town hall, the tourist office, one bank (with ATM) and a 13th-century wooden market hall.

The tourist office (☎ 05 62 66 34 45, fax 05 62 66 32 17, e s.i.cantondesaintclar@wan adoo.fr) opens 9am to 12.30pm and 3.30pm to 7pm Monday to Saturday mid-June to mid-

September; 9am to 12.30pm and 2.30pm to 6pm Tuesday to Saturday other months.

Facing place Dastros is the crumbling **Vieille Église** (Old Church), parts of which date from the 11th and 12th centuries. It's ignominiously boarded up, although the tourist office runs one-hour village tours (€1.00; at 5pm on the days the office is open) during which you can have a look inside.

St-Clar is the Lomagne's main centre for the processing of *l'ail blanc* (white garlic). While its weekly Thursday morning market proceeds in place de la Mairie (year round), a **marché de l'ail** (garlic market) also goes on from 10am to 11am in place de l'Ail, 300m west of the parish church, during the garlic season (July to at least November). Naturally, St-Clar has an annual Fête de l'Ail (garlic festival), on the first Thursday of August.

Places to Stay & Eat The tourist office keeps a list of nearby *gîtes* (cottages) and *fermes auberges* (farm restaurants).

La Garlande (☎ 05 62 66 47 31, fax 05 62 66 47 70, ✉ nicole.cournot@wanadoo.fr, place de la Mairie) Doubles with WC & bath €45.75-54.90. Dinner by arrangement €13.70. St-Clar's sole chambre d'hôte is a work of art, with three huge rooms, tasteful old furniture, a garden and homemade food.

Restaurant Le Rison (☎ 05 62 66 40 21, place de la Lomagne, rear entrance place Dastros) Menus €14.95-27.45. Open midday Mon & Tues-Thurs. The Rison serves good, garlicky regional dishes in an unpretentious atmosphere; the €9.90 midday *menu* will stick to your ribs.

Gramont

Tiny Gramont (population 107), 3km east of L'Isle Bouzon on the River Arrats, is barely more than a church and a chateau.

The staid **Château de Gramont** (☎ 05 63 94 05 26, fax 05 63 94 14 63; guided tour €4.90; open 9am-noon & 2pm-6.30pm daily May-Sept; 2pm-6pm daily Feb-Apr & Oct-Nov) has been carefully restored and donated to the state. At the front is the original 14th-century Gothic mansion. The immense wing at the back, begun in 1530 and chock-full of period furnishings and Aubusson tapestries,

may represent the earliest appearance of the Italian Renaissance style in France.

The chateau is also the venue for art exhibits and a small festival of classical music from July to mid-August.

The only dining option is *Auberge le Petit Feuillant* (☎ 05 63 94 00 08, opposite the chateau) Menus €13.70-22.85. Open Thur-Sat, Sun midday, Mon-Tues. This twee place offers somewhat pricey traditional dishes to a captive audience.

Pays d'Armagnac

North-western Gers is the land of Armagnac, the southwest's answer to cognac (see the boxed text 'Armagnac' later in the chapter). Its gentle hills are a patchwork of vineyards, plum orchards and wheat fields. This is also, more or less, the historical domain of the counts of Armagnac, Gascony's godfathers until Louis XI terminated the line in 1472 (see Lectoure in the Lomagne section).

CONDOM

postcode 3210 • pop 8070 • elevation 80m
Poor Condom, whose resonant name (see the boxed text 'Put It This Way, How Did the Condom Get *Its* Name?') has made it the butt of endless English jokes. Some tourists only stop to be photographed beside the sign *'Bienvenue à Condom, Ville Propre'* (Welcome to Condom, the Clean Town). But this pretty – and indeed very clean – town beside the River Baïse is worth a visit for its cathedral and a clutch of sober neoclassical mansions, and for its access to the surrounding Ténarèze region.

History

The Vascone people – forebears of both the Gascons and the Basques (see History in the Facts about Southwest France chapter) – settled here in the early 8th century. A proper town grew around the 11th-century Benedictine Abbey of St Pierre.

Condom suffered repeatedly during the Albigensian Crusade (following which it was made a bishopric), the Hundred Years' War and the Wars of Religion. Much of the

THE GERS

'old' town dates from Condom's economic revival in the 17th and 18th centuries.

Orientation & Information

The tourist office (☎ 05 62 28 00 80, fax 05 62 28 45 46, e otsi.condom@condom.org) is on place Bossuet, in the 13th-century Tour Auger d'Andiran. The office is open 9am to 1pm and 2pm to 7pm daily in July and August; 9am to noon and 2pm to 6pm Monday to Saturday the rest of the year.

Place St-Pierre is the town's centre. Several banks here have ATMs. The Centre Hospitalier (hospital; ☎ 05 62 28 20 77) is at 21 av Maréchal Joffre. A small Maison de la Presse, at 26 rue Gambetta, sells guidebooks, maps and books on the region, plus a few foreign newspapers.

Cathédrale St-Pierre & Around

Built in less than three decades at the start of the 16th century, Condom's cathedral immediately took a severe beating in the Wars of Religion. Its finest portal faces place St-Pierre in an otherwise sombre Gothic-Renaissance facade. The Flamboyant Gothic interior has a few original stained-glass windows and many from the 19th century. The Chapelle Ste-Marie at the eastern end was there two centuries before the cathedral.

North of the cathedral is the **cloister**, now occupied by the town hall. Nearby, on place Lannelongue, the sub-prefecture occupies the 18th-century **bishop's palace**, with one fine Renaissance portal.

Armagnac

The **Musée de l'Armagnac** (*☎ 05 62 28 47 17, 2 rue Jules Ferry; adult/child €2.15/ 1.05; open 10am-noon & 3pm-5pm Wed-Mon Apr-May; 10am-noon & 3pm-7pm Wed-Mon June-Aug; 10am-noon & 3pm-6pm Wed-Mon Sept; 10am-noon & 3pm-5pm Wed-Mon Oct; 2pm-5pm Sat-Sun Nov-Mar),* in the former episcopal stables, offers a look at the traditional production of Armagnac

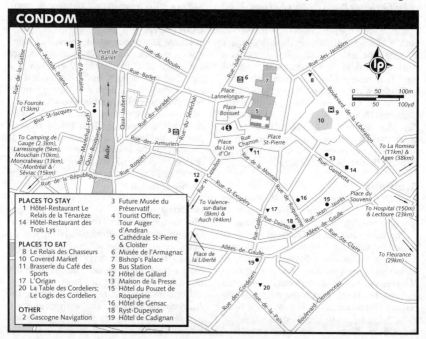

CONDOM

PLACES TO STAY
1 Hôtel-Restaurant Le
   Relais de la Ténarèze
14 Hôtel-Restaurant des
   Trois Lys

PLACES TO EAT
8 Le Relais des Chasseurs
10 Covered Market
11 Brasserie du Café des
   Sports
17 L'Origan
20 La Table des Cordeliers;
   Le Logis des Cordeliers

OTHER
2 Gascogne Navigation

3 Future Musée du
   Préservatif
4 Tourist Office;
   Tour Auger
   d'Andiran
5 Cathédrale St-Pierre
   & Cloister
6 Musée de l'Armagnac
7 Bishop's Palace
9 Bus Station
12 Hôtel de Gallard
13 Maison de la Presse
15 Hôtel du Pouzet de
   Roquepine
16 Hôtel de Gensac
18 Ryst-Dupeyron
19 Hôtel de Cadignan

(see the boxed text 'Armagnac' later in this section).

Family-run **Ryst-Dupeyron** (☎ 05 62 28 08 08, 36 rue Jean Jaurès; admission free; open 10am-noon & 2pm-6.30pm Mon-Fri year round; also 3.30pm-6.30pm Sat-Sun July-Aug) is one of several Armagnac producers offering free tastings and tours. It's in an 18th-century mansion, the Hôtel de Cugnac.

Mansions

Condom is graced with many 18th-century hôtels particuliers, quite unlike the Renaissance confections of Toulouse and Montauban. Handsomer ones include the Hôtel de Gallard (rue H Cazaubon), Hôtel de Gensac (rue de Roquepine), Hôtel du Pouzet de Roquepine (rue Jean Jaurès, along the old town walls) and Hôtel de Cadignan (allées de Gaulle). None is open to the public.

River Cruises

A 20km stretch of the Baïse between Moncrabeau and Valence-sur-Baïse can be navigated, with six bypass locks working from late March to November. **Gascogne Navigation** (☎ 05 62 28 46 46, Capitainerie, quai Bouquerie) rents small boats by the day, bigger ones by the week and, in July and August, runs 1½ hour cruises (adult/child aged 4-12 €6.85/5.35) every afternoon except Sunday.

Special Events

On the second weekend in May, Bandas à Condom (☎/fax 05 62 68 31 38) brings marching bands from all over Europe for 48 hours of singing, dancing, competitions and high jinks.

Places to Stay

The tourist office keeps a list of *chambres d'hôte* around Condom, plus several *campings à la ferme* within 5km.

Camping de Gauge (☎/fax 05 62 28 17 32, route d'Éauze) Adult/pitch €2.90/3.10 with car. Open year round. This well equipped municipal site is 2.3km south-west on the D931. Nearby is a sports centre with tennis, swimming, horse riding and bicycle rental.

Hôtel-Restaurant Le Relais de la Ténarèze (☎ 05 62 28 02 54, fax 05 62 28 46 96, 22 av d'Aquitaine) Doubles with shower €32, or €37.35/43.45 with WC & shower/bath. Breakfast €4.55. Restaurant open midday Mon-midday Sat. Credit cards not accepted. This fussy, family-run place has comfortable rooms and good home cooking.

Le Logis des Cordeliers (☎ 05 62 28 03 68, fax 05 62 68 29 03, rue de la Paix) Doubles €41.15-56.40, twins €47.25-59.45. Breakfast €5.80. Open Feb-Dec. Many of the quiet rooms in this small hotel overlook the garden and large swimming pool. The top attraction is the adjacent restaurant (see Places to Eat).

Hôtel-Restaurant des Trois Lys (☎ 05 62 28 33 33, fax 05 62 28 41 85, @ info@les -trois-lys.com, 38 rue Gambetta) Doubles €74.70-105.20. Breakfast €8.40. Indulge yourself at this deluxe, family-run hotel in

Put It This Way, How Did the Condom Get *Its* Name?

You would think from all the sniggering that the town was named after the contraceptive sheath.

Condoms have been used since the 18th century for controlling the spread of syphilis, and although a 'Dr Condom' is often identified as its inventor, no physician by that name has been traced. The word carries no overtones for French speakers, who refer to the little latex device as a *préservatif*.

Nobody is sure where Condom-the-town got its name either, though it probably derives from a Roman-era name – perhaps from the Latin *condominium*, for shared ownership or rule, as was the case with the Vascone people who first settled here.

At any rate the town is not about to let itself become an international joke. In true Gascon style it has taken the offensive, hosting exhibitions and a conference on *le préservatif*. In the works is a Musée du Préservatif, though at the time of writing there wasn't much at the site on rue du Sénéchal but a small free exhibit, in French.

an 18th-century townhouse. At the back is a swimming pool, and downstairs is a good-value restaurant (see Places to Eat).

Places to Eat

Condom's market day is Wednesday, with food in the *covered market* and clothes and bric-a-brac outside.

Brasserie du Café des Sports (☎ 05 62 28 15 26, 11 rue Charron) Open noon-7.30pm daily. If your budget's tight, this place has omelettes (€5.35) and big salads (€2.30-10.65).

Le Relais des Chasseurs (☎ 05 62 28 20 14, 3 blvd de la Libération) Menus €12.95-19.80. Credit cards not accepted. Open midday & evening Tues-Sat, midday only Mon. This down-to-earth Les Routiers eatery is a favourite of truckers, and feeds the masses with aplomb on market day. Everybody likes the plain, €9.15 midday *menu*.

L'Origan (☎ 05 62 68 24 84, 4 rue Cadéot) Pizzas €6.70-8.70, pasta €5.95-8.35. Open midday & evening Tues-Sat, evening only Mon. L'Origan is a good-value Italian restaurant with a robust choice of pizzas, pasta and non-Italian dishes.

Hôtel-Restaurant des Trois Lys (see Places to Stay) Menus €13.70-24.40. Open daily. Come here for good Gersoise cooking at mid-range prices, or a selection of big €9.15 salads.

La Table des Cordeliers (☎ 05 62 68 28 36, 1 rue des Cordeliers) Restaurant menus €29.75-44.95, brasserie menus €10.50/15.10 midday/evening. Open Thur-Tues. Les Cordeliers offers probably the finest Gascon cuisine in town, in a former 14th-century chapel.

Getting There & Away

ATR (☎ 05 62 05 46 24) has three buses to Auch (€5.65, 45 minutes) Monday to Saturday, one of which continues to Toulouse (€13.10, 2½ hours); and one daily to Bordeaux (€16.30, 2¾ hours). Citram Pyrénées' daily coach from Pau (€25.30, 2¼ hours) continues to Agen (€7.15, 45 minutes).

Getting Around

Camping de Gauge (see Places to Stay) rents bikes for €6.15 per day.

AROUND CONDOM

Condom is within reach of a spectrum of sights in the Ténarèze, from a Gallo-Roman villa to Unesco-protected waystations on the road to Santiago de Compostela.

La Romieu

postcode 32480 • pop 550 • elevation 185m

Tradition holds that two monks returning from a pilgrimage to Rome founded a monastery here in 1062. They named the place La Romieu, from the Latin *romaeus* or Occitan *roumieu* (pilgrim). A village grew up around the monastery.

Arnaud d'Aux was born into a noble family here in about 1265. When his cousin became Pope Clement V and moved the papacy to Avignon, Arnaud was made a cardinal. With the wealth that soon came his way he bought the monastery, enlarged it and built himself a collegiate church and palace, completed in 1318. Though the palace has mostly disappeared, the church and monastery remain, largely unchanged since then, with Arnaud's towers rising above folds of Gascon farmland.

In 1999 the church was, with other landmarks on the road to Compostela, granted Unesco World Heritage protection. The GR65 arcs north around the village.

The village is full of cats and cat sculptures, and a bust of its own legendary 'cat woman' (see the boxed text).

Orientation & Information The tourist office (☎/fax 05 62 28 86 33), opposite the cloister at the eastern end of the central square, place Bonet, is open 10am to noon and 2pm to 6pm daily February to May and October to December, 10am to noon and 2pm to 7pm daily in June and September and 10am to 12.30pm and 2pm to 7.30pm daily in July and August; it's closed Sunday morning and all of January.

Monastery & Church Tourist office staff will let you into the 14th-century complex (*opposite tourist office; €3.05; same hours as tourist office, no admission in the half-hour before lunch and closing*). Across the Gothic cloister – originally three storeys

The Cat Woman of La Romieu

Look around the village and you'll see life-size stone cats perched on window ledges, climbing walls, peering out of nooks and crannies. Strangest of all is the bust of a half-woman-half-cat in place Bonet.

In the 14th century an infant girl named Angeline was orphaned when her woodsman father was killed by a falling tree and her mother died of grief. Raised by a neighbour, Angeline developed a great affection for cats.

Some years later, several seasons of poor harvests and harsh winters left the people on the edge of starvation. In desperation they decided to kill and eat all the village cats. Angeline's adoptive parents, knowing how this would devastate her, secretly allowed her to keep a pair in the attic, letting them out to hunt only at night.

With the end of the famine came hope, and a cruel twist. Without cats the rat population had shot up, and before long the new harvests were being devoured by these creatures. Again the people faced starvation. Angeline at this point confessed to keeping two cats – and to the fact that there were now some twenty offspring in her attic as well.

The cats were distributed to the overjoyed villagers, the rodent population was brought under control, Angeline became a heroine and her story shaded into legend. It was said that in old age she came to resemble a cat herself.

The sculptures are a recent addition to the village, the gift of an artist from Orléans who overheard the story being told to local children.

❁ ❁ ❁ ❁ ❁ ❁ ❁ ❁ ❁ ❁ ❁

tall – is the luminous little Collégiale St-Pierre church. Along the walls are the tombs of Arnaud d'Aux and several nephews. The stained glass dates from the 1860s except for a small 16th-century head of Christ at the centre of the rose window.

Left of the altar is the **sacristy**, whose original frescoes include biblical characters, family portraits and esoteric symbols. From there, climb the double-helix stairway into the octagonal **Belvedere Tower**, with views over the countryside. The church also has a square belfry, and just to the west is the **Cardinal's Tower**, all that remains of Arnaud's palace.

Arboretum Coursiana This six-hectare arboretum (☎ *05 62 68 22 80, 600m southwest of the village centre; with/without guided tour €6.10/4.60; open 9am-7pm daily mid-Mar–Nov)* with over 600 trees and rare plants, was the personal project of a local agricultural engineer.

Places to Stay & Eat There are no rooms available in the village, but the tourist office has a list of nearby *gîtes, chambres d'hôte* and *camping à la ferme*.

Camp de Florence (☎ 05 62 28 15 58, fax 05 62 28 20 04, W www.campdeflorence .com) 2-person forfait €20.20/10.40 in the high/low season, bungalows €600/200 per week. *Menus* €14.50-25.20. Open Apr-Oct (restaurant & pool mid-May–Sept). This vast, kid-friendly camp site 700m east of the village centre has pool, sports facilities, scheduled events and a good restaurant.

Restaurant Le Cardinal (☎ 05 62 28 42 75, place Bonet) is little more than a cafe-bar, but has a €14.50 midday *menu*.

Getting There & Away No buses come here, but it's an undemanding drive or cycle ride from Condom (go north-east on the D931 Agen road for 2.7km, then turn right on the D41 for 8.1km).

Fourcès
postcode 32250 • pop 350

Fourcès (pronounce the 's'), 13km north-west of Condom beside the River Auzoue, is a heavily restored, unbearably cute bastide, founded by the English in the 13th century. What makes it interesting is that it's circular, with sturdy, arcaded medieval houses ringing the central plaza, plus a 15th- or 16th-century bell tower and fragments of a surrounding wall. There was a chateau in the middle until Charles VIII had it demolished in 1488.

A tiny tourist office (☎ 05 62 29 50 96, fax 05 62 29 47 44) on the central plaza is open

10.30am to noon and 3pm to 6pm Tuesday to Saturday mid-May to mid-October (closed the rest of the year).

The population swells to thousands during the village's Marché aux Fleurs (Flower Market) on the last weekend of April.

Places to Stay & Eat The tourist office has a list of nearby *chambres d'hôte* and *gîtes*.

Château de Fourcès (☎ 05 62 29 49 53) Doubles with shower/bath €111/148. Midday *menus* €16-22.10, evening *menus* €28.20-43. The small chateau and grounds are very grand, but most of us would have to empty our bank accounts to stay a night.

L'Auberge (☎ 05 62 29 40 10) Menus €8.40, salads & pâtés €5.35-7.60. Open midday & evening Thur-Tues, midday only Wed. Sip and snack with other foreign tourists at this bar-restaurant on the main plaza. The delicately prepared dishes won't fill you up.

Larressingle & the Pont d'Artigues

Larressingle, about 5km west of Condom on the D15, may be France's cutest fortified village. Armies of Compostela pilgrims and breathless tourists seem to have put its tiny community on the defensive. Locals, presumably with tongues deep in their cheeks, refer to it as 'the Carcassonne of the Gers'.

But it's pretty amazing, a textbook bastion bearing witness to the troubled times of medieval Gascony, driven by the Hundred Years' War. From its 12th-century founding it belonged jointly to the abbeys of Agen and Condom, and was later an official residence of the bishops of Condom.

The original walls, surrounded by a moat, are largely intact. Inside are the remains of a castle-keep, the sturdy Romanesque Église St-Sigismond (featuring a mermaid in one of its stained-glass windows), an unconvincing museum of medieval life, the *Crêperie du Château* (crepes €3-6, omelettes €2.30) and some craft shops. You can see the whole place in half an hour.

Just outside the walls is **Cité des Machines du Moyen-Age** (☎/fax 05 62 68 33 88; €1.55; open 11am-5.30pm daily Apr-

Sept; 1pm-5.30pm daily Oct-Mar), an alfresco museum of medieval war-machines. For an extra €1.55 they'll operate the things at 11.30am, 3pm, 4.30pm and 5.30pm in July and August.

About 1.5km south of the village is the **Pont d'Artigues**, a simple stone bridge with asymmetrical arches, across the River Osse. Built for Compostela pilgrims in the Middle Ages, it's part of the inventory of pilgrim sites with a joint Unesco World Heritage designation.

Montréal du Gers & Séviac

postcode 32250 • pop 1270 • elevation 124m

Montréal du Gers was probably Gascony's first bastide, begun in 1255 by Alphonse de Poitiers, although the English moved in before he had finished it. The once-fortified site, above the gorge of the River Auzoue, is all the more attractive for being largely unrestored. Its chunky Gothic church squats at the edge of the main square, thumbing its nose at the bastide's precision by aligning itself instead with the town walls.

But the town's trump card is the excavated remains of a Gallo-Roman country house, 2.3km south-west of the centre.

Orientation & Information The tourist office (☎ 05 62 29 42 85, fax 05 62 29 42 46, ℮ otsi.montrealdugers@wanadoo.fr) and an attached museum of Roman artefacts are on the main square, place Hôtel de Ville. Both are open 10am to noon and 3pm to 5pm weekdays October to December and February to April; 10am to noon and 3pm to 6pm Monday to Saturday in May, June and September; 10am to noon and 2pm to 7pm daily Monday to Saturday plus 3pm to 7pm Sunday in July and August (closed January).

Séviac The 2-hectare site at Séviac (☎ 05 62 29 48 57, route d'Éauze; €3.05, child aged under 12 free; open 10am-noon & 2pm-6pm daily Mar-June & Sept-Nov; 10am-7pm daily July-Aug) came to light in 1866, when the curate of nearby Labarrère found a patch of mosaic tiles. Further work came in 1909, though most excavation was done between 1959 and 1992.

What archaeologists found were the remnants of a luxurious villa on the agricultural estate of a 4th-century Roman aristocrat, along with other buildings dating from the 2nd to the 7th centuries. Large areas of the villa's spectacular mosaic floors – in some 30 detailed patterns – had survived intact. An attached bathing complex was equipped with a forced-air heating system – state-of-the-art for its time and the grandest ever found in a private house.

The entry ticket also admits you to the museum attached to Montréal's tourist office (you can buy it at either place). A detailed multilingual text is available to borrow. The turning to Séviac is on the D29, 900m west of Montréal; from there, follow the well signposted country road for 1.4km.

Places to Stay & Eat The tourist office has a list of nearby *chambres d'hôte*.

Le Couloume (☎ 05 62 29 44 78, fax 05 62 29 47 05, route d'Éauze) €2.30/4.60 per adult/pitch. Open year round. This spartan *camping à la ferme* is on the D29, 600m south of the Séviac turning.

La Rose d'Armagnac (☎/fax 05 62 29 47 70, e claire.owen@freesbee.fr, route de Nérac) €2/3.05/4.25 per person/small pitch/large pitch. Open May-Oct. This small, Welsh/English-run camp site 2.6km north of Montréal (turn off the D29 about 800m from the village) has field and woodland pitches and a fishing pond.

Ferme de Macon (☎ 05 62 29 42 07, fax 05 62 29 44 85, route de Séviac) Menus €15.25-27.45. Double/twin €39.65/56.45 with breakfast. Meals daily year round, reservation only; rooms Apr-Oct. Surely the finest choice for accommodation and superb Gascon meals is this ferme auberge 500m off the D29 on the country road to Séviac.

The cheapest food choice is a picnic; there's an *épicerie* (grocery), open Monday to Saturday and Sunday morning, on place Hôtel de Ville.

Getting There & Around There's no public transport. For a taxi call Taxi Daste (☎ 05 62 09 93 94).

Château de Cassaigne

You can enjoy a visit to this 13th-century chateau, ancient country-house of the bishops of Condom, and sample the Armagnac produced in its 18th-century distillery. Also worth a look is the 16th-century kitchen. The chateau (☎ 05 62 28 04 02, fax 05 62 28 41 43, Cassaigne, W www.chateaude cassaigne.com; admission free; open 9am-noon & 2pm-7pm daily year round) is 6.5km south-west of Condom on the D208. There's no public transport.

Abbaye de Flaran

Flaran Abbey (☎ 05 62 28 50 19, D142; adult/child aged 12-17 €3.80/1.85, free 1st Sun of month Nov-Dec & Jan-Mar; open 10am-12.30pm & 2pm-6pm Feb-June & Sept-Dec; 9.30am-7pm July-Aug) was founded on the banks of the Baïse in 1151, part of the Cistercian movement for a return to back-to-basics monasticism.

Despite severe damage in the Hundred Years' War, desecration by Protestant troops during the Wars of Religion, and layers of Baroque plaster applied in the 17th and 18th centuries, you can still sense its founding spirit, particularly in the beautiful church, the Église Notre Dame. This is the Gers' best-preserved Cistercian site, feasible as a day trip from Auch or Condom.

You enter through **guest quarters** dating from the 18th century (by which time the monks were spending little time in the monastery). Turn right into the **cloister**. One gallery dates from the 14th century, with capitals carved with foliage and faces, and traces of its Romanesque predecessor. The other three, trashed by the Protestants, are now supported by simple bevelled columns. Off the cloister are the kitchen, refectory, a fine vaulted chapter house and above it a dormitory with some Romanesque windows.

The best part is the early 13th-century **church**, startlingly austere but full of light, with a transept longer than the nave.

If you're looking to stay close to the abbey, you could try the following.

La Ferme de Flaran (☎ 05 62 28 58 22, fax 05 62 28 56 89, D930 route de Condom) Doubles with bath & WC €44.95. Breakfast

€6.10. Comfortable, uninspiring rooms at this Logis de France place are aimed at groups visiting the abbey, 500m away.

The nearest bus stop is in Valence-sur-Baïse, 1.5km to the south-east. Useful ATR buses depart from Condom (€1.50, 15 minutes) at 10am Monday, Thursday and Saturday, and 4pm Monday to Saturday, with return departures from Valence at 12.05pm and 6.50pm Monday to Saturday.

BAS-ARMAGNAC

The north-western corner of the Gers – with some overlap into Lot-et-Garonne and the Landes – is called the Bas-Armagnac. This is the heart of Armagnac brandy country, the zone of its best-known *appellation contrôlée* (AOC; a system of strict definition and control of quality lines and spirits). Here too is the boyhood home of the prototype Gascon, Alexandre Dumas' larger-than-life hero, D'Artagnan (see the boxed text under Lupiac, later in this chapter).

Labastide d'Armagnac

postcode 40240 • pop 710 • elevation 94m

This pocket-sized bastide – vine-covered, cobbled and unassuming – was founded in 1291 by Comte Bernard VI d'Armagnac. Though marooned since the Revolution in the Landes, it is still decidedly Gascon. Most villagers today are involved in one way or another with the production of Armagnac and floc de Gascogne (see the boxed text 'Armagnac') at nearby Château Garreau.

Information The tourist office (☎ 05 58 44 67 56, fax 05 58 44 84 15, e tourisme@labastide-d-armagnac.com) is on the central square, place Royale. It opens 10am to 12.30pm and 2pm to 6.30pm Monday to Saturday and 3pm to 6.30pm Sunday April to September; 10am to noon and 2pm to 6pm Monday to Saturday from October to March (Tuesday to Saturday in December and January).

Musée des Bastides This earnest museum of bastides *(same ☎ as tourist office, cours Maubec; €3.05, students €1.20; tourist office for hours)* has an audioguide (French only) to walk you through a pocket history of bastides and through the construction and occupation of one, complete with 'medieval street' soundtrack. The museum is in a restored Protestant *temple* (church), built outside the walls after the one inside was burned following the 1685 revocation of the Edict of Nantes. It's about 300m south-west of place Royale on the D11.

Notre Dame des Cyclistes That's right, Our Lady of the Cyclists *(same ☎ as tourist office, Géou, route de Cazaubon; admission free; usually 3pm-6pm Tues-Sun, but check with tourist office)* – a pretty 11th-century chapel, in 1959 declared by the local abbot to be a sanctuary for cyclists of both racing and tourist varieties. Inside is a mini-museum with champions' jerseys and old bikes. It's on the D626, 2.6km south-east of Labastide.

Ecomusée de l'Armagnac Château Garreau *(☎ 05 58 44 88 38, route de Mauléon; €3.80; open 9am-noon & 2pm-6pm Mon-Sat year round; 3pm-6pm Sun Apr-Oct)*, 3km south-east of Labastide d'Armagnac, has a collection of old Armagnac stills and other apparatus, as well as vineyards, woods and a small bird refuge – plus free tastings of their own floc and Armagnac. Turn right 1km south-east of Labastide on the D626, and continue for 3.2km.

Places to Stay & Eat For *chambres d'hôte* in and near the village, ask at the tourist office.

Camping Le Pin (☎/fax 05 58 44 88 91, route de Roquefort, St-Justin) 2-person *forfait* (package camping rate) €16. Open mid-Mar–Oct. This well equipped camp site (with a pool) is 5.5km north-west of Labastide on the D626.

Camp Municipal de Nauton (☎ 05 58 45 50 45, fax 05 58 45 53 63, D932, Nauton) 2-person forfait €6.70. Open June-Sept. On the more modest side (but with tennis courts) is Roquefort's municipal campsite.

Hôtel de France (☎ 05 58 44 83 61, fax 05 58 44 83 89, place des Tilleuls, St-Justin) Doubles €37.35-45.75. *Menus* cafe €10.65,

Armagnac

> O Lord, give me good health, for a long time; love, from time to time; work, not much of the time; and Armagnac, all the time.
>
> **Village prayer, Fourcès**

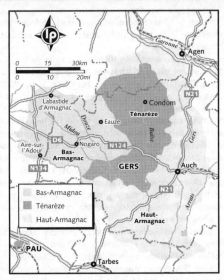

First produced as a medicine in the 15th century, Armagnac is probably France's original brandy (distilled wine).

White-wine grapes of 10 approved varieties are harvested in October, made into wine, and single-distilled over the winter into a potent, colourless *eau de vie*. This is matured in 400L oak casks – traditionally made from trees grown on the same soil as the grapes – for 10 to 40 years or more, taking from the wood its amber colour and an array of subtle aromas.

Then it's blended and bottled. Armagnac's high alcohol content (at least 40%) means that it doesn't mature further in the bottle. It can be drunk immediately, or will keep indefinitely. Its 'age' is the time spent in the cask: A *Trois Étoiles* brandy is aged at least two years; *VO*, *VSOP* and *Réserve* at least five; *Extra*, *Napoléon*, *XO* and *Vieille Réserve* at least six; and *Hors d'Age* at least 10. Vintage brandies, like vintage wines, are blended only from grapes harvested in specific years.

A gentler fortified wine called Floc de Gascogne (or Floc d'Armagnac), with the strength of sherry or port, is made by blending young Armagnac and the juice of a single grape variety from the same vineyard, and ageing it in casks for at least 10 months. This may be *floc blanc* or *floc rosé*, according to whether the juice grape is white or red.

The Armagnac area covers some 150 sq km in northwest Gers, plus a few parishes of the Landes and Lot-et-Garonne. There are three *appellations d'origine contrôlée*. From the sandy, acidic soil of the **Bas-Armagnac** come the finest brandies, delicate and fruity. The chalky clay of the **Ténarèze** produces full-bodied brandies that age well. The **Haut-Armagnac** is a 19th-century expansion with only a small fraction of the total output.

You can stop for a free taste at any number of small producers (bigger tourist offices keep lists of them). A good place for a guided walk through the process is the Domaine Départemental d'Ognoas (see the section of the same name in this chapter). Condom also has an Armagnac museum.

---

restaurant €22.85-38.85. Restaurant open midday & evening Mon-Wed, Fri-Sat, midday only Thur; midday & evening Tues-Sat July-Aug. This is the nearest hotel, 5km north-west on St-Justin's main square, with plain, comfortable rooms and a popular cafe-restaurant.

Crêperie Sucre-Paille (☎ *05 58 44 81*

43, place Royale) Menus €12.20, crepes from €3.05. Open Thur-Tues May-Sept. Sucre-Paille is Labastide's only eatery, except for picnic fare from the neighbouring *epicerie* (small grocery shop).

Getting There & Away Serag's (☎ 05 58 75 22 89) Mont de Marsan-Agen bus stops

D'Artagnan & the Three Musketeers

Many people think the reckless heroes of Alexandre Dumas' romantic novel, *Les Trois Mousquetaires* (The Three Musketeers), are pure invention. In fact they really existed, though not as Dumas portrayed them.

D'Artagnan, whose real name was Charles de Batz-Castelmore, was born around 1611 in Castelmore. At the age of 19 – and borrowing the name D'Artagnan from his mother's side of the family for its aristocratic ring – he left for Paris, enrolling as a cadet in the royal guards.

Little is known of his early years there but he gained a reputation – partly via Paris' salon society – as a brave soldier and a gallant gentleman. This brought him to the attention of Cardinal Mazarin, Louis XIV's chief minister, and before long he had become a friend and confidant of the King himself. Eventually D'Artagnan was given command of the musket-armed elite of the royal guards, the mousquetaires. Arrogant, quarrelsome, rowdy but brave and disciplined, the mousquetaires were always at the head of royal corteges.

Soon he had become Maréchal D'Artagnan, taking part in military campaigns all over Europe. He was rewarded in 1672 with the governorship of Lille, but soon grew restless for the soldier's life. He died a hero's death, of a musket-shot to the neck, in the siege of Maastricht in 1673.

Fake D'Artagnan 'memoirs', anonymously ghost-written 27 years after his death, were discovered by Dumas in a Marseille library, and served as background for the latter's now-famous novel. D'Artagnan (who apparently did have three close friends in the musketeers) had come back to life in swashbuckling, highly fictionalised form. But, as Dumas wrote, history is just 'the nail upon which I hang my stories'.

Never mind – the novel was received with enthusiasm, and over the years some 50 films have been made about the imaginary adventures of D'Artagnan and his companions Athos, Porthos and Aramis.

here (see Mont de Marsan in the Bordeaux, the Atlantic Coast & the Landes chapter), Sunday to Friday.

Domaine Départemental d'Ognoas

This is Gascony's oldest distillery, founded in 1486, and the only state-owned one in France. In 1847 the heirless owners left the *domaine* (estate) to the church. After the separation of church and state in 1905 it went to the Landes department, which now runs it like a private operation, with a quality product and all profits reinvested, but also as a showplace for Armagnac production.

The 540-hectare estate (☎ 05 58 45 22 11, fax 05 58 45 38 21, Arthez d'Armagnac; admission free; open 9am-noon & 2pm-5.30pm Mon-Fri year round; also 2pm-6pm Sat-Sun May-Sept) includes 25 hectares of vineyards and 300 hectares of dedicated forests. Armagnac is produced using a single 1804 copper still. Casks – from oak trees at least 80 years old, dried for seven years – are made in the traditional way by the only cooper in the region who still knows the art.

The estate is 4km east of Villeneuve de Marsan and 21km east of Mont de Marsan on the D1. It opens for free tours and tasting – but call first, preferably several days ahead. Non-French-speaking guides are available in the high season.

Centre d'Artagnan (Lupiac)

Tiny Lupiac's sole claim to fame is that Charles de Batz-Castelmore, better known as D'Artagnan (see the boxed text), was born and raised at Château Castelmore, 4km to the north. The chateau is closed to the public, but a small museum, the Centre D'Artagnan (☎ 05 62 09 24 09, route d'Aignan; audio-guide rental adult/child aged 10-18 €3.05/ 2.30; open 10.30am-7pm daily July-Aug; 2pm-6pm Tues-Sun Sept-June; closed 1-15 Jan) has been grafted onto the Chapelle St-Jacques, built in 1605 by D'Artagnan's uncle Charles for Compostela pilgrims.

It's essential to rent the audioguide to appreciate the museum; this and the short video which follows are available in French, English and other languages. Though jumbled and vaguely corny, they provide a good introduction to the times D'Artagnan lived in, and dispel a few of the myths promulgated by Alexandre Dumas.

The museum is a stone's throw from the arcaded centre of Lupiac. Lupiac is 9km east of Aignan on the D174. There's no public transport.

Southern Gers

MARCIAC

postcode 32230 • pop 1200 • elevation 155m
Marciac's annual jazz festival, now one of France's biggest, has put it on the map. But this is also an emblematic bastide of Southwest France, founded in 1298 for Philippe IV, and now under unhurried renovation. The town's tall steeple rises above the countryside like the spire of a lost cathedral. A nearby lake and water-sports complex make this a good place to stop with kids.

Orientation & Information

On the wide, arcaded central square, place de l'Hôtel-de-Ville, are the town hall, the post office, a bank and – on Wednesday morning – a big produce market.

The tourist office (☎ 05 62 08 26 60, fax 05 62 08 26 61, e ot.marciac@wanadoo.fr), at place du Chevalier d'Antras, a block north of the central square, is open 9am to noon and 2pm to 6pm (from 9.30am Sunday) daily April to September; Sunday to Friday during the rest of the year.

Église Notre-Dame de Marciac

Marciac's fine 14th-century Gothic church has portals and interior capitals carved in an appealing, almost Romanesque style. The 85m steeple is the highest tower in the Gers.

Les Territoires du Jazz

Les Territoires du Jazz (same address/☎/fax as tourist office; adult/those under 18 years €4.55/3.05; open 9.30am-noon & 2.30pm-6pm daily Apr-Sept; Sun-Fri only Oct-Mar) is a multi-media 'museum' of jazz from its African roots to the present. Visitors don headsets and jive through a dozen musical settings from Dixieland to the Blues. It shares space with the tourist office in a 14th-century abbey on place du Chevalier d'Antras.

Base Nautique

About 1km north of the town centre on the D3 is a water-sports complex (☎ 05 62 09 34 65, D3 route de Plaisance) on Lac de Marciac, a 30-hectare reservoir on the River Bourès, with windsurfing, sailing, boating, water-skiing and fishing.

Special Events

Jazz in Marciac is the grandfather of the Midi-Pyrénées' many jazz festivals, with big-name concerts, jam sessions and masterclasses, as well as special markets and exhibitions, for about two weeks in August. More healthy than ever, it's gradually expanding across the calendar, with guest artists throughout the year. Festival tickets cost about €10-50; for more information contact the festival organisers (☎ 08 25 08 82 30, fax 05 62 09 34 83).

Places to Stay & Eat

The tourist office has lists of nearby *chambres d'hôte* and can arrange homestays during the jazz festival.

Camping du Lac (☎/fax 05 62 08 21 19, D3 route de Plaisance) Adult €4.40 plus €3.35/4.90 per pitch with tent/caravan; cheaper outside of Aug. Open mid-Mar–mid-Nov. Dutch-run Camping du Lac, just off the highway 1.4km north of town, is tidy, shady and 400m from the Base Nautique.

Hôtel Les Comtes de Pardiac (☎ 05 62 08

20 00, fax 05 62 08 28 05, e *h.j.p.cazaban@ wanadoo.fr, 28 place de l'Hôtel de Ville)* Doubles €42.70/48.80 with WC & shower/ bath. Breakfast €5.35. A bit of foliage around the patio would help, but this freshly renovated little hotel in the town centre looks like the best value in its range.

Restaurant La Petite Auberge *(☎ 05 62 09 31 33, 16 place de l'Hôtel de Ville) Menus* €8.25-30.50. Open midday & evening Fri-Tues, midday only Wed. Carefully prepared regional dishes in a bright, quiet setting make this restaurant, a few doors from Le Comtes, a good place for indulging.

Brasserie Le Festival *(☎ 05 62 08 25 00, 23 rue St-Justin) Menus* €9.90-11.60. Open midday & evening Wed-Mon, midday only Tues. This laid-back bar-brasserie with an outdoor patio has pretty good regional dishes for modest prices (including a midday €6.85 *menu*).

Restaurant La Péniche *(☎ 05 62 09 38 46, D3 route de Plaisance) Menus* €15.25-22.85. Open Tues to midday Sun. This isn't a *péniche* (barge) but it does float, moored at the edge of Lac de Marciac. The Gascon dishes are good but the setting is the main thing.

The main square has several mini-markets that stay open until about 12.30pm, perfect for rustling up a picnic.

Getting There & Away
Surprisingly, there are no regular bus services. The nearest useful bus stop is in Laas, 16km south-east on the Auch-Tarbes route (N21), with three SNCF buses daily (one Sunday); Auch-Laas takes 45 minutes. The nearest useful train stations are at Tarbes (40km) and Auch (45km).

The tourist office organises a special Auch-Mirande-Marciac evening bus service during the jazz festival, which can be booked along with concert tickets. For a taxi, call ☎ 05 62 09 38 05 or 05 62 08 20 36.

MIRANDE
postcode 32300 • pop 4040 • elevation 175m
Founded on the River Baïse in 1281 by a royal *sénéchal* (seneschal) named Eustache de Beaumarchais, cheerful Mirande served

as the capital of the medieval province of Astarac. Most visitors come to see its arresting parish church and perfect checkerboard grid, or in mid-July for its festival of country music.

Orientation & Information
Buses stop in the arcaded main square, place d'Astarac. The main landmark is the pointed tower of the church, two blocks north.

Across rue de l'Évêché from the church is the tourist office (☎ 05 62 66 68 10), open 9am to noon and 2pm to 6pm Monday to Saturday (from 10am Saturday), plus Sunday morning in July and August.

At least three banks with ATMs are on or near place d'Astarac.

For Internet access, try Internet Academy (☎ 05 62 59 05 80), 27 rue Victor Hugo. It opens 10am to 8pm daily Monday to Saturday (to midnight Friday and Saturday). Access costs €4.55 per hour.

Mirande's weekly market, in place d'Astarac, is on Monday.

Église Ste-Marie de Mirande
There's no other church in the southwest like this one *(rue Sabathé; open 9am-noon & 2pm-6pm Mon-Sat, 9.30am-noon Sun)*, a stocky Gothic thing far too big for the space, with buttresses flying right across the road, and a remarkable belfry-cum-lookout tower with pointy hats.

For a time in the 15th century there were three popes, including one in Avignon. One of the many things on which they didn't agree was where to put a new bishopric for the region. One said Mirande, so for its early years (1410–13) this was a 'cathedral' (Auch eventually took the title). It was used as a barn for almost a century after the Revolution.

The austere interior is warmed by luminous 19th-century stained glass high above the altar. One chapel on the northern side has its original window, depicting St Michael with a dragon.

Other Things to See
Arcaded **place d'Astarac** presides over one of the most perfectly regular bastide grids you'll see – the central blocks are all precise

50m squares – dotted with medieval **half-timbered houses**, the finest of them along rue de l'Évêché. A block north is the **Tour de Rohan**, a medieval watchtower. Four blocks north-east are 500m of old **town walls**.

Beside the tourist office is the municipal **Musée des Beaux-Arts et des Arts Decoratifs** (same ☎ as the tourist office, rue de l'Évêché; adult/child aged under 16 €2/1.20; open 10am-noon & 3pm-6pm Mon-Sat), with 15th- to 19th-century fine art and china.

Special Events
Mirande hosts a Festival de Country Music, complete with a motorbike and car show, Western dancing and hot-air balloons, from the Thursday to Sunday closest to Bastille Day (14 July), in the sports park south-west of the town centre. For more information contact the festival organisers (☎ 05 62 66 78 53, fax 05 62 66 82 02, **e** countrymusic mirande@wanadoo.fr).

Places to Stay & Eat
For details of *chambres d'hôte* and *fermes auberges* in the area, ask at the tourist office.

Camping L'Île du Pont (☎ 05 62 66 64 11, fax 05 62 66 69 86, Île du Pont) 2-person forfait €14; bungalows €297 per week. Open Apr-Sept. This well equipped camp site is within a riverside leisure centre a few hundred metres east of the town centre.

Hôtel Métropole (☎ 05 62 66 50 25, fax 05 62 66 77 63, 31 rue Victor Hugo) Doubles with bath with/without WC €38.90/37.35. Breakfast €4.55. *Menus* €10.30-33.55. Of the town's three hotels, best value is this Logis de France place, three blocks south of the square, tastefully furnished and restored.

Hôtel Les Pyrénées (☎ 05 62 66 51 16, fax 05 62 66 79 96, **e** hotel-des-pyrenees@ wanadoo.fr, 5 av d'Étigny) Doubles with shower €68.60-99.10, with bath €53.35-83.85. Breakfast €6.86. This is the luxury address, flash and well run; pricier rooms overlook the pool.

Europ'Hotel Maupas (☎ 05 62 66 51 42, fax 05 62 66 74 69, 2 av d'Étigny) Singles €30.50-38.10, doubles €35.05-45.75, all with shower & WC. The Maupas has old but well kept rooms.

Le Coup d'Envoi (☎ 05 62 66 52 77, 4 place d'Astarac) Plat du jour €6.10. Local young people like nursing a coffee here, and the plat du jour won't hurt your budget.

Restaurant La Villetta (☎ 05 62 66 76 24, 8 rue de Rohan) Pizzas €6.10-7.70, pasta €7.25-9.55. If you fancy a change from French, try this agreeable small Italian restaurant.

Restaurant Sông Huöng (☎ 05 62 66 84 49, 18 rue Victor Hugo) Dishes €5.65-8.40, seafood €7.95-14.50. Here's another change of pace, with an enormous menu of Vietnamese and Chinese dishes.

Getting There & Away
SNCF (☎ 08 36 35 35 35) has two to three buses daily from Auch (€4.40, 30 minutes). Claude Labriffe (☎ 05 62 66 51 20) has one to two daily Monday to Saturday.

AROUND MIRANDE
The gently folded southern Gers landscape conceals dozens of medieval villages, some restored and some not. The petite, one-street *castelnau* of Tillac seems to harbour more pigeons than people, but its twin gate-towers suggest that it was once important. Stop by early or late, sit down at the *Relais de la Tour* (☎ 05 62 70 00 81) by the western gate, and have coffee in another century (Tillac was founded in the 13th century, the church was built in the 14th, and its prettily restored houses date from the 17th).

Sleepy **Miélan** (population 1300) was founded in 1284 by Eustache de Beaumarchais, a royal seneschal with a penchant for naming bastides after southern European cities, this one for Milan. Leaning, half-timbered houses surround its central square, place Jean Sènac, with the town hall in the middle. About 2km north on the N21 is a small lake and leisure complex. SNCF buses serving Mirande also stop here.

One of the finest mountain views anywhere in the southwest is from the highest point in the Gers, a nondescript 315m rise called **Puntous de Laguian**, 6km west of Miélan on the N21. Pull over for a stunning view of some 150km of the Hautes-Pyrénées.

SAMATAN
postcode 32130 • pop 2010
• elevation 165m

This easygoing market town in the south-eastern corner of the Gers has little of historical interest but, with probably the biggest foie-gras market in France, it's pretty important to foodies and restaurant owners. For more on foie gras – the enlarged, fatty liver of a force-fed goose or duck, an essential ingredient in the southwest's renowned gastronomy – see the special section 'Food & Wine of the Southwest'. On the subject of force-feeding, refer to Treatment of Animals under Society & Conduct in the Facts about Southwest France chapter.

Orientation & Information
The town centre is, predictably, the market square, place des Halles. This is also where regional buses stop.

The tourist office (☎ 05 62 62 55 40, fax 05 62 62 50 26, e ot.samatan@wanadoo .fr), at 3 rue Chanoine Dieuzaide, two blocks to the north-east, is open 10am to noon and 4pm to 6pm Monday to Saturday and Sunday morning in July and August; 10am to noon and 3pm to 5pm Monday and Wednesday to Saturday the rest of year.

Banks with ATMs are on place des Halles and north-east around the block on rue du Pradel. The post office is a block north-west at 8 blvd des Castres.

Markets
Every Monday an open-air **produce market** fills place des Halles. On the same day the big **foie-gras market** cranks up at the Halle au Gras, a few hundred metres south-east on allée du 14 Juillet, across the canal.

Buyers mill outside while sellers set their tables; a whistle sounds, and in they go. The professionals – probably including many of the southwest's best chefs or their agents – are finished in 20 minutes. During peak foie-gras season, from October to December, 45 tonnes of carcasses and 4 tonnes of livers are sold every Monday morning. Most sellers are from the Gers, Haute-Garonne or Hautes-Pyrénées, while buyers come from all over the Midi-Pyrénées and beyond.

From October to April, carcasses are sold at 9.30am, livers at 10.30am and live birds at 11.30am. The rest of the year, it's carcasses and livers at 10am and live birds at 11am. A smaller foie-gras market takes place on Sunday from November to March at Gimont, 19km north on the D4.

Foie-Gras Museum
At the back of the tourist office is a miscellany of farmer mannequins, old gadgets for grinding maize, and more alarming ones – manual and electric – for cramming it into geese. Entry is free, and it's open the same hours as the tourist office.

Foie-Gras Farms
If you'd like to see how the geese and ducks are raised, and perhaps watch the *gavage* (force-feeding), ask at the tourist office for a list of farms that welcome visitors. One near the centre is **Conserverie Bernard Duplan** (*☎ 05 62 62 31 33, Campan; admission free)*; turn right about 1.2km west down the Lombez road (D39).

Places to Stay & Eat
The tourist office keeps a list of nearby *campings à la ferme* and *chambres d'hôte*. Alternatively, you could try one of the following.

Camp Municipal (☎ 05 62 62 02 98, just south-west of foie-gras market) €1.85 per adult plus €1.05/1.85 per pitch with car/caravan. Open mid-June–mid-Sept. The town's camp site is as spartan as the price suggests, but well kept.

Restaurant Le Castre (☎ 05 62 62 39 15, 9 blvd des Castres) Midday *menus* €9.15. Open Mon-Sat. Le Castre, a stone's throw north-west of place des Halles, has delicious, uncomplicated regional fare and cheerful service. On market day, get there by noon.

Getting There & Around
There are no buses to Samatan from Auch. Semvat's (☎ 05 61 61 67 67) Bus Nos 65, 66 or 67 makes the 1¼-hour trip from Toulouse five times daily (more Monday, fewer Sunday).

The French Basque Country

The Basque country (*Euskal Herria* in the Basque language) – today occupying the western foothills of the Pyrénées – is a land apart, stubbornly independent and profoundly different from either of the nation-states which have adopted it.

The 20% or so of Euskal Herria on the French side (called *Iparralde* in Basque or *Le Pays Basque* in French) is less populous and less industrialised than the Spanish Basque provinces (*Hegoalde* in Basque or *País Vasco* in Spanish). The French Basque Country comprises about a third of the Pyrénées-Atlantiques *département* (administrative department). The three provinces on the French side – Labourd, Basse-Navarre and Soule – no longer have any administrative function.

The administrative capital of the French Basque country, Bayonne, is the best springboard to see the region, with a fine mix of French and Basque, and vital transport links. The balance tips to Basque just down the coast at St-Jean de Luz. But to take the pulse of this region, head for inland towns such as Sare, Aïnhoa or Bidarray, or up the valley of the River Nive into the western Pyrénées.

Three useful Web sites dealing with the French Basque Country are:

Basque Explorer
(Ⓦ www.basquexplorer.com) With a full calendar of summer events (French/English)
Centre d'Information du Pays Basque
(Ⓦ www.infobasque.com) Food, accommodation, history and town links (French/English)
Guide Basque
(Ⓦ www.guide-basque.com) Links to activities, town Web pages, Basque games and shopping

History

Basques are known to be descended from a tribe the Romans called the Vascones, who were already living on both sides of the Pyrénées long before the Celts encountered them across the Garonne River in about 600 BC. Indeed, DNA research suggests that the Basques are direct descendants of the Cro-Magnon peoples of this region.

Highlights

- Indulge yourself in Bayonne or Espelette with southern Europe's finest chocolate
- Ride a cog-wheel railway to the hallowed mountaintop of La Rhune
- Watch balls and bodies hit the wall in the lightning-fast game of *cesta punta*
- Ride championship-quality surf at Anglet
- Stuff yourself with grilled sardines beside the harbour at St-Jean de Luz

Bayonne p324;-5
Biarritz p332
St-Jean de Luz p338
Hendaye p344
St-Jean Pied de Port p352

Food & Wine Highlights

axoa – a spicy veal stew of onions, garlic, tomatoes and Espelette pimentos

ttoro – the classic Basque fish chowder

piperade – a piquant mush of red and green peppers, tomatoes, garlic and whipped eggs

Irouléguy – stout red wines (plus whites and rosés) of the Basse-Navarre

Basques on both sides of the mountains defended their lands ferociously, and emerged from the turbulent Middle Ages with a fair degree of autonomy. As part of the duchy of Aquitaine, the French Basque country was under English rule from the 12th to 15th centuries. French Basque autonomy came to an end during the 1789 Revolution.

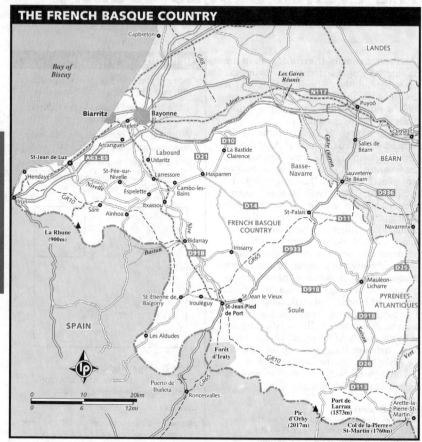

THE FRENCH BASQUE COUNTRY

After the Spanish Basque provinces (except Navarra) were stripped of autonomy in 1876, Basque nationalism gathered strength. Several provinces threw in their lot with republicans in the Spanish Civil War and Franco came down hard on them afterwards. Until Franco's death in 1975, many Spanish Basque nationalists sheltered in France.

In 1961 a group of nationalists called ETA (*Euskadi ta Askatasuna*, 'Basque Nation and Liberty') carried out its first terrorist attack, starting a cycle of violence and repression that continues today in Spain.

Converted to Christianity in the 10th century, Basques are still known for their devotion to Catholicism.

Basque Symbols

The Basque flag looks like a false-colour UK flag, with a red field, white vertical cross and green diagonal cross.

Another common symbol, often called the 'Basque cross', is a kind of rounded swastika with clockwise arms (also used, curiously enough, by Hindus and by the Navajos of North America). It represents the sun, and is used as a sign of blessing, protection or good luck.

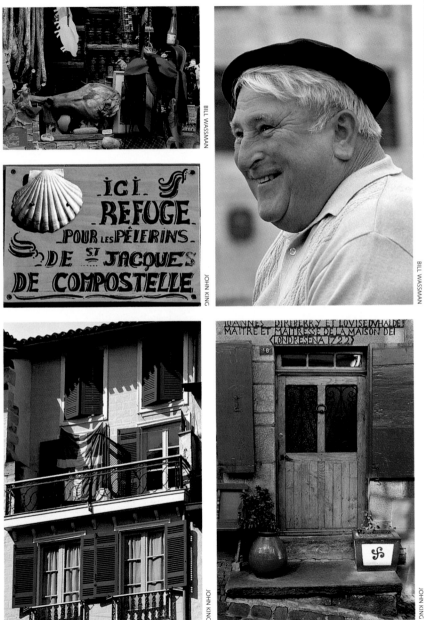

BILL WASSMAN

JOHN KING

BILL WASSMAN

IOANNES DIRIBERRY ET LOVISE DVHALDE
MAITRE ET MAITRESSE DE LA MAISON DEI
LONDRESENA 1722

JOHN KING

JOHN KING

Evidence of the pride in and strength of the Basque region's heritage is to be found in local shops, clothing, houses and flags. Even plant pots get the Basque treatment, sporting its sun symbol.

JOHN KING

Not for sufferers of vertigo: catching an unobstructed view of the scenery, vallée d'Aspe

MARTIN MOOS

A staggering five million pilgrims and travellers descend on Lourdes each year.

JOHN KING

The pretty village of Cette looks out onto the vallée d'Aspe, Haut-Béarn.

The Basque Language

Basque (Euskara) is a pre-Indo-European language, the only language in south-western Europe to have withstood the onslaught of Latin and its derivatives, and probably unrelated to any other tongue on earth. It's now spoken by about a million people in Spain and France, most of them bilingual. Two television stations in Spain and one in France broadcast in Basque. On shop doors, you will occasionally see *Hemen Euskara emaiten dugu*, which means 'Basque spoken here'.

Good morning	*Egun on*
Good afternoon	*Arratsalde on*
Good evening	*Gau on*
How are you?	*Nora zira?*
Fine/well	*Ongi*
Not well	*Gaizki*
Goodbye	*Agur* or *Ikus arte*
Thank you	*Milesker*
Pardon me	*Barkatu*
Please	*Otoi* or *Plazer baduzu*
Yes	*Bai*
No	*Ez*

A good Web site dealing with the Basque language can be found at **w** www.eirelink.com/alanking/basquep.htm.

❀ ❀ ❀ ❀ ❀ ❀ ❀ ❀ ❀ ❀ ❀ ❀ ❀

NICKY CAVEN

Pelota is an integral part of Basque life.

Basque Games

Pelote Basque Called *pelota* in Basque and English, *pelote basque* is the generic name for over 20 games played with a hard, rubber-cored ball. Most use either bare hands, a wooden paddle called a *pala*, a lighter one called a *paleta*, or a wicker scoop called a *chistera*, strapped to the wrist. Play is usually on an outdoor *fronton* (one-walled court), or a *trinquet* (three-walled indoor court). All players face the same wall. The three essential features of virtually every Basque village are a church, a town hall and a fronton.

The most common games are *eskuz huska* (French *main nue*) using bare hands; *joko garbi (petit-gant)* using a small chistera; *chistera (grand-gant)* using a bigger chistera; *pala, paleta* and lightning-fast *cesta punta*, using a big chistera on a long, three-sided indoor court called a *jaï alaï*.

Force Basque *Euskal indar-jokoak* is a Basque tournament of male muscle-power, with its origins in rural work: chopping through massive logs, running with 80kg sacks, lifting immense weights. One event that Basques probably gave to the rest of the world is *soka tira*, tug-of-war. The biggest annual Force Basque festival is held in mid-August in St-Palais, 70km south-east of Bayonne, with smaller festivals somewhere on just about every weekend from May to September.

Fishing-Boat Races Popular in the Spanish Basque country, races using *traînières* (replicas of 18th- to 19th-century tuna or herring boats) are catching on here too. Fixtures include the Régates de Traînières at St-Jean de Luz on the first weekend in July, and Hendaye's Fêtes de la Mer in mid-July.

Bullfighting

Corrida, Spanish-style bullfighting, has unapologetic fans all over the French Basque country, with several tournaments each summer. Tickets cost from €15 to €70, and advance reservations are usually necessary (ask at tourist offices). The corrida season is from July to early September.

Activities

Much of the French Basque Country's appeal comes from its opportunities for outdoor recreation, especially surfing, white-water boating and walking.

Surfing Hendaye's swells tend to be ideal for novices, while beaches that consistently serve as world championship venues include Guéthary, Biarritz's Grand Plage and Anglet's La Barre. For details, see the boxed text 'Surfing in the Southwest' under Activities in the Facts for the Visitor chapter.

White-Water Boating The main rafting river is the Nive, plunging down from the western Pyrénées. No fewer than five outfits offer trips by raft (€20 to €22 per person for about 1½ hours on the river) and smaller inflatables, plus other white-water activities.

Cocktail Adventure (☎ 05 59 54 18 69, fax 05 59 54 55 09, [e] cocktailaventure@wanadoo.fr) Résidence Laminak, St-Pée-sur-Nivelle

Évasion Eaux Vives (☎ 05 59 29 31 69, fax 05 59 29 81 62, [e] paysbasque.evasion@ wanadoo.fr) Maison Erola, Itxassou

Uhina Rafting (☎ 05 59 14 77 84, fax 05 59 84 76 45) Chemin de Burgachiloa, Cambo-les-Bains

Ur Bizia (☎/fax 05 59 37 72 37, [e] ur-bizia .wanadoo.fr) D918, Bidarray

Ur Ederra (☎/fax 05 59 37 78 01) D918, Bidarray

Walking The GR10 climbs from Hendaye's beach right up along the ridgeline of the Pyrénées, and the GR65 arrives at St-Jean Pied de Port from the Gers. Many tourist offices offer maps and booklets on local *petites randonées* (short hikes).

Bayonne

postcode 64100 • pop 40,000 • elevation 5m
If Pau weren't already prefecture of the Pyrénées-Atlantiques department, agreeable Bayonne (Baïona in Basque) would deserve the title. Unlike the upmarket beach resort of Biarritz, a short bus ride away, Bayonne retains plenty of Basque-ness. Its timber-framed, red and green-shuttered buildings are typical of the region, the beret remains *de rigueur* and you can hear almost as much Basque as French in certain quarters.

HISTORY
Bayonne, founded by the Romans at the strategic confluence of the Rivers Nive and Adour, enjoyed favour and prosperity under English rule and was one of the last English-held towns to give in to the French, in 1451.

Anxiety about the Spanish led to heavy fortification, and Bayonne mutated into a military centre. The town gave its name to the *baïonnette* (bayonet), developed here in the early 17th century. That period's hallmark is the magnificent fortifications by the Marquis de Vauban, Louis XIV's famous chief military engineer.

Bayonne went back into high gear after being declared a free port in 1759. Trade with Holland and Spain was brisk and Basque *corsaires* (pirates; see the boxed text 'The Basque Corsairs' under St-Jean de Luz later in this chapter) landed richer cargoes than did Basque cod fishermen.

A second crash came when the free-port status was abolished after the 1789 Revolution. En route from Spain in 1813 to battle Napoleon, Wellington twice laid siege to Bayonne. With Napoleon's defeat, the town's military career came to an end and commerce returned to the fore.

ORIENTATION
Bayonne is now part of a vast conurbation with Anglet and Biarritz, abbreviated BAB, sharing a public transport system (see Getting Around later in this section) and airport. The best maps of the area are Éditions Grafocarte's 1:13,500 *Bayonne Anglet Biarritz*, from bigger bookshops, and STAB's bus map, from the tourist office.

Bayonne is trisected by the Nive and Adour. The three central *quartiers* (districts) are St-Esprit north of the Adour, Petit Bayonne on the Nive's east bank, and Grand Bayonne on the west bank. Each has a riverside plaza; Grand Bayonne's is place de la Liberté, beside the town hall (Hôtel de Ville). Locals consider the town centre to be the lively shopping district between the town hall and place Louis Pasteur.

BAB's airport is 5km south-west of the town centre. Bayonne's train and bus stations are both in St-Esprit.

INFORMATION
Tourist Office
The tourist office (☎ 05 59 46 01 46, fax 05 59 59 37 55, e infos@bayonne-tourisme .com), place des Basques, is open 9am to 6.30pm on weekdays and 10am to 6pm on Saturday (9am to 7pm Monday to Saturday and 10am to 1pm on Sunday during July and August).

Among useful brochures are *Fêtes*, listing French Basque country cultural and sporting events, and *Guide Loisirs*, for walking, biking and other activities. The office runs town tours at 10am Monday to Friday (in English on Thursday) in July and August. Tours cost €4.60.

Money
Banks with exchange facilities and ATMs are numerous around the town hall and along rue Thiers in Grand Bayonne, and around place de la République and along blvd Alsace-Lorraine in St-Esprit. Many, but not all, Bayonne banks open on Saturday morning. The post office (see Post & Communication) also has exchange services.

Post & Communications
The post office, at 11 rue Jules Labat, is open 8am to 6pm on weekdays and to noon on Saturday. Poste restante items addressed to '64100 Bayonne-Labat' come here; any other poste restante mail goes to the main post office (rue de la Nouvelle Poste), 1km northwest of the town centre. A smaller post office is at 21 blvd Alsace-Lorraine in St-Esprit.

The Bureau d'Information Jeunesse (BIJ; ☎ 05 59 59 35 29, e bayonneinfojeunesse@ wanadoo.fr), 16 rue Pontrique in Petit Bayonne, offers free Internet access (maximum 30 minutes when it's busy); it opens 10am to 7pm Monday to Saturday. Cyber Net Café (☎ 05 59 50 85 10, e cyber-net-cafe@wana doo.fr), 9 place de la République in St-Esprit, charges €0.15 per minute or €4.55/6.85 per hour before/after midday; it opens 7am to 11pm daily (from noon on Sunday).

Travel Agencies
Pascal Voyages (☎ 05 59 25 48 48), 8 allées Boufflers, is Bayonne's only travel agent

serving incoming visitors. It opens 8.30am to 6.30pm on weekdays and, except in August, to noon on Saturday.

Bookshops
A vast book and music shop, Mattin Megadenda (☎ 05 59 59 35 14), place d'Arsenal, is the best source of books on Basque history and culture, maps and books for walking in the Basque Country, and Basque music. It opens 10am to 7pm Monday to Saturday.

Librairie Celhay (☎ 05 59 59 81 34), 12 rue de la Salie, stocks French titles and a modest selection of guidebooks; it opens Tuesday to Saturday and Monday afternoon. For foreign newspapers and maps, cross to Maison de la Presse, 15 rue de la Salie.

Universities
Bayonne has a branch of the Universitaire de Pau et de Pays de l'Adour, whose thousand or so students are scarce in the centre until the weekend.

Laundry
Hallwash, at 6 rue d'Espagne, is open 8am to 8pm daily. Laverie St-Esprit, 30 blvd Alsace-Lorraine, is open 11am to 8pm Monday to Saturday.

Medical Services & Emergency
The Centre Hospitalier (hospital; ☎ 05 59 44 35 35) is south-west of the town centre on av de l'Interne Jacques Loeb (take bus No 3 from the train station or town hall). The most central police station (☎ 05 59 46 22 22) is at 5 rue Vauban.

RAMPARTS
Bayonne's fortifications, completed at the end of the 17th century, are among Vauban's finest surviving work, and best viewed along blvd du Rempart Lachepaillet and rue Tour de Sault. They also provide an excuse for a lush parkland belt around the centre. By **porte d'Espagne**, the old gate on the road to Spain, are traces of Bayonne's three 'layers' of fortifications: Roman foundations along rue Tour de Sault, 16th-century walls from the time of François I, and Vauban's outer walls.

BAYONNE

PLACES TO STAY
5 Hôtel Paris-Madrid
8 Hôtel Adour
13 Hôtel Côte Basque
19 Hôtel Loustau
28 Hôtel San Miguel
35 Hôtel des Arceaux
58 Hôtel des Basques;
   Bar-Restaurant Guernika
69 Hôtel des
   Basses-Pyrénées

PLACES TO EAT
12 Restaurant Le Moulin à
   Poivre
14 Bistrot Ste-Cluque
17 Restaurant Le Koskera
20 Restaurant Agadir
27 Café Miam-Miam
29 Champion Supermarket
38 Restaurant Le Chistera
39 Monoprix
43 Restaurant My-Tho
45 Restaurant Le Bayonnais
54 Covered Market
56 Auberge du Cheval Blanc
63 Pizzeria de la Nive
64 Bar-Restaurant du
   Marché

OTHER
1 Spanish Consulate
2 Police Station
3 Citadelle (Closed
  Military Area)
4 Train Station
6 Bus Station
7 Avis Car Rental
9 ADA Car Rental
10 Open Car Rental
11 Avis Car Rental
15 Rent-a-Car Système
16 Europcar Car Rental

18 Cyber Net Café
21 Tourist Office
22 ATCRB Bus Stop
23 Post Office
24 Eurolines Office
25 STAB Office
26 Hôtel de Ville (Town
   Hall)
30 Cinéma L'Atalante
31 Post Office
32 Laverie St-Esprit
33 Pascal Voyages
34 Cazenave; Daranatz
36 Crédit Agricole
37 Château Vieux
   (Closed Military Area)
40 Portuguese Consulate
41 Musée Bonnat
42 Riverboat (Le
   Bayonne)
44 Musée Basque
46 Berrogain
47 Boutique Gîtes de
   France
48 Cathédrale Ste-Marie
49 Trinquet Moderne
50 Cloister
51 Maison Montauzer
52 Maison de la Presse
53 Librairie Celhay
55 Bureau d'Information
   Jeunesse
57 Château Neuf
59 Trinquet St-André
60 Mattin Megadenda
61 Killarney Pub
62 Pierre Ibaïalde
65 La Pompe
66 La Luna Negra
67 Gérard Léoncini
68 Hallwash
70 Porte d'Espagne
71 Stadium

Avenue des Allées Marines

To Main Post
Office (950m),
Anglet (4.5km) &
Biarritz (7.5km)

Rue Vauban

Jardin
Public

Avenue Léon Bonnat

Place
des
Basques

Rue de Gramont

Rue Jules Labat

Rue du 49ème Régiment d'Infanterie

Rue Lormand

Rue Albert-1er

Rue Thiers

R Lombard

Avenue du
Maréchal Foch

To Arènes
(800m)

Avenue des Allées
Paulmy

Avenue du 11 Novembre

Grand
Bayonne

Rue des Gouverneurs

37

Rue Port Neuf

Rue Orbe

Rue de la Monnaie

R Victor Hugo

Boulevard-Rempart-Lachepaillet

Douer

Place
Monseigneur
Vansteenberghe

Place
Louis
Pasteur

Place
des Cinq-
Cantons

49

Rue du Maréchal Lautrec

Rue des Faures

Rue Montaut

Rue de Luc

Place
Montaut

Rue Vieille Boucherie

Rue d'Espagne

Rue Poissonnerie

Place
Lacarre

Rue de la Salle

To Airport (4.5km),
Biarritz-La Négresse
Train Station (6.3km),
Biarritz (6.5km) &
St-Jean de Luz
(23km)

Avenue de Pampelune

Rue Gosse

Rue des Augustins

Rue des Basques

Quai d'Amiral-Jauréguiberry

La
Plachotte

Ave du Maréchal
Soult

Avenue F Forgues

Ave-R-des-Martres

To Hospital
(550m),
Universitaire
de Pau (800m),
A63 (5km),
Arcangues
(10km),
St-Jean Pied
de Port (40km)
& Pau
(112km)

To Camping
la Chêneraie
(5.5km), Dax (48km)
& Mont de Marsan
(98km)

Rue Tour de Sault

Pont
du
Génie

71

BAYONNE

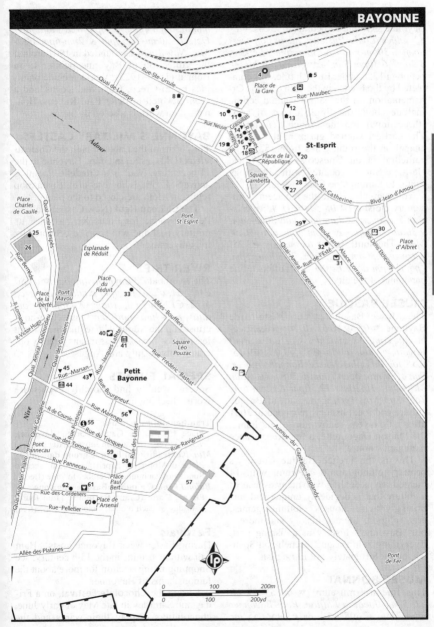

CATHÉDRALE STE-MARIE
Bayonne's Gothic cathedral (☎ 05 59 59 17 82, place Louis Pasteur; admission free; open 7.30am-noon & 3pm-7pm Mon-Sat, 3.30pm-6.30pm Sun, except during Mass), begun in 1258 under English rule, was completed by the French in the 16th century. Ornamentation on the nave's vaulted ceiling includes both the English coat of arms (three lions) and the French fleur-de-lis. The earliest stained glass, in the second chapel on the right, dates from 1531. The cathedral is on Unesco's list of World Heritage Sites associated with pilgrimage routes to Santiago de Compostela.

You can also visit the adjacent 13th-century cloister (☎ 05 59 46 11 43; admission free; open 9.30am-6pm daily June-Sept; 9.30am-12.30pm & 2pm-5pm daily Oct-May). The south tower (admission €2.25; entry at 9.30am, 10.30am, 11.30am, 3pm, 4pm & 5pm daily Easter-Sept) offers a fine panorama of the city.

MUSÉE BASQUE
The Musée Basque et de l'Histoire de Bayonne (☎ 05 59 46 61 90, W www.musee-basque.com, 37 quai des Corsaires, Petit Bayonne; adult/child €5.35/3.05, €9.15/4.55 for this plus Musée Bonnat, free 1st Sun of month; open 10am-6.30pm Tues-Sun May-Oct; 10.30am-12.30pm & 2pm-6pm Tues-Sun Nov-Apr), a museum of Basque culture and local history, reopened in 2001 after an 11-year renovation of its home, the Maison Dagourette, a fine Renaissance merchant's house.

This is the French Basque Country's primary ethnographic museum, with 14 themed rooms dealing with many aspects of a culture that is decidedly unique and surprisingly rich – houses, clothing, games, arts, religion, literary history and more – plus Bayonne's history as a fishing port. Everything is in Basque, French and Spanish, but unfortunately not in English.

MUSÉE BONNAT
This fine-arts museum (☎ 05 59 59 08 52, 5 rue Jacques Laffitte, Petit Bayonne; adult/child €3.05/1.50, or €9.15/4.55 for this plus Musée Basque, free 1st Sun of month; open 10am-6.30pm Wed-Mon May-Oct; 10.30am-12.30pm & 2pm-6pm Wed-Mon Nov-Apr) was founded in 1901 around the collection of Bayonne painter Léon Bonnat (1833–1922). Works include paintings by El Greco, Goya and Degas, and a room devoted to Peter Paul Rubens. Bonnat's own work is also on display.

BAYONNE'S MILITARY CASTLES
The counts of the Labourd built the Château Vieux (Old Castle) in Grand Bayonne in the 11th century. Vauban's Citadelle, looming above St-Esprit, is home to an elite paratroop regiment. Both are closed to the public.

The Château Neuf (New Castle), built in Petit Bayonne for Louis XI, has shed its military past and will soon be occupied by the university.

RIVER TRIPS
The riverboat Le Bayonne (mobile ☎ 06 80 74 21 51, allées Boufflers; adult/child aged 5-12 €12.20/7.60; 10am, 2.45pm & 5pm daily mid-June–mid-Sept) runs two-hour cruises on the Adour. The requirement for at least 10 to 15 passengers means it rarely operates outside July and August.

SPECIAL EVENTS
Several weekly and monthly events are worth checking out:

Traditional Basque music
  Place Charles de Gaulle (Grand Bayonne), 9.30pm every Thursday in July and August (free)
Mutxiko, traditional Basque group dancing,
  Place d'Albret (St-Esprit), 11.30am, second Sunday of each month October to June (free)
Baïona kantus, a public Basque singalong
  Place Lacarre (Grand Bayonne), 11am fourth Saturday of each month, October to June (free)

Festivals
During Easter week Bayonne hosts a Ham Fair with its origins in the 15th century; see Shopping in this section for more about the famous hams of Bayonne.

During the Chocolate Festival, on a Friday and Saturday in late May or early June, chocolatiers display their wares and the tourist office offers French-language tours on a chocolate theme.

Jazz aux Remparts features six days of 24-hour jazz and blues in mid-July.

Bayonne's most important festival is the **Fêtes de Bayonne**, from the first Wednesday in August to the following Sunday, with fireworks, Basque music, a float parade, *courses landaises* (see Spectator Sports in the Facts for the Visitor chapter), corridas, rugby and lots of jollity.

Two prestigious summer fairs with daily corridas are the **Feria de l'Assomption** in mid-August and the **Feria de l'Atlantique** in early September.

PLACES TO STAY – BUDGET
Camping
By public transport it's easier to reach camp sites in Biarritz and Anglet (see those sections later in this chapter), but if you'd rather be close to Bayonne, try the following.

Camping La Chêneraie (☎ 05 59 55 01 31, fax 05 59 55 11 17, chemin de Cazenave) 2-person *forfait* (package rate) with tent €18.60-21.65, bungalows €168-488 per week. This four-star camp site has a pool, as well as bungalows. It's on the N117, 5.5km east of the town centre in the St-Étienne *zone industrielle*.

Rural Accommodation
The tourist office keeps a list of nearby *chambres d'hôte* (B&Bs) and *campings à la ferme* (camping on farms).

Boutique Gîtes de France (☎ 05 59 46 37 00, fax 05 59 46 37 08, e gdfbayonne@ yahoo.fr, W www.gites-de-france-64.com, 12 place Louis Pasteur) will help with rural accommodation and customised holidays in the Pyrénées-Atlantiques department. It is open from 2pm to 6pm Monday, 9am to 12.30pm and 2pm to 6pm Tuesday and Saturday.

Hotels
Bayonne has a good selection of hotels to choose from.

Hôtel Paris-Madrid (☎ 05 59 55 13 98, fax 05 59 55 07 22, place de la Gare, St-Esprit) Singles/doubles €14.50/20.60; doubles with shower & with/without WC €27.45/24.40;

quads with WC & shower €39.65. Hall showers €0.75. Breakfast €3.80. Don't be fooled by the shabby exterior – this is a hospitable, family-run place with big rooms and a courtyard. The price is right, and English is spoken. It's beside the train station, so there's train noise in some rooms.

Hôtel San Miguel (☎ 05 59 55 17 82, fax 05 59 50 15 22, 8 rue Ste-Catherine, St-Esprit) Rooms €21.35, or with WC & with/without shower €28.95/25.90. The cheerfully downmarket San Miguel, over a neighbourhood bar, has plain but generously big rooms.

Hôtel des Basques (☎/fax 05 59 59 08 02, 5 rue des Lisses, Petit Bayonne) Rooms with WC €21.35-27.45, with WC, shower & TV €27.45-35.05. Breakfast €4.55. This modest but hospitable hotel offers plain rooms, the pricier, sunnier ones with views over place Paul Bert, Petit Bayonne's de facto centre.

Hôtel des Arceaux (☎ 05 59 59 15 53, 26 rue du Port Neuf) Doubles with/without bath & WC €41.15/22.85, plus larger rooms. Plain, tidy rooms at the briskly run Arceaux are a good budget bet, and bang in the centre.

PLACES TO STAY – MID-RANGE
Booking at least a week ahead is advisable from June to August.

Hôtel Adour (☎ 05 59 55 11 31, fax 05 59 55 86 40, 13 rue Ste-Ursule, St-Esprit) Rooms with WC & shower €38.10-48.80. Breakfast €5.35. The Adour offers bright rooms and a generous breakfast, plus evening meals by arrangement. Double glazing doesn't quite solve the noise problem for light sleepers. This is the only place in town that rents VTTs (see Getting Around later).

Hôtel Côte Basque (☎ 05 59 55 10 21, fax 05 59 55 39 85, 2 rue Maubec, St-Esprit) Rooms with/without shower €38.10/27.45, with WC & shower €45.45-54.90. Breakfast is overpriced at €5.80, but this is otherwise a very agreeable place, old but well kept. Upper rooms have long views, and rear ones are quiet at night.

Hôtel des Basses-Pyrénées (☎ 05 59 59 00 29, fax 05 59 59 42 02, 12 rue Tour de Sault) Rooms with shower & WC €45.75-47.25, without €24.40-32. Breakfast €5.35. Private parking €5. Plain, quiet rooms at this well run old hotel are good value in their range.

PLACES TO STAY – TOP END
If you're here to indulge yourself, try the following.

Hôtel Loustau (☎ 05 59 55 08 08 or 08 00 12 12 12, fax 05 59 55 69 36, e loustau@aol .com, 1 place de la République, entrance rue de la Chateau, St-Esprit) Singles/doubles with WC & shower €69.35/69.35. Off-street parking €7.60. The business-oriented Loustau, facing the Adour, is the best hotel in St-Esprit and part of the Quality Hotel chain, with uninspiring but very comfortable rooms.

PLACES TO EAT
Restaurants – French
French options run from tasty salads to top-of-the-line fare.

Bar-Restaurant Guernika (☎ 05 59 59 28 69, 5 rue des Lisses, Petit Bayonne) Midday *menus* €8.55. Open daily, midday only. This always-crowded bar-cafe offers one tasty lunchtime *menu*. Its chief asset is the buzz around place Paul Bert.

Bistrot Ste-Cluque (☎ 05 59 55 82 43, 9 rue Hugues, St-Esprit) Midday/evening *menus* €8.40/14.50. Open midday & evening Tues-Sun. The St-Cluque offers gourmet salads (around €6–7), a sizable choice of fish dishes (€11–13), and indoor or pavement seating. The midday *menu* is good value.

Restaurant Le Moulin à Poivre (☎ 05 59 50 16 77, 4 rue Maubec, St-Esprit) Midday *menus* €8.85, evening *menus* €10.65-13.70. Open midday & evening Mon-Sat, evening only Sun July-Aug; Thur-Fri & evening only Sun, midday only Wed Sept-Jun. This unstuffy place opposite the train station offers a nice fish selection (around €11) plus first-rate Basque, French and Moroccan dishes.

Restaurant Le Bayonnais (☎ 05 59 25 61 19, 38 quai des Corsaires, Petit Bayonne) Menus €14.95, dishes €12.95-16.75. Open midday & evening Tues-Sat & midday only Mon. Modest Le Bayonnais is tasteful, welcoming and clearly popular, with good regional fare.

Auberge du Cheval Blanc (☎ 05 59 59 01 33, 68 rue Bourgneuf, Petit Bayonne) *Menus* €20.60-54.90. Open midday & evening Tues-Sat, midday only Sun Sept-July; daily Aug. This restaurant's Michelin star guarantees first-class French cuisine, worth paying extra for.

Restaurants – Basque
The choice of distinctive Basque food is probably at its widest here in Bayonne.

Bar-Restaurant du Marché (☎ 05 59 59 22 66, 39 rue des Basques) Dishes €6.25-6.85, house specialities €4.55-8.85. Open midday only Mon-Sat. This bar-restaurant, with home-style cooking and a madly cheerful atmosphere, is one of Bayonne's most delightful eateries; try the €6.70 *piperade* (see the boxed text 'Piperade' in the Food & Wine section) with Bayonne ham.

Restaurant Le Chistera (☎ 05 59 59 25 93, 42 rue du Port Neuf) Menus €12.95, plats du jour €7-11. Open midday & evening Thur-Sun & midday only Tues-Wed Sept-June; daily June-July. The family-run, Basque-owned Chistera has superb Basque dishes along with French ones, in a traditional atmosphere.

Restaurant Le Koskera (☎ 05 59 55 20 79, 2 rue Hugues, St-Esprit) Menus around €11. Open midday only Mon-Sat. Unassuming, family-run Le Koskera, near the train station, offers inexpensive Basque and other dishes.

Café Miam-Miam (☎ 05 59 55 18 14, 3 blvd Alsace-Lorraine) Formule de jour (set meal of the day) €9.15. Open daily. Spartan, manic but cheerful Miam-Miam offers always-inventive Basque *taloas* (savoury or sweet pastry pies, €4.55) plus brochettes, omelettes and pricier dishes.

Restaurants – Other
Check out the range of low-overhead international restaurants along rue Ste-Catherine.

Restaurant Agadir (☎ 05 59 55 66 56, 3 rue Ste-Catherine, St-Esprit) Menus €15.25, couscous €9.15-12.20. Open midday & evening Tues-Sun & evening only Mon. Agadir offers Moroccan specialities, plus less exotic dishes from the grill, in an atmospheric setting with a bit of class.

Restaurant My-Tho (☎ 05 59 59 15 07, 40 rue Bourgneuf, Petit Bayonne) Menus

€10.50-12.05. Open midday & evening Mon-Sat & evening only Sun. This Chinese-Vietnamese restaurant has a daunting choice of tasty and good-value lunch and dinner plates.

Pizzeria de la Nive (☎ *05 59 25 69 52, 37 quai Amiral Jauréguiberry)* Pizza & pasta €6.55-9, midday *formule* (set meal with choice of courses) €13.55. Open midday & evening Wed-Sun & midday only Tues. This good but unexceptional pizzeria is worth a note because it opens on Sunday.

Self-Catering
Grand Bayonne's central *covered market* is open every morning (except Sunday) and all day Friday and Saturday. There are *food shops* along rue Ste-Catherine (St-Esprit). Convenient supermarkets include *Champion (8 blvd Alsace Lorraine, St-Esprit)* and *Monoprix (8 rue Orbe, Grand Bayonne)*, both open Monday to Saturday.

ENTERTAINMENT
Pubs & Bars
Students converge on the bars of rue des Cordeliers and rue Pannecau (Petit Bayonne) on Friday and Saturday nights.

Killarney Pub (☎ *05 59 25 75 51, 33 rue des Cordeliers, Petit Bayonne)* This cheerful pub, the most popular place on the block, has frequent live music and a huge choice of beers, and stays open until 2am (3am July and August).

La Luna Negra (☎ *05 59 25 78 05, rue des Augustins)* Admission prices vary, usually €7.60 (€4.55 students). Hours also vary, usually opening between 8pm and 9.30pm, closing 2am, nightly except Sunday. This cabaret (cafe-theatre) has a mind-stretching range of gigs, from jazz to improvisational theatre, bluegrass to marionettes, plus light food. Wednesday is blues night.

La Pompe (☎ *05 59 25 48 12, 7 rue des Augustins)* Open 10pm-dawn Thur-Sun nights. La Pompe is Bayonne's only discotheque.

Cinemas
Aquitaine's oldest functioning cinema is the *Cinéma L'Atalante* (☎ *05 59 55 76 63, 7 rue Denis Etcheverry, St-Esprit; adult/student tickets €5.65/3.80)*, which screens non-dubbed films.

SPECTATOR SPORTS
Pelote Basque
Weekly *main nue* matches (see under Pelote Basque in the introduction to this chapter) take place at **Trinquet St-André** (☎ 05 59 59 18 69), at the eastern end of rue des Tonneliers, at 4.10pm Thursday from October to June. Tickets cost €7.60.

Rugby
The town's rugby club, Aviron Bayonnais, plays in the stadium just south of the centre in the Parc des Sports. The tourist office has details on upcoming matches.

Bullfighting
From July to early September, corridas are held at the *arènes* (arena), 1km west of the town centre on av du Maréchal Foch. The tourist office will know of upcoming corridas and can sell you a ticket (about €12-70).

SHOPPING
Bayonne is famous throughout France for its cured ham. The lowest prices are at the covered market (see Self-Catering under Places to Eat), but the best hams are at specialist shops such as *Maison Montauzer* (☎ *05 59 59 07 68, 17 rue de la Salie)* and *Pierre Ibaïalde* (☎ *05 59 25 65 30, 41 rue des Cordeliers, Petit Bayonne)*.

Bayonne's other famous edible is chocolate (see the boxed text overleaf). Two of its finest *chocolatiers* are on rue du Port Neuf: *Cazenave* (☎ *05 59 59 03 16)* at No 19 and *Daranatz* (☎ *05 59 59 03 55)* at No 15. At Cazenave, treat yourself to the best *chocolat chaud* (hot chocolate) you've ever had.

Izarra, a potent, yellow or green Basque liqueur made from mountain herbs, spices and Armagnac, is now popular all over France. In fact it's no longer made in the Basque Country at all, but in northern France. For a look at an old Izarra still, and a taste of the stuff, visit the Ecomusée de la Tradition Basque (see under St-Jean de Luz later in this chapter).

Chocolate

Christopher Columbus brought cocoa beans back from the New World in 1502. A drink made from them, sweetened with sugar and vanilla and spiced with cinnamon, took the Spanish court by storm for its stimulant, tonic and, some said, aphrodisiac properties.

Several Sephardic Jewish families who had learned the art of brewing chocolate fled to Bayonne during the Spanish Inquisition (or arrived later via Portugal). The drink remained an upper-class privilege until the 17th century, when these *chocolatiers* began pitching it to the masses. Before long, *salons de chocolat* were sprouting all over Europe, though the Church regarded the development with suspicion.

Only in the 19th century was a way found to solidify chocolate. In the 1850s Bayonne had no fewer than 32 chocolate workshops (today there are seven). Surprisingly, the city's last genuine chocolate-maker closed its doors in the 1960s. Confectioners now begin with ingots of basic chocolate from a few national firms (but for one that starts from the bean, see Espelette later in this chapter).

The French like their chocolate *noir* – dark and strong, with 60–70% cocoa content.

Rural Pays Basque's (and Béarn's) proudest export is *fromage de brebis* (sheep's cheese, *ardi gasna* in Basque). Look for it in small food shops all over town (plus rural outlets of Ossau-Iraty, a federation of Pyrénées *fromageurs*).

Calling a *makila* a 'Basque cane' is like calling a Lamborghini a 'car'. Made from the wood of the medlar tree, engraved with runes and mottoes and fixed with a steel tip, a makila is a formidable instrument of status and self-defence. Of three French Basque families who have maintained the art, one, Gérard Léoncini, is in Bayonne.

Gérard Léoncini (☎ 05 59 59 18 20, 37 rue Vieille Boucherie; workshop open 4pm-6.30pm Mon-Fri & 10am-noon Sat) Expect to pay €150–800 and wait six months or more for a makila.

A good source of fine Basque linen and cotton goods is *Berrogain (☎ 05 59 59 16 18, place des Cinq-Cantons)*.

GETTING THERE & AWAY
Air
Aeroport de Parme (☎ 05 59 43 83 83) – usually identified in timetables as Biarritz airport – is 5km south-west of central Bayonne. Air France flies directly to Paris about eight times daily. Ryanair flies daily from London Stansted (with a second flight daily except Saturday from August to early September). See the Getting There & Away chapter for details and booking numbers.

Bus
From place des Basques, buses of ATCRB (☎ 05 59 26 06 99) follow the coast to the Spanish border, including six to 10 services daily to St-Jean de Luz (€3.50, 35 minutes) and Hendaye (€6.25, one hour). Summer beach traffic can double the travel time.

From the train station, RDTL (☎ 05 59 55 17 59) runs into the Landes – for example, Capbreton/Hossegor (€3.75, 35 minutes) and Dax (€7.40, 2½ hours). RDTL also has a daily-except-Sunday coastal service that stops at Capbreton and Hossegor every one to 1½ hours. From square Gambetta in St-Esprit, TPR (☎ 05 59 27 45 98) goes to Pau (€13.50, 2¼ hours, three a day Monday to Saturday).

Bayonne is one of three Southwest France hubs for Eurolines (see the Getting There & Away chapter). Eurolines (☎ 05 59 59 19 33), at 3 place Charles de Gaulle, is open during normal weekday business hours (plus Saturday in July and August). This is also where their buses stop.

Train
The booking office (☎ 08 36 35 35 35) at the train station is open 9am to 7pm (to 8pm July to September) Monday to Saturday. There are multiple daily services to Dax (€7.30, 40 minutes) and Bordeaux (€21.05, two hours); to St-Jean de Luz (€3.80, 25 minutes), Hendaye (€5.65, 40 minutes) and into Spain; to St-Jean Pied de Port (€7.15, one hour), Pau (€12.80, 1¼ hours) and Toulouse (€30.50, 3¾ hours).

TGVs running from Paris' Gare Montparnasse (€66.45) take five hours. Two daily non-TGV trains go overnight to Paris' Gare d'Austerlitz (€59.15) in about 6½ hours.

Car

Rental agencies cluster near the train station, including French franchises ADA (☎ 05 59 50 37 10, 11 bis quai de Lesseps), Rent-a-Car Système (☎ 05 59 50 70 60, 7 rue Hugues) and Open (☎ 05 59 55 30 29, 8 rue Ste-Ursule); plus Europcar (☎ 05 59 55 38 20, 5 rue Hugues) and Avis (☎ 05 59 55 06 56, 1 rue Ste-Ursule). All are open daily (closed Sunday outside July and August).

GETTING AROUND
To the Airport

Bus No 6 goes to the airport from the train station or the town hall, about hourly Monday to Saturday, for €1.15. A taxi from St-Esprit costs about €13, with extra charges for night or weekend trips and for lots of baggage.

Bus

BAB's bus network is called STAB. Individual tickets cost €1.15 (€9.45 for a carnet of 10). Tickets remain valid, for an onward or return trip, for an hour after being time-stamped. Buy tickets on board or at STAB's information office (☎ 05 59 59 04 61) at the town hall, open 8am to noon and 1.30pm to 6pm Monday to Saturday.

Taxi

There are taxi ranks by the town hall (☎ 05 59 59 48 48) and at the train station (☎ 05 59 55 13 15).

Bicycle

The Hôtel Adour (see Places to Stay earlier) rents VTTs for €9.15/12.20 per half/full day or longer (eg, €61 for a week).

Basque Coast

BIARRITZ
postcode 64200 • pop 30,000
The high-toned coastal town of Biarritz, 8km west of Bayonne, started as a resort in the mid-19th century when Napoleon III and his Spanish-born wife, Eugénie, began coming here. In later decades Biarritz was popular with wealthy Britons and was visited by Queen Victoria and King Edward VII. These days it's best known for its fine beaches and world-class surfing. It's easy to see everything of interest in a day trip from Bayonne.

Orientation

Long-distance ATCRB buses stop opposite the tourist office on square d'Ixelles, from where it's a 250m walk to place Clémenceau, the town centre. The beach runs north to a headland called Pointe St-Martin. West of place Clémenceau, rue Mazagran rollercoasters out to Biarritz's own headland, Pointe Atalaye. The train station and airport are both about 3km south-east of the town centre.

Information

The tourist office (☎ 05 59 22 37 10, fax 05 59 24 97 80, e biarritz.tourisme@biarritz.tm.fr, w www.biarritz.tm.fr), 1 square d'Ixelles, is open 8am to 8pm daily in July and August; 9am to 6pm Monday to Saturday and 10am to 5pm Sunday the rest of the year. A summer annexe is open at the train station 8am to 1pm and 3pm to 8pm daily in July and August only.

Place Clémenceau is surrounded by banks equipped for foreign exchange. The Bureau de Change Atollíssimo (☎ 05 59 22 27 27), at No 27, offers competitive rates.

The main post office is on rue de la Poste. Internet access is available for €5.35 per hour at Univercom (☎ 05 59 22 07 78), 13 rue du Helder, open Monday to Saturday; and for €0.15/7.60 per minute/hour at Genius Informatique (Difintel; ☎ 05 59 24 39 07), 60 av Edouard VII, open daily (except Sunday from September to June).

Beaches

In summer **La Grande Plage** and **plage Miramar**, Biarritz's main beaches, are wall-to-wall with people and lined with striped bathing tents. Beyond Pointe St-Martin the fine surfing beaches of **Anglet** stretch northwards for over 4km (get there on eastbound bus No 9 from place Clémenceau).

THE FRENCH BASQUE COUNTRY

Southwards are the long, exposed **plage de la Côte des Basques**, **plage de Marbella** and, 2km away, **plage de la Milady** (take westbound bus No 9 from place Clémenceau to the Madrid Milady or Thermes Marins stop).

Rocher de la Vierge

The mauve cliffs of Pointe Atalaye come to a head at the Rocher de la Vierge (Rock of the Virgin), a splendid outcrop topped by a statue of the Virgin Mary and accessible only by a long iron footbridge that whistles in the wind. From here on a clear day you can see north to the Landes and south to the mountains of the Spanish Basque country.

Musée de la Mer

If you're here with kids, don't miss the four-storey Musée de la Mer *(Sea Museum; ☎ 05 59 22 75 40, Esplanade du Rocher de la Vierge; adult/child aged 5-16 €7.15/4.55, €0.75 discount on tickets purchased from the tourist office; open 9.30am-midnight daily July-Aug; 9.30am-7pm daily June & Sept; 9.30am-12.30pm & 2pm-6pm Mon-Fri, 9.30am-6pm weekends & holidays May; 9.30am-12.30pm & 2pm-6pm Tues-*

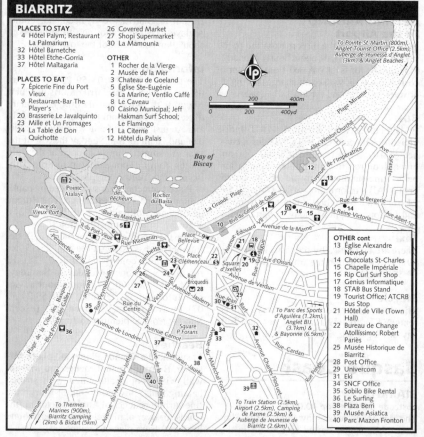

BIARRITZ

PLACES TO STAY
4 Hôtel Palym; Restaurant La Palmarium
32 Hôtel Barnetche
33 Hôtel Etche-Gorria
37 Hôtel Maïtagaria

PLACES TO EAT
7 Épicerie Fine du Port Vieux
9 Restaurant-Bar The Player's
20 Brasserie Le Javalquinto
23 Mille et Un Fromages
24 La Table de Don Quichotte

26 Covered Market
27 Shopi Supermarket
30 La Mamounia

OTHER
1 Rocher de la Vierge
2 Musée de la Mer
3 Chateau de Goeland
5 Église Ste-Eugénie
6 La Marine; Ventilo Caffé
8 Le Caveau
10 Casino Municipal; Jeff Hakman Surf School; Le Flamingo
11 La Citerne
12 Hôtel du Palais

OTHER cont
13 Église Alexandre Newsky
14 Chocolats St-Charles
15 Chapelle Impériale
16 Rip Curl Surf Shop
17 Genius Informatique
18 STAB Bus Stand
19 Tourist Office; ATCRB Bus Stop
21 Hôtel de Ville (Town Hall)
22 Bureau de Change Atollissimo; Robert Pariès
25 Musée Historique de Biarritz
28 Post Office
29 Univercom
31 Eki
33 SNCF Office
35 Sobilo Bike Rental
36 Le Surfing
38 Plaza Berri
39 Musée Asiatica
40 Parc Mazon Fronton

To Pointe St-Martin (800m), Anglet Tourist Office (2.5km), Auberge de Jeunesse d'Anglet (3km) & Anglet Beaches

Bay of Biscay

Pointe Atalaye

Place du Vieux-Port

Port des Pêcheurs

Rocher du Basta

Plage Miramar

Allée Winston Churchill

Avenue de l'Impératrice

Ave Sarasate

La Grande Plage

Rue de la Bergerie

Avenue de la Reine Victoria

Ave Albert-Ier

Blvd du Maréchal-Leclerc

Blvd du Général de Gaulle

R. du Port-Vieux

Rue Mazagran

Perspective de la Côte-Basque

Rue Gambetta

Place Bellevue

Place Clémenceau

Square d'Ixelles

Rue Broquedis

Rue Victor Hugo

Avenue-Jaulerry

Rue du Centre

Plage de la Côte des Basques

Blvd Prince des Galles

Rue Peyroloubilh

Avenue de Londres

Square P Forans

Avenue Carnot

Rue Jean-Jaurès

Avenue du Maréchal-Foch

Avenue de la République

Avenue Beaurivage

Avenue du Maréchal-Joffre

Place Édouard VII

Avenue de la Marne

Rue Gardague

Avenue d'Ossuna

Avenue de Verdun

Rue Pétrisse

Rue Jean-Bart

Avenue Charles Floquet

Rue Cardan

Avenue du Maréchal Foch

To Parc des Sports d'Aguiléra (1.2km), Anglet BIJ (3.1km) & Bayonne (6.5km)

To Thermes Marines (900m), Biarritz Camping (2km) & Bidart (5km)

To Train Station (2.5km), Airport (2.5km), Camping de Parme (2.5km) & Auberge de Jeunesse de Biarritz (2.6km)

0   200   400m
0   200   400yd

Sun Oct-Apr). The aquarium is full of beasties from the Bay of Biscay, and upstairs are exhibits on commercial fishing and whaling (Biarritz was once a whaling port). Seals are fed in their pool at 10.30am and 5pm daily.

Asiatica

With over 1000 works of art from China, Tibet, India and Nepal, this fine museum, also called the Musée de l'Art Oriental (☎ 05 59 22 78 78, 1 rue Guy Petit; €6.85, or 13-12 years/child aged 8-12/under 8 €3.80/2.25/free; open 10.30am-7pm Mon-Fri & 2pm-8pm Sat-Sun), qualifies as one of Europe's best oriental art collections.

Musée Historique de Biarritz

The Biarritz Historical Museum (☎ 05 59 24 86 28, opposite 10 rue Broquedis; adult/child €2.30/0.75; open 10am-noon & 2.30pm-6.30pm Tues-Sat), in a former Anglican church, has exhibits on the town's history.

Other Things to See

A promenade follows the coast above the **Port des Pêcheurs**, an old fishing port now filled with pleasure craft. Standing above the port is the **Église Ste-Eugénie**.

The most imposing landmark along the Grande Plage is the stately **Hôtel du Palais**, a villa built for Empress Eugénie in 1854, largely rebuilt as a luxury hotel after a fire in 1903. Across av de l'Impératrice, at No 8, is **Église Alexandre Newsky**, a Russian Orthodox church built by Russian aristocrats before the Revolution of 1917.

The **Chapelle Impériale** (same ☎ as tourist office, rue Pellot; €3.05; open 10am-noon & 3pm-7pm Mon-Sat mid-July–mid-Sept; 3pm-6pm Tues, Thur & Sat mid-Sept–mid-July) was built for Eugénie, in a striking mix of Byzantine and Moorish styles, in 1864. This is the town's only genuine survivor from that period.

To the north is the **Phare de Biarritz** (Pointe St-Martin; €1.50; open 10am-noon & 3pm-7pm Tues-Sun July-Aug; 2pm-6pm Sat-Sun May-June), the town's 73m-high lighthouse, erected in 1834. Climb its 248 steps for splendid views.

Surfing

The best rental and instruction bargains are to be found at the **Auberge de Jeunesse d'Anglet** (see under Surfing in the following Anglet section).

In Biarritz, try the **Jeff Hakman Surf School** (☎ 05 59 22 03 12, Casino Municipal; board rental €4.55/10.65/15.25 per hour/half-day/day, classes €30/150 for one/six days). The **Rip Curl Surf Shop** (☎ 05 59 24 38 40, 2 av de la Reine Victoria) has similar rates and offerings, and the tourist office has a list of half-a-dozen more surf schools in town.

Thalassotherapy

Biarritz's main thalassotherapy centre (see under Activities in the Facts for the Visitor chapter) is **Les Thermes Marins** (☎ 05 59 23 01 22, fax 05 59 23 29 17, 80 rue de Madrid).

Special Events

In July and August the town hall sponsors free Friday-night concerts in front of Église Ste-Eugénie and elsewhere (check with the tourist office).

Biarritz hosts a good many impressive international events, including:

Fêtes Musicales de Biarritz This is a five-day festival of classical orchestral music, late April
Biarritz Surf Festival This is a week-long event with competitions, demonstrations, films and concerts, mid-July
Le Temps d'Aimer This is a two-week festival of classical, modern, traditional, street and other forms of dance, mid-September
La Cita A celebration of Latin American film and culture takes place in the first week in October
Reef Biarritz Surf Trophée Surfing's 'Masters', takes place in late October or early November (dates vary)

Places to Stay

Camping *Biarritz Camping* (☎ 05 59 23 00 12, fax 05 59 43 74 67, e biarritz.camping@wanadoo.fr, 28 rue d'Harcet) 2-person forfait €16.75. Open May-Sept. This small, shady camping ground, 3km south-west of the town centre, has a swimming pool and bar-restaurant. Take westbound bus No 9 from place Clémenceau to Biarritz Camping stop.

Hostels Biarritz has an official youth hostel plus a good-value hotel with dorm beds.

Auberge de Jeunesse de Biarritz (☎ 05 59 41 76 00, fax 05 59 41 76 07, e biarritz@ fuaj.org, 8 rue Chiquito de Cambo) Dorm beds €11.30 with breakfast. Open mid-Jan–mid-Dec; reception 8.30am-10pm. Biarritz's four-star hostel is 800m west of the train station. Get there early during the summer.

Hôtel Barnetche (see Hotels) This hotel also has €18.30 beds in 12-bed dorms.

Hotels Good, cheap hotels are rare in Biarritz, and beds at any price are hard to find from June to August, but space multiplies and prices drop by as much as 30% at other times. You can book ahead with these hotels, or on the tourist office's Web site.

Hôtel Palym (☎ 05 59 24 16 56, fax 05 59 24 96 12, 7 rue du Port-Vieux) Doubles with/without WC & shower €48.80/36.60; triples and quads also available. Breakfast €4.25. The family-run Palym has sloping floors, ancient furniture and plain, bright, well kept rooms, plus a cheerful restaurant downstairs (La Palmarium; see Places to Eat).

Hôtel Etche-Gorria (☎ 05 59 24 00 74, fax 05 59 22 13 12, 21 av du Maréchal Foch) Doubles €38.10-44.20, with WC & shower €44.20-59.45, with WC & bath €59.45-74.70. This well run hotel is in a converted villa with garden and terrace.

Hôtel Maïtagaria (☎ 05 59 24 26 65, fax 05 59 24 27 37, 34 av Carnot) Doubles with WC & shower/bath €51.85/54.90, triples with WC & bath €68.60. The family-run Maïtagaria offers elegant, spacious rooms in a staid, 19th-century house with a garden at the back.

Hôtel Barnetche (☎ 05 59 24 22 25, fax 05 59 24 98 71, 5 av Charles-Floquet) Doubles with breakfast €53.35, with WC & shower/bath €61/67.10 ; half-board obligatory July-Aug, for two people €85.35/ 99.10/106.70; larger rooms with breakfast €29 per person or half-board €47.25 per person; dorms €18.30 per bed with optional €5.35 breakfast. Open May-Sept. The Barnetche's quiet, well tended rooms and home-cooked food make this a top-value choice.

Places to Eat

The food options here are good, if a little touristy.

Brasserie Le Javalquinto (☎ 05 59 24 57 37, 2 av Joseph Petit) Menus €9.90-14.50. Open midday only, daily July-Aug; Mon-Sat Sept-June. This brasserie, opposite the tourist office, does good salads and has a reasonable €8.40 lunchtime formule.

La Mamounia (☎ 05 59 24 76 08, 4 rue Jean Bart) Couscous €12-18, grills €13-15. Open Tues-Sun. La Mamounia is a good place for lunch, with couscous and other Moroccan specialities.

Restaurant-Bar The Player's (☎ 05 59 24 19 60, 2 rue Gardères) Salads €2.75-9.95, pizzas €5.95-9.15. Open daily. The Player's, opposite the Casino Municipal, is touristy but cheap, and the view is terrific.

Restaurant La Palmarium (☎ 05 59 24 25 83, 7 rue du Port-Vieux) Menus €11.45-16.15. The cheerfully touristy Palmarium, occupying both sides of the street, dishes up rich pasta concoctions (around €10), pizzas, *moules frites* (fried mussels) by the plateful and good paëlla (€12).

Self-Catering Biarritz's *covered market*, south-west of place Clémenceau, is open 7am to 1.30pm daily. Nearby food shops include a *Shopi* supermarket, at 2 rue du Centre (open Mon-Sat).

La Table de Don Quichotte (☎ 05 59 22 29 66, 12 av Victor Hugo) serves fine hams, sausages and wines. It opens midday and evenings Tuesday to Saturday and midday only Mondays. Farther along is a splendid array of cheeses at *Mille et Un Fromages* (☎ 05 59 24 67 88, 8 av Victor Hugo). *Épicerie Fine du Port Vieux* (☎ 05 59 24 13 98, 41 bis rue Mazagran) is a handy if pricey place to assemble a gourmet picnic.

Entertainment

Bars Biarritz has at least a dozen agreeable bars, typically open at least 7pm to 2am nightly except Sunday. The following are recommended.

La Citerne (☎ 05 59 22 04 32, 7 blvd du Général de Gaulle & 21 av Edouard VII) Open 7pm-3am daily. This is not so much a bar as a *café-concert* (cafe-bar with a stage), with food until 3am, live gigs Wednesday to Saturday, and plenty of fun, such as rock-n-roll 'happy-hour' 7pm to 9pm Thursday and salsa lessons 4pm to 6pm Saturday.

La Marine (☎ 05 59 24 87 71, 28 rue Mazagran) The clientele here is young and the street is always lively.

Ventilo Caffé (☎ 05 59 24 31 42, 30 bis rue Mazagran) The bar is decorated with surfboards, but you needn't be a surfer to enjoy this easy-going place.

Le Caveau (☎ 05 59 24 16 17, 4 rue Gambetta) The trendy Caveau is upstairs from a club of the same name (the latter opens 11pm to dawn).

Le Surfing (☎ 05 59 24 78 72, 9 blvd Prince des Galles) The mountain views from the terrace of this Hawaiian-flavoured surfers' haunt are a knockout.

Discos Two discotheques near the town centre are *Le Caveau (see Bars)* and *Le Flamingo (☎ 05 59 22 77 59, Casino Municipal)*.

Spectator Sports
There are pelote Basque matches at the fronton at **Plaza Berri** *(☎ 05 59 22 15 72)*, 42 av du Maréchal Foch, at 9.15pm Tuesday and Friday, and *grand chistera* matches at the fronton at Parc Mazon at 9pm Monday, July to mid-September. Tickets cost about €6.50.

At the **Parc des Sports d'Aguiléra** *(☎ 05 59 23 91 09)*, 2km east of the town centre on av Henri Haget, Euskal-Jaï has professional *cesta punta* matches at 9pm Wednesday and Saturday, from mid-June to mid-September. Tickets cost €10 to €20. Take bus No 1 from the town hall to the Aguiléra stop.

Two professional competitions staged at the Parc des Sports d'Aguiléra are the Biarritz Masters Jaï Alaï (cesta punta; two weeks in late July) and the Gant d'Or Professionnel (pelote Basque; 2½ weeks in mid-August).

See under Basque Games at the beginning of this chapter for more on these games.

Shopping
For fine chocolate and Basque sweets, head for *Chocolats St-Charles (☎ 05 59 24 14 03, 8 rue Pellot)* or *Robert Pariès (☎ 05 59 22 07 52, 27 place Clémenceau)*.

Eki (☎ 05 59 24 79 64, 21 av de Verdun) Open Tues-Sat. Basque music, crafts and guidebooks are available here.

Getting There & Away
Air The small Aeroport de Parme (☎ 05 59 43 83 83) is 3km south-east of central Biarritz, or 5km south-west of Bayonne. Air France flies directly to Paris about eight times daily. Daily Ryanair flights from London Stansted (with a second flight daily except Saturday from August to early September) are putting Biarritz back into British holiday plans. See the Getting There & Away chapter for details and booking numbers.

Bus ATCRB buses to St-Jean de Luz, Hendaye and other southern coastal points (nine daily, six on Sunday), and San Sebastián in Spain, stop outside the tourist office. For connections to southern Landes, you're better off going from Bayonne.

Train SNCF has an office (☎ 05 59 50 83 34) at 13 av du Maréchal Foch, open 9am to noon and 2pm to 6pm on weekdays. The Biarritz La Négresse train station (☎ 08 36 35 35 35) is served by three TGVs daily to Paris' Gare Montparnasse and one direct non-TGV train to Paris' Gare d'Austerlitz. Other multiple daily services include Dax, Bordeaux, St-Jean de Luz, Hendaye, Pau and Toulouse. Fares and travel times are similar to those listed under Getting There & Away in the Bayonne section.

Getting Around
To the Airport Bus No 6 runs between the town hall and the airport once or twice per hour (on Sunday and holidays, line C goes once in the morning and every 40 minutes in the afternoon), until about 7pm.

Bus For more information on the STAB bus system, see Getting Around in the Bayonne section. STAB buses stop on square d'Ixelles opposite the tourist office. Useful lines include No 1 (via Anglet to Bayonne's town hall and train station), No 2 (train station via Anglet tourist office to Bayonne's town hall and train station) and No 9 (train station to Anglet youth hostel and beaches).

Motorcycle & Bicycle Sobilo (☎ 05 59 24 94 47), 24 rue Peyroloubilh, rents mountain bikes for €12.20 a day and scooters from €30.50. It's open 8am to 7pm daily.

ANGLET

Anglet (the final 't' is pronounced) seems little more than a suburb wedged between Biarritz and Bayonne, but this is the place to be if you're here to surf. The centre of all activity is plage de Marinella, offering low-risk surfing and big crowds, and adjacent plage des Sables d'Or.

The tourist office (☎ 05 59 03 77 01, fax 05 59 03 55 91, e anglet.tourisme@wanadoo.fr) is at 1 av de la Chambre d'Amour (take bus No 7/2 from Bayonne's town hall, or No 2 from the Biarritz tourist office, to the Cinq-Cantons stop). It opens 9am to 7pm Monday to Saturday in July and August, and 9am to 12.15pm and 1.45pm to 6pm on weekdays and Saturday morning, September to June. A summer annexe at plage des Sables d'Or is open 10.30am to 7.30pm daily in July and August and at weekends from April to June.

Surfing

The tourist office publishes the good French-English *Anglet Surf Guide*, with safety tips, tournament dates, surf shops and schools, places to stay and eat, and details of the 10 best spots along Anglet's 4km of championship-quality beaches.

The **Auberge de Jeunesse d'Anglet** *(see Places to Stay)* offers popular one-week surfing courses (with room, half/full board and equipment €306/360; €280/332 if you're camping) mid-June to mid-September, with lower rates during the Easter holidays. Courses are in French, though instructors usually speak some English. Hostel guests can rent **surfboards** (€7.60/11.45/68.60 per half-day/day/week).

Thalassotherapy

Anglet's thalassotherapy centre is the **Concorde-Atlanthal** (☎ 05 59 52 75 75, fax 05 59 52 75 13) at 153 blvd des Plages, on plage des Cavaliers, 1.8km north of plage de Marinella (see under Activities in the Facts for the Visitor chapter).

Places to Stay

Camping and hostelling are the main choices in Anglet.

Camping de Parme *(☎ 05 59 23 03 00, route de l'Aviation, quartier Brindos)* 2-person forfait €19.95. This small, crowded but shady facility – BAB's only year-round camp site – has a shop, restaurant and swimming pool. It's near Lac de Brindos, 5.5km south of the Anglet tourist office. For other Bayonne, Anglet and Biarritz camp sites see Places to Stay in the relevant sections.

Auberge de Jeunesse d'Anglet *(☎ 05 59 58 70 00, fax 05 59 58 70 07, e anglet@ fuaj.org, 19 route des Vignes)* Dorm beds €7.60 with breakfast. Open mid-Feb–mid-Nov; reception 8.30am-10pm. STAB bus No 9 from Biarritz's train station or place Clémenceau to the Auberge de Jeunesse stop (bus C from the town hall on Sunday). You can also pitch a tent here for about €7 per person. In summer, get to this lively hostel early as it's very popular.

Getting There & Around

Bus Nos 7/1 and 7/2 come to plage de Marinella from Bayonne's town hall. Bus No 9, from place Clémenceau or the youth hostel in Biarritz, stops at all the beaches. Bus No 6 runs from the Biarritz tourist office via southern Anglet to the airport.

ST-JEAN DE LUZ
postcode 64500 • pop 13,200

St-Jean de Luz (Basque name Donibane Lohizune), 24km south-west of Bayonne at the mouth of the River Nivelle, is gathered round a small harbour, its long beach facing a sheltered, perfectly oval bay. Add to this its strong Basque and seafaring roots and you've got a winner. So it's no surprise that St-Jean and Ciboure (Basque name Ziburu), its twin town across the harbour, are packed to the gunwales in summer. They're expensive too, and you'll save a fair bit by making this a day trip from Bayonne. That's about what you'll need for a good look.

St-Jean de Luz is still an active fishing port, known for its large catches of sardines, anchovies and tuna.

History
There isn't much to see that's ancient – only one building survived a 1558 sacking by the Spanish, and another great bite was taken by massive storms in 1749. But traditions go back at least as far, including a colourful history of fishing and whaling, and of piracy (see the boxed text 'The Basque Corsairs').

St-Jean de Luz's single moment of glory was Louis XIV's lavish, geopolitically important marriage held here on 9 June 1660. He was married to the Spanish *infanta* Maria Teresa (Marie Thérèse), daughter of King Philip IV of Spain, as specified in the 1659 Treaty of the Pyrénées ending 24 years of war. Everywhere that the royal feet trod became hallowed ground, and 3½ centuries later people still talk about it as if it happened last year.

Orientation
St-Jean de Luz and its long beach occupy the eastern side, and Ciboure the western side, of the Baie de St-Jean de Luz, protected from the sea by three 19th-century breakwaters between the headlands of Socoa and Pointe Ste-Barbe. Before emptying into the bay, the

The Basque Corsairs
From the time of Louis XIV, many Basque shipowners supplemented their whaling or fishing income with piracy, and did so with gusto after the 1713 Treaty of Utrecht deprived France of the cod-rich waters off Newfoundland. These were no eye-patched scoundrels of the sea, but privateers, their ships fitted out for battle by royal consent, their spoils shared with the crown or with the wealthy citizens who commissioned them, and their families looked after if they should die on the high seas.

Nivelle pools in a small fishing harbour between the two towns.

The town's axis is its pedestrianised shopping precinct, rue Gambetta, 200m inland from the beach and anchored on the southwest by place Louis XIV. The train station is a further 200m inland, and across blvd du Commandant Passicot is the bus station, the Halte Routière.

Information
The good tourist office (☎ 05 59 26 03 16, fax 05 59 26 21 47, e infos.tourisme@saint-jean-de-luz.com) on place Maréchal Foch, is open 9am to 12.30pm and 2pm to 6pm Monday to Saturday (to 7pm April to October); and all day until 8pm, plus 10am to 1pm and 3pm to 7pm on Sunday, in July and August.

The town centre is full of banks with ATMs and exchange facilities, including no fewer than six along blvd Victor Hugo. The Change Plus exchange bureau, at 32 rue Gambetta, is open 9am to 12.30pm and 2pm to 7pm Monday to Saturday (9am to 8pm, plus 10am to 1pm Sunday, in July and August).

The post office is at 44 blvd Victor Hugo; Ciboure's post office is at 3 quai Maurice Ravel. A print shop called Azerty (☎ 05 59 51 22 50) at 8 blvd Thiers is open during weekday business hours with Internet access for €2.50/4/6 per 15/30/60 minutes.

Librairie Louis XIV, facing place Louis XIV, sells maps and foreign newspapers.

Place Louis XIV
On this square at the heart of town is the imposing **Maison Louis XIV** (☎ 05 59 26 01 56, place Louis XIV; admission free; open 10.30am-noon & 2.30pm-6.30pm Mon-Sat, 2.30pm-6.30pm Sun July-Aug; 10.30am-noon & 2.30pm-5.30pm Mon-Sat, 2.30pm-5.30pm Sun June & Sept), built in 1643 by a wealthy shipowner. Louis XIV lived here for over a month before his marriage. It's still furnished in 17th-century style. Guided tours (with English text) cost €3.80 (students and children €2.25).

Beside this is St-Jean de Luz's equally ancient **town hall**, erected in 1657.

THE FRENCH BASQUE COUNTRY

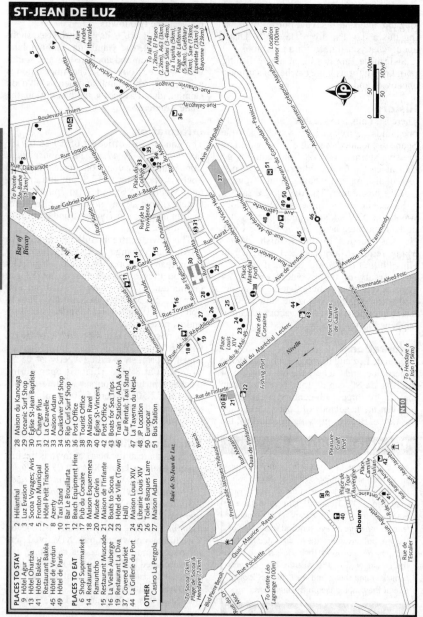

ST-JEAN DE LUZ

THE FRENCH BASQUE COUNTRY

PLACES TO STAY
9 Hôtel Agur
13 Hôtel Ohartzia
41 Hôtel Bakéa;
   Restaurant Bakéa
45 Hôtel de Verdun
49 Hôtel de Paris

PLACES TO EAT
6 Shopi Supermarket
14 Restaurant
   Ramuntcho
15 Restaurant Muscade
16 La Vieille Auberge
19 Restaurant La Diva
37 Covered Market
44 La Grillerie du Port

OTHER
1 Casino La Pergola
2 Hélianthal
3 Luz Evasion
4 Socoa Voyages; Avis
5 Fronton Municipal
7 Hôtel Petit Trianon
8 Azerty
10 Taxi Stand
11 Bar Le Brouillarta
12 Beach Equipment Hire
17 Pub du Corsaire
18 Maison Esquerrenea
20 Musée Grévin
21 Maison de l'Infante
22 Boats to Socoa
23 Hôtel de Ville (Town
   Hall)
24 Maison Louis XIV
25 Librairie Louis XIV
26 Toiles Basques Larre
27 Maison Adam
28 Maison du Kanouga
29 Oceanic Surf Shop
30 Église St-Jean Baptiste
31 Change Plus
32 La Caravelle
33 Maison Adam
34 Quiksilver Surf Shop
35 Rip Curl Surf Shop
36 Post Office
38 Tourist Office
39 Maison Ravel
40 Église St-Vincent
42 Post Office
43 Boats for Sea Trips
46 Train Station; ADA & Avis
   Car Rental; Taxi Stand
47 La Taverna du Nesle
48 JP Location
50 Europcar
51 Bus Station

Maison de l'Infante & Musée Grévin

Before her marriage to Louis XIV, Maria Teresa stayed in another shipowner's mansion, the brick-and-stone Maison Joanoenia, also called the **Maison de l'Infante** (☎ *05 59 26 36 82, quai de l'Infante; adult €2.30, child under 12 free; open 11am-12.30pm & 2.30pm-6.30pm Tue-Sat, 2.30pm-6.30pm Mon mid-June–mid-Oct*).

For the historical context, pop into the **Musée Grévin** (☎ *05 59 51 24 88, 3 rue Mazarin; adult €5.35, child under 12 & student €2.65; open 10am-noon & 2pm-6.30pm daily Apr-June, Sept & Oct; 10am-12.30pm & 2pm-8pm daily July-Aug; 2pm-6pm Sat, Sun & holidays rest of year*), with over 50 wax figures of everyone from fishwives to pirates, musketeers to Paris courtiers.

Église St-Jean Baptiste

This is France's largest and finest Basque church (☎ *05 59 26 08 81, rue Gambetta; admission free; open 8.30am-noon & 2pm-7pm daily*) – and its most famous one, where Louis XIV and Maria Teresa were married. The plain face conceals a splendid interior, dating from a major overhaul already in progress when the wedding took place.

Until the Second Vatican Council (1962–65), Basque churches like this had separate seating for men and women. Here the men sat in the three tiers of grand **oak galleries** (five tiers at the rear) and sang as a chorus. The women sat on the ground floor near the underground family sepulchres.

The stupendous gilded **altarpiece**, made in 1665–70, is a delightful mixture of classical severity and Spanish baroque madness. Above it all is a **vaulted ceiling** of painted panels, resembling an upturned ship's hull. The **model ship** hanging in the middle of the nave was presented by Empress Eugénie (wife of Napoleon III) after her own ship *L'Aigle* nearly went down on the rocks off Ciboure.

The **portal** on the church's southern side, through which Louis XIV and Maria Teresa left the church, was sealed after the ceremony; its outline can be seen opposite 20 rue Gambetta.

Ecomusée de la Tradition Basque

This Museum of Basque Tradition (☎ *05 59 51 06 06, Ferme Berrain; €5.35/2.30 adult/child under 12; open 10am-7pm Mon-Sat Sept-June; 9am-8pm Mon-Sat July-Aug, last entry two hours before closing*) features scenes of Basque life, complete with animated figures. The remnants of a former Izarra distillery (see Shopping under Bayonne) provide an excuse for tastings and sales. The museum is an awkward 3.7km east of the town centre on the N10; take any ATCRB Biarritz or Bayonne bus to the Dubonnet stop (€1.50).

Other Things to See in St-Jean de Luz

The only building that survived when the Spanish torched the town in 1558 is the **Maison Esquerrenea**, the stone building at 17 rue de la République. Narrow, closely spaced streets just south of rue Gambetta, and to the west on either side of rue Mazarin, are the town's old **fisherfolk neighbourhoods**.

Thalassotherapy

The local thalassotherapy centre (see under Activities in the Facts for the Visitor chapter) is **Hélianthal** (☎ *05 59 51 51 51, fax 05 59 51 51 54*), place Maurice Ravel, beside the Casino.

Ciboure & Socoa

Ciboure is St-Jean de Luz's quiet alter ego. Many whitewashed **Basque houses**, timber-framed and shuttered in red or green, survive along rue Agorette, rue de la Fontaine and rue de l'Escalier.

Église St-Vincent, on rue Pocalette, built in the 16th and 17th centuries, is topped by an unusual octagonal bell tower. The beautiful wood interior is typically Basque. The composer Maurice Ravel (1875–1937) was born (of a Basque mother and Swiss father) in the **Maison Ravel**, at 27 quai Maurice Ravel.

Ciboure's **Socoa** district is 2.5km farther north-west along quai Maurice Ravel and blvd Pierre Benoît. Its prominent **fort** was built in 1627 under Henri IV. You can walk out to the **Digue de Socoa** breakwater, or climb to the **lighthouse** via rue du Phare, then out along rue du Sémaphore for fabulous **coastal views**.

ATCRB buses go via Ciboure to Socoa (€1.05, 10 minutes) five times daily (except Sunday) from the Halte Routière.

Pointe Ste-Barbe

This promontory at the northern end of the Baie de St-Jean de Luz is a fine place for panoramas of town and wind-tossed sea. It is 1km north-east of St-Jean de Luz's beach, via blvd Thiers and the seaside promenade des Rochers.

Beaches & Surfing

St-Jean de Luz's family-friendly beach sprouts bathing tents from June to September. You can rent your own, at the kiosk by the northern end of rue Tourasse, for €6.10 a day. Ciboure has its own modest beach below blvd Pierre Benoît.

Plage de Socoa, 2km west of Socoa on the coastal road called the Corniche (D912), is served by ATCRB buses to Hendaye (€1.05, Socoa Centre stop). In the high season the *Lixto* (mobile ☎ 06 81 20 84 98) sails between quai de l'Infante and Socoa every 30 minutes during the day, for €1.90 one way – daily from June to September, on Saturday, Sunday and holidays in May and October, and on holidays only in April.

For prime surfing, head 4.5km north-east from the centre of St-Jean de Luz to **plage de Lafitenia**; ATCRB's Biarritz and Bayonne buses pass within 1km of the beach on the N10 (Martienia or Dubonnet stop, €1.35). Surf schools based at several surf shops – including **Rip Curl** (☎ 05 59 26 81 95, 72 rue Gambetta), **Quiksilver** (☎/fax 05 59 26 17 58, 64 rue Gambetta) and **Oceanic** (☎ 05 59 26 07 93, 16 rue Gambetta) run their own free shuttle buses.

Other Activities

From Easter to September, **École de Voile International** (☎ 05 59 47 06 32, Parking de Socoa, Ciboure) offers windsurfing lessons (one/two/three hours €9.20/15.30/22.90) plus private instruction; take ATCRB's Hendaye bus (Corniche route) to the Bordagain stop.

Tech Ocean (☎ 05 59 47 96 75, 45 av du Commandant Passicot; open year round), below Socoa Fort (Socoa stop) has introductory dives (€45 inclusive) and longer courses.

Sea Trips

From quai du Maréchal Leclerc, the *Marie Rose* (☎ 05 59 26 25 87) and *Nivelle III* (mobile ☎ 06 09 73 61 81) take visitors for deep-sea fishing trips in the morning (€24.40) or ocean cruises in the afternoon (half/one/two hours €4.60/7.70/12.20), from May to mid-September.

Special Events

Kantuaren Eguna is a Basque singing competition held on the third Sunday in June. **Festival Andalou** brings dance troupes from Andalucia on Pentecost weekend, and they come from all over the Spanish and French Basque country for **Danses des Sept Provinces Basque** in late May or early June.

St John the Baptist's day is 24 June, celebrated as the **Fêtes de la St-Jean** on the preceding or following weekend, with a choral concert at the Église St-Jean Baptiste, plus bonfires, music and dancing. **La Fête du Thon** (Tuna Festival), on the first Saturday after 1 July, brings buskers to place des Corsaires, quai du Maréchal Leclerc and Ciboure, Basque music and rock to place Maréchal Foch, and midnight fireworks. **Régates de Traînières** is a weekend of boat races on the first weekend in July.

On the second Saturday in September the **Fête du Ttoro** pits chef against chef in the preparation of this classic Basque fish soup. Église St-Jean Baptiste and other churches in St-Jean de Luz and Ciboure resound with **classical French and Basque music** during the first two weeks of September.

For tourists the town lays on a pop concert, a confetti battle and fireworks on place Louis XIV every Wednesday and Sunday evening in July and August.

Places to Stay – Budget

Camping Between St-Jean de Luz and Guéthary, 7km up the coast, are no fewer than 16 camp sites, clustered behind plage d'Erromardie in quartier Erromardie, and behind plage de Mayarkoenia in quartier Acotz. Acotz has the best access to the surfing beaches of Lafitenia and Senix.

Among the cheaper, though rather shadeless, camp sites at Erromardie are *Elgar-Erromardie* (☎ *05 59 26 85 85; two people with tent/car €9.15/10.65; open Apr-Sept)* and the municipal *Chibaou* (☎ *05 59 26 11 94, fax 05 59 51 61 70; adult/pitch €4.25/ 4.25; open June–mid-Sept)*, the latter right above the beach. In the same price range in Acotz are *Maya* (☎ *05 59 26 54 91; adult/ tent/car €3.95/3.05/1.35; open mid-June– Sept)*, by the railway line, and shady *Arena* (☎/fax *05 59 26 51 90,* [W] *www.arenacamp ing.com; €4.10/6.10; open Apr-Sept)*.

ATCRB's Biarritz and Bayonne buses (see Getting There & Away later in this section) stop within 1km of them all – get off at the Trikaldi stop for Erromardie, or the Martienia stop for Acotz. From June to September, buses A and B of the Navette Intercommunal bus (see Getting Around later in this section) go out to Erromardie.

Camp sites south-west of Ciboure include *Larrouleta* (☎ *05 59 47 37 84, fax 05 59 47 42 54, Socoa; adult/tent/car €3.65/2.60/ 1.50; open year round)* and *Suhiberry* (☎ *05 59 47 06 23, fax 05 59 47 18 93, Socoa; €3.65/3.65/1.20; open May-Sept)*.

Hostel The plain *Centre Léo Lagrange* (☎/fax *05 59 47 04 79, 8 rue Simone Menez, Ciboure)* hostel, with dorm beds for about €8, tends to get block-booked, but you might bag a bed.

Places to Stay – Mid-Range
Many hotels get the same clients year after year, so it can be hard to find a room in July and August. Rates soar and some hotels require that you take half-board. At other times of the year prices may drop by a third or more. We give peak prices.

Hôtel de Paris (☎ *05 59 85 20 20, fax 05 59 85 20 25, 1 blvd du Commandant Passicot)* Doubles with WC & shower €40.20-43.25. Nondescript and a bit noisy, the Hôtel de Paris nevertheless offers renovated rooms at modest prices.

Hôtel de Verdun (☎/fax *05 59 26 02 55, 13 av de Verdun)* Rooms €23.25, or €26.30/ 30.85 with shower/shower & WC. Breakfast €3.80. Opposite the train station, the good-value Verdun is pitched at pilgrims but open to all, with big, plain rooms.

Hôtel Bakéa (☎ *05 59 47 34 40, fax 05 59 47 48 87, 9 place Camille Julian, Ciboure)* Open Mar-Dec. Rooms with shower & WC €38.10. Rooms are plain but the food is great (see Places to Eat) at this cheerful, family-run hotel. It's across the harbour but no farther from the centre of St-Jean than some hotels there.

Places to Stay – Top End
For a particularly comfortable stay, try one of the following.

Hôtel Agur (☎ *05 59 51 91 11, fax 05 59 51 91 21,* [e] *hotel.agur@wanadoo.fr, 96 rue Gambetta)* Rooms €55.65-60.20, mini-suites with kitchenette €75.45-121.20, flats for two €335-505 per week. Accommodation at this Scots-run place runs from simple rooms to self-catering flats. Breakfast is generous and the garden is quiet.

Hôtel Ohartzia (☎ *05 59 26 00 06, fax 05 59 26 74 75, 28 rue Garat)* Rooms with shower €45.75-54.90, with bath & breakfast €59.45. The Ohartzia offers charming, sunny rooms in a quiet corner of town.

Places to Eat
Restaurants Just *look* at all the restaurants lined up waiting for you along rue de la République! There are more, plus lots of cafes, around place Louis XIV. Most shut down for a few days per week outside July and August, and for a few months outside summer.

La Grillerie du Port (☎ *05 59 51 18 29, quai Maréchal Leclerc)* Dishes €6.10-8.40, menus €15.25. Open 11.30am-2.30pm & 6pm-10pm daily mid-June–mid-Sept. You'll like this no-frills, harbourside place with simple, tasty food – salads, omelettes, tuna steaks the size of Frisbees – at minuscule prices. Order (and pay) at the door. It's staffed by students, hence the short season.

Restaurant Muscade (☎ *05 59 26 96 73, 20 rue Garat)* Salads €7.30-11.90, *tartes*

€4.55-10.65. Open daily. The Muscade is a recommended stop, specialising in big mixed salads and delicious tartes, both savoury and sweet.

Restaurant La Diva (☎ *05 59 51 14 01, 7 rue de la République) Menus* €12.20-18.30. Open Mar-Oct. The Basque fish chowder called *ttoro* (say 'tyoro'), touted all along rue de la République, is part of a good €13.70 midday *menu* at La Diva.

La Vieille Auberge (☎ *05 59 26 19 61, 22 rue Tourasse) Menus* €13.55-19.65. This place serves generous portions of traditional French and Basque cuisine, including *moules marinières* (marinated mussels) for €10.50.

Restaurant Ramuntcho (☎ *05 59 26 03 89, 24 rue Garat) Menus* €14.50-24.40. Here you'll find a unique mix of regional dishes; house specialities include duck and fish. The *patron* is from Normandy so sauces are rich with fresh cream.

Hôtel Bakéa (see Places to Stay) Menus €16.75-23.65. With superb seafood, this hotel restaurant is a great place for a splurge. See if you can get through their €26-per-person *plateau de fruits de mer* (seafood platter).

Self-Catering Rue Gambetta is lined with *food shops*. The *Shopi* supermarket, at 87 rue Gambetta, is open until 7pm Monday to Saturday.

Tuesday and Friday (plus Saturday during July and August) are market days at the *covered market* on blvd Victor Hugo. Ciboure's *market* is on Sunday morning on place Camille Julian.

Entertainment

Bars & Discos Laid-back pubs near the town centre, open 4pm to 3am daily (5pm to 2am Monday to Saturday in winter), include the following.

Bar Le Brouillarta (☎ *05 59 51 29 51, 48 promenade Jacques Thibaud)* A pricey beachside brasserie by day, the Brouillarta is a breezy, agreeable bar by night.

Pub du Corsaire (☎ *05 59 26 10 74, 16 rue de la République)* The Corsaire is a bit more olde-worldy atmospheric than the others.

La Taverna du Nesle (☎ *05 59 26 60 93, 5 av Labrouche)* This is a cheerful, unpretentious neighbourhood pub.

St-Jean de Luz has two discos: *El Paseo* (☎ *05 59 26 04 28, 48 av André Ithurralde)*, 2km east of the Halte Routière, and *La Tupiña* (☎ *05 59 54 73 23, N10)*, 5km east of the town centre.

Casino The town's grand beachside *Casino La Pergola* (☎ *05 59 51 58 58, place Maurice Ravel)* has slot machines from 11pm to 3am daily and gaming from 9pm to 3am Tuesday to Sunday.

Spectator Sports

Cesta punta matches take place at 9pm every Tuesday and Friday at Jaï Alaï Campos Berri (☎ 05 59 51 65 30), opposite 43 av André Ithurralde. Tickets cost around €8 to €19. Look out for daytime matches on Monday and Thursday at the Fronton Municipal, at the eastern end of rue St-Jacques.

Shopping

St-Jean de Luz is a good place to buy Basque linen, for example, at *La Caravelle (62 rue Gambetta)*, or *Toiles Basques Larre (4 rue de la République)*. Or those with a sweet tooth could investigate the following.

Maison du Kanouga (9 rue Gambetta; open 8.30am-12.45pm & 2pm-7.30pm Tues-Sun, 9am-12.45pm & 3pm-7.30pm Mon) Bust your budget here with *mouchous* (almond biscuits), *kanouga* (chewy chocolate or coffee candy) or *gâteau Basque* (Basque cake).

Maison Adam (49 rue Gambetta & 6 rue de la République; open Tues-Sun) If that's not enough, the town's most venerable sweet shop (founded 1660) has two branches.

Getting There & Away

Bus From the Halte Routière, ATCRB (☎ 05 59 08 00 33) buses run up the coast to Biarritz (€2.75, 30 minutes, nine daily) and Bayonne (€3.50, 35 minutes, six to 10 daily); and down to Hendaye (€2.75, 20 minutes) 10 to 12 times daily (four Sunday), with three weekday departures taking the Corniche coastal route.

Basque Bondissant (☎ 05 59 26 30 74) runs regular buses from the Halte Routière to the cog-wheel railway at La Rhune and on to the Grottes de Sare (see under Sare later in this chapter).

Train There are at least 20 trains daily to Biarritz (€2.45, 12 minutes) and Bayonne (€3.80, 25 minutes), and to Hendaye (€2.45, 12 minutes) from where shuttle trains continue into Spain (see Hendaye later in this chapter). A TGV/non-TGV ticket to Bordeaux costs €24.40/22.85.

Car The budget-rate agency ADA (☎ 05 59 26 26 22) is open daily at the train station. International agencies include Europcar (☎ 05 59 26 82 40), open only in July and August, at 3 blvd du Commandant Passicot; and Avis, with an office (☎ 05 59 26 76 66) at the train station and one (☎ 05 59 26 17 43) at Socoa Voyages, 31 blvd Thiers.

Getting Around
Bus From June to September ATCRB runs a local service called Navette Intercommunal (☎ 05 59 26 06 99) from the Halte Routière, with connections to Socoa (line D) and to Erromardie (lines A and B) three to six times a day (except Sunday). Get timetables at the tourist office or the Halte Routière.

Bicycle JP Location (☎ 05 59 26 14 95), 7 av Labrouche, rents road bikes for €9.15/44.80 per day/week and VTTs (mountain bikes) for €12.20/55.65, as well as scooters and motorbikes. The shop is open daily except Saturday afternoon, Sunday and Monday (daily except Sunday in July and August).

The Hôtel Petit Trianon (☎ 05 59 26 11 90), 56 blvd Victor Hugo, charges €13.70/61 per day/week. Other outlets include Luz Evasion (☎ 05 59 26 43 88), 4 rue Dalbarade, and Location Aiknor (☎ 05 59 26 32 26), 12 av de Habas. In summer, Sobilo (☎ 05 59 26 75 76) rents out VTTs (mountain bikes) for €12.20 a day and scooters from €30.50, from a kiosk situated at the train station.

HENDAYE
postcode 64700 • pop 13,000

Hendaye's main claim to fame is as Southwest France's main border crossing point and rail link into Spain (to Irún on the other side), although it's also a pleasant, if unexceptional, beach resort. If you've come this far, don't miss a walk around the clifftop Domaine d'Abbadia.

Orientation
Hendaye sits beside the River Bidassoa – the frontier – across which is the twin Spanish resort of Fuenterrabía and, just upstream, the Spanish border post and rail terminus of Irún. The Bidassoa has silted up enough to form a natural harbour, the Baie de Txingudi, just before it empties into the Atlantic.

There are three distinct Hendayes – the train station and border area, the town centre, and the beach – too far apart for easy walking but linked by local bus services. ATCRB buses from up the coast also stop in all three areas.

Le Croisière, the Moorish-style building sticking out onto the beach, started out in 1884 as a casino. Today it includes a shopping centre, apartment complex and several restaurants.

Information
The tourist office (☎ 05 59 20 00 34, fax 05 59 20 79 17, e tourisme.hendaye@wanadoo.fr) is at 12 rue des Aubépines. It opens 9am to 7.30pm daily (10am to 1pm on Sunday) in July and August; 9am to 12.30pm and 2pm to 6.30pm Monday to Friday, and Saturday morning during the rest of the year. The post office is next door.

Château d'Abbadie & Domaine d'Abbadia
East of town on a rugged plateau above the sea stands a neo-Gothic castle, built in the 1860s for an Irish-Basque explorer named Antoine d'Abbadie d'Arrast. The Château d'Abbadie (*☎ 05 59 20 04 51, route de la Corniche; adult/child €5/2.50; open 10am-2pm Mon-Sat & 2pm-6pm Sun June-mid-Sept; 10am-noon Mon-Fri Feb-May & mid-Sept–mid-Dec*), complete with observatory

THE FRENCH BASQUE COUNTRY

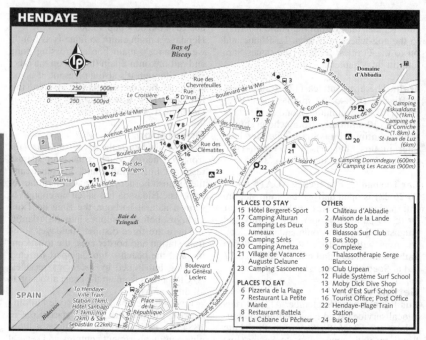

HENDAYE

PLACES TO STAY	OTHER
15 Hôtel Bergeret-Sport	1 Château d'Abbadia
17 Camping Alturan	2 Maison de la Lande
18 Camping Les Deux	3 Bus Stop
Jumeaux	4 Bidassoa Surf Club
19 Camping Sérès	5 Bus Stop
20 Camping Ametza	9 Complexe
21 Village de Vacances	Thalassothérapie Serge
Auguste Delaune	Blanco
23 Camping Sascoenea	10 Club Urpean
	12 Fluide Système Surf School
PLACES TO EAT	13 Moby Dick Dive Shop
6 Pizzeria de la Plage	14 Vent d'Est Surf School
7 Restaurant La Petite	16 Tourist Office; Post Office
Marée	22 Hendaye-Plage Train
8 Restaurant Battela	Station
11 La Cabane du Pêcheur	24 Bus Stop

and the eclectic furnishings of a wealthy traveller to the Orient, is also open for guided visits (€6/3; 3pm-5.30pm Mon-Sat June–mid-Sept, 3pm & 4pm Mon-Fri Feb-May & mid-Sept–mid-Dec).

Domaine d'Abbadia, the windswept estate, is a protected area, owned since 1979 by the Conservatoire du Littoral. Its lawns, moors and cliffs are open, via the Maison de la Lande visitor centre (☎ 05 59 20 37 20; admission free; 9.30am-12.30pm & 2.30pm-6.30pm daily July-Aug; 9am-noon & 2pm-6pm Tues-Sat, afternoon only Mon Sept-June). The centre also has an exhibit on the estate's rich flora and fauna.

Thalassotherapy
One of the Basque coast's bigger centres for thalassotherapy (see Activities in the Facts for the Visitor chapter) is the **Complexe Thalassothérapie Serge Blanco** (☎ 05 59 51 35 35, fax 05 59 51 36 00, 125 blvd de la Mer), beside the marina. Pool, hammam

(steamhouse), sauna, Jacuzzi and other facilities are available on a drop-in basis for €13.70/18.30 for one/two hours.

Fuenterrabía
The pretty Spanish resort of Fuenterrabía (Fontarrabie to the French) has a charming old centre full of timber-frame houses, a castle and baroque church, its own beach, modest accommodation and good food. Behind it rises the 500m peak of Jaizkibel. Several boats shuttle to and from Hendaye's marina every 15 to 30 minutes into the evening, for €1.37 each way.

Activities
The swells along Hendaye's 3km beach will please novice surfers. Hendaye has at least three surf schools (typically two/10/20 hours of instruction for about €17/15/14 per hour): **Fluide Système** (☎ 05 59 20 67 47, 4 rue des Orangers), **Vent D'Est** (☎ 05 59 48 14 08, e vendest@aol.com, 69 blvd du Général

Leclerc) and **Bidassoa Surf Club** *(☎ 05 59 48 32 80, 1 bis route de la Corniche).*

A dive shop called **Moby Dick** *(☎/fax 05 59 20 45 33,* e *mbdck@aol.com, 5 rue des Orangers)* runs introductory dives (€27.45) and rents out sailboats (about €900-1800 per week). Across the road is another dive shop, **Club Urpean** *(☎ 05 59 20 55 55, 10 rue des Orangers).*

From the marina, the *Hendayais II (mobile ☎ 06 14 85 72 65)* will take you deep-sea fishing all morning (€24.40), or on a one/ two-hour afternoon ocean cruise (€4.55/ 12.20).

The GR10 trail, which runs the length of the Pyrénées, starts roughly in front of Le Cruisière.

Places to Stay

Hendaye has at least 11 camp sites. Following are two good-value options – both open from April to September, with 2-person forfait for €15 (20% less outside July to August), within the sound of passing trains but rambling and shady.

Les Acacias (☎/fax 05 59 20 78 76, w *www.les-acacias.com, rue de Glacière)* This spacious, 311-pitch camp site has a swimming pool, bar and restaurant.

Camping Dorrondeguy (☎/fax 05 59 20 26 16, rue de la Glacière) Though a bit crowded, Dorrondeguy is well equipped with a bar-restaurant and bicycle rental.

Village de Vacances Auguste Delaune (☎ 05 59 20 07 07, fax 05 59 48 02 52, rue Hélène Boucher) 4-bed bungalow with kitchen about €30 per weekday or €75 for a weekend. Open Apr-Oct. The plain bungalows here are for groups in July and August but at other times may be available to all.

Hôtel Bergeret-Sport (☎ 05 59 20 00 78, fax 05 59 20 67 30, 4 rue des Clématites) Doubles with WC €30.50-38.10, without WC €42.70-57.95. Breakfast €5.65. Open May-Oct. This good-value hotel, with big, bright rooms, is around the corner from the tourist office and close to the beach.

Hôtel Santiago (☎ 05 59 20 00 94, fax 05 59 20 83 26, 29 rue Santiago) Doubles with WC & shower €30.50-35.90. Breakfast €4.55. The friendly Santiago, two blocks

east of Hendaye-Ville train station, has well kept rooms, its own bar and a small restaurant. Free off-street parking is available.

Places to Eat

Three places for good seafood at modest prices (evening *menus* around €9–12) are *Restaurant La Petite Marée (☎ 05 59 20 77 96, 2 av des Mimosas)*, closed Wednesday outside July and August; *La Cabane du Pêcheur (☎ 05 59 20 38 09, quai de la Floride)*; and *Restaurant Battela (☎ 05 59 20 15 70, 5 rue d'Irún)*, closed Monday and Tuesday outside July and August, and in December and January.

Pizzeria de la Plage (☎ 05 59 48 04 18, Le Croisière, 2 blvd de la Mer) Midday plates €6.90-11.50. Open daily. Unexceptional but right on the beach is this busy brasserie with €6 salads, €7 pizza and pasta, and fish dishes for €10–27.

The Hôtel Bergeret-Sport and Hôtel Santiago (see Places to Stay) also have restaurants.

Getting There & Away

Bus ATCRB uses the same beach, centre and train station stops as local buses (see Getting Around later in this section). Services to St-Jean de Luz (€2.75, 20 minutes) operate at least 10 times daily (four on Sunday), including three weekday runs via the Corniche (see Car later in this section). Most continue to Bayonne (€6.25, one hour).

Train Six to nine trains daily (except Sunday) link Hendaye-Ville station to St-Jean de Luz (€2.45, 10 minutes), Biarritz (€4.25, 25 minutes) and Bayonne (€5.65, 40 minutes). About half of these also serve Hendaye-Plage station, near the beach. Daily Paris-Bordeaux-Irún TGVs also stop at Hendaye-Ville.

From Hendaye-Ville station a Spanish-gauge shuttle train called EuskoTren crosses the border to San Sebastián (€1.50 return, 30 minutes) every half-hour from 7am to 9pm. Another runs twice daily via San Sebastián to Bilbao (€12.80 return, 2½ hours).

Car Treat yourself to the slow but spectacular drive from St-Jean de Luz (D912) atop the seaside cliffs called the Corniche, where the Pyrénées tumble into the sea. The views along the Basque coast are superb.

Getting Around

An unnumbered local bus (€0.90) runs every half-hour from 10am to 8pm, daily from mid-June to mid-September, linking the beach, the town centre and the train station.

The Navette Plage is a shuttle-bus that takes campers down to the beach from the remotest of Hendaye's camping grounds (including Dorrondeguy). It costs €0.50 each way and runs hourly from 2pm to 7pm daily.

Labourd

SARE

postcode 64310 • pop 2260 • elevation 70m

Sare (Sara in Basque), 14km south-east of St-Jean de Luz, is a handsome Basque town set in a lush Labourd landscape on the flanks of La Rhune mountain. The picture-postcard scene has earned town and mountain some heavy tourist traffic.

Sare's centre is dominated, as in most Basque villages, by its severe church, with five gilded altars and typical gallery seating, and a tall fronton that serves as the focus of most social events. The GR10 passes through the middle of town.

Half of La Rhune is in the Spanish Basque Country. The Basques have never paid much attention to the border, and the people of Sare have a history of cheerful, matter-of-fact smuggling here, over a network of remote tracks.

Orientation & Information

Sare spreads endlessly along rambling roads through a dozen *quartiers*, less like a township than an ultra-low-density suburb. Beyond the central square, place du Fronton, it's hell to find your way around, and the tourist-office map is of little use.

The tourist office (☎ 05 59 54 20 14, fax 05 59 54 29 15, e otsi.sare@wanadoo.fr) is in the town hall, at the corner of the square. It opens 9.30am to 12.30pm and 2pm to 6.30pm weekdays, 10am to 12.30pm and

3pm to 6.30pm Saturday and 10am to 12.30pm Sunday in July and August; 9am to 12.30pm and 2pm to 6pm weekdays and 2pm to 6pm Saturday in April, May, June and September; and 1.30pm to 5.30pm weekdays November to March.

La Rhune

Antenna-topped, 905m La Rhune (Larrun in Basque) is something of a Basque symbol. Indeed, it was sacred as early as the Stone Age, as witnessed by the many stone circles, dolmens, barrows and tumuli in its middle reaches. Ever since Empress Eugénie visited in 1859 it has been a must-see.

There are stunning views of the Lower Pyrénées, the Spanish Basque province of Navarra and the Bay of Biscay from the summit, which can be reached on foot or via a **train à crémaillère** *(cog-wheel railway;* ☎ *05 59 54 20 26, Col de St-Ignace; adult/child €9.90/6.10; open 9am daily Easter-June & Sept–mid-Nov; 8.30am daily July-Aug).* The train, built in 1924, runs from the Col de St-Ignace, 3km north-west of place du Fronton on the D4 (St-Jean de Luz road), with departures roughly every 35 minutes. The 4km trip takes 30 minutes each way. The last train up usually departs from the Col about 6pm, though there may be later runs depending on weather and demand. Waits of an hour or more are common in July and August.

En route, watch for the shaggy, shy feral ponies called *pottok* (po-**tyok**), once used in local mines and crossbred for drayage, now mainly sought after for pony trekking. There's a brisk local trade in them (see Espelette later in this chapter), as well as a private nature reserve for them (see Bidarray later in this chapter). For more on efforts to protect this unique animal, see Endangered Species in the Facts About Southwest France chapter.

Les Grottes de Sare

Through a yawning cave mouth 6km south of Sare, via the D306, is a network of underground passages, galleries and a huge central chamber. Bones and tools found here show that these limestone caves had long-term occupants some 20,000 years ago. Local lore says the underground river that formed them emerges in Spain and that smugglers used to pass *under* the border here!

Admission to the caves (☎ *05 59 54 21 88, route des Grottes; adult/child €5.35/ 2.30; open 2pm-4pm daily Jan-Carnaval; 2pm-5pm daily Carnaval-Easter & mid-Nov–Dec; 10am-6pm daily Easter-June & Sept; 10am-7pm daily July-Aug; 10am-5pm daily Oct–mid-Nov)* includes an obligatory, multilingual guided tour.

Special Events

Everything happens at the fronton. In July and August, there's weekly pelote Basque at 9pm Monday and Basque dancing at 9.30pm Wednesday. Seasonal events include handicrafts and food fairs on the Sunday after 14 July (Bastille Day) and on the Sunday after 18 August. The latter is usually preceded on the Saturday by a Fête de la Pelote.

Places to Stay & Eat

Alas, the only places that are easy to find around Sare are the priciest. Everything is clean and quiet and everyone is polite; it's like an episode from *The Prisoner*.

Camping La Petite Rhune (☎ *05 59 54 23 97, fax 05 59 54 23 42, quartier Lehenbiscaye)* 2-person forfait €12.95 (€14.50 July). Open May-Sept. This deluxe camp site, with pool and tennis courts, is 3km south of place du Fronton.

Hôtel Pikassaria (☎ *05 59 54 21 51, fax 05 59 54 27 40, quartier Lehenbiscaye)* Doubles €35.05-44.20. Open mid-Mar–mid-Nov. Opposite the camp site is this equally well managed hotel with spotless rooms.

Hôtel Arraya (☎ *05 59 54 20 46, fax 05 59 54 27 04,* [e] *hotel@arraya.com, place du Fronton)* Rooms with WC & bath €80 (€90 Aug–mid-Sept). *Menus* €20.60-29.75. Open Apr–mid-Nov. Tops in Sare, and with the best food (and famous gâteau Basque), is this three-star hotel.

Restaurant Lastiry (☎ *05 59 54 20 07, place du Fronton)* *Menus* €14.50-25.15. Open Wed-Mon. Despite stiff competition from across the road, the Lastiry has its own good reputation for quality Basque cooking.

Getting There & Away

Unless you have a car or bike, Sare is conveniently visited only from St-Jean de Luz. Basque Bondissant (☎ 05 59 26 30 74) runs regular buses from St-Jean de Luz to Col de St-Ignace (€1.85, 20 minutes), Sare (€2.30, 30 minutes) and the Grottes de Sare (€3.05, 45 minutes) – one to three times a day Monday to Saturday. Most arrive at the Col in time to catch the cog-wheel railway. The timetable depends on the day of the week and whether it's school holiday time or not; contact the St-Jean de Luz or Sare tourist office for current information.

Two St-Jean de Luz agencies offering half-day tours to La Rhune, for around €13/8 adult/child, are Basque Bondissant (daily Monday to Saturday) and Bruno Francisco (☎ 05 59 51 23 40; Tuesday and Saturday).

AÏNHOA

postcode 64250 • pop 550 • elevation 120m

Aïnhoa (Ainhoa in Basque) is the most southwesterly bastide in France, jointly founded around 1230 by Premonstratensian monks, keen to make a buck from Compostela pilgrims, and Juan Pérez de Baztan, a Navarre signeur worried about the English. The Spanish trashed it in 1629 so almost everything dates from the late 17th and 18th centuries.

This is the place in which to see classic Labourd Basque village architecture. The single main street, the route d'Espagne, is lined with stout, half-timbered, brightly painted houses, some with unnerving outward tilts. Facades on the western side are noticeably finer than those opposite. The latter are actually backsides, according to a tradition that houses should face away from the sea, source of stormy weather.

Many bear stone lintels engraved in Latin or French with the essentials of their founding. One of the most detailed of these, on the building called Maison Gorritia, notes that the house was paid for with money earned overseas. The confidence implicit in these permanent declarations arises from another Basque tradition (now overruled by French law), that houses cannot be sold out of the family after the second generation.

The paint and whitewash are renewed

annually. The overall effect is dignified and harmonious: this must be one of the southwest's most photogenic villages. Of course everybody from everywhere wants to see it, so it's wall-to-wall with visitors all summer.

Information

There's no tourist office, though you may find a few brochures at the little town hall on the route d'Espagne opposite the church. It opens 9am to noon and 2pm to 6pm on weekdays.

Things to See & Do

Aïnhoa's fortified church, parts of which date from the 14th century, contains two tiers of wooden galleries and a grand, gilded altarpiece. It shares an outer wall with the village fronton and has has a small cemetery full of melancholy Basque grave markers.

The GR10 passes through town: Sare is a 3½-hour walk to the west, Bidarray seven hours to the east. For a 45-minute climb that will reward you with lofty views as far as Navarra and St-Jean de Luz, follow signs east from the town hall to a pilgrims' chapel called Vierge d'Ainhoa (the Aïnhoa Virgin).

Places to Stay & Eat

Aïnhoa offers a few options for camp sites and hotels.

Camping Harazpy (☎ *05 59 29 89 38, fax 05 59 29 73 82, 300m west of town centre*) 2-person forfait €10.20 (hikers €4.90). Open July–mid-Sept. This little municipal site is little more than a tree-lined field, though the views are super.

Camping Xokoan (☎ *05 59 29 90 26, fax 05 59 29 73 82, Dancharia*) 2-person forfait €9.90, doubles with shared facilities €33.55. *Menus* €12.95-16.75. Open year round; restaurant open 12.15pm-7pm daily. This shady little camp site is as peaceful a spot as you could want, with a bar and modest restaurant, plus a few rooms to rent. Across the stream is Spain. It's 2.6km south of Aïnhoa.

Hôtel Ohantzea (☎ *05 59 29 90 50, route d'Espagne*) Rooms with WC & bath €45.75. Breakfast €5.35. Rooms in this well kept 16th-century building are plain but carefully renovated.

Hôtel Oppoca (☎ *05 59 29 90 72, fax 05 59 29 81 03, route d'Espagne*) Doubles with WC & bath €35.05-48.80, less outside July-Aug. Breakfast €5.35. *Menus* €15-25. Restaurant open midday & evening Tues-Sat, midday only Sunday mid-Dec–mid-Nov. Opposite the church is this Logis de France property with small, pretty rooms and the only restaurant on the road.

ESPELETTE

postcode 64250 • pop 1920 • elevation 72m
The dark red peppers called pimentos, which arrived from Mexico and Spain in the 17th century, are now an essential part of Basque cuisine. The best known variety – now with its own *appellation d'origine contrôlée* (AOC; a system of strict definition and control of quality wines and spirits) – is grown around Espelette (Basque name Ezpeleta), and for two months after the late-August harvest, chains of *le piment d'Espelette* are hung out to sun-dry on the village's traditional Basque facades, faultlessly trimmed in the same blood-red colour.

At the edge of the town is a little stone chateau with bits going back to the 11th century. There's also a boxy, 17th-century church with some of the region's most exuberant interior woodwork and a churchyard dotted with traditional disk-shaped Basque markers (and the grave of Agnes Souret, a local young woman who became the first Miss France in 1920). Espelette has lots of handicrafts shops, and one of the Basque Country's few genuinely traditional chocolatiers.

Be prepared for heavy tourist traffic here in July and August.

Orientation & Information

Espelette's heart is place du Marché, around which are the post office, trinquet, covered market and bus stand. Off the north-eastern corner is the chateau, with the town hall on the ground floor, the tourist office on the 1st floor and a free photographic exhibition on chilli peppers around the world on the 2nd floor.

The tourist office (☎ 05 59 93 95 02, fax 05 59 93 89 71), and the pimento exhibition, are open 9.30am to 12.30pm and 2pm to

THE FRENCH BASQUE COUNTRY

6pm Monday to Saturday, year round (closed Monday morning July to September).

Peppers & Chocolate
The shelves of every food shop in town groan under piment d'Espelette and its derivative products.

Among the few chocolatiers in the Basque Country who still begin with the bean – and offer free tastings – is **Chocolats Antton** (☎ 05 59 93 80 58, place du Marché; open Mon-Sat year round, plus Sun afternoon Apr-Oct & Sun morning July-Aug). For more on the region's most famous confection, see the boxed text 'Chocolate' earlier in this chapter.

Horse Riding
At **Poney Club Ichtaklok** (☎ 05 59 93 82 13, chemin de Lapitxague), 500m north of place du Jeu de Paume, a half-day's riding costs €21.35/18.30 per adult/child.

Special Events
Espelette's weekly market is held at place du Marché on Wednesday (plus Saturday in July and August).

The French Basque country's last big festival of the year is the **Fête du Piment**, held here on the last weekend in October, with a blessing of the peppers, processions and the selection of a *chevalier du piment* (knight of the pimento).

Pottoks, the shaggy ponies of the Basque high country (see La Maison du Pottock later in this chapter), are bought and sold at Espelette's **Foire aux Pottoks**, held throughout the town on the last Tuesday and Wednesday in January.

Places to Stay & Eat
There are several options for those interested in staying after the tour buses have left.

Camping Biper Gorri (☎/fax 05 59 29 81 82, chemin de Lapitxague) 2-person forfait €15.25, bungalow/chalet €300/480 per week (less outside the high season). Open Apr-Oct. This small, shady camp site is about 1km north of town.

Hôtel-Restaurant Chilhar (☎ 05 59 93 90 01, fax 05 59 93 93 25, rue Principale)

Rooms with WC & shower/bath €31.25/35.85. Breakfast €4.55. Hotel open Apr-Nov, restaurant open Fri-Wed year round. *Menus* €12.95-20.60. The Chilhar, tucked in a cool side-street, has quiet rooms and a covered terrace.

Hôtel-Restaurant Euzkadi (☎ 05 59 93 91 88, fax 05 59 93 90 19, rue Principale) Singles/doubles €33.55/42.70. *Menus* €15.25-25.90, plat du jour €9.90. Hotel open mid-Dec–Oct, restaurant open Wed-Sun year round. This is the place for a comfortable room at the centre of town, and for good Basque and traditional French meals. There are also tennis courts and a pool.

Restaurant Pottoka (☎ 05 59 93 90 92, place du Jeu de Paume) Menus €10.65-19.80. Open midday & evening Tues-Sat & midday only Sun. Another local speciality is *axoa* (French *hachoa*), a spicy veal stew with onions, garlic, tomatoes and, of course, pimentos. This is a good place to try it, for €9.

Café Central (☎ 05 59 93 91 62, rue Principale) Menus €11.45-20.60. Open Sat-Wed & morning only Thur Oct-May; daily June-Sept. If your budget looks shaky, fill up with a combination plate (€10–11), salad or omelette at this cheerful cafe.

Getting There & Away
Espelette is 30 minutes from St-Jean de Luz. Hasparren-bound buses of Lata (☎ 05 59 54 11 37) depart St-Jean de Luz at 11am Tuesday to Friday and 5.30pm Monday to Saturday (€3.75; daily except Wednesday and Saturday in winter), and from Espelette at 7.20am Monday to Saturday (weekdays only in winter), at 1.55pm on Tuesday and Friday.

Basse-Navarre

BIDARRAY
postcode 64780 • pop 650 • elevation 480m
Now you're into the Basse-Navarre and its main artery, the valley of the River Nive. Typical of rural Basque settlements, little Bidarray (Bidarrai in Basque) is not so much a village as a scattering of farmsteads and hamlets, perched on its own plateau where the River Bastan joins the Nive.

Orientation & Information

From the D918, bus stop or train station, cross the bridge over the railway and the river (noticing, upstream, the graceful 14th-century Pont Noblia, the Nive's first bridge). Turn right for 700m, then left for a steep 800m up to the centre, place de l'Église – little more than the customary town hall/church/fronton.

The tourist office (☎/fax 05 59 37 74 60), beside the church, is open 9am to 12.30pm and 3pm to 8pm daily (except Sunday October to March).

Bidarray Village

There's little to do except snoop around Bidarray's tiny Romanesque church (built in 1132 as the chapel of a long-gone priory and now fronted by an outsize, 17th-century belfry-wall), soak up the silence and the view over deliciously rolling, fertile countryside, or set out on the GR10, which runs past.

La Maison du Pottok

This private nature reserve in the hills above Bidarray was opened in 1993 to preserve breeds of the shaggy wild pony of the Basque Country, the pottok (see also La Rhune in this chapter, and Endangered Species in the Facts about Southwest France chapter). La Maison du Pottok (☎ 05 59 52 21 14, W www.maisondupottok.com; admission & year's membership €6.10/4.55 adult/child aged 6-13; open 10am-6pm daily July-Aug) offers video presentations, exhibits, guided visits and fine views across the Basque Country. The reserve is 5km up a signposted road, near the train station on the D918.

Activities

A year-round youth activity centre called Auñamendi (☎/fax 05 59 37 71 34, west end of village) organises VTT trips (€10.65/15.25 rental plus €7.60/12.20 per half/full day), climbing (€12.20/21.35), horse-riding (€10.65 per hour), canyoning (€38.10 per day), white-water rafting (€13.70 per half day) and more. Several outfits down on the D918 near the Bidarray turning offer rafting and other white-water activities; see under Activities in the introduction to this chapter.

Places to Stay & Eat

Auñamendi (see Things to See & Do earlier) has a year-round *gîte d'étape* (dormitory accommodation) for its activity groups – and others if there is space – for €8.40 per bed. Meals are only available for groups.

Hôtel-Restaurant Noblia (☎ 05 59 37 70 89, fax 05 59 37 93 16, Halte du Pont Noblia) Room with WC €22.85, shower €30.50-33.55, both €35.06-39.65. *Menus* €12.95-16.75. Of several hotels near the train station, this is the only one with any character, an unpretentious Logis de France place with good regional dishes in its tiny dining room, and charming, well kept rooms.

Hôtel Barberaenea (☎ 05 59 37 74 86, fax 05 59 37 77 55, place de l'Église) Rooms with shared facilities €28.95, twins/quad with WC & shower €51.05/70.15. Breakfast €6.10. *Menus* €14.50-20.60. Open mid-Dec–mid-Nov. Opposite the church is this hotel with a few very comfortable rooms (most with eye-popping views) and a small *restaurant*. Book well ahead.

Auberge Iparla (☎ 05 59 37 77 21, place du Fronton) *Menus* €14.50-22.10. Open Wed-Mon. This oversize place, the only full-scale eatery in the village centre, offers reasonable Basque dishes.

Getting There & Around

SNCF has at least three daily trains (two Sunday) from Bayonne to Pont-Noblia station (€5.35, 40 minutes).

VTTs can be hired for €10.65/15.25 per half/full day, from a shop called Estekaenea (☎ 05 59 37 76 47), sharing space with the tourist office.

ST-JEAN PIED DE PORT

postcode 64220 • pop 1800 • elevation 170m

You can't arrive in St-Jean Pied de Port (Basque name Donibane Garazi) without feeling a little surprised. Here at the head of the rustically beautiful valley of the River Nive, 6km from the Spanish border, is a handsome, stoutly fortified town with an important look to it.

Indeed it has been very important. The French name means 'St John at the Foot of the Pass' and this is the northern gateway to the Puerto de Ibañeta, the pass of Ronces-valles (Roncevaux), a funnel for history for centuries. Many of the French pilgrim routes to Santiago de Compostela coalesced here at the final stop before Spain. And through here passed Visigoths, Muslim raiders, Charlemagne, and Basque refugees from the Spanish Civil War.

The town was founded in the 13th century by the last great Basque king, Sancho VII (The Strong) of Navarre, after its predecessor (at present-day St-Jean le Vieux, 5km to the east) was razed by Richard the Lion-Heart (see the boxed text in the History section of the Facts about Southwest France chapter). Jeanne d'Albret's Protestant troops desecrated the town in 1569.

The capital and main market town of the Basse-Navarre has now bitten the golden apple of tourism. In summer it's choked with day-trippers, and residents have a besieged look. Although it's a straightforward day trip from Bayonne, consider staying the night and exploring before breakfast, or come in the low season.

Half the reason for coming is the journey itself, by train or car up the dreamy valley of the Nive. If you want more, rent a bike and head off into the hills.

Orientation

The town centre is place Charles de Gaulle, 500m south of the train station via place du Trinquet, where buses stop. Enter the walled town from place Charles de Gaulle through the old porte de Navarre, or from place du Trinquet through the porte de France, to the medieval main street, rue de la Citadelle. To the left this climbs steeply through the prettiest part of town to the Citadelle. From 2pm to 7pm in summer it's pedestrians-only here.

Information

The tourist office (☎ 05 59 37 03 57, fax 05 59 37 34 91, e saint.jean.pied.de.port@wana doo.fr), 14 place Charles de Gaulle, is open 9.30am to 12.30pm and 2pm to 7pm Monday to Saturday and 10.30am to 12.30pm and 3pm to 6pm Sunday in July and August, and 9.30am to noon and 2pm to 6.30pm Monday to Saturday September to June.

Among banks in the centre with ATMs are Crédit Agricole, up av Renaud from place du Trinquet, and Caisse d'Épargne, near Camping d'Arraddoy.

The post office is just off the road from the train station. Internet access is available for €0.15 per minute at Maison E Bernat (see Places to Stay).

Old Town

The town's ancient heart is at the bottom of rue de la Citadelle by the river. The church leaning heavily against the restored **porte de Notre Dame** gate-tower is the **Église Notre Dame du Bout du Pont** – Our Lady at the End of the Bridge – with foundations as old as the town but thoroughly rebuilt in the 17th century. That's John the Baptist, the town's original patron saint, in the niche on the inner side of the belfry.

From the **Vieux Pont** (Old Bridge) check out the photogenic whitewashed houses with balconies leaning out above the water. Fishing is forbidden where the crystal-clear Nive passes through town, and the fat trout seem to know it. On the other side is the commercial artery of **rue d'Espagne**.

Now climb **rue de la Citadelle**, a gauntlet of bright, well tended 16th- to 18th-century houses trimmed in red or brown, on foundations of pink granite. The lintels of many are carved with the date of construction (the oldest is 1510).

A common motif is the scallop shell, symbol of the pilgrims of Compostela. Pilgrims would enter the town at the top, through the **porte de St-Jacques** (part of Unesco's list of Compostela-related World Heritage Sites), and some days later leave for Spain – refreshed and probably a little poorer – through the **porte d'Espagne** on the other side of the river.

La Citadelle

From the top of rue de la Citadelle, a rough cobblestone path climbs to the massive Citadelle, offering fine views of the town, the Nive and the surrounding hills. Often attributed to Vauban, the fortress was actually completed in 1628 before the great man was born, although his military engineers beefed

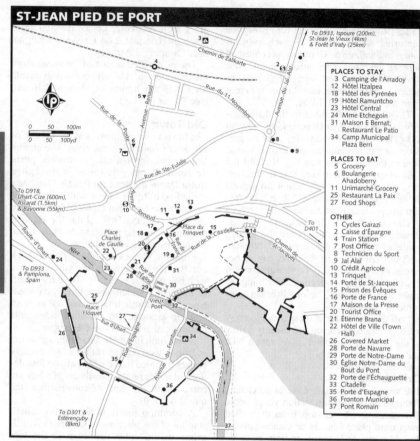

ST-JEAN PIED DE PORT

To D933, Ispoure (200m),
St-Jean le Vieux (4km)
& Forêt d'Iraty (25km)

Chemin de Zalikarte

Rue du 11-Novembre

Avenue du Jaï-Alaï

Rue-de-la-Poste

Rue de Ste-Eulalie

Avenue Renaud

To D918,
Uhart-Cize (600m),
Ascarat (1.5km)
& Bayonne (55km)

Place
Charles
de Gaulle

Nive

Route d'Uhart

To D933
& Pamplona,
Spain

Place du
Trinquet

Rue de la Citadelle

Chemin de
St-Jacques

To
D401

Rue de l'Église

Rue d'Espagne

Vieux
Pont

Place
Floquet

Rue d'Uhart

Avenue du Fronton

To D301 &
Estérençuby
(8km)

PLACES TO STAY
3 Camping de l'Arradoy
12 Hôtel Itzalpea
18 Hôtel des Pyrénées
19 Hôtel Ramuntcho
23 Hôtel Central
24 Mme Etchegoin
31 Maison E Bernat;
   Restaurant Le Patio
34 Camp Municipal
   Plaza Berri

PLACES TO EAT
5 Grocery
6 Boulangerie
   Ahadoberry
11 Unimarché Grocery
25 Restaurant La Paix
27 Food Shops

OTHER
1 Cycles Garazi
2 Caisse d'Épargne
4 Train Station
7 Post Office
8 Technicien du Sport
9 Jaï Alaï
10 Crédit Agricole
13 Trinquet
14 Porte de St-Jacques
15 Prison des Évêques
16 Porte de France
17 Maison de la Presse
20 Tourist Office
21 Étienne Brana
22 Hôtel de Ville (Town
   Hall)
26 Covered Market
28 Porte de Navarre
29 Porte de Notre-Dame
30 Église Notre-Dame du
   Bout du Pont
32 Porte de l'Échauguette
33 Citadelle
35 Porte d'Espagne
36 Fronton Municipal
37 Pont Romain

0   50   100m
0   50   100yd

it up around 1680. Under renovation for years, it presently serves as a high school.

A more interesting route up is from the river just behind the church, through the Gothic **porte de l'Échauguette** (Watchtower Gate) and up a narrow staircase clinging to mossy ramparts that predate the Citadelle.

The tourist office runs **fortress tours** (*€1.50, child under 12 free*) every Friday morning.

Prison des Évêques

The so-called Bishops' Prison, a vaulted cellar that is now a museum (☎ 05 59 37 03 57,

41 rue de la Citadelle; adult €2.30, child under 12 free; open 10am-12.30pm & 3pm-6pm daily Easter–mid-Oct), is a bit of Gothic hyperbole. It certainly feels like a dungeon, with damp walls and one tiny, barred window, and dates from the 13th century when St-Jean Pied de Port was a bishopric of the Avignon papacy. But the building above it dates from the 16th century, by which time the bishops were gone. It did serve as town jail from 1795, and a military brig from the 19th century. In WWII the Germans used it to intern people caught trying to flee to Spain and North Africa.

Pont Romain
This pretty stone bridge on the pastoral outskirts of the town, 500m upriver from the Vieux Pont, is a perfect picnic spot, though it's probably not Roman (what you see dates from the 17th century).

Walking & Cycling
This is a splendid place from which to walk or cycle into the Pyrénéan foothills, where the loudest sounds you'll hear are cowbells and the wind. The GR10 and the GR65 pass right through town.

The tourist office sells an excellent French-language booklet (€6.10) describing and mapping 25 walking and cycling routes from St-Jean Pied de Port and surrounding towns into the Vallées de Garazi, including the beech woods of the **Forêt d'Iraty**, 25km south-east on the Spanish border. Also available is a more basic free brochure.

The Maison de la Presse, at 23 place Charles de Gaulle, has every IGN map you could want.

You can bring bicycles free of charge on certain trains from Bayonne and cycle back down, or you can hire a bike locally (see Getting Around later in this section).

Special Events
Five summer **handicraft and food fairs** take place in the covered market: on the third Tuesday in July; on the Wednesday of the following week; and on the first, second and fourth Tuesdays of August.

The fronton municipal hosts a festival of **force Basque** (see the introduction to this chapter) on the third Sunday in July. See under Entertainment for additional, weekly Basque games. In July and August, **Basque music and dancing** feature at the jaï alaï at 9.30pm on Thursday.

Places to Stay
Camping There are several camping options in and around the town.

Camp Municipal Plaza Berri (☎ 05 59 37 11 19, av du Fronton) Adult/pitch/car €2/1.20/1.20. Open Easter-Sept. How about camping inside the old town walls? You can do it at this shady, riverside camp site.

Camping de l'Arradoy (☎ 05 59 37 11 75, 4 chemin de Zalikarte) Adult/pitch/car €1.85/1.50/0.75. Open Mar-Sept. This camp site, shady but small and overcrowded, is near the train station.

About 2km north-west down the D918 at Ascarat are two large, well equipped sites with pools: *Camping de la Truite* (☎ 05 59 37 31 22, route de Bayonne), open mid-June to mid-September, at €2/1.50 per adult/pitch; and *Camping Narbaïtz* (☎ 05 59 37 10 13, fax 05 59 37 21 42, route de Bayonne), open March to September, at €11.90 for a two-person forfait.

Gîtes d'Étape & Chambres d'Hôtes
There's a heavy emphasis here on hostel and B&B accommodation, for both walkers and pilgrims, and the tourist office maintains a long list of non-hotel accommodation.

Mme Etchegoin (☎ 05 59 37 12 08, 9 route d'Uhart) Dorm beds €7.60. Open year round. This favourite gîte d'étape is just beyond the old town walls on the Bayonne road.

Maison E Bernat (☎ 05 59 37 24 07, fax 05 59 37 23 10, ✉ elmh@wanadoo.fr, 20 rue de la Citadelle) Rooms with WC & bath €48.80-61, breakfast included. This carefully restored house (built 1662) has four rooms, finished to the smallest detail; a hillside garden; a generous breakfast with homemade pastries and preserves; and a first-rate restaurant, *Le Patio* (see Places to Eat).

Hotels St-Jean is oversupplied with hotels, whose high rates increase in July and August. Rooms are generally similar in all the lower-end places.

Hôtel Itzalpea (☎ 05 59 37 03 66, fax 05 59 37 33 18, 5 place du Trinquet) Doubles/twins with WC & shower €33.55/38.10. Breakfast €6.10. This is good value in its range, with well kept rooms and a modest restaurant.

Hôtel Ramuntcho (☎ 05 59 37 03 91, fax 05 59 37 35 17, 1 rue de France) Doubles with WC & shower €40.40-55.65. This Logis de France is the only hotel within the old walls, and consequently the quietest.

Hôtel Central (☎ 05 59 37 00 22, fax 05 59 37 27 79, 1 place Charles de Gaulle) Doubles €50.30-74.70. Breakfast €7.45.

Open March-mid Dec. The back rooms at this venerable hotel look out on the Nive.

Hôtel des Pyrénées (☎ *05 59 37 01 01, fax 05 59 37 18 97, 19 place Charles de Gaulle)* Doubles €88.40-144.80. This is a top-of-the-line hotel, with deluxe rooms to match the acclaimed *restaurant (see Places to Eat)*.

Places to Eat

Restaurants & Brasseries This is a town that seems to have more eateries than street corners. Every hotel also has a restaurant, though only a few rise above 'adequate'.

Restaurant La Paix (☎ *05 59 37 00 99, 4 place Floquet)* Menus €10.35-21.05. Open July-Aug. Budgeteers will like this place, with salads and pizzas for around €6, plus accessible versions of French and Basque regional cooking.

Restaurant Le Patio (Maison E Bernat; see Places to Stay) Menus €14.95-25.15. Open midday & evening daily July-Aug; midday Fri-Mon & evening Fri-Sat Apr-June & Sept. You'd never know it from outside (or the prices) but the small restaurant here has food, prepared with fresh local ingredients, to rival anything in town.

Hôtel Itzalpea (see Places to Stay) Menus €10.65-14.50. Open daily (except Sat Sept-June). Among the town's abundant hotel restaurants, this family-friendly one comes up with tasty regional dishes for quite reasonable prices.

Hôtel Ramuntcho (see Places to Stay) Menus €10.06-15.55. Open Thur-Tues. Good French and Basque dishes are priced surprisingly modestly at this Logis de France hotel restaurant.

Hôtel des Pyrénées (see Places to Stay) Menus €36.60-79.25. Open daily except Mon evening & Tue Nov-Mar, and except Tue Apr-June; closed mid-Nov–mid-Dec & most of Jan. The price is no typo: The restaurant here has two Michelin stars, and the *menus* of classical French and Basque cuisine are priced to match.

Self-Catering St-Jean Pied de Port's *weekly market* is held in place Charles de Gaulle on Monday (or Tuesday if Monday

is a holiday). Small *groceries* at 35 av Renaud and on place du Trinquet are open until 7.30pm (to at least 12.30pm at the weekend). *Boulangerie Ahadoberry (2 rue de la Poste)* stays open until 8pm (to 1pm Sunday). Several other *food shops* are along rue d'Espagne.

Spectator Sports

There's a busy line-up of **pelote Basque** matches (see under Basque Games earlier in this chapter) year round, including main nue at the trinquet at 5pm Monday; joko garbi at the fronton municipal at 9.30pm Wednesday; grand chistera at the fronton municipal at 5pm Friday; and cesta punta at the jaï alaï at 9pm Saturday. Tickets cost about €8.

A two-hour **course landaise** (see Spectator Sports in the Facts for the Visitor chapter) takes place at the jaï alaï at 9pm every Monday from mid-July to early September.

Shopping

The town is awash with 'Basque souvenir' shops, but a better investment is a few bottles of the region's good Irouléguy white, rosé and red wines. A local grower, Domaine Brana, has its own shop, *Étienne Brana* (☎ *05 59 37 00 44, rue d'Église; open 10am-noon & 2.30pm-6.30pm, Mon-Fri 15-30 June & 1-15 Sept; daily July-Aug)*, where you can taste before you buy.

Getting There & Away

The best way to get here from Bayonne is by train, a lovely trip beside the Nive to the end of the line (€7.15, one hour), with at least two daily trains, and another daily except Sunday in July and August – an easy day trip if you leave Bayonne by about 9am (times vary from season to season). Getting here by bus is a headache, as you must go via St-Palais, 30km out of your way.

Getting Around

VTTs can be hired from Cycles Garazi (☎ 05 59 37 21 79, 1 place St-Laurent). Another source of VTTs is Technicien du Sport (☎ 05 59 37 15 98), just down the road at 18 av du Jaï Alaï.

Béarn

The history and culture of the ancient province of Béarn are as un-French as those of the Basque country, but the Béarnais – being landlocked, fairly modest and without tendencies to terrorism – are less well known in the wider world. They dislike it if you confuse Béarn with the French Basque country, or lump them together. The language of their ancestors is a cousin of Occitan, not of Basque. Béarn had Catholicism imposed upon it, while the Basques embraced it.

But it's no accident that Béarn is lumped together with the French Basque Country in the same *département* (administrative department), that of Pyrénées-Atlantiques. Had the viscounts of Béarn not got their act together early on, this might well be Basque Country too. The Béarnais, like the Basques, have historical links south of the border, and their traditions have been shaped by the mountains. They certainly have a distrust of outside authority equal to the Basques, and the men wear berets at their festivals as comfortably as the Basques do (indeed most 'Basque' berets are made in the Béarn!).

Béarn's biggest attractions for tourists are the mountains and the activities available in them: trekking above all, plus river sports, skiing, cycling, horse riding and fishing.

This chapter also includes the world-famous pilgrimage centre of Lourdes. Although Lourdes falls within the neighbouring Hautes-Pyrénées department, it's an easy drive or bus ride from Pau.

Orientation

Béarn has three traditional parts: Béarn des Gaves, the lowlands along its main rivers, the Gave de Pau and Gave d'Oloron (*gave* is Béarnaise for river); the Marches de Béarn, hilly and dotted with castles, like the Gers; and the mountainous Haut-Béarn. Béarn's capital, Pau, sits beside the Gave de Pau.

History

Béarn first appears in history in 820, with the conquest of the region by Charlemagne

Highlights

- Admit the Needles of Ansabère can't be captured on film and just savour one of the southwest's most stupendously photogenic spots, at Lescun
- Get lost in the 13th century in the gentle fortified town of Sauveterre de Béarn
- Eavesdrop on the family life of a vulture at Aste-Béon
- Go parasailing at picturesque Accous, one of the Pyrénées' main venues for the sport
- Ponder the visions of St Bernadette at Lourdes

- Pau p359
- Oloron-Ste-Marie p368
- Lourdes p383

Food Highlights
poule au pot – traditional Pyrénéan dish of chicken stuffed with vegetables

brebis d'Ossau – superb summer-season sheep's cheese

Jurançon – fruity white wines (dry or sweet) from south-west of Pau

✳ ✳ ✳ ✳ ✳ ✳ ✳ ✳ ✳ ✳ ✳ ✳

and the founding of a viscountcy, with its capital at Lescar. Before long the title had become hereditary. Many of its holders seem to have been named Gaston.

When Lescar was sacked by the Moors in 841 the capital was moved to Morlaás. The first important Gaston was Gaston IV, who in the early 11th century signed a charter called

BÉARN

BÉARN

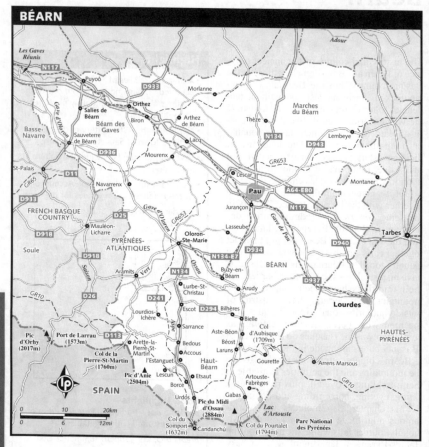

the *For de Morlaás,* establishing the limitations of the law and setting, for centuries to come, the tone of Béarnais distrust of central authority. Gaston VII de Moncade moved the capital to Orthez in the late 13th century.

In 1290 the House of Foix (in the Ariège) absorbed the viscountcy through marriage. The best known Gaston was Gaston the Hunter (1331–91), also called Gaston Fébus (the Golden) for his long blonde locks. This was the Gaston who moved the capital to Pau.

By the 16th century, judicious marriages had given a minor Gascon family named

d'Albret control of the lands and titles of Foix, Basse-Navarre and Béarn. Henri d'Albret and Marguerite d'Angoulême were the parents of Jeanne d'Albret, who – as the staunchly Calvinist queen of Navarre – was to have a major hand in prolonging France's Wars of Religion.

Jeanne's son was Henri of Navarre, the future Henri IV of France. Even on the throne, Henri would regard Béarn as a separate kingdom. But his son, Louis XIII, finally seized it in the name of France in 1620 and filled it with Catholic settlers and monasteries.

Pau

**postcode 64000 • pop 90,000
• elevation 207m**

Pau (pronounced po), capital of Béarn and prefecture of the Pyrénées-Atlantiques department, is famed for its mild climate, flower-filled public parks and magnificent views of the Pyrénées. In the 19th century it was a favourite wintering spot for wealthy English and Americans, and is proud of its Anglophone heritage.

The city owes its present prosperity to a high-tech industrial base, the huge natural gas field at Lacq, 20km to the north-west, and an abundance of Spanish tourists and shoppers. If French highway planners have their way (see Vallée d'Aspe later in this chapter), it may one day become an important gateway city from Spain.

Though it has some of the roughness of a city twice its size, Pau is still an agreeable place to visit, well supplied with cheap hotels, and an obvious base for forays into the mountains.

HISTORY

For centuries a feature of life here has been transhumance – the seasonal movement of livestock between lowlands north of the Gave de Pau and summer pastures in the Pyrénées (see the boxed text 'Transhumance & Cheese' later in this chapter). Pau began as a stockade at an easy ford of the river, and by the 11th century the town was important enough for the count of Foix to build a castle there.

Strategic marriages gradually transformed the family into an important dynasty in southern France. In the 14th century Gaston Fébus enlarged the castle, fortified the town and eventually made it Béarn's capital. By 1484 it presided over the entire kingdom of Navarre – and then in 1512 lost everything south of the Pyrénées to Ferdinand of Aragon.

After the Revolution of 1789, the English handed Napoleon a major defeat near Orthez in 1814 and, while they were here, discovered the charms of Pau (see the boxed text 'Anglophone Pau'). Over the next 75 years the town grew into an international winter resort. The Great Depression put an end to the fun and by WWII Pau was lost in obscurity.

A surge in wartime and postwar industrial development gave Pau a new lease of life, and its population quadrupled in 20 years. Its greatest expansion dates from the 1960s, since when the population has again quadrupled. But thanks to a legacy of gardens – both monastic and English – it boasts an extraordinarily high per capita endowment of green space.

ORIENTATION

Pau's ancient heart is the *vieille ville* (old town) beside Gaston Fébus' chateau. Its axis is the thoroughfare of rue Maréchal Joffre, rue Maréchal Foch and cours Bosquet. The 'English' centre is the promenade along blvd des Pyrénées, with its Cinemascope views of the mountains.

Long-distance and local buses converge on place Clémenceau, the train station is just below the promenade by the river and the airport is 10km north-west of the centre.

INFORMATION
Tourist Offices

The tourist office (☎ 05 59 27 27 08, fax 05 59 27 03 21, e omt@ville-pau.fr), on place Royale, is open 9am to 6pm daily in July and August; and 9am to 12.30pm and 1.30pm to 6pm Monday to Friday (to 5.30pm Saturday, and 9am to 1pm Sunday September to June). A good free resource here is the *Béarn Guide des Loisirs,* a detailed summary of almost everything there is to do in the area.

For general information about the Béarn, visit the Pau office of the Comité Départemental du Tourisme Béarn-Pays Basque (☎ 05 59 30 01 30, fax 05 59 84 10 13, e cdt @cg64.fr), at 22 ter rue JJ-de-Monaix, open 8.30am to 12.30pm and 2pm to 6pm Monday to Thursday (until 5pm Friday).

Money

Rue Maréchal Foch and its eastern and western extensions are lined with banks, all with ATMs and/or exchange facilities. Exchange

BÉARN

Anglophone Pau

The first British to 'discover' Pau were Wellington's soldiers, fresh from thrashing Napoleon at Orthez in 1814. Many soon returned as tourists and some retired here. After falling ill with typhus, a Scots physician named Alexander Taylor came here, kicked it in three weeks and in 1842 wrote enthusiastically of Pau's curative climate.

Upper-class Britons flooded in and by the 1850s were numerous enough to dominate local society. They built the blvd des Pyrénées promenade and scores of grand villas. They gave Pau a taste for fine gardens and for sports – steeplechase, polo, fox hunting, angling, tennis – and in 1856 founded the Continent's first golf club. They gave France its first gas-lamps and its first sewer system.

Americans arrived soon afterwards and by the 1860s formed a substantial community. At its peak, the foreign population was perhaps 10,000.

When Queen Victoria's attention turned to Biarritz and the seaside, off went the English, leaving Anglophone Pau to the Scots, Welsh and especially the Americans. Two Americans whose careers took off here were the Wright brothers, attracted by Pau's almost windless climate. In 1908 they founded the world's first flying school and an aeroplane factory here – perhaps sowing the seeds for the region's current prominence in aeronautics.

The entire expatriate community fled in the Great Depression. But to this day, a segment of upper-class Béarnaise society still hunts foxes and plays golf at exclusive clubs, and Pau has a high per-centage of English speakers. The Pau Golf Club (at Billère, about 3.5km to the west of the city centre) is straight out of upper-class England, right down to the cravats and cashmere.

The big estates of the English and Americans were sold off for smaller villas, but many of the old mansions, especially in the surrounding hills, survived. Several big English gardens survive as parks, such as **Parc Beaumont** and **Parc Lawrence**.

The city's grand old hotels have been chopped into flats, for example, the **Hôtel de France** on place Royale – which once welcomed the likes of the Prince of Wales and the King of Spain – and the **Hôtel de Gassion** on blvd des Pyrénées.

Rue Gaston Fébus was a typical middle-class neighbourhood in the 19th century. The **Église St-André** (Church of St Andrew), on rue O'Quinn, is still Church of England, part of the Gibraltar diocese.

services are also available at the main post office.

Post & Communications

The main post office is at 21 cours Bosquet.

Pau's cheapest Internet access costs €3.05 per hour, at Logis Michel Hounau (☎ 05 59 27 44 59), a workers' hostel at 30 ter rue Michel Hounau, open 9am to 10pm daily. At €3.80 per hour is Cyber Coyote (☎ 05 59 27 04 03), 11 rue Duboué, open 10am to 8pm weekdays, 10am to 2am Saturday and 2pm to 8pm Sunday. Two others charge €4.55 per hour and keep hours similar to Coyote's: L'Arobase (☎ 05 59 98 44 16), 5 rue Mathieu Lalanne, and Cyber Café (☎ 05 59 98 06 17), 20 rue Lamothe. Pricier alternatives are the Cyberposte terminal at the post office and the pay-by-card terminal at the tourist office.

Bookshops

One of Southwest France's most complete bookshops for walkers and travellers is the Librairie des Pyrénées (☎ 05 59 27 78 75), 14 rue St-Louis, which also has a back room devoted to the Occitan language. Librairie Marrimpouey (☎ 05 59 27 52 11), 2 place de la Liberation, is Southwest France's oldest 'cultural' bookshop, full of resources on re-gional languages and traditions (in French). Both shops are open until 7pm, Monday to Saturday.

Universities

The Universitaire de Pau et de Pays de l'Adour has some 50,000 students, most of them at a spacious campus 2km north of the centre (from place Clémenceau take bus No 4 to the Facultés or Cité Universitaire stop;

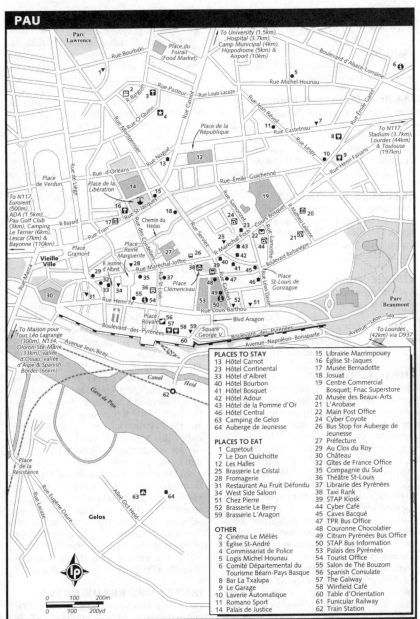

PAU

PLACES TO STAY
13 Hôtel Carnot
23 Hôtel Continental
33 Hôtel d'Albret
40 Hôtel Bourbon
41 Hôtel Bosquet
42 Hôtel Adour
43 Hôtel de la Pomme d'Or
46 Hôtel Central
63 Camping de Gelos
64 Auberge de Jeunesse

PLACES TO EAT
1 Capetout
7 Le Don Quichotte
12 Les Halles
25 Brasserie Le Cristal
Fromagerie
31 Restaurant Au Fruit Défondu
34 West Side Saloon
51 Chez Pierre
52 Brasserie Le Berry
59 Brasserie L'Aragon

OTHER
2 Cinéma Le Méliès
3 Église St-André
4 Commissariat de Police
5 Logis Michel Hounau
6 Comité Départemental du
Tourisme Béarn-Pays Basque
8 Bar La Txalupa
9 Le Garage
10 Laverie Automatique
11 Romano Sport
14 Palais de Justice

15 Librairie Marrimpouey
16 Église St-Jaques
17 Musée Bernadotte
18 Josuat
19 Centre Commercial
Bosquet; Fnac Superstore
20 Musée des Beaux-Arts
21 L'Arobase
22 Main Post Office
24 Cyber Coyote
26 Bus Stop for Auberge de
Jeunesse
27 Préfecture
29 Au Clos du Roy
30 Château
32 Gîtes de France Office
35 Compagnie du Sud
36 Théâtre St-Louis
37 Librairie des Pyrénées
38 Taxi Rank
39 STAP Kiosk
44 Cyber Café
45 Caves Bacqué
47 TPR Bus Office
48 Couronne Chocolatier
49 Citram Pyrénées Bus Office
50 STAP Bus Information
53 Palais des Pyrénées
54 Tourist Office
55 Salon de Thé Bouzom
56 Spanish Consulate
57 The Galway
58 Winfield Café
60 Table d'Orientation
61 Funicular Railway
62 Train Station

BÉARN

alternatively, take No 2 or 6 to the Commune de Paris, Leclerc or Monge stop).

Laundry

Laverie Automatique, 66 rue Émile Garet, is open 7am to 8pm daily.

Medical Services & Emergency

The Centre Hospitalier (hospital; ☎ 05 59 92 48 48), 4.5km north-east of the city centre at 4 blvd Hauterive, is the last stop on the northbound Nos 3 and 6 bus lines. The Commissariat de Police (☎ 05 59 98 22 22) is north of the city centre on rue O'Quinn.

PYRÉNÉES PANORAMA

From blvd des Pyrénées on a clear day you can see a breathtaking panorama of Pyrénéan peaks. Opposite No 20 is a *table d'orientation* to tell you where you are and what you're looking at.

VIEILLE VILLE

Pau has preserved little of its labyrinthine old centre – an area no more than 300m in diameter – but what is left is dignified and handsome, full of restored medieval and Renaissance buildings, and streets that cross over and under one another.

CHÂTEAU DE PAU

Gaston Fébus' 14th-century castle was transformed into a Renaissance chateau and surrounded by gardens by Marguerite d'Angoulême in the 16th century. Marguerite's grandson, the future Henri IV, was born here. Neglected in the 18th century and used as a barracks after the Revolution, the chateau was a mess by 1838, when King Louis-Philippe ordered a complete interior renovation, which was then completed by Napoleon III.

The result is a chilly, unconvincing imitation of medieval and Renaissance architecture, now open as the **Musée National du Château de Pau** (*☎ 05 59 82 38 14, rue du Château; adult/those aged 18-25 €4.10/2.60, child under 18 free, admission free to all 1st Sun of each month; open 9.30am-11.45am & 2pm-4.15pm daily Nov-Mar; 9.30am-11.45am & 2pm-5pm daily Apr–mid-June &*

mid-Sept–Oct; 9.30am-12.15pm & 1.30pm-5.45 daily mid-June–mid-Sept).

Most of the furniture, including an oak dining table big enough to seat 100, dates from this time. The chateau's pride and joy is one of Europe's finest collections of 16th- to 18th-century Gobelins tapestries. In the room where Henri IV was born is an upturned tortoise shell said to have been his cradle.

On the river side of the chateau are a 33m-high brick tower erected by Gaston Fébus, and the medieval, brick-and-stone Tour de la Monnaie.

The chateau is owned by the Ministry of Culture and Communication, whose aim is to preserve it, not to show it off. The entrance fee includes an obligatory, often tedious, one- to two-hour guided tour in rapid French or Spanish (though a printed narrative in English is available).

MUSÉE BERNADOTTE

The Bernadotte Museum (*☎ 05 59 27 48 42, 8 rue Tran; adult/child €1.50/0.75; open 10am-noon & 2pm-6pm Tues-Sun*) is devoted to the curious story of how a French general, born in this building in 1763, became king of Sweden and Norway.

Jean-Baptiste Bernadotte enlisted in the French army at the age of 17 and went on to a distinguished career as a general and diplomat, serving both the Revolutionary government and Napoleon. Sweden was at the time in the throes of a dynastic crisis, and the Riksdag, having concluded that the only solution was to install a foreigner on the throne, turned to Bernadotte, electing him crown prince in 1810.

Against the expectations of Napoleon, Bernadotte did not follow a pro-French line; indeed Swedish troops under his command at the 1813 Battle of Leipzig helped deal Napoleon his first major defeat. In 1818 Bernadotte became King Charles XIV John of Sweden and Norway, dying in office in 1844. The present king of Sweden is the seventh ruler in the Bernadotte dynasty.

MUSÉE DES BEAUX-ARTS

Pau's Fine Arts Museum (*☎ 05 59 27 33 02, enter opposite 15 rue Mathieu Lalanne;*

adult/child & student €1.50/0.75; open 10am-noon & 2pm-6pm Wed-Mon) is one of the southwest's better provincial museums. Among works on display are 17th- to 20th-century European paintings, including some by Rubens, El Greco and Degas.

SPECIAL EVENTS

The **Festival de Pau** is a three-week extravaganza of dance, music and theatre, held from mid-June to early July at the Théâtre St-Louis and other venues. The **Festival de Dance** (modern dance) runs from mid-March to mid-April and the **Festival de Flamenco** for 15 days in early April. Pentecost weekend sees the **Formula 3000 Grand Prix** in the city's streets.

PLACES TO STAY

Pau's hotels offer some of France's best value for money. Peak season is April to October – except, curiously, July and August – but you can always find a room if you arrive in the morning.

PLACES TO STAY – BUDGET

Camping There are at least three camp sites in the Pau vicinity.

*Camping Municipal de Gelos (☎ 05 59 06 57 37, fax 05 59 06 38 39, **e** bearn .camping@wanadoo.dr, Base de Plein Air, Gelos)* Bus No 1 from place Clémenceau to Mairie de Gelos stop. Adult/tent/car €2.60/3.80/0.90. Open June-Sept. Small and functional, this camp site across the river in Gelos region has basic facilities and a bar-cafe.

Camp Municipal de la Plaine des Sports et des Loisirs (☎ 05 59 02 30 49, fax 05 59 82 85 55, blvd du Cami-Salié) Bus No 4 to end of line. Adult/pitch €2.65/5.10. Open June–mid-Sept. This crowded, no-frills camp site is 4km north of the town centre, in the shadow of the massive Palais des Sports.

*Camping Le Terrier (☎ 05 59 81 01 82, fax 05 59 81 26 83, **e** camping.terrier@ wanadoo.fr, av du Vert Galant)* Bus No 8 to Laou stop plus 1.5km walk. Adult/pitch €3.80/4.90. Open year round. Spacious, shady Le Terrier, 7km west beside the Gave de Pau, is the most comfortable option near Pau. Facilities include a pool and cafe.

Hostels In summer, one *university dormitory* in the complex at the north-west corner of the campus (the modern-looking one at the east end of the row) is open to non-French students with student ID.

*Auberge de Jeunesse (☎ 05 59 06 53 02, fax 05 59 11 05 20, **e** fjt@ldjpau.org, Base de Plein Air, Gelos)* Dorm beds €8.10 with breakfast. Reception 4pm-11pm; open year round. The hostel, beside Camping de Gelos (see Camping), was temporarily closed for renovation at the time of writing.

Rural Accommodation The tourist office keeps a list of nearby *chambres d'hôte* (B&Bs), *gîtes d'étape* (basic accommodation for hikers and pilgrims) and *campings à la ferme* (camping on farm fields).

*Gîtes de France (☎ 05 59 11 20 64, fax 05 59 11 20 60, **e** gites.de.france64@wanadoo .fr, **w** www.gites-de-france-64.com, Maison de l'Agriculture, 20 rue Gassion)* Open 8.30am-6pm Mon-Sat. You can stop here for information on, and help with, rural accommodation and tailormade holidays in the Pyrénées-Atlantiques department.

Hotels Centrally located, budget hotels include the following.

Hôtel d'Albret (☎/fax 05 59 27 81 58, 11 rue Jeanne d'Albret) Rooms with/without shower €18.30/13.70, with shower & WC €22.10. Breakfast €2.75. This family-run hotel is the town centre's best lower-end bargain, a clean, well tended place with big rooms and friendly folks.

Hôtel de la Pomme d'Or (☎ 05 59 11 23 23, fax 05 59 11 23 24, 11 rue Maréchal Foch) Doubles €15.25-18.30, with shower €19.05-22.85, with shower & WC €20.60-24.40. Breakfast €3.05. Credit cards not accepted. The Pomme d'Or is the cheapest acceptable option in Pau. You couldn't ask for anything more central, though walls are thin.

Hôtel Carnot (☎ 05 59 27 88 70, 13 rue Carnot) Singles €15.30-16.80, doubles/twins €18.95/20.50. Breakfast €3.35. Plain but spacious rooms at this friendly, no-frills hotel are good value. Rooms do not come with shower or WC.

BÉARN

PLACES TO STAY – MID-RANGE & TOP END

Two clean, characterless places offering doubles with shower for €33.55 (€38.85/41.15 with WC & shower/bath) face one another in the town centre: *Hôtel Adour* (☎ 05 59 27 47 41, fax 05 59 83 86 49, 10 rue Valéry Meunier) and *Hôtel Bosquet* (☎ 05 59 27 76 38, 11 rue Valéry Meunier).

Hôtel Central (☎ 05 59 27 72 75, fax 05 59 27 33 28, 15 rue Léon Daran) Singles €28.20-42.70, doubles €36.60-47.25, twins €41.15-53.35. Breakfast €5.35. The Central has large, plain but well tended doubles; double-glazing keeps street noise at bay. All rooms have WC and shower.

Hôtel Bourbon (☎ 05 59 27 53 12, fax 05 59 92 80 99, 12 place Clémenceau) Doubles with shower & WC €48.80, doubles/twins with bath & WC €50.30/51.85. Breakfast €5.80. This central hotel offers very comfortable rooms, some with air-conditioning.

Hôtel Continental (☎ 05 59 27 69 31, fax 05 59 27 99 84, 2 rue Maréchal Foch) Doubles €61/83.85 with WC & shower/bath. Breakfast €6.10 (buffet €9.15). This is as good as it gets in Pau, a three-star Best Western operation, stuffy but posh.

PLACES TO EAT
Brasseries

Pau has some good brasseries that won't break your budget.

Brasserie Le Cristal (☎ 05 59 27 61 08, 20 rue Maréchal Foch) Dishes €3.35-5.35. Open Mon-Sat. Simple, stylish Le Cristal is a handy lunch oasis, with omelettes, quiches, sandwiches and good pastries as well as quick service.

Brasserie Le Berry (☎ 05 59 27 42 95, 4 rue Gachet) Specialities €6.85-22.85. Open midday & evening daily. The Berry is top value, with Béarnaise specialities, lots of fish dishes under €12 and cheery, professional service. It keeps restaurant-like hours and it has a loyal clientele, so arrive early (noon to 2pm lunch, 7.30pm to 11pm dinner).

Brasserie L'Aragon (☎ 05 59 27 12 43, 18 blvd des Pyrénées) Cold entrees & salads €7.75-11.90, meat platters €10.35-22.55, seafood platters €14.95-30.35. Open daily.

Popular and professional, this brasserie does very good French and international dishes. Keep your budget intact with the €8.85 midday special.

Restaurants – French

Spanish influence may account for unnervingly late dinnertimes here; most restaurants remain deserted until after 8pm.

Capetout (☎ 05 59 62 40 34, 3 rue Viard) Menus €21.35. Tiny Capetout, in a nowhere neighbourhood north of the centre, may be the best place in Pau for an introduction to high-quality, traditional Béarnaise cooking. Opening hours and days are unpredictable, however, so call ahead.

Restaurant Au Fruit Défondu (☎ 05 59 27 26 05, 3 rue Sully) Fondues €11.60-14.50, *pierrades* €12.95-14.50, *menus* (set menus) €17.05-22.85. Open evenings daily. For a change, try cheese, fish or chocolate fondue or grill-it-yourself *pierrades* here.

Chez Pierre (☎ 05 59 27 76 86, 16 rue Louis Barthou) Menus €30.50. Open midday & evening Mon-Fri, evening Sat. This is the highest-rated French restaurant in town. For a treat, try lobster and saffron *cassoulet* (casserole).

Restaurants – International

Pau's international fare includes:

Le Don Quichotte (☎ 05 59 27 63 08, 30 rue Castetnau) Main dishes €4.90-7.30, combination plates €8.85. Open midday Tues-Fri, evening Mon-Sat. A nice change of pace is this tiny restaurant, plastered with bullfight posters and serving sparky Basque and Spanish dishes and snacks.

West Side Saloon (☎ 05 59 82 90 78, 5 place Reine Marguerite) Menus €12.95, Mexican combination plates €10.35-11. Open 9am-2am Mon-Sat. Over the years this place has shifted from all-American to Tex-Mex, but you can still get a good burger (€8.85-9.90) or salad (€5.50-7.60). Mexican beers are available.

Le Garage (☎ 05 59 83 75 17, 49 rue Émile Garet) Menus €6.10-6.85. Open 6pm-1am daily. Le Garage is mainly a bar, filling student tummies with Tex-Mex and other food every evening.

BÉARN

Self-Catering
Les Halles, the big covered market on place de la République, is open Monday to Saturday (closed 1pm to 3.30pm except Saturday). On Wednesday and Saturday morning there's also a *food market* at place du Foirail.

A central supermarket is **Champion**, in the Centre Commercial Bosquet at 14 cours Bosquet. Several *food shops* cluster around place Reine Marguerite in the old town, and there is also a good *fromagerie* at 24 rue Maréchal Joffre.

ENTERTAINMENT
Pubs & Bars
The centre of student nightlife is a laid-back zone known as *le Triangle*, bounded by rue Henri Faisans, rue Émile Garet and rue Castelnau. One or more bars may offer live music at the weekend, and they all stay open until 2am. Being student hangouts they have a sizable concentration of English speakers, and there's nothing touristy about them.

Le Garage *(see Places to Eat)* Open 6pm-2am daily. Irish-owned Le Garage is probably the best of the lot. It's straightforward, friendly and open to the street. Tex-Mex food also supplements the beer until 1am.

Bar La Txalupa (☎ 05 59 98 06 73, 34 rue Émile Garet) This bodega-style bar is done all in wood and shaped like an upturned boat.

On blvd des Pyrénées is a line of decidedly touristy but welcoming cafe-bars open all day and until 2am nightly. The best choices are a self-styled Australian bar called the **Winfield Café** (☎ 05 59 27 80 60, 20 blvd des Pyrénées) and an Irish-style pub, **The Galway** (☎ 05 59 82 94 66, 20 blvd des Pyrénées).

There aren't many appealing bars in the town centre, and the ones in the old town are pricey, but a good spot in between is the **West Side Saloon** *(see Places to Eat)*, open 9am to 2am Monday to Saturday with good beer, Tex-Mex decor and food.

Classical Music & Dance
The main venue in the town centre is

Théâtre St-Louis (☎ 05 59 27 85 80, 1 rue St-Louis), around the corner from the tourist office. Tickets can be purchased at the box office or the tourist office.

Cinema
For cinema with nondubbed English films, try the following.

Cinéma Le Méliès (☎ 05 59 27 60 52, 6 rue Bargoin) Tickets adult/student/child €5.35/4.25/3.05, €4.25 for all on Wed, €3.35 for all after 10pm. Closed mid-July–mid-Aug.

SPECTATOR SPORTS
Pau is France's biggest horse-training centre after Chantilly in Paris, and horse racing and steeplechase are big here. The **Hippodrome du Pont Long** (☎ 05 59 13 07 07, blvd du Cami-Salié) is 5km north of the city centre; take bus No 3 (direction Perlic) to the Hippodrome stop. The horse-racing season is from late autumn to March.

Rugby union is popular, with matches played at a stadium 4km north-east of the city centre; ask the tourist office about upcoming matches. Tickets are available at the Fnac superstore at the Centre Commercial Bosquet (see Shopping).

SHOPPING
Pau's trendiest shops are along rue des Cordeliers and rue Serviez. Another place for general shopping is the big Centre Commercial Bosquet at 14 cours Bosquet.

Two *caves* (cellars) where you can taste and buy the area's best-known wine, Jurançon (for details refer to the special section on Food & Wine), are **Au Clos du Roy** (☎ 05 59 98 48 02, 50 rue Maréchal Joffre) and **Caves Bacqué** (☎ 05 59 27 31 95, 1 place St-Louis de Gonzague).

Pau, like Bayonne, has a sweet-tooth. Two of the city's best chocolatiers are **Couronne** (☎ 05 59 82 83 77, 20 Palais des Pyrénées) and **Josuat** (☎ 05 59 27 65 67, 23 rue Serviez).

Salon de Thé Bouzom (☎ 05 59 27 70 88, 6 rue Henri IV) Open Tues-Sun. Treat yourself to sublime *chocolat chaud* (hot chocolate) here.

BÉARN

GETTING THERE & AWAY
Air
The Pau-Pyrénées airport (also known as Uzein; ☎ 05 59 33 33 00) is 10km northwest of central Pau. Air France flies directly to Paris at least six times daily; for details see the Getting There & Away chapter.

Bus
Eurolines coaches (see the Getting There & Away chapter) stop at the train station.

TPR, with a stand and ticket office (☎ 05 59 82 95 85; open weekdays plus Saturday morning) on rue Gachet, has connections around Béarn and the Basque Country – for example, Bayonne (€13.50, 2¼ hours, three daily except Sunday) via Orthez and Salies de Béarn.

The main operator to the vallée d'Ossau is Citram Pyrénées (☎ 05 59 27 22 22; information office open daily except Monday morning, Saturday afternoon and Sunday) in the Palais des Pyrénées, opposite TPR. Most Citram buses go only as far as Laruns (see the Haut-Béarn section). Citram also goes to Mont de Marsan (€12.65, two hours, one daily except Sunday). Buy tickets on board.

The main operator into the vallée d'Aspe is SNCF, with trains and buses to Oloron-Ste-Marie and buses onwards from there; see under Train.

Train
The information office (☎ 08 36 35 35 35) at the train station is open 9am to 6pm daily. SNCF has four to five trains and three to five buses daily Monday to Saturday (fewer Sunday) via Arudy to Oloron-Ste-Marie – with onward bus connections from Arudy into the vallée d'Ossau and from Oloron-Ste-Marie into the vallée d'Aspe (see Haut-Béarn later in this chapter). Some vallée d'Aspe buses continue to the big Spanish railhead of Canfranc-Estación, from where there are trains to Saragossa and elsewhere in Spain.

Long-haul destinations served by direct trains from Pau include Bayonne (€12.80, 1¼ hours, six daily); Toulouse (€22.55, 2¾ hours, five daily); Dax (€11, 55 minutes) and Bordeaux (€23.80, 2¼ hours), six to nine daily.

Car
Eurorent (☎ 05 59 27 44 41) is at 15 rue d'Étigny. ADA (☎ 05 59 72 94 40), 3 bis route de Bayonne in Billère, will deliver cars to Pau. Citer (☎ 05 59 33 25 00) is at the airport.

GETTING AROUND
To/From the Airport
The only way to get to the airport is by taxi, for about €19 (€23 Sunday). Pau's municipal taxis can be booked at ☎ 05 59 02 22 22, or picked up at the taxi rank on place Clémenceau.

Bus
The local bus company, STAP (☎ 05 59 14 15 16), has an office on rue Gachet and a kiosk at the corner of place Clémenceau (both open 9am to 12.15pm and 1.45pm to 5.30pm weekdays with information, bus maps and tickets). Maps are also available from the tourist office. Bus No 7 links the train station with place Clémenceau, though it's easier to take the funicular (see Funicular Railway).

Local buses run from 6am to at least 7pm daily except Sunday and holidays, and each stops somewhere on place Clémenceau (see the map at the kiosk). Single tickets, sold on board, cost €0.90, and are valid for an hour after they've been time-stamped.

Funicular Railway
The train station is linked to blvd des Pyrénées by a free *funiculaire*, a stately contraption that saves you about four minutes of easy uphill walking. It was built in 1908 by the hotels along blvd des Pyrénées. Cars leave every five minutes 7am to 9pm Monday to Saturday, and 1.30pm to 9pm Sunday.

AROUND PAU
Lescar
postcode 64230 • pop 6000
• elevation 183m
Lescar is today a suburb of Pau, reached via a sea of factories and discount furniture stores. But this was once the heart of Béarn, and its first capital. Its Roman predecessor, Beneharnum, was obliterated by the Vikings but bequeathed its name to Béarn. On a hill

adjacent to the ruins a new town grew from the 10th century.

At the top is a quiet ensemble of old buildings, centred around the Romanesque **Cathédrale Notre Dame** *(☎ 05 59 81 15 98, place Royale; admission free; open 9am-noon & 2pm-6pm daily high season; 9am-noon & 2pm-5pm daily low season; 1½-hour guided tours 3pm Fri and 2pm Sat, €3.05),* completed in 1140. The exterior was smashed during the Wars of Religion, but inside capitals brim with carved foliage, mythical animals and biblical scenes. The apse is tiled with original mosaics, which were rediscovered in the 19th century, with curiously secular subjects like boar-hunting (note the archer with a peg-leg).

Behind the altar are the graves of many princes of Foix-Béarn and kings and queens of Navarre, including Henri II d'Albret and saintly Marguerite d'Angoulême, as well as their daughter Jeanne d'Albret, sword of Calvinism and mother of the future Henri IV of France.

Opposite the north-west entrance, two towers from the 13th and 14th centuries mark the extremities of the bishop's palace, wholly rebuilt in the early 18th century and almost destroyed during the Revolution. Here also is a little archaeological museum.

Just south of the cathedral is the 16th-century **Tour du Presbytère**, now the tourist office (☎ 05 59 81 15 98, fax 05 59 81 12 54), which is open 10am to noon and 2pm to 6pm Monday to Friday (to 5pm Saturday).

Surrounding the whole ensemble are remnants of Lescar's medieval fortifications.

Getting There & Away Lescar is 8km north-west of Pau. From place Clémenceau, STAP's No 9 bus goes there throughout the day (€0.90; Mariotte stop) and TPR's Biarritz buses call by three times daily (once on Sunday from mid-June to August only).

Haut-Béarn

The Pyrénées form a 430km natural boundary between France and Spain. Some of their most spectacular landscapes are in or near the Parc National des Pyrénées (see the boxed text), which runs along the border.

Haut-Béarn (or the vallées Béarnaises), that part of the Pyrénées range lying within the traditional borders of Béarn, is only marginally less dramatic than the central range, and considerably less tamed. The most accessible of its deeply cut valleys, the vallée d'Ossau and the beautiful vallée d'Aspe, converge at Oloron-Ste-Marie. Haut-Béarn's highest peak – and the one that sticks out in every view of the Pyrénées from Béarn and the Gers – is 2884m Pic du Midi d'Ossau, at the head of the vallée d'Ossau.

From the railway line between Pau and Oloron-Ste-Marie, bus services run into both valleys (see Getting There & Away under Vallée d'Aspe and Vallée d'Ossau).

ACTIVITIES

The possibilities will make your head spin. Before you set out, visit a tourist office for the free French-language booklets *Béarn: Guide Loisirs* and *Béarn et Pays Basque: Randonnées de Rêve,* stuffed with ideas for things to do and people to help you do them.

Walking

The two valleys are laced with hundreds of kilometres of walking trails – including the GR10 and GR653 – some of which link up with trails in Spain.

The upper valleys are dotted with *refuges* (basic hikers' accommodation), which are open roughly from July to September with dorm beds for €8-15 and meals for €12-15. Some are run by the National Park but most by Club Alpin Français. You can't usually book ahead. In winter some are open on a limited basis. A useful listing is in *Hébergement en Montagne,* published by Éditions Randonnées, available in many bookshops.

Pau's Librairie des Pyrénées (see Bookshops earlier in this chapter) is the best bookshop for maps and detailed topoguides. The best general walking map is IGN's 1:50,000 *Béarn* (€9.90); more detailed is the 1:25,000 TOP 250 *Ossau/Vallée d'Aspe* (€9). The handsomest of many walking guides is *Le Guide Rando: Aspe-Ossau* (€16.75).

If you've got kids or a heavy load, you

Parc National des Pyrénées

JANE SMITH

The 450-sq-km Pyrénées National Park, created in 1967, runs in a narrow strip along the Spanish border from the vallée d'Aspe eastwards for about 100km, sharing part of the border with a Spanish national park, the Parque Nacional Ordesa y Monte Perdido. Some 40% of the park is within the Pyrénées-Atlantiques department. A park-managed buffer zone takes in most of the Aspe and Ossau Valleys.

Important animal species under the park's protection include chamois (a kind of mountain goat), large birds of prey including the royal eagle, and most urgently, some of southern Europe's very last brown bears (see the boxed text, 'L'Ours Brun', later in this section). Among protected plants are the park's extensive beech forests (about 12% of the park is forested).

If you're lucky, you may catch a glimpse of the sure-footed chamois

National park visitor centres in the Béarn are at Etsaut and (from summer 2001) at Laruns. There's also a park office (☎ 05 59 39 75 55) at 14 rue Adoue, Oloron-Ste-Marie. Park headquarters (☎ 05 62 44 36 60, fax 05 62 44 36 70) are at 59 route de Pau, 65000 Tarbes. Among park regulations worth noting are:

VTTs (mountain bikes) These are forbidden except on designated tracks; these include cross-country ski routes at Brousset (vallée d'Ossau) and Somport (vallée d'Aspe).

Camping This is prohibited, except for a small tent, pitched during the hours of darkness, at least an hour's walk from any road, for a maximum of one night.

Dogs Pet dogs may not be brought into the park, even on a lead.

can hire a donkey from La Garbure in the vallée d'Aspe (see Places to Stay & Eat under Etsaut).

Compagnie du Sud *(☎ 05 59 11 10 00, fax 05 59 11 10 09, e compagnie.du.sud@ wanadoo.fr, 27 rue Maréchal Joffre, Pau)* runs guided, small-group treks with English-speaking guides in the French and Spanish Pyrénées (about €500-600 for a one-week trip). **Romano Sport** *(☎ 05 59 98 48 56, 1 rue Jean-Réveil, Pau)* rents hiking boots for €7.60 per day.

For weather information in the Pyrénées-Atlantiques department, try calling the *météo* (weather bureau) on ☎ 08 36 68 02 64, or Pau weather station on ☎ 05 59 33 32 00.

White-Water Rafting

Haut-Béarn boasts some of France's finest white water, with the added advantage of fairly steady flow throughout the year.

The choicest reach for rafting is the Gave

d'Oloron from Oloron to Sauveterre de Béarn. Reliable outfits offering trips (adult/child about €30/25 for one day with lunch) and other activities include:

A Boste Sport-Loisirs (☎/fax 05 59 38 57 58), rue Léon Bérard, Sauveterre de Béarn

Centre Nautique de Soeix (☎ 05 59 39 61 00, fax 05 59 39 65 16) quartier Soeix, Oloron-Ste-Marie

Rafting Eaux Vives Le Pont (☎ 05 59 66 04 05, fax 05 59 66 01 78) Navarrenx

Also popular is the Gave de Pau, where the biggest operator is **Maison pour Tous Léo Lagrange** *(☎ 05 59 06 67 00, fax 05 59 06 91 51, 41 rue du Colonel Gloxin, Pau)*.

Cycling

Dedicated cyclists like riding the mountain routes of the Tour de France (eg, the Col de Marie-Blanque and Col d'Aubisque), but anybody in reasonable shape can do short trips. Among places where you can hire a VTT (about €15 per day) are:

Béarn VTT (☎/fax 05 59 39 33 43), 24 bis rue Auguste Peyré, Oloron-Ste-Marie
CPL Sports (☎/fax 05 59 05 82 28), place Camps, Louvie-Juzon (vallée d'Ossau)
Cycles Igouassel (☎ 05 59 39 06 00), 3 rue Despourrins, Oloron-Ste-Marie
Montagne Nature (☎/fax 05 59 34 75 77), place Sarraillé, Bedous (vallée d'Aspe); also guided cycling trips (about €40 per day including bike and transport); open July-August only
Romano Sport (☎ 05 59 98 48 56), 1 rue Jean-Réveil, Pau

Parasailing

Accous (vallée d'Aspe) is one of the Pyrénées' biggest centres for *parapente*. Two places for flights and lessons (15-minute accompanied introductory flight about €60, five-day introductory course €350 plus board and lodging) are:

Ascendance (☎ 05 59 34 52 07, fax 05 59 34 53 33, **e** info@ascendance.fr) rue de la Poste, Accous – Haut-Béarn's oldest parasailing school; open daily July-Sept, weekends Oct-June
Abélio (☎/fax 05 59 34 58 07, **e** abelio@abelio .com) Accous

Rock-Climbing

There are at least half a dozen small, reputable companies here who can teach you *escalade* (rock-climbing) and show you where to do it, for around €25/40 per half/full day. Many also organise nature-study, walking, caving, canyoning and combination trips.

Skiing

Haut-Béarn's biggest *ski de piste* or *ski alpin* (downhill ski) resort is at **Gourette** in the vallée d'Ossau. Up the valley is another at **Artouste-Fabrèges**, with a big snowboarding centre. **Arette-la-Pierre-St-Martin** (vallée d'Aspe) is good for beginners and kids. At the head of the vallée d'Aspe is the fairly basic **Le Somport** cross-country skiing *(ski de fond)* area.

You can hire alpine or cross-country ski gear at Romano Sport in Pau, L'Evasion in Accous and La Garbure in Etsaut (see those sections).

For a general look at skiing in the Pyrénées, see Activities in the Facts for the Visitor chapter.

OLORON-STE-MARIE
postcode 64400 • pop 12,000
• elevation 225m

Poor Oloron-Ste-Marie (or just Oloron) – everybody hurries through, bound for the mountains. But this attractive town at the confluence of Haut-Béarn's two main rivers, the Gave d'Aspe and Gave d'Ossau, has much to offer. Give it a few hours while you wait for your bus into the mountains.

Before the mid-19th century this was two separate towns. Oloron was probably founded by the Romans. Its important position led the viscounts of Béarn to fortify it at the end of the 11th century, about the time Ste-Marie was created on the ruins of another Roman settlement.

Oloron's best known export is the beret; in fact most *chapeaux Basques* are made here.

Orientation

The oldest part of town is the quartier Ste-Croix, on a hill like a ship's prow above the point where the two rivers unite as the Gave d'Oloron. The centre of quartier Notre-Dame, on the Oloron side, is place de la Résistance, where long-distance buses stop. The heart of quartier Ste-Marie is the cathedral of the same name, and 800m north of this is the train station.

Information

The keen tourist office (☎ 05 59 39 98 00, fax 05 59 39 43 97, **e** oloron-ste-marie@ fnotsi.net, **w** www.ot-oloron-ste-marie.fr) is in the middle of place de la Résistance. It opens 9am to 7pm Monday to Saturday and 9am to noon Sunday July to mid-September, and 9am to 12.30pm and 2pm to 6.30pm Monday to Saturday the rest of the year. In 2002 a branch office (same ☎ and fax) is to open in Villa Bordeu, on rue de la Poste in the quartier Ste-Marie.

A Parc National des Pyrénées office (☎ 05 59 39 75 55, fax 05 59 39 58 76), 14 rue Adoue, is open 10am to 12.30pm and 3pm to 7.30pm weekdays.

BÉARN

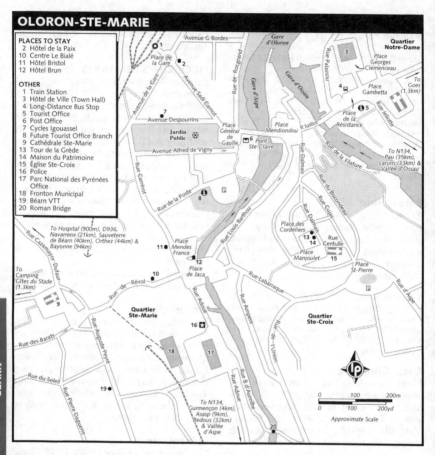

OLORON-STE-MARIE

PLACES TO STAY
2 Hôtel de la Paix
10 Centre Le Bialé
11 Hôtel Bristol
12 Hôtel Brun

OTHER
1 Train Station
3 Hôtel de Ville (Town Hall)
4 Long-Distance Bus Stop
5 Tourist Office
6 Post Office
7 Cycles Igouassel
8 Future Tourist Office Branch
9 Cathédrale Ste-Marie
13 Tour de la Grède
14 Maison du Patrimoine
15 Église Ste-Croix
16 Police
17 Parc National des Pyrénées Office
18 Fronton Municipal
19 Béarn VTT
20 Roman Bridge

Quartier Ste-Croix

At the heart of the tiny medieval quarter is the 11th- to 12th-century **Église Ste-Croix** – Romanesque but with a great ribbed dome, perhaps an inspiration from Moorish Spain.

Down rue Dalmais, the ancient main street, there are several handsome Renaissance houses and the 13th- or 14th-century **Tour de la Grède**.

Beside this, in a 17th-century mansion, is the **Maison du Patrimoine** (*☎ 05 59 39 10 63, 52 rue Dalmais; admission €3.05, child free; open 10am-12.30pm & 3pm-7.30pm Tues-Sun July-Sept*), a very modest museum of the archaeology, ethnography and geology of Oloron-Ste-Marie and Béarn. The collection includes artefacts from the ruins of a Roman villa unearthed at Goes, 2km to the north-east.

Quartier Ste-Marie

Quartier Ste-Marie feels less ancient, though not by much. The town's centrepiece is the **Cathédrale Ste-Marie** (*admission free; open 9am-7pm daily except during Mass*), mainly Gothic (14th century) but with a Romanesque pedigree of its own, evident at the western end. The cathedral is on Unesco's list of

World Heritage sites associated with the pilgrimage routes to Santiago de Compostela.

The best part is the 12th-century **portal** under the belfry porch – easily a rival for the one at Moissac (see under Moissac in the Toulouse, Tarn-et-Garonne & Tarn chapter) for sheer exuberant imagination. Beneath St John's vision of the Apocalypse are visions of a life of happy industry down on earth (hunting, fishing, cheese-making, goose-plucking); a man-eating monster to remind us of the Day of Judgement; and a mounted Emperor Constantine (or perhaps a Gaston IV of Béarn, who founded the church when he returned triumphant from the First Crusade).

There's more to the building than this, however. Recent work has uncovered an extraordinary relief – possibly of the Roman god Mars – bricked up in the wall behind the portal and dating from the 2nd century AD, suggesting that the cathedral may have been founded upon a pre-Christian temple.

Special Events
Oloron-Ste-Marie is best known for its Festival du Folklore (☎ 05 59 39 37 36, fax 05 59 39 80 79), one and a half weeks of international dance, music and theatre in late July and early August. It's held here in even years and at Jaca, in the Spanish province of Aragón, in odd years.

Since 1995, the town has hosted Jazz Oloron on the first weekend in July (bookings through the tourist office).

Places to Stay & Eat
The quartier Ste-Marie has two Logis de France hotel-restaurants, both with comfortable doubles that come with shower and WC (about €40) and good food in a pleasant setting (*menus* about €10-13): **Hôtel Bristol** (☎ 05 59 39 43 78, fax 05 59 39 08 19, 9 rue Carrérot) and **Hôtel Brun** (☎ 05 59 39 64 90, fax 05 59 39 12 28, 5 place de Jaca). Other options include the following.

Camping Gîtes du Stade (☎ 05 59 39 11 26, fax 05 59 36 12 01, chemin de Lagravette, quartier Soeix) 2-person forfait (package rate) with tent/caravan €9.90/10.50, bungalows €381 per week. Open mid-Mar–Sept.

This shady, three-star camp site is 2km west in the municipal sports complex.

Centre Le Bialé (☎ 05 59 39 15 29, fax 05 59 39 35 95, 10 rue de Révol) Dorm beds €8.25. Open year round. This spartan hostel for sports and school groups is also open to visitors, though booking ahead is advisable.

Hôtel de la Paix (☎ 05 59 39 02 63, fax 05 59 39 98 20, 24 av Sadi-Carnot) Doubles €30.50-39.65. Open daily July–mid-Sept, Monday to Saturday mid-Sept–June. The Hôtel de la Paix, opposite the train station, is good value in its range, with functional, well kept rooms.

Getting There & Away
SNCF (☎ 05 59 39 00 61) has four to five trains and three to five buses Monday to Saturday (fewer Sunday) from Pau (€5.65, 40 minutes), plus daily onward connections into the vallée d'Aspe (see the following Vallée d'Aspe section). Citram Pyrénées buses from Pau (€5.50, 50 minutes) come to the train station three to five times daily during term time (twice daily during school holidays), Sundays excepted.

Getting Around
Drivers take note: Old right-of-way rules still apply (ie, entering drivers have priority) at the place Gambetta roundabout. Parking is free everywhere in town.

VALLÉE D'OSSAU
In its 60km journey from the 1794m Col du Pourtalet to Oloron-Ste-Marie, the Gave d'Ossau (River Ossau) cuts a more stately figure than its sibling. The valley is broader, the peaks rounder and the villages less rough-cut.

The tourist office with the most to tell you about the valley is at Laruns. A National Park visitor centre was due to open there in 2001.

Getting There & Away
SNCF goes to Buzy-en-Béarn on the Oloron-Ste-Marie line (four to five trains and three to five buses daily, fewer Sunday), and from there has bus connections into the valley, mainly as far as Laruns (€6.10, one hour, three to four a day Monday to Saturday,

Transhumance & Cheese

Haut-Béarn is not only seriously scenic but is perhaps the most 'authentic' border area in the south of France, with still-healthy pastoral traditions.

A long-standing feature of life in the western Pyrénées, and especially the vallée d'Ossau, is transhumance, the annual movement of livestock to high pastures. Some 92% of land in this valley is in communal hands, and many decisions are taken – as they have been for centuries – in common. Every spring the valley's mayors jointly decide when the summer migration of sheep is to begin. The date is usually in early July, and nobody may start before that. The carefully coordinated, valley-wide operation is over in two or three days, with sheep trucked beyond Gabas and herded the rest of the way. There's a similar but less-regimented transfer of cattle, typically in the last half of June. Herders can bring their animals back down when they choose.

A closely allied tradition is that of cheese production. The finest sheep's cheese is made from the relatively small quantities of milk obtained when sheep are in rich summer meadows. Shepherds prepare these summer cheeses on the spot and bring them down to designated *saloirs* – facilities, mainly in Gabas, where they're salted and stored. The return of sheep and shepherds after months in the mountains is celebrated with merry *foires aux fromages* (cheese fairs), where summer cheeses are presented and judged. See Special Events under Laruns for examples of this and other events based on transhumance in the valley.

fewer Sunday). Citram Pyrénées has buses directly from Pau to Laruns (€6.95) two to three times a day Monday to Saturday, with Sunday services in July and August and in the ski season (mid-December to April).

In July and August, and in the ski season, SNCF has two buses each on Saturday and Sunday, direct from Pau to Artouste-Fabrèges (€8.40); and Canonge (Laruns ☎ 05 59 05 30 31) runs two each weekday from Laruns to Artouste-Fabrèges (€3.80).

Aste-Béon

There's just one reason to stop off at Aste-Béon (population 231, elevation 480m): to be a vulture voyeur (see the boxed text 'La Falaise aux Vautours'). The riverside grounds of La Falaise aux Vautours also make a great picnic spot.

Places to Stay & Eat Aste-Béon has relatively few options for food and accommodation.

Camping Le Toussaü (☎ 05 59 34 91 01, D290, Aste) Adult/site €2.25/3.05. Open June-Sept. This plain camp site, with limited shade, is 2.5km south of La Falaise au Vautours, just beyond the Aste part of the village.

L'Étape du Berger (☎ 05 59 82 65 58, D290, Béon) Menus €8.55-27.45. Open midday daily, evening Thur-Mon. A stone's throw from La Falaise au Vautours in Béon, this restaurant-bar, offers modest Béarnaise specialities; service is snail-like.

Getting There & Away Citram Pyrénées buses stop on the D934 road, en route from Pau (€6.95, 55 minutes) to Laruns. They leave Pau at around 9.30am Monday to Saturday, and call at Aste-Béon about 2pm on their return. In July and August there's an additional run, and Sunday services, but get current times from Citram or the Pau tourist office.

Laruns

postcode 64440 • pop 1500 • elevation 536m
Laruns, 19km to the south of Buzy-en-Béarn, is vallée d'Ossau's best source of information and supplies, and the best place to experience several traditional festivals. The mountain setting is also an absolute knockout.

Orientation & Information The valley tourist office, La Maison de la Vallée d'Ossau (☎ 05 59 05 31 41, fax 05 59 05 35 49, e ossau.tourisme@wanadoo.fr), is on place de la Mairie, on the D934 through town. It opens 9am to 12.30pm and 2pm to 6.30pm daily in July and August, and 9am to noon and 2pm to 6pm daily except Sunday after-

La Falaise aux Vautours

The griffon vulture (Gyps folvus) is one of France's largest birds of prey. The huge bird – with an adult wingspan of around 2.8m – is a familiar sight over the Pyrénées, with its stately gliding flight. It is unique in feeding exclusively on carrion, which nowadays means mainly livestock killed by predators, disease or age.

In 1974 the villages of Aste-Béon, Bielle, Bilhères and Castet established a 92-hectare reserve for the protection of seven to 10 griffon vulture pairs nesting in the limestone cliffs above the villages, and threatened by egg poachers and careless photographers. A measure of its success is that there are now about 120 nesting pairs, along with other raptors and five pairs of migratory Egyptian vultures. This is not a park operation but a private one, under the control of the mayor of Aste-Béon, and all the more amazing for succeeding without government 'help'.

A public information and education centre called **La Falaise aux Vautours** (Cliff of the Vultures; ☎ 05 59 82 65 49, fax 05 59 82 65 65, Béon; adult/child aged 5-12 €5.95/3.80; open 10.30am-12.30pm & 2pm-7pm daily June-Aug) was inaugurated in 1993, centred on a video theatre showing live images of 10 griffon vulture nests from a remote-controlled camera installed on the cliffs just 30m away, and from a fixed camera right beside one of the nests. Visitors can thus look in on nesting, hatching and feeding in real time, an extraordinary achievement. There's also a child-friendly interactive museum (including English captions) about vultures.

The centre keeps limited hours outside the summer season (check with the Laruns or Pau tourist office), and is closed to the public for much of the winter.

❀ ❀ ❀ ❀ ❀ ❀ ❀ ❀ ❀ ❀ ❀ ❀

noon September to June. Check out their booklets of VTT circuits and local walks, each €4.55.

At the time of writing a National Park visitor centre was to open near the tourist office in summer 2001, replacing one closed at Gabas. It was to be open daily in summer (hours similar to the tourist office's); winter hours had not been set.

Within sight of the tourist office are two banks and a Maison de la Presse, which sells maps. The Auberge L'Embaradère (see Places to Stay & Eat) has a pay-by-card Internet terminal.

Special Events The Fête de la Montagne (Mountain Festival), on the first weekend in May, brings together professionals and organisations – from fisheries officers to hydroelectric engineers, shepherds' groups to the Club Alpin Française – to present just about every side of the mountains through trips, films and a concert of traditional Ossau music.

The Fête Ossaloise, usually on the first Saturday in July at the height of the annual movement of sheep to the high valleys, is an evening of traditional song and dance. The Hesta de Noste Dama (Béarnaise for Festival of Our Lady), on a Wednesday in mid-August, features a Mass with traditional chants and costumes, a parade, traditional games and an evening of dance and fireworks.

Laruns holds a medieval fair on the first Saturday in October, complete with period costume, traditional music and dance, horse trials and more. Local restaurateurs make enough *poule au pot* (a traditional Pyrénéan dish – chicken stuffed with vegetables and prepared with tomato sauce) to feed 8000 people. The next day sees the valley's all-important Foire aux Fromages, when the long-awaited summer cheeses are presented and judged.

Places to Stay & Eat Laruns has at least eight camp sites within 2km of the town centre, though many are just dreary little patches for caravans.

Camping du Valentin (☎ 05 59 05 39 33, fax 05 59 05 65 84, ancienne route d'Eaux-Bonnes) Adult €3.05, pitch €4.75-6.25 plus €0.60 per vehicle. Open May-Oct. This spacious camp site rises above the others, literally and figuratively. It's on a hillside 2.4km south of town, with fine views. Tenters won't feel hemmed in by caravans.

BÉARN

Camping de Geteu (☎ *05 59 05 37 15, D934, 1.8km north of Laruns*) Adult/site €2/3.05. Open year round. This informal, plain camp site between the river and the roadway has showers and a little shop, but few other amenities.

Auberge L'Embaradère (☎ *05 59 05 41 88, 13 av de la Gare*) Dorm beds adult/children under 12 €9.15/6.85 (reservations recommended); B&B €12.95 per person; half-board €22.85. *Plat du jour* (dish of the day) €6.85, *menus* €9.90-15.25. Open year round. About 200m east of the tourist office is this switched-on inn and hikers' *refuge*. The auberge offers tasty local dishes.

Hôtel d'Ossau (☎ *05 59 05 30 14, fax 05 59 05 47 00, place de la Mairie*) Rooms €39.95. Breakfast €4.55. *Menus* €12.20-16.75. This is Laruns' only hotel, staid and well kept. Among four eateries on place de la Mairie is the hotel's own serviceable restaurant.

There's a small *food shop* on place de la Mairie.

Getting There & Away Citram's direct buses from Pau (€6.95, one hour) stop two to three times a day Monday to Saturday (Sunday services in July, August and ski season only). SNCF buses from Pau (€6.10), with a change at Buzy-en-Béarn, stop three to four times a day Monday to Saturday (less often Sunday).

Gabas
postcode 64440 • pop 36 • elevation 1027m
Tiny Gabas, 13km south of Laruns, is for visitors mainly a trekking base. For locals it's one of the valley's most important settlements – an entrepôt to Spain, at the confluence of major high valleys, and the site of three *saloirs* where summer cheese is stored and salted (see the boxed text 'Transhumance & Cheese' earlier in this chapter).

Places to Stay & Eat There are a variety of places to stay for walkers.

Chalet-Auberge du CAF (☎ *05 59 05 33 14, D934 route de Col du Pourtalet*) Dorm beds €7.30, breakfast €3.95, half-board €21.35. Open weekends and summer holi-days. This Club Alpin Français *refuge*, 800m south out of Gabas, sleeps 45 and will do meals or picnic lunches on request. Booking ahead is essential in summer.

The following places, within 100m of one another along the D934, also serve as saloirs. Not surprisingly they all offer tastings and sales of sheep's cheese, along with more or less identical local dishes.

Hôtel Le Biscaü (☎ *05 59 05 31 37, fax 05 59 05 43 23, D934*) Doubles with WC & shower/bath €33.55/39.65, half-board €28.95/32 per person. Breakfast €3.80. Open mid-Dec–mid-Nov.

Hôtel-Restaurant Vignau (☎ *05 59 05 34 06, fax 05 59 05 46 12, D934*) Doubles with WC €22.85-27.45, with WC & bath €30.50-33.55. *Menus* €8.40-18.30.

Restaurant Le Pic du Midi (☎ *05 59 05 33 00, D934*) *Menus* €8.85-21.35. This is the best bet for a modest midday meal and a taste of sheep's cheese.

From Gabas, a sharp 4km climb to the **Lac de Bious-Artigues** reservoir (1422m) will reward you with superb views, southeast to Pic du Midi d'Ossau and south-west to 2288m Pic d'Ayous. There are two accommodation options here.

Camping de Bious Oumettes (☎ *05 59 05 38 76, Parc National*) Adult/pitch €2/1.85. Open mid-June–mid-Sept. This 60-pitch camp site, 1km before you reach the lake, has showers and a little shop.

Chalet Pyrénéa-Sport (☎/fax *05 59 05 12 42, Lac de Bious-Artigues*) B&B €12.20, half-board €23.65. Open year round.

Le Petit Train d'Artouste
About 1.5km east of Gabas on the D934 is the settlement of Artouste-Fabrèges (postcode 64440, elevation 1250m), devoted mainly to maintaining the **Lac de Fabrèges** reservoir and to sending tourists in a cable car up the flanks of 2032m Pic de la Sagette. From there they ride for 10km to another reservoir, **Lac d'Artouste** (1991m), in the open-topped Little Train of Artouste, built for dam workers in the 1920s. It's touristy, popular and crowded, but great for kids, and the ride is gorgeous.

The train runs 9.30am to 3pm from the

last week in May to the first week in July and from the last week in August to the end of September; 9am to 4pm during the remainder of July; and 8.30am to 5pm in August (closed the rest of the year). The price depends on your age and the season, from €7.95 for kids aged between 4 and 10 years in the lowest season, to €16.75 for adults in the highest season (August). Kids under the age of four ride free.

Give yourself four hours to get up and back, and dress warmly. In July and August you're only allowed to stay 1½ hours at the upper lake. If you want to stay longer, consider walking up – a two-hour trip from lower to upper lake. Beside the upper lake is *Refuge d'Arrémoulit* (☎ 05 59 05 31 79, Lac d'Artouste), open mid-June to mid-September plus weekends in April, May and September.

For current information on the train, call ☎ 05 59 05 36 99. There's a tourist office at Artouste-Fabrèges (☎ 05 59 05 34 00, fax 05 59 05 37 55). Overpriced snack bars are at both ends of the cable car and train rides.

Up the D934 from Artouste-Fabrèges is the 1794m **Col du Pourtalet** into Spain, normally clear of snow only from July to October.

Getting There & Away In July and August, and in the ski season, SNCF buses run twice each on Saturday and Sunday from Pau (€8.40), and Canonge buses run twice each weekday from Laruns.

VALLÉE D'ASPE
The Gave d'Aspe (River Aspe) flows for some 60km from the Col du Somport down to Oloron-Ste-Marie, through a lush, exceedingly lovely valley. This has been a trans-Pyrénéan artery since the legionaries of Julius Caesar marched through, and the Col du Somport is the central Pyrénées' only all-weather pass. Nevertheless this valley remains one of the Pyrénées' remotest corners, with fewer than 3000 souls in its 13 villages. Away from the valley bottom it still seems untouched by the 20th century.

Public transport is limited but accommodation is inexpensive and food is downright cheap. The valley's official tourist office at

Bedous (see Bedous later in this section) is the place to ask about camp sites, *refuges* and gîtes d'étape, as well as walking itineraries and local events.

Getting There & Away
The N134 runs the length of the valley. European Union (EU) planners have designated it the E7 and want to see it become a major road link between Spain and France. Work has already begun to upgrade the road, though not everybody is happy about it (see the boxed text 'You Want to Build a *What* Here?' later in this chapter).

SNCF goes from Pau to Oloron-Ste-Marie (four to five trains and three to five buses a day Monday to Saturday, fewer Sunday; see those sections for details), and from there has at least three bus connections a day Monday to Saturday into the valley (fewer Sunday) via Bedous (€8.25, one hour 10 minutes from Pau) to the Spanish railhead of Canfranc (€11.45, 2¼ hours from Pau). There are no direct buses into the valley from Pau.

Escot
postcode 64490 • pop 122 • elevation 330m
Escot, 15km above Oloron-Ste-Marie, was the valley's first village. From here the D294 climbs for 20km over the 1035m Col de Marie-Blanque to Bielle in the vallée d'Ossau.

Sarrance & Lourdios-Ichère
At Sarrance (postcode 64490, population 228, elevation 400m), 7km south of Escot, is a 17th-century cloister, Notre-Dame de la Pierre.

From here the D241 climbs westward for 12km to **Lourdios-Ichère** (postcode 64490, population 175, elevation 450m). Here is a first-rate museum of the valley's pastoral traditions, **Lourdios-Ichère, Un Village se Raconte** (A Village Tells Its Story; ☎ 05 59 34 44 84; open 10am-noon & 2pm-7pm daily July–mid-Sept; 2pm-6pm Sat & Sun mid-Sept–June).

Also here is what must be the southwest's most remote auberge de jeunesse: *Estivade* (☎ 05 59 34 46 39, fax 05 59 34 48 04, Maison Pelou) Dorm beds €7.60. Open

BÉARN

year round; reception 9am-7.30pm (9am-8pm weekends & holidays).

Bedous

postcode 64490 • pop 560 • elevation 416m
The valley's biggest village, 25km south of Oloron-Ste-Marie, sits commandingly in a wide basin. This is the place to get your bearings, the starting point for some fine lower-elevation hikes and a good place to stock up on food.

Orientation & Information Buses stop at the car park in front of the police station. A N134 bypass is now under construction; meanwhile the N134 charges through the village, where it's called rue Gambetta.

The tourist office (☎ 05 59 34 71 48, fax 05 59 34 52 51, ⓔ aspe.tourisme@wanadoo .fr) is in the town hall on place Sarraillé (also called place du Marché and place de l'Église). It opens 8.30am to 7.30pm Monday to Saturday and 10am to 1pm Sunday in July and August, and 9am to 12.30pm and 2pm to 6pm Monday to Saturday the rest of the year.

Exchange money at Caisse d'Épargne on the square, or Crédit Agricole on rue Pierre Portes. The post office is on rue Gambetta.

Activities The prettiest short walk from here is eastwards for 6km up the valley of the tumbling River Gabarret to Aydius (population 74, elevation 780m). Follow the signs to Plateau d'Ourdinse for excellent views up and down the valley. Aydius also has a very good restaurant (see Places to Eat).

The tourist office has produced its own packet (€1.50) of map-leaflets on nine excellent walks in the vallée d'Aspe.

Montagne Nature (☎/fax 05 59 34 75 77), on place Sarraillé, rents VTTs and runs guided cycling trips (see Activities at the start of this section), plus canyoning, climbing, mountain skiing and winter mountaineering trips. It opens daily except Saturday and Sunday mornings, in July and August only.

Arette-la-Pierre-St-Martin Fifteen tortuous kilometres west of Bedous is the ski resort of **Arette-la-Pierre-St-Martin** *(☎ 05 59 66 20 09; open Dec-Apr)*; for details see

You Want to Build a *What* Here?

The vallée d'Aspe once had its own railway – a 1928 marvel of bridges, viaducts and an extraordinary spiral tunnel that worked its way up below the Col du Somport and then tunnelled for 8km beneath it to the Spanish railhead at Canfranc.

What nobody had thought of was the need for a reliable link from the bottom of the valley to the existing network of roads and railroads. Then one day in 1970 a bridge at l'Estanguet, south of Accous, collapsed under the weight of an overloaded train. Everybody got cold feet and the railway line was abandoned.

Since then, as part of a EU initiative to improve road links between France and Spain, a road tunnel has been driven under the Col du Somport, close to the old rail tunnel. At the time of writing the new tunnel had been closed indefinitely in response to safety fears after the 1999 Mt Blanc tunnel inferno in the Alps, though the road over the pass remains open. The N134 (now also called the E7) is being widened, and bypasses have been completed or are under construction around several valley towns.

The project has generated lots of local anxiety about the effects of a multilane highway on this narrow, fragile valley (not to mention the impact on its vanishing brown bears). In any case, now that heavy lorries are starting to use it, the present narrow road is clearly dangerous, and there have been numerous accidents.

One alternative to widening it is to shift cargo onto a revitalised rail link. While either option would shatter the valley's calm and mar its beauty, the latter has the advantage that the railway is already part of the scenery. So far the French response has been political gridlock, and the EU has shown little interest in studying the rail option. A wider road is starting to look inevitable.

under Activities in the introduction to the Haut-Béarn section.

Places to Stay Bedous has a fair range of modestly priced, rambler-friendly accommodation.

Camp Municipal de Bedous (Camping Carole; ☎ 05 59 34 59 19, route d'Osse) Adult/pitch/vehicle €2.15/0.75/0.75. Open Easter–mid-Sept. Bedous' municipal camp site – small, plain, quiet and fairly shady – is 500m west of the square.

Le Choucas Blanc (☎ 05 59 34 53 71, fax 05 59 87 19 88, 4 rue Gambetta) Dorm beds €7.30 with 6-month €0.75 membership. Open year round. The folks at this spartan gîte d'étape on the N134, opposite the bus stop, are generous with good advice. There's no food but you can use the kitchen for €0.75.

Le Mandragot (☎ 05 59 34 59 33, place Sarraillé) Dorm beds €7.60, breakfast €3.05, half-board €21.35, children under 10 half-price. Open year round. Le Mandragot is a peaceful, friendly gîte d'étape opposite the tourist office.

Maison Laclède (☎ 05 59 34 70 19, route d'Aydius) B&B doubles €30.50. This chambres d'hôte, 200m from the square along the Aydius road, has quiet rooms with shower and Louis XVI furniture.

Places to Eat You can find basic food in the village and good eating not far away.

Restaurant-Crêperie du Gabarret (☎ 05 59 34 76 22, place Sarraillé) Menus €9, crepes about €6. Open noon-10pm daily during school holidays; 7pm-10pm Tues & Thur-Fri & noon-10pm Sat-Sun at other times. Tucked south-east of the church, this place offers crepes, grills and salads in a rustic setting.

Pimparela (☎ 05 59 34 52 23, Osse-en-Aspe, vallée d'Osse) Open midday & evening daily, reservation only. At this ferme auberge, 3km west up the Osse Valley, treat yourself to first-class home cooking or buy pâtés, cheeses or other products to take away.

Restaurant des Cols (☎ 05 59 34 70 25, Aydius) Menus €12.20-22.85. Open Tues-Sat & Sun midday. This snug bar-restaurant,

6.5km east up the Gabarret Valley, is known for excellent, traditional-style food at reasonable prices, and perhaps for its bric-a-brac and stuffed, mounted wild animals. There are also three rooms (B&B €32 for two).

Food shops in Bedous include *Casino* at 5 rue Gambetta (open Monday to Saturday and Sunday morning) and *Guyenne et Gascogné* two doors down. Bedous' weekly *market* is on Thursday morning.

Accous
postcode 64490 • pop 400 • elevation 460m
Accous, 2.5km south of Bedous and 800m east of the highway, sits at the yawning mouth of the vallée Berthe, with a splendid backdrop of 2000m-plus peaks. Above Accous the vallée d'Aspe closes in dramatically.

Activities Look up – this is the home of two parasailing schools, Ascendance (700m off the N134) and Abélio (just off the N134). For details see Activities at the start of the Haut-Béarn section.

From May to December you can hire a horse at **Auberge Cavalière** *(see Places to Stay & Eat; €11.45 per hour, €39.65/63.25 half/full day; advance booking essential)*. They're specialists in long mountain treks, including into Spain.

At *L'Evasion (☎ 05 59 34 50 40)*, a tiny bar on the N134 near the Accous turning, you can rent downhill/cross-country skiing gear for about €8/10 per day. Hours are variable but they'll open up if you call them.

Places to Stay & Eat There are a couple of options in Accous, including camping.

Camping Despourrins (☎ 05 59 34 71 16) Adult/pitch €2.35/2.50. Open Mar–mid-Nov. This small, plain, tidy camp site is opposite Abelio, just off the N134.

Hôtel Le Permayou (☎ 05 59 34 72 15, fax 05 59 34 72 68) Singles/doubles €36.60/41.15. Breakfast €4.55. Also just off the N134 is this hotel with uninspiring but fully equipped rooms.

Auberge Cavalière (☎ 05 59 34 72 30, fax 05 59 34 51 97, l'Estanguet) Doubles €36.60. Breakfast €5.35. *Menus* €15.55-32.80. Open year round. All the rooms have a shower and WC. Auberge Cavalière stirs up good Pyrénéan specialities, such as *poule au pot* (boiled chicken), over a wood fire. It's 3.2km south of Accous.

Lescun
postcode 64490 • pop 198 • elevation 900m
About 4km south of Bedous is the bridge at l'Estanguet, whose collapse in 1970 brought an end to train traffic in the valley. Here also is the turning for a steep, twisting 5.5km ride up to Lescun, whose slate roofs once sheltered a leper colony. In a valley already too beautiful for its own good, here's a view to take your breath away and blow your film budget: **Les Aiguilles d'Ansabère** (the Needles of Ansabère), an amphitheatre of jagged limestone peaks rising at the back to 2504m Pic d'Anie, one of Haut-Béarn's highest.

Walks The GR10 passes through Lescun, and perhaps the best of many fine walks takes it west up the valley of the River Lauga, over the Pas d'Azuns to Arette-la-Pierre-St-Martin, a strenuous half- to full-day trek.

Places to Stay You might want to soak this up for a day or two – certainly the perfect time to be here is for sunrise on those peaks.

Camping Municipal du Lauzart (☎/fax 05 59 34 51 77) Gîte d'étape €9. Camping mid-Apr–Sept, gîte Jan-Sept. Lescun's plain municipal camp site, 1.5km south-west of the village, also has hikers' accommodation.

Refuge de l'Labérouat (☎/fax 05 59 34 50 43) Dorm beds €12/15 in summer/winter, half-board €24/27. Open Jan-Sept. This comfortable *refuge*, with rooms for one to six people, is roughly 5km north-west, on the GR10 towards Arette-la-Pierre-St-Martin.

Maison de la Montagne (☎/fax 05 59 34 79 14, place de la Mairie) Dorm beds €9.90, half-board €24.40. Here is a place to linger. In a restored house beside the *mairie* (village hall) is a tasteful, comfortable Rando'Plume gîte d'étape (see under Accommodation in the Facts for the Visitor chapter for more on Rando'Plume).

Hôtel du Pic d'Anie (☎ 05 59 34 71 54, fax 05 59 34 53 22) Hotel: rooms €40, half-board €37 per person; *refuge*: dorm beds

€9, B&B €14, half-pension €26. Open mid-Apr–mid-Sept. This is a comfortable, hiker-friendly hotel, right in the village.

Etsaut
postcode 64490 • pop 92 • elevation 590m
About 12km south of Bedous is tiny Etsaut, the valley's highest village of any size. This and Borce (postcode 64490, population 195, elevation 700m), just across the N134, are obvious bases for higher-elevation hikes. Borce also has a pretty medieval centre.

Orientation & Information Etsaut is 500m east of the N134. The bus stop is in the main square, which doubles as a car park. You can exchange money at the post office, just east off the square beside the church.

The Maison du Parc National des Pyrénées (☎ 05 59 34 88 30) is a national park visitor centre in the old train station, 200m north of the square. It opens 9.30am to 12.30pm and 2pm to 6.30pm daily mid-May to mid-November (closed the rest of the year). It has a small, free exhibit (in French) on the park's rapidly disappearing brown bears (see the boxed text 'L'Ours Brun').

Walks About 3km south of Etsaut is the **Fort du Portalet**, an early 19th-century fortress overlooking a particularly narrow and defensible bit of the valley. From 1941 to 1945 the Germans and the Vichy government used it as a prison. It was recently purchased by the valley's 13 *communes* (districts), who have not yet decided what to do with it.

From Etsaut you can walk south and then east along part of the GR10 known as the **Chemin de la Mâture**, partly hacked out of solid rock and used in the 18th century to harvest timber for Bayonne shipyards. With unprotected sheer drops, this is not for the faint hearted. You can see the Fort du Portalet from along the trail.

A strenuous segment of the trail continues south-eastwards to the **Lacs d'Ayous** at the foot of Pic du Midi d'Ossau, five to six hours walking from Etsaut. Alternatively, the lakes can be reached in about two hours from the Col du Somport.

Places to Stay & Eat Food and accommodation here is modest but more than adequate for walkers.

La Garbure (☎ *05 59 34 88 98, fax 05 59 34 50 86,* e *pyrenees.aspe@wanadoo.fr)* Dorm bed €9.15, breakfast €3.05, half-pension €19.05, evening *menus* €9.90. This family-friendly hostel has dormitories with en suite showers (hall WCs), an informal evening auberge (fixed menu), a kitchen for guests' use and even a little swimming pool. You can rent alpine, touring or mountain skis (€5.35 per day), take one of the hostel's donkeys on a trek (€11/22/33 per hour/half-day/day) and arrange other activities. The hostel is 100m down the lane beside the church.

Maison de l'Ours (Centre d'Hébergement Léo Lagrange; ☎/*fax 05 59 34 86 38,* W *www .club-internet.fr/perso/giteours, main square)*

L'Ours Brun

The upper vallée d'Aspe and vallée d'Ossau are the last Pyrénéan home of the brown bear *(Ursos arctos)*. But tourism, roadbuilding and forest management, plus a long (two-year) breeding cycle, has driven its numbers relentlessly and tragically down. From a population of 2000 in 1967, there are now an estimated *five* indigenous adult bears left in the National Park, including just one female.

The Institution Patrimonial du Haut-Béarn (IPHB), a heritage agency that gets 40% of its support from the EU, has proposed stocking the region with more females, but the project is gridlocked by politics and tradition. The French Environment Ministry has agreed to the plan, provided local organisations agree to participate in EU scientific surveys. But Béarn's historical hostility to centralised authority has predisposed local farmers and politicians to say no. Without their agreement, the IPHB doesn't get its 40%, and there it stands.

Slovenian brown bears imported some years ago into the high Pyrénées, well to the east of Béarn, have bred successfully there. Now a few have been sighted in the Haut-Béarn, and farmers here are not pleased.

Dorm bed €12.20 with breakfast, €21.35 half-board. Open year round. This plain, family-oriented gîte d'étape in the village centre organises bike trips and other activities for guests.

Hôtel des Pyrénées (☎ *05 59 34 88 62, fax 05 59 34 86 96, main square)* Doubles with/without shower & WC €37/24, half-board €27/35 per person. *Menus* €11.60-16.75. Open year round. For those looking for more comforts, this is the village's only hotel, with rooms to Logis de France standards.

The *grocery* on the main square is open daily.

Two basic national park *refuges* are on trails from Etsaut.

Refuge d'Arlet (☎ *05 59 34 76 88, fax 05 59 34 70 72, three to four hours from Borce)* Dorm beds with/without breakfast €11/8, half-board €24. Open mid-June–mid-Sept.

Refuge d'Ayous (☎ *05 59 05 37 00, Lacs d'Ayous)* Dorm beds €8.25, advance reservations essential. Open mid-June–mid-Sept. This one is actually over in the vallée d'Ossau.

Béarn des Gaves

ORTHEZ
postcode 64300 • pop 10,900
• elevation 60m

Viscount Gaston VII of Béarn made Orthez his capital in the late 13th century, though even when Gaston Fébus moved it to Pau he often held court here. The town's two claims to fame are Gaston VII's striking fortified bridge over the Gave de Pau, and an earnest Museum of Protestantism. Surprisingly, one of the town's big exports is Bayonne ham!

Orientation & Information
Buses stop along the south side of the central square, place d'Armes.

The tourist office (☎ 05 59 69 02 75, fax 05 59 69 12 00, e tourisme.orthez@wana doo.fr, rue Bourg-Vieux) is a block west of the square in a 16th-century townhouse called Maison Jeanne d'Albret (though it's unlikely she ever stayed there). It opens

BÉARN

9am to 12.30pm and 2pm to 7pm Monday to Saturday and 9.30am to 12.30pm Sunday in July and August; and 9am to noon and 2pm to 6pm Monday to Saturday the rest of the year. From the train station it's an 800m walk north-west to the tourist office.

The post office is on the east side of place d'Armes. Orthez's BIJ, called Espace Info Jeunes (☎ 05 59 69 31 30, fax 05 59 69 31 12), was at the time of writing about to offer Internet access, but no further information was available. It's at 10 place Brossers, one and a half blocks north of the post office, and is open 8am to 1pm and 2pm to 6pm Sunday to Friday.

Gaston VII's Town

The axis of the old town is rue Bourg-Vieux and its northward extension, rue de l'Horloge and rue Moncade. Little remains of Gaston's fortress but a tower, the **Tour Moncade** (☎ 05 59 69 37 50, rue Moncade; adult/child €1.85/0.90; open 2.30pm-6.30pm Tues-Sun May; 10am-noon & 3pm-7pm Tues-Sun June & end-Aug; 3pm-6pm Tues-Sun mid-July–mid-Aug & Sept), 500m north of the tourist office. Townsfolk knocked off the top for building materials before the town council blew the whistle in the 19th century.

Gaston's fortified bridge – and Orthez's trademark – the **Pont Vieux**, crosses the Bayonne-Pau TGV line and the churning river, three blocks south and a block west of the tourist office. Once it had a second tower and guarded the entrance to the town, stopping the Duke of Wellington himself in 1814. Across the river is one of the town's prettiest streets, rue du Pont Vieux.

The only photogenic vantage point for the bridge is from the riverside, but beware the dangerously unprotected TGV line!

Musée du Protestantisme Béarnais

If you grew up Protestant, or among Protestants, you may find it hard to take this staid museum seriously, though most French people – 98% of whom have never seen the inside of a *temple* (Protestant church) – will find it pretty interesting. Aside from a few remote villages in the Haut-Béarn where

Protestants number as many as 50%, Orthez has an unusually large Protestant community (about 10%) for France.

The museum (☎ 05 59 69 14 03, 1st floor, Maison Jeanne d'Albret, rue Bourg-Vieux; adult/child €2.30/1.50; open 10am-noon & 2pm-6pm Mon-Sat) – upstairs from the tourist office – consists of a reconstructed 19th-century Protestant church, an exhibit of tiny chalices, miniature hymnals and other concealable paraphernalia of worship, and a few too many exhibits on the tolerant years after the Revolution. Some staff speak English and are keen to tell visitors all about Protestantism in France and Europe.

Places to Stay & Eat

Good choices for food and accommodation in Orthez include the following.

Camping de la Source (☎ 05 59 67 04 81, blvd Charles de Gaulle) Adult/tent/car €2.45/1.20/0.90. Open Apr-Sept. Peaceful and shady, this small camp site is 1.5km east of the town centre.

Hôtel Moulia (☎ 05 59 69 02 82, 18 rue Pierre Lasserre) Doubles €18.30-27.45. This staid hotel beside the bus stop has comfortable but unexciting rooms facing place d'Armes.

Hôtel Godfroy (☎ 05 59 69 08 90, 20 av Pont-Neuf) Rooms with WC/shower €22.85/ 30.50, with both €33.55-38.10. Menus €7.60-15.25. The Godfroy is the best-value choice in the centre, with well kept, quiet rooms and a cheerful bar-grill. It's around the left side of the Hôtel Moulia.

Hôtel La Reine Jeanne (☎ 05 59 67 00 76, fax 05 59 69 09 63, ⓔ reine.jeanne .orthez@wanadoo.fr, 44 rue Bourg-Vieux) Doubles with WC €45/49 with shower/bath. Menus about €14-43. This Logis de France hotel occupies 17th- and 18th-century quarters opposite the tourist office. The very good restaurant runs its own annual cookery course (see Courses in the Facts for the Visitor chapter). On selected winter weekends jazz groups play in the restaurant.

Auberge Saint-Loup (☎ 05 59 69 15 40, 20 rue du Pont Vieux) Menus €15-30. Open midday & evening Tues-Sat, midday only Sun. Across the old bridge in an equally old inn is one of the best places in Béarn for quality regional specialities.

If all this is too much for your pocket, the *Café de la Place d'Armes* (☎ 05 59 69 10 08, 2 place d'Armes) does coffee and €4 sandwiches daily.

Getting There & Away

TPR buses stop here en route from Pau (€5.85, 45 minutes) to Bayonne, three times daily, and SNCF runs one or two daily buses. Trains from Pau (€6.10, 25 minutes) stop here about 10 times daily.

SALIES DE BÉARN

postcode 64270 • pop 5000 • elevation 53m

This is one of the Béarn's most postcard-pretty villages – its half-timbered, brightly painted, hygienically whitewashed houses festooned with flower boxes and washing, and its compact, well marked centre a network of sun-washed lanes. Wooden balconies lean picturesquely out over the River Saleys. Here you may refresh yourself, or you may perish from boredom.

Hyper-saline, 50°C springs gave Salies its name and its vocation. Back in the mists of time, says a legend, an injured wild boar stumbled into a swamp and died, only to be discovered the following year, encrusted with salt and perfectly preserved. For centuries Salisiens made their living from this salt. Curing with it is deemed essential to the taste of famous Bayonne hams. When the competition from sea-salt got tough, Salies reinvented itself as a thermal spa.

Orientation & Information

From the bus stop on place du Général de Gaulle walk south over the bridge, to the end of rue Loumé. Turn right and cross another bridge to the tourist office, or turn left into place de la Trompe and place du Bayaá, the heart of town.

The tourist office (☎ 05 59 38 00 33, fax 05 59 38 02 95, e salies-de-bearn.tourisme@ wanadoo.fr), on rue des Bains, is open 9.30am to noon and 2pm to 6pm Monday to Saturday (9.30am to 12.30pm and 2pm to 6.30pm, plus Sunday morning, in July and August).

There's a Crédit Agricole bank, with ATM, on place du Bayaá. A publicity firm called Bagur Création (☎/fax 05 59 38 17 02), 11 place de la Trompe, offers Internet access for €0.10/6.85 per minute/hour. It opens Tuesday to Saturday.

Things to See & Do

The **station thermale** (☎ 05 59 38 10 11, place du Jardin Public; open 9am-1pm & 2pm-6.30pm Tues-Fri, 9am-2pm Sat) is just north of the tourist office. Hot, super-salty pools are for spa patients, but visitors can soak in cooler (32°C), diluted pools for one/1½/two hours at a cost of €7.60/9.15/ 12.20.

Off to one side of place du Bayaá is a little saline **fountain** in the shape of a boar's head, with a Béarnaise motto, 'If I hadn't died here, nobody would live here'.

North off place de la Trompe is a 17th-century house containing a little **Musée du Sel** *(rue des Puits Salants)* with a reconstruction of a traditional salt workshop. Near the boar's head fountain in place du Bayaá is a folklore museum, the **Musée des Arts et Traditions**. Both are open 3pm to 6pm Tuesday to Saturday from mid-May to mid-Oct (closed the rest of the year). A single ticket (€2.30, free for under-12s), from the tourist office or either museum, admits you to both.

Places to Stay

Accommodation here is an odd mix of top and bottom-end places.

Auberge de Jeunesse (☎ 05 59 65 06 96, Stade 'Al Cartero', chemin du Padu) Dorm beds €6.85. Open year round. Guests can use the kitchen at this small, unheated hostel, and there's space to pitch a tent. Walk south-west out of place du Bayaá on rue du Canal and rue Félix Pécaut for 600m.

Camp Municipal de Mosqueros (☎ 05 59 38 12 94, fax 05 59 38 06 43, Base de Plein Air de Mosquéros, av Al Cartero) Adult/pitch €2.40/2.45. Open June-Sept. Salies' municipal camp site is 1.2km west on the Bayonne road (D17).

Hôtel Hélios (☎ 05 59 38 37 59, fax 05 59 38 16 41, D933 route d'Orthez) Rooms €27.45-36.60. Breakfast €6.10. Open year round. Golfers will like this hotel, in a country house beside a golf course and clubhouse on the grounds of the Domain d'Hélios, 1km east of town. Most other guests are spa patients.

Places to Eat
Place du Bayaá comes alive with *markets* every Thursday morning (food and clothing) and Saturday morning (food).

Pizzeria Il Capitello (☎ 05 59 65 04 17, 16 place du Bayaá) Pizzas & pasta €5.50-9, *menus* €4.55-22.85. Open Thur-Tues (daily in July-Aug). Budgeteers can fill up Italian-style at little Il Capitello.

Restaurant La Terrasse (☎ 05 59 38 09 83, rue Loumé) Menus €12.95-19.80. Open midday & evening Tues-Sun, evening only Mon (daily July-Aug). La Terrasse is one of Béarn's top places for regional cooking, and has outdoor riverside dining. Rescue your budget with the €6.40 plat du jour.

Getting There & Away
Salies is midway between Pau and Bayonne, just over an hour to either by bus (€8.25); TPR's Pau-Bayonne bus stops here three times daily. The nearest train station is 7km to the north at Puyoô, on the Pau-Bayonne line (€7.60, 35 minutes either way), with about five services daily (fewer at the weekend).

SAUVETERRE DE BÉARN
postcode 64390 • pop 1300 • elevation 70m
Here's a town good for strolling through, and letting your imagination go – fortified in stone and cloaked in greenery, with plenty of well preserved and interesting architecture, set on a cliff above a peaceful, sighing river. Like Orthez, Sauveterre has a fortified bridge, but only half of one, full of mystery. The longer you wander, the more you find: vine-covered stairways and landings, little courtyards, old fountains.

History
Viscount Centule IV of Béarn chartered the town in 1090 as a *sauveterre*, a free zone from the miseries of war, and – just to make sure – fortified it to the hilt, perhaps because of its position on routes between Béarn and its tumultuous neighbours, Navarre and Aquitaine. Much of what you see now are 12th- to 14th-century improvements by his descendants, Gaston VII and Gaston Fébus.

Orientation & Information
The old town sits on the high north bank of the River Oloron. The tourist office (☎ 05 59 38 58 65, fax 05 59 38 94 82) is in the shadow of the town hall, at the eastern end of town on place Royale. It opens 10am to 1pm and 3pm to 7pm Monday to Saturday mid-June to August, and 10am to 1pm and 3pm to 6pm Tuesday to Friday the rest of the year. Here you'll find a good, English-language *Guided Tour of Sauveterre* (€3.05).

Also on place Royale are the post office and a Crédit Agricole bank.

Pont de la Légende
It's thought that this bridge – down chemin du Pont de la Légende at the south-western end of the old town – was built by Gaston VII in the 13th century, and fixed with a drawbridge by Gaston Fébus. Once upon a time it presumably crossed the river via the little Île de la Glère.

Of course the bridge has a legend attached to it – literally, on a plaque by the tower door. Sancie, wife of Gaston V, gave birth to a dead child while her husband was away on a campaign. Rumours of witchcraft spread. Sancie's brother Sanche, king of Navarre, had her put to trial by water – tie her up, throw her in the river (from this bridge, goes the story) and see if God saves her. Of course He does and the story ends happily. The only problem is that the bridge was built decades after Sancie and Gaston lived here.

Église St-André
The St Andrew Church, on place d'Église within sight of the tourist office, was consecrated in the 12th century. It is Romanesque outside – including a simple, inventive tympanum over the door – and plain, more or less Gothic inside. But look for Romanesque columns framing both little side-chapels; a scattering of charming carved capitals; and, just to the right of the

main door as you enter, a little door for the use of *les cagots*, a curious medieval 'untouchable' caste – possibly ostracised for deformity, illness or ancestry – about which bits of evidence appear in the older towns throughout the region.

Other Things to See

There's more to see, though most buildings of interest are closed to the public.

The so-called **Château Gaston Fébus**, in the town centre and above the river, was almost certainly built by Gaston VII. Originally it was entered through a barbican (a covered outer gate) and drawbridge on the western side.

The stark 12th-century **Tour Monréal** behind the church is probably the ancient keep, with metre-thick walls and slit windows. Beside it is one of several stairways leading down to the riverside, from where you get a good look at the **ramparts**, some of the sturdiest of any town in Béarn des Gaves.

Just inside the ancient **porte de Datter**, on the western side, are the heavy walls of the old **armoury**. Across the lane is a **fortified house** that may once have been a guardhouse.

Up an alley just north of the church is the **Fort de Tolose**, a 16th-century addition to the northern ramparts, which run through the middle of the block here.

East of the tourist office is a former **Carmelite convent**, built at the request of Gaston Fébus.

Places to Stay & Eat

The tourist office keeps a list of modest local *chambres d'hôte*.

Camp Municipal Le Gave (☎ 05 59 38 50 17, fax 05 59 38 94 82, chemin du Pont de la Légende) Adult/pitch/tent €1.55/2.20/ 1.10. Open June-Sept. This plain, shady municipal facility is perfectly sited beside the Oloron.

At the time of writing, both of Sauveterre's hotels had closed down, though there were hopes that under new ownership the good-value *Hostellerie du Château* (☎ 05 59 38 52 10, fax 05 59 38 96 49, rue Léon Berard), right behind the chateau, would reopen.

Getting There & Away

Sauveterre sits in a crook of the D933, the St-Jean Pied de Port to Orthez road. The only public buses are SNCF's, from Dax (€7.75, 50 minutes) to Mauléon-Licharre, running twice a day (once Saturday).

Hautes-Pyrénées

LOURDES
postcode 65100 • pop 15,000
• elevation 400m

Lourdes, 44km south-east of Pau, was just a sleepy Pyrénées market town until 1858, when Bernadette Soubirous (1844–79), a near-illiterate, 14-year-old peasant girl, saw the Virgin Mary in a series of 18 visions in a grotto near the town. These were eventually investigated by the Vatican, which confirmed them as bona fide apparitions. Bernadette, who lived out her short life as a nun, was in 1933 canonised as St Bernadette.

These events were to turn Lourdes into one of the world's most important pilgrimage sites. Some five million visitors now come here annually from all over the world. Well over half are pilgrims, including many sick people seeking cures. Some 45% now come from beyond France's frontiers.

Accompanying the fervent, almost medieval, piety of these pilgrims is an astounding display of tacky commercial exuberance – wall thermometers, shake-up snow domes and other 'religious art' (ie, souvenirs) are on sale everywhere you turn. It's easy to mock, but bear in mind that some people have spent their life savings to come here. For many of the Catholic faithful, Lourdes is as sacred as Jerusalem is to Jews, Mecca to Muslims or the Ganges to Hindus.

Lourdes has over 350 hotels – in all of France, only Paris has more – so you shouldn't need help finding a bed. There's plenty of lower-end accommodation. You may have to look harder than usual during Easter, Whitsuntide, Ascension Day, during May and from August to early October. Rooms are scarcest in mid-August during France's Pèlerinage Nationale (National Pilgrimage), either side of Assumption Day

(15 August). In winter the town practically hibernates, and most hotels shut down.

The whole town is unbearably tidy, and picturesque at a distance, though it's only really worth a detour if you're here because of St Bernadette, as it were. It's just over the line from Béarn, in the Hautes-Pyrénées department.

Orientation

Lourdes' main east–west streets are rue de la Grotte and blvd de la Grotte. Both lead west across the Gave de Pau to the Sanctuaires Notre Dame de Lourdes, the vast complex that has grown up around the original cave where Bernadette had her visions.

The north–south axis, called av du Général Baron Maransin (or Chaussée Maransin) near the town centre, connects the train station with place Peyramale, where the tourist office is.

Information

Tourist Offices The spiffy tourist office (☎ 05 62 42 77 40, fax 05 62 94 60 95, e lourdes@sudfr.com), on place Peyramale, is open 9am to 7pm Monday to Saturday May to October (plus 10am to 6pm Sunday, Easter to mid-October), and 9am to noon and 2pm to 6pm Monday to Saturday mid-October to April (except to 7pm mid-March to April).

For multilingual information and brochures on the Sanctuaires Notre Dame de Lourdes, go to the Forum Information office (☎ 05 62 42 78 78, e saccueil@lourdes-france.com), on Esplanade des Processions. It opens 8.30am to 12.30pm and 1.30pm to 6.30pm daily April to mid-October (no lunch break in July and August), and 9am to noon and 2pm to 6pm daily for the rest of the year.

Lourdes is one big traffic jam in summer. If you have a vehicle, leave it near either the train or bus station, where parking is free, and walk.

Money There are branch banks with ATMs along rue de la Grotte, blvd de la Grotte, Chaussée Maransin and elsewhere. The post office also has exchange facilities.

Post & Communications The main post office, at 1 rue de Langelle, has Cyberposte. Lourdes' BIJ, at the Forum Centre Social (☎ 05 62 94 94 00, fax 05 62 94 12 14, e bij.lourdes@wanadoo.fr), on place du Champ Commun, has Internet access for €3.05 per hour (free on Wednesday; book ahead) and is open 9am to noon and 2pm to 4pm weekdays. Difintel (☎ 05 62 42 30 68), 7 rue de la Grotte, charges €5.35 per hour, Monday to Saturday.

Bookshops Some walking maps are available at Librairie Lettres et Images (☎ 05 62 94 00 29), 7 rue St-Pierre. The Maison de la Presse, at 23 rue de la Grotte, stocks some foreign newspapers. The Book Shop (☎ 05 62 42 27 94), 5 rue du Bourg, has lots of English-language books, mainly on religious topics but with some English classics, travel titles and Pyrénées maps.

Laundry Laverie Libre Service is situated on Chaussée Maransin, opposite the Hôtel Ibis. It opens 7am to 9pm daily.

Medical Services & Emergency The Centre Hospitalier Général (hospital; ☎ 05 62 42 42 42) is at 3 av Marqui. The police station (☎ 05 62 42 72 72) is at 7 rue Baron Duprat.

Sanctuaires Notre Dame de Lourdes

Development began at the site of Bernadette's visions within a decade of the events of 1858, and has continued ever since. It's hard to see how the gaudy architecture of the time – more reminiscent of Disneyland than of Gothic cathedrals – inspires awe and devotion, but it clearly does.

The holiest site is known variously as the **Grotte de Massabielle**, the Grotte Miraculeuse or the Grotte des Apparitions. Its walls have been worn smooth by millions of hands over the years. Nearby are 17 **pools** in which 400,000 people immerse themselves each year. The last medically certifiable cure took place in 1987 and after a 12-year investigation was recognised by the church as a miracle.

LOURDES

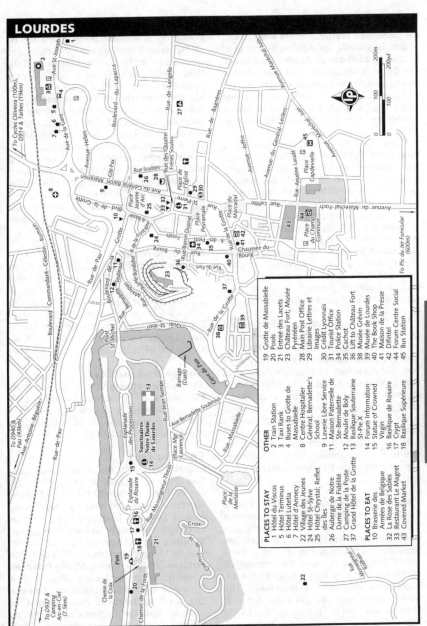

PLACES TO STAY
1 Hôtel du Viscos
5 Hôtel Terminus
6 Hôtel Lutetia
7 Hôtel d'Annecy
22 Village des Jeunes
24 Hôtel St-Sylve
25 Hôtel Chrystal; Reflet des Îles
26 Auberge de Notre Dame de la Fidélité
27 Camping de la Poste
37 Grand Hôtel de la Grotte

PLACES TO EAT
10 Brasserie des Armées de Belgique
32 La Rose des Sables
33 Restaurant Le Magret
43 Covered Market

OTHER
2 Train Station
3 Taxi Rank
4 Buses to Grotte de Massabielle
8 Centre Hospitalier Général; Bernadette's School
9 Laverie Libre Service des Îles
11 Maison Paternelle de Ste-Bernadette
12 Moulin de Boly
13 Basilique Souterraine St-Pie X
14 Forum Information
15 Statue of Crowned Virgin
16 Basilique de Rosaire
17 Crypt
18 Basilique Supérieure
19 Grotte de Massabielle
20 Pools
21 Entreé des Lacets
23 Château Fort; Musée Pyrénéen
29 Librairie Lettres et Images
30 Crédit Lyonnais
31 Tourist Office
34 Police Station
35 Cachot
36 Lift to Château Fort
38 Musée Grévin
39 Musée de Lourdes
40 The Book Shop
41 Maison de la Presse
42 Difintel
44 Forum Centre Social
45 Bus Station

BÉARN

384 Hautes-Pyrénées – Lourdes

The 19th-century part of the Sanctuaries has three main sections. At the western end of the Esplanade du Rosaire is the neo-Byzantine **Basilique du Rosaire** (Basilica of the Rosary), inaugurated in 1889. Above and beyond this is the **crypt**, opened in 1866 and reserved for silent worship. Above that is the spire-topped, neo-Gothic **Basilique Supérieure** (Upper Basilica), completed in 1876.

From April to at least mid-October, a **Procession Eucharistique** (Blessed Sacrament Procession), in which pilgrims carry banners along the Esplanade des Processions, takes place daily at 5pm, and there is a solemn **torch-light procession** nightly at 9pm from the Massabielle Grotto.

When it's wet, the Procession Eucharistique is held in the bunker-like **Basilique Souterraine St-Pie X** (Underground Basilica of St Pius X), built in 1959 and big enough to hold 20,000. It's somewhat redeemed by fine, back-lit works of *gemmail* – superimposed pieces of coloured glass embedded in colourless enamel.

The Grotte de Massabielle can be visited 24 hours a day via the Entrée des Lacets on rue Monseigneur Theas. The Pont St-Michel entrance, and all four places of worship, are open 5am to midnight daily, year round. Visitors should dress with relative modesty – very short skirts, even shorts and a T-shirt, are out, for example. Smoking is also strictly forbidden throughout the complex.

Bus No 1 links the train station with the Grotte de Massabielle every 20 minutes 7am to 6.30pm (to 10.30pm in July and August), for €1.70.

Chemin de la Croix The 1.5km Way of the Cross, also known as the Chemin du Calvaire (Calvary Way), leads up the forested hillside from close to the Basilique Supérieure. Inaugurated in 1912, it is lined with life-size versions of the Stations of the Cross. The especially devout mount the stairs to the first station on their knees. The path is open 6am to 7pm from April to October and 9am to 5pm for the rest of the year.

Other Bernadette Sites

Four other places that figure in the life of St Bernadette are open to the public at no charge. Her birthplace, **Moulin de Boly** (Boly Mill), can be found at 12 rue Bernadette Soubirous. On the same road is the **Maison Paternelle de Ste-Bernadette**, the house furnished by the town after the apparitions. The **Cachot**, a former prison at 15 rue des Petits Fossés, is where Bernadette was living when she had her visions.

Bernadette's school, where she studied and lived from 1860 to 1866 with the Sœurs de Notre Dame de Nevers (Sisters of Our Lady of Nevers), is now part of the town's Centre Hospitalier Général. West of the train station on Chaussée Maransin, it contains some of her personal effects.

Musée Grévin

This commercial wax museum (☎ 05 62 94 33 74, at 87 rue de la Grotte; adult/child aged 6-12 €5.35/2.65; 9am-11.30am & 1.30pm-6.30pm Mon-Sat, 10am-11.30am & 1.30pm-6.30pm Sun Apr–mid-Nov; 8pm-10pm daily July-Aug) has life-size dioramas of important events in the lives of Jesus Christ and of St Bernadette.

Musée de Lourdes

The Lourdes Museum (☎ 05 62 94 28 00, Parking de l'Égalité; adult/child €4.90/2.45; 9am-noon & 1.30pm-6.45pm daily Apr-Oct) portrays the life of St Bernadette and the history of Lourdes.

Château Fort

Legend has it that the eyrie-like Château Fort (Fortified Castle; ☎ 05 62 42 37 37, rue du Fort; adult/child €4.90/2.45; 9am-noon & 1.30pm-6pm daily Apr-Sept; 9am-noon & 2pm-6pm Wed-Mon Nov-Mar) was taken by Charlemagne. It has also served as a military fort and a prison. Most of the present buildings date from the 17th and 18th centuries. Inside is a small **Musée Pyrénéen** (same hours; no additional admission) of Pyrénéan folk art and traditions. You can take a lift up from rue Baron Duprat, or walk up from the northern end of rue du Bourg.

Pic du Jer

The Pic du Jer, whose 948m summit affords a panoramic view of Lourdes and the central Pyrénées, can be reached by a six-minute ride in a funicular (☎ 05 62 94 00 41, 59 av F Lagardère; return ticket adult/child €6.70/3.35; 1.30pm-6.30pm daily Apr & Oct; 9.30am-noon & 1.30pm-6.30pm daily May-June & Sept; 9.30am-12.30pm & 1.30pm-6.30pm daily July-Aug). The lower terminus is on blvd d'Espagne, 1.5km south of the tourist office (bus No 2 from place Marcadal, €1.70).

Alternatively, a fine walk to the summit (three hours return) starts from near the lower station.

Places to Stay

Camping There are several camp sites, with one in the town centre. The tourist office has a map-brochure with information on other nearby sites.

Camping de la Poste (☎ 05 62 94 40 35, 26 rue de Langelle) Adult/pitch €2.25/3.50. Open Easter–mid-Oct. As it's bang in the middle of town, this friendly, pocket-size camp site is often full in summer.

Camping Arc-en-Ciel (☎/fax 05 62 41 81 54, D937 route de Bétharram, Peyrouse) Adult/pitch €2.60/2.60; 4-person bungalow/gîte €275/335 per week. Open Easter-Sept. This tidy, roadside farm site 8km west of Lourdes has minimal shade, but there's a pool. They also rent bungalows and gîtes.

Village des Jeunes (☎ 05 62 42 79 95, ⓔ village.jeunes@lourdes-france.com, av Monseigneur Rodhain) €2.75 per person. Open Mar-Sept. Young pilgrims (but not ordinary tourists) can pitch a tent at this Youth Village 1km south-west of the Sanctuaries.

Hostels The hostels in Lourdes, like some of the camping facilities, are primarily for religious visitors.

Village des Jeunes (see Camping) Dorm/private bed €4.25/5.50; bring your own sleeping sheet or bag. Young pilgrims staying here can join a range of religious activities. Reception is staffed round the clock.

Auberge de Notre Dame de Fidélité (☎ 05 62 42 14 91, 15 rue Soubies) B&B €9.15, showers €1.20, bed-linen €1.55. Evening meal €6.10. Notre Dame de la Fidélité is a convent, so you'll have to behave yourself; doors shut sharply at 9pm.

Hotels Lourdes has lots of cheap hotels. The area around the train station is a good place to find value for money. In the 'lower town' – the semi-pedestrianised streets just west of the tourist office – there are also many small and modestly priced family-friendly places. Moneyed visitors stay in the top-end hotels close to the Sanctuaires.

Camping de la Poste (see Camping) rents a few excellent-value rooms with shower and WC for €22.85.

Hôtel du Viscos (☎ 05 62 94 08 06, fax 05 62 94 26 74, 6 bis av St-Joseph) Doubles with/without WC €30.50/24.40; hall showers free. Open Feb–mid-Nov. Rooms in this unpretentious, family-run hotel near the train station are plain, but service is personal.

Hôtel d'Annecy (☎ 05 62 94 13 75, 13 av de la Gare) Doubles with WC/shower/both €22.85/25.90/28.95; hall showers €1.50. Breakfast €3.80. Open Apr-Oct. Spruce and set back from the road, the Annecy has everything from hostel-like rooms (showers in adjacent building) to en suite facilities, plus off-street parking.

Hôtel Lutetia (☎ 05 62 94 22 85, fax 05 62 94 11 10, 19 av de la Gare) Doubles €21.35, with WC €26.70, with WC & shower €35.05; hall showers €2.75. Breakfast €4.90. Open mid-Mar–mid-Nov. This well run hotel near the train station has simple but comfortable rooms.

Hôtel Terminus (☎ 05 62 94 68 00, fax 05 62 42 23 89, ⓔ terminuslourdes@aol .com, 31 av de la Gare) Singles/doubles €25.90/28.95. Open Easter–mid-Nov. The Terminus, right beside the train station, has big old rooms with shower and WC, and there is a downstairs brasserie (see Places to Eat).

Hôtel St-Sylve (☎/fax 05 62 94 63 48, 9 rue de la Fontaine) Doubles with/without shower €27.45/19.80. Breakfast €3.80. Open Apr-Sept. Right in the town centre, the St-Sylve is snug and cheerful downstairs, yet rooms are big.

BÉARN

Hôtel Chrystal (☎ *05 62 94 00 36, fax 05 62 94 80 32, 16 rue Basse*) Doubles with/without WC €24.40/21.35. Breakfast €3.80. Open Feb-Oct. This pokey but cheerful place in the centre has plain rooms, all with shower, and a simple restaurant (see Places to Eat).

Grand Hôtel de la Grotte (☎ *05 62 94 58 87, fax 05 62 94 20 50, 66 rue de la Grotte*) Singles €61-103.65, doubles €65.55-122. Open Apr-Oct. This is one of Lourdes' finer spots, in *fin de siècle* quarters in the heart of the 'souvenir district', with balconies, mod cons and a gorgeous garden.

Places to Eat

Most hotels at mid-range or higher offer half- or full-board, sometimes obligatory in the high season. It tends to work out cheaper than eating out, though the food is rarely inspiring. The best-value brasseries and restaurants are in the narrow streets west and north-west of the tourist office.

Brasserie-Restaurant Terminus (see *Places to Stay*) Menus €11.45-19.65. Open daily. This bright, airy place by the train station does pizzas and has a convenient though unexceptional €7.60 plat du jour.

Brasserie des Armées de Belgique (☎ *05 62 94 00 07, 22 blvd de la Grotte*) Midday menus €7.45-12.20. Open Thur-Tues. In among legions of streetside eateries around place Jeanne d'Arc, this brisk one does anything from pizzas to pretty good regional dishes. Fill up with the €6.85 plat du jour.

Reflet des Îles (*Hôtel Chrystal; see Places to Stay*) Main dishes around €10. For a change, try a mildly spicy curry or massala from the Indian Ocean island of La Réunion in this modest upstairs restaurant; helpings are small.

Restaurant Le Magret (☎ *05 62 94 20 55, 10 rue des Quatre Frères Soulas*) Menus €12.95-30.50. Open Tues-Sun. Opposite the tourist office, Le Magret has versatile a la carte dishes and *menus*, both very good value for money.

La Rose des Sables (☎ *05 62 42 06 82, 8 rue des Quatre Frères Soulas*) Couscous with 1-5 meats €11.90-18.60. Open Tues-Sun, plus Mon July-Aug. This North African restaurant – a bold Muslim presence in this fervently Catholic town – offers a good three-course dinner for €14.95.

The *covered market (place du Champ Commun)* is open 7am to 1pm Monday to Saturday (daily Easter to October).

Getting There & Away

From the bus station on place Capdevielle, TPR (Pau ☎ 05 59 82 95 85) has at least three daily services to Pau (€6.70, 1¼ hours).

Lourdes is well connected by rail – there are links to all of France. Regional links – all with multiple daily services – include the Bayonne (€16.45, 1¾ hours), Bordeaux (€26.85, 2½ hours), Pau (€6, 30 minutes) and Toulouse (€19.35, 2¼ hours) lines. For those going to Paris there are five daily TGVs to Gare de Montparnasse (€63.40, six hours) plus an overnight train to Gare d'Austerlitz.

Getting Around

There's a taxi stand (☎ 05 62 94 31 30) outside the train station.

Between the months of May and August, Cycles Oliveira (☎ 05 62 42 24 24) – 14 av Alexandre Marqui, near the train station – rents out both VTTs (mountain bikes) and cheaper street bikes.

Language

Modern French developed from the *langue d'oïl*, a group of dialects spoken north of the River Loire that grew out of the vernacular Latin used during the late Gallo-Roman period. The langue d'oïl – particularly the Francien dialect spoken in the Île de France – eventually displaced the *langue d'oc*, the dialects spoken in the south of the country and from which the Mediterranean region of Languedoc got its name.

Standard French is taught and spoken in France, but its various sub-dialects and accents are an important source of identity in certain regions. In addition, some of the peoples subjected to French rule many centuries ago have preserved their traditional languages. These include Flemish in the far north; Alsatian in Alsace; Breton (a Celtic tongue similar to Cornish and Welsh) in Brittany; Basque (a language unrelated to any other) in the Basque Country; Catalan in Roussillon (Catalan is the official language of nearby Andorra and the first language of many in the Spanish province of Catalonia); Provençal in Provence; and Corsican on the island of Corsica.

Around 122 million people worldwide speak French as their first language; it is an official language in Belgium, Switzerland, Luxembourg, the Canadian province of Quebec and over two dozen other countries, most of them former French colonies in Africa. It is also spoken in the Val d'Aosta region of north-western Italy. Various forms of Creole are used in Haiti, French Guiana and parts of Louisiana. France has a special government ministry (Ministère de la Francophonie) to deal with the country's relations with the French-speaking world.

While the French rightly or wrongly have a reputation for assuming that all human beings should speak French – until WWI it was *the* international language of culture and diplomacy – you'll find that any attempt to communicate in French will be much appreciated. Probably your best bet is always to approach people politely in French, even if the only sentence you know is *Pardon, madame/monsieur/mademoiselle, parlez-vous anglais?* (Excuse me, madam/sir/miss, do you speak English?).

For a more comprehensive guide to the French language get hold of Lonely Planet's *French phrasebook*.

Grammar

An important distinction is made in French between *tu* and *vous*, which both mean 'you'. *Tu* is only used when addressing people you know well, or children or animals. When addressing an adult who is not a personal friend, *vous* should be used unless the person invites you to use *tu*. In general, younger people insist less on this distinction and they may use *tu* from the beginning of an acquaintance.

All nouns in French are either masculine or feminine and adjectives reflect the gender of the noun they modify. The feminine form of many nouns and adjectives is indicated by a silent *e* added to the masculine form, as in *étudiant* and *étudiante*, the masculine and feminine for 'student'. In the following phrases we have indicated both masculine and feminine forms where necessary. The masculine form comes first, separated from the feminine by a slash. The gender of a noun is often indicated by a preceding article: 'the/a/some', *le/un/du* (m), *la/une/de la* (f); or a possessive adjective, 'my/your/his/her', *mon/ton/son* (m), *ma/ta/sa* (f). With French, unlike English, the possessive adjective agrees in number and gender with the thing possessed: 'his/her mother', *sa mère*.

Pronunciation

Most letters in French are pronounced more or less the same as their English equivalents. A few which may cause confusion are:

j   as the 's' in 'leisure', eg, *jour* (day)

c before e and i, as the 's' in 'sit'; before **a**, **o** and **u** it's pronounced as English 'k'. When undescored with a 'cedilla' (ç) it's always pronounced as the 's' in 'sit'.

French has a number of other sounds that are difficult for Anglophones to produce. These include:

- The distinction between the 'u' sound (as in *tu*) and 'oo' sound (as in *tout*). For both sounds, the lips are rounded and projected forwards, but for the 'u' the tongue is towards the front of the mouth, its tip against the lower front teeth, whereas for the 'oo' the tongue is towards the back of the mouth, its tip behind the gums of the lower front teeth.

- The nasal vowels. With nasal vowels the breath escapes partly through the nose and partly through the mouth. There are no nasal vowels in English; in French there are three, as in *bon vin blanc* (good white wine). These sounds occur where a syllable ends in a single **n** or **m**; the **n** or **m** is silent but indicates the nasalisation of the preceding vowel.

- The **r**. The standard **r** of Parisian French is produced by moving the bulk of the tongue backwards to constrict the air flow in the pharynx while the tip of the tongue rests behind the lower front teeth. It's similar to the noise made by some people before spitting, but with much less friction.

Basics

Yes.	*Oui.*
No.	*Non.*
Maybe.	*Peut-être.*
Please.	*S'il vous plaît.*
Thank you.	*Merci.*
You're welcome.	*Je vous en prie.*
Excuse me.	*Excusez-moi.*
Sorry/Forgive me.	*Pardon.*

Greetings

Hello/Good morning.	*Bonjour.*
Good evening.	*Bonsoir.*
Good night.	*Bonne nuit.*
Goodbye.	*Au revoir.*

Small Talk

How are you?	*Comment allez-vous?* (polite) *Comment vas-tu?/ Comment ça va?* (informal)
Fine, thanks.	*Bien, merci.*
What's your name?	*Comment vous appelez-vous?*
My name is ...	*Je m'appelle ...*
I'm pleased to meet you.	*Enchanté/ Enchantée.* (m/f)
How old are you?	*Quel âge avez-vous?*
I'm ... years old.	*J'ai ... ans.*
Do you like ...?	*Aimez-vous ...?*
Where are you from?	*De quel pays êtes-vous?*

I'm from ...	*Je viens ...*
Australia	*d'Australie*
Canada	*du Canada*
England	*d'Angleterre*
Germany	*d'Allemagne*
Ireland	*d'Irlande*
New Zealand	*de Nouvelle Zélande*
Scotland	*d'Écosse*
Wales	*du Pays de Galle*
the USA	*des États-Unis*

Language Difficulties

I understand.	*Je comprends.*
I don't understand.	*Je ne comprends pas.*
Do you speak English?	*Parlez-vous anglais?*
Could you please write it down?	*Est-ce que vous pouvez l'écrire?*

Getting Around

I want to go to ...	*Je voudrais aller à ...*
I'd like to book a seat to ...	*Je voudrais réserver une place pour ...*

What time does the ... leave/arrive?	*À quelle heure part/arrive ...?*
aeroplane	*l'avion*
bus (city)	*l'autobus*
bus (intercity)	*l'autocar*
ferry	*le ferry(-boat)*
train	*le train*
tram	*le tramway*

Where is (the) ...?	Où est ...?
bus stop	l'arrêt d'autobus
metro station	la station de métro
train station	la gare
tram stop	l'arrêt de tramway
ticket office	le guichet

I'd like a ... ticket.	Je voudrais un billet ...
one-way	aller-simple
return	aller-retour
1st class	première classe
2nd class	deuxième classe

How long does the trip take?	Combien de temps dure le trajet?

The train is ...	Le train est ...
delayed	en retard
on time	à l'heure
early	en avance

Do I need to ...?	Est-ce que je dois ...?
change trains	changer de train
change platform	changer de quai

left-luggage locker	consigne automatique
platform	quai
timetable	horaire

I'd like to hire ...	Je voudrais louer ...
a bicycle	un vélo
a car	une voiture
a guide	un guide

Around Town

I'm looking for ...	Je cherche ...
a bank	une banque/
an exchange office	un bureau de change
the city centre	le centre-ville
the ... embassy	l'ambassade de ...
the hospital	l'hôpital
my hotel	mon hôtel
the market	le marché
the police	la police
the post office	le bureau de poste/ la poste
a public phone	une cabine téléphonique
a public toilet	les toilettes
the tourist office	l'office de tourisme

Signs

Entrée	Entrance
Sortie	Exit
Ouvert	Open
Fermé	Closed
Chambres Libres	Rooms Available
Complet	No Vacancies
Renseignements	Information
Interdit	Prohibited
(Commissariat de) Police	Police Station
Toilettes, WC	Toilets
Hommes	Men
Femmes	Women

Where is (the) ...?	Où est ...?
beach	la plage
bridge	le pont
castle/mansion	le château
cathedral	la cathédrale
church	l'église
island	l'île
lake	le lac
main square	la place centrale
mosque	la mosquée
old city/town	la vieille ville
the palace	le palais
quay/bank	le quai/la rive
ruins	les ruines
sea	la mer
square	la place
tower	la tour

What time does it open/close?	Quelle est l'heure d'ouverture/ de fermeture?

I'd like to make a telephone call.	Je voudrais téléphoner.

I'd like to change ...	Je voudrais changer ...
some money	de l'argent
travellers cheques	chèques de voyage

Directions

How do I get to ...?	Comment dois-je faire pour arriver à ...?
Is it near/far?	Est-ce près/loin?
Can you show me on the map/ city map?	Est-ce que vous pouvez me le montrer sur la carte/le plan?

Go straight ahead.	*Continuez tout droit.*
Turn left.	*Tournez à gauche.*
Turn right.	*Tournez à droite.*

at the traffic lights	*aux feux*
at the next corner	*au prochain coin*
behind	*derrière*
in front of	*devant*
opposite	*en face de*
north	*nord*
south	*sud*
east	*est*
west	*ouest*

Accommodation

I'm looking for ...	*Je cherche ...*
the youth hostel	*l'auberge de jeunesse*
the campground	*le camping*
a hotel	*un hôtel*
Where can I find a cheap hotel?	*Où est-ce que je peux trouver un hôtel bon marché?*
What's the address?	*Quelle est l'adresse?*
Could you write it down, please?	*Est-ce vous pourriez l'écrire, s'il vous plaît?*
Do you have any rooms available?	*Est-ce que vous avez des chambres libres?*
I'd like to book ...	*Je voudrais réserver ...*
a bed	*un lit*
a single room	*une chambre pour une personne*
a double room	*une chambre double*
a room with a shower and toilet	*une chambre avec douche et WC*
I'd like to stay in a dormitory.	*Je voudrais coucher dans un dortoir.*
How much is it ...?	*Quel est le prix ...?*
per night	*par nuit*
per person	*par personne*
Is breakfast included?	*Est-ce que le petit dé-jeuner est compris?*
Can I see the room?	*Est-ce que je peux voir la chambre?*

Where is ...?	*Où est ...?*
the bathroom	*la salle de bains*
the shower	*la douche*
Where is the toilet?	*Où sont les toilettes?*
I'm going to stay ...	*Je resterai ...*
one day	*un jour*
a week	*une semaine*

Shopping

How much is it?	*C'est combien?*
It's too expensive for me.	*C'est trop cher pour moi.*
Can I look at it?	*Est-ce que je peux le/la voir? (m/f)*
I'm just looking.	*Je ne fais que regarder.*
Can I pay by credit card?	*Est-ce que je peux payer avec ma carte de crédit?*
Can I pay by travellers cheques?	*Est-ce que je peux payer avec des chèques de voyage?*
It's too big/small.	*C'est trop grand/petit.*
more/less	*plus/moins*
cheap	*bon marché*
cheaper	*moins cher*
bookshop	*la librairie*
chemist/pharmacy	*la pharmacie*
laundry/laundrette	*la laverie*
market	*le marché*
newsagency	*l'agence de presse*
stationers	*la papeterie*
supermarket	*le supermarché*

Time & Dates

What time is it?	*Quelle heure est-il?*
It's (two) o'clock.	*Il est (deux) heures.*
When?	*Quand?*
today	*aujourd'hui*
tonight	*ce soir*
tomorrow	*demain*
day after tomorrow	*après-demain*
yesterday	*hier*
all day	*toute la journée*
in the morning	*du matin*
in the afternoon	*de l'après-midi*
in the evening	*du soir*

Monday	*lundi*
Tuesday	*mardi*
Wednesday	*mercredi*
Thursday	*jeudi*
Friday	*vendredi*
Saturday	*samedi*
Sunday	*dimanche*

January	*janvier*
February	*février*
March	*mars*
April	*avril*
May	*mai*
June	*juin*
July	*juillet*
August	*août*
September	*septembre*
October	*octobre*
November	*novembre*
December	*décembre*

Numbers

1	*un*
2	*deux*
3	*trois*
4	*quatre*
5	*cinq*
6	*six*
7	*sept*
8	*huit*
9	*neuf*
10	*dix*
11	*onze*
12	*douze*
13	*treize*
14	*quatorze*
15	*quinze*
16	*seize*
17	*dix-sept*
18	*dix-huit*
19	*dix-neuf*
20	*vingt*
100	*cent*
1000	*mille*

one million	*un million*

Health

I'm sick.	*Je suis malade.*
I need a doctor.	*Il me faut un médecin.*

Emergencies

Help!	*Au secours!*
Call a doctor!	*Appelez un médecin!*
Call the police!	*Appelez la police!*
Leave me alone!	*Fichez-moi la paix!*
I've been robbed.	*On m'a volé.*
I've been raped.	*On m'a violée.*
I'm lost.	*Je me suis égaré/ égarée. (m/f)*

Where is the hospital?	*Où est l'hôpital?*
I have diarrhoea.	*J'ai la diarrhée.*
I'm pregnant.	*Je suis enceinte.*

I'm ...	*Je suis ...*
diabetic	*diabétique*
epileptic	*épileptique*
asthmatic	*asthmatique*
anaemic	*anémique*

I'm allergic ...	Je suis allergique ...
to antibiotics	*aux antibiotiques*
to penicillin	*à la pénicilline*
to bees	*aux abeilles*

antiseptic	*antiseptique*
aspirin	*aspirine*
condoms	*préservatifs*
contraceptive	*contraceptif*
medicine	*médicament*
nausea	*nausée*
sunblock cream	*crème solaire haute protection*
tampons	*tampons hygiéniques*

FOOD

breakfast	*le petit déjeuner*
lunch	*le déjeuner*
dinner	*le dîner*
grocery store	*l'épicerie*

I'd like the set menu.	*Je prends le menu.*
I'm a vegetarian.	*Je suis végétarien/ végétarienne.*
I don't eat meat.	*Je ne mange pas de viande.*

Basics

beurre	butter
chocolat	chocolate
confiture	jam
crème fraîche	cream
farine	flour
huile	oil
lait	milk
miel	honey
œufs	eggs
poivre	pepper
sel	salt
sucre	sugar
vinaigre	vinegar

Utensils

bouteille	bottle
carafe	carafe
pichet	jug
verre	glass
couteau	knife
cuillère	spoon
fourchette	fork
serviette	serviette (napkin)

Meat, Chicken & Poultry

agneau	lamb
aiguillette	thin slice of duck fillet
andouille or	sausage made from
andouillette	pork or veal tripe
bifteck	steak
bœuf	beef
bœuf haché	minced beef
boudin noir	blood sausage (black pudding)
brochette	kebab
canard	duck
caneton	duckling
cervelle	brains
charcuterie	cooked or prepared meats (usually pork)
cheval	horse meat
chèvre	goat
chevreau	kid (goat)
chevreuil	venison
côte	chop of pork, lamb or mutton
côtelette	cutlet
cuisses de grenouilles	frogs' legs

entrecôte	rib steak
dinde	turkey
épaule d'agneau	shoulder of lamb
escargot	snail
faisan	pheasant
faux-filet	sirloin steak
filet	tenderloin
foie	liver
foie gras de canard	duck liver pâté
gibier	game
gigot d'agneau	leg of lamb
jambon	ham
langue	tongue
lapin	rabbit
lard	bacon
lardon	pieces of chopped bacon
lièvre	hare
mouton	goose
pieds de porc	pigs' trotters
pigeonneau	squab (young pigeon)
pintade	guinea fowl
porc	pork
poulet	chicken
rognons	kidneys
sanglier	wild boar
saucisson	large sausage
saucisson fumé	smoked sausage
steak	steak
tournedos	thick slices of fillet
tripes	tripe
veau	veal
venaison	venison
viande	meat
volaille	poultry

Fish & Seafood

anchois	anchovy
anguille	eel
brème	bream
brochet	pike
cabillaud	cod
calmar	squid
carrelet	plaice
chaudrée	fish stew
chipirons	cuttlefish
colin	hake
coquille Saint-Jacques	scallop
crabe	crab

crevette grise	shrimp	*citrouille*	pumpkin
crevette rose	prawn	*concombre*	cucumber
écrevisse	small, freshwater crayfish	*cornichon*	gherkin (pickle)
		courgette	courgette (zucchini)
fruits de mer	seafood	*crudités*	small pieces of raw vegetables
gambas	king prawns		
goujon	gudgeon (small fresh water fish)	*échalotte*	shallot
		épice	spice
hareng	herring	*épinards*	spinach
homard	lobster	*estragon*	tarragon
huître	oyster	*fenouil*	fennel
langouste	crayfish	*fève*	broad bean
langoustine	very small saltwater 'lobster'; (Dublin Bay prawn)	*genièvre*	juniper
		gingembre	ginger
		haricots	beans
maquereau	mackerel	*haricots blancs*	white beans
merlan	whiting	*haricots rouge*	kidney beans
morue	cod	*haricots verts*	French (string) beans
moules	mussels	*herbe*	herb
oursin	sea urchin	*laitue*	lettuce
palourde	clam	*légume*	vegetable
poisson	fish	*lentilles*	lentils
raie	ray	*maïs*	sweet corn
rouget	mullet	*menthe*	mint
sardine	sardine	*navet*	turnip
saumon	salmon	*oignon*	onion
sole	sole	*olive*	olive
thon	tuna	*origan*	oregano
truite	trout	*panais*	parsnip
		persil	parsley
		petit pois	pea
		poireau	leek
		poivron	green pepper
		pomme de terre	potato
		ratatouille	casserole of aubergines, tomatoes, peppers and garlic

Vegetables, Herbs & Spices

ail	garlic		
aïoli or *ailloli*	garlic mayonnaise		
aneth	dill		
anis	aniseed	*riz*	rice
artichaut	artichoke	*salade*	salad or lettuce
asperge	asparagus	*sarrasin*	buckwheat
aubergine	aubergine (eggplant)	*seigle*	rye
avocat	avocado	*tomate*	tomato
basilic	basil	*truffe*	truffle
betterave	beetroot		
cannelle	cinnamon		
carotte	carrot		
céleri	celery	**Fruit & Nuts**	
cèpe	cep (boletus mushroom)	*abricot*	apricot
		amande	almond
champignon	mushroom	*ananas*	pineapple
champignon de Paris	button mushroom	*arachide*	peanut
chou	cabbage	*banane*	banana

cacahuète	peanut
cassis	blackcurrant
cerise	cherry
citron	lemon
datte	date
figue	fig
fraise	strawberry
framboise	raspberry
grenade	pomegranate
groseille	red currant/gooseberry
mangue	mango
marron	chestnut
melon	melon
mirabelle	type of plum
myrtille	bilberry (blueberry)
noisette	hazelnut
noix de cajou	cashew
orange	orange
pamplemousse	grapefruit
pastèque	watermelon
pêche	peach
pistache	pistachio
poire	pear
pomme	apple
prune	plum
pruneau	prune
raisin	grape

Cooking Methods

à la broche	spit-roasted
à la vapeur	steamed
au feu de bois	cooked over a wood-burning stove
au four	baked
en croûte	in pastry
farci	stuffed
fumé	smoked
gratiné	browned on top with cheese
grillé	grilled
pané	coated in breadcrumbs
rôti	roasted
sauté	sautéed (shallow fried)

Starters (Appetisers)

assiette anglaise – plate of cold mixed meats and sausages

assiette de crudités – plate of raw vegetables with dressings

entrée – starter

fromage de tête – pate made with pig's head set in jelly

soufflé – a light, fluffy dish made with egg yolks, stiffly beaten egg whites, flour and cheese or other ingredients

Soup

bouillabaisse – Mediterranean-style fish soup originally from Marseille, made with several kinds of fish, including *rascasse* (spiny scorpion fish); often eaten as a main course

bouillon – broth or stock

bourride – fish stew; often eaten as a main course

croûtons – fried or roasted bread cubes, often added to soups

potage – thick soup made with pureed vegetables

soupe au pistou – vegetable soup made with a basil and garlic paste

soupe de poisson – fish soup

soupe du jour – soup of the day

ttoro – (French tïoro) chunky Basque fish soup, a kind of fish ragout

Common Meat & Poultry Dishes

axoa d'Espelette (French *hachoa*) – Basque veal stew with onions, garlic, tomatoes and peppers

blanquette de veau or *d'agneau* – veal or lamb stew with white sauce

bœuf bourguignon – beef and vegetable stew cooked in a red wine (usually burgundy)

cassoulet – Languedoc stew made with goose, duck, pork or lamb fillets and haricot beans

chapon – capon

chou farci – stuffed cabbage

choucroute – sauerkraut with sausage and other prepared meats

confit de canard/d'oie – duck or goose preserved and cooked in its own fat

coq au vin – chicken cooked in wine

civet – game stew

fricassée – stew with meat that has first been fried

grillade – grilled meats

marcassin – young wild boar

poulet Basquaise – chicken sauteed with onions, peppers and tomatoes

quenelles – dumplings made of a finely sieved mixture of cooked fish or (rarely) meat

steak tartare – raw ground meat mixed with onion, raw egg yolk and herbs

thon basquaise – tuna grilled with peppers and tomatoes, Basque style

tripotxa – blood pudding or little lamb or veal sausages (Basque)

Ordering a Steak

bleu – nearly raw

saignant – very rare (literally, 'bleeding')

à point – medium rare but still pink

bien cuit – literally, 'well cooked', but usually like medium rare

Sauces & Accompaniments

béchamel – basic white sauce

huile d'olive – olive oil

mornay – cheese sauce

moutarde – mustard

pistou – pesto (pounded mix of basil, hard cheese, olive oil and garlic)

provençale – tomato, garlic, herb and olive oil dressing or sauce

tartare – mayonnaise with herbs

vinaigrette – salad dressing made with oil, vinegar, mustard and garlic

Desserts & Sweets

crêpe – thin pancake

crêpes suzettes – orange-flavoured crêpes flambeed in liqueur

bergamotes – orange-flavoured confectionery

dragée – sugared almond

éclair – pastry filled with cream

far – flan with prunes (a Breton speciality)

flan – egg-custard dessert

frangipane – pastry filled with cream and flavoured with almonds or a cake mixture containing ground almonds

galette – wholemeal or buckwheat pancake; also a type of biscuit

gâteau – cake

gateau Basque – a shortbread crust filled with almond cream or cherry preserves

gaufre – waffle

gelée – jelly

glace – ice cream

glace au chocolat – chocolate ice cream

île flottante – literally 'floating island'; beaten egg white lightly cooked, floating on a creamy sauce

macarons – macaroons (sweet biscuit made from ground almonds, sugar and egg whites)

sablé – shortbread biscuit

farine de semoule – semolina flour

tarte – tart (pie)

tarte aux pommes – apple tart

yaourt – yogurt

Snacks

croque-monsieur – a grilled ham and cheese sandwich

croque-madame – a croque-monsieur with a fried egg

frites – chips (French fries)

quiche – quiche; savoury egg, bacon and cream tart

Glossary

Refer to the boxed text 'The Basque Language' in the French Basque Country chapter for some Basque words and phrases.

(m) indicates masculine gender, (f) feminine gender and (pl) plural

accueil (m) – reception; welcome
alimentation (f) – grocery shop
aller-retour – return (round) trip
aller-simple or **aller** – one way (single)
appellation d'origine contrôlée (AOC) or **appellation contrôlée** (f) – a system of strict definition and control of quality wines, spirits and some other products
auberge (f) – inn (generally family-run)
auberge de jeunesse (f) – youth hostel

balade (f) – stroll, short excursion
barrage (m) – dam
base/parc de loisirs (f) – leisure centre with outdoor activities
bastide (f) – fortified 'new town' built in the 13th to 14th centuries, usually on a grid surrounding an arcaded square
billet (m) – ticket
billeterie (f) – ticket office or counter
bodéga (f) – literally 'cellar'; a Spanish-style bar serving wine from the barrel
boisson (f) – drink
boulangerie (f) – bakery, bread shop
boules (f pl) – bowls; a game played with heavy metal balls on a sandy pitch; also called *pétanque*
bornes (f pl) – taxi ranks
BP (f) – *boîte postale;* post-office box
brasserie (f) – restaurant, usually serving food all day
brocante (f) – second-hand item or bric-a-brac

camping à la ferme (m) – farm camping
carnet (m) – a book of bus, tram or metro tickets sold at a reduced rate
carrefour (m) – crossroads
carte (f) – card; menu; map
cassolette (f) – plate

causse (m) – limestone plateau
cave (f) or **chai** (m) – wine cellar or above-ground storage area for fermentation casks
centre (de) hospitalier (m) – hospital
chambre (f) – room
chambre d'hôte (f) – B&B
charcuterie (f) – delicatessen
col (m) – mountain pass
commissariat (m) – police station
commune (f) – district, parish
composteur (m) – ticket-punching machine
consigne (f) – left-luggage office
consigne automatique (f) – left-luggage locker
couchette (f) – sleeping berth on a train or ferry
courses landaises (m pl) – 'running of the bulls', during which cows are taunted, chased and dodged in an arena
cuisine du terroir (f) – country cooking

DAB (m) – *distributeur automatique de billets;* automated teller machine (ATM)
dégustation (f) – tasting
demi-pension (f) – half-board (B&B plus either lunch or dinner)
demi-tarif (m) – half-price
département (m) – department of a *région*, with its own local council
domaine (m) – estate, property
dortoir (m) – dormitory
douane (f) – customs

église (f) – church
épicerie (f) – small grocery shop
équitation (f) – horse riding
escalade (f) – rock-climbing

ferme auberge (f) – farm restaurant offering home-cooked meals
fête (f) – festival
fête patronale (f) – saint's day
foire (f) – fair
forfait (m) – inclusive price, eg, for two people plus car and tent/caravan at a camping ground
formule or **formule rapide** (f) – like a

menu, but with a choice of two out of three courses (eg, starter and main course or main course and dessert)
foyer (m) – workers' or students' hostel
fromagerie (f) – cheese shop
fronton (m) – a one-walled court used for *pelote Basque*, usually outdoors

gabarre (f) – flat-bottomed river boat once used to transport wine
gare or **gare SNCF** (f) – railway station
gare routière (f) – bus station
gave (f) – river (Béarnaise)
gendarmerie (f) – police station/force
gîte (m) – cottage
gîte d'étape (m) – simple accommodation for hikers or pilgrims
GR (f) – *grande randonnée;* long-distance hiking trail

halles (f pl) – covered food market
halte routière (f) – bus stop
hébergement chez l'habitant (m) – homestay
horaire (m) – timetable
hôtes payants (m pl) – homestay
hôtel de ville (m) – city or town hall
hôtel particulier (m) – town house, typically of a 16th- or 17th-century merchant

jardin (m) – garden; park
jour férié (m pl) – public holiday

lac (m) – lake
Langue d'Oc (f) – the medieval language of southern France, also called Occitan
laverie (f) or **lavomatique** (m) – laundrette
lits jumeaux (m pl) – twin beds
location (f) – rental

mairie (f) – town or village hall
Maison de la Presse (f) – common newsagent
marché (m) – market
marché couvert (m) – covered market
menu (m) – fixed-price meal with two or more courses
meublé (m) – furnished accommodation
musée (m) – museum

navette (f) – shuttle bus, train or boat

nom de famille (m) – surname, family name
numéro vert (m pl) – toll-free telephone number

Occitan – see Langue d'Oc
office de/du tourisme (m) – tourist office run by local government

parapente (f) – parasailing
patisserie (f) – pastry shop
pelote Basque (f) – generic name for Basque court games using bare hands or racquets and a hard, rubber-core ball (*pilota* in Basque)
pétanque (f) – see *boules*
piste cyclable (f) – bicycle path
place (f) – square
plage (f) – beach
plan (m) – city map
planche à voile (f) – windsurfing
plat du jour (m) – daily special in a restaurant
plongée (f) – diving
point d'argent (m) – automated teller machine (ATM)
pont (m) – bridge
port de plaisance (m) – pleasure-boat marina or harbour
porte (f) – gate in a city wall
pourboire (m) – tip
préfecture (f) – prefecture, capital of a département
prénom (m) – first or given name
pression (f) – draught beer
produce du terroir (m) – local produce

quai (m) – quay; railway platform
quartier (m) – quarter, district

randonnées pédestres (f pl) – hikes; hiking
refuge (m) – mountain hut, basic shelter for hikers
région (f) – the largest French administrative division
riverain (m) – local resident
routier (m) – long-distance trucker or truckers' restaurant

sentier (m) – trail, footpath

SNCF (f) – Société Nationale des Chemins de Fer; state-owned railway company
sortie (f) – exit
sous-préfecture (f) – sub-prefecture
spéléologie (f) – caving
supplément (m) – surcharge, supplement
syndicat d'initiative (m) – tourist office founded by local merchants

tabac (m) – tobacconist (also sells bus tickets, phonecards etc)
table d'hôte (f) – meals in a private house
tapas (f pl) – Spanish-style snacks, usually served at a *bodéga* or other bar
tarif réduit (m) – reduced price
taxe de séjour (f) – municipal tourist tax
télécarte (f) – phonecard
téléférique (m) – cable car
temple (m) – protestant church
terroir (m) – land, soil, earth (eg, see *cuisine du terroir*)
TGV (m) – *train à grande vitesse;* high-speed train
timbre (m) – stamp

tour (f) – tower
tour d'horloge (f) – clock tower
trinquet (m) – three-walled indoor court for playing *pelote Basque*
troubadour (m) – medieval poet-musician

ULM (m) – *ultraléger motorisé;* microlight aircraft

vélo (m) – bicycle; cycling
vendange (f) – wine harvest
vente en détaxe (f) – duty-free sales
v.f. (f) – *version française;* refers to a film dubbed in French
vieille ville (f) – old town/city
vin de pays (m) – local wine
v.o. (f) – *version originale;* refers to a non-dubbed film
voile (f) – sail; sailing
vol (m) – theft; flight
vol à voile (m) – gliding
v.o.s.t. (f) – *version originale sous-titrée;* refers to a film with subtitles
VTT (m) – *vélo touts terrain;* mountain bike

LONELY PLANET

You already know that Lonely Planet produces more than this one guidebook, but you might not be aware of the other products we have on this region. Here is a selection of titles that you may want to check out as well:

Cycling France
ISBN 1 86450 036 0
US$19.99 • UK£12.99

Walking in France
ISBN 0 86442 601 1
US$19.99 • UK£12.99

World Food France
ISBN 1 86450 021 2
US$12.99 • UK£7.99

Corsica
ISBN 1 86450 313 0
US$15.99 • UK£9.99

Provence & the Côte d'Azur
ISBN 1 86450 196 0
US$17.99 • UK£11.99

Normandy
ISBN 1 86450 098 0
US$15.99 • UK£9.99

France
ISBN 1 86450 151 0
US$24.99 • UK£14.99

Paris
ISBN 1 86450 125 1
US$15.99 • UK£9.99

French Phrasebook
ISBN 0 86442 450 7
US$5.95 • UK£3.99

Mediterranean Europe
ISBN 1 86450 154 5
US$27.99 • UK£15.99

Europe on a shoestring
ISBN 1 86450 150 2
US$24.99 • UK£14.99

Read This First: Europe
ISBN 1 86450 136 7
US$14.99 • UK£8.99

Available wherever books are sold

Lonely Planet Guides by Region

Lonely Planet is known worldwide for publishing practical, reliable and no-nonsense travel information in our guides and on our Web site. The Lonely Planet list covers just about every accessible part of the world. Currently there are 16 series: Travel guides, Shoestring guides, Condensed guides, Phrasebooks, Read This First, Healthy Travel, Walking guides, Cycling guides, Watching Wildlife guides, Pisces Diving & Snorkeling guides, City Maps, Road Atlases, Out to Eat, World Food, Journeys travel literature and Pictorials.

AFRICA Africa on a shoestring • Botswana • Cairo • Cairo City Map • Cape Town • Cape Town City Map • East Africa • Egypt • Egyptian Arabic phrasebook • Ethiopia, Eritrea & Djibouti • Ethiopian Amharic phrasebook • The Gambia & Senegal • Healthy Travel Africa • Kenya • Malawi • Morocco • Moroccan Arabic phrasebook • Mozambique • Namibia • Read This First: Africa • South Africa, Lesotho & Swaziland • Southern Africa • Southern Africa Road Atlas • Swahili phrasebook • Tanzania, Zanzibar & Pemba • Trekking in East Africa • Tunisia • Watching Wildlife East Africa • Watching Wildlife Southern Africa • West Africa • World Food Morocco • Zambia • Zimbabwe, Botswana & Namibia
Travel Literature: Mali Blues: Traveling to an African Beat • The Rainbird: A Central African Journey • Songs to an African Sunset: A Zimbabwean Story

AUSTRALIA & THE PACIFIC Aboriginal Australia & the Torres Strait Islands •Auckland • Australia • Australian phrasebook • Australia Road Atlas • Cycling Australia • Cycling New Zealand • Fiji • Fijian phrasebook • Healthy Travel Australia, NZ & the Pacific • Islands of Australia's Great Barrier Reef • Melbourne • Melbourne City Map • Micronesia • New Caledonia • New South Wales • New Zealand • Northern Territory • Outback Australia • Out to Eat – Melbourne • Out to Eat – Sydney • Papua New Guinea • Pidgin phrasebook • Queensland • Rarotonga & the Cook Islands • Samoa • Solomon Islands • South Australia • South Pacific • South Pacific phrasebook • Sydney • Sydney City Map • Sydney Condensed • Tahiti & French Polynesia • Tasmania • Tonga • Tramping in New Zealand • Vanuatu • Victoria • Walking in Australia • Watching Wildlife Australia • Western Australia
Travel Literature: Islands in the Clouds: Travels in the Highlands of New Guinea • Kiwi Tracks: A New Zealand Journey • Sean & David's Long Drive

CENTRAL AMERICA & THE CARIBBEAN Bahamas, Turks & Caicos • Baja California • Belize, Guatemala & Yucatán • Bermuda • Central America on a shoestring • Costa Rica • Costa Rica Spanish phrasebook • Cuba • Cycling Cuba • Dominican Republic & Haiti • Eastern Caribbean • Guatemala • Havana • Healthy Travel Central & South America • Jamaica • Mexico • Mexico City • Panama • Puerto Rico • Read This First: Central & South America • Virgin Islands • World Food Caribbean • World Food Mexico • Yucatán
Travel Literature: Green Dreams: Travels in Central America

EUROPE Amsterdam • Amsterdam City Map • Amsterdam Condensed • Andalucía • Athens • Austria • Baltic States phrasebook • Barcelona • Barcelona City Map • Belgium & Luxembourg • Berlin • Berlin City Map • Britain • British phrasebook • Brussels, Bruges & Antwerp • Brussels City Map • Budapest • Budapest City Map • Canary Islands • Catalunya & the Costa Brava • Central Europe • Central Europe phrasebook • Copenhagen • Corfu & the Ionians • Corsica • Crete • Crete Condensed • Croatia • Cycling Britain • Cycling France • Cyprus • Czech & Slovak Republics • Czech phrasebook • Denmark • Dublin • Dublin City Map • Dublin Condensed • Eastern Europe • Eastern Europe phrasebook • Edinburgh • Edinburgh City Map • England • Estonia, Latvia & Lithuania • Europe on a shoestring • Europe phrasebook • Finland • Florence • Florence City Map • France • Frankfurt City Map • Frankfurt Condensed • French phrasebook • Georgia, Armenia & Azerbaijan • Germany • German phrasebook • Greece • Greek Islands • Greek phrasebook • Hungary • Iceland, Greenland & the Faroe Islands • Ireland • Italian phrasebook • Italy • Kraków • Lisbon • The Loire • London • London City Map • London Condensed • Madrid • Madrid City Map • Malta • Mediterranean Europe • Milan, Turin & Genoa • Moscow • Munich • Netherlands • Normandy • Norway • Out to Eat – London • Out to Eat – Paris • Paris • Paris City Map • Paris Condensed • Poland • Polish phrasebook • Portugal • Portuguese phrasebook • Prague • Prague City Map • Provence & the Côte d'Azur • Read This First: Europe • Rhodes & the Dodecanese • Romania & Moldova • Rome • Rome City Map • Rome Condensed • Russia, Ukraine & Belarus • Russian phrasebook • Scandinavian & Baltic Europe • Scandinavian phrasebook • Scotland • Sicily • Slovenia • South-West France • Spain • Spanish phrasebook • Stockholm • St Petersburg • St Petersburg City Map • Sweden • Switzerland • Tuscany • Ukrainian phrasebook • Venice • Vienna • Wales • Walking in Britain • Walking in France • Walking in Ireland • Walking in Italy • Walking in Scotland • Walking in Spain • Walking in Switzerland • Western Europe • World Food France • World Food Greece • World Food Ireland • World Food Italy • World Food Spain **Travel Literature:** After Yugoslavia • Love and War in the Apennines • The Olive Grove: Travels in Greece • On the Shores of the Mediterranean • Round Ireland in Low Gear • A Small Place in Italy

Lonely Planet Mail Order

L onely Planet products are distributed worldwide. They are also available by mail order from Lonely Planet, so if you have difficulty finding a title please write to us. North and South American residents should write to 150 Linden St, Oakland, CA 94607, USA; European and African residents should write to 10a Spring Place, London NW5 3BH, UK; and residents of other countries to Locked Bag 1, Footscray, Victoria 3011, Australia.

INDIAN SUBCONTINENT & THE INDIAN OCEAN Bangladesh • Bengali phrasebook • Bhutan • Delhi • Goa • Healthy Travel Asia & India • Hindi & Urdu phrasebook • India • India & Bangladesh City Map • Indian Himalaya • Karakoram Highway • Kathmandu City Map • Kerala • Madagascar • Maldives • Mauritius, Réunion & Seychelles • Mumbai (Bombay) • Nepal • Nepali phrasebook • North India • Pakistan • Rajasthan • Read This First: Asia & India • South India • Sri Lanka • Sri Lanka phrasebook • Tibet • Tibetan phrasebook • Trekking in the Indian Himalaya • Trekking in the Karakoram & Hindukush • Trekking in the Nepal Himalaya • World Food India **Travel Literature:** The Age of Kali: Indian Travels and Encounters • Hello Goodnight: A Life of Goa • In Rajasthan • Maverick in Madagascar • A Season in Heaven: True Tales from the Road to Kathmandu • Shopping for Buddhas • A Short Walk in the Hindu Kush • Slowly Down the Ganges

MIDDLE EAST & CENTRAL ASIA Bahrain, Kuwait & Qatar • Central Asia • Central Asia phrasebook • Dubai • Farsi (Persian) phrasebook • Hebrew phrasebook • Iran • Israel & the Palestinian Territories • Istanbul • Istanbul City Map • Istanbul to Cairo • Istanbul to Kathmandu • Jerusalem • Jerusalem City Map • Jordan • Lebanon • Middle East • Oman & the United Arab Emirates • Syria • Turkey • Turkish phrasebook • World Food Turkey • Yemen **Travel Literature:** Black on Black: Iran Revisited • Breaking Ranks: Turbulent Travels in the Promised Land • The Gates of Damascus • Kingdom of the Film Stars: Journey into Jordan

NORTH AMERICA Alaska • Boston • Boston City Map • Boston Condensed • British Columbia • California & Nevada • California Condensed • Canada • Chicago • Chicago City Map • Chicago Condensed • Florida • Georgia & the Carolinas • Great Lakes • Hawaii • Hiking in Alaska • Hiking in the USA • Honolulu & Oahu City Map • Las Vegas • Los Angeles • Los Angeles City Map • Louisiana & the Deep South • Miami • Miami City Map • Montreal • New England • New Orleans • New Orleans City Map • New York City • New York City City Map • New York City Condensed • New York, New Jersey & Pennsylvania • Oahu • Out to Eat – San Francisco • Pacific Northwest • Rocky Mountains • San Diego & Tijuana • San Francisco • San Francisco City Map • Seattle • Seattle City Map • Southwest • Texas • Toronto • USA • USA phrasebook • Vancouver • Vancouver City Map • Virginia & the Capital Region • Washington, DC • Washington, DC City Map • World Food New Orleans **Travel Literature**: Caught Inside: A Surfer's Year on the California Coast • Drive Thru America

NORTH-EAST ASIA Beijing • Beijing City Map • Cantonese phrasebook • China • Hiking in Japan • Hong Kong & Macau • Hong Kong City Map • Hong Kong Condensed • Japan • Japanese phrasebook • Korea • Korean phrasebook • Kyoto • Mandarin phrasebook • Mongolia • Mongolian phrasebook • Seoul • Shanghai • South-West China • Taiwan • Tokyo • Tokyo Condensed • World Food Hong Kong • World Food Japan **Travel Literature:** In Xanadu: A Quest • Lost Japan

SOUTH AMERICA Argentina, Uruguay & Paraguay • Bolivia • Brazil • Brazilian phrasebook • Buenos Aires • Buenos Aires City Map • Chile & Easter Island • Colombia • Ecuador & the Galapagos Islands • Healthy Travel Central & South America • Latin American Spanish phrasebook • Peru • Quechua phrasebook • Read This First: Central & South America • Rio de Janeiro • Rio de Janeiro City Map • Santiago de Chile • South America on a shoestring • Trekking in the Patagonian Andes • Venezuela **Travel Literature**: Full Circle: A South American Journey

SOUTH-EAST ASIA Bali & Lombok • Bangkok • Bangkok City Map • Burmese phrasebook • Cambodia • Cycling Vietnam, Laos & Cambodia • East Timor phrasebook • Hanoi • Healthy Travel Asia & India • Hill Tribes phrasebook • Ho Chi Minh City (Saigon) • Indonesia • Indonesian phrasebook • Indonesia's Eastern Islands • Java • Lao phrasebook • Laos • Malay phrasebook • Malaysia, Singapore & Brunei • Myanmar (Burma) • Philippines • Pilipino (Tagalog) phrasebook • Read This First: Asia & India • Singapore • Singapore City Map • South-East Asia on a shoestring • South-East Asia phrasebook • Thailand • Thailand's Islands & Beaches • Thailand, Vietnam, Laos & Cambodia Road Atlas • Thai phrasebook • Vietnam • Vietnamese phrasebook • World Food Indonesia • World Food Thailand • World Food Vietnam

ALSO AVAILABLE: Antarctica • The Arctic • The Blue Man: Tales of Travel, Love and Coffee • Brief Encounters: Stories of Love, Sex & Travel • Buddhist Stupas in Asia: The Shape of Perfection • Chasing Rickshaws • The Last Grain Race • Lonely Planet ... On the Edge: Adventurous Escapades from Around the World • Lonely Planet Unpacked • Lonely Planet Unpacked Again • Not the Only Planet: Science Fiction Travel Stories • Ports of Call: A Journey by Sea • Sacred India • Travel Photography: A Guide to Taking Better Pictures • Travel with Children • Tuvalu: Portrait of an Island Nation

Index

Text

Bold indicates maps.

MAP LEGEND

BOUNDARIES

.... International
.... Regional
.... Suburb

HYDROGRAPHY

.... Coastline
.... River, Creek
.... Lake
.... Canal

⊛ .... Park, Gardens
.... Urban Area

TOULOUSE .... City
Biarritz ..... City or Large Town
● Arcachon .... Large Town
● Dax .... Town
● Irún .... Village

● .... Point of Interest
▪ .... Place to Stay
⬛ .... Camp Site
▼ .... Place to Eat
⬛ .... Pub or Bar

⊠ .... Airport
...... Ancient or City Wall
ⓢ .... Bank
⌘ .... Beach

ROUTES & TRANSPORT

.... Autoroute
.... Primary Road
.... Secondary Road
.... Tertiary Road
.... Unsealed Road
.... City Autoroute
.... City Primary Road
.... City Road
.... City Street, Lane

AREA FEATURES

.... Building
.... Market

MAP SYMBOLS

🦢 .... Bird Sanctuary
⌂ .... Cave
🚌 🚏 .... Bus Stop, Station
🏰 .... Castle or Château
⛪ 🕌 ..... Cathedral or Church
🎭 🎬 .... Theatre, Cinema
.... Cliff or Escarpment
🏛 .... Embassy
⛲ .... Fountain
✚ .... Hospital
🖥 .... Internet Cafe
🗼 .... Lighthouse
🗿 .... Monument
▲ ∧ ⌒ ..... Mountain, Range
🏛 .... Museum

.... Pedestrian Area
⟩═══ ═ .... Tunnel
●—Ⓞ— .... Train Route & Station
—Ⓜ— ...... Metro & Station
●●●🚋●● .... Tramway
ʜ—ʜ—ʜ—ʜ— ... Cable Car or Chairlift
———————— .... Walking Track
············ .... Walking Tour
——————🚢—— . Ferry Route & Terminal

.... Beach
.... Cemetery

→ .... One Way Street
🅿 .... Parking
)(.......................... Pass
⊙ ...... Petrol or Gas Station
⊞ .... Police Station
✉ .... Post Office
⊠ .... Ruins
⊗ .... Shopping Centre
🏛 .. Stately Home or Palace
🏄 .... Surf Beach
🏊 .... Swimming Pool
✡ .... Synagogue
🚕 .... Taxi Rank
☎ .... Telephone
🚻 .... Toilet
🛈 .... Tourist Information

Note: not all symbols displayed above appear in this book

LONELY PLANET OFFICES

Australia
Locked Bag 1, Footscray, Victoria 3011
☎ 03 8379 8000 fax 03 8379 8111
email: talk2us@lonelyplanet.com.au

USA
150 Linden St, Oakland, CA 94607
☎ 510 893 8555 TOLL FREE: 800 275 8555
fax 510 893 8572
email: info@lonelyplanet.com

UK
10a Spring Place, London NW5 3BH
☎ 020 7428 4800 fax 020 7428 4828
email: go@lonelyplanet.co.uk

France
1 rue du Dahomey, 75011 Paris
☎ 01 55 25 33 00 fax 01 55 25 33 01
email: bip@lonelyplanet.fr
www.lonelyplanet.fr

World Wide Web: www.lonelyplanet.com *or* AOL keyword: lp
Lonely Planet Images: lpi@lonelyplanet.com.au